Routledge History of World Philosophies

Volume 1

Routledge History of World Philosophies

Since the publication of the first volumes in 1993, the prestigious *Routledge History of Philosophy*, edited by G.H.R. Parkinson and S.G. Shanker, has established itself as the most comprehensive chronological survey of Western philosophy available. It discusses all the most important philosophical movements from the sixth century B.C. up to the present day. All the major figures in Western philosophy are covered in detail in these volumes. These philosophers are clearly situated within the cultural and scientific context of this time.

Within the main corpus of the *Routledge History of Philosophy*, the Jewish and Islamic traditions are discussed in the context of Western philosophy, with which they are inextricably linked. *The History of Islamic Philosophy* and *The History of Jewish Philosophy* are designed to supplement the core volumes by dealing specifically with these two philosophical traditions; they provide extensive analysis of all the most significant thinkers and concepts. In keeping with the rest of the series, each additional volume has a comprehensive index and bibliography, and includes chapters by some of the most influential scholars in the field. They will form the first volumes of a new series, Routledge History of World Philosophies.

Routledge History of World Philosophies
Volume I

History of Islamic Philosophy

Part II

EDITED BY

Seyyed Hossein Nasr
and Oliver Leaman

ROUTLEDGE
London and New York

First published 1996
by Routledge
11 New Fetter Lane, London EC4P 4EE

Simultaneously published in the USA and Canada
by Routledge
29 West 35th Street, New York, NY 10001

Reprinted 1997 and 1999

Typeset in Garamond by Florencetype Ltd,
Stoodleigh, Devon

Printed and bound in Great Britain by
T. J. International Ltd., Padstow, Cornwall

British Library Cataloguing in Publication Data
A catalogue record for this book is available from
the British Library

Library of Congress Cataloguing in Publication Data
A catalogue record for this book has been requested

ISBN 0–415–13159–6 (Part I)
0–415–13160–X (Part II)
0–415–05667–5 (Set)

Contents

Part II

VII Philosophy and its parts

X Interpretation of Islamic philosophy in the West

XI Bibliography

Transliteration and style

Transliteration has normally been carried out in accordance with the schedule set out here. This has not always been done, though, especially for terms very frequently used, and it seemed more natural to allow authors slight differences in transliteration, particularly in the sections on Jewish philosophy. The original attempt to apply the transliteration schedule strictly proved unsatisfactory, since it resulted in a text which often looked rather strange. Authors have followed their own preferences in some respects for spelling and capitalization of key terms. Some additional bibliographical material has been supplied by the editors.

ARABIC CHARACTERS

ء	’	غ	gh
ب	b	ف	f
ت	t	ق	q
ث	th	ك	k
ج	j	ل	l
ح	ḥ	م	m
خ	kh	ن	n
د	d	ه	h
ذ	dh	و	w
ر	r	ي	y
ز	z	ة	ah; at (construct state)
س	s	ال	(article) al- and ’l- (even before the anteropalatals)
ش	sh		
ص	ṣ		
ض	ḍ	long vowels	
ط	ṭ	اى	ā
ظ	ẓ	و	ū
ع	‘	ي	ī

short vowels

……َ	a
……ُ	u
……ِ	i

diphthongs

و……َ	aw
ي……َ	ai (ay)
ـيّـ	īy (final form ī)
ـُوّ	uww (final form ū)

Persian letters added to the Arabic alphabet

پ	p
چ	ch
ژ	zh
گ	g

VII

Philosophy and its parts

CHAPTER 47

Metaphysics

Charles Genequand

Whereas the other great divisions of philosophy (logic, physics, ethics, etc.) are defined in relation to a clearly identifiable object or field of study, metaphysics owes its name to a book, Aristotle's *Metaphysics*, whose title refers to the treatises placed after the *Physics* in the collection of his works. Moreover, the proper subject-matter of that book is largely problematic: unlike the *Physics*, for instance, which studies the material world of generation and decay, the bulk of the *Metaphysics* is devoted to looking for its subject matter and trying to define it. An important consequence of this is that for a long time metaphysical writings mostly assumed the form of commentaries on the founding text of Aristotle. The existence of a metaphysical reflection in Islam is thus closely dependent on the availability of translations of that work, although other sources were also used. A nearly complete translation of Aristole's work (some books seem never to have been translated at all) was made by a certain Usṭāt (Eustathius?) about the time of al-Kindī and is preserved in the commentary of Ibn Rushd (Averroes). Several other translations followed, all fragmentary.[1] Owing to the difficulty of the text, the Muslim philosophers often preferred to use paraphrases and summaries, among which those by Alexander of Aphrodisias and Themistius were especially appreciated.[2]

Neoplatonic texts were also translated, but their influence on the *falāsifah* was not as profound as might be expected. Some treatises by Plotinus and Proclus were made available to Muslims in the days of al-Kindī,[3] extracts from Plotinus' *Enneads* were patched together under the title of *The Theology of Aristotle*, and a number of propositions from Proclus' *Elements of Theology* were adapted in various guises, such as the *Book of the Pure Good*, and falsely ascribed to Aristotle. The confusion (or should we say the deception?) was made easier by the fact that the more specific Neoplatonic tenets had been watered down to the point of being almost unrecognizable. The basic hierarchical structure, intellect–soul–nature, could be deduced from those texts, but the very special status of the One beyond intellect and being was totally erased.

While it is important to be aware of the genealogy of the concepts used by the *falāsifah*, this should not blind us to the new meanings these were often given by being inserted into different contexts. In the same way as the early mosques are unmistakably mosques even though elements of their technical features can be traced back to ancient churches or other monuments, the synthesis achieved in Islamic philosophy assumes a clearly recognizable form which differentiates it from its parent despite the general likeness.

WHAT IS METAPHYSICS?

Metaphysics is variously designated in Arabic philosophical literature by the expressions *mā ba'd* (*fawq, warā'*) *al-ṭabī'ah* (what is after (above, beyond) nature), *al-falsafat al-ūlā* (first philosophy), *ilāhiyyāt* (theology, divinity) or even *ḥikmah* (wisdom). All these terms except the last derive historically from Greek equivalents and their use, in the first stages of philosophical reflection in Islam, seems to have been dictated by the usage of the respective Greek sources or models of the Muslim authors more than by their literal meaning or their correctness. Thus, at the beginning of his treatise *On First Philosophy* (*Fi'l-falsafat al-ūlā*), al-Kindī explains that first philosophy is so called because it is the science of the first Reality (*ḥaqq*) which is the cause of all reality, and knowing a thing requires knowing its cause.[4] A little further on he mentions the study of the things above nature (*fawq al-ṭabī'ah*), i.e. immaterial things, the relation between the First Cause and immaterial things in general remaining so far unexplained. What is clear, however, is the contrast between natural things, which have both matter and motion, and immaterial ones, which have neither.[5] The third chapter of the same tract is devoted to a long discussion of unity and multiplicity culminating in the renewed affirmation of the existence of a First Cause "higher and nobler than all things and prior to them which is the cause of their being and permanence".[6] One of the reasons for this is that it is impossible to postulate an infinite series of causes. The First Cause, moreover, is one; it is neither motion, nor soul, nor intellect, nor any other thing, but it is the cause of all other things. This causality is also described as creation (*ibdā'*) and emanation (*fayḍ*). In the epistle *On the Number of Aristotle's Books*, metaphysics (*mā ba'd al-ṭabī'ah* or *mā fawq al-ṭabī'ah*) is the science of immaterial things and of God as efficient and final cause of the universe.[7]

In his *Philosophy of Aristotle* al-Fārābī explains in a few lines that metaphysics (*mā ba'd al-ṭabī'ah*) investigates the existents from a point of view different from that of natural philosophy.[8] But another passage of the same work affords us a glimpse of his conception of the relation between the two disciplines: the study of the heavenly bodies' essence does not belong to natural philosophy because the latter deals only with beings falling under the ten categories. But there are beings which fall outside the categories, such as the Active Intellect or the thing which imparts their motion to the heavenly bodies.[9] It is thus necessary to study beings in a more comprehensive fashion than that of natural philosophy, and this more comprehensive study, which represents humanity's highest achievement and highest goal, is metaphysics.

In his short epistle *On the Aims of Aristotle's Metaphysics* (*mā ba'd al-ṭabī'ah*), al-Fārābī shows himself to be aware of a duality of purpose in the work of the master: it contains a general science of being and a theology. Many people, he says, have wrongly imagined that the subject-matter of this book is God, the intellect, the soul and what pertains to these entities; but only book *Lām* (= *Lambda* = XII) corresponds to this definition. Metaphysics is a universal science (*'ilm kullī*) investigating such general concepts as being, unity, species, accidents and so on. But theology (*al-'ilm al-ilāhī*) is a part of this science because God is the principle of being in general.[10]

The fullest treatment of the problem of determining the exact subject-matter(s) of metaphysics is, as expected, that of Ibn Sīnā (Avicenna). The term he favours to designate this discipline is that of *ilāhiyyāt*, which is the title of the metaphysical part of his main philosophical encyclopedia *al-Shifā'*. But he is careful to accommodate the other traditional denominations of metaphysics and attempts a synthesis of the different views taken of the matter, showing them to be but different ways of envisaging the same discipline. Thus, theology (*ilāhiyyāt*) inquires into the things which are separate from matter, the first cause of natural beings and the cause of causes and principle of principles which is God. There is in addition a "first philosophy" which provides the principles of the other sciences: it is also properly called "wisdom" (*ḥikmah*): the object of this science is variously described as (1) the best science of the best object of science; (2) the truest and most certain science; (3) the knowledge of the first causes of the universe. But these are merely three different descriptions of the same science.[11]

Here Ibn Sīnā introduces a distinction between a science's subject-matter (*mawḍū'*) and its object, or goal (*maṭlūb*). The subject-matter of any one science is taken for granted (*musallam*) in that science which merely investigates its "modes" (*aḥwāl*). God is the goal, not the subject-matter, of this science,[12] and so are the ultimate causes (*asbāb quswā*). What is then the subject-matter of metaphysics? It must be something which is taken for granted in this science: no science can demonstrate its own subject-matter, for this would imply the existence of a higher science as starting-point of the demonstration. Being as being (*al-mawjūd bi-mā huwa mawjūd*) is therefore the primary subject-matter of this science, because the study of the properties of being is at the same time the study of its principles. Moreover, the principle is not the principle of the whole of being, because in that case it would be the principle of itself, which is impossible. The whole of being has no principle: the principle is the principle of the *caused* being (*maʿlūl*) only.[13] In this way, Ibn Sīnā tries to escape from the pitfall of infinite regress.

This science is subdivided into several parts: (1) the ultimate causes, i.e. the causes of every caused being; (2) the First Cause from which every caused being emanates (*yafīḍu*); (3) the properties of being; (4) the principles of the particular sciences. It deserves the name of "first philosophy" in two senses: as science of the first in being, i.e. the First Cause, and as science of the first in generality (or inclusiveness), i.e. being and unity. As knowledge of God and of the immaterial causes of the universe, it is a "divine" science. As to the term "metaphysics", literally "what is after nature", it refers to the fact that natural, or sensible, bodies are what we perceive first. If we consider the essence of this science it should rather be called "what is before nature".[14]

What Ibn Sīnā sketches thus in the first pages of his *Ilāhiyyāt* is an attempt to reconcile the two apparently conflicting aspects of Aristotle's metaphysics: a science of being as such, and a study of the divine and immaterial causes of the physical world. How the programme is to be fulfilled we shall consider in more detail later on.

One of the most striking features of Ibn Rushd's metaphysical works and particularly his so-called *Great Commentary* (*Tafsīr*)[15] is the complete failure to distinguish different aspects or parts of the science of metaphysics corresponding to the different terms that traditionally serve to designate it and which he uses quite interchangeably.[16] It is true that the form of the commentary is not conducive to the expression of personal opinions, and Ibn Rushd for one tends to take over in each case the term which Aristotle himself is using in the passage commented upon, thus reproducing to a large extent the ambiguities of the Aristotelian metaphysics. For instance, he uses the name *ʿilm ilāhī* in the only passage of the *Metaphysics* where Aristotle explicitly defines its subject-matter as *theologikè*.[17] Metaphysics is there regarded as the science of the substance that is both unmoved and separate from matter, as opposed to physics or natural philosophy which deal with the movable and material substance, and to mathematics which deals with the substance that is unmoved but separate from matter in definition only. Ibn Rushd insists that the "separate" substance is the proper subject-matter of metaphysics, but a distinction must be maintained between the movable eternal things (i.e. the heavenly bodies) and their causes which are unmoved and eternal; both, however, are the objects of metaphysics as understood by Ibn Rushd.[18] This comes out very clearly in a crucial passage where Aristotle does not mention theology or separate substances at all:

> he [Aristotle] said concerning natural philosophy that it is second in respect to first philosophy and its task,[19] for the separate things which are the proper subject-matter of first philosophy are the principles of the subject-matter of natural science, and natural science is second in rank with regard to it, and its subject-matter is one of the tasks of the subject-matter of first philosophy which is the divine things (i.e. the heavenly bodies).

Thus the proper subject-matter of first philosophy or metaphysics is the realm of the divine, separate things, i.e. the heavenly bodies and their causes or principles.

What the concrete content of this philosophy is we shall see presently. The question which now arises concerns the place and function assigned by Ibn Rushd to the general study of being, or the study of being as being (*mawjūd bi-mā huwa mawjūd*), and its relation to the "divine science". Such a question is difficult to answer because Ibn Rushd is mostly concerned to follow Aristotle's text step by step without raising the general problem of the coherence of his model. Ibn Rushd however states clearly that metaphysics deals with the principles of all kinds of substance, because the latter is eminently being. Metaphysics studies all kinds of substance, both movable and eternal, but from a standpoint different from that of natural philosophy. Moreover the eternal and unmoved substance is eminently the object of metaphysics.

But in order to define more precisely the relation obtaining between the two kinds of substance and between the two disciplines we must turn to the cosmology of the *falāsifah*.

THE COSMOLOGICAL PROBLEM AND THE THEORY OF EMANATION

There is a general consensus among the Muslim philosophers about the existence of two realms: the material world of nature, of the things subject to generation and decay, and an immaterial, separate world. One of the main problems of Islamic philosophy is to determine the kind of relationship linking the two realms together. Aristotle had admitted the existence of such a link in vague and tantalizing allusions, but apart from the obvious fact that the yearly motion of the sun along the ecliptic, by causing the seasonal differences, is the source of the life-cycle of generation and decay, his views on the subject remained programmatic.

The basic idea that the heavenly bodies and especially the planets (including of course the sun and the moon) occupy an intermediate position between the wholly immaterial being, normally identified with God, and the natural world of generation and decay appears in different guises in all the philosophical systems of Classical Islam.

For al-Kindī, the only real cause is God who created the world *ex nihilo*; all other causes are so called only metaphorically *bi'l-majāz*).[20] This real cause, or First Cause, is also called ultimate (*ba'īdah*) cause, as opposed to the proximate (*qarībah*) cause. The heavenly world, from the moon to the ultimate sphere (that of the fixed stars) is entirely devoid of the primary qualities (hot, cold, moist and dry) as well as of generation and decay which are found only in the sublunary world composed of the four elements (fire, air, water and earth). All changes occurring in the world of nature are due to the motions of the heavenly bodies, their different velocities and distances, their conjunctions and oppositions. This is particularly obvious in the case of the sun which influences even the physical make-up of the population living in the torrid zone. But all this happens only by the Will of the Creator.[21] There is a close connection between the four primary qualities, the four elements and the four seasons.[22] The moon and the planets, and also the larger stars and constellations, although their influence is less conspicuous, also play an important role in the seasonal variations observed between one year and another.

The stars, or the sphere (*falak*), are thus the cause of all that occurs in the world of nature, but al-Kindī points out insistently that this is so only by God's Will, because God so arranged it.[23] The real efficient cause of all is God. It is all the more interesting, in view of such a voluntaristic theory of creation, to note that we also encounter in al-Kindī the term "emanation" (*fayḍ*) coupled with "generosity" (*jūd*).[24] Creationism and emanationism are often regarded as mutually exclusive solutions to the problem of becoming. This clearly is not the case for al-Kindī, for whom emanation results from the will and goodness of the Creator. The problem of emanation will be taken up later.

Al-Kindī's God is the First Cause and as such it is essentially one; it is the only real One, all other things which are said to be one being so in a metaphorical sense (*bi'l-majāz*) only. At the end of the preserved part of his treatise *On First Philosophy* al-Kindī provides one of the first and most perfect examples of negative theology in Islam: the One is none of the intelligible things and none of the terms that can be applied to any thing can be applied to it. The unity which flows from it (*fayḍ*) is at the same time the cause of the coming into being (*takawwin*) of all sensible things. It is also agent (*fā'il*), creator (*mubdi'*) and mover (*muḥarrik*), all these terms denoting apparently for al-Kindī different aspects of the One. If unity deserted the universe the latter would perish.[25]

The metaphysical realm for al-Kindī is that which extends from the Active Intellect upwards, including the heavens and, as a matter of course, God. If we want to discover what conception al-Fārābī formed of this world we have to turn to his politico-cosmological treatises, particularly the *Opinions of the Inhabitants of the Ideal State*.[26] This and his other works of similar content must be taken to put forward his personal philosophy, and although many elements in it undoubtedly derive from Greek sources, the overall construction and the way in which these elements have been combined may be considered as authentically Fārābīan. As noted above, al-Fārābī in his exposition of Aristotle's philosophy almost entirely ignored his metaphysics. It has been suggested, quite plausibly, that this is because al-Fārābī was dissatisfied with it, particularly with its unsystematic order, and wanted to replace it by a theory of his own.[27]

Al-Fārābī begins with a description of the First Cause, or more simply the First, and its main attributes. The First is the source of all further being; it is absolutely perfect; it is unique (*wāḥid*), knowing (*ʿālim*), wise (*ḥākīm*), real (*ḥaqq*) and living (*ḥayy*). The influence of Muʿtazilite *kalām* may be detected in these epithets.[28] Like Aristotle's God it thinks itself. It must be noted that al-Fārābī, with the majority of the Peripatetic Islamic philosophers, does not accept the Neoplatonic distinction between the Intellect and the One: such a notion of a One above and beyond being and intellection must have been inconceivable for them.

From the First all other beings and the heavenly world in the first place derive by a process generally designated by the name of emanation (*fayḍ*, lit. "flowing" or "overflowing"). This emanation results from the mere existence of the First; it is the necessary consequence of the First's existence. Terms expressing the necessary character of this process (*yalḥaqu*, *yalzamu*, *yatbaʿu*) are commonly used as synonyms of *yafīḍu* (emanates). The First neither gains nor loses anything by it, nor does it cause it in order to achieve a specific aim, for this would be contrary to its own perfection by implying that it is in need of something outside itself. The notion of will, on which al-Kindī lays such great stress, is conspicuously absent from al-Fārābī's description of emanation. There is also a hierarchical order of the entities emanating from the First down to the lowest grade of being.

From the First emanates the Second (intellect); by thinking the First, it gives rise to the Third, and by thinking itself it gives rise to the first heaven. The Third in turn, by thinking the First, produces the Fourth and by thinking itself produces the second sphere, that of the fixed stars. The same process repeats itself ten times, thus giving rise to the ten heavenly spheres and to the ten entities (intellects) following the first. The tenth intellect is the so-called Active Intellect (*al-ʿaql al-faʿʿāl*) which is the last of the immaterial entities. It has not only a cognitive function as in the Greek tradition, but also physical and cosmological ones. By implanting the forms in matter it constitutes the final link between the heavens and the world of nature. In spite of superficial analogies, the function of these heavenly intellects is quite different from that of the movers postulated by Aristotle in his *Metaphysics*. Not only has al-Fārābī reduced their number by adopting a simpler astronomical theory with ten entities instead of forty-seven or fifty-five; their function is to give existence, not merely motion, to the heavenly bodies.

Al-Fārābī thus meets the objection he had himself made to Aristotle's scheme on the grounds that it did not account for the existence of the heavens, but only for their motion. The reason for the latter is explained a little later in the same work:[29] each of the heavenly bodies also has a form, which is an Intellect, by means of which it thinks the First and the Intellect from which it derives its own existence. This secondary Intellect is situated within the heavenly body; it is not completely immaterial and thus has something in common with man. This emphasizes once again the intermediate position occupied by the heavenly bodies between the purely intelligible realm and the human world. But when it comes to explaining the circular motion of the heavens, al-Fārābī resorts to a curiously mechanical solution: since the heavenly bodies are spherical, and no part of them is more entitled than another to the place it occupies, their parts have to succeed each other in each part of the space occupied by the sphere, thus producing an eternal circular motion. The heavenly motions and the ever-changing positions of the heavenly bodies in relation to each other are the causes of sublunar matter and of the continuous flux of the forms in matter. But this belongs to natural philosophy.[30]

When we turn to Ibn Sīnā, we find that he mostly builds on the foundations laid by al-Fārābī but gives to the latter's theses an immensely ampler development. In the first place he wants to prove the existence of the first cause whereas al-Fārābī was content to assume it. Ibn Sīnā's proof is based on the impossibility of admitting an infinite series of causes. Any causal series, however long it may be, presupposes the existence of an upper and a lower limit (*ṭaraf*). The upper limit is the cause which has no cause, or First Cause. Structurally this proof is analogous to Aristotle's proof (in the *Physics*) from the impossibility of assuming an infinite series of movers. But Ibn Sīnā characteristically replaces the cause of motion by the cause of being. Al-Fārābī had already expressed some dissatisfaction at not finding in Aristotle's writings an explanation of the origin of being, as opposed to motion. Ibn Sīnā is the first to undertake a full refutation of the Aristotelian conception of God as prime mover and source of motion rather than of being. Even the eternity of the sphere's motion is regarded by Ibn Sīnā as unproven.[31]

Ibn Sīnā makes a completely new start from the basic divisions, or modes, of being. These are the necessary, the possible (or contingent) and the impossible which imply each other so that all definitions given of these terms are open to the charge of circularity. Among the three, "necessary" has precedence in our understanding.[32] The necessary existent is uncaused, whereas the possible has a cause. Furthermore, the necessary existent is one: it does not admit of any multiplicity either as the species of a genus or as the individuals of a species. It is not a notion (*ma'nā*) common to a multiplicity of beings. The First Principle alone, then, is necessarily existent, and every other thing derives its existence from it, that is, not only its form, but also its matter is created. The First has no other quiddity (or definition: *māhiyyah*) than being (*inniyyah*), but it emanates (causes to emanate: *yufīḍu*) existence on the essences of the quiddities which by themselves are merely possible.[33] According to a practice well established since al-Kindī it is described in purely negative terms.[34] There is no apodictical demonstration of it (*burhān*), but it is the apodictical demonstration of everything. It can be conceived of only by clear indications (*al-dalā'il al-wāḍiḥah*), i.e. by induction, not by the demonstrative or syllogistic method. It is pure good (*khayr maḥḍ*), the reality (*ḥaqq*), pure intellect and intelligible, being itself the object of its own intellection, without this entailing in any way the presence in it of duality or multiplicity. The Neoplatonic distinction between the One and the Intellect is therefore clearly rejected by Ibn Sīnā as it had been by al-Kindī and al-Fārābī.

Being good, the Necessary Being is also the aim or perfection, i.e. the final cause of everything, or that which everything desires (*yatashawwaqu*). As such, it is the object of love (*maḥbūb*, *ma'shūq*). At this point, Ibn Sīnā's argument links up with the physical demonstration of the eternity of motion as evidenced in the circular motion of the heavenly bodies. This motion is not natural but voluntary (*'an irādah*);[35] its proximate mover must be a soul, not an intellect, and this soul is not separate from the matter of the sphere. It is also necessary to postulate the existence of an intellect as final cause (*ghāyah*, *gharaḍ*) of the soul which is moved towards it by desire and love; but this desire is of a purely rational kind and may therefore be defined as choice (*ikhtiyār*) or will (*irādah*), which is properly the desire of the rational part of the soul. The kinds of desire belonging to the two inferior parts of the soul, namely passion (*ghaḍab*) and appetite (*shahwah*) are not fitting for an unchangeable body like the heavenly sphere. The good desired by the soul is not such that it could be attained by motion, for in that case motion would cease when the good had been reached.[36] The good therefore subsists by itself and cannot be reached; but the intellect strives to become similar (*tashabbuh*) to it in so far as this is possible,[37] and this is the cause of its eternal motion. Furthermore, the power belonging to a finite body is necessarily finite, so that the infinite motion of the heavens must be bestowed by an infinitely powerful source which is the First.

Ibn Sīnā's explanation of the circular motion is clearly derived from that of al-Fārābī; if a part of the heavenly body is actually in a certain place, it is potentially in another; but since it strives to free itself of all potentiality, it moves in order to be in all parts of the sphere in actuality in so far as this is possible. In other words, what is not possible for an individual may be possible in succession.[38] This motion is also compared by Ibn Sīnā to a kind of angelical or celestial worship (*'ibādah malakiyyah aw falakiyyah*). The first mover and first beloved is one and cannot be more than one, but each one of the nine spheres (Ibn Sīnā explicitly adopts the Ptolemaic system) has a proximate mover of its own (i.e. a soul) and an object of desire and love of its own. By desiring and loving its own principle each one of the spheres acquires its own particular motion, and by desiring and loving the First they all share in the common circular motion (the daily motion). The tenth Intellect (eleventh including the First) is the Active Intellect which is in the same relation to the human souls as each of the heavenly intellects to the corresponding heavenly soul.

The theory of emanation is set forth by Ibn Sīnā in conclusion of his astronomical and cosmological scheme. All beings derive from the First, but not as a result of deliberate intention; the First cannot will anything other than itself, because this would be tantamount to an admission of its own imperfection. The First contemplates itself and this thought produces other beings. By contemplating itself, it produces the first Intellect (that of the starless sphere). The First Intellect contemplates its own essence as possible in itself and from this intellection the first sphere results necessarily (*yalzam*). It also contemplates its own essence as necessitated by the First and from this intellection the soul of the first sphere results necessarily. Finally, by contemplating the First it produces the next Intellect, that which is immediately below itself. This ternary process repeats itself at the level of each of the ten heavenly spheres down to the Active Intellect.[39]

There appear to be several reasons explaining why Ibn Sīnā, after al-Fārābī, adopted this curious emanationist scheme. It is designed to account for the heavenly motions in accordance with the astronomical theory of Ptolemy, although it disregards some of its intricacies. It also explains the emergence of multiplicity out of absolute unity. Furthermore, there must be more than one intermediary between the First and the world of nature: out of the One only a one can arise, which is the first Intellect. But out of the first Intellect only a specific multiplicity, not a numerical multiplicity, can arise, as the latter presupposes the existence of matter. The multiplicity of the individual human souls cannot therefore arise directly from the first caused or any of the separate Intellects. Like all the forms of the physical world embedded in matter they emanate from the tenth Intellect, the Giver of Forms (*wāhib al-ṣuwar*).[40] Ibn Sīnā's account of the origin of matter and the four elements is not very clear; he seems to regard them as produced by the heavenly motions and Intellects.

The theory of emanation is commonly regarded as typical of *falsafah* and as an element of paramount importance in it. While it is true that it appears in one form or another in the majority of the Islamic philosophical systems, its importance, particularly in the case of Ibn Sīnā, has generally been exaggerated. It is set forth summarily at the end of what is by contrast an extremely detailed exposition of the mechanics of the heavenly bodies' motions in their loving aspiration towards the First Cause. The upward drive of the whole cosmos is indeed one of the outstanding characteristics of Ibn Sīnā's philosophy which is comparable in this respect to the Aristotelian teleology. The purpose of the theory of emanation is to establish between the First Cause, the heavenly movers and the physical world the link which was missing in Aristotle's system, as was already noted and deplored by some of his Greek successors. It may of course be questioned whether the very notion of timeless creation or causality which is at the basis of the theory can reasonably be upheld in any other sense than that of finalistic causality. Creation understood as efficient causality seems to imply a time lag between cause and effect. But this is not to say that the idea of emanation is irreconcilable with the transcendence of the First Cause:[41] rather it is the device whereby the *falāsifah* and Ibn Sīnā in particular thought that they could reconcile the two notions. In any case there is a much stronger emphasis in Ibn Sīnā's cosmology on the ascending order of the lower entities' longing for the higher and their desire to become similar to them than on the descending order of efficient causality. In this respect it is fully consistent with his psychology which culminated in the soul's ascent towards the Creator. In spite of his proclaimed intention of substituting a metaphysics of being (an ontology) for the Aristotelian metaphysics of motion, Ibn Sīnā retained a privileged role for motion in his system as it appears from the fact that it is through motion that the lower entities express their love of the higher ones, and through motion also that the heavenly bodies are the cause of the ordered and regular changes occurring in the material world. This may point to the difficulty of admitting any kind of change other than locomotion in an eternal universe.

Ibn Rushd rejected most innovations introduced by Ibn Sīnā in what remained a basically Aristotelian system. The notion of a being contingent by itself, but necessary by something else, seemed absurd to him. However, this distinction can be maintained in the case of motion: the motion of the heavenly bodies is in itself contingent, that is to say they would stop if left to their own resources, but it is eternal and necessary through the action of the First Mover, which is unceasing.[42] Their substance is eternal because they are not composed of matter and form, or because they have no contrary. It follows from this that the only demonstration of the First Mover's (i.e. God's) existence is the Aristotelian proof by way of motion, and that Ibn Sīnā's attempt to derive not only the motion but also the existence of the heavenly bodies from the immaterial Intellects must be discarded.[43] Motion constitutes the link between nature and the divine, heavenly realm. Moreover, since there can be no demonstration of the first principles (a point on which Ibn Rushd agrees with Ibn Sīnā, although he blames him for applying it too rigidly), it is only by a kind of inductive, dialectical reasoning starting from their effects in the world of becoming that their existence and properties can be established. This explains why so much of Aristotle's *Metaphysics* is taken up by discussions concerning the sensible substance.

As in al-Fārābī and Ibn Sīnā, so with Ibn Rushd the heavenly bodies are intermediaries between the first unmoved mover and the world of nature: they are moved by their desire to become similar (*tashabbuh*) to the First Mover,[44] and this motion in turn is the cause of the processes taking place in the physical world. Each heavenly body has an Intellect which desires the First Mover, and this desire is the cause of the circular motion of those bodies. Furthermore, all heavenly bodies are moved by the same final cause, in other words they desire the same beloved, namely the First Mover. It is not necessary to assume different final causes for each heavenly body; they may all desire the same object and nevertheless have different motions according to their own different natures, or according to their thinking and desiring different aspects of the First Mover.[45] On this point, Ibn Rushd distances himself from Ibn Sīnā as he does on the question of emanation, which is emphatically rejected.[46] The main reason alleged by Ibn Rushd in this is that the very idea of emanation implies the presence of potentiality in the thing which proceeds, or emanates, from something else. The notion of an eternal procession thus appears to him to be a contradiction in terms. He also denies the existence of a First above and distinct from the mover of the first heaven: nothing exists in vain and the sole justification for the existence of the heavenly Intellects is their being the movers of the spheres. In Ibn Sīnā's system the First is merely the source of the existence of the first heaven's Intellect, but is not itself a mover: it is consequently useless from Ibn Rushd's viewpoint.[47] If he rejects both the theory of emanation and the Ibn Sīnan demonstration of the First on the basis of the distinction between necessary and possible being, it is not because he is a doctrinaire Aristotelian, as is commonly asserted, but because the two tenets of the eternity of the world and of the primacy of motion are intimately bound up with each other; in other words, the only way in which a relation between an eternal God and an eternal universe can express itself is an eternal, and hence circular, motion.[48]

EMANATION

The very notion of emanation and the meaning of this term as used with reference to the cosmological system of Islamic philosophy are problematic. For al-Fārābī and Ibn Sīnā the heavenly bodies and their intellects arise one from the other as a consequence of their intellection (*ta'aqqul*).[49] But the term *fayḍ* which properly corresponds to emanation (overflow) suggests something quite different, namely a kind of spontaneous outpouring independent from any conscious activity; so also do the verbs *inbaʿatha* and *inbajasa* which are commonly found in the *Theology of Aristotle* and related texts where the light metaphor is also widespread as it is in Plotinus. But the continuous process evoked by those images appears hardly compatible with the hierarchy and discontinuous succession of discrete entities constituted by the heavenly spheres and their intellects found in al-Fārābī and Ibn Sīnā. The *falāsifah* were influenced, perhaps unwillingly, by creationist patterns which induced them to reflect in a more ontological sense the essentially cognitive processes of Greek Neoplatonism.

A much clearer idea of the distinction between creation (*ibdāʿ*) and emanation (*inbijās*, *inbiʿāth*) emerges in the developed form of the Ismāʿīlī system as we encounter it in the works of al-Sijistānī and al-Kirmānī in particular. Although the terminology of these authors in the cosmological field has much in common with that of the *falāsifah*, their conceptions differ from those of the latter in some important respects: God is described by them in more consistently negative terms than is the case with the philosophers. He cannot even be called a cause (*ʿillah*), for this implies the existence of an effect (*maʿlūl*), whereas He exists independently of His creation. Creation from nothing (*ibdāʿ*) is His exclusive prerogative. Through His word or command He creates the first intellect which is therefore also called the first created (*al-mubdaʿ al-awwal*). But the levels of being from the intellect downwards arise through emanation: the universal soul, nature, the heavenly spheres and the elements. Al-Kirmānī's system is more elaborate and complex in some respects than al-Sijistānī's, but the basic features, and in particular the distinctive functions of creation and emanation, are the same in both authors. The main innovation al-Kirmānī brought into the system inherited from al-Sijistānī, namely the double process of emanation giving rise on the one hand to the heavenly Intellects and on the other to the spheres[50] seems to be due to the influence of Ibn Sīnā.

As happened in Greek Neoplatonism, the number of hypostases ema-nating from the First tended in Islam to increase with time. A spectacular instance of this phenomenon is offered by Suhrawardī. The hierarchies of intellects and spheres are replaced in his cosmology by pure lights, and the First itself has become the light of lights (*nūr al-anwār*). But the Ibn Sīnan concepts have not been entirely discarded for all that: the expression *wājib al-wujūd* occurs in Suhrawardī, as well as the double movement of descending emanation and ascending desire (*shawq*). The proof of God's existence based on the impossibility of admitting an infinite series of contingent lights[51] is nothing but a reformulation of Ibn Sīnā's argument, derived itself from Aristotle. However, his exclusive use of light imagery, his "ontology of light", brings him closer to Plotinus than any of his predecessors.

The starting-point of some of the philosophical or theosophical onceptions underlying Ibn 'Arabī's system is also to be sought in the metaphysics of Ibn Sīnā; this appears for instance in his definition of God as necessarily being by Himself (*wājib al-wujūd bi-dhātihi*).[52] The central intuition of Ibn 'Arabī which commands the whole development of his thought is the idea of unity: not only God's absolute unity, but the unity of the totality of being considered as the epiphany of God. In a sense, this doctrine can be viewed as the logical outcome of emanationism carried to its ultimate consequences. This is the doctrine of the unity of being (*waḥdat al-wujūd*), in which all individual beings are conceived as mere manifestations (*tajalliyyāt*) of God. The question whether such a doctrine is open to the charge of pantheism cannot be discussed here, but should probably be answered in the negative. Ibn 'Arabī's idea appears to be that nothing can exist without being somewhat related to the source of all being, and to that extent can be regarded as an adaptation of the doctrine of eternal creation present in one form or another in the thought of all the *falāsifah*. But the manifestations of Ibn 'Arabī's cosmos are much more closely linked with the deity than are for instance the heavenly intellects of al-Fārābī or Ibn Sīnā; they do not have any ontological reality but are mere reflections of God in the human soul. Nevertheless the first (in a non-temporal sense) manifestations of God are described in terms which are borrowed from the traditional Neoplatonic hierarchy of hypostases (intellect, universal soul, nature).[53] The fact that the sequence of emanations closes upon itself in a circle and returns to God is quite consistent with the general structure of Neoplatonic metaphysics in which the return (*epistrophè*) is the necessary counterpart of procession (*proodos*).[54]

CONCLUSION

Concerning the place of philosophy in general, and of its metaphysical and cosmological doctrines in particular, within the civilization of Islam, three types of considerations are commonly expressed which reflect widely divergent viewpoints and are hard reconcile.

Firstly, Islamic philosophy is dominated and the course of its development has been largely shaped by the problem of harmonizing the Greek tradition with the monotheistic revelation of Islam.

Secondly, the thought of the *falāsifah* is in essence irreconcilable with certain tenets of Islamic theology especially in its Sunni form and in consequence became prematurely stifled after a short and brilliant flowering.

Thirdly, the Islamic philosophers worked under the threat of intellectual persecution and were therefore compelled to disguise their real thought or to present it in an allusive or allegorical form.

From the beginning, philosophy was regarded with suspicion by the traditional and conservative circles of Islam. But it is important to distinguish between different disciplines: large sections of philosophy, such as logic, ethics and politics, were quietly and lastingly absorbed into the mainstream of Islamic thought. The most dangerous discipline, as was already pointed out by al-Ghazzālī,[55] is metaphysics (in the sense of divine science, *ilāhiyyāt*) which can enter into direct conflict with traditional conceptions of God. But even within this rather narrow field it is important to note that of the three tenets which according to al-Ghazzālī should be branded with the accusation of unbelief (*kufr*), only one, namely the assertion of the eternity of the world, is really central in Greek and Islamic philosophy. The denial of God's knowledge of particular things and of the resurrection of the body are inferences drawn by Muslim scholars from some basic principles of Greek philosophy rather than philosophical doctrines expressly upheld by the philosophers. In the first stages of the development of philosophy in Islam, traditional Islamic thinking and philosophical speculation for the most part did not overlap. Some of the more important debating points were elaborated in Islam inreaction to philosophical principles (for instance occasionalism versus natural causality), very much in the same way as some Islamic practices seem to have developed as a conscious reaction against Christianity (e.g. image worship).[56] The Islamic philosophers followed the dicta of reason while seeking to create harmony between reason and revelation.[57] For example, the curious doctrine of emanation, as we have seen, may be regarded as an attempt to reconcile the idea of the eternity of the world with some form of creationism, and is linked with Ibn Sīnā's insistence that God is cause not only of motion but of being as well. But this notion of God as efficient cause of the world is already present in the last pagan philosophers of antiquity, notably Ammonius and Simplicius. The main themes taken up again and again in Islam link up directly with the debates of late Neoplatonism.

The first hostile reactions to philosophy that we know of, directed against al-Kindī, are probably to be related to the intra-Muslim controversy of traditionalism versus Mu'tazilism and to the philosopher's association with the Mu'tazilite caliphs. In some cases, as in the celebrated Sīrāfī-Mattā controversy, a kind of nationalistic reflex is perceptible whereby the old Arabic culture asserted itself against the new fangled disciplines borrowed from the Greeks.[58] The conscience of a substantial incompatibility between Qur'ānic revelation and philosophical rationalism arose in fact astonishingly slowly. But as traditionalist juridical Islam was growing aware of its own specificity, it could no longer tolerate any rival in the field of learning and education, with the exception of very technical disciplines such as mathematics or astronomy. Even medicine was suspicious, to say nothing of *kalām*. That the rise of the *'ulamā'*, the creation of *madrasah*s and the anti-philosophical reaction, all phenomena epitomized in the person of al-Ghazzālī, happened roughly at the same time is no coincidence.

As for the view that the *falāsifah* concealed their real convictions under the veil of symbols and feigned allegiance to Islam, it is not only intrinsically implausible but also in plain contradiction with the ascertainable facts. Such an esoteric approach makes sense only if the latent meaning of the texts can be made out by a discriminating reader; the proponents of this interpretation have not been able to bring forward any conclusive evidence in its favour.[59]

Philosophy did not die in Islam with Ibn Rushd. What may have died with him is philosophy as a fully autonomous discipline linking up without interruption with the Greek tradition. In order to survive, it had to merge with other currents of thought more thoroughly integrated in Islam such as Sufism, Shī'ī spirituality or *kalām*. To that extent the attacks of al-Ghazzālī and others led philosophy to achieve some sort of harmony with the *Sharī'ah*. Just as the development of *falsafah* had helped the *'ulamā'* to reach a deeper understanding of the specificity of Islam, so the progress of Islam led to the adaptation of philosophy to the needs of a different culture.

NOTES

1 The fullest account of the Arabic translations of Aristotle's *Metaphysics* is given by Bouyges, *Notice*, in Averroes (1952): cxv–cxxiv.
2 Excerpted by Ibn Rushd, see Averroes (1948): 1393ff., and Badawī (1947): 12–21 and 329–33.
3 On these texts see in particular Endress (1973).
4 Al-Kindī (1950): 95ff. = (1978): 26ff.
5 *Ibid.*: 110ff. = (1978): 42ff.
6 *Ibid.*: 142–3 = (1978): 82.
7 *Ibid.*: 384.
8 Al-Fārābī (1961): 132.
9 *Ibid.*: 130.
10 Al-Fārābī, *Fī aghrāḍ al-ḥakīm fī kull maqālah min al-kitāb al-mawsūm bi'l-ḥurūf*, in al-Fārābī (1890): 35.
11 Ibn Sīnā (1960): 14–15.
12 *Ibid.*: 6.
13 *Ibid.*: 13–14.
14 *Ibid.*: 21–2.

15 Averroes (1938–48).

16 Averroes (1948): 1424 provides a particularly clear instance of the complete equivalence of *al-'ilm al-ilāhī* or *al-falsafat al-ūlā* with the study of *al-mawjūd bi-mā huwa mawjūd* or *al-jawhar bi-mā huwa jawhar.*

17 Aristotle, *Metaphysics,* E.1.1026a,19.

18 Averroes (1942): 710, 5–712, 15.

19 *Ibid.*: 935, 16–14. The word translated as "task" is *'amal.* The sentence is slightly confused because Ibn Rushd is paraphrasing an erroneous translation of Aristotle, *Metaphysics,* Z.11.1037a.14–16.

20 Al-Kindī (1950): 183 = (1978): 135.

21 *Ibid.*: 226, 231, etc.

22 *Ibid.*: 330.

23 *Ibid.*: 255.

24 *Ibid.*: 162, 260.

25 *Ibid.*: 162 = (1978): 106–7.

26 Al-Fārābī (1985).

27 See on this Druart (1987).

28 Walzer (1985): 345, 348, 362.

29 *Ibid.*: 118–34.

30 See Druart (1981).

31 Badawī (1947): 24.

32 Ibn Sīnā (1960): 36.

33 *Ibid.*: 347.

34 *Ibid.*: 354.

35 *Ibid.*: 383.

36 *Ibid.*: 387–8.

37 *Ibid.*: 389. This is the celebrated formula of Plato's *Theaetetus,* 176b which became one of the standard definitions of philosophy in late Greek and Arabic commentaries. See e.g. Ibn al-Ṭayyib (1975): 18.

38 Ibn Sīnā (1960): 390.

39 *Ibid.*: 406–7.

40 *Ibid.*: 413.

41 Netton (1989): 167.

42 Averroes (1948): 1630–2.

43 *Ibid.*: 1423.

44 See above, n. 37.

45 Averroes (1948): 1649. Kogan (1985): 200 wants to separate the spheres' desire from their intellects, but this interpretation is in complete contradiction with Ibn Rushd's statements. See Averroes (1948): 1596–8.

46 *Ibid.*: 1652.

47 *Ibid.*: 1648.

48 Concerning the importance of motion in Ibn Rushd's metaphysics see Kogan (1985): 206ff.

49 For the idea of contemplation as source of being in Greek philosophy see Plotinus, *Enneads,* 3.8; Proclus (1963): prop. 174 and Dodds's note on this passage. It is interesting to note that the main texts setting forth this fundamental doctrine do not appear to have been translated into Arabic. There have

clearly been other channels than the translations known to us through which Neoplatonic conceptions percolated into the Islamic world.

50 Netton (1989): 225–9.

51 *Ibid.*: 258.

52 *Ibid.*: 270.

53 *Ibid.*: 281–2.

54 I cannot understand Netton's remark (1989): 280, following Afifi, that the Neoplatonic system "moves in a straight line".

55 Al-Ghazzālī (1959): 23.

56 Grabar (1987): 132–8.

57 Even in the case of a late work like Ibn Ṭufayl's *Ḥayy ibn Yaqẓān* the earlier view of Gauthier that it was concerned above all with the harmony of philosophy and religion has been refuted by Hourani (1956).

58 Mahdi (1970); Zimmermann (1986): 111.

59 For a decisive rebuttal of such theories see Leaman (1985): 182–201.

BIBLIOGRAPHY

Averroes (1938–48) *Tafsīr mā ba'd aṭ-ṭabī'at*, ed. M. Bouyges (Bibliotheca Arabica Scholasticorum 5–7 (Beirut).

— (1952) *Notice* by M. Bouyges (Beirut).

Badawī, A. (1947) *Arisṭū 'ind al-'arab* (Cairo).

Druart, T. A. (1981) "Al-Fārābī's causation of the heavenly bodies", *Islamic Philosophy and Mysticism*, ed. P. Morewedge (New York): 35–45.

— (1987) "Al-Farabi and Emanationism", *Studies in Philosophy and the History of Philosophy*, 17: 23–43.

Endress, G. (1973) *Proclus Arabus* (Beiruter Texte und Studien 10) (Beirut).

Al-Fārābī (1961) *Falsafah Arisṭūṭālīs*, ed. M. Mahdi (Beirut).

— (1890) *Philosophische Abhandlungen*, ed. F. Dieterici (Leiden).

— (1985), *see* Walzer (1985).

Al-Ghazzālī (1959) *al-Munqidh min al-ḍalāl* ("The Deliverer from Error"), ed. F. Jabre (Beirut).

Grabar, O. (1973) *The Formation of Islamic Art* (New Haven).

Hourani, G. (1956) "The Principal Subject of Ḥayy ibn Yaqẓān", *Journal of Near Eastern Studies*, 15: 40–6.

Ibn Rushd, *see* Averroes.

Ibn Sīnā (1960) *Al-Shifā'. Al-Ilāhiyyāt*, ed. G. C. Anawati and S. Zayed, 2 vols (Cairo).

Ibn al-Ṭayyib (1975) *Commentary on Porphyry's Eisagoge*, ed. K. Gyekye (Beirut).

Al-Kindī (1950) *Rasā'il falsafiyyah*, ed. M. Abū Rīdah, 1 (Cairo).

— (1978) *Rasā'il falsafiyyah*, ed. M. Abū Rīdah, 2nd ed. (Cairo).

Kogan, Barry S. (1985) *Averroes and the Metaphysics of Causation* (New York).

Leaman, O. (1985) *An Introduction to Medieval Islamic Philosophy* (Cambridge).

— (1988) *Averroes and his Philosophy* (Oxford).

Mahdi, M. (1970) "Language and Logic in Classical Islam", *Logic in Classical Islamic Culture* (First Giorgio Levi della Vida Conference), ed. G. E. von Grunebaum (Wiesbaden).

Netton, I. (1989) *Allah Transcendent* (London).
Proclus (1963) *The Elements of Theology*, ed. E. R. Dodds, 2nd ed. (Oxford).
Walzer, R. (1985) *Al-Farabi on the Perfect State* (Oxford).
Zimmermann, F. W. (1986) "The Origins of the so-called *Theology of Aristotle*", *Pseudo-Aristotle in the Middle Ages* (Warburg Institute Surveys and Texts 11) (London).

CHAPTER 48

Logic

Shams Inati

The task of this chapter is extremely difficult, not only because it is impossible to cover in one short chapter the long history of the field of Arabic logic and the enormous quantity of material encompassed by it but also because many Arabic logical writings have not reached us. In addition, of those works that have reached us, many are still in manuscript form. Thus, it must be stressed at the outset that this is not the full story of Arabic logic or even the recounting of all its important elements, as a comprehensive study of the field is not possible at this point. Rather, this is a modest attempt to trace the outline of the history of Arabic logic, pointing out within the space allowed some of the essential features of this field which are accessible to us.

Historians differ regarding the date of the beginning of the movement of the translation of Greek logic into Arabic, a movement that helped shape Arabic logic and philosophy. Some are of the opinion that this took place during the Umayyad period (*c.* 40/661–133/750); others believe it took place in the first century of the ʿAbbāsid period (*c.* 133/750–235/850). Regardless of when this activity began, however, the following points concerning the history of the development of Arabic logic remain uncontested.

The highest point in the movement of translation of Greek logic into Arabic occurred during the third/ninth and fourth/tenth centuries. This was achieved primarily at the House of Wisdom, established in 217/832 by the ʿAbbāsid caliph al-Maʾmūn (199/813–218/833).

For the most part these translations were made from Syriac, not directly from Greek. Even as early as a few centuries before the advent of Islam, Nestorians in the East and Jacobites in the West engaged in translating Greek scientific and philosophical works into Syriac. The Syriac translation movement was enhanced especially after some of the Syriac-speaking people, such as the well-known Jacob of Edessa (d. 708) and

George, bishop of the Arabs (d. 724), studied at Alexandria, where Greek culture flourished. These Syriac translations were made mainly at schools and monasteries in Persia, Iraq, Syria and Egypt, the first countries with which Arabs came into contact in the early period of the Islamic conquests.[1]

The most prominent translators of Greek logic into Arabic were 'Abd Allāh ibn al-Muqaffa' (d. 139/757);[2] Yaḥyā (Yuḥannā) ibn al-Biṭrīq (d. 215/830);[3] Ḥunayn ibn Isḥāq (d. 877);[4] his son, Isḥāq ibn Ḥunayn (d. 910); his nephew, Ḥubaysh ibn al-Ḥasan al-Dimashqī, known as Ḥubaysh al-A'sam (d. 890); Abū Bishr Mattā ibn Yunus (d. 940);[5] Abū Zakariyyā' Yaḥyā ibn 'Adī (d. 973);[6] Ibrāhīm ibn 'Abd Allāh (d. 297/940); and Abū 'Uthmān Sa'īd ibn Ya'qūb al-Dimashqī (d. 308/920).

In its early stages, the movement of translation of Greek logical works into Arabic focused on Porphyry's (d. 304) *Isagoge*,[7] as well as Aristotle's *Categories*, *De interpretatione* and *Prior Analytics*. Aristotle's *Posterior Analytics* was not introduced into Arabic before the tenth century. Its introduction into Arabic and the high place it occupied in Arabic logic, as will be seen later, mark a break with the Syriac tradition that did not seem to go beyond *Prior Analytics*.[8] In this period, attention was also given to Galen's (d. 200) *Introduction to Logic*, and the works of Aristotle's commentators, such as Theophrastus (d. 287 B.C.), Alexander of Aphrodisias (d. 222), Themistius (d. 387), Ammonius (d. 520) and John Philoponus (d. 540). Other works, or parts of them, were translated and were not considered as important. Such works include Aristotle's *Topics, Sophistics, Rhetoric* and *Poetics*.

The ninth and tenth centuries witnessed not only what may in some cases be the first translations of Greek logical works into Arabic but also further improvements upon these translations, and even summaries and expansions of, and commentaries on, these works. The commentaries, which were emulated by future commentators, such as Ibn Rushd (d. 595/1198), were of three types: great, middle and short. Basically, these commentaries were similar in structure to those of the Syriac tradition. A great commentary consists of a quoted passage from the text in view followed by a long discussion of this passage. A middle commentary is a paraphrase of a passage from the text followed by a discussion of this passage. A short commentary is primarily a summary of the main ideas of the text.[9] In contrast to the Syriac tradition, however, Arabic commentaries of this and later periods modify this basic form either by adding to or subtracting from the text certain ideas.[10]

Arabic commentaries on Greek logic (excluding those of al-Kindī) and, more importantly, the creativity in Arabic logic flourished from the tenth to the fourteenth centuries – first in the East and then in the West. Some of the important commentators were Abū Bakr al-Rāzī (d. 313/925), al-Fārābī (d. 339/950), Ibn Sīnā (d. 429/1037) and Ibn Rushd.

Almost up to the end of the tenth century, the leading logicians, with the exception of al-Fārābī, were Christians.[11] After that, logic took on an Islamic guise, as it became a tool employed by eminent Muslim thinkers against each other and against non-Muslims, such as Christians and Jews, in an attempt to defend Islamic causes. In fact, in early Islam the main reason for Muslims' interest in Greek logic seems to have been their need for debating with each other over issues such as those of freedom and determinism, and for debating with others, like the Christians, over issues such as that of the Trinity.

Approximately from the end of the fourteenth century on, Arabic logic is marked by lack of creativity, appearing to have become in the main a reiteration of previous views, commentaries on commentaries, or syllabi for class use. In particular, *al-Risālat al-shamsiyyah* by al-Qazwīnī (d. 675/1276) and *Maṭāli' al-anwār* by al-Urmawī (d. 682/1283)[12] and even commentaries on these works became the subject of the commentaries of this period. One may say, therefore, that the development of Arabic logic ends by the fourteenth century, as the field continues its stagnation from that period.

In Islamic circles, Greek logic had its proponents, who made every effort to point out its value and defend its use, but it also had its opponents, who saw no value in it. Of the first group, some, such as Ibn Rushd, accepted it almost in its entirety and played the role of the commentator on, and explicator of, Aristotle's logical writings. Others, such as al-Fārābī, Ibn Sīnā, Ibn Ḥazm (d. 454/1064), al-Ghazzālī (d. 505/1111) and Ibn Khaldūn (d. 808/1406), accepted most of its basic principles but expanded it in ways that befitted their culture, language and religious beliefs. The second group, such as Ibn Taymiyyah (d. 728/1328) and al-Ṣuyūṭī (d. 911/1505), rejected it in its entirety.

Since this chapter is a part of a history of Islamic philosophy, we will concentrate primarily on the first group, which includes the most prominent Muslim philosophers, and pay special attention to al-Fārābī and Ibn Sīnā, who seem to have been the first and most eminent Arabic logicians to modify Greek logic to suit their linguistic and cultural purposes. Thus, they may be said to have introduced some original elements into Greek logic and to have set the ground for the further development of logic.

Like most other Arabic logicians, al-Fārābī and Ibn Sīnā began their logical works not with a discussion of the *Categories*, as dictated by the Aristotelian tradition, but with discussions called for primarily by the nature of the Arabic language, the Islamic religion and the philosophical trends of the day that were to a great measure shaped by the Alexandrian and Syriac traditions. In some cases, these introductory discussions appear in works considered introductions (*madkhal*) to logic. This is not to say that such works were not considered a part of logic. Ibn Sīnā's *Madkhal*, for example, includes such discussions and is considered by its author to be the first of the nine parts of logic.[13] In other cases, however, such discussions appear in works or sections of works that do not seem to be intended as a part of logic. An example of this is al-Fārābī's *al-Alfāẓ al-musta'malah fi'l-manṭiq* ("Book of Expressions Used in Logic"). Furthermore, these discussions did not follow the same order even in the different writings of the same author. Regardless, they seem to focus primarily on the meaning of the term *logic*, the function and benefit of logic, the relation of logic to grammar and to language in general, the relation of logic to philosophy and, finally, the predicables, i.e., the subject of Porphyry's *Isagoge*.

It is primarily in such discussions that Arabic logicians exhibited originality. For this reason, a large portion of this chapter will be devoted to a study of these matters. Let us, therefore, first explicate the meaning of logic as understood by Arabic logicians and then move on to study briefly the rest of these introductory elements, beginning with the function and benefit of logic and ending with the predicables. This will be followed by a brief account of the *Organon*,[14] or the parts of logic, and their essential elements as understood by these logicians.

THE MEANING OF *MANṬIQ* (LOGIC)

The Arabic word *manṭiq* meant in the Arabic language *kalām* (speech).[15] Prior to the development of Arabic logic, this word was in use in its Greek form, which also gave it the added logical meaning it acquired in Islamic philosophy. In the Qur'ān, for example, the word *manṭiq* is used in the sense of speech.[16] The verb form of the word is also mentioned in the Qur'ān in the same sense.[17]

To facilitate the translation of the Greek logical writings into Arabic and the summaries, commentaries on and expansion of these works, Arabic thinkers felt the need to coin new words or to give new meaning to words that already existed in the Arabic language. Al-Kindī, for example, coined the words *huwiyyah* (essence), *māhiyyah* (quiddity), *al-ays* (existence) and *al-lays* (non-existence).[18] The word *manṭiq* was among the Arabic words that took on added meanings. Thus, the word *al-nuṭq* (utterance), from which the word *manṭiq* is derived, acquired three meanings, which it had for the ancients, as al-Fārābī observes:[19]

> (1) The power with which a human being grasps the intelligibles. This is the power with which one acquires the sciences and crafts, and by means of which one can distinguish between good and bad deeds. (2) The intelligibles that occur to the human soul by virtue of comprehension. These intelligibles are called by the

> ancients "internal utterance". (3) The expression of thought by the tongue.[20] This is called by the ancients "external utterance".[21]

The "craft" under consideration came to be known as *al-manṭiq* because

> it provides the rational power with rules concerning internal utterance, i.e., the intelligibles, and rules common to all tongues with regard to external utterance, i.e., the expression, and gives the rational power good direction towards the truth in both matters and rescues it from falsehood in both of them.[22]

Therefore, the meaning of the name of the field under consideration indicates the purpose of this field.[23]

THE FUNCTION AND BENEFIT OF LOGIC

Muslim philosophers found it necessary to justify the enormous attention and energy they devoted to the study of logic and to point out the reasons for opening their philosophical works with this study. They did so by discussing and elaborating the important function and the indispensable use of this field. Building on the views of his predecessors, especially al-Fārābī, Ibn Sīnā took the lead in this regard.[24] He argued that logic is the key to knowledge,[25] and knowledge is the key to happiness, the ultimate human objective. Thus, logic is the key to happiness and must be fully understood and properly utilized at the outset if happiness is to be achieved. The understanding of this claim requires the understanding of three points: firstly, the nature of knowledge, secondly, the reason why logic is necessary for knowledge and, thirdly, the manner in which knowledge leads to happiness. While the first and second points are discussed in detail in the logical writings of these philosophers, the third is only touched upon there and is detailed in their metaphysical and mystical writings.[26]

Firstly, along Aristotelian lines, knowledge is divided into two types, conception (*taṣawwur*) and assent or judgment (*taṣdīq*).[27] This bipartite division of knowledge is a common feature of Arabic logical writings, whether earlier or later, whether belonging to the philosophical circle or to the religious one.[28] Conception is defined as the mental grasping of an object apart from any assertion as to whether or not the object corresponds to the external reality it is supposed to represent.[29] This mental object is the concept and can be of three kinds: simple, that is, without possibility for having parts; single, that is, if having parts (which it may), these parts cannot have separate meanings inasmuch as they are its parts; and composite, that is, with no less than one single concept as a part of it. An example of a simple concept is "God"; an example of a single concept is "human being"; and an example of a composite concept is "mortal, rational animal". Assent is also the mental grasping of an object, but with the assertion that the relation of correspondence between this object and the external reality it represents is true.[30] This does not mean that assent is always true but only that it is an assertion of the truth. In itself, assent can be either true or false. It must be mentioned though that occasionally the term *assent* is used in the sense of true judgment,[31] but this is not the general use of the word in Arabic logic.

Secondly, the objects of conception, or concepts, are either known or unknown, as are the objects of assent. Furthermore, an object, whether of conception or assent, is known relative to a mind.[32] This is to say that an object can be known by George but not by Jerry. This is so with the exception of a small number of concepts and assents that are evident to any healthy-minded individual.[33] Such concepts are exemplified by "being" and "thing". And such assents are exemplified by "the angles of every triangle are equal to two right angles"[34] and "every 3 is an odd number".[35] These self-evident objects al-Fārābī calls "the customary, primary, well-known knowledge, which one may deny by one's tongue, but which one cannot deny by one's mind since it is impossible to think their contrary".[36] In contrast to the known objects of conception and of assent, which are not the subject of inquiry, the unknown objects of conception and of assent are the subject of inquiry but, of course, only to the individuals to whom these objects are unknown. The more one reduces the number of unknown objects, whether of conception or of assent, the higher the degree of knowledge one achieves.

This reduction in the number of unknown objects can be made by means of movement from what is known to what is unknown. The movement from a known object of conception to an unknown one is through the "explanatory phrase", and the movement from a known object of assent to an unknown one is through the "proof". The explanatory phrase is of two types: definition and description, both of which will be discussed later. Suffice it to say here that the purpose of a real and a complete definition[37] is to determine the essence of a thing.[38]

Before the proof is discussed, a presentation is given of the proposition, a true or false phrase and which is a part of the proof. While not ignoring the Aristotelian categorical or predicative propositions, Arabic logicians, including Ibn Rushd, the strongest defender of Aristotle among them, follow in the footsteps of Themistius and the Stoics in studying conditional propositions.[39] The proof, which consists of propositions (which in turn consist of concepts either conjoined or separated by certain particles), is of three types: analogy, induction and syllogism.

Analogy is a judgment about a particular thing. This judgment is drawn from the similarity between that thing and another particular one.

But while a particular judgment may be useful in certain practical matters, it does not give knowledge. Knowledge is only of the universal, as we shall see later. That is why analogy is considered the weakest form of proof. Induction is a judgment about a universal. This judgment is drawn from judgments about particular cases. If the judgment of the induction applies to all the members of the class, the conclusion is certain and the induction demonstrative. If the judgment applies to the majority of the members of the class, the conclusion is probable and the induction is an incorrect science. However, in either type of induction, the universality of the subject makes this type of proof more reliable than analogy.

Like Aristotle, Arabic logicians consider the syllogism the most reliable form of the proof and demonstration the most reliable form of the syllogism. A syllogism is a discourse in which the premisses necessarily lead to the conclusion. A demonstration is a syllogism in which the certainty of the premisses necessarily leads to the certainty of the conclusion. The definition employed as a principle in the demonstration identifies the cause of the essence of the subject, this cause being the middle term. For this reason, the definition on which the demonstrative conclusion is based is of the real and incomplete type.[40] Given the limitation of space, much has been omitted from this discussion of the proof. Our purpose here was just to give a brief overview of the role of the types of proof in knowledge and the link between definition and knowledge of the type of assent.

The concepts in the explanatory phrase and the assents in the proof must already be known; otherwise, the explanatory phrase and the proof cannot lead us to knowledge.[41] Not all such primary knowledge is necessary for logic, however. Rather, some of it is necessary for logic, while the rest is necessary for one or the other of the remaining sciences.[42]

In addition to known concepts in the explanatory phrase and known assents in the proof, the attainment of knowledge requires certain rules in accordance with which the explanatory phrase and the proof are properly formed. Logic provides the rules for determining the properly formed or valid from the improperly formed or invalid explanatory phrase and proof. By the distinction it makes between the true and the false, the valid and the invalid, it protects human thought from falling into falsehood and, therefore, secures for us the path to knowledge.[43] As a set of rules that governs thought, logic is called, among other things, *mīzān* (the scale),[44] *mi'yār* (the standard)[45] and *miḥakk al-naẓr* (the test of thought).[46]

Thirdly, the knowledge that is necessary for happiness is not the grasping of just any object. Rather, it is the grasping of the essences or natures of things, primarily the essence or nature of God. This is so because essences are the eternal, most complete and most beautiful aspects of the universe, and to grasp them is to become like them, since the knower and the known are identical. It is in the mirroring of eternity, completion and beauty that metaphysical perfection and, hence, happiness lies. The grasping of the external elements of things is not useless for the pursuit of happiness; on the contrary, it helps to prepare the way for this theoretical knowledge.[47] But, in itself, this type of grasping cannot lead to happiness, as its objects are perishable and deficient.

From the above, it should be clear that Arabic logic is not simply a theoretical science or an exercise in reasoning purely for the sake of the exercise of reasoning. Rather, it has a strong metaphysical bent that gives it practicality and applicability to the most important human concern, namely that of self-perfection, or happiness.[48]

It is worth noting that some religious scholars, such as Ibn Ḥazm and al-Ghazzālī, agree with the philosophers that logic is of great value. While these religious scholars do not specifically advocate the idea that logic is necessary for the ultimate human happiness, they still find it useful not only for secular but also for religious studies,[49] rejecting the claims that it can be harmful to religion. Ibn Ḥazm, for example, says that logic not only distinguishes us from other animals but also helps us understand God's intention as conveyed to us through His speech.[50] He believes that logic has been wrongly charged with helping the cause of disbelief, claiming this charge is made by those who have neither understood the concepts incorporated in Aristotle's logical works nor even read those works.[51] He cites passages from the Qur'ān calling on people not to argue over issues they do not understand and for which they have no evidence.[52] Ignorance, according to Ibn Ḥazm, has also led some to consider Aristotle's logical works as incomprehensible nonsense and idle talk.[53] Others have also rejected these works, not having understood them because of reading them after having "already accepted the ignorants' view that these are books of disbelief".[54]

If, on the other hand, one turns to these works with a "pure" and a "healthy" mind, "one will be enlightened by them and will understand their objectives; thus one will be guided by their light, and God's oneness will be proven to one through inevitable, necessary demonstrations. One will also witness the division of creatures, God's effect on them, and His management of them."[55] Claiming to speak as one who desires one's God and who does not know other than what God taught us, Ibn Ḥazm asserts that explicating Aristotle's logical works will perhaps earn him the pleasure of God, owing to "the great benefit of these works".[56]

Both Ibn Ḥazm and al-Ghazzālī agree that among the reasons that led to the ignorance of Greek logical works, and hence to the rejection of these works, is the unfamiliar language in which these works were introduced.[57] Realizing that not all language can be comprehended by everybody, they were determined to correct this matter by presenting logic in simple, ordinary language which could be understood by everybody, including, as Ibn Ḥazm puts it, "the commoner and the elite, as well as the knower and the ignorant".[58] Before moving on to the next issue, it must be said that the acceptance of logic by Muslim thinkers of the stature of Ibn Ḥazm and al-Ghazzālī was no doubt a main factor in the reconciliation between logic and the religious studies. This reconciliation, in turn, helped the flourishing of logic in the twelfth and thirteenth centuries.

THE RELATION OF LOGIC TO GRAMMAR

As soon as logic was introduced into Arabic and began to permeate the various branches of Islamic studies, it was faced with a strong resistance by different Islamic groups, among the first of whom were the grammarians. These groups saw in logic an element of a non-Islamic foreign civilization that threatened their religion, language and grammar. The grammarians' resistance to logic reached its highest point in the tenth century. The best-known grammarian opponents to logic included Abu'l-'Abbās al-Nāshī';[59] Ibn Qutaybah;[60] Ibn al-Athīr;[61] and Abū Sa'īd al-Sīrāfī (d. 979), best known for his debate against the leading logician of his day, Abū Bishr Mattā, which is said to have taken place in 932. This debate was recorded by Abū Ḥayyān al-Tawḥīdī in his works *al-Imtā' wa'l-mu'ānasah* and *al-Muqābasāt*.[62]

This debate consists of a severe attack on the logicians for their high regard for an innovation introduced by a Greek[63] in accordance with conventions of the Greek language, even though the logicians did not master the Greek language, while at the same time admitting that language is a necessary means for doing logic.[64] On more than one occasion in this debate we see al-Sīrāfī challenging Mattā to give the meanings of the same expression put in different grammatical forms to show that the grammar of a specific language is necessary for grasping the meanings, or intelligibles, as the logicians call them, and that knowledge of Aristotle's logic will not help them do so.[65] The approval with which al-Sīrāfī's success in this debate was met, even by the vizier, Abu'l-Fatḥ al-Faḍl ibn Ja'far ibn al-Furāt, indicates that the general mood at that time was against logic and logicians.

The points advanced by the grammarians were mainly of three types: (1) the frequent use of dialectical discourse or of instructions in geometry and the science of number – in short, in reasoning – suffices for logic;[66] (2) logic is an unnecessary additional good, for it is possible for a person with a perfect native intelligence to have sound thought without any prior knowledge of logic;[67] and (3) contrary to grammar, which is self-sufficient, logic is dependent on, and can be replaced by, language and, more particularly, grammar.[68] As such, the grammarians argued that logic is unnecessary for the sciences, since the frequency of reasoning, native intelligence or grammar can replace it.

The logicians, headed by al-Fārābī and Ibn Sīnā, responded to these objections and also defended the necessity of logic for the pursuit of philosophy and hence happiness, pointing out the role that language and, more particularly, grammar play in this regard. Al-Fārābī, for example, responds to the first objection by saying that to make such a claim is similar to claiming that the frequent use of poetry memorization and recitation suffices for grammatically sound discourse and protects one against committing grammatical errors.[69] Again, the second claim, he says, is similar to the claim that grammar is unnecessary, for there may be somebody who does not deviate from the correct use of the language without any prior knowledge of the rules of grammar.[70]

Ibn Sīnā goes further in responding to the second objection. He contends that it is possible for a proper definition and a proper proof to emerge in one's natural mind, but this would not be the result of a skill and, thus, could not protect one against falsehood in other circumstances. Rather, such an act would be like hitting the target unintentionally.[71] If natural intelligence were sufficient to develop such a skill, there would have been neither the disagreements among thinkers nor the self-contradiction that we see within particular thinkers' work.[72] He realizes that even if one has acquired such a skill, one would not be fully protected against falsehood. This is because it is possible for one at times not to use this skill effectively owing to incomplete mastery of it, negligence or other incapacitating factors. However, one who has this skill and who uses it does not fall into as much falsehood as does one who lacks it.[73] Ibn Sīnā draws a contrast between logic on the one hand and grammar and metre on the other. He says that it is possible for a good natural intelligence to play the role of grammar in securing sound discourse, as it is possible for good taste to play the role of metre for composing poetry. But nothing can play the role of logic in securing sound thought except the guidance of God.[74]

Before discussing the logicians' response to the third objection, it may be helpful to consider their stand concerning the manner in which the functions of grammar and logic compare and differ. Al-Fārābī, for example, asserts that there is a similarity between logic and grammar, but he reminds us that there is also a difference between the two. Logic and grammar are similar in that as logic is a set of rules governing thought or the intelligibles, so is grammar a set of rules governing expressions.[75] They differ, however, in that logic is a set of universal rules that apply to human thought and the expressions that signify human thought, regardless of time, place or language; while grammar is a set of particular rules that apply only to specific languages.[76] In other words, logic deals with language, but only inasmuch as language has common conditions. Such conditions are exemplified in the fact that expressions are either single or composite, and that the single is either a noun, a verb or a particle. However, logic does not deal with the Arabic language, for example, inasmuch as the agent is in the nominative and the object in the accusative.[77]

Al-Fārābī's response to the third objection can be found in *Kitāb al-tanbīh 'alā sabīl al-sa'ādah*, where he recognizes that grammar can play an important role in facilitating the logical process. Primary knowledge, he tells us, which is instinctive, i.e., present to all minds from the beginning of their existence, may not be perceived by the individual who has it. However, when hearing expressions that signify this knowledge, one realizes that such knowledge was already present in one's mind. Furthermore, the elements of such knowledge may not be distinct in one's mind such that one comprehends every one of these elements separately. However, when one hears expressions that signify such elements, one comprehends them as distinct in the mind. In short, if one is unaware of the presence of some primary notions or is unaware of their distinctness, then one must enunciate the expressions that signify these notions.[78] From this the conclusion is drawn that: "Since the craft of grammar . . . includes the various types of signifying expressions, it must, therefore, have some kind of worth for the study and understanding of the primary principles of logic."[79] It is important to note that al-Fārābī here does not say that grammar is necessary for logic, as the grammarians claim, but that it has "some worth" for it. This worth consists in its governing the *common elements* of the *signifying expressions*, for such expressions form a part of the subject of logic. Al-Fārābī identifies the subject or subjects of logic in this way: "The subjects of logic concerning which the rules of logic are given, are the intelligibles inasmuch as they are signified by the expressions, and the expressions inasmuch as they signify the intelligibles."[80]

In addition to being a clear rejection of the grammarians' positions, Ibn Sīnā's response to the third objection constitutes an expansion of some aspects of al-Fārābī's view and a rejection of some of its other aspects. He clearly states that it is necessary for the logician to study expressions. However, inasmuch as one is a logician, one has no primary preoccupation with expressions except for the purpose of grasping the intelligibles and facilitating dialogue and communication.[81] He continues:

> Were it possible to learn logic through pure thought in which only intelligibles by themselves are recognized, that would be sufficient. Also, were it possible for the interlocutor in logic to grasp the intelligibles in his soul through a means other than language, this would be sufficient for dispensing with expressions altogether. However, since it is necessary to use expressions,

> especially in that reason cannot arrange the intelligibles without imagining their expressions, . . . it is necessary that the different states of expressions result in different states of the intelligibles that correspond to these expressions. As such, these intelligibles acquire conditions, which they would not have had, were it not for the expressions.[82]

It is for this reason alone, according to Ibn Sīnā, that some parts of logic came to be concerned "with the study of the states of expressions".[83] He is convinced that any discourse about expressions that have corresponding intelligibles is similar to a discourse about those intelligibles.[84] However, he maintains that it would be inappropriate to conclude from this that such expressions form the subject or a part of the subject of logic; for, after all, even the corresponding intelligibles to these expressions cannot play that role. He puts it thus: "There is no merit in the statement of those who say that the subject of logic is the study of expressions inasmuch as they signify the intelligibles, and that the logician's craft is to discuss expressions inasmuch as they signify the intelligibles."[85]

In short, according to Ibn Sīnā, neither language as governed by grammar forms the subject of logic, as grammarians claimed, nor even the expressions that signify their corresponding intelligibles form a part of the subject of logic, as al-Fārābī claimed. Rather, logic is concerned with expressions only inasmuch as they have different states due to which the states of the intelligibles in the soul become different. The very subject of logic is identified as nothing other than "the intelligibles inasmuch as they are employed in the composition by means of which they induce in our minds the acquisition of some things which were not in our minds, and not inasmuch as they are things".[86] The same idea is expressed in *al-Madkhal*, where it is said that logic is not concerned with things inasmuch as they exist externally or in the mind, or inasmuch as they are separate quiddities, "but inasmuch as they are predicates and subjects, universal and particular, etc.".[87]

This amounts to saying that the subject of logic is the intelligibles, not inasmuch as they are intelligibles and are signified by expressions, but inasmuch as they have different states whose composition in the explanatory phrase and proof leads from the known to the unknown. Therefore, while the expressions are not the concern of the logician because they signify intelligibles, they are his or her concern because they have states, the difference among which reflects the difference among the states of the intelligibles. To put it another way, neither language nor grammar is the ultimate objective of the logician. Rather, language is necessary for logic, but inasmuch as it is the only vehicle that reflects or mirrors states and interrelations of the intelligibles. In other words, language is a necessary means for reaching the object of logic, but it is accidental to the nature of this object. Thus it does not enter in the definition of the subject of logic.

Another group of Arabic thinkers took a middle ground concerning the conflict between the grammarians and logicians. This group, headed by al-Tawḥīdī and his teacher, al-Sijistānī (d. *c.* 378/988), argued that whatever is true of logic is true of grammar, and vice versa. This is so because logic and grammar are two sides of the same thing, the former governing the internal aspect of expressions, and the latter governing their external aspect.[88]

THE RELATION OF LOGIC TO PHILOSOPHY

One of the issues that preoccupied Arabic logicians was whether logic is a part of or an instrument of philosophy. The controversy over this issue emerged in ancient times. The Platonists considered logic both a part and an instrument of philosophy; the Peripatetics considered it only an instrument of philosophy; and the Stoics considered it only a part of philosophy.

The history of Arabic logic is full of references to the idea that logic is an instrument (*ālah*) of philosophy.[89] However, some, such as Ibn Sīnā, spoke of logic at times as an instrument and at other times as a science, i.e., as a part of philosophy.[90] This is because he finds no conflict in considering logic both as an instrument of and as a part of philosophy. The conflict, he asserts, arises from using the term *philosophy* in two different senses. If *philosophy* is used in the sense of the study of "things inasmuch as they exist and are divided into the two types of existence", meaning the external and the mental, then logic is not "a part of philosophy. But inasmuch as logic is useful for this study, it is an instrument of philosophy." If, on the other hand, *philosophy* is used in the sense of the study of "every theoretical matter and from every point of view", then logic is "a part of philosophy and an instrument of the other parts of philosophy".[91] According to him, to engage in a dispute over such a matter is to engage in falsehood, because the two positions are not contradictory, and in futility, because concerning oneself with such a matter leads to no benefit.[92]

THE FIVE PREDICABLES

On the whole Porphyry's predicables, or universal terms (genus, species, difference, property and common accident), are adhered to in Arabic logic, both in number and in basic meaning. It is true that a sixth term, the individual (*al-shakhṣ*), is added to Porphyry's terms by the Ikhwān al-Ṣafā', but the term does not seem to have acquired acceptance in Arabic circles.[93] However, Arabic logicians elaborated these terms extensively, disagreeing at times with earlier views over certain details concerning these terms. Ibn Sīnā, for example, rejects the ancients' idea that a concomitant which attaches to more than one universal subject – as "two-footed" attaches to "human being" – is a property in the real sense.[94] Thus, he dismisses this type, considering it unworthy even of discussion.[95]

Arabic logicians seem to have been interested in studying the five predicables extensively, not just for the purpose of understanding these terms in themselves but primarily for a higher purpose, namely, that of determining the role these terms play in knowledge. This higher purpose required them to distinguish first between the single and the composite, the universal and the particular, the essential and the accidental to isolate the basic components of the definition and the other principles of knowledge. Ibn Sīnā's distinction among these terms is particularly detailed, well structured and clear. Therefore, a brief account of it will be helpful, especially as it is representative of the general Arabic tendency.

Single and composite concepts were defined earlier in this chapter. A single term is said to signify the former, and a composite term is said to signify the latter. In the course of discussing the predicables, only the single term and its concept are discussed. A single concept is one in which either more than one can participate, such as the concept "human being", or no more than one can participate, such as the concept Zayd. The former is a single concept in which all human individuals participate; the latter is a single concept in which nobody but one can participate. Participation of more than one in the latter concept can occur only in the sound of the expression and not in the concept Zayd. The former concept and the term signifying it are universal; the latter concept and the term signifying it are individual.[96] We are told that it is the universal concepts and terms that concern the logician, for the individual ones are infinite in number and, therefore, cannot be determined. However, even if they were finite in number, knowledge of them inasmuch as they are individual is not conducive to the ultimate philosophical perfection,[97] which is the grasping of the essences of things.

An essential term is said to signify either the essence or a part of the essence of a thing.[98] The former answers the question: "What is it?" and the latter answers the question: "Which is it?" The former is of two types: a term that signifies the more general essence, the genus, and a term that signifies the more particular essence, the species. The latter is a term that signifies a part of the essence – this part being the difference.[99] For example, in relation to a human being, "animal" is a genus, "human being" is a species and "rational" is a difference.

A term that signifies anything other than the essence or a part of the essence – whether or not this thing is a necessary concomitant – is an accidental term which signifies an accidental concept.[100] An accident is something that can be removed from a thing both in existence and in the mind, or something that can be removed from it only in the mind, or something that can be removed from it only in existence. In no case does this removal cause the removal of the essence. An example of the first is "sitting"; an example of the second is "black" for an Ethiopian; an example of the third is "capacity for laughter" for a human being.[101] The first is a particular accident and does not concern the logician; the second and third are universal accidents, and as such they concern the logician – the second being the common accident, which is separable from its subject, and the third, the property, which necessarily attaches to its subject. Like the constituents of an essence, the property, being a necessary concomitant, is something without which the essence cannot be conceived.[102] However, "this must not be taken to mean that the elimination of such necessary concomitants leads to the elimination of the essence, but that their removal indicates that there is no essence to which they attach".[103]

These terms signify concepts that are such neither in themselves nor in relation to all things. "Animal", for example, is a genus in relation to all the species that participate in it and not in itself or in relation to all things. "Human being" is a species in relation to all human individuals. "Rational" is a difference in relation to a certain being inasmuch as it distinguishes it from other beings under the same genus. "Laughter" is a property in relation to what occurs to the human nature only. Finally, "black" is a common accident for an Ethiopian and anything else which is black.[104]

In sum, the predicables are of two main types: essential and accidental. The essential is also of two types: either that which signifies the essence, or that which signifies a part of the essence. The former is further divided into that which signifies the more general essence and that which signifies the more particular essence. Universal accident is also of two types: common accident, which belongs to more than one thing; and property, which belongs to one thing only.

This helps us determine the explanatory phrase and the proof, the two pillars of knowledge according to Arabic thought, by helping us determine the simple elements of the former and the parts of the latter. As mentioned, there are two types of explanatory phrase: the definition and the description. The definition determines the essence of a thing, which is made up of the genus and difference or differences. Therefore, by implication, the definition determines the genus and the difference or differences of a thing.[105] If a thing has more than one difference, its identifying phrase is not a real definition unless it indicates its genus and all its differences. If, in the case of this thing, the identifying phrase indicates the genus and one difference of this thing only, the phrase gives an essential distinction between this thing's essence and those under the same genus.[106] A thing that has no genus and at least one difference cannot be defined. From this it follows that God is indefinable since He has no parts. The description, on the other hand, signifies by implication the genus and the properties of a thing.

Errors in forming the definition and the description can result from the following: including unfamiliar expressions in the identifying phrase; identifying a thing by another thing, which is equally known or equally unknown to it; identifying a thing by another thing, which is more unknown than it; identifying a thing by itself; identifying a thing by another thing, which is identified by it; identifying a thing by another thing, which is unnecessary; identifying a thing by its correlative.[107]

THE PARTS OF LOGIC

Traditionally the Aristotelian *Organon* was thought to consist of only the following parts: *Categories*, *De interpretatione*, *Prior Analytics*, *Posterior Analytics*, *Topics* and *Sophistics*. But in keeping with the Syriac tradition, which was influenced by the views of some members of the Alexandrian school, many Arabic logicians also considered *Rhetoric* and *Poetics* as parts of logic.[108] Here is how al-Fārābī puts it:

> The parts of logic are eight. This is because the kinds of syllogism and the kinds of phrase, which one can use to correct an opinion or an object in general, are three. Also, the kinds of crafts, whose function comes after the acquisition of the use of syllogism in speech, are in general five: demonstrative, dialectical, sophistical, rhetorical and poetical.[109]

According to al-Fārābī, the demonstrative syllogism expresses certitude, the dialectical expresses presumptiveness, the sophistical expresses delusion (falsehood), the rhetorical expresses persuasiveness and the poetical expresses imaginativeness.[110] Every one of these five syllogisms is used to correct something in some type of discourse.[111]

Every kind of syllogism has some things that are proper to it and some things that it shares with the other kinds of syllogisms. A syllogism is always composite, whether in the soul or in language. A syllogism in the soul is composed of a number of intelligibles joined together and arranged just for the purpose of securing the soundness of a certain matter. Similarly, a syllogism in language is composed of a number of expressions joined together and arranged to signify these intelligibles for the purpose of securing the soundness of a certain matter for the hearer.[112] The smallest composite unit of a syllogism is composed of two expressions in the case of the linguistic syllogism, and of two intelligibles in the case of the mental syllogism. These smallest composite units are referred to as "simple".[113] These simple units are in turn composed of single intelligibles and single expressions signifying these intelligibles.[114]

From this it follows, according to al-Fārābī, that the parts of logic must be eight, each part constituting a book. The first, *al-Maqūlāt* (*Categories*), includes the rules that govern single intelligibles and their signifying expressions. The second, *al-'Ibārah* (*De interpretatione*), includes the rules that govern what was called above "simple" units. The third, *al-Qiyās* (*Syllogism*, i.e., *Prior Analytics*), includes the rules governing the common elements of the syllogism of any craft. The fourth, *al-Burhān* (*Demonstration*, i.e., *Posterior Analytics*), includes the rules governing demonstrative discourse. The fifth, *al-Mawāḍi' al-jadaliyyah* (*Topics*), includes the rules governing dialectical discourse. The sixth, *al-Ḥikmah al-mumawwahah* (*Sophistics*), includes the rules governing delusive matters and an enumeration of all the things that can be used in the craft of delusion and an enumeration of all the matters that protect against falsification. The seventh, *al-Khaṭābah* (*Rhetoric*), includes the rules governing rhetorical discourse, the various kinds of discourse and the statements of rhetoricians to determine whether or not these statements are in accordance with the rules for rhetorical discourse. All the principles on which this craft is based are also enumerated as are all the procedures for perfecting this craft in the various disciplines. The eighth, *al-Shi'r* (*Poetics*), includes the rules governing poetry, the kinds of poetic discourse, an enumeration of all the principles on which the craft of poetry is based, the types of this craft and the principles that help perfect this craft.[115]

Al-Fārābī states that the ultimate object of logic is the fourth part, which is why it is considered the most noble of the parts of logic. The three parts that precede it are mere introductions to it, and the four that follow it have a double purpose: firstly to act as instruments for the fourth part; and secondly, to help distinguish the various types of discourse and their functions.[116]

Other Arabic logicians considered the parts of logic to be nine, adding to the above-mentioned parts *Īsāghūjī* or *al-Madkhal* (*Isagoge*) as the introductory or first part.[117] Ibn Sīnā tells us that this is the part concerned with some expressions inasmuch as they signify universal concepts.[118] Most Arabic logicians, including those who did not consider the *Isagoge* a part of logic, still considered it an introduction to the whole *Organon* and not just to the *Categories*.[119] As such, it includes discussions relating not only to the five predicables but also to logic in general. Examples of such general discussions have already been given, namely, those relating to the meaning of logic, the use and benefit of logic, the relation of logic to grammar, the relation of logic to philosophy, etc.[120]

Ibn Rushd remained more true to the Aristotelian tradition than did his fellow Muslim thinkers. He began his commentaries on Aristotle's logical works with *Categories* and ended them with *Sophistics*. This is not to say that he did not concern himself with other subjects with which other Arabic logicians were concerned. He commented, for example, on *Rhetoric*, *Poetics* and even Porphyry's *Isagoge*. However, he did not consider these works to be parts of logic.

By way of concluding this chapter, we must say that Arabic logicians not only kept Aristotle's logic alive but also went beyond it. In doing so, they did not necessarily introduce new elements, as in the discussions of the conditional syllogism, regarding which we find mere hints in Aristotle and detailed discussions in the Stoics.[121] However, even in adhering to Greek logic, whether Aristotelian or not, they showed independence from earlier thinkers and, at times, from each other, at least in organizing, subtracting from and adding to the Greek logical works. Besides, no doubt they were pioneers in certain areas, such as that of reconciling Greek logic with Arabic grammar and Islamic religious studies, and perhaps in much more. However, the exact degree of originality in the various areas of Arabic logic is not possible to determine at this point, because much of Arabic logic and much of what preceded it is lost, and much of what is not lost is still unpublished.

NOTES

1 The most important schools in the East are that of Naṣibin (Nisibis) in Iraq; that of Jundīshāpur, established in Persia (555) by Chosroes I; that of the Pagan school of Ḥarrān in northern Syria. The latter produced, among others, the prominent scholar Thābit ibn Qurrah (d. 901). The most important school in the West was that of Alexandria. Finally, the most important monastery was that of Qinnisrin, established on the Euphrates in the first half of the sixth century by John bar Aphtonia (d. 538).

2 According to some Arabic sources, Ibn al-Muqaffa' was among the first to translate into Arabic some Greek logical works, including Aristotle's *Categories*, *De interpretatione* and *Prior Analytics*, as well as Porphyry's *Isagoge*. This he did from Persian, into which these works had already been translated, at the request of the 'Abbasid caliph, Abū Ja'far al-Manṣūr (136/754–159/775). (See, for example, Ibn al-Nadīm, *al-Fihrist*, trans. Bayard Dodge (New York, 1970): 581; al-Qifṭī, *Tārīkh al-ḥukamā'*, ed. Julius Lippert (Leipzig, 1903): 36.)

3 Among other things, he is said to have translated *Prior Analytics*. (See Majid Fakhry, *History of Islamic Philosophy* (New York, 1983): 9.)

4 The most prominent translator of Greek works into Syriac and Arabic, and the head of the House of Wisdom.

5 A prominent Nestorian logician who was the teacher of al-Fārābī. He was the first to translate into Arabic Aristotle's *Posterior Analytics* (Nicholas Rescher, *The Development of Arabic Logic*, hereafter *Development* (Pittsburgh, 1964): 44).

6 A prominent Jacobite logician known for his debates with Nestorians over the Divine nature and with Muslims, especially al-Kindī (d. 873), over the concept of the Trinity.

7 This work played a very important role in Arabic logic. It was considered the *madkhal* (introduction) to Aristotle's logical works and was taught at schools and is still taught at Azhar, one of the oldest universities in the world.

8 See Rescher, *Development*: 44.

9 See *Al-Fārābī's Short Commentary on Aristotle's "Prior Analytics"* (hereafter *Short Commentary*), trans. Nicholas Rescher (Pittsburg, 1963): 22.

10 *Ibid.*: 23.

11 For this reason, it is better to refer to the logic in medieval Islam as "Arabic logic" instead of "Islamic logic", and to the logicians as "Arabic logicians" instead of "Muslim logicians".

12 Al-Qazwīnī and al-Urmawī are two of the best logicians of the thirteenth century.

13 A discussion of the parts of logic will be given in the final section of this chapter.

14 This title was given in the last three centuries B.C.E. to Aristotle's logical writings and means "instrument".

15 Ibn Manẓūr, *Lisān al-'arab*, 10 (Beirut, 1956): 354.

16 Qur'ān, 28: 16.

17 *Ibid.* 23: 62; 45: 29; 37: 92; 51: 23; 21: 63; 27: 85; 77: 35.

18 See Ibn Rushd, *Talkhīṣ manṭiq Arisṭū* (hereafter *Talkhīṣ*), 1, ed. Jirār Jahāmī (Beirut, 1982): 108.

19 Al-Fārābī, *at-Tawṭi'ah* in *al-Manṭiq 'ind al-Fārābī*, 1, ed. Rafīq al-'Ajam (Beirut, 1958): 59.

20 By "expression" Muslim philosophers do not mean just any external sound, but, as Ibn Sīnā says, it is "a human-made composition of letters" (Ibn Sīnā, *al-Shifā'*, *al-Manṭiq*, *al-'Ibārah*, hereafter *al-'Ibārah*, ed. Maḥmūd al-Khūḍayrī (Cairo, 1970): 9). This means that an expression is "a freely chosen composition of letters" (*ibid.* 10). The expression is what Ibn Ḥazm refers to as the intended sound (Ibn Ḥazm, *al-Taqrīb li-hadd al-manṭiq*, hereafter *al-Taqrīb*, in *Rasā'il Ibn Ḥazm al-Andalusiy*, 4, ed. Iḥsān 'Abbās (Beirut, 1983): 105–6). This is to be distinguished from a mere sound, which is any non-human or non-freely made vocal emission (Ibn Sīnā, *al-'Ibārah:* 10).

21 Al-Fārābī, *al-Tawṭi'ah*: 59; *Iḥṣā' al-'ulūm* (hereafter *Iḥṣā'*), ed. 'Uthmān Amīn (Cairo, 1949): 62–3. For the internal and external utterance, see al-Fārābī *al-Alfāẓ al-musta'malah fī'l-manṭiq* (hereafter *al-Alfāẓ*), ed. Muḥsin Mahdī (Beirut, 1968): 103; Ibn Sīnā, *al-Shifā'*, *al-Manṭiq*, *al-Madkhal* (hereafter *al-Madkhal*), eds George Anawātī, Maḥmūd al-Khuḍayrī and Fu'ād al-Ahwānī (Cairo, 1952): 20.

22 Al-Fārābī, *al-Tawṭi'ah*: 59–60.

23 Al-Fārābī, *Iḥṣā'*: 62.

24 For al-Fārābī's discussion of this matter, see, for example, *Kitāb al-tanbīh 'alā sabīl al-sa'ādah* (hereafter *al-Tanbīh*), ed. Ja'far Āl-Yāsīn (Beirut, 1985): 77–9; *Iḥṣā'*: 53ff.

25 Except in the case of a prophet's knowledge, which is received by God's grace. But prophets are a very small minority; therefore, in the case of the majority of people logic is necessary for the acquisition of knowledge.

26 See, for example, Ibn Sīnā, *al-Ishārāt wa'l-tanbīhāt, Part Four*, tenth class, for an elaboration of the third point.

27 For a fuller analysis of *taṣawwur* and *taṣdīq*, see Ibn Sīnā, *Remarks and Admonitions, Part One: Logic* (hereafter *Remarks*), trans. Shams Inati (Toronto, 1984): 5–6 and 49–50. Compare with Aristotle, *Posterior Analytics*, i.1.71a.11–15.

28 See, for example, al-Ghazzālī, *Mi'yār al-'ilm* (hereafter *Mi'yār*), ed. Sulaymān Dunyā (Cairo, 1961): 66; Muḥammad A'lā ibn 'Alī al-Tahānawī, *Kashshāf iṣṭilāḥāt al-funūn*, 2 (Calcutta, 1863): 2.

29 Ibn Sīnā, *Remarks*: 49.

30 Ibn Sīnā, *Manṭiq al-mashriqiyyīn* (hereafter *Manṭiq*) (Cairo, 1910): 60.

31 Ibn Sīnā, *Remarks*: 5.

32 Al-Fārābī, *al-Tanbīh*: 81.

33 *Ibid.*

34 Ibn Sīnā, *Remarks*: 49.

35 Al-Fārābī, *Iḥṣā'*: 53.

36 Al-Fārābī, *al-Tanbīh*: 81.

37 A definition can be real, but not complete if it determines something that relates to the essence of a thing, such as its cause, but not the whole essence. The fact that the cause relates to the essence makes the definition real. The fact that not the whole essence is determined makes the definition incomplete (see Ibn Sīnā, *Remarks*: 41).

38 *Ibid.*: 40; Ibn Rushd, *Talkhīṣ*: 111.

39 See Ibn Rushd, *Talkhīṣ*: 105–7 and 234ff.

40 The foregoing discussion of analogy, induction and syllogism is based on Ibn Sīnā, *Remarks*: 34–41.

41 A vague reference to this idea is made in al-Fārābī, *al-Tanbīh*: 81–2.

42 *Ibid.*: 82.

43 Ibn Sīnā, *Remarks*: 47.

44 Ibn Sīnā, *al-Qaṣīdat al-muzdawijah* in *Manṭiq*: 3; al-Ghazzālī, *Mi'yār*: 59.

45 As seen in a previous note, al-Ghazzālī gives *mi'yār* as the title of a whole logical work; see also al-Ghazzālī, *Tahāfut al-falāsifah* where logic is referred to as *Mi'yār al-'aql* (the standard for reason) (al-Ghazzālī, *Tahāfut al-falāsifah* (hereafter *Tahāfut*), ed. Maurice Bouyges (Beirut, 1962): 45.

46 Again, al-Ghazzālī gives one of his logical works the title *Miḥakk al-naẓar* (ed. Muḥammad Badr al-Dīn al-Ni'sānī (Beirut, 1966)).

47 For an explanation of this point, whose details are unnecessary for this chapter, see Shams Inati, *Ibn Sīnā's Analysis of the Notion of Evil* (Ph.D. dissertation, State University of New York at Buffalo, 1979), chapter 2.

48 For an elaboration of this tendency in Ibn Rushd, see Ibn Rushd, *Talkhīṣ*: 109ff.

49 See, for example, Ibn Ḥazm, *al-Taqrīb*: 100 and 102–3; al-Ghazzālī, *Mi'yār*: 60.

50 Ibn Ḥazm, *al-Taqrīb*: 99.

51 *Ibid.*: 98.

52 *Ibid.*

53 *Ibid.*: 99.

54 *Ibid.*

55 *Ibid.*: 100.

56 *Ibid.*: 98.
57 *Ibid.*: 100; al-Ghazzālī, *Tahāfut*: 45.
58 Ibn Ḥazm, *al-Taqrīb*: 100. Compare with al-Ghazzālī, *Mi'yār*: 61.
59 Al-Nāshī''s opposition to Aristotelian logic is known from the writings of others, such as Abū Ḥayyān al-Tawḥīdī (d. 1023), as none of al-Nāshī''s own writings on the subject has reached us (see al-Tawḥīdī, *al-Imtā' wa'l-mu'ānasah* (hereafter *al-Imtā'*), 1, eds Aḥmad Amīn and Aḥmad al-Zayn (Cairo, 1953): 24).
60 See Ibn Qutaybah, *Adab al-kātib*, ed. M. al-Daynūrī (Beirut, 1967): 6.
61 A linguist and historian who suggests that neither the Greeks nor Ibn Sīnā considered the rules of logic before composing poetry. In his opinion, this amounts to saying that logic is unnecessary for the soundness of poetry and perhaps for discourse in general (see Muḥammad 'Abd al-Sābir Aḥmad Naṣṣār, *al-Madrasah al-salafiyyah wa mawqif rijālihā min al-manṭiq wa 'ilm al-kalām* (Cairo, 1979): 272–3.
62 Al-Tawḥīdī, *al-Imtā'*: 108ff.; *al-Muqābasāt*, ed. Ḥasan al-Sandūbī (Cairo, 1929): 68ff.
63 I.e., Aristotle.
64 Al-Tawḥīdī, *al-Imtā'*: 110–11.
65 See, for example, *ibid.*: 114.
66 Al-Fārābī, *Iḥṣā'*: 58.
67 *Ibid.*: 59.
68 Al-Tawḥīdī, *al-Imtā'*: 113ff.
69 Al-Fārābī, *Iḥṣā'*: 58–9.
70 *Ibid.*: 59.
71 Ibn Sīnā, *al-Madkhal*: 19.
72 *Ibid.*; Ibn Sīnā *al-Najāt*, ed. Majid Fakhri (Beirut, 1985): 43.
73 Ibn Sīnā, *al-Madkhal*: 19–20.
74 *Ibid.*: 19; Ibn Sīnā, *al-Najāt*: 43. The idea that nothing can replace logic except the guidance of God is also expressed by al-Ghazzālī (see al-Ghazzālī, *Mi'yār*: 65).
75 Al-Fārābī, *Iḥṣā'*: 59. Compare with al-Ghazzālī, *Mi'yār*: 59–60.
76 Al-Fārābī, *Iḥṣā'*: 59.
77 *Ibid.*: 60–2.
78 Al-Fārābī, *al-Tanbīh*: 82–3. For a similar point, see al-Fārābī, *Iḥṣā'*: 59–60.
79 Al-Fārābī, *al-Tanbīh*: 83. Ellipsis points indicate omission of the word *allatī* (which).
80 Al-Fārābī, *Iḥṣā'*: 59.
81 Ibn Sīnā, *al-Madkhal*: 22.
82 *Ibid.*: 22–3.
83 *Ibid.*: 23.
84 *Ibid.*
85 *Ibid.*
86 Ibn Sīnā, *Manṭiq*: 10.
87 Ibn Sīnā, *al-Madkhal*: 21.
88 Al-Tawḥīdī, *al-Muqābasāt*: 169–172.
89 See, for example, al-Fārābī, *al-Alfāẓ*: 107; Ibn Sīnā, *Remarks*: 47; *Manṭiq*: 5, 8 and 10; al-Ghazzālī, *Tahāfut*: 45; 'Alī ibn Muḥammad al-Sharīf al-Jurjānī, *Kitāb al-ta'rīfāt* (Beirut, 1969): 351.

90 Ibn Sīnā, *Remarks*: 47.
91 Ibn Sīnā, *al-Madkhal*: 15–16.
92 *Ibid.*: 16.
93 See *ibid.* (introduction by Ibrāhīm Madkūr): 50.
94 A discussion of the nature of property will be given shortly.
95 Ibn Sīnā, *al-Madkhal*: 83–4.
96 *Ibid.*: 26–7. Compare with al-Fārābī, *al-Alfāẓ*: 58–9.
97 Ibn Sīnā, *al-Madkhal*: 27–8.
98 *Ibid.*: 30.
99 *Ibid.*: 46.
100 *Ibid.*: 30.
101 *Ibid.*: 32.
102 Ibn Sīnā, *Remarks*: 56–7.
103 *Ibid.*: 16.
104 Ibn Sīnā, *al-Madkhal*: 46.
105 Ibn Sīnā, *Remarks*: 19.
106 *Ibid.*: 20.
107 *Ibid.*: 21.
108 See, for example, al-Fārābī, *Iḥṣā'*: 63ff.; Ibn Ḥazm, *al-Taqrīb*: 98.
109 Al-Fārābī, *Iḥṣā'*: 63–4. Compare with al-Fārābī, *al-Alfāẓ*: 104–6.
110 Al-Fārābī, *Iḥṣā'*: 69.
111 *Ibid.*
112 *Ibid.*
113 *Ibid.*
114 *Ibid.*: 70.
115 *Ibid.*: 70–2.
116 *Ibid.*: 72ff.
117 See, for example, Ibn Sīnā, *Risālah fī aqsām al-'ulūm al-'aqliyyah*, in *Tis' rasā'il fi'l-ḥikmah wa'l-ṭabī'iyyāt*, ed. Ḥasan 'Āṣī (Beirut, 1986): 92–4.
118 *Ibid.*
119 See, for example, Ibn Ḥazm, *al-Taqrīb*: 104.
120 Ibn Sīnā's *Madkhal* is an excellent illustration of pursuing such discussions, and thus carrying his *Madkhal* way beyond Porphyry's *Isagoge*.
121 See al-Fārābī, *Short Commentary*: 38–41; Nicholas Rescher, "Avicenna on the Logic of Conditional Syllogisms", *Notre Dame Journal of Formal Logic*, 4 (1963): 48–58.

CHAPTER 49

Epistemology

Sari Nuseibeh

GENERAL QUESTIONS

Perhaps two major questions relating to knowledge characterize intellectual efforts to address this subject in the Islamic period. The first question is: In what sense does human knowledge detract from, or resemble, God's knowledge? The second question is: What is the role of the person who has knowledge?

It is possible with these two questions as terms of reference to understand much of the intellectual debate – implicit or explicit – that went on in the Islamic milieu on the subject of knowledge. The first question is especially pertinent given two widely held beliefs: (1) that one of God's major attributes and abilities – besides life and power – is knowledge, and (2) that true knowledge is attainable only if and when one has knowledge of the divine cause or secret of the universe (because how otherwise, in the context of the widely held belief in God as the first and final cause of the universe, can one be said to have knowledge about the minutest item in the ontological order?). In a nutshell, these two beliefs are that one of God's distinctive traits is His knowledge, and that true knowledge is of God. Given these beliefs, to say that human beings can attain true knowledge is to say (1) that they can acquire an ability that God possesses, and (2) that God can be to a human being *qua* knowledge almost what a human being is *qua* God (notwithstanding ontological differences). To understand these implications is to understand the underlying tensions and apprehensions which characterized the debates that took place among intellectuals about this subject. On the one hand we find views claiming that knowledge of God or the first cause – whether philosophically or mystically – is possible, and so is "union" with God in one form or another; and on the other hand we find views that a human being, because of his or her inbuilt intellectual and existential limitations, is bound at the outer reaches of the mind to make the leap from personal capabilities (whether rational or mystical) to faith in the pursuit of understanding the universe. On this second view "revealed knowledge" (the Qur'ānic text) assumes a literal importance – with varieties of this view at one end upholding a totally literal understanding of the Qur'ān; while on the first view the revealed text assumes a symbolic importance – with varieties of this view at one end upholding a totally metaphorical understanding of the Qur'ān. Yet more poignantly, on the first view revelation (hence prophecy) can be argued to be unnecessary for the attainment of true knowledge, while on the second view knowledge which is humanly possible is attainable only through revelation and prophecy.

The second question, relating to function or role, was addressed in literature which one could retrospectively read as "political", in the sense that, once it was established what kind of person possessed knowledge (e.g., a philosopher, a mystic, a preacher, a Qur'ānic exegetist, etc.), the next step was to establish what function such a person ought to have in society. Views varied from those espousing Platonic "leadership" roles, to those favouring the retired and reclusive roles. Intellectuals finding themselves in disagreement over who is to be defined as possessing real knowledge may here be in agreement on espousing an active political role for such a person, or a reclusive, advisory role. Inevitably, tensions would arise if both agree that wise men should be rulers but disagree on who is to be defined as wise. Ultimately, if it can be said that there was any tension between a secularist and a religious school of thought with respect to the state in Islam, it was only in relation to this conflict over power between the jurisprudent and the philosopher. It is in this context that one can appreciate the treatise *Faṣl al-maqāl* by Ibn Rushd (Averroes), for whom a resolution of the apparent conflict between revelation and reason (or the attempt to rehabilitate reason through the revealed text) was perhaps more importantly an effort to rehabilitate the political stature of the philosopher in the context of a religious state.

In any case, any debate concerning knowledge in that period could be described as one concerning the abilities and limits of the human mind, and therefore concerning the essence and *raison d'être* of the human being. To what extent is the human mind free to "seek newer and newer worlds", until the limitless has been accomplished? Or to what extent is the human mind limited, not free to question and ordained only to serve? Seen from one perspective, the call is to seek to be as close to perfection and to God as possible. Seen from the opposite perspective, this unholy quest simply reinforces the "original" sin: the sin, as al-Shahrastānī describes it in the introduction to his *Milal wa'l-niḥāl* which Satan committed by asking "Why?" All later dissensions and disagreements, al-Shahrastānī claims, originate from this intellectual act of rebelliousness (of transcending the written text in search of an individual opinion).

Within these two extreme poles one may comfortably find most of the views expressed by intellectuals living in the Islamic period concerning the subject of knowledge. In what follows, a brief outline of the four main intellectual schools will be presented, followed by a closer look at some of the operating concepts in two of them.

METHODS OF KNOWLEDGE: SCHOOLS

What were the major "epistemological" trends in the Islamic period, and how can one give a general characterization of them? Our initial characterization might seem too general, but it is important to keep it in mind as a general framework of reference before one addresses the more specialized distinctions. Briefly, it is possible to characterize four general trends or attitudes with respect to knowledge.

Firstly, one can talk about a conservative approach, according to which every humanly attainable truth can be found in the revealed text or can be logically extrapolated from truths that are found in that text. According to this view, not every truth is humanly attainable, and it is the mark of a believer to accept that one can only have faith in the more elevated truths. The Qur'ān is specific and reiterant about the contrast between those that have faith (*īmān*) in the divine truths and those who claim to have contrary knowledge (*'ilm*) but are wrong. It is basically God who knows, and who teaches. The first lesson begins with Adam, who is taught "the names of things" before the crowd of angels who are totally without that knowledge (2: 30ff.). However, the lessons continue through the generations and history (e.g., 2: 151), and through the various prophets (e.g., 2: 251). Indeed, the Qur'ān is replete with references to the fact that it is itself the repository of truth, and that it is God who transmits knowledge (*'ilm*) and wisdom (*ḥikmah*). The Qur'ān is also replete with references to the fact that nature is full of "clues" (*āyāt*) indicating God's wisdom and wholistic plan which it is the task of human reason to unravel. Above all to be a Muslim believer – to submit – is to accept that the human intellect is limited, and therefore to resort to faith. In this frame of reference, the domain of epistemic intellectual exercise is limited to the Qur'ānic text, either by way of direct and comprehensive acquaintance with it or by way of developing the necessary skill to extrapolate from it. This latter skill (analogy, or *qiyās*) is developed by the jurisprudents, who are called upon to make judgments over specific events which are covered in the Qur'ān only in a general sense. Analogy becomes the skill to apply the principle to the newly arising situation.

In his characterization of Islamic intellectual schools of thought Ibn Khaldūn describes this trend as the "knowledge-through-transmission" (*'ulūm naqliyyah*) category, and he subsumes under it all those skills which are associated directly with a working knowledge of the Qur'ān, as the exegesists, the jurisprudents, the grammarians and the linguists share. One should assume that the practitioners of these sciences, and the general milieu to which they belonged, constituted the mainstream of thought in the Islamic period. Politically, it is they who dominated the scene. Their derogation of any other kind of scientist, in particular those who relied on "foreign" texts in their pursuit of truth, is none more salient than in Abū Ḥayyān al-Tawḥīdī's famous dramatic presentation of the "argument" which takes place between a logician and a grammarian in the company of a political ruler, in which the logician is seen to be reduced to a stuttering idiot before the astute grammarian. One assumes that this dramatic exchange typified the general intellectual atmosphere which prevailed at the time rather than literally or scrupulously adhering to the actual minutes of the exchange.

Secondly, a more vivacious approach to, and use of, the human intellect was adopted by the practitioners of *kalām*, or theology. Ibn Khaldūn places this epistemic pursuit along with the previously mentioned sciences (as a knowledge-through-transmission item). Indeed, in so far as the Qur'ānic text defines the frame of reference for the theologian in the exercise of his intellect, *kalām* shares with the transmitted sciences a major characteristic. *Kalām* is conceived as a defensive theology, or a polemical art whose explicitly defined objective is the defence of the Islamic doctrine against would-be detractors – whether agnostics or theologians of other religions. However, while bound to the revealed text as a fixed frame of reference for developing answers and positions, *kalām*'s vivacity is derived from having to address questions and doctrines which originate from a variety of frames of reference. Thus, if the jurisprudent (who is a practitioner of the first set of sciences, and who shares with the theologian the faith that the revealed text constitutes the frame of reference to all answers) exercises his or her powers of reasoning by addressing new questions which arise from the need to maintain the direct relevance of the Qur'ān to unfolding daily events, the theologian goes a step beyond this to address questions which originate from entirely different theological and philosophical frames of reference. This makes the operating theatre of the theologian much wider.

The dialectical skills developed by theologians in their pursuit to address a wide spectrum of ideological challenges involved not only a unique set of logical relations (e.g., distinctive interpretations of causal relations) but also a unique universe of discourse (i.e., a special vocabulary or terminology containing references to items or objects not generally found in other disciplines, such as *ma'nā*, *ḥāl*, *mawḍū'ī*, etc.). These polemical skills, abstracted from any specific subject matter to which they may be applied, come close to being a unique logic or method of reasoning. Indeed, if one abstracts from the specific doctrines or positions adopted by the two main schools of *kalām* (the Muʿtazilites and the Ashʿarites), one finds that what is common to both is precisely this unique logic (causal relations and objects of discourse), thus rendering al-Shahrastānī's reference to *kalām* as being synonymous with "logic" quite understandable, notwithstanding the derogatory attitude to *kalām* expressed by the so-called "Second Master" of Greek logic in Islam, al-Fārābī.

The classical characterization of *kalām*'s distinctive methodology is its dialectical approach (as opposed to what is regarded generally as the "deductive" approach of the "Classical" logicians in Islam). However, it would be misleading to rely too heavily on this distinguishing feature, as it is not always precisely clear what is meant by it. There is certainly no presumption by its practitioners that the ultimate answers are unknown, and the argumentative nature of its literature is explanatory, not exploratory. Counter-arguments for *kalām* doctrines are formulated, and are then addressed and undermined. It is true that the modern-day reader faces the task of having to reconstruct the general position of the *kalām* practitioners on various subjects (as epistemology, perception, free will, etc.) on an argument-by-argument basis, but this seems to be more of an expository or stylistic problem rather than a substantive logical problem. If one had to focus on a truly distinguishing methodological mark, it is far safer to consider the above-mentioned universe of discourse (both ontological items as well as relations), and to determine in what precise way this differs from the "Classical" logical approach of the Aristotelian school. However, a second and related distinguishing mark of the *kalām* discipline is its ontology: that the world is made up ultimately of primary, indivisible and indistinguishable atoms, which are held together through an external cause. This is a fascinating theory on more than one level, but one suspects that it also provided the ontological foundation for those claiming that even the essence of an object is accidental to it, and is therefore held to it by an external cause (meaning, ultimately, by God of course). Thus one cannot help feeling as one reads al-Ghazzālī's (d. 505/1111) discourse on how God can intervene in the universe in such a way as to make fire, as fire, incapable of burning a combustible object (or how God can therefore intervene not only in determining *whether* things are but also, given that they are, in what they are – the explanation of miracles) that he must have been influenced by his *kalām* teacher al-Juwaynī (d. 478/1085). Certainly the atomist theory, unlike the Classical Aristotelian theory on the infinity of matter, is far more amenable to the belief in divine omnipotence, as it provides for far more room for God's intervention in the universe, including enough for the operation of miracles. One suspects also that perhaps it is this theory which is at the backbone of some of the Classical philosophers' theories on identity or unity (being a one, or a this), such as the theories of al-Kindī as expressed in his *Epistle on First Philosophy*, or Avicenna. Both these philosophers also express views that seem to indicate a bifurcation between essence and existence, or its being accidental to a thing that it is *a* thing, an individual, and therefore being *what* it is. (Discourse on unity/identity/essence in this context seems analogous to the discourse on knowledge, because the same apprehensions relating to the discussion about whether knowledge is the same in both God and humans obtain in relation to the discussion about whether a thing is necessarily what it is.)

Thirdly, there is what generally goes under the name of "philosophy", or *falsafah*, and is assumed as a discipline to be detached from the Islamic milieu, and more influenced by the "foreign" sciences of the Greeks, etc. It is mostly the practitioners of this discipline that are the object of derogation and criticism by the mainstream intellectual schools of thought. What bound them together was perhaps less a set of doctrines than their respect for, and readiness to learn from, the Greek philosophers. To distinguish them from the other disciplines (in particular from the disciplines which depended heavily on the so-called "knowledge-by-transmission" method), Ibn Khaldūn called them adherents of the "knowledge-by-intellect" method. In other words, they were supposed in theory to be adherents – even worshippers of reason, and unbound by any framework of reference. But in practice they were in general bound by their own framework of reference, namely, the received set of philosophical and scientific works transmitted to them from the Greek and Syriac. Indeed, it is arguable that they were as bound to their specific framework of reference, and as bound to its parameters for the exercise of their reason, as were the practitioners of *kalām* bound to the revealed text. Put differently, they worked from a transmitted body of knowledge analogously to the way the theologians worked. But because this body of knowledge was foreign, and generally seemed to be being presented as a substitute for, if not a superior replacement of, the traditional Islamic body of knowledge, the philosophers were a constant target of criticism and suspicion. The claim of *falsafah* to be the repository of real truth drew scathing attacks by leading Muslim thinkers, such as al-Ghazzālī and Ibn Taymiyyah. Indeed, *falsafah* never flourished except among its own practitioners, and it was generally marginal to mainstream Islamic society.

However, it is difficult to claim (as their opponents assumed) that all philosophers defended the same set of received doctrines. Nor are the differences between the main figures of Islamic philosophy (e.g., al-Fārābī and Avicenna) attributable only to different Greek and neo-Hellenistic schools of thought (e.g., Aristotelian, Neoplatonic, etc.). Indeed one finds that even on theories of epistemology (see below) there is a gulf dividing these thinkers. In the general context of *falsafah* versus the traditional disciplines, the differences between the philosophers might have seemed like an irrelevant detail. But in the context of *falsafah* itself, the different theories are what distinguish one philosopher from another. In his writings al-Ghazzālī picks out al-Fārābī and Avicenna as heretics for claiming, among other things, that God does not know particulars. It is doubtful that al-Ghazzālī was unaware of Avicenna's theory on God's knowledge of particulars (see below), but in any case it is telling that he does not think it worthwhile to point out the differences between al-Fārābī and Avicenna on this issue. In short *falsafah* was – and to some extent it still is – treated as a uniform discipline with individual distinguishing features being regarded as a marginal detail, and at best as clues for determining pre-Islamic influences on this philosopher or that. Generally, we have not succeeded yet in taking the philosophers in Islam seriously.

There were various attempts by the practitioners of *falsafah* to reconcile – at least ostensibly – their "body of knowledge", or their "truth", with that of the traditionalists. Regardless of the sincerity of their intentions, an entire body of epistemic discourse developed as a result of that attempt. Drawing partly on the Platonic imagery of the cave (where different shades of reality are postulated), and partly on Qur'ānic verses which confirm the need to use imagery for communicating truths, the philosophers attempted to show that there are different grades of truth, not different or conflicting truths. They also tried to show that rational truth was real truth, while other truths (including religious) were images of this truth. Naturally, this did not appease the committed practitioners of the religious sciences, but it seemed to satisfy the philosophers' quest for a compromise formula. (This imagery, by the way, was to be used by the fourth epistemic school, i.e., the mystics, to distinguish their kind of knowledge from that of the philosophers.)

Fourthly, there were the mystics. Theirs is a truly defiant theory, because it can be neither tested nor even described. There are different schools and shades of Sufi knowledge, but what is common to all of them is the claim that language obstructs, rather than communicates, understanding. To them, knowledge is a form of individual "taste". It is the difference between being able to give a precise scientific definition of health and being healthy, or "to know" medically what being inebriated is and experiencing drunkenness, or to know down to the minutest detail what a town looks like and being able to walk in its streets and to see it as it really is. Inevitably, their theories are communicated through metaphor and imagery, rather than through definitive linguistic mechanisms. Often, poetry and stories are used to convey meanings rather than straightforward expositions. While frustrating to those trained in philosophy, their methods of communication draw upon precisely that imagery which the philosophers used to reconcile their "truth" with that of the practitioners of the religious sciences.

THE EPISTEMOLOGY OF *KALĀM*

Two major problems confront one when one attempts to provide at least a brief outline of *kalām* epistemology. The first problem has to do with the diversity of views held on the subject, not only between the two Classical schools (Muʿtazilites and Ashʿarites) but also between adherents of the same school. The second problem is technical, in that we do not as yet possess a complete and consensus account of a *kalām* theory of knowledge. However, if one were to look beyond the details distinguishing one view from the next, and were to attempt to throw light on the main operating concepts and words that constituted the language of discourse in the subject, one could perhaps begin with the following itinerary: (1) disposition (*ḥāl*), meaning to-be-in-a-state-of-such-and-such; (2) generation (*tawlīd*), meaning in this context the rational operation which produces knowledge; and (3) repose (*sukūn al-nafs*), meaning the psychological state of mind which is associated with the dispositional attitude (of being in a state of knowing). There may have been differences between various thinkers (whether in the same school or belonging to the two opposite schools) on how to understand or to explain these operating concepts, yet a definitive outline and appreciation of the significance of the different interpretations can be understood fully only against the entire intellectual frame of reference which the different thinkers operated in. For example, to appreciate why a specific thinker claimed that knowledge is or cannot be a disposition, one has to have a fuller view of his intellectual frame of reference, in which different ontological categories other than dispositional attitudes (e.g. substance, accident, cause, condition, etc.) were featured in specific ways. One often also finds that a particular thinker's definition of *ḥāl* (or disposition) – for example, whether it is an effect, a cause or a condition – is a function of that thinker's general intellectual frame of reference. Therefore, the following discussion must be viewed only as a tentative introduction to the universe of discourse in *kalām* epistemology, and not as a definitive outline of specific schools of thought in that universe.

How does *ḥāl* feature in a discussion about knowledge? Perhaps the simplest and most direct route to answer this question is to view it in the context of a subject (perhaps even a substance) and a state (perhaps even an accident). One asks oneself the question, in what sense is the state attributable to the subject? (Or in what sense does this kind or category of accident pertain to this kind or category of substance?) To ask such a question would be as much as to ask, in what sense is knowledge attributable to a person?

Ḥāl can perhaps best be described as the being-in-such-and-such-a-state. Among the thinkers who asserted the meaningfulness or existence of such a category, there were differences concerning whether such a category had the same application to living agents as to inanimate objects. Some would argue, for example, that the accident's-being-an-accident, or the substance's-being-in-existence, or even the accident's-being-a-colour, are all on a par with a living organism's-being-alive, its-being-in-a-state-of-hearing, or its-being-in-a-state-of-knowing. Others would claim that the last three examples are distinct from the first three, in that they clearly presuppose life in the substance/subject to which they pertain. In general, those who wished to give *ḥāl* a distinct status in their intellectual frames of reference would argue that *ḥāl* (plural *aḥwāl*) can be said to pertain only to living agents. The rest would better be described as attributes, or at best – if further specifications are needed – as *akwān* (singular, *kawn*), which are specific attributes/accidents of movement, rest, conjunction and separation.

Yet to have made this distinction as one which, in the final analysis, seems to be that of different ontic categories of accidents, is only to have introduced the rich variety of subtle distinctions used in this discipline. Primarily, however, it was generally agreed that states (dispositional attitudes) attributable to live agents had to fulfil certain specifications relating to their causal mode. The issue therefore was, given the subject (the agent) and the disposition (the state-of-knowing), in what sense can we understand the coming-to-be of the disposition in the subject? The being-white of a table is caused, and the-being-in-a-state-of-knowing is also caused, but surely the modes of causality in the two examples are different. It is to address these questions that the concept of generation (*tawlīd*) seems to have been evolved, as a specific type of causal implication.

To recapitulate: to know something, or "the-knowing-of-something" is an accident that comes to pertain to a subject. However, accidents are of different categories. If the accident in question is a dispositional attitude that pertains to a living agent, then it can be called a *ḥāl*. Even so, distinctions can still be made out between various sub-groups of such dispositional attitudes. For example, to be in a state of pain, or to feel pain, is not the same as to be in a state of knowledge, or to be in a state of believing such-and-such: in the first example, pain can be sensed in a particular location (the *maḥall*, or location, where the *ḥāl* so to speak subsists and can be physically identified), whereas in the second example the *maḥall* of knowledge/belief is said to be the person (the *jumlah*) as a whole rather than a specific physical location in that person. To be in a state of desire (to desire such-and-such) can analogously to the pain example be argued to relate at least in some instances to a physical location: thus to say "I know such-and-such", or "So-and-so finds himself in a state of believing such-and-such" is not quite the same as to say "I feel such-and-such" or "So-and-so finds herself in a state of desiring/feeling such-and-such" since one cannot or should not identify a physical location as the subject of the state of knowledge/belief, whereas one can at least in some cases identify physical locations wherein the desire/feeling is experienced. Perhaps, to make out the distinction in clearer or more contemporary terms, one can point out that it is possible in one case to say *where* it hurts (one senses the pain), or *which part* of the body senses the feeling of, say, hunger, whereas such localizations in the case of knowledge are less appropriate to make.

These sub-distinctions are perhaps relevant only to the extent that they underline the primarily operational nature of knowledge/belief: that the state of knowledge is an active dispositional state of the person, as opposed perhaps to its being a passive or perhaps even a neutral dispositional state. Above all, the distinctions set out knowledge in terms of *dispositional states*. Perhaps one should point out here that, contrary to *kālam* epistemologists, the philosophers and even mystics spoke of knowledge in terms of *final* states, or as the end-products of a process (see below). According to them knowledge is *something* which one acquires after or through a process (the subject being the mind or the soul rather than the person). Thus, although being an attribute, it is somehow made out as something (an existential category) which is distinct from the person, and which the person comes to acquire, in part or in whole. Such a description obviously lends knowledge an objective status, whereas the *kalām* description ties it very tightly to subjective states.

Typically, a dispositional state (a *ḥāl*) is one which agents find themselves as having. Thus agents find themselves as being in the state of knowing, and are able to distinguish themselves as being in such a state partly by their ability to distinguish their being in such a state from their not being in such a state, and partly by their ability to distinguish this state from others which they find themselves as being in. Such abilities to distinguish are argued by *kalām* thinkers to be direct or immediate. This is like saying that one just happens to know when one believes something, is thinking about it or knows it. The question, therefore, What is knowledge?, or What is it to know something? is first answered in terms of a dispositional state which is immediately distinguishable by the person who experiences it. One simply *finds* oneself being in such a state.

In order to address the second main question, namely, how to explain the acquisition of such a state, or how does one happen to come by finding oneself in such a state after not having had it first, the concept of generation (*tawlīd*) was introduced, as a process of reasoning leading to knowledge. *Kalām* thinkers distinguished naturally between immediate and acquired knowledge, but did not expend too much effort on trying to make the distinction in terms of the objects of knowledge in the Classical way that the philosophers did (for example by saying that some truths are by their nature immediately perceptible). Their main concern was to try to explain how one comes by knowledge. How is it that one comes by finding oneself being in such-and-such-a-state? Their answer was that reason generates knowledge, in the sense that the state of knowing such-and-such can be acquired only if a methodical process of considering the right kind of evidence in the right kind of way is applied. On this view, "aborted" generation can be due only to one or another of these conditions being absent: that methodical reasoning was not used, that not the right evidence was considered, or that not the right manner of considering this evidence was used. Strictly speaking, on this view, to "learn a truth" from someone else cannot be considered as acquiring knowledge. Similarly, "to recollect a truth" is not necessarily the same as recalling a state of knowledge. Assuming normal conditions, so to speak, only a person engaged methodically in reasoning about the right kind of evidence will find himself or herself in the state of knowing such-and-such. Merely to recollect a truth without the reasoning that led to it, or to be told a truth, is thus not to be in a state of knowledge.

The third operative concept in this discourse about knowledge sheds still further light on the subject: *sukūn al-nafs*, or repose of the soul, is the psychological confidence a person feels which is associated with being in a state of knowledge. This is the confidence that what one believes to be the case is in fact the case, or that no further search is needed. Indeed, more explicitly, knowledge is depicted by *kalām* thinkers as a kind of belief, distinguished partly by its having been arrived at in a specified methodical manner, and partly by the additional psychological criterion of confidence that the person feels regarding this belief.

One does not find in *kalām* literature too much concern for establishing – or arguing for or explaining – for example a correspondence relation between subject and object, or between a person's believing such-and-such to be the case and its being in fact the case. Knowledge is primarily addressed as a dispositional attitude, a subjective state of the mind, and the effort to explain it is made precisely in terms of its being such a subjective state. Thus it is first of all distinguished from other dispositional states of the person (*aḥwāl*, *akwān*, *ṣifāt*, etc. – see above) and then from other dispositional states of the mind (being ignorant of, suspecting, doubting, etc.). Having thus depicted it as an attitudinal state of the mind which one finds oneself as experiencing (rather than as an object itself whose knowledge presupposes and explains knowledge of items other than itself), it is then simply explained in terms of the confidence an agent feels in the truth of what he or she believes (which makes knowledge similar to ignorance), as well as in terms of the method used by the agent in acquiring this belief.

FALSAFAH EPISTEMOLOGY

Unlike *kalām* thinkers, whose intellectual efforts in the subject give the impression at least of being indigenous, the philosophers operated within the framework of a transmitted system or systems, and their contributions or originality can be understood against this background. Broadly speaking, one can perhaps distinguish between two main streams of thought in *falsafah* epistemology, represented by al-Fārābī and Avicenna. In many ways, Avicenna's epistemology is closer to *kalām*, while al-Fārābī's is closer to the Neoplatonic system. In al-Fārābī, the epistemic order reflects or corresponds to the ontic order. The world is neatly described in terms of a terrestrial and an extraterrestrial order. The extraterrestrial order consists of a progressively elevated ontology of heavenly bodies and minds (intellects) whose pinnacle is the Prime Mover, or God. The sublunar order consists of a progressively regressing ontology of animate and inanimate objects reaching as far down as the four main elements. At the top of the sublunar ontological order stands humanity, while at the beginning of the extraterrestrial order the moon stands associated with the Active Intellect, God's contact with the terrestrial world. Everything in the world is made up of matter and form, the essence and meaning of each object being its form. Terrestrial forms originate in the Active Intellect and subsist there eternally, there being virtually no epistemic difference between the totality of forms originating in the Active Intellect as an object of knowledge and the Active Intellect itself as an eternally active cognizant subject. Standing at the top of the terrestrial pyramid humanity strives for and can achieve perfection (happiness, eternality) through the pursuit of knowledge. As knowledge is knowledge of meanings/essences/forms, the more a human being cognizes and collects forms the more similar he or she becomes to the Active Intellect. This similarity, reaching almost total fusion, is a function partly of the sameness of forms as objects of knowledge in both cases, and partly of the principle adopted by al-Fārābī that in acts of cognizance the subject and object of knowledge are fused into one.

The epistemic journey towards fusion with the Active Intellect and the achievement therefore of happiness begins at the bottom of the ladder with a material intellect that stands ready to cognize material forms (forms subsisting in matter) but has not yet done so. It is thus a potential intellect rather than an intellect-in-act. Once a form is cognized (thus undergoing a transformation in its own status, *qua* the intellect cognizing it, from being an intelligible-*in-potentia* to becoming an intelligible-in-act), the intellect becomes an intellect-in-act. This intellect-in-act is material because the form it has cognized subsists in matter. However, as the intellect transcends in its epistemic journey, apprehending material forms and then, through a series of abstractions, beginning to cognize immaterial (or abstract) forms, it becomes an immaterial intellect. Given the finite framework of reference in which the intellect operates, the epistemic quest has an end which is the acquisition of all or nearly all the forms that are potentially cognizable. At that stage, the human intellect comes to be in possession of the same "data" as that inhering in the Active Intellect, and a state of fusion or sameness between the two is achieved, explained by the principle of the fusion or sameness of the subject and object of knowledge. There may be some subtle distinctions introduced at this stage (the distinction between the acquired intellect as a perfection of the human immaterial intellect and the Active Intellect as a part of the heavenly order, as well as the additional possession, by the Active Intellect, of forms abstracted from a higher ontological order), but the bottom line is that the human intellect can achieve a sense of fusion with the Active Intellect, and can thus acquire its characteristics of eternity and happiness.

Avicennan epistemology, in contrast, denies the principle of fusion between subject and object of knowledge (thus forestalling Fārābīan conclusions and theories relating to the achievement of final happiness and eternity). Furthermore, and in a series of ideas that can be truly described as ingenious, Avicenna tries to depict a theory of knowledge that is distinctively subjectivist. Whatever the ontological status of forms in the material world, forms in the intellect in any case have a distinct ontological status, in such a way that the immediate objects of intellectual cognition are not what exist in the external world. These intellectual forms are further transformed once they become logically categorized, so that the logical objects of thought and discourse are quite distinct from external as well as mental/intellectual objects. In a sense, the categorization of logical objects in a certain way (the framework of knowledge) is not a reflection of sacrosanct or eternal truths in the world (an ontic order), and it is not set up the way it is owing to an inner code of relations of essences, but it is a causal and contingent product of the intellectual effort at understanding the world. Even in the world itself objects or relations are not the way they are because of an inner code of essences, but are a causal and contingent product of God's Providence. Avicenna does not deny forms as essences, but after ascribing to them the status of subsistence as indeterminate things, their subsistence in the material or logical worlds in specific ways ceases to be regarded as *essentially* necessary, and retains only a *causal* necessity. The "Classical" school would have argued that objects might or might not have existed, but their being *what* they are is due to an inner cause which is their essence. Fire might not have existed, but given that it exists its essence necessitates that it have such-and-such qualities. In contrast, Avicenna held that not only is an object's essence contingent to it, but more radically that the essence being of such-and-such a description is also a contingent matter. Therefore, not only is fire's existence contingent on God's causing it to come to be, but also the character of its essence is also contingent on God's causing it to have this description. In the al-Fārābīan model the formal order in the Active Intellect becomes manifest in the external world and is then imprinted as that order in the human intellect. In the Avicennan model forms have no order in the Active Intellect, and their manifestation in a specific order in the external world or their categorization in a specific order by the human intellect is an expression of one of several logical possibilities. Indeed, the forms (the essences) themselves subsist as such only in the Active Intellect, but not in the material world. They are not therefore abstracted (as in the Fārābīan model) from the external material world. Images of particulars are indeed cognized, and the intellect performs the active function of unification and differentiation. However, this function is integrated with the Active Intellect, in that the presentation of a particular image enables the human intellect to cognize an abstract form emanating from above. Given that neither particular images from the material world nor abstract forms from the Active Intellect are relational in themselves (that they do not have an inherent order), the construction of the objects of knowledge (the logical order) by the human intellect becomes a non-definitive exercise, i.e., an exercise in opinion-formation rather than in the acquisition of knowledge strictly so-called. Like *kalām* thinkers, Avicenna thus subsumes knowledge under the category of belief.

Perhaps because of the absence of a formal order, the intuitive faculty (the capability to be inspired) plays a major part in the Avicennan epistemic system. Intellects vary in their receptivity to intuition, and these variations (whether in terms of number or of speed) explain the movement from premisses to conclusions (i.e., the acquisition of knowledge). The intellect has to apply itself methodically to evidence, but there is no internal or independent mechanism associated with this application that guarantees the arrival at results. Avicenna's point here seems to be that inspiration is a necessary condition for the arrival at a result, and that perspiration alone is not sufficient. There are various degrees in this intuitive ability, reaching the point where the human intellect is ever-ready to receive forms emanating from the Active Intellect, or where it is in a state of semi-constant inspiration. This intuitive faculty, at its zenith, is a holy or prophetic faculty. Avicenna argues in this context that once the human intellect reaches this point it would not be impossible for it to start perceiving images of particulars from other times, in particular from the future. However, in general Avicenna argues that the human intellect is almost always burdened by its association with bodily matters, and it cannot therefore achieve epistemic perfection (or happiness, etc.) until after becoming relieved, as a soul, from the human body. Once again, in this Avicenna seems to hold a view that is at variance with that of al-Fārābī, and closer to the Islamic tradition.

For Avicenna the knowledge of something must proceed on the basis of methodical reasoning, the result must be inspired, and ideally the intellect must be cognizant of this step-by-step process to be truly said to have knowledge. However, such knowledge can be recollected without detailed cognizance of the steps that led to it, and it can be transmitted to others. One assumes that this variety of categories of knowledge in Avicenna is possible given the overall framework of knowledge being a form of belief, which can therefore be manifested in different epistemic states of the mind.

GOD'S KNOWLEDGE OF PARTICULARS

One cannot end this brief presentation on epistemology without quickly referring to the controversy which arose concerning God's own knowledge of the material world. Once again, two main views can be distinguished here, the "Classical" Fārābīan view which held that God cannot know particulars, and the Avicennan view which tried to explain how God in fact knows particulars through the intermediation of that particular's species. In trying to put up a theory explaining how God knows particulars in a universal way (that not an atom's worth in the heavens or earth escapes his knowledge), Avicenna was once again closer than al-Fārābī to the Muslim/religious tradition.

The theory Avicenna seems to have evolved consists of several elements, parts of which have some points in common with the Theory of Descriptions. The first element in the theory, however, has something to do with "causal knowledge", or with knowledge of particular effects through knowledge of principles or general causes. Given that God knows these general principles and their interaction with one another, He can therefore also know the particular effects these lead to in the context of time (i.e., their occurrence in time). This causal knowledge, Avicenna claims, is universal (presumably since it is a knowledge of a conditional). However, Avicenna seems to distinguish here between knowledge *of* a particular and knowledge *about* a particular. The distinction has to do with whether the particular is one of a kind. If it is (e.g., like the sun) then God can have knowledge of it (through its description). If, however, it is not one of a kind, then God can know about it through a description, but God cannot be ascribed with knowledge *of* it, since this can only be acquired through ostensive reference in the first place.

In this second case, the ability according to which reference to (and therefore knowledge about) a particular can be achieved is explained through postulating two related "universal" truths or items of knowledge. The example Avicenna uses in this context is that of an eclipse: of any particular eclipse it is possible to provide (know) an entire account of specific descriptions (spatial as well as temporal). In God's case, this account is presumably possible in the causal sense already referred to. The condition here is that these spatial and temporal descriptions are part of the knowledge (the predicate), and are not limiting parameters of the intellect having that knowledge (the subject). Avicenna argues, in another context, that even particular statements are eternally true if their particularity is regarded as a feature of the predicate instead of its being a condition which is external to the statement or a characterization of the subject.

This entire account of specific descriptions, however, is universal in that it is predicable of more than one eclipse. In order for this description or universal account to be said to have a reference function, Avicenna adds a second item, namely, the knowledge that this described eclipse is only one. God can thus be said to know a particular by knowing that particular's description and by knowing, in addition, that this description happens to be true of only one. Interestingly, it is the combination of these two items as an explanation that is reminiscent of the Theory of Descriptions. Avicenna pointedly adds that, even armed with this knowledge, it would be impossible to determine of this particular eclipse whether it is the eclipse one had knowledge *about*. This is like arguing that I could know everything about the thief who broke into my house, but I cannot determine of this person, whom I now see before me, if he or she is the person who did it. Clearly, knowledge based on ostention is different from knowledge based on description, but both kinds can still be argued to be knowledge about particulars.

SELECT BIBLIOGRAPHY

Bakar, O. (1992) *Classification of Knowledge in Islam*, (Kuala Lumpur).

Daud, W. (1989) *The Concept of Knowledge in Islam* (London).

Ha'iri Yazdi, Mehdi (1992) *The Principles of Epistemology in Islamic Philosophy; Knowledge by Presence* (Albany).

Matsumoto, A. (1986) "On the Theory of the Cognizant and the Cognizable", *Bulletin of Mid Eastern Culture Centre in Japan*: 35–57.

Nasr, S. H. (1968a) *The Encounter of Man and Nature* (Cambridge, Mass.).

—— (1968b) *Science and Civilization in Islam* (Cambridge, Mass.).

—— (1976) *Islamic Science: an Illustrated Study* (London).

—— (1987) "Science Education: the Islamic Perspective", *Muslim Education Quarterly*, 5(1): 4–14.

Nusseibeh, S. (1989) "Al-'Aql al-Qudsī: Avicenna's Subjective Theory of Knowledge", *Studia Islamica*, 49: 39–54.

Rosenthal, F. (1970) *Knowledge Triumphant: The Concept of Knowledge in Medieval Islam* (Leiden).

Sardar, Z. (ed.) (1984) *The Touch of Midas: Science, Values and Environment in Islam and the West* (Manchester).

—— (ed.) (1988) *The Revenge of Athena: Science, Exploitation and the Third World* (London).
—— (ed.) (1989a) *An Early Crescent: the Future of Knowledge and the Environment in Islam* (London).
—— (1989b) *Explorations in Islamic Science* (London).
—— (ed.) (1991) *How We Know: Ilm and the Revival of Knowledge* (London).

CHAPTER 50

Political philosophy

Hans Daiber

As leader of the new Islamic community (*ummah*)[1] the Prophet Muḥammad combined religious interests with requirements of politics (*siyāsah,* literally "government").[2] In the so-called Constitution of Medina the community of the believers declared their solidarity against common enemies and accepted Muḥammad as prophet and arbiter between rival clans.[3] His leadership was legitimized by the divine revelation.

This legitimacy of the leader appeared to be replaced among the successors of the Prophet, the caliphs, by an appointment through the community either because of their merits or because of their affiliation to the family of the Prophet. There was, however, no consensus on the legitimacy of the caliphs. Early debates starting immediately after the death of the Prophet[4] created among Muslims a consciousness of community and leadership, of hierarchical structures in society and of dependence and responsibility within the individual freedom of man as a member of the new Islamic community. The traditional deterministic character of the Islamic conception of belief in an Almighty God induced members of this Islamic *ummah* to reflect again and again on the role of man as related to the leader of a religious state and to define the task and qualities of the leader, who became *khalīfah* by God's decree. Among the Umayyads we therefore find tendencies of *jabr*, divine omnipotence, and *qadar*, human freedom, as description of a polarization resulting from a developing critical attitude towards rulers: one is free to rebel against them if they are sinful rulers, that is, disobey the Qur'ān, God's Book, or the *Sunnah* of the Prophet.[5] Simultaneously, it became evident that political leadership is dependent upon divine inspiration: it is based on the revelation of the Qur'ān, the ethical guiding principle of the community for what is good and just.[6]

This ideological background of early Islam was the starting-point of political philosophy, which from the third/ninth century onwards developed under the influence of Hellenism and integrated political thoughts and ideas reflected in the early mirrors of princes, written in the second/eighth century, and in Islamic theology. The Persian Ibn al-Muqaffaʿ (d. 140/757), one of the early famous writers of Arabic literary prose, gives in his *Kitāb al-adab al-kabīr = al-Durrat al-yatīmah*, his *Risālah fi'l-ṣaḥābah* and in his version *Kalīlah wa Dimnah*, originally a collection of Indian fables, practical advice to the prince.[7] The texts give a picture of society as consisting of a minority of people with excellent judgment, solid friendship, integrity and fraternity, the *khāṣṣah* in contrast to the masses, the *ʿāmmah*;[8] they reveal a rather rationalistic morality aimed at *savoir vivre*; in the domination of political authority over Islamic *Sharīʿah* they show a rationalistic-critical and perhaps Manichaean-inspired attitude against religion, without, however, totally denying the value of religion: religion gives people what they deserve and directs them to what is their duty.[9] The prince, the ruler, appears to be a worldly and a religious leader; he should be prudent and just, but at the same time the ruled should be distrustful towards him. This sceptical attitude against religious and political authority seems to have revived the value of friendship as creating community and improving human character.[10]

Ibn al-Muqaffaʿ was indebted to Indian material; mainly, however, like later authors of mirrors of princes[11] or authors of political thought,[12] he followed Persian–Sassanian ethical traditions. They were combined with gnomological sayings by the wise men of the past: Sassanian wisdom literature is corroborated by sayings of wise men from the Greek, pre-Islamic and Islamic past.[13] Aristotle's pupil Alexander the Great becomes the ideal figure of a king[14] and appears as addressee in a collection of advice said to be by Aristotle.[15] These letters are based on Byzantine handbooks on warfare and on administration; they include material from classical and later Hellenistic–hermetical literature; they were translated from Greek at the suggestion of Sālim Abu'l-ʿAlā', the secretary of the caliph Hishām (reigned 106–126/724–743) and used in Arabic revisions like the famous pseudo-Aristotelian *Sirr al-asrār*,[16] a mirror of princes from the fourth/tenth century, which in its Latin version played a major role in the Middle Ages.[17]

Ethical literature of Islam is classified as *adab* and aims at the moral education of man, ruler and ruled; authorities of the past, Islamic and non-Islamic, justify practical advice in contemporary political situations. Above all, Greek gnomological literature became integrated in Arabic compilations like the *Nawādir al-falāsifah* by the famous translator Ḥunayn ibn Isḥāq (d. 260/873), which was widely used in later times.[18] The Greek heritage became a guiding-line for popular philosophical ethics which relied on gnomological sayings and, in addition, on translations of Greek texts like the pseudo-Aristotelian *De virtutibus et vitiis*,[19] Plutarch's *De cohibenda ira*,[20] Galen's treatise on ethics, of which only an Arabic summary is preserved,[21] Themistius' letter to Julian on *Politics*,[22] the *Oikonomikos* by the neo-Pythagorean Bryson[23] and a treatise on the banishment of sorrow, perhaps by Themistius or by Plutarch.[24] The material of these books was integrated in Islamic philosophical ethics and formed the basis of political philosophy in Islam: it elaborated the political idea of justice[25] and the hierarchical structure of society in which the position of people is determined by their behaviour (virtues and self-control) and achievement and in which friendship is a key factor of its holding together; friendship and love are central themes in Miskawayh (see below) and continue the discussion begun by Ibn al-Muqaffaʿ (see above).

These ethical traditions formed the basis of Islamic political philosophy, which began to arise in the third/ninth century. The origin of Islamic political philosophy is correlated with the translation of political writings mainly by Plato (summaries of his *Republic*, *Laws* and *Politics*)[26] and by Aristotle's *Nicomachean Ethics*, which was available to the Arabs in the translation by Isḥāq ibn Ḥunayn and in a translation of a lost Greek summary perhaps by Nicolaus Damascenus, the *Summa Alexandrinorum*; in addition, the Arabs knew Porphyry's commentary on the *Nicomachean Ethics*.[27]

Finally, besides the early development of the caliphate and ethical Islamic and non-Islamic traditions, the theological discussions on the just Imāmate by Shiʿites and Muʿtazilites from the second/eighth century and by the Ashʿarites from the fourth/tenth century (cf. e.g. al-Bāqillānī)[28] redefined the role of the leader, the Imām, and his function in the community. He is liable for the community and must have knowledge of law, moral and religious matters and must be independent in his judgment; only the most excellent can be a rightful Imām. The Twelver Shīʿah based their Imāmi doctrine on the necessity of an infallible leader for humanity, an Imām who is a God-inspired teacher of religion and thus comparable to the Prophet, without, however, being the transmitter of a holy book.[29] This conception of a divinely guided leadership deeply impressed political philosophers of Islam from the fourth/tenth century.

Their forerunners in the third/ninth century restricted themselves to the ethics of the single individual in a community and continued the tradition of Islamic and non-Islamic gnomological sayings: although the first great philosopher of the Arabs, al-Kindī (*c.* 185/801–252/866),[30] and more clearly his younger contemporary Qusṭā ibn Lūqā (*fl.* about 205/820–300/912)[31] knew the Aristotelian tripartition of practical philosophy in ethics, economics and politics and attribute to Aristotle works in these fields, the works themselves apparently were not available to them; the *Nicomachean Ethics* was translated later[32] and from Aristotle's treatise on *Politics* only a part seems to have been available to the Arabs in a paraphrase or abridgement made in the Hellenistic or Roman period.[33]

Nevertheless, the *Fihrist* by Ibn al-Nadīm lists several "political books" (*kutubuhū al-siyāsiyyāt)* by al-Kindī,[34] among them a treatise on politics (*siyāsah*) and another one on the government of the people (*siyāsat al-ʿāmmah*); both are lost. The rest of the listed treatises primarily discuss ethical themes, including the virtues of the individual. This interest of al-Kindī in ethics as the main feature of politics can be confirmed from his preserved works. In his *Risālah fī ḥudūd al-ashyāʾ wa-rusūmihā*[35] al-Kindī betrays knowledge of the Platonic–Aristotelian anthropology,[36] of the soul–body dichotomy and of the Platonic tripartion of the soul into reasonable, desiring and irascible parts; these parts cause the four Platonic cardinal virtues:[37] wisdom (*ḥikmah*), temperance (*ʿiffah*) and manliness (*najdah*); if the equilibrium (*iʿtidāl*) in them is disturbed, the opposite of them, i.e. vices, are caused; "real virtue" (*al-faḍīlah al-ḥaqqiyyah*) is part of "ethics in the soul" and also part of its "righteous" (*ʿadl*) acting (*afʿāl al-nafs*).[38] This Platonic–Aristotelian conception of ethics also appears in the sayings ascribed to al-Kindī.[39] His *Risālah fī alfāẓ Suqrāṭ*[40] and his *Risālah fī Alcibiades wa-Suqrāṭ*[41] describe Socrates as an ideal of moderation and spiritual values, which are superior to worldly possessions.[42] Al-Kindī's interest in the figure of Socrates reveals his sympathy with this conception of ethics. In a similar manner, his treatise *On the Means to Drive Away Sorrow* (*Risālah fi'l-ḥīlah li-dafʿ al-aḥzān*), which in fact reproduces a lost Hellenistic treatise,[43] advises the neglect of worldly things and concentration on the intelligible world by "imitating God".[44] This is attained through the human virtues, by our goodness in behaviour and acts. If we neglect worldly things, we will not be "unlucky" (*shaqīy*) in the hereafter, we will be "near to our creator" and will "know him".[45]

Al-Kindī's political philosophy combines Platonic–Aristotelian features with Neoplatonic trends and appears to be restricted to an individualistic ethics of the divine soul, to the behaviour of man as striving for happiness[46] in the hereafter by neglecting the world and by increasing knowledge of spiritual things, of his Creator. It is not exclusively contemplative; in its concept of wisdom (*ḥikmah*) it implies man's righteous action in relation to his fellow-citizen, as a means to a higher, spiritual goal.

After al-Kindī and before al-Fārābī (d. 339/950), the political philosopher par excellence, the following authors of books on politics (*siyāsah*) are listed by the *Fihrist* of Ibn al-Nadīm: the historian Aḥmad ibn Abī Ṭāhir Ṭayfūr (b. 205/819), the already mentioned Christian translator Qusṭā ibn Lūqā (b. c. 205/820), al-Kindī's student as-Sarakhsī (b. *c*. 220/835), his contemporary ʿUbayd Allāh ibn ʿAbd Allāh ibn Ṭāhir (b. 223/838) and Abū Zayd al-Balkhī (c. 236/850–323/934).[47] As far as the preserved fragments allow a judgment, they do not take up and develop al-Kindī's Platonic–Aristotelian idea of politics as ethics and seem to follow mainly the above-described Persian heritage as reflected in the mirror of princes: good people can be guided by making them interested (*targhīb*) through pleasurable things and lower-class people by means of intimidation (*tarhīb*).[48] To this manner of leading Abū Zayd al-Balkhī added the concept[49] of *maṣlaḥah* (welfare) of the people, which is the concern of the ruler.[50] Finally, al-Balkhī's classification of politics as one of the most important "crafts", because it allows the cultivation (*'imārah*) of a country and the protection (*ḥimāyah*) of its people, is directly or indirectly inspired by Aristotle's *Nicomachean Ethics* (1094a27ff.).[51] As in Aristotle the end of politics is not one single person, but all the people and their country. Here, the welfare of the community outweighs the interests of individuals. In contrast to al-Kindī's approach to the ethical behaviour of the individual, the virtue of humanity as a means to happiness is neglected in the available fragment of al-Balkhī's treatise. Contrary to al-Balkhī's pupil Abu'l-Ḥasan al-'Āmirī[52] the available text does not mention the importance of religion, especially of the Islamic religion, which according to al-'Āmirī is superior to other religions and is a moral guide of the individual in the perfect state, leading to individual improvement.

Al-Balkhī's realistic attitude reappears in Qudāmah ibn Ja'far (b. 260/873), *Kitāb al-kharāj*, chapter 8 (on *al-Siyāsah*);[53] like al-Balkhī he combines Persian, Islamic and Greek traditions.[54] His definition of politics, however, is different and emphasizes the necessity of a leader because of the differences between men,[55] the role and ethical qualities of rulers[56] and their subjects[57] as well as the necessity of the consolidation of people into one community, as they need each other.[58] Reflection on the science of politics and their bases (*asbāb/'ilal* "causes") is necessary for the leader.[59]

The treatment of politics by Qudāmah ibn Ja'far presupposes an advanced stage of discussion. State, ruler and ruled call for a new definition and evaluation, inspired by and orientated to new developments in Islamic intellectual history. Politics became a part of ethics, a development which, under the influence of Aristotle had already started in al-Kindī and was built up to a unique system of political philosophy by Qudāmah's contemporary al-Fārābī (259/873–339/950). This philosopher (see below) developed, under the influence of Aristotle, the Peripatetic tradition, Plato and Neoplatonic trends, a philosophical system which at the same time is a reaction to current discussions on the role of the Imām, i.e. must his knowledge be based on divine inspiration and does prophecy confirm political authority? These problems arose in discussions between the Ismā'īlī Abū Ḥātim al-Rāzī and the well-known physician and philosopher Abū Bakr al-Rāzī, which took place in Rayy between 318/930 and 320/932–3 or perhaps already before 313/925 in the presence of the governor Mardawījī. These discussions are mirrored in Abū Ḥātim al-Rāzī's book *The Proofs of Prophecy* (*A'lām al-nubuwwah*).[60] It shows that Abū Bakr al-Rāzī denied the existence and value of prophecy; man can obtain knowledge on his own, has no need of an authority, for example a prophet, and can learn from the ancestors, previous scholars and philosophers, even from their mistakes.[61] An example is Socrates, who is called "our Imām" in Abū Bakr al-Rāzī's *al-Sīrat al-falsafiyyah*: [62] Even if Socrates is not the perfect man as he is commonly described, he is a philosophical model for man's way from extremism to moderation (through asceticism), to morality by acquiring knowledge and practising justice in society; this way frees man's soul from the darkness of this world, and might save him for the world to come; the *Sīrat al-falsafiyyah,* "the philosophical way of life", is once described in a Neoplatonic manner as "becoming Godlike as far as man is capable to that" (*"al-tashabbuh billāh – 'azzah wa-jallah – bi-qadri mā fī ṭāqati'l-insān"*).[63] Abū Bakr al-Rāzī did not develop these soteriological aspects in his other available works, nor their relevance for political philosophy. His *Spiritual Physic* (*al-Ṭibb al-rūḥānī*)[64] expounds Plato (especially *Timaeus*) and Galen,[65] and within a "hedonistic" philosophy the moral virtues of the soul are shown to restrain desire with reason as the only guide to human conduct. Pleasure is the abolition of pain, of distress caused by desire; as such it is a return to the original state of relaxation by moderation and by minimization of desire.[66] This ethics of the soul can harmonize with leadership (*ri'āsah*) and assist and strengthen it; actions based on it belong to *The Symptoms of Fortune and Political Success,* as Abū Bakr al-Rāzī entitled a small political treatise.[67] According to this treatise, which is our only source of his remarks on political philosophy, additional symptoms are intuitive knowledge,[68] love for leadership, justice (*'adl*), excellent truthfulness (*ṣidq*), perception (*ḥiss*) and memory (*iddikār*) of the soul; whoever is "successful" (*muwaffaq*) and "shown the right way" (*musaddad*) through "a divine power" (*quwwah ilāhiyyah*) becomes an "outstanding" person (*fāḍil*) and leader, who is needed by the people. There must be a conformity between them and their leader. Abū Bakr al-Rāzī's remark is interesting on the "divine power" which makes man a leader: he is dependent on it and at the same time needs his own insight, the intuition of reason.

Abū Bakr al-Rāzī's high estimation of reason as a principle of ethical philosophy and his not uncritical high esteem of ancient philosophers, especially of Socrates as guide (*Imām*), was strongly contradicted by his Ismā'īlī opponent Abū Ḥātim al-Rāzī in the above-mentioned book *The Proofs of Prophecy.* The author follows Mu'tazilite,[69] Zaidite[70] and Ismā'īlī[71] tradition according to which people are imperfect and therefore require a leader, whose perfect knowledge is based on prophetic inspiration.[72] People have different opinions and are commanded by God (Qur'ān 3:93/87) to "examine" (*al-naẓar*) and to "follow what is most excellent, suitable, true, and necessary".[73] There is no equality among men, in contrast to the Kharijites, who in accordance with ancient Arab egalitarianism defended the equality of men and did not attribute to the leader of a community any charisma or make him *primus inter pares*.[74] In accordance with the Ḥanbalites[75] Abū Ḥātim al-Rāzī explicitly criticized here the Kharijites, their radicalism in belief (*ta'ammuq fi'l-dīn*), which according to him cannot be compared with independent judgment (*ijtihād*).[76] He concludes that

> there are different classes of men as concerns their intelligence, insight, and power of distinction and perception. For men are not created equal to each other in their natures, as are animals, for instance, which do not differ [*tatafāḍalu*] in their perception of what is needed by them. Since every class of animals is equal by nature, as regards their consciousness of the obligation to look for food and to reproduce, they do not differ in a comparable fashion as is the case with the mentioned diversity of classes as regards their intelligence and insight.[77]

Men can be divided into two classes, into those who know (*'ālim*) and those who learn (*muta'allim*), into leaders (*imām*) and people guided by them (*ma'mūm*).[78] God forgives the weak, who have not the same obligation as the strong;[79] "it is possible that God bestows his wisdom and mercy on men, chooses them from his creation, makes them prophets, helps them, and gives them prophecy".[80] Because of their intellectual differences people require a leader, who is elected by God and equipped with divine knowledge; the Prophet is the divinely inspired leader par excellence. People must obey him, the teacher of the divinely revealed law;[81] otherwise they must be "forced" to "accept the external forms of (the prophetic) prescriptions".[82] Nevertheless, men have the capacity to choose.[83] Who does not obey the prophetic guidance is ignorant (*jāhil*), vicious (*ṭāliḥ*), desecrating (*muntahik*) and unwise[84] and causes enmity and injustice.[85] People without knowledge love power and struggle for wordly things,[86] "they have preferred the world to religion, even though they are convinced of the reward and punishment of those to whom these are promised and threatened".[87] Wars do not arise primarily for the sake of belief, but because of the insatiability and avarice of men for worldly things. They are "kept in check" (*yuqhar*) by religion, by the divinely inspired religious leader.[88] Men cannot attain knowledge and judgment by their own "inventiveness" (*istinbāṭ*).[89] The divinely inspired leader teaches them to distinguish between truth and error and to find the true meaning of the religious symbols, of the "external" forms by way of "interpretation" (*ta'wīl*).[90] Among the prophetic leaders the Prophet Muḥammad has the highest rank and is perfect in his intellect (*'aql*), magnanimity, patience, leadership and guidance of all people".[91] In his good qualities (*shamā'il, ḥilyah*) the Prophet appears as an ideal of perfect moral life;[92] he is the bearer of prophetic knowledge, equipped with the

Platonic cardinal virtues of wisdom, abstinence, courage and justice, which appear combined with the Aristotelian happy mean (*mesotes*).[93] Whoever follows him understands the meaning of the religious laws, avoids error and controversy, and so can attain salvation (*najāt*).[94] Abū Ḥātim al-Rāzī keeps to the superiority of the Prophet Muḥammad, but at the same time defends the universality of religions in their belief in one single God and in the justness of his laws. Religion and prophetic knowledge are common to all people and nations and not a privilege of one nation.[95]

The idea of the inequality of people in society, who therefore require a leader, a "teacher" of universal knowledge, which is not the result of his own inventiveness but based on divine revelation, reappears shortly after Abū Ḥātim al-Rāzī's discussions with Abū Bakr al-Rāzī in the political philosophy of al-Fārābī (d. 339/950), also called "the Second Teacher" (after Aristotle). Al-Fārābī developed these ideas into an elaborate system of political philosophy[96] which in its originality betrays a unique combination of Platonic and Aristotelian elements on the basis of Ismā'īlī doctrines about the Imāmate.[97]

Like Abū Ḥātim al-Rāzī, al-Fārābī distinguishes in society between different classes, which can be grouped into "knowing" and "learning" people. Even more than Abū Ḥātim al-Rāzī he stresses among the listed twelve qualifications[98] besides the ethical features the intellectual qualities of the "first ruler" and "Imām", who is "understanding and conceiving very well all he is told, so that it becomes comprehensible to him according to the matter itself".[99] To the Ismā'īlī notion of interpretation of religious symbols, of parables indicating the same universal meaning of differing external forms, the laws,[100] al-Fārābī adds the Aristotelian doctrine of conception and understanding based on Aristotle's *Organon* and *Rhetoric*.[101] According to him "religion" (*millah*) is a description of the "opinions" and "actions" which are imposed upon society by its rulers in the shape of laws.[102] This explanation is combined with doctrines taken from Aristotle's epistemology, psychology and ethics and from Alexander of Aphrodisias as commentator on Aristotle's *De anima*.[103] Religion is an imitation, a picture of philosophy, which can prove and justify the "opinions" of religion; it mirrors Aristotle's practical prudence (*sophrosyne*) as developed in the *Nicomachean Ethics*. Religion is an aspect of philosophy, which uses religion as its instrument: through religion philosophy realizes itself, becomes moral insight, practical prudence leading to supreme happiness (*al-sa'ādah al-quṣwā*).[104]

Here, al-Fārābī presupposes the epistemological and Aristotle-inspired doctrine, that the universals of philosophy are only imaginable to human thinking by using the imaginative powers, which conceive them through imitation (*muḥākāt*) of the perceptible things, the particulars; on the basis of the Aristotelian interrelation between thought and perception man can only think, be a philosopher, by using pictures "imitating" the intelligible things. Ultimately, they are inspired by the divine *intellectus agens*; he transmits them to the prophet, who thus – in Platonic terms in his "assimilation" to God[105] – becomes authorized as ruler of the "perfect state". In this doctrine philosophy appears as practical philosophy in the shape of religion, of "opinions" and "actions" imposed on society in the shape of laws by the divinely inspired ruler, the prophet.[106] In contrast to Abū Ḥātim al-Rāzī, who considered Muḥammad as a prophet with the highest rank, al-Fārābī is silent on the best prophet and speaks only in general terms of the "prophet", "Imām" and "first ruler". Apparently he did so because he strictly kept to the Ismāʿīlī notion of the universality of true religion, of the belief in one single God and in the justness of His laws, common to all nations.[107]

Al-Fārābī also took up the Ismāʿīlī concept of society as consisting of differing ranks, which apparently induced him to modify similar ideas[108] from Plato's *Republic* and *Laws*.[109] At the same time he stressed the Aristotelian notion of man as *zōon politikon*, who wants to be part of an association, of the city-state, and needs his fellow-citizens.[110] The co-operation of people, who obey the divinely inspired philosopher-king, leads to real happiness in the utopian perfect state[111] through virtues, primarily intellectual virtues and through good deeds by keeping to the law, the *Sharīʿah*. Therefore, the study of politics becomes a guide to man's good actions and behaviour[112] and is necessary as a means to individual ultimate happiness; it enables man to distinguish between good and bad.[113] At the same time, philosophers like Plato and Aristotle prove the correctness and justness of the religious law, the *Sharīʿah*.

This islamization of Greek political philosophy implies the already mentioned universal validity of religious laws; therefore, al-Fārābī does not restrict himself to the Platonic description of the ideal state and the imperfect states;[114] he is more interested in the description of the perfect philosopher-ruler and legislator, who bases his knowledge on the prophetic inspiration from God and thus becomes a guide to the perfect virtuous behaviour of man in society, in the perfect state. As a teacher of man, the perfect ruler is not only addressing philosophically minded elites. Because true philosophy is practical philosophy in the state and as such "religion", aimed at the fulfilment of the law (*Sharīʿah*) in the virtuous behaviour of the individual, religion is no more than a disguise of his real opinion, of philosophy. It appears as an alternative language in al-Fārābī's summary of Plato's *Laws*.[115] Religion in the perfect state is the cornerstone of politics and the means of the individual to reach ultimate happiness with the co-operation of the fellow-citizen. The final stage is the release of the soul from matter and its eternal afterlife.[116]

This aim of al-Fārābī's political philosophy is slightly later shared by the *Rasāʾil Ikhwān al-Ṣafāʾ* ("Epistles of the Sincere Brethren"), an encyclopedia compiled before 349/959–60 by anonymous authors and sympathizers of the Ismāʿīlīs. Their didactic purpose is to purify the soul and to improve character by knowledge of "intellectual things" (*al-umūr al-ʿaqliyyah*).[117] Knowledge leads to salvation in the hereafter. In addition, the *Rasā'il* contain incidental passages, which reveal rather complex ideas of political philosophy based on al-Fārābī.[118] People are divided into three groups: the elite (*khawāṣṣ*), which can know the "mysteries of religion"; the masses (*ʿawāmm*), which have access to the exoteric aspect of religion, namely the religious obligations like prayer, fasting, etc.; finally the "middle" class, the *mutawassiṭūn*, who can contemplate the religious dogma, interpret the Qur'ān in its literal and allegorical sense and can use independent judgment (*ijtihād*). The inequality of people induces the Ikhwān to distinguish seven classes: craftsmen, businessmen, construction engineers, rulers, servants, unemployed and scholars of religion and other sciences. The privileged and rich people are attacked because they have no moral responsibility to the poor neighbour, who is content with little, and strongly believes in the hereafter. The Ikhwān criticize social conditions of their time and the immorality of people; they list the imperfections of several professions, including the unjust ruler and the caliph, who is not appointed by designation of the Prophet.[119] Social and moral grievances are caused by the inequality of living beings,[120] who do not help each other. This necessitates a ruling authority, the Prophet, who establishes the Divine Law, the *Nāmūs*, which he received through divine revelation.[121] As with al-Fārābī[122] he must have twelve qualities.[123] He and his designated successors of prophetic descent, the Imāms,[124] are assisted by eight classes of people: the reciters and transmitters of the Qur'ān; the transmitters of prophetical sayings; the experts of the Divine Law; the commentators on the text of the Qur'ān; the warriors; caliphs and leaders of the community; the ascetics and the worshippers of God; the allegorical interpreters of the Qur'ān and the theologians.[125]

Contrary to the Shiʿite doctrine of *ghaybah* (occultation), the Ikhwān maintain that people have an Imām even when they refuse to acknowledge (*munkirūn*) his existence.[126] Imāms are the caliphs who combine in their persons the functions of prophecy and kingship, like David, Solomon, Joseph and Muḥammad (who, however, is not imām).127 But the Ikhwān are aware that a prophetic state like that of Muḥammad must still be fulfilled; under the influence of the Shiʿite Imamate and al-Fārābī's Platonic–Aristotelian political philosophy they developed a utopian state, the "virtuous spiritual state" (*madīnah fāḍilah rūḥāniyyah*)[128] in contrast to the "government of evil people"; this utopian state consists of virtuous, wise and sincere men, who in a hierarchy of "artisans", "leaders", "kings" and "divine people" help each other to reach the ultimate happiness in the hereafter.[129] People, the artisans, need the guidance of the Divine Law, the *Nāmūs*, because man is a combination of four souls, the vegetative, animal, rational and angelic souls, which reflect four stages of man's way to perfection and which let man waver between good and bad; in accordance with man's varying natural disposition (*jibillah*) including his intelligence,[130] his rational soul induces him to acquire knowledge, to obey the Divine Law as revealed to the Prophet and taught by the Imāms and to realize the "virtuous spiritual state".[131] In their view of the utopian perfect state the Ikhwān indicate some optimism as regards their belief in progress of mankind and in cyclical revolutionary changes; things are in motion and change, primarily because man can mould his environment with his will and with his increasing knowledge of "prophetic" (*al-siyāsat al-nabawiyyah*) and "kingly politics" (*al-siyāsat al-mulūkiyyah*), of "popular politics" (*al-siyāsat al-'āmmiyyah*) related to the ruling of the masses, of "individual politics" (*al-siyāsat al-khāṣṣiyyah*), i.e. economy, and of "personal politics" (*al-siyāsat al-dhātiyyah*), i.e. ethics of man.[132] At the same time, however, his natural disposition depends on the constitution of his body, on the geographical environment, on his cleaving to transmitted ideas of religion and on the astrological ordinances.[133] The political philosophy of the Ikhwān al-Ṣafā' appears to be a complex amalgamation of contemporary politics and Fārābīan notions of the perfect state in a system which is orientated at traditional Islamic eschatology and at the Neoplatonic notion of the soul. In the virtuous state where the Divine Law of the Prophet or his successors is obeyed, the soul frees itself from the body and thus reaches ultimate happiness in the hereafter. The first beginning is a fraternal community in this world, a community which remains united in its obedience to the Divine Law and thus strives, with the co-operation of its members, after the "welfare of religion and the world" (*ṣalāḥ al-dīn wa'l-dunyā*).[134]

In their discussions on the community, its ruler and ruled, the Ikhwān al-Ṣafā' did not pay too much attention to the individual and his ethical behaviour.[135] The main purpose of their *Rasā'il* was an encyclopedic education of man to a new consciousness, which should enable him to avoid the blind following of wicked rulers, to develop an independent judgment (*ijtihād*) and thus find the way to ultimate happiness by growing knowledge of the "intellectual things".

As the political ideas of the Ikhwān al-Ṣafā' are rather scattered in the *Rasā'il*, they did not influence later authors very much, although they share with al-Fārābī the originally Ismā'īlī[136] ideas of the universality of prophecy as the ultimate source of human knowledge, the inequality of people and the notions of ruler and ruled.

A new approach can be found in Miskawayh (born in Rayy *c.* 320/932 and said to have died 421/1030), who – as will be shown – stressed "personal politics" (a term used by the Ikhwān al-Ṣafā', see above) and developed an ethical model of the individual in the community. His *Tahdhīb al-akhlāq*,[137] like the Ikhwān al-Ṣafā', aims to educate man to good actions based on the Platonic cardinal virtues and in accordance with knowledge, "wisdom" (*ḥikmah*), which leads him to the "spiritual things",[138] to happiness (*al-sa'ādah*)[139] and "calmness of the soul"[140] by purification of his soul from "the physical things" (*al-umūr al-ṭabī'iyyah*) and from the "bodily desires" (*shahawāt al-abdān*).[141] Therefore, Miskawayh called his ethics also *Book on the Purification (of the Soul)* (*Kitāb al-ṭahārah*).[142] As in Plato and above all in Aristotle,[143] virtues are defined as means (*i'tidāl*) between two extremes. Thus man's justice to God, to his fellow-citizens and to the ancestors, plays a crucial role in Miskawayh's ethics.[144] The virtues are prescribed by wisdom (*al-ḥikmah*), law (*al-sharī'ah*) and tradition (*al-sunnah*).[145] Miskawayh is convinced that man's character can be formed by practice (*'ādah, tadarrub*),[146] but because of the inequality of people[147] man needs the assistance of his fellow-citizen[148] and must live together with him in love (*maḥabbah*) and friendship (*ṣadāqah*).[149] In addition, the inequality of people is the very reason why everyone must seek his own happiness[150] through the development of a perfect character (*al-kamāl al-khulqī*).[151] Here the welfare of the individual prevails against the welfare of the state.

With his combination of Greek, Persian and Arabic traditions Miskawayh deeply impressed later authors like Rāghib al-Iṣfahānī (d. perhaps 502/1108), al-Ghazzālī (d. 505/1111), Ibn Abī'l-Rabī' (wrote 655/1256),[152] Naṣīr al-Din al-Ṭūsī (d. 672/1274), al-Dawānī (d.908/1502) and even Muḥammad 'Abduh (d. 1322/1905).[153] Here we should pay special attention to Miskawayh's younger fellow-citizen of the town of Isfahan, Rāghib al-Iṣfahānī.[154] His comprehensive book on *al-Dharī'ah ilā makārim al-sharī'ah* combines essential ideas of Miskawayh with those of al-Fārābī[155] and the *Rasā'il Ikhwān al-Ṣafā'* and offers a unique integration of Qur'ānic passages confirming his philosophical ethics. Because of the inequality of people, who as in the *Rasā'il Ikhwān al-Ṣafā'* (see above) can be divided into elite, masses and middle class,[156] people need each other;[157] as in Miskawayh the harmony among people is based on love/friendship and justice.[158] In addition, Rāghib follows al-Fārābī's political philosophy of the divinely inspired ruler; people need prophets (*anbiyā'*),[159] because "most of the people are not able to get knowledge of what is useful and harmful to them in the hereafter".[160] Miskawayh's notion of law is specified as "the honourable actions of law" (*makārim al-sharī'ah*), as "most honourable religious duties" (*ashraf al-'ibādāt*), as knowledge and action, which both require purity of the soul and make man a "viceroy" (*khalīfah*) of God;[161] Rāghib refers to Qur'ān 2:30 and 6:165 and develops the Neoplatonic and Fārābīan notion of ruling as "assimilation" to God: to be *khalīfah* means "to imitate the Creator in ruling according to human ability, namely by applying the noble qualities of law".[162] A precondition of *khilāfah* and *'ibādah* is man's earning (*taḥṣīl*)[163] of his livelihood (*ma'āsh*), which is classified in accordance with Qur'ān 11:61/64 as "cultivation of earth" (*'imārat al-arḍ*).[164] Thus, the task of man in society becomes *'imārah*, *'ibādah* and *khilāfah*.[165] The ultimate aim is happiness of the individual in the hereafter, which cannot be reached without assistance of the fellow-citizen, and happiness in this world, in a community with harmony, love and friendship. Rāghib's ideas deeply impressed Ghazzālī (*Mīzān al 'amal*,[166] *Iḥyā' 'ulūm al-dīn*) and by this became widespread in the Islamic world. Ghazzālī aimed at a synthesis of the Sufi virtues of love of God, of Qur'ānic ethics and of the Aristotelian doctrine of virtue as golden mean.[167] The mystical path of the believer, who inside an essentially Qur'ānic–eschatological world view keeps to the Islamic law, is the only way to perfection and happiness in the hereafter. This notion thrusts al-Fārābī's notion of society as the means to happiness of the citizen into the background; it mirrors a development, which after al-Fārābī increasingly gave political philosophy new accents. It is akin to the Neoplatonic *apragmōn-bios* ideal of the philosopher, who preferably retreats from society.[168] Already the *Rasā'il Ikhwān al-Ṣafā'* included mysticism in their philosophy[169] and influenced the great philosopher Ibn Sīnā (Avicenna) with their philosophical–scientific explanation of Sufism as a means to purify the human soul.[170]

Ibn Sīnā (370/980–428/1037) from Bukhara gives in his allegory *Ḥayy ibn Yaqẓān*[171] and in his poem *On the Soul*[172] symbolical descriptions of the way the soul returns from the chains of the body, and the darkness of matter compared to the heavenly light of the pure divine intellect. Therefore, the prophet is a Sufi, who proclaims the divine laws as a way to the mystical path,[173] which frees the rational soul from the body and leads to the vision (*mushāhadah*) of God.[174] He has spontaneous perceptions and intuitions, and therefore is higher than the philosopher and not identical with al-Fārābī's philosopher-king, Imām and first ruler; he administers man's life in this world and in the hereafter.[175] Man, however, "cannot lead a proper life when isolated as a single individual".[176] He needs society, and because of the hierarchical structure of society – as in Plato it can be divided into rulers, artisans and guardians[177] – its members are dependent on each other. Therefore, there must be between men social relations and justice; man must obey the lawgiver, the Prophet, by fulfilling his duties to God (*'ibādāt*) and men (*mu'āmalāt*).[178] Different from Plato's *Laws*, the Islamic *Sharī'ah* is the only way of life in this world to the hereafter.[179]

Life on earth as the precondition of life in the hereafter explains Ibn Sīnā's interest in politics. Thus, much more than can be found in al-Fārābī, society as the context of man's life is a precondition of human perfection; therefore "citizens are made good so that cities can exist", whereas "for Alfarabi, cities exist to make men good".[180] Besides the remarks in his *Fī aqsām al-'ulūm al-'aqliyyah*,[181] in his *Fī ithbāt al nubuwwāt*[182] and above all in the *Shifā', al-Ilāhiyyāt*[183] an idea of Ibn Sīnā's political philosophy can be found in his treatise *Fi'l-siyāsah al-manziliyyah*.[184] In accordance with his division of practical philosophy into politics, ethics and economics in *Aqsām al-'ulūm al-'aqliyyah*, he first discusses the inequality of men, who need a ruler,[185] then ethics[186] and finally[187] economics with the subdivisions successively discussing the administration of money, women, children and servants. Ibn Sīnā follows Bryson's *Oeconomica*,[188] however with a slightly differing sequence,[189] new formulations and Islamic examples. Ibn Sīnā handled his sources independently and adds new considerations:[190] for example in his *Shifā', al-Ilāhiyyāt*, Ibn Sīnā recommends taking care of the sick and infirm and of those unable to earn their livelihood. He explains that rebellion is allowed, even against the virtuous caliph, if he is inferior in power and intelligence: here, political power appears to be more important than the virtue of a pious but weak caliph. This realistic attitude does not contradict, however, the necessity of a harmony between state and religion.

The legislator must excel in the cardinal virtues of temperance, practical wisdom (related to actions in this world) and courage, which together result in justice (*'adālah*), the golden mean (*wasāṭah*).[191] If he combines with it "theoretical wisdom" (*al-ḥikmat al-naẓariyyah*) through the study of philosophy, "he is happy" (*fa-qad sa'idah su'idah*);[192] and if he in addition has prophetical qualities, he becomes *khalīfat Allāh*, God's deputy on earth. Although there might be other "praiseworthy laws" (*sunnah ḥamīdah*), the revealed divine laws (*al-sunnah al-nāzilah*) should be preferred to any other law and even imposed on other cities by war, in case this can "restore the conditions of corrupted cities to welfare [*ṣalāḥ*]".[193] Here, Ibn Sīnā presupposes the inequality of men in religion, which reminds us of a similar statement by al-Bīrūnī: according to this contemporary of Ibn Sīnā, Hindus, Christians and Muslims cannot understand each other, because of their inequality in religion, although there might be general equality between man and man, and a common belief in one God.[194] As in al-Fārābī's political philosophy, the ideal ruler remains a prophet or someone with prophetical qualities. He becomes perfect not through his "theoretical wisdom" but through his additional actions as lawgiver and ruler; those ought to direct man on his way of life in society in this world and thus pave the way, the mystical path to his life in the hereafter, to the spiritual world of the intellect.[195] Who seeks after God thus becomes an ascetic (*zāhid*), someone who worships God by ritual (*'ābid*) and finally "knows" (*'ārif*) God. The ultimate consequence of this doctrine, the total retreat from society, is not yet drawn and remains for the Andalusian philosophers Ibn Bājjah and his younger contemporary Ibn Ṭufayl.

Ibn Bājjah (Avempace), who was born in Saragossa and died 533/1138,[196] knew Plato and Aristotle and the political philosophy of al-Fārābī. He is, however, less interested in the preceding discussions on ruler and ruled, on law, justice and welfare of the community. He is convinced that virtuous men as "experts" (*'urafā'*)[197] might improve imperfect states "because social relations [*al-mu'āsharah*], which perfect the state, can be improved by ethical virtues [*al-faḍā'il al-shakliyyah*]".[198] State and society, however, are no longer preconditions for the attainment of ultimate happiness[199] by the indvidual. Resuming al-Fārābī's notion of the virtuous man and philosopher, who sometimes lives under a vicious rule and is "like a stranger in the world",[200] the notion of the solitary philosopher, the Sufi, receives a positive accentuation: not solely by moral virtue as ultimate end, but exclusively in isolation from society, as *mutawaḥḥid*, through "self-government" (*tadbīr*)[201] and contemplation of truth he can seek after ultimate happiness.[202] Although people of the state need the authority of the *'urafā'*, regents who have philosophical knowledge, separation from society might become under certain circumstances (*bi'l-'araḍ*) good,[203] especially in imperfect states, which do not assist the individual in his search for happiness. Mystical ascension to higher forms of knowledge, to liberation of the soul from matter and to union (*ittiṣāl*) with the divine active intellect,[204] an emanation of God, is possible only for the *mutawaḥḥid*. He may, however, profit from the encounter (*liqā', iltiqā'*) with others and from striving after intellectual perfection in the perfect state by emulating each other. The perfect state thus becomes indispensable for the attainment of happiness – not as guarantor of physical life but as a place of "encounter, which assists for [one's] benefit".[205] The most perfect state is the "Imām-state" (*al-madīnah al-imāmiyyah*), which excels states of timocracy (*madīnat al-karāmah*),[206] democracy (*al-madīnah al-jamā'iyyah*) and tyranny (*madīnat al-taghallub*).[207] According to Ibn Bājjah these states are often corrupted by the ruling of children descending from people living in ease and luxury (*al-mutrafūn*) or from people with noble descent (*dhawū' l-aḥsāb*).[208] There might be, however, in them individuals who have "true opinions" (*arā' ṣādiqah*) and whom Ibn Bājjah identifies with al-Fārābī's *nawābit*[209] and with the "strangers" (*al-ghurabā'*) of the Sufis.[210] Ibn Bājjah makes them a separate class besides the judges (*ḥukkām*) and physicians (*aṭibbā'*).[211]

Upon the aforementioned "assisting encounter", which is also called "the political encounter of man" (*al-liqā' al-madanī al-insānī*), follows "the encounter of reason" (*al-liqā' al-'aqlī*) "for the sake of teaching and learning" (*li'l-ta'līm wa'l-ta'allum*) and "the divine encounter" (*al-liqā' al-ilāhī*), which presents "theoretical knowledge" (*al-'ilm al-naẓarī*).[212] Here, as in al-Fārābī, man appears to be in need of the assistance of divinely inspired persons, of prophets, who would grant him knowledge.[213] He must isolate himself from society, if the above mentioned kinds of encounter are not possible in it. He can do so, because he is gifted with free will (*ikhtiyār*) based on reflection;[214] he can reach different "spiritual forms" (*ṣuwar ruḥāniyyah*)[215] depending upon his "opinions" and ethical virtues as he developed them in one of these four forms of states. The highest form of spiritual knowledge can be reached in the Imām state, the perfect state, which can contribute to man's increasing knowledge and happiness in a most perfect manner and thus becomes indispensable.[216] Contrary to Plato, the citizen is not at the service of the community; a community might, however, assist the individual in his search for spiritual knowledge.[217]

A younger contemporary of Ibn Bājjah, the Andalusian philosopher Ibn Ṭufayl (d. 580/1185 or 1186) took over Ibn Bājjah's thesis of the solitary philosopher in his philosophical romance *Ḥayy ibn Yaqẓān*.[218] Strongly inspired by the mystical views of Ibn Sīnā's allegory *Ḥayy ibn Yaqẓān* (on this see above), Ibn Ṭufayl narrates the story of Ḥayy, who on an island without help of society educates himself to mystical contemplation of God. His mystical knowledge of God appears to be identical with the inner meaning of imaged symbolic forms, which the monotheistic religion on a nearby island had developed. This religious community, to which Salāmān belonged, kept to a literal interpretation of religion. Absāl, however, studied its inner meaning; he and Ḥayy were unable to teach it to the "literalists" and therefore returned to the island of Ḥayy. Ibn Ṭufayl turned out to be radically proscriptive of society; he deviated from al-Fārābī in a much stricter sense than Ibn Bājjah, who had admitted the perfect state as assisting individual seekers after divine spiritual knowledge. According to Ibn Ṭufayl the only possible form of society appears to be a religious community, which does not understand the inner meaning of religious symbols but can content itself with following the ritual prescriptions of religion, which turns out to be a Fārābīan mirror-picture of philosophy. Only the solitary "philosopher" has access to the inner meaning of religious symbols; he cannot teach it to the religious community. At the same time, the community cannot assist the seeker after divine knowledge. Philosophy of the solitary and religion of the community do not contradict each other; at the same time they cannot assist each other and are independent of each other.

Ibn Ṭufayl's anti-Fārābīan attitude was not shared by his twenty-years-younger contemporary Ibn Rushd (Averroes) from Cordova (520/1126–595/1198).[219] In his Epistle on the *Possibility of Conjunction with the Active Intellect*[220] he declares that "felicity will not be attained by study alone or by action alone, but it will be attained by both things together; and that it is only attainable in this life". However, as man in this life is part of society, he can reach felicity and attain "theoretical sciences", which "are indeed useful for action and necessary for action"[221] and are reflected in the laws as God's will,[222] as long as society does not impede this.[223] Man needs society for his life, but only the virtuous society is an aid in the attainment of felicity. Thus, neither happiness of the solitary as proposed by Ibn Bājjah and Ibn Ṭufayl exists nor happiness in the virtuous city as described by al-Fārābī. According to Ibn Rushd happiness is immortality of the soul, which can be attained in a growing conjunction of man's acquired knowledge with the Active Intellect, the connective link between absolute simplicity and the eternity of God's knowledge and the multiplicity of acquired knowledge of the visible and perishable world.[224] Man's "progress from science to science"[225] leads to conjunction (*ittiṣāl*) with the active intellect, to happiness, and is declared by Ibn Rushd a task of mankind.[226] Philosophical knowledge and happiness are not any longer the aim of a single individual, either the ruler-philosopher who is inspired by the divine intellect (al-Fārābī) or the solitary (Ibn Bājjah, Ibn Ṭufayl). Happiness of the individual as the ultimate aim of man is specified by the universal knowledge of mankind, because man's soul, which is striving for immortality, can attain its conjunction with the active intellect only through its form, which according to Ibn Rushd is a universal *intellectus materialis*, a potentiality and disposition, to connect acquired knowledge with the active intellect. Philosophy is the highest form of universal human knowledge of religious truth as reflected in the *Sharī'ah*.[227] But like al-Fārābī, Ibn Sīnā, Ibn Bājjah and Ibn Ṭufayl he holds the view that it is not accessible to everyone; even philosophers might err.

This realistic attitude is reflected in Ibn Rushd's commentary on Plato's *Republic*,[228] in which he also referred to Aristotle's *Nicomachean Ethics*, Ibn Bājjah and above all al-Fārābī. As in al-Fārābī (see above) the virtuous ruler is qualified as king, philosopher, lawgiver and Imām[229] with cogitative and moral virtues.[230] The starting-point is the diversity of people, who can be divided into ruler and ruled;[231] this diversity necessitates the joining together and formation of a community in society as proposed by Plato.[232] Here, Ibn Rushd concedes: it is "perhaps impossible" that there is "only one rank of humans in a city"; therefore, only some people can attain "all or most of [the human perfections]".[233] Anywhere else this is explained with the lack of submission of citizens to the ruler and the "defectiveness of most of those giving themselves to wisdom".[234] Here Ibn Rushd has in mind the city of his own time, in which the true philosopher is like a man "among perilous animals" and therefore "turns to isolation and lives the life of a solitary".[235] The role of the city is restricted to something "necessary for man's existence", a "necessity-association".[236] Based on al-Fārābī, Ibn Rushd distinguishes between virtuous governance, timocratic governance (primacy of honour), oligarchy (primacy of the vile, love of money), democracy (primacy of the assembly of the multitude, love of liberty[237]) and tyranny (love of power).[238] According to Ibn Rushd, only in the time of Muḥammad and the first four caliphs the Arabs "used to imitate the virtuous governance", based on the *nomos* (= *Sharī'ah*). Thus, the best Muslim state is only an imitation of a philosophical state, which Ibn Rushd considered as something including all mankind.[239]

Ibn Rushd maintains, that after the four caliphs, in the time of Mu'āwiyah, the Muslims became timocrats, as also happened during his own time, the period of the Almohad dynasty and its predecessors, the Almoravids,[240] and finally (after 540/1145) in Cordova they changed democratic governance into hedonistic tyranny.[241] Therefore, Ibn Rushd could say that "citizens today receive no advantage from the wise who are truly wise".[242] This might have confirmed his conviction that man's "progress from science to science" is a task for all mankind and not only for single nations or individuals. As in al-Fārābī,[243] such a duty might justify war with the intention of bringing wisdom to those who cannot be persuaded through rhetorical and poetical or demonstrative arguments[244] and who thus are not able to adopt virtues except through coercion.[245]

Ibn Rushd's theories strongly influenced the political philosophy of Ibn Khaldūn (732/1332–808/1406), as reflected in his *Muqaddimah*.[246] The striving for supremacy, for domination over others, becomes an aspect of *'aṣabiyyah*, social "solidarity", a central notion in Ibn Khaldūn's philosophy of the state.[247] In addition, the solidarity in tribes is based on man's longing for affiliation (*ṣuḥbah*) with others, which includes desires for companionship, co-operation and friendship.[248] Thus, human society and its development in its correlation to the environment[249] needs the existence of a community, of the *polis*, the state.[250] If the life of society becomes easier and luxury increases in the "sedentary" period, the community might become weak and die.

As in al-Fārābī, Ibn Sīnā and Ibn Rushd, we find in Ibn Khaldūn the distinction between the elite (*khāṣṣah*) and the masses (*'āmmah*);[251] as with al-Fārābī the leader of the virtuous, law-based community (which after the rise of the Umayyad dynasty ceased to exist)[252] should be a prophet with practical wisdom, including political and legal wisdom.[253]Accordingly, politics is concerned with the behaviour of man as part of the household[254] and the city "in accordance with ethical and philosophical requirements, for the purpose of directing the masses towards behaviour that will result in the preservation and permanence of the [human] species";[255] the prophet must instruct mankind in the law, of what is the best for it and protects it.[256]

What is remarkable here is the universalistic attitude. The perfect city cannot be realized; it becomes a standard, which is the permanent aim of mankind.[257] Here the message of the prophet, the lawgiver, becomes philosophy for mankind,[258] which should guide mankind and lead to the "improvement of mankind" (*iṣlāḥ al-bashar*).[259] In the shape of "political laws" (*aḥkām al-siyāsah*) it is concerned with "worldly interests" (*maṣāliḥ al-dunyā)* of mankind,[260] but also with its "welfare in the other world" (*ṣalāḥ ākhiratihim*).[261] This utterance appears to be a compromise, combining the interests of society and individual: the Utopian state is a model for man's behaviour in the society of this world; at the same time the religious laws of the ruler-prophet became a guide-line to welfare in the other world, to "happiness" (*sa'ādah*).[262] Religion and its laws remain an indispensable tool of society.[263] They regulate the behaviour of the individual, make it conformable to ethics, which is the first part of practical philosophy and in agreement with the requirements of politics, its second part. Moral wisdom and wisdom of the ruler (including economics, management of the household) lead to the noble things, to happiness of man in society.

In this manner, by shaping the consciousness of man, Islamic philosophers contributed to the formation of Islamic society and its ruling powers, the caliphs, sultans, viziers, jurists and theologians. They were scarcely influential in Latin political thought.[264] With their metaphysical world view they supported the traditional Islamic nexus between religion and politics. This link is provided with a rational, scientific basis presupposing the universality of values. They are revived in the modern self-image of Islam.[265]

NOTES

1 On the concept of *ummah* cf. Lambton (1981): 13ff.

2 On the term and its history see E. I. J. Rosenthal (1971a): 20ff.; Lewis (1984); Najjar (1984).

3 Cf. Watt (1968): 4ff.

4 Cf. Watt (1968).

5 Cf. Murad (1991).

6 Cf. Sherwani (1977): 21ff.; Denny (1985); Hourani (1985): 23ff.

7 Several editions are available, e.g. in *Āṭār ibn al-Muqaffaʿ* (1978). The *Kitāb al-adab al-kabīr* is translated into German by Rescher (1917). The *Risālah fi'l-ṣaḥābah* is available in an edition, French translation and glossary by Ch. Pellat (1976). For details see Richter (1932): 4ff.; Lambton (1981): 43ff.; F. Gabrieli, "Ibn al-Muḳaffaʿ", in *Encyclopedia of Islam*, 2nd ed. (Leiden, 1965), III: 884f. and the references given there.

8 Cf. Charles-Dominique (1965): 53f.

9 Richter (1932): 6; cf. Charles-Dominique (1965): 62f.

10 Ibn al-Muqaffaʿ, *Kitāb al-adab al-kabīr* chapter 3; cf. Charles-Dominique (1965): 53ff.

11 Cf. Richter (1932): 33ff.; Salinger (1956) (on Qāḍī al-Nuʿmān, *Daʿāʾim al-islām*; see also al-Qāḍī (1978)); Busse (1968); Lambton (1954); (1963); (1971); Butterworth (1980): 21ff.; Chittick (1988) and the bibliography by Dāneshpačūh (1988). An until now neglected example, which shows the influence of the old mirror of princes and of philosophical ethics (cf. Miskawayh's Platonic doctrine of the virtues of the soul, ed. Zurayk, pp. 16ff.) is Abu'l-Qāsim al-Ḥusaynī ibn ʿAlī al-Maghribī (d. 418/1027 or 428/1037), *Kitāb fi'l-siyāsah* (ed. ad-Dahhān (1948) and ʿAbd al-Munʿim Aḥmad (1982). 35–60).

12 Like al Māwardī (d. 450/1058), on whom cf. E. I. J. Rosenthal (1962): 27ff.; Laoust (1968); Riḍwān al-Sayyid (1985).

13 Cf. Gutas (1990): 347ff.

14 Cf. Richter (1932): 93ff.

15 See Grignaschi (1967a); (1967b); cf. Stern (1968). The texts are in Bielawski/Plezia (1970) and in Grignaschi (1975).

16 Ed. Badawī (1954): 65–171 and Sāmī Salmān al-A'war (1986). Cf. Grignaschi (1976).

17 See Manzalaoui (1974); Grignaschi (1980).

18 The text is available only in a summary by Muḥammad ibn 'Alī ibn Ibrāhīm ibn Aḥmad ibn Muḥammad al-Anṣārī, which is edited by Badawī (1985); cf. Walsh (1976) and Gutas (1990): 350–2.

19 Peters (1968): 74f.; the translations are edited by Kellermann (1965).

20 Gutas (1975): 320f.

21 *Perì ethōn* = *Kitāb al-akhlāq*. The Arabic summary is edited by Kraus (1939) and by Badawī (1981): 190–211; it is translated into English by Mattock (1972). On the text cf. the studies listed in Ullmann (1970): 63; Rundgren (1976); Fakhry (1991): 63f.

22 *Risālah ilā Julian al-malik fi'l-siyāsah wa'l-tadbīr al-mamlakah*, ed. Cheikho (1920–2); Muḥammad Salīm Sālim (1970) and (with Latin translation) Irfan Shahid (1974). The text is lost in the Greek original. Some remarks can be found in Bouyges (1924).

23 Lost in the Greek original. The Arabic translation is edited by H. Plessner (1928), together with a German version and with the medieval Arabic–Hebrew and Arabic–Latin translations. As Plessner has shown, the text was highly influential in Islamic texts on economics (*tadbīr al-manzil*), especially through the revised version by Naṣīr al-Dīn Ṭūsī in his *Akhlāq*. Less known to the Arabs was the pseudo-Aristotelian *Economics*, of which an Arabic paraphrase, perhaps by Abu'l-Faraj ibn al-Ṭayyib, book 1 (1343a1–1345b4) is preserved; the text is preserved in a collection of texts by Ibn al-Ṭayyib in MS. Escorial no. 888, fols 145v–149v and Nuruosmaniye 3610 (new number 3095), fols 138r–140v, and is edited by Ma'lūf (1921). Both texts are different from the *Maqālah fi'l-tadbīr* ascribed to Aristotle and said to be translated by 'Īsā ibn Zur'ah (ed. Cheikho (1903)). The text seems to be an Arabic compilation and is a general discussion of the ways to deal with other persons of differing ranks. On two Hebrew translations see Pines (1954–5).

24 The title of the lost Greek text was perhaps *Peri alypias*. The text is transmitted by al-Kindī (ed. Walzer/Ritter (1938); Ṭuraiḥī (1962): 110–25; Badawī (1973): 6–32 and Fakhry (1979), 2: 13–26) and excerpted (with changes) from al-Kindī's version by Miskawayh and in the anonymous *Risālah fi'l-khawf min al-mawt* (see n. 153). A paraphrase of the beginning of the Kindī text (ed. Walzer/Ritter (1938): 31.8–32.2) is separately transmitted with the title *Risālah fī māhiyyat al-ḥuzn wa asbābihī* and ascribed to Ibn Sīnā (ed. Tura 1937); cf. on this and on other later excerpts Walzer/Ritter (1938): 8ff. and F. Rosenthal in his review in *Orientalia*, n.s., (1940): 9, 182–91. Rosenthal considers Plutarch as a possible author. Pohlenz (1938) and Gätje (1956): 228 refrain from any identification, without, however denying its Hellenistic origin. According to Pohlenz the author might indirectly be influenced by Epictetus (*c.* A.D. 50–120).

25 On the concept of justice among Mu'tazilites, Ash'arites and Māturidites in Averroes and Ibn 'Arabī cf. the survey by Kassem (1972).

26 On the reception of Plato in the Islamic world see F. Rosenthal (1940); Klein-Franke (1973) and *s.v.*, "Aflāṭūn" by R. Walzer in *Encyclopedia of Islam*, 2nd ed.

Cf. also Mahdi (1991): 14ff. Some Arabic fragments from Plato's works are collected by Badawī (1974): 121–70. On the quotations in al-Bīrūnī see Gabrieli (1951). Not mentioned by Badawī and still insufficiently known is the relation of Aḥmad ibn Yūsuf ibn Ibrāhīm ibn al-Dāyah (d. 340/951), *Kitāb al-'uhūd al-yūnāniyyah al-mustakhrajah min rumūz kitāb al-siyāsah li-Aflāṭūn* (ed. Badawī (1954): 1–64; ed. al-Mālikī (1971): 45–126; cf. Anawati (1955): 61–3 and al- Mālikī's introduction, pp. 33ff.) to Plato's political works. Ibn al-Dāya's work is a compilation, which tries to show the superiority of the Greeks to the Persians in politics; it is said to be an extract from Plato's *Politics*. The text was used in the eighth/fourteenth century by the Granadine historian Lisān al-Dīn ibn al-Khaṭīb, *Kitāb al-ishārah ilā adab al-wizārah* (ed. Zamāmah); see Dunlop (1959): 52–4; al-Qāḍī (1976): 206f.

27 On the *Nicomachean Ethics*, its afterlife in Arabic and on the Arabic–Latin translation of the *Summaria Alexandrinorum* by Hermannus Alemannus see Dunlop (1971); (1983) and the references given in Daiber (1990a). Dunlop prepared an extensive study, in which he showed that the text inserted after book 6 in the only available MS. in Fez (ed. Badawī (1979): 363–87) can be identified with the first part of Porphyry's commentary on the first half of the *Nicomachean Ethics*. The Arabic texts are edited by Badawī (1979).

28 Cf. Ibish (1966): 97ff.

29 Cf. Madelung, *s.v.*, "Imāma", in *Encyclopedia of Islam*, 2nd ed., 3 (1971).

30 *Risālah fī kammiyyat kutub Arisṭāṭālīs*, ed. Guidi/Walzer: 403, 12ff,; ed. Abū Rīdah: 384, 11ff. On the text cf. Hein (1985): 318f.

31 *Min kalām Qusṭā ibn Lūqā*, ed. and trans. Daiber (1990b): 80v.15–81r.4; cf. the commentary by Daiber (1990b): 124 and 128.

32 See above.

33 See Pines (1986): 146–56.

34 Ed. Flügel: 260.1–6; ed. Riḍā Tajaddud: 319, 8–12; Engl. trans. Dodge: 623; cf. Atiyeh (1966): 195f.

35 Ed. Abū Rīdah, *Rasā'il al-Kindī al-falsafiyyah*, I: 177–99; French commented translation by D. Gimaret in *Al-Kindī, Cinq épîtres* (1976): 37 and 65–8. The passage is not in the version edited by Klein-Franke (1982).

36 Cf. Plato, *Rep.*, 4.435.Bff.; *Laws*, 653A–C: Aristotle, *On the Soul*, 432a25 and above all *Nicomachean Ethics*, 1102b28ff.; 1116b23ff. and 1119b.

37 Cf. Plato, *Rep.*, 4.435.Bff.

38 Ed. Abū Rīdah, *Rasā'il*, I: 179.4ff.; cf. Atiyeh (1980).

39 Preserved in Abū Sulaymān al-Sijistānī, *Muntakhab ṣīwān al-ḥikmah*, ed. Dunlop: 246–8, esp. 248; English trans. in Atiyeh (1966): 239–57.

40 Fakhry (1977): 45–50

41 MS. Köprülü 1608, fols 21v11–22r1.

42 Cf. Atiyeh (1966): 123ff. esp. 133ff.; Alon (1991): 131ff. (references quoted with the abbreviations KAS and KKS).

43 Editions: see above, n. 24.

44 Cf. Atiyeh (1966): 129ff.

45 Abū Sulaymān, al-Sijistānī, *Muntakhab*, ed. Dunlop: 248, 264–8ff.; English trans. by Atiyeh (1966): 225; cf. 127.

46 On the concept of happiness in al-Kindī (al-Fārābī, Ibn Bājjah and Ibn Rushd) see Abdul Haqq Ansari (1964).

47 See F. Rosenthal (1989): 296 and 287ff.
48 See F. Rosenthal (1989): 294 and the references given there. Rosenthal compares the terms *targhīb* and *tarhīb* with Qur'ān 21: 90
49 Ultimately, it recurs to the Persian tradition of the mirror of princes (See F. Rosenthal (1989): 293f.); at the same time, there is some parallelism with a doctrine of the Muʿtazilites, who described God's creative act as "welfare" (*maṣlaḥah*; cf. *aṣlaḥ*) of man: See Daiber (1975): 220f.; cf. 232.
50 See the fragment in Abū Ḥayyān al-Tawḥīdī, *al-Baṣā'ir*, ed. Keilani, 2/2: 763–5 trans. F. Rosenthal (1989): 289f. and the comments by Rosenthal.
51 Cf. F. Rosenthal (1989): 290.
52 See F. Rosenthal (1956); the text by al-ʿĀmirī, his *Kitāb al-iʿlām* (trans. Rosenthal: 46–52), can be found in the edition by Ghurāb: 151–61; on al-ʿĀmirī's view of religion as superior to knowledge and on his harmonization of philosophy and religion see Rowson (1988): 19ff.
53 Ed. by Muṣṭafā al-Ḥiyārī: *al-Siyāsah min kitāb al-kharāj wa ṣināʿat al-kitābah;* the complete version of Qudāmah's *Kitāb al-kharāj* is now available in a facsimile edition (1986).
54 See Ḥiyari (1983): 91ff. and F. Rosenthal (1989): 296f.
55 See ed. Ḥiyari: 49ff.
56 Ed. Ḥiyari: 59ff.
57 Ed. Ḥiyari: 97ff.
58 Ed. Ḥiyari: 41ff.
59 Ed. Ḥiyari: 53ff. Cf. Ḥiyari (1983): 97f.
60 Ed. by Salah al-Sawy (1977). On it cf. Daiber (1989).
61 Daiber (1989): 91
62 Ed. Kraus in Abū Bakr al-Rāzī, *Rasā'il falsafiyyah*: 97–111; a reprint with introduction by Mehdi Mohaghegh appeared in Tehran 1964. English trans. in Arberry (1967). On the text cf. here F. Rosenthal (1940): 388; Goodman (1971); Shawer (1973): 38ff.; 62 and 68; Strohmaier (1974); Bausani (1981): 9–13; Alon (1990): 48 and 51f.
63 *Al-Sīrat al-falsafiyyah,* ed. Kraus (*Rasā'il falsafiyyah*): 108, 8f.
64 Ed. Kraus, *Rasā'il falsafiyyah*: 1–96; Fakhry (1979): 27–64; trans. Arberry (1950); text critical notes: see Gutas (1977). On the text cf. Mohaghegh (1967) and the interpretation by Goodman (1971; 1972: 31ff.). The text by Abū Bakr al-Rāzī inspired Miskawayh's chapter on "health of the soul", *Tahdhīb al-akhlāq*, ed. Zurayk: 175ff. (see Lauer (1984): 76f.) and was refuted by the Ismāʿīlī Ḥamīd al-Dīn al-Kirmānī (d. *c.* 411/1020–1), *al-Aqwāl al-dhahabiyyah* (several editions: see bibliography).
65 On the Galenic sources (above all *Perì alypías* = *Maqālah fī nafy al-ghamm* = *Kitāb fī ṣarf al-ightimām*, which is lost in the Greek original and of which only fragments are preserved; see Ullmann (1970): 65, and above, n.24) of Rāzī's ethics see de Boer (1920): 3ff. and now Bar-Asher (1989).
66 Cf. Goodman (1971 and 1972).
67 *Maqālah fī amārat al-iqbāl wa'l-dawlah* (ed. Kraus, *Rasā'il*: 135–8): 137.3ff. An Italian summary can be found in Bausani (1981): 21f. On the translation of *dawlah* see F. Rosenthal, *Encyclopedia of Islam*, 2nd ed., 2: 178a.
68 Ed. Kraus, *Rasā'il*: 136.6f.

69 Cf. al-Jāḥiẓ, *Maqālat al-zaidiyyah*, ed. Hārūn, *Rasā'il al-Jāḥiẓ*, 4: 320.3ff. German trans. Pellat (1967): 104ff.
70 Cf. e.g. al-Qāsim ibn Ibrāhīm (d. 246/860): see Abrahamov (1987).
71 Cf. Madelung (1977): 54ff.; Makarem (1967); (1972): 35ff.; a later example is the Ismā'īlī Abu'l-Fawāris Aḥmad ibn Ya'qūb, *Risālah fi'l-imāmah*: see edition and translation by Makarem (1977).
72 Cf. *A'lām*, ed. al-Sawy, 301.11ff.; 314ff.
73 *Ibid.*: 36.4–6.
74 Goldziher (1888): 138f. (= *Muslim Studies*, 1: 130f.); Watt and Marmura (1985): 27ff.
75 Cf. Laoust (1958): 55f.
76 *A'lām*, ed. al-Sawy: 43.6ff.
77 *Ibid.*: 185.6–10; cf. 61.3ff.
78 *Ibid.*: 6.21ff.; 8.7f.; 55; 72.5ff.; 184.12ff.
79 *Ibid.*: 64f.
80 *Ibid.*: 8.8–10; cf. 183.15ff.; 185.2ff.
81 *Ibid.*: 110.14ff.
82 *Ibid.*: 111.9ff., with reference to Qur'ān 8: 39–40.
83 *Ibid.*: 111.13ff., with reference to Qur'ān 2: 256–7.
84 *Ibid.*: 111.7ff.
85 *Ibid.*: 111.2ff.,
86 Cf. *ibid.*: 173.4f.; 186.6ff.
87 *Ibid.*: 187.1ff.
88 *Ibid.*: 189.1f.; cf. 189.14f. and 188.13ff.
89 *Ibid.*: 273ff.
90 Cf. Daiber (1989): 97f.
91 *A'lām*, ed. al-Sawy: 73.17–19.
92 Cf. *ibid.* 77–93; Abū Ḥātim keeps to the orthodox picture of the Prophet (see Andrae (1918): 190ff.; 245ff.).
93 Cf. Daiber (1989): 98f. and on the term *mesotes* = *i'tidāl* (cf. *A'lām*, ed. al-Sawy: 85f.) Bürgel (1967).
94 Cf. *A'lām*, ed. al-Sawy: 110.9ff.
95 Cf. Daiber (1989): 95f.; 99f.
96 Cf. the articles by Najjār (1958; 1960; 1961; 1978; 1980); Mahdi in *History of Political Philosophy*, 182ff.; Galston (1990). A survey of the relevant Fārābīan texts can be found in E. I. J. Rosenthal (1955); (1962): 122–42.
97 On the Ismā'īlī background of Fārābī's political philosophy see Daiber (1991b).
98 Cf. Walzer (1985): 445f.; Daiber (1986a): 6f.
99 *al-Madīnah al-fāḍilah*, ed. Dieterici: 59.16ff. ed. Walzer: 246.12ff.; cf. Daiber (1991b). On the edition and translation by Walzer see Mahdi (1990).
100 Cf. above.
101 Cf. Daiber (1986b): 7f. and (1991b): 145f.
102 Cf. Daiber (1986b): 11f.; Butterworth (1987): 232ff.
103 For details here and in the following see Daiber (1986a) and (1986b).
104 On the concept of happiness in al-Fārābī see Shahjahan (1985).
105 Cf. Daiber (1986a): 17 n. 79 and on the Platonic notion of "assimilation" to God cf. Plato, *Theaet.*, 176B; Berman (1961).
106 Cf. Daiber (1986a): 11ff.

107 Cf. Daiber (1991b): 147f.
108 Cf. Walzer (1985): 424ff.
109 Cf. Sankari (1970); Sajjad (1983). On al-Fārābī's hierarchical structure of the feudalistic city (and cosmos) and on the Porphyrian principle of its division see Maroth (1978).
110 Cf. Walzer (1985): 429ff.
111 Al-Fārābī is the first Muslim philosopher to have developed the utopian idea of the perfect state; see Simon (1963); (1971).
112 Cf. al-Fārābī, *Falsafat Aflāṭūn*, ed. Rosenthal and Walzer: chapter iv ff.; trans. Mahdi (1969): 57ff. The text used various Platonic sources: cf. besides the notes by Rosenthal and Walzer also Isaac Rabinowitz, *American Journal of Philology*, 67 (1946): 76–9.
113 Cf. besides al-Fārābī, *al-Madīnah al-fāḍilah* the following works: *Kitāb al-tanbīh 'alā sabīl al-sa'ādah* (French trans. Mallet (1989); *Kitāb taḥṣīl al-sa'ādah* (trans. Mahdi (1969): 13–50); *Fuṣūl muntaza'ah*, trans. into Persian in Quṭb al-Dīn al-Shīrāzī (634/1236–710/1311), *Durrat al-tāj li-ghurrat ad-dubāj*, ed. Mishkat (see Nasr (1974): 249); *Kitāb al-siyāsah al-madaniyyah* and his *Risālah fi'l-siyāsah* (German trans. Graf (1902)), an ethical treatise on man's behaviour against those who are above him, below him or equal to him in rank and on man's own conduct.
114 Cf. E. I. J. Rosenthal (1972): 164–6.
115 *Talkhīṣ nawāmīs Aflāṭūn*. Cf. Gabrieli (1949); Strauss (1957); Leaman (1985): 195ff. and Daiber (1986b): 17f. On a summary of this *Talkhīṣ*, written by Abu'l-Faraj ibn al-Ṭayyib, see Druart (1977).
116 Cf. al-Fārābī, *al-Madīnah al-fāḍilah*, ed. Walzer, chapter 5: 16 and commentary: 457ff.
117 *Rasā'il*, 3: 241.6; cf. German trans. and commentary by Diwald (1975): 203 and 206–8.
118 See on the following the details in Enayat (1977) and for a detailed comparison of Ikhwān al-Ṣafā' and al-Fārābī, Abouzeid (1987).
119 See Enayat (1977): 34ff.
120 Cf. the parable on the animal rebellion against human domination in *Rasā'il*, 2: 182ff.; English trans. Goodman (1978); Spanish version by Tornero Poveda (1984) and German version by Giese (1990).
121 Cf. Enayat (1977): 39ff.
122 *al-Madīnah al-fāḍilah*, ed./trans. Walzer: 246–7. Cf. above, n. 98.
123 *Rasā'il*, 4: 128f.; cf. Enayat (1977): 42.
124 Cf. Marquet (1962).
125 *Rasā'il*, 1: 249f.; cf. Enayat (1977): 42.
126 *Rasā'il*, 4: 199.20ff.
127 Cf. Enayat (1977): 45.
128 *Rasā'il*, 4: 220.7.
129 *Ibid.*, 4: 220f.; cf. Enayat (1977): 44.
130 Enayat (1977): 29.
131 Cf. *ibid.*: 40f. and on the conflicting parts of the soul Diwald (1972): 49ff. (lists the parallels in al-Fārābī, a source of the *Rasā'il Ikhwān al-Ṣafā'*).
132 *Rasā'il*, 1: 207; cf. Enayat (1977): 32–4. This division clearly shows the Aristotelian tripartition of practical philosophy in politics, economy and ethics

(see above, n. 31), with an additional beginning section on prophetic and kingly politics.

133 *Rasā'il*, 1: 229.12ff. Cf. Enayat (1977): 26ff.

134 *Rasā'il*, 1: 223.16.

135 Cf. Faruqi (1960).

136 See above. The Ismā'īlī impact on the *Rasā'il Ikhwān al-Ṣafā'* seems to be much greater than could be concluded from Netton (1991): chapter 6.

137 Ed. Zurayk (1966); English trans. Zurayk (1968). Cf. Daiber, *Orientalistische Literaturzeitung*, 67 (1972), cols 370–3; Arkoun (1970).

138 Ed. Zurayk: 83.

139 Cf. also Miskawayh's monograph *al-Sa'ādah fī falsafat al-akhlāq*, ed. al-Ṭūbjī. On the concept of *sa'ādah* in Miskawayh see 'Abdulḥaqq Ansari (1963).

140 Ed. Zurayk: 40.5.

141 Ed. Zurayk: 91.18. Cf. Plotinus, *Enn.* 1.6.

142 Ed. Zurayk: 91f.

143 Cf. pseudo-Aristotle, *De virtutibus et vitiis*, Arabic trans. Ibn al-Ṭayyib ed. Kellermann (1965): 59.18–58; trans. 77–9 (not preserved in Greek). On the history of mean (*mesotes*) in Islamic philosophical ethics see Bürgel (1967): 101.

144 Ed. Zurayk: 105ff.; cf. Miskawayh, *Risālah fī māhiyyat al-'adl*, ed./trans. Khan; Fakhry (1975).

145 Ed. Zurayk: 62.11.

146 *Ibid.*: 31.8.

147 *Ibid.*: 46ff.

148 As Miskawayh (ed. Zurayk: 29.8) formulates: "*inna'l-insāna madanī bi'l-ṭab'*" (cf. *Zōon politikon*, Aristotle, *Pol.*, 1.1.1253a2ff).

149 Ed. Zurayk: 135ff.

150 *Ibid.*: 72, 10ff.

151 *Ibid.*: 40, 9.

152 In his mirror of princes, the *Sulūk al-mālik fī tadbīr al-mamālik*: see edition and study by Takrītī (1980). On the text cf. also Plessner (1928): 30ff.; Richter (1932): 105f.; Dunlop in his edition of al-Fārābī's *Fuṣūl muntaza'ah*: 6 (on al-Fārābī's *Fuṣūl* as source) and Sherwani (1977): 35–57 (considers wrongly Ibn Abī'l-Rabī' as a thinker of the ninth century).

153 S. M. Arkoun, s.v. "Miskawayh" in *Encyclopedia of Islam*, 2nd ed., 7 (1991): 143b and on the mentioned authors E. I. J. Rosenthal (1962): 210ff.; Rahman (1985); Sprachman (1985); Wickens (1985); Fakhry (1991); on Naṣīr al-Dīn al-Ṭūsī cf. also Badie (1977). On the influence of Miskawayh on Ghazzālī see also Zurayk (1968): 207, n. 2 on p. 157, l. 10. As *Risālah fī daf' al-ghamm min al-mawt* the text in *Tahdhīb*, ed. Zurayk: 209.5–217.9 is transmitted separately as a work attributed to Ibn Sīnā (ed. Mehren (1891)); see Zurayk (1968): 209, n. 18 on p. 185, l. 10) and as anonymous *Risālah fi'l-khawf min al-mawt wa ḥaqīqatihī wa ḥāl al-nafs ba'dahū*, which from MS. Paris 4946 is edited by L. Cheikho (1911), *Maqālāt falsafiyyah*, pp. 103–14, with an additional passage (= ed. Cheikho, pp. 114–17), which is derived from Miskawayh (= ed. Zurayk: 217.10–221.19); both texts are identical with al-Kindī, *Risālah fi'l-ḥīlah li-daf' al-aḥzān* (see above n. 24).

154 On him see Fakhry (1991): 176ff.; Daiber (1991a).

155 Very influential appears to be al-Fārābī's *Kitāb al-tanbīh 'alā sabīl al-sa'ādah*; see Khalīfat (1990): 149.
156 *Al-Dharī'ah* ed. 'Ajamī: 163.
157 *Ibid.*: 374.
158 *Ibid.*: 364f.
159 *Ibid.*: 204f.
160 *Ibid.*: 204.4.
161 Cf. *ibid.*: 59.
162 *Ibid.*: 91.5f.; cf. 96.8f.
163 Cf. *takassub* in *ibid.*: 380f.
164 *Ibid.*: 90.11–13.
165 *Ibid.*: 90.11–91.6.
166 Ed. Sulaymān Dunyā; trans. Hachem (1945).
167 Cf. Chahine (1972): 105ff.
168 This topic is discussed by the Nestorian Christian Ibn al-Khammār (d. 1017) in his *Maqālah fī ṣifat al-rajul al-faylasūf*, ed. and trans. Lewin (1955); cf. on the text also Kraemer (1986): 128.
169 On their conception of philosophy see *Rasā'il*, 3: 325ff. and trans. Diwald (1975): 427ff.
170 On Ibn Sīnā's knowledge of the *Rasā'il Ikhwān al-Ṣafā'* see Diwald (1981).
171 Ed. by Amīn: 40–9, trans. Goichon (1959); cf. "Ḥayy B. Yakẓān", in *Encyclopedia of Islam*, 2nd ed., 3.
172 Ed. and commented by Fatḥallāh Khulayf (1974): 129–31, French trans. Noureddine (1961): 30–6.
173 Cf. Marmura (1963); (1964).
174 Cf. Marmura (1985): 363.
175 Cf. E. I. J. Rosenthal (1962): 144ff.; cf. 152ff. on the qualities of the prophet and ruler.
176 Ibn Sīnā, *al-Shifā', al-Ilāhiyyāt*, 2: 441.4f.; trans. Marmura in *Medieval Political Philosophy* (1963): 99.
177 *Al-Shifā', al-Ilāhiyyāt*, 2: 447.4ff.; trans. Marmura in *Medieval Political Philosophy*: 104.
178 E. I. J. Rosenthal (1962): 154f.
179 Cf. *ibid.*: 148ff.
180 Galston (1979): 570.
181 Published in *Tis' rasā'il* (1298/1881): 71–80; Shamsaddīn (1988): 261–72; English trans. Mahdi in *Medieval Political Philosophy*: 95–7; analysis by Baur (1903): 346–9 (based on the Latin translation by Andreas Alpago, *Avicennae opera* (Venice, 1546) (repr. Westmead, 1969), fols 139–46).
182 Ed. Marmura; ed. Shamsaddīn (1988): 298–309, English trans. Marmura in *Medieval Political Philosophy*: 112–21.
183 Part 2: 441–55; English trans. Marmura, *Medieval Political Philosophy*: 98–111; German trans. in Horten (1907). Cf. the comments by Kohler (1908–9) and by Galston (1979), who gives a comparison with al-Fārābī's more idealistic political philosophy. Avicenna's political ideas described in this text influenced the medieval author Francese Eiximenes, *Regiment de la cosa publica* (Valencia, 1383); see Lindgren (1980).

184 Several editions (see bibliography); the latest edition is in Shamsaddīn (1988): 232–60. Cf. the remarks in Shamsaddīn (1988): 60ff.; Plessner (1928): 42ff. and Ibrahim (1980).
185 Ed. Shamsaddīn (1988): 233–9.
186 Ed. Shamsaddīn: 240–5. On Ibn Sīnā's views about ethics see 'Abdul ḥaqq Ansari (1962–3); Butterworth (1987): 238ff. and Fakhry (1991): 85ff.; 207ff.
187 Ed. Shamsaddīn: 246–58.
188 On this see above, n. 23.
189 On which see Plessner (1928): 43.
190 Cf. E. I. J. Rosenthal (1962): 152ff.
191 On the mentioned terms and their Aristotelian origin see above, n. 93.
192 *Al-Shifā', al-Ilāhiyyāt*, 2: 455.14.
193 *Al-Shifā', al-Ilāhiyyāt*, 2: 453.14; cf. E. I. J. Rosenthal (1962): 155f. (instead of *jamīlah* read *ḥamīdah*; the interpretation given there slightly differs from ours).
194 Khurshid (1979); cf. Strohmaier (1979).
195 Avicenna discussed his eschatological views mainly in his *al-Risālat al-aḍḥawīyyah fi'l-ma'ād* (ed. and trans. F. Lucchetta (1969) and in his *al-Mabda' wa'l-ma'ād* (ed. Nūrānī). Cf. now the monograph by Michot (1986), esp. pp. 190ff.
196 On him cf. here the discussion in E. I. J. Rosenthal (1937; 1951); (1962): 158–174; Chemlin (1969); Allard (1974); Zainaty (1979); Leaman (1980). On Ibn Bājjah's (and Ibn Ṭufayl's) influence in Jewish medieval philosophy (Moses Narboni) see Hayoun (1989); (1990): 39ff.; 77ff.; 137ff.; 168ff.; 188ff. and (on politics) see 242ff.
197 The guardians in Plato: see E. I. J. Rosenthal (1962): 287 n. 9.
198 *Risālat al-wadā'* ed. Fakhry, *Rasā'il*: 136: 11–13; quoted by E. I. J. Rosenthal (1962): 161.
199 On Ibn Bājjah's concept of ultimate happiness see Altmann (1969).
200 Cf. al-Fārābī, *Fuṣūl muntaza'ah*, ed. Najjār: 95; *Kitāb al-millah*, ed. Mahdi: 56f.; cf. Marmura in Watt and Marmura (1985): 354 and Endress (1986): 233ff.
201 Accordingly Ibn Bājjah wrote a treatise called *Tadbīr al-mutawaḥḥid* (ed. Fakhry, *Rasā'il:* 37–96; ed. Ma'n Ziyādeh; the first two chapters (= ed. Fakhry: 37–48) are edited with English trans. by Dunlop (1945). On the concept of *tadbīr* in this text cf. E. I. J. Rosenthal (1962): 164ff.
202 This thesis by Ibn Bājjah, a polarization of moral virtue in society and contemplation in solitude, reappears in Maimonides (see Kraemer (1983)) and above all in Ibn Falaquera: see Jospe (1986). Maimonides remains more indebted to al-Fārābī: cf. also the comparison by E. I. J. Rosenthal (1968); Galston (1978); Kraemer (1979); Pines (1979); Macy (1982; 1986) and Berman (1988).
203 Ibn Bājjah, *Tadbīr*, ed. Fakhry, *Rasā'il*: 91.1ff. Cf. E. I. J. Rosenthal (1962): 170; Leaman (1980): 118f.; Marmura (1985): 375f.; Endress (1986): 236.
204 This is the subject of Ibn Bājjah's *Risālat ittiṣāl al-'aql bi'l-insān* (ed. Fakhry, *Rasā'il*: 155–73). Cf. Chemli (1969); Zainaty (1979); Kraemer (1983).
205 *al-iltiqā' al-mu'āwin 'alā'manāfi'*: Ibn Bājjah, *Risālat al-wadā'*, ed. Fakhry, *Rasā'il*: 142, 16f.; cf. 142, 13ff.; E. I. J. Rosenthal (1962): 161f.
206 E. I. J. Rosenthal (1962): 166: "oligarchy (?)". However, cf. al-Fārābī, *al-Siyāsah al-madaniyyah*, ed. Najjar: 89, 14ff. Eng. trans. Najjar in *Medieval Political Philosophy*: 43f.

BIBLIOGRAPHY

ʿAbd al-Munʿim Aḥmad, Fu'ād (1982) *Majmūʿ fi'l-siyāsah li-Abī Naṣr al-Fārābī, li-Abi' l-Qāsim al-Ḥusayn ibn ʿAlī al-Maghribī, li'l-shaykh al-Ra'īs Ibn Sīnā* (Alexandria).

ʿAbdul Haqq Ansari, M. (1962–3) "Ibn Sīnā's Ethics", *Bulletin of the Institute of Islamic Studies*, 6–7: 72–82.

—— (1963) "Miskawayh's Conception of Saʿādah", *Islamic Studies*, 2: 317–35.

—— (1964) "The Conception of Ultimate Happiness in Muslim Philosophy", *Studies in Islam*, 1: 165–73.

Abouzeid, Ola Abdelaziz (1987) *A Comparative Study between the Political Theories of al-Fārābī and the Brethren of Purity* (thesis, University of Toronto).

Abrahamov, Binjamin (1987) "Al-Ḳāsim ibn Ibrāhīm's Theory of the Imamate", *Arabica*, 34: 80–105.

Abū Bakr al-Rāzī (1939) *Rasā'il falsafiyyah*, ed. Paul Kraus (Cairo). (Reprint Tehran, n.d.)

—— (1950) *see* Arberry.

—— (1964) *al-Sīrat al-falsafiyyah*, ed. P. Kraus, in *Rasā'il falsafiyyah*: 97–111 = reprint, with introduction and commentary by Mehdi Mohaghegh (Tehran).

—— (1986) *al-Ṭibb al-rūḥānī*, ed. P. Kraus, in *Rasā'il falsafiyyah*: 1–96. Also edited by Sulaymān Salīm al-Bawwāb (Damascus and Beirut).

Abū Ḥātim al-Rāzī (1977) *Aʿlām al-nubūwwah*, ed. with introduction and notes by Salah al-Sawy (Tehran).

Abu'l-Qāsim al-Ḥusayn ibn ʿAlī al-Maghribī (1948) *Kitāb fi'l-siyāsah*, ed. Sāmī al-Dahhān (Damascus). Also in: ʿAbd al-Munʿim Aḥmad (1982): 35–60.

Abū Sulaymān al-Sijistānī (1979) *The Muntakhab ṣiwān al-ḥikmah*, Arabic text, introduction and indices ed. D. M. Dunlop (The Hague, Paris and New York).

Allard, M. (1974) "Ibn Bāǧǧa et la politique", in *Orientalia hispanica sive studia F. M. Pareja octogenario dicata*, edenda curavit J. M. Barral, I/1 (Leiden): 11–19.

Alon, Ilai (1990) "Fārābī's Funny Flora: al-Nawābit as 'Opposition'", *Arabica*, 37: 56–90. (Also in: *Journal of the Royal Asiatic Society* (1989): 222–51.)

—— (1991) *Socrates in Medieval Arabic Literature* (Leiden and Jerusalem) (= Islamic Philosophy, Theology and Science, 10).

—— (1995) *Socrates Arabus. Life and Teachings*. Sources, translations, notes, and indices (Jerusalem) (= The Max Schloessinger Memorial Series, 8).

Altmann, A. (1969) "Ibn Bājja on Man's Ultimate Felicity", in *Studies in Religious Philosophy and Mysticism* (London): 73–107. (Also in: *Harry Austryn Wolfson Jubilee Volume*, English Section, I (Jerusalem, 1965): 335–55.)

al-ʿĀmirī, Abu'l-Ḥasan (1967) *Kitāb al-iʿlām bi-manāqib al-islām*, ed. Aḥmad ʿAbd al-Ḥamīd Ghurāb (Cairo).

Anawati, G. C. (1955) "Sources grecques de la philosophie politique de l'Islam", in *Revue du Caire*, 34: 60–70.

Andrae, Tor (1918) *Die Person Muhammeds in Lehre und Glauben seiner Gemeinde* (Stockholm) (= Archives d'Etudes Orientales, 16).

Arberry, A. J. (1950) *The Spiritual Physick of Rhazes*, translated from the Arabic (London).

—— (1967) *Aspects of Islamic Civilization as Depicted in Original Texts* (Ann Arbor).

Aristotle (1979) (*Nicomachean Ethics*, summary, Arabic) *Kitāb al-Akhlāq*, ed. ʿAbdarraḥmān Badawī (Kuwait).

Pseudo-Aristotle (1921) (*Economics*, book 1, Arabic) *Risālat tadbīr al-manzil li-Aritū al-faylasūf*, ed. ʿĪsā Iskandar Maʿlūf, *Majallat al-majmaʿ al-ʿilmī al-ʿarabī bi-Dimashq*, 1: 377–85.

—— (1903) *Maqālah fi'l-tadbīr, Naqalahā ʿĪsā ibn Abī Zurʿah*, ed. L. Cheikho, *al-Mashriq*, 6: 316–18.

—— *Risālat Ariṭāṭālīs ilā l-Iskandar fī siyāsat al-mudun*, *see* Bielawski and Plezia (1970), Grignaschi (1967b).

—— *Sirr al-asrār*, see Badawī (1954): 65–171. Also edited by Sāmī Salmān al-Aʿwar (Beirut, 2nd ed., 1986).

Arkoun, Mohammed (1970) *Contribution à l'étude de l'humanisme arabe au IVe siècle: Miskawayh (320/325–421) = (932/936–1030) philosophe et historien* (Paris) (2nd ed., 1982) (= Etudes musulmanes, 12.)

—— (1977) "Ibn Ṭufayl ou le philosophe dans la cité almohade", *Les Africains*, 6: 261–87.

Atiyeh, George N. (1966) *Al-Kindi, the Philosopher of the Arabs* (Rawalpindi) (repr. 1984).

—— (1980) "Al-Kindī's Concept of Man", *Hamdard Islamicus*, 3.2: 35–46.

Averroes, *see* Ibn Rushd.

Avicenna, *see* Ibn Sīnā.

Badawī, ʿAbdarraḥmān (1954) *al-Uṣūl al-yūnāniyyah li-naẓariyyāt al-siyāsiyyah fi'l-islām*, 1 (Cairo).

—— (1973) *Rasā'il falsafiyyah li'l-Kindī wa'l-Fārābī wa ibn Bājjah wa ibn ʿAdī* (Benghazi) (2nd ed., Beirut, 1980).

—— (1974) *Aflāṭūn fi'l-islām* (Tehran) (2nd ed., Beirut, 1980).

—— (1979) *see* Aristotle, *Nicomachean Ethics*.

—— (1981) *Dirāsāt wa nuṣūṣ fi'l-falsafah wa'l-ʿulūm ʿind al-ʿarab* (Beirut).

Badie, Bertrand (1977) "La philosophie politique de l'hellénisme musulman: l'oeuvre de Nasered-Din Tusi", *Revue française de science politique*, 27: 290–304.

Bar-Asher, Meir M. (1989) "Quelques aspects de l'éthique d'Abū-Bakr al-Rāzī et ses origines dans l'oeuvre de Galien", *Studia Islamica*, 69: 5–38; 70: 119–47.

Baur, Ludwig (1903) *Dominicus Gundissalinus de divisione philosophiae* (Münster) (= Beiträge zur Geschichte der Philosophie des Mittelalters, Texte und Untersuchungen, 4/2–3).

Bausani, Alessandro (1981) *Un filosofo "laico" del medioevo musulmano: Abū Bakr Muḥammad Ben Zakariyyā Rāzī (Rhazes, n. 850/m. 923–925)* (Rome).

Berman, Lawrence V. (1961) "The Political Interpretation of the Maxim: the Purpose of Philosophy is the Imitation of God", *Studia Islamica*, 15: 53–61.

—— (1988) "The Ideal State of the Philosophers and Prophetic Laws", in *A Straight Path: Studies in Medieval Philosophy and Culture. Essays in Honor of Arthur Hyman*, ed. Ruth Link-Salinger (Washington): 10–22.

Bertman, Martin A. (1971a) "Philosophical Elitism: the Example of Averroes", *Philosophical Journal*, 8: 115–21.

—— (1971b) "Practical, Theoretical and Moral Superiority in Averroes", in *International Studies in Philosophy: a Yearbook of General Philosophical Inquiry*, 3 (Turin): 47–54.

Bielawski, Jozef and Plezia, Marian (1970) *Lettre d'Aristote à Alexandre sur la politique envers les cités [Risālat Arisṭūṭālis ilā l-Iskandar fī siyāsat al-mudun]*, texte arabe établi et traduit par J. Bielawski, commentaire de M. Plezia (Wroclaw, Warsaw and Krakow) (= Archiwum filologiczne, 25).
de Boer, Tj. (1920) *De "Medicina mentis" van den arts Rāzī* (Amsterdam) (= Mededelingen der Koninklijke Akademie van Wetenschappen, afd. Letterkunde, deel 53, ser. A, nr 1).
Bouyges, M. (1924) "Notes sur des traductions arabes d'auteurs grecs", *Archives de Philosophie*, 21: 349–71.
Bryson, *see* Plessner (1928).
Bürgel, Christoph (1967) "Adab und i'tidāl in ar-Ruhāwīs *Adab aṭ-Ṭabīb*", *Zeitschrift der deutschen morgenländischen Gesellschaft*, 117: 90–102.
Busse, Heribert (1968) "Fürstenspiegel und Fürstenethik im Islam", *Bustan*, 9(1): 12–19.
Butterworth, Charles (1972a) "Averroes: Politics and Opinion", *American Political Science Review*, 66: 894–901.
—— (1972b) "Rhetoric and Islamic Political Philosophy", *International Journal of Middle East Studies*, 3: 187–98.
—— (1980) "Philosophy, Stories and the Study of Elites", in *Elites in the Middle East*, ed. I. William Zartman (New York): 10–48.
—— (1986) *Philosophy, Ethics and Virtuous Rule: a Study of Averroes' Commentary on Plato's "Republic"* (New York and Cairo) (= Cairo Papers on Social Science, 9, monograph 1).
—— (1987) "Medieval Islamic Philosophy and the Virtue of Ethics", *Arabica*, 34: 221–50.
—— (1992) "The Political Teaching of Averroes", *Arabic Sciences and Philosophy*, 2: 187–202.
—— (1993a) "Die politischen Lehren von Avicenna und Averroes"' in *Pipers Handbuch der politischen Ideen*, ed. I. Fetscher and H. Münkler, II (München and Zürich): 141–73.
—— (1993b) "The Book of the Philosophic Life. Abū Bakr Muḥammad Ibn Zakariyyā Al-Rāzī", *Interpretation* 20/3: 227–36.
—— (1993c) "The Origins of al-Razī's Political Philosophy", *Interpretation* 20/3: 237–57.
The Cambridge History of Medieval Political Thought c. 350–c. 1450 (1988) ed. J. H. Burns (Cambridge).
Chahine, O. E. (1972) *L'originalité créatrice de la philosophie musulmane* (Paris).
Charles-Dominique, Paule (1965) "Le Système éthique d'Ibn al-Muqaffa' d'après ses deux épîtres dites 'al-ṣagīr' et 'al-kabīr'," *Arabica*, 12: 45–66.
Cheikho (1903); see Pseudo-Aristotle: *Maqālah fi'l-tadbīr*.
—— (1911) *Maqālāt falsafiyyah* (Paris).
Chemli, Mongi (1969) *La Philosophie morale d'Ibn Bajja (Avempace) à travers le Tadbīr al-Mutawaḥḥid* (Tunis).
Chittick, William C. (1988) "Two Seventeenth-Century Persian Tracts on Kingship and Rulers", in *Authority and Political Culture in Shi'ism*, ed. Said Amer Arjomand (New York): 267–304.
Cruz Hernández, Miguel (1960) "La libertad y la naturaleza social del hombre según Averroes", in *L'Homme et son destin d'après les penseurs du moyen âge*. (Actes

du premier congrès international de philosophie médiévale, Louvain–Bruxelles, 28 aout–4 septembre 1958) (Louvain and Paris): 277–83.

Daiber, Hans (1975) *Das theologisch-philosophische System des Mu'ammar Ibn 'Abbād as-Sulamī (gest. 830 n. Chr.)* (Beirut and Wiesbaden) (= Beiruter Texte und Studien, 19).

—— (1986a) *The Ruler as Philosopher: a New Interpretation of al-Fārābī's View* (= Mededelingen der Koninklijke Nederlandse Akademie van Wetenschappen, afd. Letterkunde, n.r. d. 49/4) (Amsterdam, Oxford and New York).

—— (1986b) "Prophetie und Ethik bei Fārābī (gest. 339/950)" in *L'Homme et son univers au moyen âge* (Actes du 7e congrès international de philosophie médiévale (Louvain-la-Neuve, Leuven, 30.8.–4.9.1982), 1–2) (Louvain-la-Neuve) (= Philosophes médiévaux, 26–7): 729–53.

—— (1989) "Abū Ḥātim ar-Rāzī (10th century A.D.) on the Unity and Diversity of Religions" in *Dialogue and Syncretism: an Interdisciplinary Approach*, ed. J. Gort, H. Vroom *et al.* (Amsterdam): 87–104.

—— (1990a) "Die Autonomie der Philosophie im Islam", in *Knowledge and the Sciences in Medieval Philosophy* (Proceedings of the Eighth International Congress of Medieval Philosophy, Helsinki 24–29 August, 1987), I, ed. M. Asztalos, J. E. Murdoch and I. Niiniluoto (Helsinki): 228–49.

—— (1990b) "Qosṭā ibn Lūqā (9. Jh.) über die Einteilung der Wissenschaften", *Zeitschrift für Geschichte der Arabisch-Islamischen Wissenschaften*, 6: 93–129.

—— (1991a) "Griechische Ethik in islamischem Gewande: Das Beispiel von Rāġib al-Iṣfahānī (11. Jh.)", in *Historia philosophiae medii aevi: Studien zur Geschichte der Philosophie des Mittelalters. Festschrift für Kurt Flasch zu seinem 60. Geburtstag*, eds Burkhard Mojsisch and Olaf Pluta, 1–2 (Amsterdam and Philadelphia): 181–92.

—— (1991b) "The Ismaili Background of Fārābī's Political Philosophy: Abū Ḥātim ar-Rāzī as a Forerunner of Fārābī," in *Gottes ist der Orient – Gottes ist der Okzident: Festschrift für Abdoljavad Falaturi zum 65. Geburtstag*, ed. Udo Tworuschka (Cologne and Vienna): 143–50.

Daneshpačūh, Mohammad Taqi (1988) "An Annotated Bibliography on Government and Statecraft", in *Authority and Political Culture in Shi'ism*, ed. Said Amer Arjomand (New York): 213–66.

Denny, Frederick M. (1985) "Ethics and the Qur'ān: Community and World View", in *Ethics in Islam*: 103–21.

Diwald, Susanne (1972) "Die Seele und ihre geistigen Kräfte", in *Islamic Philosophy and the Classical Tradition*: 49–61.

—— (1975) *Arabische Philosophie und Wissenschaft in der Enzyklopädie Kitāb Iḫwān aṣ-Ṣafā' (III): Die Lehre von Seele und Intellekt* (Wiesbaden).

—— (1981) "Die Bedeutung des Kitāb Iḫwān aṣ-Ṣafā' für das islamische Denken", in *Convegno sugli Ikhwān aṣ-Ṣafā'* (Roma 25–26 ottobre 1979) (Rome) (= Accademia Nazionale dei Lincei, Fondazione Leone Caetani): 5–25.

Druart, Thérèse-Anne (1977) "Un sommaire du sommaire Farabien des 'Lois' de Platon", *Bulletin de Philosophie Médiévale*, 19: 43–45.

—— (1993) "Al-Kindī's Ethics", *Review of Metaphysics*, 47: 329–57.

Dunlop, D. M. (1945) "Ibn Bājjah's Tadbīru'l-Mutawaḥḥid (Rule of the Solitary)", *Journal of the Royal Asiatic Society*: 61–81.

—— (1959) "A Little-Known Work on Politics by Lisān al-Dīn b. Al-Khaṭīb", *Miscelanea de estudios arabes y hebraicos*, 8: 47–54.
—— (1961) see al-Fārābī: *Fuṣūl muntaza'ah*.
—— (1971) "Observations on the Medieval Arabic Version of Aristotle's Nicomachean Ethics", *Atti dei convegni (Fondazione Alessandro Volta, Accademia Nazionale dei Lincei)*, 13 (= Oriente e Occidente nel medioevo. Filosofia e scienze): 229–49.
—— (1983) "The Arabic Tradition of the Summa Alexandrinorum", *Archives d'Histoire Doctrinale et Littéraire du Moyen Age*, 49: 253–63.
Enayat, Hamid (1977) "An Outline of the Political Philosophy of the *Rasā'il* of the Ikhwān al-Ṣafā'", in *Ismā'īlī Contributions*: 23–49.
Endress, G. (1986) "Wissen und Gesellschaft in der islamischen Philosophie des Mittelalters", in *Pragmatik: Handbuch pragmatischen Denkens*, ed. Herbert Stachowiak, I (Hamburg): 219–45.
Ethics in Islam (1985) ed. Richard G. Hovannisian (Malibu).
Fakhry, Majid (1975) "Justice in Islamic Philosophical Ethics: Miskawayh's Mediating Contribution", *Journal of Religious Ethics*, 3: 243–54.
—— (1977) *Dirāsāt fi'l-fikr al-'arabī* (Beirut).
—— (1979) *al-Fikr al-akhlāqī al-'arabī*, 1–2 (Beirut).
—— (1988) "The Devolution of the Perfect State: Plato, Ibn Rushd, and Ibn Khaldūn", in *Arab Civilization: Challenges and Responses. Studies in Honor of Constantine K. Zurayk*, ed. G. N. Atiyeh and Ibrahim M. Oweiss (Albany): 88–97.
—— (1991) *Ethical Theories in Islam* (Leiden, etc.) (= Islamic Philosophy, Theology and Science, 8).
al-Fārābī (1943) *Falsafat Aflāṭūn wa ajzā'uhā wa marātib ajzā'ihā min awwalihā ilā ākhirihā*, ed. F. Rosenthal and R. Walzer: *Alfarabius de Platonis philosophia* (London) (= Plato Arabus, 2). Also ed. in Badawī (1974): 3–27. English trans.: see Mahdi (1969).
—— (1971) *Fuṣūl muntaza'ah*, ed. Fauzi M. Najjar (Beirut). Also ed. with English trans. D. M. Dunlop: *Al-Fārābī, Fuṣūl al-madanī: Aphorisms of the Statesman* (Cambridge, 1961).
—— (1968) *Kitāb al-millah*, ed. M. Mahdi (Beirut). English trans.: see Stuart Rosenthal (1981).
—— (1983) *Kitāb al-siyāsat al-madaniyyah al-mulaqqab bi-mabādi' al-mawjūdāt*, ed. F. M. Najjar (Beirut, 2nd ed.).
—— (1985) *Kitāb al-tanbīh 'alā sabīl al-sa'ādah*, ed. Ja'far Āl Yāsīn (Beirut). Also ed. Ṣaḥbān Khalīfāt (Ammān, 1987). French trans.: *see* Mallet (1989).
—— (1981) *Kitāb taḥṣīl al-sa'ādah*, ed. Ja'far Āl Yāsīn (Beirut). English trans.: see Mahdi (1969).
—— (1895) *al-Madīnah al-fāḍilah* (= *Mabādi' ārā' ahl al-madīnah al-fāḍilah*), ed. F. Dieterici: *Alfarabi's Abhandlung der Musterstaat* (Leiden; repr. 1964). Also ed. and trans. R. Walzer: *al-Farabi On the Perfect State* (Oxford, 1985).
—— (1901) *Risālah fi'l-siyāsah*, ed. L. Cheikho, *al-Mashriq*, 4: 648–53; 689–700. Reprinted in *Maqālāt falsafiyyah qadīmah*: 18–34. Also ed. in: 'Abdalmun'im (1982): 21–34. German trans.: *see* Graf (1902).
—— (1952) *Talkhīṣ nawāmīs Aflāṭūn*, ed. with Latin translation by F. Gabrieli: Alfarabius, *Compendium Legum Platonis* (London) (= Plato Arabus, 3). Also

ed. in Badawī (1974): 34–83.
Faruqi, I. R. (1960) "On the Ethics of the Brethren of Purity", *Moslem World*, 50: 109–21; 193–8; 252–8; 51 (1961): 18–24.
de Fouchécour, Charles-Henri (1986) *Moralia. Les notions morales dans la littérature persane du 3e/9e au 7e/13e siècle* (Paris) (= Institut Français de Recherche en Iran. Bibliothèque Iranienne, 32. = "Synthèse", 23).
Gabrieli, Francesco (1949) "Un compendio arabo delle leggi di Platone", *Rivista degli Studi Orientali*, 24: 20–4.
—— (1951) "Le citazione delle leggi platoniche in Al-Bīrūnī", in *Al-Bīrūnī Commemoration Volume* (Calcutta): 107–10.
Gätje, Helmut (1956) "Avicenna als Seelenarzt", in *Avicenna Commemoration Volume* (Calcutta): 225–8.
Galen *Perì ethōn, see* Badawī (1981); Kraus (1939); Mattock (1972).
Galston, Miriam, (1978) "Philosopher-King V. Prophet" *Israel Oriental Studies*, 8: 204–18.
—— (1979) "Realism and Idealism in Avicenna's Political Philosophy", *Review of Politics*, 41: 561–77.
—— (1990) *Politics and Excellence: The Political Philosophy of Alfarabi* (Princeton, NJ).
al-Ghazzālī (1964) *Mīzān al-'amal*, ed. Sulaymān Dunyā (Cairo). French trans.: *see* Hachem (1945).
Giese, Alma (1990) *Mensch und Tier vor dem König der Dschinnen* (German trans. of *Rasā'il Ikhwān al-Ṣafā'*, part) (Hamburg) (= Philosophische Bibliothek, 433).
Goichon, A. M. (1959) *Le Récit de Ḥayy ibn Yaqẓān* (Paris).
Goldziher, Ignaz (1888) *Muhammedanische Studien*, I (Halle) (repr. New York and Hildesheim, 1971). [English version: *Muslim Studies*, ed. S. M. Stern, I (London, 1967).]
Goodman, Lenn Evan (1971) "The Epicurean Ethic of Muḥammad ibn Zakariyā' ar-Rāzī", *Studia Islamica*, 34: 5–26.
—— (1972), *see* Ibn Ṭufail.
—— (1973) "Rāzī's Psychology", *Philosophical Forum*, 4/1 (new series, Fall 1972): 26–48.
—— (1978) *The Case of the Animals versus Man before the King of the Jinn: A Tenth-century Ecological Fable of the Pure Brethren of Basra* (English trans. of *Rasā'il Ikhwān al-Ṣafā'*, part), (Boston) (= Library of Classical Arabic Literature, 3).
Graf, Georg (1902) "Farabi's Traktat 'Über die Leitung'", *Jahrbuch für Philosophie und spekulative Theologie*, 16: 385–406.
Grignaschi, Mario (1967a) "Le Roman épistolaire classique conservé dans la version arabe de Sālim Abū l-'Alā'", *Le Muséon*, 80: 211–64.
—— (1967b) "Les 'Rasā'il 'Arisṭāṭālīsa 'ilā-l-Iskandar' de Sālim Abū-l 'Alā' et l'activité culturelle à l'époque omayyade", *Bulletin d'Etudes Orientales*, 19 (1965–6): 7–83.
—— (1975) "La Siyāsatu-l-'Ammiyah", in J. Duchesne-Guillemin (ed.) *Monumentum H. S. Nyberg*, 3 (= Acta Iranica 6 = sér. 2, 3) (Tehran, Liège and Leiden): 33–287.
—— (1976) "L'Origine et les metamorphoses du 'Sirr-al-asrār'", *Archives d'Histoire Doctrinale et Littéraire du Moyen Age*, 43: 7–112.
—— (1980) "La Diffusion du 'secretum secretorum' (Sirr-al-asrār *dans l'Europe occidentale*", *Archives d'Histoire Doctrinale et Littéraire du Moyen Age*, 47: 7–70.

Gutas, Dimitri (1975) *Greek Wisdom Literature in Arabic Translation: A Study of the Graeco-Arabic Gnomologia* (New Haven).

—— (1977) "Notes and Texts from Cairo Mss. 1: Addenda to P. Kraus's Edition of Abū Bakr al-Rāzī's Al-Ṭibb al-Rūḥānī", *Arabica*, 24: 91–3.

—— (1990) "Ethische Schriften im Islam", *Neues Handbuch der Literaturwissenschaft*, 5 (= Orientalisches Mittelalter, ed. W. Heinrichs (Wiesbaden)): 346–65.

Hachem, Hikmat (1945) *Critère de l'action* (Paris).

Ḥamīd al-Dīn al-Kirmānī (1977) *al-Aqwāl al-dhahabiyyah*, ed. Salah al-Sawy, English introduction by Seyyed Hossein Nasr (Tehran). Also ed. Muṣṭafā Ghālib (Beirut, 1977) and 'Abd al-aṭīf al-'Abd (Cairo, 1978).

Hayoun, Maurice-Ruben (1988) "Le Commentaire de Moise de Narbonne (1300–1362) sur le Ḥayy ibn Yaqẓān d'Ibn Ṭufayl (mort en 1185)", *Archives d'Histoire Doctrinale et Littéraire du Moyen Age*, 63 (Paris 1989): 23–98.

—— (1989) *La Philosophie et la théologie de Moise de Narbonne (1300–1362)* (Tübingen) (= Texts and Studies in Medieval and Early Modern Judaism, 4).

—— (1990) "Ibn Bājja et Moise de Narbonne: edition de l'Iggeret Ha-Petirah", in *'Alei Shefer: Studies in the Literature of Jewish Thought presented to Rabbi Dr Alexandre Safran*, ed. Moshe Ḥallamish (Bar-Ilan): 75–93.

Hein, Christel (1985) *Definition und Einteilung der Philosophie: Von der spätantiken Einleitungsliteratur zur arabischen Enzyklopädie* (Frankfurt am Main, Bern and New York) (= Europäische Hochschulschriften, Reihe 20, 177).

History of Political Philosophy (1972), 2nd ed., ed. Leo Strauss and Joseph Cropsey (Chicago).

Hiyari, Mustafa (1983) "Qudāma b. Ǧa'fars Behandlung der Politik: Das Kapitel As-siyāsa aus seinem Vademecum für Sekretäre Kitāb al-ḫarāǧ wa-ṣanā'at al-kitāba", *Der Islam*, 60: 91–103.

Hoff, Tineke (1993) *Avicenna over het beheer van huis en haard [= Fi'l-siyāsah al-manziliyyah]. Ingeleid, vertaald en van commentaar voorzien* (Kampen-Kapellen).

Horten, Max (1907) *Buch der Genesung der Seele* [*ash-Shifā'*]: *eine philosophische Enzyklopädie. Serie 2: Philosophie. Gruppe 3, Teil 13: Metaphysik, Theologie, Kosmologie und Ethik* (Halle an der Saale and New York 1907; Leipzig 1909) (repr. 1960).

Hourani, G. F. (1976) *Averroes: On the Harmony of Religion and Philosophy*, trans., with introduction and notes, of Ibn Rushd's *Kitāb Fāṣl al-maqāl*, with its appendix (*Ḍamīma*) and an extract from *Kitāb al-Kashf 'an manāhij al-adilla* (London, 1961; repr. 1976).

—— (1985) *Reason and Tradition in Islamic Ethics* (Cambridge, London, etc.).

Ḥunayn ibn Isḥāq (1985) *Ādāb al-falāsifah*, ed. 'Abd al-Raḥmān Badawī (Kuwait).

Ibish, Yusuf (1966) *The Political Doctrine of al-Baqillani* (Beirut) (= American University of Beirut, Publication of the Faculty of Arts and Sciences, Oriental Series, no. 44).

Ibn Abi'l-Rabī': *see* Takrītī (1980).

Ibn Bājjah (1985) *Rasā'il Ibn Bājjah al-ilāhiyyah*, ed. M. Fakhry (Beirut).

—— (1978) *Tadbīr al-mutawaḥḥid*, ed. Ma'n Ziyādeh (Beirut). (Also in: *Rasā'il Ibn Bājjah al-ilāhiyyah*, ed. M. Fakhry: 155–73.)

Ibn al-Dāya: *Kitāb al-'uhūd al-yūnāniyyah al-mustakhrajah min rumūz kitāb al-siyāsah li-Aflāṭūn*, *see* Badawī (1954); al-Mālikī (1971).

Ibn al-Khaṭīb, *see* Lisānaddīn.

Ibn Khaldūn, *see* Quatremère; F. Rosenthal.

Ibn al-Muqaffa' (1978) *Āthār* (Beirut).

Ibn al-Nadīm (1871–2) *Kitāb al-fihrist*, ed. G. Flügel, 1, 2 (Leipzig; repr. Beirut, 1964). Also ed. by Riḍā-Tajaddud (Tehran, 1971). English trans. Bayard Dodge: *The Fihrist of al-Nadīm: a Tenth-Century Survey of Muslim Culture*, 1–2 (New York and London, 1970) (= Records of Civilization: Sources and Studies, 83).

Ibn Rushd (Commentary on Plato's *Republic*), *see* Lerner (1974); E. I. J. Rosenthal (1956).

—— (1982) *The Epistle on the Possibility of Conjunction with the Active Intellect by Ibn Rushd with the Commentary of Moses Narboni*, a critical edition and annotated translation by Kalman P. Bland (New York).

—— (1959) *Faṣl al-maqāl fīmā baynal-ḥikmah wa'l-sharī'ah min al-ittiṣāl*, ed. G. F. Hourani (Leiden). English trans.: *see* Hourani (1976).

Ibn Sīnā (1968) *Fī Ithbāt al-nubuwwāt*, ed. with introduction and notes by M. Marmura (Beirut).

—— (1906) *Fi'l-siyāsah al-manziliyyah*, ed. L. Ma'lūf, *al-Mashriq*, 9: 967–73; 1037–42; 1073–78. Reprint in: *Maqālāt falsafiyyah qadīmah*: 1–17. Also ed. 'Abd al-Mun'im Aḥmad (1982): 61–111. Also ed. Shamsaddīn (1988): 232–60.

—— (1966) *Ḥayy ibn Yaqẓān*, ed. Aḥmad Amīn: *Ḥayy ibn Yaqẓān li-ibn Sīnā wa-ibn Ṭufayl wa'l-Suhrawardī* (Cairo).

—— (1984) *al-Mabda' wa'l-ma'ād*, ed. 'Abd Allāh Nūrānī (Tehran). (= Wisdom of Persia, 36).

—— *al-Risālah al-aḍḥawiyyah fi'l-ma'ād*, *see* Lucchetta (1969).

—— (1960) *al-Shifā', al-Ilāhiyyāt*, 1–2, ed. Muḥammad Yūsuf Mūsā, Sulaymān Dunyā and Sa'īd Zāyid (Cairo). German trans.: *see* Horten. English trans. of a section: *see Medieval Political Philosophy*.

Pseudo-Ibn Sīnā (1891) *Risālah fī daf' al-ghamm min al-mawt*, ed. and French trans. M. A. F. Mehren, in *Traités mystiques d'Abou Alī al-Hosain b. Abdallāh b. Sīnā ou d'Avicenne*, 3rd fasc. (Leiden): 49–57 (French trans.: 28–32).

—— (1937) *Risālah fī māhiyyat al-ḥuzn wa asbābihī*, ed. and Turkish trans. Mehmet Hazmi Tura, in *Büyük Türk Filozof ve Tib Ustadi ibni Sina* (Istanbul) (= Türk Tarih Kurumu yayinlarindan, 7 ser., no. 1) (3 pages separate pagination).

Ibn Ṭufayl (1936) *Ḥayy ibn Yaqẓān*, ed. L. Gauthier, 2nd ed. (Beirut); ed. A. Nader, 2nd ed. (Beirut, 1968). English trans. L. E. Goodman: *Ibn Tufayl's Ḥayy ibn Yaqẓān* (New York, 1972) (repr. Los Angeles, 1983).

Ibrahim, Ahmad (1980) "Ibn Sina and the Philosophy of Law and the State", *Jernal Undang-Undang*, 7: 175–199.

Ikhwān al-Ṣafā', *see Rasā'il Ikhwān al-Ṣafā'*.

Islamic Philosophy and the Classical Tradition: Essays presented by his Friends and Pupils to Richard Walzer on his Seventieth Birthday, ed. S. M. Stern *et al.* (Oxford, 1972).

Ismā'īlī Contributions to Islamic Culture, ed Seyyed Hossein Nasr (Tehran, 1977).

al-Jāhiẓ (1970) *Rasā'il*, ed. 'Abd al-Salam Hārūn, 1–4 (Cairo).

Jospe, Raphael (1986) "Rejecting Moral Virtue as the Ultimate Human End", in *Studies in Islamic and Judaic Traditions: Papers presented at the Institute for Islamic–Judaic Studies*, ed. William M. Brinner and Syephen D. Ricks (Atlanta): 185–203.

Kassem, Hammond (1972) "The Idea of Justice in Islamic Philosophy", *Diogenes*, 79: 81–108. (French version in: *Diogène*, 79 (Paris, 1972): 81–107.)
Kellermann, Mechthild (1965) *Ein pseudoaristotelischer Traktat über die Tugend*, Edition und Übersetzung der arabischen Fassungen des Abū Qurra und des Ibn aṭ-Ṭayyib (thesis, Erlangen–Nürnberg).
Khalifat, Sahban Mahmoud (1990): "New Lights on al-Fārābī's *Risāla al-Tanbīh 'alā sabīl al-Sa'ādah*", in *Acts of the International Symposium on Ibn Turk, Khwārezmī, Fārābī, Beyrūnī, and Ibn Sīnā (Ankara, 9–12 September 1985)* (Ankara) (= Atatürk Culture Center Publications, no. 41): 147–50.
Khan, M. S., *see* Miskawayh, *Risālah fī māhiyat al-'adl.*
Khulaif, Fatḥ Allāh (1974): *Ibn Sīnā wa-madhhabuhū fi'l-nafs* (Beirut).
Khurshid, Abdus Salam (1979) "Al-Bīrūnī's Political Role and Philosophy", in *Al-Biruni Commemoration Volume* (Karachi): 357–61.
al-Kindī (1976) *Cinq épîtres* (Paris).
—— (1950–3) *Rasā'il al-Kindī al-falsafiyyah*, ed. Muḥammad 'Abd al-Hādī Abū Rīdah, 1–2 (Cairo) (2nd ed., 1978).
al-Kirmānī, *see* Ḥamīd al-Dīn.
Klein-Franke, Felix (1973) "Zur Überlieferung der platonischen Schriften im Islam", *Israel Oriental Studies*, 3: 120–39.
Kohler, Josef (1908–9) "Avicenna's Rechtsphilosophie", *Archiv für Rechts-und Wirtschaftsphilosophie*, 2: 465–70.
Kraemer, Joel (1979) "Alfarabi's Opinions of the Virtuous City and Maimonides' Foundation of the Law", in *Studia Orientalia memoriae D. H. Baneth dedicata* (Jerusalem): 107–53.
—— (1983): "Ibn Bajja y Maimonides sobre la perfección humana", in *I congreso internacional "Encuentro de las tres culturas" (3–7 octubre 1982)* (Toledo): 237–45.
—— (1986) *Humanism in the Renaissance of Islam* (Leiden).
—— (1987) "The *Jihād* of the *Falāsifah*", *Jerusalem Studies in Arabic and Islam*, 10: 288–324.
Kraus, P. (1939) "*Dirāsāt fī ta'rīkh at-tarjamah fī l-islām.* I: *Kitāb al-Akhlāq li-Jālīnūs*", *Bulletin of the Faculty of Arts of the Egyptian University*, 5(1): 1–51.
Lambton, Ann K. S. (1954) "The Theory of Kingship in the *Naṣīḥat ul-mulūk* of Ghazālī", *Islamic Quarterly*, 1: 47–55. (Also in Lambton (1980).)
—— (1963) "Justice in the Medieval Persian Theory of Kingship", *Studia Islamica*, 17: 91–119. (Also in Lambton (1980).)
—— (1971) "Islamic Mirrors for Princes", in *La Persia nel medioevo (Roma, 31 marzo–5 aprile 1970)* (Rome) (= Accademia Nazioanle dei Lincei, Anno 368, 1971): 419–42. (Also in Lambton (1980).)
—— (1980) *Theory and Practice in Medieval Persian Government* (London) (= Variorum Reprints).
—— (1981) *State and Government in Medieval Islam* (Oxford).
Laoust, Henri (1958) *La Profession de foi d'Ibn Baṭṭa* (Damascus).
—— (1968) "La Pensée et l'action politiques d'al-Māwardī (364–450/974–1058)", *Revue des Etudes Islamiques*, 36: 11–92. (Also in Laoust (1983).)
—— (1981) "La Pensée politique d'Ibn Khaldoun, in *A'māl nadwat Ibn Khaldūn: Bi-munāsabat murūr sittat qurūn 'alā ta'līf al-Muqaddimah*". *Ayyām Jāmi'iyyah, 14–17 fabrāyir 1979* (Rabat): 466–49.

—— (1983) *Pluralismes dans l'Islam (Recueil d'articles parus entre 1932 et 1980)* (Paris).

Lauer, Hans H. (1984) "Ethik und ärztliches Denken im arabischen Mittelalter", in *Bausteine zur Medizingeschichte: H. Schipperges zum 65. Geburtstag* (Wiesbaden) (= Sudhoffs Archiv, Beiheft 24): 72–86.

Lazar, Louis (1980) "L'Education politique selon Ibn Roshd (Averroes)", *Studia Islamica,* 52: 135–66.

Leaman, Oliver (1980) "Ibn Bājja on Society and Philosophy", *Der Islam,* 57: 109–19.

—— (1985) *An Introduction to Medieval Islamic Philosophy* (Cambridge, etc.).

—— (1988) *Averroes and his Philosophy* (Oxford).

Lerner, Ralph (1974) *Averroes on Plato's Republic,* trans. with introduction and notes (Ithaca and London).

—— *see Medieval Political Philosophy.*

Lewin, Bernhard (1955) "L'Idéal antique du philosophie dans la tradition arabe: un traité d'éthique du philosophe Bagdadien Ibn Suwār", *Lychnos* 1954–5: 267–84.

Lewis, Bernard (1984) "Siyāsa", in *In Quest of an Islamic Humanism: Arabic and Islamic Studies in Memory of Mohamed al-Nowaihi* (Cairo): 3–14.

Lindgren, Uta (1980) "Avicenna und die Grundprinzipien des Gemeinwesens in Francese Eiximenis' Regiment de la cosa publica (Valencia 1383)", in *Soziale Ordnungen im Selbstverständnis des Mittelalters,* 2, ed. A. Zimmermann and G. Vuillemin-Diem (Berlin and New York) (= Miscellanea mediaevalia, 12/2): 449–59.

Lisān al-Dīn ibn al-Khaṭīb: *Kitāb al-ishārah ilā adab al-wizārah fi'l-siyāsah,* ed. 'Abd al-Qādir Zamāma, *Majallat al-majma' al-'ilmī al-'arabī,* 47 (Damascus 1972): 76–91.

Lucchetta, Francesca (1969) *Avicenna, Epistola sulla vita futura: ar-Risāla al-aḍḥawīya fī l-ma'ād,* 1, testo arabo, traduzione, introduzione e note (Padua).

Macy, Jeffrey (1982) "The Theological–Political Teaching of Shemonah Peraqim: a Reappraisal of the Text and of its Arabic Sources", in *Proceedings of the Eighth World Congress of Jewish Studies (Jerusalem, August 16–21, 1981),* division C (Jerusalem): 31–40.

—— (1986) "The Role of Law and the Rule of Wisdom in Plato, al Fārābī, and Maimonides", in *Studies in Islamic and Judaic Traditions: Papers presented at the Institute for Islamic–Judaic Studies,* ed. William M. Brinner and Stephen D. Ricks (Atlanta): 205–32.

Madelung, Wilferd (1977) "Aspects of Ismā'īlī Theology: the Prophetic Chain and the God Beyond Being", in *Ismā'īlī Contributions to Islamic Culture*: 51–65. (Reprint in Madelung, *Religious Schools and Sects* (London, 1985) = Variorum Reprints.)

Mahdi, Muhsin (1957) *Ibn Khaldūn's Philosophy of History* (London) (2nd ed., Chicago, 1971).

—— (1962) "Die Kritik der islamischen politischen Philosophie bei Ibn Khaldūn", in *Wissenschaftliche Politik: eine Einführung in Grundfragen ihrer Tradition und Theorie,* ed. Dieter Oberndörfer (Freiburg im Breisgau): 117–51.

—— (1964) "Averroes on Divine Law and Human Wisdom", in *Ancients and Moderns: Essays on the Tradition of Political Philosophy in Honor of Leo Strauss,* ed. Joseph Cropsey (New York and London): 114–31.

—— (1969) *Alfarabi's Philosophy of Plato and Aristotle,* trans. with an introduction, rev. ed. (Ithaca and New York).

—— (1978) "Alfarabi et Averroès: Remarques sur le commentaire d'Averroès sur la République de Platon", in *Multiple Averroès* (Paris): 91–102.

—— (1990) "Al-Fārābī's Imperfect State", *Journal of the American Oriental Society*, 110: 691–726.

—— (1991) "Philosophy and Political Thought: Reflections and Comparisons", *Arabic Sciences and Philosophy*, 1(1): 9–29.

Makarem, Sami N. (1967) "The Philosophical Significance of the Imām in Ismā'īlism", *Studia Islamica*, 27: 41–53.

—— (1972) *The Doctrine of the Ismailis* (Beirut).

—— (1977) *The Political Doctrine of the Ismā'īlīs (The Imamate)* (Delmar, New York).

al-Mālikī, 'Umar (1971) *al-Falsafah al-siyāsiyyah 'ind al-'arab (La Philosophie politique chez les arabes)* (Algiers) (2nd ed., 1980).

Mallet, D. (1989) "Le Rappel de la voie a suivre pour parvenir au bonheur de Abū Naṣr Al-Fārābī. Introduction, traduction et notes", *Bulletin d'Etudes Orientales*, 39–40: 113–46.

Ma'lūf (1921), *see* Pseudo-Aristotle: *Economics*.

Manzalaoui, Mahmoud (1974) "The Pseudo-Aristotelian *Kitāb Sirr al-Asrār*", *Oriens*, 23–4: 147–257.

Maqālāt falsafiyyah qadīmah li-ba'ḍ mashāhīr falāsifat al-'arab al-muslimīn wa'l-naṣārā ma'a ta'rīb Isḥāq ibn Ḥunayn li-maqālāt Arisṭū wa Aflāṭūn wa Fithāghūras (Beirut, 1911) (repr. Frankfurt, 1974).

Marmura, M. (1963) "Avicenna's Psychological Proof of Prophecy", *Journal of Near Eastern Studies*, 22: 49–56.

—— (1964) "Avicenna's Theory of Prophecy in the Light of Ash'arite Theology", in *The Seed of Wisdom: Essays in Honor of T. J. Meek*, ed. W. S. McCullough (Toronto): 159–78.

—— (1979) "The Philosopher and Society: Some Medieval Arabic Discussions", *Arab Studies Quarterly*, 1: 309–23.

—— (1983) "The Islamic Philosophers' Concept of Islam", in *Islam's Understanding of Itself*, ed. R. G. Hovannisian and Speros Vryonis (Malibu) (= Giorgio Levi della Vida Biennial Conference, 8): 87–102.

—— (1985) *see* Watt and Marmura.

Maroth, M. (1978) "Griechische Theorie und orientalische Praxis in der Staatskunst von Al-Fārābī", *Acta Antiqua*, 26: 465–9.

Marquet, Yves (1962) "Imamat, résurrection et hiérarchie selon les Ikhwan Aṣ-Ṣafa", *Revues des Études Islamiques*, 30: 49–142.

al-Ma'ṣūmī, Ṣaghīr Ḥasan (1961) "Ibn Bajjah on Prophecy", *Pakistan Philosophical Journal*, 5(1): 31–7. (Also in: *Sind University Journal*, 1 (1961): 22–9.)

Mattock, J. N. (1972) "A Translation of the Arabic Epitome of Galen's Book ΠΕΡΙ ΗΘΩΝΙ", *Islamic Philosophy and the Classical Tradition*: 235–60.

Medieval Political Philosophy: a Sourcebook (1962), ed. Ralph Lerner and Muhsin Mahdi (Glencoe).

Michot, Jean R. (1986) *La Destinée de l'homme selon Avicenne: le retour à Dieu (ma'ād et l'imagination)* (Louvain).

Miskawayh (1964) (*Risālah fī Māhiyat al-'adl*) *An Unpublished Treatise of Miskawaih on Justice*, ed. with notes, annotations, English translation and an introduction by M. S. Khan (Leiden).

—— (1928) *al-Sa'ādah*, ed. 'Alī al-Ṭūbjī (Cairo).

—— *Tahdhīb al-akhlāq*, ed. Constantine K. Zurayk (Beirut). Also ed. by Ḥasan Tamīm (2nd ed. Beirut, 1978). English trans. C. K. Zurayk: *The Refinement of Character* (Beirut, 1968). French trans. Mohammed Arkoun: *Miskawayh (320/ 21–420): Traité d'éthique* (Damascus, 1969) (2nd ed., 1988).

Mohaghegh, Mehdi (1967) "Notes on the 'Spiritual Physick' of al-Rāzī", *Studia Islamica,* 26: 5–22. (Also in Mohaghegh *Fīlsūf-i-Rayy Muḥammad Ibn-i-Zakariya-i-Razi,* 2nd, enlarged ed. (Tehran, 1974): 5–27.)

Murad, Hasan Qasim (1991) "Jabr and Qadar in Early Islam: a Reappraisal of their Political and Religious Implications", in *Islamic Studies presented to Charles J. Adams,* ed. Wael B. Hallaq and Donald P. Little (Leiden, etc.): 117–32.

Najjar, Fauzi M. (1958) "Al-Fārābī on Political Science", *Moslem World,* 48: 94–103.

—— (1960) "On Political Science, Canonical Jurisprudence and Dialectical Theology", *Islamic Culture,* 34: 233–41.

—— (1961) "Fārābī's Political Philosophy and Shī'ism", *Studia Islamica,* 14: 57–72.

—— (1978) "Political Philosophy in Islam", *Islamic Quarterly,* 20–2: 121–32.

—— (1980) "Democracy in Islamic Political Philosophy", *Studia Islamica,* 51: 107–22.

—— (1984) "Siyāsa in Islamic Political Philosophy", in *Islamic Theology and Philosophy: Studies in Honor of George F. Hourani* (Albany): 92–110.

Naṣīr al-Dīn Ṭūsī (1971) *Akhlāq-i nāṣirī,* ed. Mujtabā Mīnuwī and 'Alī Riḍā Ḥaydarī (Tehran). English trans. *The Nasirean Ethics by Naṣīr al-Dīn Ṭūsī,* trans. from the Persian by G. M. Wickens (London, 1964).

Nasr, Seyyed Hossein (1974) "Quṭb al-Dīn al-Shīrāzī", in *Dictionary of Scientific Biography,* 11 (New York): 247–53.

Netton, Ian Richard (1991) *Muslim Neoplatonists: an Introduction to the Thought of the Brethren of Purity (Ikhwān al-Ṣafā'),* new edition with corrections (Edinburgh) (= Islamic Surveys, 19).

Noureddine, A. (1961) *Anthologie de textes poétiques attribués à Avicenne* (Algiers).

Oweiss, Ibrahim M. (1988) "Ibn Khaldun, the Father of Economics", in *Arab Civilization: Challenges and Responses. Studies in Honor of Constantine K. Zurayk,* ed. G. N. Atiyeh and Ibrahim M. Oweiss (Albany): 112–27.

Pellat, Charles (1967) *Arabische Geisteswelt: ausgewählte und übersetzte Texte von al-Ǧāḥiẓ* (Zürich).

—— (1976) *Ibn al-Muqaffa', mort vers 140/757, "conseilleur" du calife* (Paris) (= Publications du département d'islamologie de l'université de Paris – Sorbonne, 2).

Peters, F. E. (1968) *Aristoteles Arabus* (Leiden).

Piaia, Gregorio (1973) "Filosofia e politica in Ibn Tufail e in Averroe", in *Filosofia e politica e altri saggi,* ed. Carlo Giacon (Padua): 33–54.

Pines, Shlomo (1954–5) "A Note on the History of a Pseudo-Aristotelian Text", *Tarbiz,* 24: 406–9. (In Hebrew, with English summary.)

—— (1957) "Notes on Averroes' Political Philosophy", *Iyyun,* 8: 65–84; 128–30. (In Hebrew, with English summary.)

—— (1971) "The Societies Providing for the Bare Necessities of Life According to Ibn Khaldūn and to the Philosophers", *Studia Islamica,* 34: 125–38.

—— (1978) "La Philosophie dans l'économie du genre humain selon Averroès; une reponse à al-Fārābī?", in *Multiple Averroès* (Paris), 189–207.

—— (1979) "The Limitations of Human Knowledge According to Al-Farabi, ibn Bajja, and Maimonides", in *Studies in Medieval Jewish History and Literature,* ed. Isadore Twersky (Cambridge, Mass. and London): 82–109. (Also in *Maimonides: a Collection of Essays*, ed. J. A. Buijs (Notre Dame, 1988): 91–121.)

—— (1986) *Studies in Arabic Versions of Greek texts and in Mediaeval Science* (Jerusalem and Leiden) (= The Collected Works of Shlomo Pines, 2).

Plessner, Martin (1928) *Der ΟΙΚΟΝΟΜΙΚΟΣ des Neupythagoreens "Bryson" und sein Einfluss auf die islamische Wissenschaft* (Heidelberg) (= Orient und Antike, 5).

—— *see* Bielawski.

Pohlenz, M. (1938) "Die Araber und die griechische Kultur", *Göttinger gelehrte Anzeigen*, 200: 409–16.

The Political Aspects of Islamic Philosophy. Essays in Honor of Muhsin Mahdi, ed. C. E. Butterworth (Cambridge, 1992) (= Harvard Middle Eastern Monographs, 27).

al-Qāḍī, Wadād (1976) "Lisān al-Dīn Ibn al-Ḥaṭīb on Politics", in *La Signification du bas moyen âge dans l'histoire et la culture du monde musulman: Actes du 8me congrès de l'Union européenne des arabisants et islamisants. Aix-en-Provence septembre 1976*: 205–17.

—— (1978) "An Early Fāṭimid Political Document", *Studia Islamica*, 48: 71–108.

Quatremère, Etienne Marc (1858) *Prolégomènes d'Ebn Khaldoun* (Paris) (repr. Beirut, 1970).

Qudāmah ibn Ja'far: *Kitāb al-kharāj wa ṣina'at al-kitābah*, ed. F. Sezgin in collaboration with M. Amawi, A. Jokhosha, E. Neubauer (Frankfurt, 1986) (= Publications of the Institute for the History of Arabic–Islamic Science, series C, 42).

—— (1981) *al-Siyāsah min kitāb al-kharāj wa ṣina'at al-kitābah*, ed. Muṣṭafā al-Ḥiyārī (Amman).

Quṭb al-Dīn al-Shīrāzī (1938–44) *Durrat al-tāj li-ghurrat al-dubāj (Introduction, Logic, Metaphysics, Theodicy)*, ed. S. M. Mishkāt (Tehran).

Rabī', Muhammad Mahmoud (1967) *The Political Theory of Ibn Khaldūn* (Leiden). (Arabic trans.: *al-Naẓariyyah al-siyāsiyyah li-Ibn Khaldūn* (Cairo, 1981.)

al-Rāghib al-Iṣfahānī (1987) *Kitāb al-Dhari'ah ilā makārim al-sharī'ah*, ed. Abu'l-Yazīd al-'Ajamī (Cairo).

Rahman, F. (1985) "Aḵlāq", in *Encyclopaedia Iranica*, 1/2 (London, Boston and Henley): 719b–723a.

Ramon Guerrero, Rafael (1986) *Obras filosoficas de Al-Kindī*, trans. Emilio Poveda (Madrid).

Rasā'il Ikhwān al-Ṣafā', (1928) ed. Khayr al-Dīn al-Ziriklī, 1–4 (Cairo).

—— *see* Diwald; Giese; Goodman; Tornero Poveda.

Rescher, O. (1917) "Das kitāb 'el-adab el-kebīr' des Ibn el-Moqaffa'", *Mitteilungen des Seminars für orientalische Sprachen*, 20(2): 35–82.

Richter, Gustav (1932) *Studien zur Geschichte der älteren arabischen Fürstenspiegel* (Leipzig) (= Leipziger semitistische Studien, N. F. 3) (repr. New York, 1968).

Riḍwān al-Sayyid (1985) "Abū-'l-Ḥasan al-Māwardī. Dirāsah fī ru'yatihi-l-ijtimā'iyyah", *al-Abḥāth*, 33: 55–97.

Rosenthal, E. I. J. (1932) *Ibn Khalduns Gedanken über den Staat* (Munich and Berlin) (= Historische Zeitschrift, Beiheft 25).

—— (1937) "Politische Gedanken bei Ibn Bāǧǧa", *Monatsschrift für Geschichte und Wissenschaft des Judentums*, 81 (N.F., 45). 153–68; 185–6.

—— (1951) "The Place of Politics in the Philosophy of Ibn Bajja", *Islamic Culture*,

25: 187–211. (Also in (1971c): 35–59.)
—— (1953) "The Place of Politics in the Philosophy of Ibn Rushd", *Bulletin of the School of Oriental and African Studies*, 15: 246–78. (Also in (1971c): 60–92.)
—— (1955) "The Place of Politics in the Philosophy of al-Farabi", *Islamic Culture*, 29: 157–78. (Also in (1971c): 93–114.)
—— (1956) *Averroes' Commentary on Plato's Republic*, ed. with an introduction, translation and notes (Cambridge) (repr. 1969).
—— (1958) "Der Kommentar des Averroes zur Politeia Platons", *Zeitschrift für Politik*, N.F., 5: 38–51.
—— (1962) *Political Thought in Medieval Islam* (Cambridge, 2nd ed.).
—— (1968) "Political Philosophy in Islam and Judaism", *Judaism*: 17 430–40.
—— (1971a) "Some Aspects of Islamic Political Thought", in (1971c): 17–33.
—— (1971b) "Ibn Khaldun: a North African Muslim Thinker of the Fourteenth Century", in (1971c): 3–16.
—— (1971c) *Studia Semitica*, 2 (Cambridge).
—— (1972) "Politisches Denken im Islam – Kalifatstheorie und politische Philosophie", *Saeculum*, 23: 148–171.
—— (1973) "The Role of the State in Islam: Theory and the Medieval Practice", *Der Islam*, 50: 1–28.
—— (1980) "Political Ideas in Moshe Narboni's Commentary on Ibn Ṭufail's Ḥayy b. Yaqẓān", in *Hommage à Georges Vajda: études d'histoire et de pensée juives*, ed. Gérard Nahon et Charles Touati (Louvain): 227–34.
Rosenthal, Franz (1940) "On the Knowledge of Plato's Philosophy in the Islamic World", *Islamic Culture*, 14: 387–422. (Repr. in 1990).
—— (1956) "State and Religion According to Abū'l-Ḥasan al-'Āmirī", *Islamic Quarterly*, 3: 42–52. (Repr. in *Muslim Intellectual and Social History* (London, 1990) = Variorum Collected Studies series.)
—— (1958) *Ibn Khaldūn: The Muqaddima. An Introduction to History*, translated from the Arabic (London).
—— (1989) "Abū Zayd al-Balkhī on Politics", in *The Islamic World: From Classical to Modern Times. Essays in Honor of Bernard Lewis*, ed. C. E. Bosworth, Ch. Issawi, *et al.* (Princeton): 287–301.
—— (1990) *Greek Philosophy in the Arab World* (Aldershot) (= Variorum Collected Studies series, SC 322).
Rosenthal, Stuart (1981) *Al-Fārābī's Kitāb al-Milla. Translated, with Notes and Introductory Essay* (M. Phil. thesis, Oxford University).
Rowson, Everett K. (1988) *A Muslim Philosopher on the Soul and its Fate: al-'Āmirī's kitāb al-amad 'alā l-abad* (New Haven) (= American Oriental Series, 70).
Rubio, L. (1981) "El filósofo autodidacto: Su posición dentro del sufismo neoplatónico y su doctrina acerca de las relaciones entre la razón y la revelación", *Cuadernos Salmantinos de filosofía*, 8: 105–36.
Rundgren, Frithiof (1976) "Das Muxtaṣar min kitāb al-Axlāq des Galenos", *Orientalia Suecana*, 23–4: 84–105.
Sajjad, Saiyid Ali (1983) "Al-Fārābī's Classification of States with Particular Reference to his Imam-State", *Islamic Culture*, 57: 253–61.
Salinger, Gerard (1956) "A Muslim Mirror for Princes", *Moslem World*, 46: 24–39.
Sankari, Farouk A. (1970) "Plato and Alfarabi: a Comparison of Some Aspects of their Political Philosophies", *Vivarium*, 8: 1–9. (Also in *Moslem World*, 60

(1970): 218–25 and in *Studies in Islam*, 7 (1970): 9ff.)
Shahjahan, Muhammad (1985) "An Introduction to the Ethics of al-Fārābī", *Islamic Culture*, 59: 45–52.
Shamsaddīn, 'Abd al-Amīr (1988): *al-Madhhab al-tarbawī 'ind Ibn Sīnā min khilāl falsafatihi'l-'amaliyyah* (Beirut).
Shawer, Chere Winnek (1973) *Abu Bakr Muhammad ibn Zakariya al-Razi on Reason and Nature* (thesis, University of Missouri).
Sherwani, Haroon Khan (1977) *Studies in Muslim Political Thought and Administration* (Philadelphia) (repr. of 4th rev. ed., Lahore, 1963).
al-Sijistānī, *see* Abū Sulaymān al-Sijistānī.
Simon, Heinrich (1959) *Ibn Khaldūn's Wissenschaft von der menschlichen Kultur* (Leipzig) (English trans.: *Ibn Khaldun's Science of Human Culture*, trans. with preface by Fuad Baali (Lahore, 1978).
—— (1963) "Arabische Utopien im Mittelalter", *Wissenschaftliche Zeitschrift der Humboldt-Universität zu Berlin. Gesellschafts- und sprachwissenschaftliche Reihe*, Vol. 12: 245–52.
—— (1971) "Elements of Utopian Thought in Mediaeval Islamic Philosophy", in *Ve congrès international d'arabisants et d'islamisants. Bruxelles 1970. Actes* (Brussels) (= Correspondence d'Orient, 11).
Sprachman, P. (1985) "Aklāq Al-Ašrāf", in *Encyclopaedia Iranica*, 1(2) (London, Boston and Henley): 723a–724a.
Stern, S. M. (1968) *Aristotle on the World State*, (Oxford).
Strauss, Leo (1957) "How Farābī read Plato's Laws", *Mélanges Louis Massignon*, 3 (Damascus): 319–44. (Also in *What is Political Philosophy And Other Essays* (New York, and London, 1959) (repr. 1988): 134–54.)
Strohmaier, Gotthard (1974) "Die arabische Sokrates-Legende und ihre Ursprünge", in *Studia Coptica*, ed. Peter Nagel (Berlin) (= Berliner Byzantinistische Arbeiten, 45): 121–36.
—— (1979) "Elitetheorien bei arabischen Philosophen", in *Arabische Sprache und Literatur im Wandel*, ed. M. Fleischhammer (Halle an der Saale): 221–7.
Takrītī, Nājī (1980) *al-Falsafat al-siyāsiyyah 'ind Ibn Abi'l-Rabī' ma'a taḥqīq kitābihī sulūk al-mālik fī tadbīr al-mamālik* (Beirut).
al-Tawḥīdī: *al-Baṣā'ir wa'l-dhakhā'ir*, ed. Ibrāhīm al-Kaylānī, 1–4 (Damascus, 1964) (new ed. by Wadād al-Qāḍī, Beirut, 1988).
Themistius (1920–3) *Risālah ilā Julian al-malik fi'l-siyāsah wa tadbīr al-mamlakah*, ed. Louis Cheikho, in *Anciens traités arabes contenant La politique de Themistius, L'Economie domestique de Probus (?), Les Récits amusants de Barhebraeus et L'Exclusion de la tristesse, attribué à Platon (Majmū'at arba'a rasā'il li-qudamā' falāsifat al-yūnān wa li-Ibn al-'Ibrī)* (Beirut) 1–11. Also edited by Muḥammad Salīm Sālim (Cairo, 1970) and by Irfan Shahid, in *Themistii orationes quae supersunt*, rec. H. Schenkl, opus consummaverunt G. Downey et A.-T. Norman, 3 (Leipzig, 1974) (= Bibliotheca scriptorum graecorum et romanorum Teubneriana): 73–119.
Tis' rasā'il fi'l-ḥikmah wa'l-ṭabī'iyāt, Ta'līf al-shaikh al-Ra'īs Abī 'Alī al-Ḥusayn ibn 'Abd Allāh ibn Sīnā, wa-fī ākhirihā qiṣṣat Salāmān wa Absāl (Istanbul, 1881).
Tornero Poveda, Emilio (1984) *La disputa de los animales contra el hombre* (Madrid).
—— (1992) *Al-Kindī. La transformación de un pensamiento religioso en un pensamiento racional* (Madrid).

Ṭurayḥī, M. K. (1962) *al-Kindī, faylasūf al-'Arab al-awwal* (Baghdad).
al-Ṭūsī, *see* Naṣīr al-Dīn al-Ṭūsī.
Ullmann, Manfred (1970) *Die Medizin im Islam* (Leiden and Cologne) (= Handbuch der Orientalistik, 1. Abteilung, Ergänzungsband, 6, 1).
Victor, Ulrich (1983) [Aristotle] *OIKONOMIKOS. Das erste Buch der Ökonomik – Handschriften, Text, Übersetzung und Kommentar – und seine Beziehungen zur Ökonomieliteratur* (Königstein/Ts.) (= Beiträge zur klassischen Philologie, 147).
von Sivers, Peter (1968) *Khalifat, Königtum und Verfall: Die politische Theorie Ibn Khaldūns* (Munich).
Walbridge, John Tuthill (1992) *The Science of Mystic Lights: Quṭb al-Dīn Shīrāzī and the Illuminationist Tradition in Islamic Philosophy* (Cambridge, Mass).
Walsh, John K. (1976) "Versiones peninsulares del 'Kitāb Ādāb al-Falāsifa' de Ḥunayn ibn Isḥāq", *Andalus*, 41: 355–84.
Walzer, Richard (1985) *see* al-Fārābī: *al-Madīnah al-fāḍilah.*
Walzer, R. and Ritter, Helmut (1938–9) "Studi su Al-Kindī 2: Uno scritto morale inedito di Al-Kindī. Temistio peri alypias?", in *Atti della Reale Accademia Nazionale dei Lincei. Memorie della Classe di Scienze morali, storiche e filologiche*, Series 6, 8 (Rome): 5–63.
Watt, W. Montgomery (1968) *Islamic Political Thought* (Edinburgh) (repr. 1980) (= Islamic Surveys, 6).
—— (1988) *Islamic Fundamentalism and Modernists* (London and New York).
Watt, W. M. and Marmura, M. (1985) *Der Islam*, 2 (Stuttgart, etc.) (= Die Religionen der Menschheit 25, 2).
Wickens, G. M. (1985) "Aḵlāq-e Jalālī; Aḵlāq-e Moḥsenī; Aḵlāq-e Nāṣerī", in *Encyclopaedia Iranica*, 1(2) (London, Boston and Henley): 724a–725b.
Zainaty, Georges (1979) *La Morale d'Avempace* (Paris) (= Etudes musulmanes, 22).
Zonta, Mauro (1995) *Un interprete ebreo della filosofia di Galeno. Gli scritti filosofici di Galeno nell'opera di Shem Tob ibn Falaquera* (Turin) (= Eurasiatica. Quaderni del Dipartimento di Studi Eurasiatici, Università degli Studi di Venezia, 39).

CHAPTER 51

Literature

Shams Inati and Elsayed Omran

The determination of the relation of Islamic philosophy to literature first requires a clear delineation of the meaning of *philosophy* and of *literature.*

The most common definition of *falsafah* (philosophy) in Arabic thought stresses that philosophy determines the realities of all things and that it does so in accordance with human capacity.[1] *Adab,* which is commonly translated as literature, has been used in a number of different ways to mean: (1) guidance to good deeds and diversion from bad ones; (2) proper behaviour;[2] (3) knowledge of the art of poetic composition;[3] (4) knowledge of the Arabic language: knowledge that helps one avoid error in verbal or written Arabic discourse;[4] and (5) knowledge in an unrestricted sense.[5] The first two of the above definitions of *adab* can be reduced to that which leads to good conduct; the last three, to knowledge, but knowledge of rather different sorts – of poetic composition (3), of the soundness of the Arabic language (4), or of just anything (5). Thus, there are two aspects to *adab*: a practical one, referring to good conduct, and a theoretical one, referring to knowledge.

A study of *falsafah* and *adab,* therefore, focuses on the subject of the human grasp of the realities of things and its relation to the practical aspect of *adab* and/or to one or more of its theoretical aspects.

The major Arabic extant philosophical writings that concern themselves with one or more literary aspects are those of al-Fārābī, Ibn Sīnā (Avicenna) and Ibn Rushd (Averroes).[6] Because these three figures were primarily philosophers, their main concern was to investigate human knowledge of the realities of things, a type of knowledge they believed to be essential to ultimate human happiness. Such knowledge, however, must be preceded, according to them, by the performance of good deeds. This performance is, in turn, enhanced by the use of a certain type of language – a type of language that reflects a certain type of reality. For reasons that will be elaborated later in this chapter, these three philosophers believed that this type of language would have to be primarily poetic in order to be most effective with the majority of people.

To study their understanding of the relation of philosophy to literature is thus in part to study their concept of the relation of human knowledge of the realities of things to that which leads to good conduct and language, particularly, poetic composition. Their view of the relation of philosophy to language in general is touched upon in the chapter on logic. The present chapter will concentrate on the relation of philosophy to poetry and on how the latter can lead to good deeds, although reference to other forms of linguistic composition will be made when relevant.

In order to understand these philosophers' view of human knowledge of the realities of things and the manner in which poetry relates to the good deeds necessary for such knowledge, it is important first to examine their view of the structure of the human soul and the function of its parts.

STRUCTURE AND FUNCTION OF THE HUMAN SOUL

According to Muslim philosophers, the human soul consists of three parts or souls: the plant soul, the animal soul and the rational soul. The first is responsible for nourishment, growth and reproduction; the second for sensation and movement; the third for knowledge. To say this, however, is not to say that no powers of the human soul other than those of the rational soul are needed for knowledge. The animal soul plays a significant role in preparing the way for the attainment of knowledge, and at least one of its powers (the imagination) is said to be able to attain some form of knowledge to be specified later.

Sensation is of two types: that of the external senses or faculties and that of the internal ones. Al-Fārābī, Ibn Sīnā and Ibn Rushd agree that there are five external senses: those of touch, taste, smell, hearing and sight. The function of these faculties is to collect material and, hence, particular forms from external objects, a function these faculties can perform only if such objects are present to them. The internal senses, however, vary in number, according to these philosophers. For al-Fārābī and Ibn Sīnā, for example, there are five: those of common sense, representation, imagination, estimation and memory.[7] Ibn Rushd, like his teacher, Ibn Bājjah, reduces their number to three: those of common sense, imagination and memory.[8] The function of the internal senses is more varied and more complex than that of the external ones. Because of this variation and complexity – especially in the works of Ibn Sīnā – only a general view of the function of the internal senses will be given here. The details and differences of opinion among the philosophers studied will, therefore, not be dealt with except when relevant to the present subject.

In part the function of the internal senses is to receive the material forms from the external senses and to purify them from material attachments as much as possible. For the internal senses to do this, the external objects need not be present to them.

The common sense faculty receives all the material forms from the external senses. It differs from the external senses though in that it collects the various types of external sensations instead of only one and does not require the presence of the external objects. The imagination plays two roles, an epistemological one and an ethical one, both of which will be discussed in some detail.

The epistemological function of the imagination consists in its acting as a central post office, where it receives information from all its neighbouring faculties and then distributes it in different directions after having stamped it with its own character. From the common sense, it receives the material forms of external objects (whether through the representational faculty that stores such objects, as al-Fārābī and Ibn Sīnā have it, or directly, as Ibn Rushd has it). From memory, it receives nonsensible, particular notions of external objects, such as the sheep's fear of the wolf. According to al-Fārābī and Ibn Sīnā, such notions are first grasped by the estimative faculty and then stored in memory.

The rational soul, which is a superior neighbour to the imagination and from which the imagination can also receive information in a manner to be mentioned later, possesses two faculties or intellects, the theoretical and the practical. The proper function of the theoretical intellect is to know the realities also called natures, quiddities or essences. Such realities are the universal aspects of the universe. They are simple and eternal; that is why when the theoretical intellect grasps them it becomes like them, since the knower and the known are one.[9] The theoretical intellect, which is potential at first, attains its actuality by receiving the realities of things. How this happens, however, is not fully clear. At times, for example, al-Fārābī and Ibn Sīnā seem to think that the objects of the imagination, which are somewhat material and particular and cannot therefore be grasped by the theoretical intellect, are finally stripped of their materiality when the light of the agent intellect, the lowest celestial intelligence,[10] shines over them. This light, as it were, makes the objects of the imagination, which are still in mud and darkness, completely visible to the theoretical intellect. In other words, the light of the agent intellect casts the universal aspect of the objects of the imagination on the theoretical intellect, leaving behind their particularity and materiality. This is the Aristotelian tendency that locates the original source of the universals in the outside world, from which they are taken by the external senses. From the external senses, the universals are then taken by the common sense that conveys them to the imagination, which finally hands them to the intellect. Ibn Rushd is a strong advocate of this tendency. Al-Fārābī and Ibn Sīnā, on the other hand, seem at times to speak as if the imagination only prepares the rational soul for accepting the universals that overflow to it from the agent intellect.[11] But the manner and nature of this preparation are not fully clear. Still, whether the objects of the imagination are themselves abstracted from matter and then grasped by the theoretical intellect or whether these objects simply prepare the way for the overflow of the universals from the agent intellect to the theoretical one does not change the fact that the imagination plays a very important role in the attainment of theoretical knowledge.

While the theoretical intellect looks upward to learn the essences of the universe, the practical intellect looks downward to manage worldly affairs. Its proper function is to know the principles of the practical crafts as well as those of ethics and the manner in which they must be applied. The practical intellect requires that virtue consist in acting in accordance with reason, something which calls for moderation in action and results in knowledge and happiness. In grasping such principles and their manner of application, the practical intellect relies on the imagination for providing repeated instances of particular things on the basis of which the practical intellect draws its conclusions. After all, the practical intellect perfects itself through experience and habits, which require particular instances as prerequisites. Without knowledge and application of the principles of the practical intellect, there would be disorder in the life of the individual, society and state. Such disorder, however, can distract the theoretical intellect from performing its function by calling for its attention downward. The imagination, therefore, can help in the attainment of theoretical knowledge also by providing the practical intellect with the information necessary for disciplining the individual.

The ethical role of the imagination consists in its directing the locomotive powers of the animal soul. These powers are of two types: those that move other things (the desiderative parts, including instincts, inclinations and reactions) and those that are moved by other things (the parts of the body, such as muscles). The desiderative parts cause motion either in the direction of something or away from it.[12] How the imagination portrays an object to the desiderative power determines whether or not the latter moves in the direction of, or away from, that object. If the imagination portrays an object as suitable, the desiderative power moves in the direction of that object. If, on the other hand, the imagination portrays an object as unsuitable, the desiderative power moves away from that object.[13]

The imagination generates desire for or against an object either in accordance with the principles of the practical intellect or independently.

If the principles of the practical intellect guide the imagination, human action is rational, that is, it follows the real good and avoids the real bad. If the imagination acts independently, however, human action is blind, that is, it follows suggestions of the imagination that are at best described as half true and half false. If one finds oneself wanting to do something but also not wanting to do it, it is because there is a conflict, as is the case quite often, between the imagination, trying to act independently, and the practical intellect, trying to govern it.

It is primarily during sleep that the imagination is set free from the restraints of the practical intellect. That is why in sleep the imagination is more free to co-operate with the demands of the body, which it supplies with images that satisfy those demands.[14] Diseases, fears, insanity and the like can also set the imagination free from the bounds of reason even during the wakeful state.[15] But what is the role of poetry in all of this? To be able to answer this question, one must first understand the nature of poetry. Thus, we must now turn to a study of what poetry is.

THE NATURE OF POETRY

Muslim philosophers assert that poetry is an imaginative discourse.[16] Poetry, however, differs from other imaginative compositions in that it is essentially an imitation (*muḥākāt*).[17] However, there are two main types of imitation – one that is in action, and one that is in words.[18] Poetry is of the latter type.

In order to clarify imitative discourse by discussing imitation in general, al-Fārābī points out that imitation in action is further divided into two types: making something that resembles something else, such as making a statue that resembles a certain person; or doing something that mimics something else, such as mimicking a neighbour's walk. Imitation in words, on the other hand, uses a discourse composed of objects that resemble the subjects of the discourse. This is to say that the discourse must signify things that resemble the subject of the discourse.[19] Whether in action or in discourse, imitation can represent either something that resembles the thing itself or something that resembles something else that resembles the thing itself. For example, one may make a statue that resembles Zayd himself or a mirror that reflects the statue that resembles Zayd.[20] But whether the imitation is of the thing itself or of something that imitates the thing itself, it can identify the thing itself, regardless of whether this imitation is in action or in words.[21]

Which type of imitation, though, is better, that which requires no intermediaries or that which does? To this issue, al-Fārābī, for example, responds not by giving his own opinion but simply by saying, "Many people consider the imitation of a thing by means of the more remote thing more complete and preferable than its imitation by means of the more proximate one."[22] Perhaps the reason al-Fārābī and other Muslim philosophers do not give their own opinion regarding this matter is their conviction that the discussion of the more complete and the less complete imitation is not for philosophers, who must be concerned with universal principles. Rather, such a discussion, as al-Fārābī asserts, is the concern of poets and those knowledgeable about poetry, in particular languages.[23]

In his *Treatise on the Canons of the Art of Poets*, al-Fārābī distinguishes imitative discourse from other types of expressions. He asserts:

> that expressions are either significant or non-significant; that significant expressions are either single or composite; that composite expressions are either discourses or non-discourses; that discourses are either categorical or non-categorical; that categorical discourses are either true or false; that false categorical discourses represent in the minds of the hearers either something expressed which is other than the subject of the discourse, or something that imitates the real thing – the last being the poetic discourse.[24]

Poetry, therefore, is said to be false, but only in the sense that it gives an imitation of the thing and not the thing itself. Imitation is to be distinguished from sophistry. The objective of the former is to represent in the minds of the hearers that which resembles the real thing; the objective of the latter is to represent in the minds of the hearers the contrary of the thing.[25] An example of imitation is one's picture in the mirror; an example of sophistry is seeing things external to a ship as moving just because one is on a moving ship.[26] The well-known Arabic saying, "The best poetry is that which is most false", can, therefore, be understood by Muslim philosophers to mean that the best poetry is that which embodies the most complete imitation of reality.

This link to reality is the reason why poetic discourse is an analogy (*tamthīl*), that is, a potential syllogism.[27] But syllogisms differ from each other in terms of the degree of their truth. Al-Fārābī points out that:

> discourses are either unavoidably completely true; unavoidably completely false; true for the major part, false for the minor one; the contrary of this; or equal in truth and falsity. That which is unavoidably completely true is demonstrative discourse; that which is true for the major part is dialectical discourse; that which is equal in truth and falsity is rhetorical discourse; that which is true for the minor part is sophistical discourse; and that which is unavoidably completely false is poetic discourse.[28]

One must keep in mind, though, that poetic discourse is to be considered completely false, not just in any sense, but in the sense stated above, namely, that it is an imitation. It must be remembered, however, that it is an imitation of reality. Al-Fārābī insists that poetry is a branch of logic, for to him it is a syllogism or "what follows the syllogism"; the latter is exemplified in induction and analogy.[29]

Ibn Sīnā, too, considers *Poetics* a part of logic, contrary to the Aristotelian tradition, which is thought not to include *Rhetoric* and *Poetics*, as pointed out in the chapter on logic.[30] Being faithful to the Aristotelian tradition, Ibn Rushd, however, does not consider *Rhetoric* and *Poetics* as parts of logic. Interestingly enough, though, he too speaks of poetry as a logical art. When distinguishing the imaginative arts in his own *Poetics*, for example, he says:

> The imaginative art, or that which does what the imagination does, is three in kind: the art of harmony, the art of metre, and the art of making imitative discourse. The last is the logical art which is the subject of our study in this book.[31]

It must be remembered, however, that not every imaginative art is poetic or logical, but only that which is imitative, as pointed out in this passage from Ibn Rushd. Thus, when Ibn Sīnā says, "It is only inasmuch as poetry is an imaginative discourse that it concerns the logician",[32] or "The logician studies poetry, inasmuch as it is imaginative",[33] he is referring specifically to the imitative imaginative aspect of the poetic discourse.

But what is the imaginative? To this question, Muslim philosophers respond:

> The imaginative is that to which the soul submits such that it is relaxed owing to certain things and is depressed owing to certain other things, without any reasoning, thought, or choice, . . . regardless of whether the object of discourse is true or false.[34]

The imaginative is not the same as the true; a thing may be imaginative but not true and vice versa. A discourse has more power to move the soul by the aspect of its imaginativeness than by the aspect of its truth.[35] Ibn Sīnā's insight into human nature reveals that, contrary to expectation, "people are more apt to abide by the imaginative than by the truth. In fact, many people dislike and avoid true statements, when hearing them."[36] This is because of the element of marvel found in imitation, or falsehood, but not in truth.[37] The reason is that truth is either known or unknown. If it is known, it is taken for granted; if it is unknown, it is not paid any attention.[38] The way to make truth more appealing and, hence, more effective, is to merge it with the marvellous. This can be done by presenting it with a moderate degree of unfamiliarity of metre, linguistic expressions, concepts or a combination of these.[39] Unlike Greek poetic imitation, whose sole purpose was to urge the soul to do or not to do a certain thing, Arabic poetic imitation was used either for that purpose or simply for generating marvel.[40]

An important question may now be raised. If poetry is an imaginative art, and if an imaginative art affects the soul apart from any rational consideration and regardless of the truth of the object, then how can Muslim philosophers consider poetry a logical discipline, when logic is said by them to be a set of rules for distinguishing the true from the false and for drawing the unknown from the known? To answer this question one must remember what has been stated earlier, namely that the imagination can either function independently or as bound by the rules of the practical intellect. If it functions in the former way, it is free from any rational restraints; if it functions in the latter way, it enters the sphere of logic. In other words, the definition of the imaginative as given above applies to the object or act of the imagination when this faculty acts independently. But even when the imagination is guided by the practical intellect, it does not lose its effect on the soul. Its effect on the soul is instead in line with reason, and not simply based on blind emotions. It is primarily inasmuch as poetry can play this important ethical role that Muslim philosophers took interest in it.

Another perplexing issue is the following. If the benefit of poetry lies in the rational grip of the practical intellect over the soul, a grip that is mediated by the imagination, would it not be better to maintain such a grip directly with no form of imitative imaginative mediation? After all, imitation does not give us the thing itself, but only its resemblance, something which, at least to some extent, veils the light of reason and hence the reality of a thing. The answer becomes clear when it is remembered that, to Muslim philosophers, people have different capacities for grasping things. There is, for example, an elite group, the purely philosophical, who can grasp the realities of things as they are and by means of nothing but reason. There is also the multitude who cannot grasp the realities of things as they are but can grasp the semblance of these realities, or their imaginative or symbolic form. Poetry is the link between reason and universality, on the one hand, and action and particularity, on the other – a link that can be grasped by the greater number of people. In other words, it is only through such veiling of reason that the multitude can be guided by the light of reason. For example, Ibn Sīnā's poetry on logic, medicine and the soul can be taken to be intended to educate the public about truths which, if explicated in a non-poetic form, would be inaccessible to them.

While the most important function of poetry is to help the multitude not to stray from the right path of conduct, this function is an outcome, and not an essential element, of poetry. This function cannot be perfected except by metre.[41] As we will soon see, however, it is not metre but universality and reality that are the distinguishing marks of poetry itself. Ibn Sīnā discusses such distinguishing marks in a rather obscure passage in which he seems to be making the following points, with which Ibn Rushd seems to agree.

Imitation in proverbs, tales and fables must be distinguished from imitation in poetry. The latter "touches only upon that whose existence in things is possible, or that which existed and, thus, entered the realm of necessity".[42] If metre were the only thing that differentiated proverbs, tales and fables from poetry, as one might think, then a fable, for example, would become poetic if it were given metre, and a poetic discourse would become a fable, if it lost its metre. But this is not the case. Rather, the primary difference between these types of discourse is that fable has an unreal subject, while poetry has a real one.[43] "Real" here means something which existed, exists or will exist; that is, something which is either necessary or possible – the unreal being the contrary of this. Put another way, the subject of a fable has verbal existence only; the subject of poetry has external existence.[44] A poet is thus like a painter, in that they are both imitators of something real.[45] Owing to this and to the universality of the poetic subject, poetry is closer to philosophy than is the other type of discourse.[46]

In spite of this assertion, Muslim philosophers recognize that in some instances proverbs, tales and fables may have subjects that have external existence, as does history. But such a subject, they say, must be particular and non-imaginative.[47] As such, this type of discourse cannot move the soul, as does poetry, but can only give an opinion.[48] They also recognize that poetry can, as it did in Greek times, have an invented particular subject, but they hasten to add that this is so only in rare cases when the state of affairs in existence corresponds to those invented.[49] In other words, poetry differs essentially from fables and the like in that the subject of the former is both real and universal, while the subject of the latter is not. The fact that the subject of poetry is real no doubt facilitates the ethical function of poetry. For one to be affected by a thing, one must realize that that thing is not unreal, but at least possible. As Ibn Sīnā puts it: "The existent and the possible are more persuasive to the soul than the non-existent and the non-possible. Also, if an experience is supported by something that exists, it is more persuasive than if it were supported by an invented thing."[50]

Stressing the reality of the poetic subject, whether in existence or in possibility, leads to the conclusion that not taking such a reality into consideration is an error on the part of a poet. Such an error is of two types: essential and accidental. The former is to imitate what has no existence or possibility; the latter is to imitate something that exists, but whose existence has been distorted.[51] Jubrān's poem about *al-'anqā'* (a non-existent bird) should, therefore, count as an essential error. An accidental error is exemplified in a poetic discourse that resembles a painting that portrays a horse as having its hind legs in front or on the side instead of the rear.[52] Ibn Rushd adds to the above two types of error the following four: (1) imitation of a rational being by something non-rational; (2) imitation of a thing by something which resembles its contrary, or by something which is the contrary of itself; (3) using a word that signifies both the subject and its contrary; and (4) moving from poetic imitation to persuasive discourse, especially when the poetic discourse is far-fetched.[53] Ibn Sīnā's *Ode on the Soul*, in which the human soul is compared to a pigeon, might be considered by Ibn Rushd as an example of type (1), an imitation of a rational thing by something non-rational.

To be a poet does not require being rationally knowledgeable of the nature of poetry and the rules that govern it. One can be a poet for one of three reasons: because one has the natural capacity for composing one or more types of poetry; or because one knows all the properties of, and rules for, all types of poetry – these are the syllogistic poets; or because one imitates the poetic acts of the above two types. Since the third type has neither the poetic nature nor the knowledge of poetic rules, they are more apt to be in error than the first two.[54]

The purpose of Muslim philosophers in their poetics was to set *universal* poetic rules to help reduce the degree of poetic error, considering the ethical value of poetry in human society. No doubt they contributed mightily to a better understanding of Arabic poetry, especially by the distinction they made between it and Greek poetry and by the examples of Arabic verses they provided to explicate the universal poetic rules. Nevertheless, their ultimate objective was simply to focus on the universal poetic rules to the exclusion of those that relate to particular languages.[55] That is why they did not concern themselves with the study of metre or rhyme, even though the latter was a property of Arabic poetry, but only with the imitative imaginative aspect of poetic discourse.[56]

Since Muslim philosophers considered their works in poetics as commentaries on Aristotle's *Poetics*, they left these works incomplete, as is the latter. This fact is interesting even though their works in this area can hardly count as commentaries on Aristotle's *Poetics* regardless of their assertion that they are.[57] For example, with the exception of a short discussion concerning the types of poetry, al-Fārābī's *Qawānīn* has nothing to do with Aristotle's *Poetics*, nor has most of the material in the first chapter of Ibn Sīnā's *Fann al shi'r*. Al-Fārabī goes so far as to claim that it would be inappropriate for someone like him to complete a study that was left incomplete by the wise and skilful Aristotle.[58] While Ibn Sīnā confirms the incompleteness of his *Poetics*, he indicates that he may produce another deeper and more detailed study of this area.[59] There is no evidence, however, that he ever produced anything of the sort.

Finally, it is worth noting that some Muslim philosophers did not only do philosophy of poetry but also poetic philosophy. Ibn Sīnā, whose poems on the soul, logic and medicine constitute excellent examples of poetic philosophy, is the best example of this.[60]

NOTES

1 Ibn Sīnā, *al-Shifā', al-Manṭiq, al-Madkhal*, ed. G. C. Anawātī, M. al-Khuḍayrī and A. F. al-Ahwānī (Cairo, 1952): 12.
2 Ibn Manẓūr, *Lisān al-'Arab*, 1 (Beirut, 1956): 206–7; al-Fayrūzābādī, *al-Qāmūs al-muḥīṭ*, 1 (Cairo, 1977): 36; Buṭrus al-Bustānī, *Muḥīṭ al-muḥīṭ* (Beirut, 1977): 5.
3 Buṭrus al-Bustānī, *Muḥīṭ al-muḥīṭ*: 5.
4 *Ibid.*
5 *Ibid.*
6 Al-Kindī is said to have written two works on poetics, a commentary on Aristotle's *Poetics* and an essay on poetics, but so far these have not been discovered (Ibn al-Nadīm, *al-Fihrist* (Cairo, 1929): 359).
7 See, for example, Ibn Sīnā, *al-Ishārāt wa'l-tanbīhāt, Part Three*, ed. S. Dunyā (Cairo, 1950): 373–86.
8 See, for example, Ibn Rushd, *al-Ḥāss wa'l-maḥsūs*, in *Arisṭūṭālīs fi'l-nafs*, ed. 'A. R. Badawī (Cairo, 1954): 208–12.
9 Ibn Sīnā, *Risālat al-'arūs*, ed. C. Cuns, in *Majallat al-kitāb*, 11 (Cairo, 1952): 396.
10 For the function of the agent intellect, see Chapter 16 above on Ibn Sīnā, p. 239.
11 See, for example, Ibn Sīnā, *Risālah fī bayān al-mu'jizāt wa'l-karāmāt wa'l-a'ājīb*, in *al-Madhhab al-tarbawī 'ind Ibn Sīnā min khilāl falsafatih al-'amaliyyah*, ed. 'Abd al-Amīr Shams al-Dīn (Beirut, 1988): 404.
12 Al-Fārābī, *Ārā' ahl al-madīnat al-fāḍilah* ed. A. N. Nādir (Beirut, 1959): 72; Ibn Sīnā, *'Uyūn al-ḥikmah*, ed. A. R. Badawī (Cairo, 1954): 39; Ibn Rushd, *Talkhīṣ kitāb al-nafs*, ed. A. F. al-Ahwānī (Cairo, 1950): 92.
13 Ibn Sīnā, *Risālah fi'l-nafs wa baqā'ihā wa ma'ādihā*, in *Rasā'il Ibn Sīnā*, ed. H. D. Ülken (Istanbul, 1953): 120; Ibn Rushd, *Talkhīṣ kitāb al-nafs*: 60.
14 Al-Fārābī, *Ārā' ahl al-madīnah al-fāḍilah*: 89–91; Ibn Sīnā, *al-Nafs*: 195; Ibn Rushd, *al-Ḥāss wa'l-maḥsūs*: 231–2.
15 Al-Fārābī, *Ārā' ahl al-madīnah al-fāḍilah*: 95; Ibn Sīnā, *al-Ishārāt wa'l-tanbīhāt, Part Four*, ed. S. Dunyā (Cairo, 1958): 876; Ibn Rushd, *al-Ḥāss wa'l-maḥsūs*: 223.
16 Al-Fārābī, *Kitāb al-shi'r*, ed. M. Mahdi, in *Majallat shi'r*, 12 (Beirut, 1959): 94–5; Ibn Sīnā, *al Shifā', al-Manṭiq, Fann al-Shi'r* (hereafter *Fann al-Shi'r*), in *Arisṭūṭālīs: Fann al-shi'r*, ed. A. R. Badawī (Cairo, 1953): 161; Ibn Rushd, *Talkhīṣ kitāb Arisṭūṭālīs fi'l-shi'r* (hereafter *Talkhīṣ*, in *Arisṭūṭālīs: Fann al-shi'r*: 203–4.
17 Al-Fārābī, *Kitāb al-shi'r*: 92; Ibn Sīnā, *Fann al-shi'r*: 168; Ibn Rushd, *Talkhīṣ al-shi'r*: 203–4.
18 Al-Fārābī, *Kitāb al-shi'r*: 93; Ibn Sīnā, *Fann al-shi'r*: 168.
19 Al-Fārābī, *Kitāb al-shi'r*: 93.
20 *Ibid.*: 93–5.
21 *Ibid.*: 95.
22 *Ibid.*

23 Al-Fārābī, *Risālah fī qawānīn ṣinā'at al-shu'arā'* (hereafter *Qawānīn*), in *Arisṭūṭālīs: Fann al-shi'r*: 150.
24 *Ibid.*
25 *Ibid.*
26 *Ibid.*: 150–1.
27 *Ibid.*: 151
28 *Ibid.*; for the nature and function of these various types of discourse, see Chapter 48 above on logic, p. 802ff.
29 Al-Fārābī, *Qawānīn*: 151.
30 See p. 802ff. above.
31 Ibn Rushd, *Talkhīṣ al-shi'r*: 203.
32 Ibn Sīnā, *Fann al-shi'r*: 161.
33 *Ibid.*
34 *Ibid.* See also al-Fārābī, *Kitāb al-shi'r*: 94.
35 Ibn Sīnā, *Fann al-shi'r*: 161–2.
36 *Ibid.*: 162.
37 *Ibid.*
38 *Ibid.*
39 *Ibid.*: 162–3.
40 *Ibid.*: 170.
41 *Ibid.*: 183; Ibn Rushd, *Talkhīṣ al-shi'r*: 214.
42 Ibn Sīnā, *Fann al-shi'r*: 183; Ibn Rushd, *Talkhīṣ al-shi'r*: 214–15.
43 Ibn Sīnā, *Fann al-shi'r*: 183.
44 *Ibid.*
45 *Ibid.*: 196.
46 *Ibid.*: 184; Ibn Rushd, *Talkhīṣ al-shi'r*: 214.
47 Ibn Sīnā, *Fann al-shi'r*: 183
48 *Ibid.*
49 *Ibid.*: 184.
50 *Ibid.*; see also Ibn Rushd, *Talkhīṣ al-shi'r*: 214, 219.
51 Ibn Sīnā, *Fann al-shi'r*: 196; Ibn Rushd, *Talkhīṣ al-shi'r*: 247–8.
52 Ibn Sīnā, *Fann al-shi'r*: 196; Ibn Rushd, *Talkhīṣ al-shi'r*: 248.
53 Ibn Rushd, *Talkhīṣ al-shi'r*: 248–9.
54 Al-Fārābī, *Qawānīn*: 155–6.
55 See al-Fārābī, *Qawānīn*: 158.
56 Ibn Sīnā, *Fann al-shi'r*: 161.
57 Al-Fārābī, *Qawānīn*: 149; Ibn Sīnā, *Fann al-shi'r*: 198; Ibn Rushd, *Talkhīṣ al-shi'r*: 201.
58 Al-Fārābī, *Qawānīn*: 149–50.
59 Ibn Sīnā, *Fann al-shi'r*: 198.
60 It would be most interesting to study the content of these poems, especially the one on the soul, and to compare it with those of Shawqī and al-Ghaḍbān which address the same subject with the same metre, rhyme, spirit and terminology. An even more important inquiry resulting from the present study, though, would be the determination of whether or not such philosophical poems are governed by the rules set in Islamic poetics. There is no room, however, to explore such subjects here.

CHAPTER 52

Language[1]

Shukri B. Abed

Throughout fourteen centuries of history, Islam as a civilization has faced major external cultural challenges on two separate occasions. The first of these occurred during the early days of Islam, when Greek, Indian and Persian philosophy and science were transmitted to the Islamic world cotemporaneously with the rise of the Muslims as a power in the Middle East region; the second began about two hundreds years ago with European colonization of the Middle East. On both occasions, the Arabs found it advisable and even necessary to re-evaluate certain aspects of their own indigenous culture in light of the cultural and scientific challenges presented by the West. The Arabic language, the language of the holy Qur'ān, was not only the medium through which these challenges were debated but also itself a central subject matter of the debates.

The purpose of this chapter is to characterize the debates concerning the development of the Arabic language (*al-'arabiyyah*) and to identify the specific mechanisms through which linguistic accommodations have been (and are being) made in the Arabic language to adapt to evolving circumstances. The first section will deal with the reaction of Arab intellectuals to the introduction of Greek, Indian and Persian philosophy and science into the Islamic world beginning in the second/eighth century. This reaction was mirrored in a series of debates concerning the relative merits of (Greek) logic and (Arabic) grammar. These culminated in a particularly important debate, documented toward the middle of the fourth/tenth century, which will serve as a focus for discussion in the first section of the chapter. The second and third sections will address the impact of the two external cultural confrontations cited above on the Arabic language, during the classical and the modern periods of Islam, respectively. The fourth and final section will briefly summarize contemporary debates concerning the future of the Arabic language.[2]

LANGUAGE AND LOGIC IN CLASSICAL ISLAM

The question of the relationship of the Arabic language to Greek logic arose during the early stages of the "philosophical movement" in the Islamic world. Al-Kindī's student Aḥmad ibn al-Ṭayyib al-Sarakhsī (d.286/899), for example, was reportedly the first in the Arab world to write about the difference between logic and Arabic grammar. Although his treatise on "the difference between the grammar of the Arabs and logic" is not extant, al-Sarakhsī, we are told, considered logic to be a *universal grammar* and as such superior to Arabic grammar and to any other particular grammar, for that matter.[3]

This view – according to which logic is superior to language because the former is a necessary science dealing with meanings and with what is universal, whereas the latter is conventional and accidental – is a view that prevailed among Arab logicians throughout the tenth and eleventh centuries. In fact, according to the Arab logicians of this period, language should not even be considered an issue for logicians in their logical inquiries. Logic, they claimed, is concerned with utterances (*alfāẓ*) only accidentally and only in so far as these utterances signify the concepts (*ma'ānī)* themselves, which (in the logicians' view) are the only proper subject matter of logic.

This theme is clearly stated in a debate concerning the relative merits of logic and grammar that took place in Baghdad in 331/932 between grammarians (represented by Abū Sa'īd al-Sīrāfī) and logicians (represented by the Nestorian Christian Abū Bishr Mattā). A second theme formulated during this debate and relevant to our discussion is the Arab grammarians' claim that, in order to introduce Greek philosophy and science into the Islamic arena, the Arab philosophers had resorted to "building a language within a language";[4] that is, they were distorting the original and pure Arabic language as revealed in the Qur'ān in an unnecessary and irresponsible manner. This debate, translated into English toward the beginning of the fourteenth/twentieth century,[5] has been the subject of several scholarly studies in recent years.[6] I nevertheless propose to summarize briefly herein those sections of the debate which suggest that the linguistic arguments upon which the opposing positions are ostensibly based may in fact mask socio-political arguments identifiable just beneath their surface.

At the outset of this debate, Abū Bishr Mattā is quoted by the vizier Ibn al-Furāt as having claimed that "there is no way to know truth from falsehood, verity from lying, good from bad, proof from sophism, doubt from certainty except through logic".[7] Mattā, present when the vizier attributed this claim to him, attempted to defend his position as follows:

> The logician has no need of grammar, whereas the grammarian does need logic. For logic enquires into the meaning, whereas grammar enquires into the utterance. If, therefore, the logician deals with the utterance, it is accidental, and it is likewise accidental if the grammarian deals with the meaning. Now, the meaning is more exalted than the utterance, and the utterance humbler than the meaning.[8]

Statements of this sort clearly belittled the study of Arabic grammar and the status of the Arab grammarians. It is not difficult, therefore, to comprehend why the logicians' position drew a strong reaction from the circle of Arab grammarians, a reaction later endorsed by certain influential theologians (such as Ibn Taymiyyah in the seventh/thirteenth century). The grammarians criticized Mattā and the other logicians on the grounds that the intelligible meanings they present as universal and eternal can be achieved only through the mastering of a specific language.

Abū Sa'īd al-Sīrāfī, described by al-Tawḥīdī as a dignified, pious and earnest man,[9] undertook the challenge of open debate with Mattā to defend the grammarians' point of view. Towards the beginning of the debate, al-Sīrāfī asked Mattā to define what he means by logic so that their discussion concerning logic would be "according to accepted rules and a defined method".[10] Mattā replied as follows:

> I understand by logic an "instrument" [*ālah*] of "speech" [*kalām*], by which correct "speech" is known from incorrect, and unsound "meaning" [*ma'nā*] from sound: like a balance, for by it I know overweight from underweight and what rises from what sinks.[11]

Speaking for the grammarians, al-Sīrāfī criticized Mattā on the grounds that there is no such thing as "language" in general, rather we speak and express meanings by using a particular language, and each language has its own tools and instruments by which one determines what is correct and what is incorrect when that language is used.

> Abū Sa'īd [al-Sīrāfī] said: You are mistaken, for correct speech is distinguished from incorrect by the familiar rules of composition and by the accepted inflection [*i'rāb*] when we speak in Arabic; unsound meaning is distinguished from sound by reason when we investigate meanings.[12]

According to al-Sīrāfī, then, on *the language level*, correct speech is distinguished from incorrect speech by following the standard rules of Arabic grammar and syntax, rather than the formal rules of logic; whereas on *the level of intelligibles*, unsound meaning is distinguished from sound meaning by utilizing reason. In other words, al-Sīrāfī rejects the notion that one instrument (logic) can be used simultaneously on two different levels: the language level and the level of intelligibles or concepts.

Al-Sīrāfī further attacks the very analogy of "balance" employed by Mattā:

> Suppose you determine the relative weight of two or more objects, how can you know which one of the things weighed is iron, which gold, which copper and which lead? Hence, after you know the weight, you still need to know the substance of what is weighed, its value and the rest of its qualities.[13]

Al-Sīrāfī's point seems to be the following. Even if we grant you that logic is capable of distinguishing between correct and incorrect language usage, as well as between sound and unsound meanings, there are still many aspects of both the utterances and the meanings that cannot be known by logic. Furthermore, al-Sīrāfī argues,

> not everything in this world can be weighed. Some things are weighed, others are measured with respect to their volume, others with respect to their length, . . . and still others can be guessed at. And if this is the case in the realm of visible bodies, this applies also to the domain of intelligibles.[14]

Elsewhere in the debate, the logicians are urged to concentrate on the knowledge of a particular language (Arabic, in this case) as a necessary condition for mastering the art of logic. Knowledge of the Arabic language is required if logicians wish to convey the logical theories of the Greeks to speakers of the Arabic language, al-Sīrāfī concludes.

> This [Arabic] language in which you dispute or agree with us, you should instruct your friends in accordance with the way it is understood by those who speak it, and interpret the books of the Greeks according to the custom of those whose language it is. For then you will come to know that you can dispense with the meanings of the Greeks as well as you can dispense with the language of the Greeks.[15]

According to al-Sīrāfī, then, there is no distinction between logic and language.[16] Logic for him is the logic of a particular language, and there is no such thing as "universal logic". The logic the logicians are promoting is a purely Greek logic, derived from Greek language and grammar.[17]

Al-Sīrāfī moves on to argue against the very notion that other nations should accept a logical system based on a specific language:

> Furthermore, since logic was established by a Greek man [i.e., Aristotle] according to the language of his country's people, according to their understanding of it and their conventions

> regarding its definitions and properties, why should the Turks, the Indians, the Persians and the Arabs study it and take it as their judge and arbitrator, who decides for them and against them such that they must accept what he agrees to and reject what he denies?[18]

In other words, al-Sīrāfī rejects the notion that logic transcends national and language boundaries (rendering it a universal instrument), a notion that is the cornerstone of the logicians' position, as is clear from the following counter-argument by Mattā:

> This follows since logic investigates the intellegibles, the intentions and the conceived meanings . . . As far as intelligibles are concerned, all human beings are equal, as is evident from the fact that [the sum of] four plus four is the same for all nations.[19]

Again, al-Sīrāfī accuses Mattā of offering a misleading example. For al-Sīrāfī, this mathematical example fails to reflect the complex nature of the problems for which logic is presumed to be the solution or the means to a solution. He in fact charges Mattā and his fellow logicians with a conscious effort to mislead people:

> If the things conceived by the mind and expressed by words with all their various divisions and diverse paths could be reduced to the level of simplicity [in the statement] "four plus four equals eight", then the disputes [among people] would disappear and there would be total agreement. But this is not the case. Your example is misleading, and you [logicians] are accustomed to misleading others.[20]

Later on in the debate,[21] al-Sīrāfī in fact accuses the logicians of purposely using invented terminology (such as the Arabic counterparts for "genus", "species", "essence", etc.) – terms with which most people are not familiar – in order to confuse the ignorant and create the impression that logic is a magical solution to the problems of the world.

For al-Sīrāfī this logic which Mattā and his fellow logicians hold in such high regard is nothing more than *Greek* logic and as such it cannot be employed by other nations, since it is based on and derived from the Greek language. Al-Sīrāfī charges that in essence Mattā is asking the Arabs to study not a universal logic but the Greek language. Yet this same Greek language Mattā wants them to study "perished long ago, its speakers have disappeared and the community that used to communicate their intentions by means of its inflections are now extinct".[22]

Although al-Sīrāfī seriously doubts Mattā's assertion that the translations from Greek to Arabic have managed to preserve the meanings and the truth, he is nevertheless willing, for the sake of argument, to grant that this is the case. Al-Sīrāfī is perfectly willing to ignore the question of the reliability of these translations, since he detects that Mattā's assertion is in fact based on a quite different assumption, and one he categorically rejects. "You seem to be implying," al-Sīrāfī says, "that there is no reliable authority [*ḥujjah*] other than the intellects of the Greeks, no demonstration except what they have established and no truth except what they brought to light."[23]

Al-Sīrāfī strongly criticizes Mattā's blind support of the Greeks, thereby implicating all the other defenders of Greek culture. He completely rejects Mattā's insinuation that the Greeks are a special nation and that "of [all] [nations], it was they who applied themselves to the pursuit of wisdom [*ḥikmah*] and to the investigation of the apparent and hidden aspects of the world", and that "the discovery and propagation of every kind of science and art is due to them, something we cannot attribute to other [nations]".[24] Accusing Mattā of being prejudiced [*ta'aṣṣabta*] and of committing an error by making such a statement, al-Sīrāfī goes on to explain that the Greeks are not different from any other nation, as "they were right about certain issues and wrong about others, they knew certain things and were ignorant of other things".[25]

At this point, al-Sīrāfī's strategy becomes clear. He means to discredit the entire Greek culture, considered by its defenders in the Arab world as superior to other cultures, including the Arab/Islamic culture. Al-Sīrāfī seems to single out Aristotle and his teachings, above all his logic, for particular disparagement. The reason for this is clear, as well. Aristotle was considered by his defenders *the authority*. It was, in fact, customary for the Arab philosophers to refer to Aristotle as "the First Teacher", a designation with quasi-religious connotations. Yet Aristotle, in al-Sīrāfī's view, cannot be identified with the Greek nation. He is only one man, who learned from his predecessors just as his successors learned from him. Nor can he be considered "an authority [*ḥujjah*] over all God's creation . . . he has opponents among the Greeks and among other nations".[26]

The logicians' reported defeat [27] in this particular confrontation with the Arab grammarians did not alter their position that logic is concerned with meanings rather than with utterances as such, while Arabic grammar [*naḥw*] is concerned exclusively with utterances.[28] It did, however, lead them to take the grammarians and their field of endeavour more seriously. The Achilles' heel of the first generation of Arab logicians had been their profound ignorance of the discipline they so summarily dismissed.[29]

The next wave of logicians – including al-Fārābī, Yaḥyā ibn 'Adī (both disciples of Mattā) and Abū Sulaymān al-Sijistānī (a disciple of Ibn 'Adī) – was broader in its analysis of the relationship between logic and language. These philosophers still believed that logic is a universal grammar and therefore more significant than any particular language which, by definition, is restricted to a particular nation. But the defeat of Abū Bishr

Mattā, whose openly admitted ignorance of Arabic grammar had left him vulnerable to the Sirāfian attacks, suggested that serious logicians might do well to master their own language as a firm basis from which to pursue their logical studies. Al-Fārābī, Ibn 'Adī and al-Sijistānī all engaged in serious study of Arabic grammar and were able to argue their positions much more convincingly than Mattā, leader of the fourth/tenth-century Baghdad logicians, had been able to do. These logicians continued to maintain that logic is superior to grammar, with the only utterances seriously considered by the logician being those that signify universal concepts or meanings. Yet, unlike their predecessors, these men accorded the beauty and intricacies of the Arabic language due respect, realizing that language and logic are closely, indeed inextricably, interrelated.[30]

While the details of these debates are fascinating in and of themselves, what is important to realize is the context they form for the language development issues to be dealt with in our subsequent discussion. At the time these debates took place, the Arabic language was being deluged by a tremendous influx of new terminology required to convey the scientific and philosophical ideas and discoveries of other nations. The grammarians and their supporters genuinely feared an attempt by the logicians of fourth/tenth-century Baghdad to ravage the Arabic language, while importing foreign ideas and modes of thought that were not only ill-suited but also downright contradictory to certain essential tenets of the Arabic/Islamic culture. This fear is clearly reflected in the grammarians' charge that the logicians, in response to the linguistic and philosophical developments of the period, were threatening to "build a language within a language [which is already] well defined among its native speakers [*muqarrarah bayna ahlihā*]"[31] – an attack levelled not only at the introduction of foreign terminology but also at the imposition of new and artificial structures on the Arabic language.[32]

Al-Sīrāfī's attempt to discredit the Greeks and their major supporters among the Arab philosophers clearly has implications above and beyond a single debate concerning the relative merits of logic and language. Al-Sīrāfī's criticism penetrates deeply into the question of the Muslim attitude towards foreign cultures and the perceived threat they pose to the Arabic/Islamic culture. In other words, it is an attempt to combat the influence of the Greeks and other foreigners on the Arabic culture, a battle that was to continue into the thirteenth and fourteenth centuries, ultimately pitting the philosophers against the Islamic religious establishment. In fact, as we shall see, the battle rages on to this day, enveloping religious, political and artistic dimensions along with the linguistic.

With this theoretical background, we will now examine in concrete terms the linguistic process that took place as a result of the medieval philosophical movement in Islam and continued in a similar form with the advent of Western colonialist expansion in the Middle East.

THE MEDIEVAL PERIOD – THE TRANSMISSION OF GREEK PHILOSOPHY AND SCIENCE TO THE ARAB WORLD

The Qur'ān, the holy book of Islam, was revealed to the Prophet Muḥammad during the first part of the first/seventh century and is considered by Muslims as the word of God. Among other things, it includes thoughts about humanity and knowledge. The term *'ilm*, which in Arabic has two closely related meanings ("knowledge" and "science"), appears repeatedly in the Qur'ān, as well as in the *Ḥadīth*. All believers, male and female, old and young are obliged by the teachings of the Qur'ān to acquire knowledge; knowledge is to be sought and acquired from cradle (birth) to grave (death). Muslims are urged to pursue knowledge even if they must travel to China for that purpose.

Scientific activity in Islam, however, did not begin when the Qur'ān was revealed during the first part of the first/seventh century, nor when it was assembled several decades later; rather it did not begin in earnest until the third/ninth and fourth/tenth centuries.[33] Thus, while clearly encouraging the followers of Islam in the pursuit of knowledge, the Qur'ān in and of itself was *not* a sufficient condition to stimulate scientific activity. Initially, the inhabitants of the Arabian peninsula, to whom the Qur'ān was first revealed, were simply not prepared to engage in scientific activity, nor were they in the least aware of the scientific and philosophical developments that had taken place in Greece, Persia and India more than a thousand years before the appearance of Islam. The early Muslims of Arabia excelled in poetry and in warfare, but were blissfully ignorant of Euclid's theorems in geometry, Ptolemy's astronomy and the philosophical treatises of Plato and Aristotle.

Even the Arabic language was not equipped to function as a scientific language. At the time, for instance, its writers and speakers had not yet begun to exploit the *-iyyah* ending later so productive in generating the abstract nouns required to discuss philosophy and scientific theories. The Qur'ān itself included no more than two terms with this ending: *rahbāniyyah* (monasticism) in *Al-Ḥadīd* (27); and *jāhiliyyah* (ignorance [of God]) in *Āl-'Imrān* (154), *al-Mā'idah* (50), *al-Aḥzāb* (33) and *al-Fatḥ* (26).

The translation of Greek philosophical works into Arabic, however, presented an opportunity for a fresh, new look at the Arabic language. Faced with the task of creating equivalent terms to express meanings conveyed in the original Greek (and other language) texts, the translators set about developing the means to expand the Arabic language and enhance its ability to adjust to changing realities. These translators, most of whom were Nestorian Christians, translated Greek works into Arabic primarily via their native language of Syriac.

Following is a summary of the linguistic techniques these early translators employed in order swiftly and effectively to close the gap between the Arabic language as it then was and the barrage of new concepts and ideas they wished to express by means of it.

Formation of abstract nouns (the suffix -iyyah)

One of the most productive word generation techniques employed by the early translators was the aforementioned formation of new abstract terms by means of the suffix *-iyyah*, a mechanism that has become an integral part not only of the Arabic philosophical language, where it finds the majority of its uses, but also of the Arabic language in general.

In Arabic, the relative adjectives (*al-asmā' al-mansūbah* or *al-nisbah*) are formed by adding the termination *-iyy* to the words from which they are derived. They denote the fact that a person or thing belongs to or is connected with the thing from which its name is derived (in respect to origin, family, birth, sect, trade, etc). According to W. Wright, Arabic abstract nouns of the form *-iyyah* are morphologically derived from relative adjectives.[34]

Using the *-iyyah* suffix to generate abstract nouns not only solved a major problem for the translators in their work with philosophical and other texts but also proved productive in everyday life during the translation period and thereafter. The *-iyyah* suffix could be used with question particles, such as *kam* (how many or how much?) and *kayfa* (how?), to create abstract nouns such as *kamiyyah* (quantity) and *kayfiyyah* (quality). It could be used with pronouns, such as *huwa* (he), to create a noun such as *huwiyyah* (being). It could be used with particles, such as *inna* (truly) to create a noun such as *inniyyah*[35] (nature [of a thing]), etc.

Despite the alternatives suggested by several scholars of the time,[36] then, the translators and subsequently the Arab philosophers had no need to look beyond the Arabic language in order to find a suffix with which to produce abstract nouns. All they did was *broaden* the scope of application for an *existing* suffix. The only new element introduced was the idea that this suffix might be applied to terms that were not nouns – such as *huwa* (a pronoun), *kayfa* and *mā* (question particles) – and even to semi-verbs such as *ays*[37] (there is, existence) and *laysa* (there isn't, negation of existence, it is not the case), to create *aysiyyah* (being) and *laysiyyah* (non-being), respectively,[38] or to terms such as *ghayr* (other), to create *ghayriyyah* (otherness).[39]

The use of the suffix *-iyyah* as a means to generate abstract nouns is discussed by several leading philosophers of medieval Islam, primarily by al-Fārābī (fourth/tenth century) and Ibn Rushd/Averroes (sixth/twelfth century). Both al-Fārābī and Ibn Rushd discussed this issue in relation to the term *huwiyyah*, derived from the pronoun *huwa* in order to render the Greek *ousia* (being).

Al-Fārābī states, for example, that *-iyyah* is the form of the *maṣdar* of certain nouns that are both non-declinable and prototypal[40] (*fa-inna hādha'l-shakl fi'l-'arabiyyah huwa shakl maṣdar kull ism kān mithāl*[an] *awwal*[an] *wa-lam yakun lah taṣrīf*), such as *insāniyyah* (humanity), which is the abstract noun of the non-declinable prototype *insān*.[41] This is a somewhat surprising statement, since *maṣdar* generally refers to the infinitive (or verbal noun), and it hardly seems appropriate to categorize a noun such as *insāniyyah* as an infinitive. However, given that another (more essential) meaning of the term *maṣdar* is 'source', the statement begins to make sense.

In al-Fārābī's view, although we arrive at the abstract concepts (which are second order concepts) during a (chronologically) later stage in the language acquisition process, these forms are nevertheless *ontologically prior* to the first order concepts. It is in this sense, then, that the form *insāniyyah* can be considered a 'source' (*maṣdar*) for the term *insān*, just as the second order concept *ṭūl* (tallness, length) is ontologically prior, in al-Fārābī's view, to the particular *ṭawīl* (tall, long), although we first become acquainted with the latter and later abstract to the former.

Therefore, al-Fārābī can state (as he does in his *Kitāb al-ḥurūf* ("Book of Letters") that when the suffix *-iyyah* is added to *substantive nouns* (both non-declinable and prototypal), it produces a *maṣdar* (or 'source'). The examples given by al-Fārābī to illustrate this point are: *insān* (man) from which *insāniyyah* (humanity) is derived; *ḥimār* (donkey) from which *ḥimāriyyah* (donkeyness) is derived; and *rajul* (man) from which *rujūliyyah* (manhood) is derived. Al-Fārābī seems to take the liberty of identifying "abstract nouns" with *maṣādir* because this serves his purpose. Having once been coined, the abstract nouns, as second order terms that correspond to second order concepts, become *sources* (*maṣādir*) from which everything else (linguistically speaking) is derived.

Averroes, as mentioned above, also addresses this question in his *Tafsīr mā ba'd al-ṭabī'ah* ("Commentary on Aristotle's *Metaphysics*").[42] In essence, he repeats al-Fārābī's explanation that *huwiyyah* was derived from the pronoun *huwa* following the pattern of deriving (abstract) nouns from nouns. It is unusual for the Arabic language to derive a noun from a pronoun, and Averroes explains that it was done in this case in order to replace the term *mawjūd* used by the translators (mainly in the *Posterior Analytics*). It is clear that Averroes, like al-Fārābī before him, speaks of this pattern of derivation as a natural phenomenon in the Arabic language. Neither suggests that the *-iyyah* suffix is modelled on similar suffixes in other languages.

The use of the suffix *-iyyah* was only one of several linguistic devices used by the translators of that period in order to expand the Arabic language to encompass the new ideas pouring into the Arab world from the Greek and other cultures. These included borrowing, altering the meaning of existing terms, abbreviating, producing compound terms and creating new terms from existing roots.[43]

Borrowing terms from other languages (al-taʿrīb, *i.e. "arabicization" or* al-muʿarrab, *the "arabicized")*

This method, which refers to the generation of arabicized words or *al-dakhīl* (foreign or strange [words and expressions]),[44] was already in use during the pre-Islamic period, primarily involving borrowings from Aramaic, Hebrew and Persian. The Qur'ān itself includes several terms the origin of which can be traced back to other languages.[45] This fact in itself apparently legitimized the method of borrowing terms from other languages as the need arises.

During the philosophical and scientific movement in Islam, many more loan-words were introduced into Arabic from Greek and Persian, primarily in the fields of pharmacology and medicine. According to Josef Bielawski, Greek and Persian loan-words "are particularly numerous among the names of plants and mineralogy, but very rare in the [fields] of jurisprudence, philosophy, theology and philology".[46] Words – such as *jawhar* ("substance", borrowed from the Persian), *falsafah* (from the Greek *philosophia*),[47] *safsaṭah* (from the Greek *sophistry*), *hayūlā'* (from the Greek *hylé*, meaning "matter", *usṭuqussāt* (from the Greek for "elements") and *qāṭīghūriyāt* (from the Greek for "categories") – became assimilated into works of the Islamic philosophers, even when an Arabic term had also been coined for them.[48] Once a term was assimilated, the rules of derivation for pure Arabic terms were applied to the borrowed term as well.[49]

The pros and cons of accepting loan-words into Arabic was discussed by Sībawayh, the second/eighth-century founder of the study of Arabic grammar, in his definitive work entitled *al-Kitāb*.[50] The topic was taken up again by grammarians of the fourth/tenth century (al-Sīrāfī's view that the philosophers were building a language within a language was meant to address precisely this point) and is still a subject of debate today. Apart from purely linguistic considerations (such as the suitability of borrowed words for Arabic nominal or verbal patterns), the assimilation of foreign words into Arabic has social, religious and political implications that have occasioned strong objections, then as now.

It is worth noting that many of the "arabicized" words (i.e., those accepted as loan-words) were modified in order to fit certain noun or verbal patterns.[51] For example, the term *falsafah* (derived in the Classical period of Islam from the Greek *philosophia*) was adjusted to fit the pattern *fa'lalah* (like *'arqalah* (impeding, hindering), and the term *dirham*[52] (derived from the Greek *drakhme*) was modified to fit the pattern *fi'lal* (like *'iṣba'* (a finger)). Other terms, however, were modified without accommodation to an existing Arabic pattern (for example, *jughrāfiā* (derived from the Greek *geō graphia*, meaning literally *earth description*; the combination of the two words produces *geographia*, i.e., geography)), and still others were borrowed without any change whatsoever even though they did not follow any Arabic pattern (for example, *asṭurlāb* or *usṭurlāb* (astrolabe)).[53]

As we shall see, the derivation of new terms from Arabic roots generally follows a certain pattern native to the Arabic language. This does not mean, however, that every word that fits such a pattern is an Arabic (i.e., non-borrowed) term; as noted above, some loan-words were adjusted to fit Arabic patterns. Rather, we can conclude only that every term that does not fit an Arabic language pattern is an arabicized term [*mu'arrab*]. This is the basis for one of seven criteria developed by the Arab grammarians to distinguish between Arabic words and foreign words adopted by the Arabs: "If a term does not fit one of the Arabic nominal patterns [*awzān al-asmā' al-'arabiyyah*], such as *ibrīsam* [the term should be considered foreign]."[54]

*Altering the meaning of existing terms (*al-majāz*)*

This technique takes an existing Arabic term and modifies or expands it to encompass a new meaning. In essence, this method is what Arab grammarians refer to as *majāz* (figurative speech), which basically means going beyond the original (usually concrete material) meaning of a term and attaching to it a new meaning.[55] Whereas in the previous method [*ta'rīb*] terms are borrowed from other languages to be used generally within the same discipline, this method often involves borrowing terms from the same language to be used in different disciplines. Examples of this include *ḥadd* (essential definition), *rasm* (description), *jins* (genus), *naw'* (species), *'araḍ* (accident), *faṣl* (differentia), *madhhab* (discipline) and *'irq* (vein). Each of these terms existed before the transmission of Greek philosophy and science to the Muslims, but all were given new – and in most cases, technical – meanings to augment or complement any existing meaning(s).

The term *ḥadd*, for example, acquired the technical logical meaning conveyed by the Greek term *horos*. Both terms – the Greek *horos* and the Arabic *ḥadd* – mean in ordinary usage "boundary", "border" or "limit". But just as the Greek term acquired the meaning of the Aristotelian notion of "essential definition" (i.e., a definition by means of a thing's "essential difference" and its "genus", two further terms that acquired technical meanings of their own), the parallel Arabic term also became identified with the technical concept of "essential definition". This type of definition is based on the notion of defining objects by delineating the boundaries that separate them from one another in an essential way as opposed to a non-essential way (i.e., by means of their "accidental properties"). In this latter (non-essential) case the distinction between the objects is made through "description" (*rasm*) rather than through "definition".

Similarly, the term *'irq* (pl. *'urūq*), originally meaning "root of a plant", acquired the medical meaning of "vein", probably owing to analogy of form and function.

To provide yet another example, the verbal noun *manṭiq* (logic) is derived from the root *n-ṭ-q*, the basic meaning of which is "to speak". The term *manṭiq* appears already in the Qur'ān,[56] although not yet in its technical meaning as "logic". Yet as "logic" and "language" are so closely related, it was but a small cerebral step for the translators to assign the term its new technical meaning.[57]

*Compound construction through abbreviation (*naḥt ikhtizālī*)*[58]

The technique of fusing words together to produce new meanings is used to construct new terms in many languages (English, German and even modern Hebrew). In Arabic, one can distinguish two variations of this device, which I will term "abbreviated compounds" (*naḥt ikhtizālī*) and "joined compounds" (*naḥt bi-wāṣiṭāt al-tarkīb al-mazjī*).

Strictly speaking, *naḥt* is the derivation of one term from two or more other terms (*istikhrāj kalimah wāḥidah min kalimatayn aw akthar*).[59] In some cases, *naḥt* involves a truncation of the terms forming the composite. An example of this would be the abbreviation of certain recurrent (primarily religious) phrases, as in the reduction of *lā ḥawl^a^ wa-lā quwwat^a^ illā bi-Llāh* ("There is no power and no strength save in God") to the verb *ḥawlaqa* (the act of pronouncing this phrase); or the reduction of *bi-ism Allāhi al-raḥmān al-raḥīm* ("In the Name of Allāh, Most Gracious, Most Merciful") to the verb *basmạlah* (the act of pronouncing this phrase).[60] In this sense, then, *naḥt* is a kind of abbreviation, as the fourth/tenth-century grammarian Ibn Fāris rightly observes,[61] and as such requires morphological changes in the original terms.

However, just as in borrowing a term from a foreign language (*ta'rīb*) one should attempt to conform it to the verbal or nominal patterns of the Arabic language, so in constructing this type of abbreviated compound term (*naḥt ikhtizālī*), one must also try to follow Arabic language rules to the extent possible. These include:

1 To use in this process, as much as possible, original letters of the terms involved in this process.
2 If the derived term is a noun, it must agree with one of the noun patterns.
3 If the derived term is a verb, it must follow the pattern *fa'lala* or *tafa'lala*.[62]

As stated earlier, this type of abbreviated compound was reserved primarily for religious phrases, rather than to derive new scientific or philosophical terminology. The limited use made of it was principally confined to expressions from the religious realm.

*Compound construction through joining (*naḥt bi-wāsiṭat al-tarkīb al-mazjī*)*

Yet *naḥt* has a broader usage, as well. It can also refer to a phrase resulting from the combining of two terms without causing any morphological change to either. The resulting combination must be considered "one term [*ism*[an], lit. 'a noun'] in terms of inflection and structure, whether the [combined] terms are of Arabic origin or arabicized".[63] Modern Arab linguists refer to this process as *al-tarkīb al-mazjī* (the compound construction), and we will follow them in treating this broader sense of *naḥt* as a separate category.[64]

A clear example of this type of derivation is the compound numbers (such as *ithnā 'ashara*, lit. "two-ten", meaning "twelve"), but the scope of this method of word formation is much broader, including adverbs of time (such as *ṣabāḥ*[a] *masā'*[a], lit. "morning-evening", meaning "all the time", "non-stop"); adverbs of place (such as *bayn*[a] *bayn*[a], lit. "between-between", meaning "in the middle").

This method was used extensively during the translation period to translate *literally* philosophical terms that represented similar compound terms in the original language (generally, Greek). The majority of these compound terms consisted of a negation particle along with a noun. Examples include *lā-wujūd* (non-existence); *lā-nihāyah* [lit. "no-end", meaning "infinity"]; *al-ghayr maḥsūs* (the intangible); *al-ghayr mutaḥarrik* (the immobile); *al-ghayr māddī* (the immaterial).

However, there are also examples of compound expressions without negation particles, as well. An example would be *mā ba'd al-ṭabī'ah* (lit. "that which is beyond nature", meaning "metaphysics").[65]

*Derivation or the creation of new terms from existing roots (*ishtiqāq*)*

Important as they were, the methods thus far discussed – formation of abstract nouns (using the suffix *-iyyah*), use of borrowed terms (*ta'rīb*), semantic change of existing words (*majāz*), abbreviation (*naḥt*) and (the closely related method of) creating compound terms (*tarkīb mazjī*) – were used only for a relatively limited number of terms. These methods alone would not have been able to produce the full range of new technical terms needed to convey ideas transmitted from Greek science and philosophy without "building a language within a language", the charge levelled by the Arab grammarians against the logicians. The translators of the second/eighth, third/ninth and fourth/tenth centuries, realizing the limitations of the methods previously discussed,[66] ultimately made a maximum use of the unique richness of the Arabic language in terms of *derivability*. The Arabic language, like other Semitic languages and even more so, offers the means to derive from any given root a significant number of related words according to patterns. This characteristic of Arabic, called *ishtiqāq* (derivation), has been the single most productive method used by Arab philologists, past and present, to meet the influx of new terminology and ideas through "neologisms". We will provide two extended examples to illustrate this method and then list some of the most common patterns employed to produce new terms during the Classical period of philosophical and scientific activity in Islam.

Firstly, the term *qiyās* (syllogism) is a verbal noun derived from the root *q-y-s*, the basic meaning of which is "to measure" or "to compare". As the Aristotelian syllogism basically "measures" or "compares" against each other premisses considered to be true, in order to reach a conclusion, the verbal noun *qiyās* ("measuring" or "comparing") was selected to convey the technical meaning of "syllogism". *Qiyās*, while used in logical contexts to render "syllogism", was employed by both Arab grammarians and Muslim jurists in their respective fields to mean "analogy".

Secondly, the term *iṣṭilāḥ* or its synonym *muṣṭalaḥ*[67] is derived from the root *ṣ-l-ḥ* the basic meaning of which is "to be suitable" or "to be in good condition, without defects". The eighth form of this verb (*iṣṭalaḥa*) means "to agree, accept, adopt". The verbal noun of the eighth form (*iṣṭilāḥ*) and the passive participle (*muṣṭalaḥ*) were both adopted to mean "a technical term", since it is something agreed upon and accepted.

This derivation method sometimes employed a given pattern to derive terms of the same category. The pattern *fu'āl*, for example, was used to derive terms relating to sickness *ṣudā'* ("headache", from *ṣ-d-'*, meaning "to split, to separate"); *zukām* ("cold", from *z-k-m*, meaning "to cool, get cold"), *duwār* ("dizziness", from *d-w-r*, meaning "to turn around" or "to move in a circular motion"), and *su'āl*, ("cough", from *su'ala*, "to cough").

Similarly, as the tenth form (*istaf'ala*) often expresses "taking", "seeking" or "asking for" that which is referred to by the simple (first) form, the verbal noun of this form (*istif'āl*) was used in various disciplines to deduce terms expressing the concept of "seeking". In logic, for example, the term *istiqrā'* (induction) was derived according to this principle from the root *q-r-w*. The tenth form of this root (*istaqrā'*) means: to pursue things and examine their conditions and properties.[68] Consequently, the verbal noun of this form, *istiqrā'*, was chosen to mean "induction" since in induction "one examines the individual cases in order to reach an affirmative universal judgment".[69] Similarly, *istintāj* (reaching a conclusion) was derived from *n-t-j* (to result).[70] The medical term *istisqā'* (derived from *saqā* which means "to water" or "to give to drink") was coined to refer to the disease "hydropsy" (or "dropsy"), involving an excessive accumulation of fluid in the cellular tissues.

Maṣādir (verbal nouns) of various forms were used in the classical period to derive new terms, such as *khiṭābah* (rhetorics), a verbal noun derived from the root *kh-ṭ-b*, the basic meaning of which is to "give a speech", "to preach"; and *jadal* (dialectics), a verbal noun derived from the root *j-d-l*, the basic meaning of which is "to twist [a rope] firmly; to braid". This term acquired the meaning "dialectics" (*jadal*), since in dialectical discussions it is "as though each of the two parties twisted the other from his opinion: or, as some say, it originally means the act of wrestling, and throwing down another upon the *jadālah* (or ground)".[71] Similar analysis leads us to the rationale behind assigning new technical, philosophical meanings to already existing verbal nouns such as *taḥlīl* (analysis), from the second form of *ḥ-a-l-l* (i.e., *ḥallala*, "to resolve into the component parts of a thing"), *tarkīb* (classification), from the second form of *r-k-b* (i.e., *rakkaba*, "to construct, assemble, to put together"), and *qismah* (division), from the root *q-s-m* (the basic meaning of which is "to divide, split, separate").[72]

THE SECOND CONFRONTATION WITH THE WEST – COLONIZATION BY WESTERN POWERS

For historical and internal reasons, the details of which go beyond the scope of this chapter, the Arab/Islamic culture lost its momentum after the ninth/fifteenth century and began to decline in terms of scientific and intellectual achievement and development. This stagnation continued throughout, and perhaps was further enhanced by, the Ottoman rule of most of the Arab world for over four centuries. The occupation of Egypt by the French in 1798 and later by the British in 1882, however, marked the beginning of a new phase of confrontation between the Arabs and the West, a confrontation with both political and intellectual dimensions.

Given the influx of new concepts and terms entering from other cultures over the past two hundred years, contemporary Arab linguists, like their counterparts from the Classical period, have attempted to coin equivalent new terms in Arabic using various methods. They have essentially employed the methods elaborated upon earlier in this chapter: borrowing words from other languages, modifying the meaning of existing terms, abbreviating, forming compound terms and deriving new words from existing roots. As in the Classical period, the latter method has experienced the most frequent use, whereas borrowing has been the method least often employed.

*Borrowing terms from other languages (*al-taʿrīb*)*[73]

It is interesting to note that – in contrast to other Middle Eastern languages, such as Persian, Turkish, Hebrew and even colloquial Arabic – written Arabic (or what has become known as Modern Standard Arabic) has been very conservative when it comes to accepting borrowed terms (loan-words).[74] This can probably be attributed to cultural/religious as well as political considerations. In the words of Charles Issawi:

> the intense Arab nationalism has, quite rightly, fastened on the Arabic language as the main bond – together with Islam – holding the otherwise rather diverse Arab peoples and the one differentiating them from their non-Arab Muslim neighbours and has further strengthened their attachment to and jealousy for their language; hence any borrowing that might increase the diversity of the Arabic used in various parts is looked upon with deep suspicion as a disruptive factor.[75]

None the less, many terms have been borrowed by the Arabs in the thirteenth/nineteenth and fourteenth/twentieth centuries. Among the first wave of European terms the Arabs encountered in the modern period were terms of a primarily political nature. Borrowed political terms include *dīmuqrāṭī/dīmuqrāṭiyyah* (democratic/democracy); *barlamān* (parliament); *qunṣul/qunṣuliyyah* (consul/consulate); *diktātūr/diktātūrī* (dictator/dictatorial).[76]

Following closely on the heels of these political loan-words were borrowed terms from Western science and technology, such as *rādyu* (radio); *tilfizion* (television); *sīnamā* (cinema); *film* (film); *vīdyū* (video); *talafon* (telephone); *kombūtar* (computer); and the names of the chemical elements, such as *uksūjin* (oxygen) and *haydrujīn* (hydrogen).

Arabic terms coined to replace many of these loan-words were either rejected or used interchangeably with the foreign term they were meant to replace. The term *mirnāt*, for example, coined to replace *telfizion*, was totally ignored by the speakers of the language, as well as by those using the written language; whereas *hātif*, coined to replace *talafun*, has managed to exist alongside its foreign counterpart.[77] The borrowed term *kumbūtar* has evinced itself particularly resistant to supplantation by indigenous Arabic substitutes. Jamīl al-Malāi'kah documents as many as ten suggested replacements for the tenacious term, ranging from *al-'aql al-iliktronī* (lit., "the electronic mind") to *al-naẓẓāmah* (lit., "the machine that organizes", generated according to the *fa''ālah* pattern discussed under "Derivation" below).[78]

Altering or expanding the meaning of existing terms

The second method of semantically modifying existing words[79] has also been employed during the modern period. According to Bernard Lewis, Arabic made much "use of an important new vocabulary coined by the Ottoman scholars, officials and journalists".[80] These were often words of Arabic origin adapted by the Ottomans for use in translating terms of European origin and later on re-adopted back into Arabic, gaining virtually universal acceptance in their newly acquired meanings. Examples of such terms include *jumhūriyyah* (republic), *qawmiyyah* (nationality), *ishtirākī* (socialist), *iqtiṣādī* (economic), *khārijiyyah* (foreign affairs), *dākhiliyyah* (domestic or internal affairs), and *baladiyyah* (municipality).[81]

Examples of other terms produced by this means include *ḥukūmah* (government),[82] *azmah* (classical meaning, "shortage or famine"; modern meaning, "crisis (political or economic)"); *muḥarrik* (originally used to express the Aristotelian term "prime mover" or "God" as the first cause; modern meaning, "motor or engine"); *dharr* (originally, "small particles"; modern meaning, "atoms").[83]

The formation of compound terms

The method of producing compound terms in its broader sense (i.e., *tarkīb mazjī*, rather than *naḥt*) has actually gained momentum during the modern period. Whereas in the Classical period only isolated compound terms were produced by means of this method, a relatively long list of compound terms has been compiled in the modern period. Examples include: *lā-silkī* (wireless); *al-'aql al-lā wā'ī* (the subconscious mind); *al-ashi''ah fawq al-hanafsajiyyah* (lit., "the rays that are above the violet", i.e., "ultraviolet rays").

The above examples closely resemble those presented in this same category for the Classical period, i.e., they represent literal translations of foreign compound terms. It is worth noting, however, that a new trend has appeared in the modern period representing non-literal, which is to say, conceptual translations of new or foreign terms. The more conceptually (i.e., non-literally) translated compounds rely heavily on a powerful construct in Arabic called *iḍāfah*, which suggests through the positioning of two nouns in a sentence (or compound) a relationship of possession between the second and the first. Examples of these more conceptually translated compounds include *'ilm al-nafs* ("science of the soul", i.e., "psychology"); *'ilm al-ijtimā'* ("science of society", i.e., "sociology"); *maraḍ al-nafs* (lit., "sickness of the soul", i.e., "mental illness"); *naṭīḥat al-saḥāb* (lit., "that which butts against the sky", i.e., "skyscraper"); *jawāz safar* (lit., "permit to travel", i.e., "passport"); and many more.

Derivation or the creation of new terms from existing roots

Just as in the Classical period, however, *ishtiqāq* (derivation of new terms from existing roots according to certain patterns) has been the main method used by modern Arabic speakers to generate new terms. There follow illustrations of two of the more common patterns in current use.[84] Firstly, the pattern *fa''ālah*, the basic meaning of which is "capable of doing", is employed in the feminine form to indicate "instruments capable of doing". Thus, *thallājah* (refrigerator) is derived from *th-l-j* (snow); *ghawwāṣah* (submarine) is derived from *gh-w-ṣ* (diving). Second is the pattern *mif'al*, the basic meaning of which is "to perform the act involved in the meaning of the root". Thus, from the verb *ṣa'ida* (to ascend) the term *miṣ'ad* (lift, elevator) is derived; from the verb *jahara* (to reveal, make public, or make known) the term *mijhar* (microscope) is derived.

CONTEMPORARY DEBATES CONCERNING THE FUTURE OF THE ARABIC LANGUAGE

This concludes our discussion of the methods by which new terms have been generated in the Arabic language, past and present. There are, however, further topics relating to the development of the language that are relevant to the modern period but were not really at issue during the Classical period.

Although the French occupation of Egypt lasted only about three years, European influence spread rapidly in Egypt and later throughout the rest of the Arab world. Muḥammad 'Alī, a Turk sent with Ottoman forces to battle the French forces in Egypt, ruled the country between 1805 and 1848. During these years, he instituted scientific and social reforms aimed at improving the economy and the standard of living in Egypt. His modernization plans occasioned the first real encounter with Western civilization in the modern era, a turning point in terms of the Arabs' self-esteem and their view of their own culture. Since that time, the Arabs have been literally overwhelmed militarily, politically and technologically by the West.

The Arabs' political and military impotence and their social backwardness have prompted serious questions and inquiries concerning the ability of the Arab–Islamic culture to cope with the challenges of the modern period, marked as it is by a clear superiority of the West. A major task Arab intellectuals have set for themselves is that of divining solutions for their peoples' predicament. These attempts have in turn led to divisions within the Arab intellectual community, the effects of which go far beyond the intellectual realm.

The debates that have taken place regarding the Arabic language and its ability to reflect the scientific and technological innovations of the modern period clearly illustrate these deep divisions. Sāṭiʿ al-Ḥuṣrī (1882–1968), a leading member of one of the intellectual factions and regarded as the spiritual father of Arab nationalism, summarizes these current philological debates in his *al-Lughah* as follows:

> Whereas some Arab philologists go to the lengths of declaring *ʿArabiyyah* to be the richest language in the world, other [Westernized] authors go to the other extreme, asserting that Arabic is incapable of adopting the scientific terminology necessary for our generation. We share neither of these extremes.[85]

Al-Ḥuṣrī himself represents a third trend between the two extremes, which calls for modernization of the Arabic language, roughly along the lines adopted during the medieval period.[86]

Yet contemporary debates concerning the Arabic language centre not only on the question of how to coin or incorporate new terminology into the existing linguistic network but also on the problem of how to reduce or eliminate the degree of alienation that exists between the language and its speakers. For almost any language, there is a more or less pronounced dichotomy between the language as it is spoken and the language as it is written. For Arabic, the gap between the two levels more closely resembles a chasm. Spoken Arabic consists of a set of widely differing (and in some cases mutually unintelligible) regional dialects, whereas written Arabic is essentially the language of the Qur'ān. A major challenge faced by contemporary Arab linguists, then, is to devise means for narrowing the gap between *ʿāmmiyyah* (the spoken language) and *fuṣḥā* (the written language).

Prominent intellectuals – such as the Egyptians Ṭaha Ḥusayn (1889–1973), Salāmah Mūsā (1887–1958), and Yūsuf Idrīs (1927–1991); and the Lebanese Mīkhā'īl Nu'aymah (1889–1987) and Anīs Frayhah – strongly suggest that the gap between the spoken and the written language must be closed so that Arabic speakers may express themselves in a language closer to their hearts, a language they use every day. Ṭaha Ḥusayn, for example, has repeatedly demanded that the written form of Classical Arabic, as well as its grammar, should be simplified in order to make it accessible to everyone in Egypt and the Arab world in general.[87] Salāmah Mūsā, too, has argued that the language should be simplified, lest it become a language of monks, which only a few people know and use.[88]

Others, such as Mīkhā'īl Nu'aymah, have gone even further, demanding that plays, for example, should be "written" in the spoken language. Otherwise one is artificially imposing a language on the characters that real people would not use.[89] Yūsuf Idrīs has actually written many of his plays and short stories in colloquial Arabic, precisely because he believes that Classical (or written) Arabic is an alien tongue to the majority of his readers and that it would be unrealistic to impose on the characters in his drama and fiction a language they would not use in daily life. Idrīs was the first writer in the Arab world to follow the practice of using both colloquial Arabic (for the language of his characters) and classical Arabic (in his descriptive matter) in one and the same story.

Those who oppose the use of colloquial Arabic in writing are not only anxious about violating the purity of the language of the Qur'ān, but also fear the political consequences of abandoning Classical Arabic as the written language. Since the Arabic language is perhaps the single most important aspect of the Arab identity, the promotion of colloquial Arabic would undermine the potency of this unifying factor. The future of the Arab countries, these intellectuals fear, would be similar to that of Europe, where many languages, and consequently many nations, emerged with the disappearance of Latin as a living language.[90] Even those who advocate the use of colloquial Arabic in writing are aware of this dilemma (*al-'uqdah*, lit., "the complexity") and seem unable to offer a solution to it.[91]

There is no doubt that the linguistic issues facing the Arab world today are exceedingly complex, with compelling arguments on both sides. It is too soon to tell what course the future development of the Arabic language will take, but one thing is sure, the philosophers, theologians and other important thinkers for whom Arabic is a native tongue will be in the forefront of the debate, just as they were during medieval times. They must help guide the community of speakers of the language in preserving their rich linguistic heritage, while also contributing to and benefiting from the fact that they are citizens of a larger and rapidly evolving global community.

NOTES

1 I would like to acknowledge the invaluable assistance of my former teacher and mentor Wolfhart Heinrichs of Harvard University, who read a draft of this chapter and offered numerous insightful comments and suggestions, many of which have been incorporated in this final version.

2 Owing to space limitations, other important linguistic issues, such as the discussion of the nature and the origin of language (i.e., whether it is conventional or inspired) cannot be dealt with here. A summary of various views on these subjects in the writings of medieval Islamic intellectuals may be found in J. al-Dīn al-Suyūṭī (n.d.): 7ff. For the origin of the term *lughah* (language), consult the *Encyclopaedia of Islam*, new edition, *s.v.* "*Lughah*", contributed by A. Hadj-Salah.

3 G. Endress (1977): 110.

4 Abū Ḥayyān al-Tawḥīdī (n.d.): 122, p. 15.

5 English translation with an introduction by D. S. Margoliouth, "The Discussion between Abu Bishr Matta and Abu Sa'id al-Sirafi on the Merits of Logic and Grammar", *Journal of the Royal Asiatic Society* (1905): 79–129. For further details regarding this translation consult Muḥsin Mahdī (1970): 55 n. 12.

6 Mahdi (1970); Gerhard Endress (1977) and (1986); A. El Amrani-Jamal, *Logique Aristotelienne et grammaire Arabe: Etude et documents* (Paris, 1983). Concerning the general attitude to logic and science in medieval Islam, one should consult Goldziher's "Mawqif Ahl al-Sunnah al-Qudama' Bi-iza' 'Ulum al-Awa'il" in 'Abd al-Raḥmān Badawī (ed.) *al-Turāth al-yūnānī fi-l-ḥaḍārah al-islāmiyyah* (Cairo, *al-nahḍah al-miṣriyyah* 1940): 123–72.

7 *Ibid.*: 108. 10–12. A very similar view was held by the fifth/eleventh-century philosopher Ibn Sīnā (980–1037). See, for example, his *al-Najāt* (Book of Deliverance'), ed. al-Kurdī (Cairo, 1938): 3.

8 *Imtā'*: 114, ll. 6–9.

9 *Ibid.*: 129, l. 2.

10 *Ibid.*: 109, ll. 9–10.

11 *Ibid.*: 109, ll. 11–13.

12 *Ibid.*: 109, ll. 14–16.

13 *Ibid.*: 109, l. 16; 110, ll. 1–3.

14 *Ibid.*: 110, ll. 7–10.

15 *Ibid.*: 113, ll. 13–16.

16 *Ibid.*: 115, ll. 1–2.

17 *Ibid.*: 111, para. 11, where he states, "You are not, therefore, asking us [to study] the science of logic, but rather to study the Greek language." Al-Sīrāfī's position on this issue represents what some contemporary philosophers of language call a "naturalistic" (rather than a "constructionistic") point of view and can be summed up in the words of Fred Sommers as follows: "The naturalist believes with Aristotle and Leibniz that logical syntax is implicit in the grammar of natural language and that the structure attributed by grammarians to sentences of natural language is in close correspondence to their logical form" (Sommers (1982): 2).

18 *Imtā'*: 110, ll. 11–14.

19 *Ibid.*: 111, ll. 1–3.

20 *Ibid.*, ll. 4–7.

21 *Ibid.*: 123, ll. 7ff.

22 *Ibid.*: 111, ll. 13–14. Al-Sīrāfī seems here unaware of the close relationship between the Byzantine Greek spoken by his contemporaries (*al-rūmiyyah*) and the ancient Greek of Aristotle and his contemporaries (*al-yūnāniyyah*).

23 *Ibid.*: 112, ll. 5–6. The translation of this particular passage is by Muḥsin Mahdī (1970): 67.

24 *Ibid.*: 112, ll. 7–10. See Mahdī (1970): 67.

25 *Ibid.*: 113, ll. 4ff.

26 *Ibid.*: 113, ll. 8ff.

27 At least this is the picture painted in al-Tawḥīdī's description of this debate. At various junctures, in response to particularly incisive points made by the grammarian Abū Sa'īd al-Sīrāfī, the logician Mattā "was bewildered" (*Imtā'*: 114, l. 5) or "was troubled and hung his head and was choked by his saliva" (*ibid.* 119, l. 2), unable to produce counter-arguments.

28 Utterances not in the sense of speech-acts but rather of composite utterances, i.e., utterances in the context of sentences.

29 Witness the following blunt admission by Abū Bishr Mattā in the debate that took place between him and the grammarian al-Sīrāfī: "This is grammar, and I have not studied grammar "(*Imtā'* : 114, l. 6). This position was also defended by Avicenna. Cf. Ibn Sīnā (1970): 5. Elsewhere Avicenna says that logicians need natural languages only in order to be able to address logical issues and to communicate with others about these issues. Logic, according to him, does not deal with utterances per se because these are only a tool and can theoretically be replaced by some other device (*ḥīlah*) through which one can express logical relations without the mediation of a natural language. Ibn Sīnā (1952): 22.

30 Abū Naṣr al-Fārābī was the most thorough and systematic among the second generation of Arab logicians in analysing the relationship between Arabic grammar and Greek logic. For further details concerning al-Fārābī's views on this issue, see S. Abed (1991), introduction and conclusion.

31 *Imtā'*: 122, 1. 15.

32 Although the details of this argument exceed the scope of this chapter, let one example suffice to demonstrate, namely, the issue of the copula. The tenth-century logician and student of Mattā, Abū Naṣr al-Fārābī (258/870–339/950), conducted a logical analysis of the language that led him to assume the implicit presence of the copula in Arabic sentences where it would naturally not be present, such as "*Zayd (yūjad) 'ādil*[an]". In making this assumption, he was following Aristotle's assertion that every sentence must have a verb. Al-Fārābī knew, of course, that Aristotle's rule did not accurately describe the Arabic language. He therefore applied the rule only to the logical form of the sentence, arguing that the copula exists in the *logical* structure of every Arabic sentence.

33 By "scientific activity" I here refer to activity in the *natural* sciences. As early as the eighth century, legal reasoning and linguistic thinking were already quite well developed.

34 W. Wright (1975), 1. 149, 165: "The feminine of the relative adjective serves in Arabic as a noun to denote the abstract idea of the thing, as distinguished from the concrete thing itself, e.g., *ilāhiyyah* (divine nature), *insāniyyah* (humanity)."

35 For a discussion of the origin and meaning of this term, see R. M. Frank (1956): 181–201.

36 For example, L. Massignon and P. Kraus, "La formation des noms abstraits en arabe", *Revue d'Etudes Islamiques* (1934): 507ff., where it is suggested that "this suffix was copied from the Syriac, which in turn adopted it from the Greek =*ia*, the common suffix denoting abstraction". S. M. Afnan (1964), from whom the last quotation was adopted, suggests (p. 32) that the inclination of the Arabs to form abstract nouns of the *-iyyah* variety is likely to have been influenced by Pahlawi and Persian. The holder of this opinion bases his assumption on the observation that there are far more abstractions in the writings of philosophers of Persian origin (probably a reference to the works of philosophers such as Ibn Sīnā and Mullā Ṣadrā) than in those of philosophers of Arab origin. He also observes that in Persian the mere addition of the suffix *-ī* makes a perfectly good abstraction out of almost any word in the language. This last observation is supported by al-Fārābī, who in *Kitāb al-ḥurūf* ("Book of Letters") (1970: 111, l. 82) illustrates this linguistic feature of the Persian language by means of the terms *hast* (is) and *mardum* (men), each of which becomes an abstract noun through the simple addition of the Persian suffix *-ī*. See Abed (1991): 155ff. for a reply to these views.

37 This is a rare word in Arabic philosophical terminology; see, however, al-Kindī's use of this term in *Rasā'il al-Kindī al-falsafiyyah* ("Al-Kindī's Philosophical Essays") (1950: 182); see also Abū Rīdah's commentary on this term (*ibid.*).

38 These too are rare; see, however, the list produced by al-Sīrāfī in his critique of the philosophers, in al-Tawḥīdī (n.d.): 123, ll. 8–10. Al-Sīrāfī mentions in that list abstract terms such as *ḥāliyyah*, which is derived from the question particle *ḥāl* ("is it the case?"; an interrogative particle introducing direct and indirect questions), and *ayniyyah* (derived from *ayna*, which is also a question particle meaning "where?").

39 See al-Kindī (1950): 174–5.

40 For the meaning of *mithāl awwal* (prototype), consult F. W. Zimmermann (1981): xxxf, cxxxvi; and Abed (1991): 146ff.

41 Al-Fārābī (1970): 112, l. 83.

42 Ibn Rushd (1938–48), 2: 557.

43 For a detailed study of these methods, consult J. Bielawski (1956): 263–320.

44 Cf. al-Jawālīqī (1867). The term *al-dakhīl* is contrasted by al-Jawālīqī with *al-ṣarīḥ* (i.e., the pure [Arabic]), p. 3. There are also several relatively modern works dealing with this question. Cf. Al-Sayyid Adday Shir (1908); Tūbyā al-Ḥalabī (1932).

45 The sixteenth-century scholar Jalāl al-Dīn al-Suyūṭī lists several Qur'ānic terms as foreign, mentioning (though not always accurately) their respective origin; al-Suyūṭī (n.d.): 1: 268. Later grammarians developed seven criteria through which to determine whether a word is of Arabic origin or borrowed (*ibid.*: 270). For a comprehensive study of foreign words in the Qur'ān consult A. Jeffrey (1938).

46 Bielawski (1952): 285.

47 More accurately, *falsafah* is an Arabic derivation from *faylasūf* which in turn is derived from the Greek via Syriac (*philosophia*), likewise *safsaṭah* in relation to *sufisṭā'ī*, etc.

48 *Falsafah* = *ḥikmah*; *hayūlā* = *māddah*; *qāṭīghūriyāt* = *maqūlāt*; etc.

49 For example, the past tense verb *tafalsafa* (philosophized) was derived from *falsafah*. See Bielawski (1952):

50 Sībawayh (1966–77), 4: 303ff.

51 Arabicized words, i.e., those accepted as loan-words from other languages, do *not* violate the "truth of the Kuran's being [altogether] Arabic; for when a foreign word is used by the Arabs, and made by them comfortable with their language in respect of desinential syntax and determinateness and indeterminateness and the like, it becomes Arabic". Lane (1980), under the term *qusṭus* (balance – arabicized from Greek). See the discussions on this issue in al-Suyūṭī (n.d): 268–9.

52 See Sībawayh (1966–77): 303.

53 Al-Suyūṭī (n.d.): 269–70. With the exception of *dirham*, however, the examples are not from al-Suyūṭī.

54 *Ibid.*: 270.

55 This is true of other related methods used by Arab grammarians and philologists, such as *isti'ārah* (metaphor), *ittisā'* (extension, which is a subcategory of *majāz*), and *tasāmuḥ* (licence), all of which are used to expand the meanings of existing terms. Ibn Jinni, in his *al-Khaṣā'iṣ*, for example, claims that terminology derived by *majāz* comprises most of the terms used in a language (*al-Khaṣā'iṣ*, 2: 447). For al-Fārābī's view of these concepts see Abed (1991): 171.

56 For example, "We have been taught the speech [*manṭiq*] of birds" (27: 16). In two other passages in the Qur'ān the verb *naṭaqa* is associated with "saying the truth": "Before us is a record which clearly speaks the truth [*yanṭuq[u] bi'l-ḥaqq*]" (23: 62); "This our record speaks about you with truth [*yanṭuq[u] 'alaykum*]" (45: 29).

57 Bielawski (1952): 278 classifies this term among the derived terms, rather than among the terms that have acquired new meaning.

58 Literally, "carving (usually a stone or a piece of wood)". Al-Suyūṭī (n.d.), 1: 482, quotes the following definition of *al-manḥūt* (passive participle of *naḥt*): "[A word is called] *manḥūtah* [carved] from two words just as the carpenter carves two pieces of wood and combines them into one."

59 I. Anīs (1966): 71.

60 For further examples see Anīs (1966): 72ff.

61 Ibn Fāris (1977): 461. In his definition, Ibn Fāris mentions only "two terms" rather than "two or more", and then adds that *naḥt* is "a kind of abbreviation [*ikhtiṣār*]".

62 M. Khalaf Allāh Aḥmad and M. Shawqī Amīn (eds) *Kitāb fī uṣūl al-lughah* ("A Book Concerning the Principles of the (Arabic) Language") (Cairo, 1969): 49.

63 *Ibid.*: 52, 61.

64 Apparently this terminology is a latecomer to Arabic linguistics. It cannot be traced in the writings of Arab grammarians until the fourteenth century. See *ibid.* p. 58.

65 See Bielawski (1952): 284–5.

66 The method of "borrowing" has the further drawback of introducing non-Arabic elements into the Arabic language. This is something the Arabs tend to be uneasy about, as it may corrupt the purity of the language, which is after all the holy language of the Qur'ān.

67 This example is analysed by Bielawski (1952): 278.

68 Lane (1980); *s.v. q-r-'*. See also al-Tahānawī (1966), 5: 1229.

69 *Ibid.*

70 For further details, the reader is referred to Bielawski (1952): 279ff.

71 Lane (1980), *s.v. jadal.*
72 For the technical meaning of these last two terms see Abed (1991): 95–100.
73 One should distinguish here between two senses of the term *ta'rīb*: "borrowing" as opposed to "arabicization". The first of these senses refers to the borrowing of terms from foreign languages for use in Arabic, usually with some adaptation to Arabic patterns. The second sense refers to a comprehensive change of the official language used in a country – from the tongue of the colonizers to that of the native Arab inhabitants. This second process – politically, as well as culturally motivated – is currently under way in the former French colonies of North Africa (Algeria, Tunisia and Morocco), which for decades have employed French as their official language but are now in the process of converting to Arabic. A similar conversion took place during the early days of the Arab empire when the Umayyads established Arabic as the official imperial language, replacing other languages then in use (such as Persian). See, for example, N. Aḥmad (1986).
74 Charles Issawi studied the European loan-words in a Nagīb Maḥfūẓ trilogy and, on the basis of his findings, he evaluated "the Arabic response to the challenge of the foreign vocabulary by comparing it with that of three other Middle Eastern languages – Persian, Turkish, and Uzbek" (1967: 110–33). Issawi summarizes his study as follows (p. 128): "The conclusion of this study may be briefly stated. Modern Arabic has shown a very marked reluctance to take in European (or other) loan-words, Persian has been somewhat more receptive, Turkish has been very hospitable and Uzbek has been flooded with such words."
75 *Ibid.*: 110.
76 For a comprehensive study of political terms in Arabic in the modern period, see Ayalon (1989): 23–42.
77 This occurred also during the Classical period. Al-Suyūṭī, for example, devotes an entire chapter to "arabicized terms that have names in the language of the Arabs" (n.d.: 283–5).
78 J. al-Malā'ikah (1984): 52.
79 Bernard Lewis (1973): 285–6 refers to this method as "semantic rejuvenation or resemanticization", which he describes as follows: "This occurs where an old word, which may or may not be obsolete, is given, more or less arbitrarily, a new meaning different from those which it previously expressed."
80 *Ibid.*: 283.
81 *Ibid.*: 283–5. See also Ami Ayalon (1989): 23: "In meeting the challenge, the Arabs could largely benefit from the experience of their Turkish counterparts who, as rulers of the empire, were first to encounter European political ideas and to respond to the resultant linguistic needs."
82 See Lewis (1973): 286, for the semantic change in this case, as well as in the case of the term *dustūr* (constitution).
83 For a relatively detailed list, see Bielawski (1952): 294–5.
84 For further details, see Bielawski (1952): 294ff.
85 Quoted in Bassam Tibi (1990): 96.
86 This debate regarding the future of the Arabic language mirrors a deeper undercurrent of divisions in the Arab world concerning the future not only of the Arabic language but also of the Arabic culture in general. There are those who wish to

transform the culture via cultural revolution, others who believe that the Arabic culture is "viable for modern life if only understood and interpreted better, and if certain of its elements are developed in light of modern needs and the experience of modern nations", and still others who seek "to return to the Islamic roots of their culture". For futher details, consult I. Boullata (1990): 3–4.

87 See, for example, his lecture *Mushkilat al-iʿrāb* ("The Problem of Declension"), delivered in 1955 before the Academy of the Arabic Language in Cairo (1981).

88 See, for example, his book *al-Balāghah al-ʿaṣriyyah wa'l-lughat al-ʿarabiyyah* "The Contemporary Art of Composition and the Arabic Language" (Cairo, 1964), particularly 43–6, "*Al-Lughah wa'l-mujtamaʿ*" (Language and Society").

89 See, for example, Mīkhā'īl Nuʿaymah (1967): 15.

90 See, for example, N. Aḥmad (1986): 27.

91 See, for example, Nuʿaymah (1967): 15–16.

BIBLIOGRAPHY

Abed, S. (1991) *Aristotelian Logic and the Arabic Language in Alfārābī* (Albany).

Afnan, S. (1964) *Philosophical Terminology in Arabic and Persian* (Leiden).

Aḥmad, N. (1986) *Al-Taʿrīb wa'l-qawmiyyah al-ʿarabiyyah fī al-Maghrib al-ʿarabī* ("Arabicization and Arab Nationalism: (The Case of) Arab North Africa") (Beirut).

Aḥmad, M. Khalaf Allāh and Amīn, M. Shawqī (eds) (1969) *Kitāb fī uṣūl al-lughah* ("A Book Concerning the Principles of the [Arabic] Language") (Cairo).

Anīs, I. (1966) *Min asrār al-lughah* ["Secrets of the [Arabic] Language"] (Cairo).

Ayalon, A. (1989) "*Dīmuqrāṭiyya, Ḥurriyya, Jumhūriyya*: the Modernization of the Arabic Political Vocabulary", *Asian and African Studies* (Journal of the Israel Oriental Society), 23(1) (March): 23–42.

Bielawski, J. (1956) "Deux periodes dans la formation de la terminologie scientifique arabe", *Rocznik Orientalistyczny* 20: 263–320.

Boullata, I. (1990) *Trends and Issues in Contemporary Arab Thought* (Albany).

The Encyclopedia of Islam (1913–38) (Leiden and Leipzig).

The Encyclopedia of Islam, new edition (Leiden and London, 1960ff.).

Endress, G. (1977) "The Debate Between Arabic Grammar and Greek Logic", *Journal for the History of Arabic Science*, 1(2) (November).

—— (1986) "Grammatik und Logik: Arabische Philologie und griechische Philosophie im Widerstreit", in *Sprachphilosophie in Antike und Mittelalter*, Bochumer Studien zur Philosophie, 3 (Amsterdam).

al-Fārābī, A. N. (1970) *Kitāb al-ḥurūf* ("Book of Letters"), ed. Muḥsin Mahdī (Beirut).

Frank, R. M. (1956) "The Origin of the Arabic Philosophical Term *aniyyah*", *Cahiers de Byrsa*, 6: 181–201.

Goichon, A. M. (1938) *Lexique de la langue philosophique d'Ibn Sina* (Paris).

Al-Ḥalabī, T. (1932) *Tafsīr al-alfāẓ al-dakhīlah fi'l-lughah al-ʿarabiyyah* ("Interpretation of Foreign Words in Arabic"), 2nd ed. (Cairo).

Ḥusayn, Ṭ. (1981) *Mushkilat al-iʿrāb* ("The Problem of Declension"), delivered in 1955 before the Academy of the Arabic Language in Cairo, in *Al-majmūʿat al-kāmilah li-muʾallafāt Ṭaha Ḥusayn* ("The Complete Works of Taha Hussein") (Beirut), 16: 380–96.

Ibn ʿAdī, Y. (1978) "On The Difference Between Philosophical Logic and Arabic Grammar", *Journal for the History of Arabic Science*, 2.
Ibn Fāris, A. (1977) *Al-Ṣāḥibī fī fiqh al-lughah* ("Semantic Studies"), ed. al-Sayyid Aḥmad Ṣaqr (Cairo).
Ibn Rushd (1938–48) *Tafsīr mā baʿd al-ṭabīʿah* ("Averroes' Commentary on Aristotle's Metaphysics"), ed. Maurice Bouyges, 3 vols (Beirut).
Ibn Sīnā (1938) *Al-Najāt* ("Book of Deliverance"), ed. M. al-Kurdī (Cairo).
—— (1952) *Al-Shifāʾ, al-Manṭiq, 1: al-Madkhal* ("Isagoge: Book of Healing, part 1"), eds G. Anawati, M. al-Khodairī and F. al-Ahwānī (Cairo).
—— (1970) *al-Shifā, al-Manṭiq, 3: al-ʿIbārah* ("De interpretatione: Book of Healing, part 3"), ed. M. al-Khodairī (Cairo).
Issawi, C. (1967) "European Loan-Words in Contemporary Arabic Writing: a Case Study in Modernization", *Middle Eastern Studies,* 3 (January): 110–33.
Al-Jawālīqī, (1867) *Al-Muʿarrab min al-kalām al-aʿjamī* ("Arabicized Foreign Words"), ed. E. Sachau (Leipzig).
Jeffrey, A. (1938) *The Foreign Vocabulary of the Qurʾan* (Baroda).
Al-Kindī (1950) *Rasāʾil al-Kindī al-falsafiyyah* ("al-Kindī's Philosophical Essay"), ed. M. Abū Rīḍah (Cairo).
Lane, E. (1980) *Arabic–English Lexicon* (Beirut).
Lewis, B. (1973) *Islam in History* (New York).
Mahdi, M. (1970) "Language and Logic in Classical Islam", in G. E. Von Grunebaum (ed.) *Logic in Classical Islamic Culture* (Wiesbaden).
Al-Malāʾikah, J. (1984) *Al-Muṣṭalaḥ al-ʿilmī wa-waḥdat al-fikr al-qawmī* ("The Formation of Scientific Concepts and the Unity of National Thought"), *al-Mustaqbal al-ʿArabī* ("The Arab Future"), 60 (February).
Mūsā, S. (1984) *Al-Balāghat al-ʿaṣriyyah waʾl-lughat al-ʿarabiyyah* ("Contemporary Art of Composition and the Arabic Language"), (Cairo) particularly pp. 43–6 ("*al-Lughah waʾl-mujtamaʿ*" ("Language and Society")).
Nuʿaymah, M. (1967) *Al-Ābāʾ waʾl-banūn* ("Fathers and Sons") (Beirut).
Al-Sayyid Addy Shīr (1908) *Al-Alfāẓ al-fārisiyyah al-muʿarrabah* ("The Arabicized Persian Words") (Beirut).
Sībawayh, ʿAmr ibn ʿUthmān (1966–77) *Al-Kitāb*, 5 vols, ed. ʿA. S. M. Harūn (Cairo).
Sommers, F. (1982) *The Logic of Natural Language* (Oxford).
Al-Suyuṭı, J. D. (n.d.) *Al-Muẓhir fī ʿulūm al-lughat wa-anwāʿihā* ("The Luminous in the Sciences of [Arabic] Language and its Various Kinds") (Cairo), 2nd ed. 1: 7ff.
Al-Taḥānawī (1966) *Kashshāf iṣṭilāḥāt al-funūn* ("A Dictionary of the Technical Terms"), eds Mawlawies Moḥammad Wajīh, Abd al-Ḥaqq and Gholām Kadir (Beirut).
Al-Tawḥīdī, A. H. (n.d.) *al-Imtāʿ waʾl-muʾānasah*, 2 vols, eds A. Amin and A. al-Zayn (Beirut), 1: 104–29.
Tibi, B. (1990) *Islam and the Cultural Accommodation of Social Change*, trans. Clare Krojzl (San Francisco).
Wright, W. (1975) *A Grammar of the Arabic Language,* 2 vols (Cambridge).
Zimmermann, F. W. (1981) *Al-Farabi's Commentary and Short Treatise on Aristotle's De Interpretatione* (Oxford).

CHAPTER 53

Science

Osman Bakar

INTRODUCTION

The main aim of this chapter is to discuss the position of science in relation to philosophy as it has been viewed within the religious and intellectual culture of Islam. In other words, it is concerned primarily not with the history of science in Islamic culture, which is now popularly known as Islamic science, but rather with its philosophy, the writing of which, however, necessarily presupposes a sufficient knowledge of the latter.

By "philosophy" we mean *falsafah* or *ḥikmah*. As it has been commonly understood in Islamic philosophical tradition, either term is used to refer to a particular form of knowledge as well as in the sense of a generic noun comprising several disciplines. And by "science" we mean that domain of knowledge traditionally covered under the disciplines known among Muslim scholars as (1) mathematical sciences (*'ulūm al-ta'ālīm*, or *al-'ulūm al-riyāḍiyyah*) such as arithmetic, geometry, astronomy and music and (2) natural sciences (*al-'ulūm al-ṭabī'iyyah*), including physical sciences, biological sciences and cognitive sciences (faculty psychology).

In the Islamic intellectual tradition these groups of disciplines were collectively known by different names among different groups of scholars. Among philosophers and scientists who were mainly responsible for the cultivation of these sciences, the usual term used is philosophical sciences. Among religious scholars, however, various terms like ancient sciences, foreign sciences, intellectual sciences and non-religious sciences have often been used.

Each of these names reflects to a certain extent the philosophical or intellectual attitudes of individual scholars or schools who have adopted it towards those sciences. Moreover, although science was generally presented as a branch of philosophy, there were many perspectives that shaped Muslim views concerning relations of philosophy and science. Consequently, we will present here a broad spectrum of traditional Muslim views, representing various schools of thought, concerning the nature and characteristics of science, its epistemological paradigm and its role and function in relation to the goals of both individual and social life.

SCIENCE AS A BRANCH OF PHILOSOPHY

Martin Plessner has stated correctly that "a concern for the ancient sciences in Islam began long before the period of translations; the constant dialogue with Christians and the newly converted bearers of Hellenic culture could not fail to stimulate an interest in science".[1] Muslim interest in the Hermetic sciences of alchemy and astrology, both of which were closely allied to medicine, predates the Ḥunayn translation school by more than a century.

The Umayyads founded an astronomical observatory in Damascus as early as 700. During the second half of the second/eighth century, the second 'Abbasid caliph, al-Manṣūr, was known to have gathered a number of men of science in Baghdad, including physicians from Jundishapur in Persia and astronomers from India. The second/eighth-century works of the celebrated alchemist Jābir ibn Ḥayyān (d. *c.* 800) already displayed a sound familiarity with many aspects of pre-Islamic scientific knowledge.[2] As asserted by Nasr, "the Hermetic sciences were early integrated into the Shī'ite perspective".[3]

Notwithstanding all these early manifestations of Islamic scientific and philosophic interest, Muslims did not really begin to cultivate science in the form of complete academic disciplines until after the first translations into Arabic of older philosophical, scientific and medical texts inherited mainly from the Greeks but also from Indians and Persians. Al-Kindī (*c.* 185/801–260/873), the first Muslim to cultivate philosophy and science in a serious and systematic manner, was also the first to define the epistemic position of science within the total scheme of philosophic knowledge.

It was on the basis of his firm belief in the possibility of a synthesis of Greek philosophical ideas and Islamic religious thought that al-Kindī sought to investigate the nature and scope of scientific knowledge, its philosophical foundation and the aims and methods of each of its various branches. In his work *Fī aqsām al-'ulūm* ("On the Divisions of the Sciences"), he reaffirms the Aristotelian division of philosophy into its theoretical and practical parts, and the position of science as a branch of theoretical philosophy.[4]

Consequently, an investigation into the nature of science has to be preceded by a similar kind of inquiry into the nature of philosophic knowledge. This is what al-Kindī did precisely in his treatise *On First Philosophy* (*Fi'l-falsafah al-ūlā*). There he begins by presenting *falsafah* as the highest form of human intellectual activity and of human knowledge. He defines philosophy as "knowledge of the true nature of things in so far as is possible for man".[5] Elsewhere, he defines it as "the knowledge of the eternal, universal things, of their existence, essence and causes".[6]

The two definitions are equivalent. By "the true nature of things" (*al-ashyā' bi-ḥaqā'iqiha*) al-Kindī means their existence, essence and causes, or, in short, their truths. The word *ḥaqq*, which is the singular form of the word *ḥaqā'iq* that he had used in the phrase, and which is abundantly found in the Qur'ān, means both truth and reality. And the truth or reality of a thing refers to its existence, essence and causes. As al-Kindī himself expressed it, "we do not find the truth we are seeking without finding a cause; the cause of the existence and continuance of everything is the True One [*al-Ḥaqq*], in that each thing which has being has truth".[7]

Al-Kindī's definitions of philosophy were a restatement of those given by Plato, Aristotle, and their Alexandrian commentators. Plato speaks of philosophy as the activity of "becoming like God insofar as is possible for man". And Aristotle describes philosophy as "a knowledge of the truth" which he understands as being equivalent to the ultimate nature of things or the first principles of being.[8]

Science as an academic discipline with a special kind of inquiry and as a special kind of organized knowledge has its rational basis, ontological and epistemological, in the above conception of philosophy. This assertion at least holds true for the Peripatetic school of philosopher-scientists founded by al-Kindī and whose philosophy of science was further developed, systematized and articulated by al-Fārābī and Ibn Sīnā. In this school, there are precise ontological and epistemological reasons for accepting mathematics and natural science and all their branches as parts of the philosophical sciences, and for maintaining the necessary link between science and philosophy, or more particularly the inseparability of science and metaphysics.

Al-Kindī maintains that "knowledge of the true nature of things includes knowledge of Divinity, unity and virtue, and a complete knowledge of everything useful, and of the way to it, and a distance from anything harmful, with precautions against it".[9] Philosophy thus includes metaphysics, the science of divine things, which falls under theoretical philosophy, and ethics, the science of virtues and of useful and harmful things, which forms part of practical philosophy.

In al-Kindī's ontological scheme, we encounter several different divisions of beings. First, there is the broad twofold division of beings into

(1) material (*al-jismāniyyāt*) and (2) immaterial entities. The latter he further divides into (2a) those things which have the property of being associated with matter but which are not matter in themselves, and (2b) those entities which have no matter and which are never joined to matter. As an example of immaterial objects belonging to class (2a) al-Kindī mentions in one instance geometrical shape[10] and in another instance he mentions the soul.[11]

Then there is another broad twofold division of beings into (1) divine and (2) created. The two divisions correspond to one another. In the first division, all beings belonging to class (1) and class (2a) are created while in the remaining class (2b) we have both created and divine beings. Similarly, beginning with the second division, we may arrive at the first. Divine beings are immaterial in the sense of (2b) and created beings are comprised of both material and immaterial entities.

In yet another division, al-Kindī divides beings into (1) the movables and (2) the immovables.[12] Here he identifies things which move with physical or material objects and things which do not move with immaterial entities. The three kinds of division of beings given by al-Kindī are in fact equivalent, and these represent different ways of looking at the anatomy of Reality. Any of the three divisions would be sufficient to provide him with the ontological criterion for accepting metaphysics, mathematics and natural science as the main branches of theoretical philosophy.

Metaphysics deals with divine things, the immovables, or immaterial entities which are absolutely separable from matter. Natural science investigates material things, the movables, or created beings. Although the domain and scope of mathematics is left ambiguous, and the relation of mathematical objects to both metaphysics and natural science is left undetermined, al-Kindī's acceptance of mathematics as a branch of theoretical philosophy is implied in his reference to geometrical shape as an example of immaterial entities which have the property of being associated with matter.

Moreover, in mentioning geometrical shape and the soul as entities that are a kind of intermediate in nature between material things and absolutely immaterial entities, as seen from the point of view of their respective relations with matter, al-Kindī seems to entertain the idea of mathematics and psychology as two sciences occupying an intermediary position between natural science and metaphysics. However, not only is this idea left undeveloped, but al-Kindī's tendency to go for a more simplified twofold division of beings in which the "intermediate" immaterial objects are absorbed into metaphysical entities has led some scholars to the view that in his philosophy of science the domain of mathematics is hardly distinguishable from that of metaphysics.[13]

It was left to his successors, notably al-Fārābī and Ibn Sīnā, to explore further the idea of mathematics as an intermediate science between metaphysics and natural science, to secure a stronger ontological foundation for mathematics and to remove certain ambiguities in al-Kindī's thought concerning the relation between mathematics and the other two theoretical philosophical sciences.

Muslim philosopher–scientists were generally interested in the problem of classification of the sciences, especially the theoretical philosophical sciences, and in the discussion of the relative merits and positions of these sciences in the hierarchy of knowledge. Some, however, were more detailed than others in their treatment of the problem. But they shared many common views concerning the hierarchy of the philosophical sciences and the place of mathematics and natural science in that hierarchy.

For example, they all accept the idea that the philosophical sciences admit of degrees of excellence. And they all maintain that metaphysics is the most excellent philosophical science. According to al-Fārābī, there are three criteria by means of which the hierarchy of the sciences may be established:[14]

> The excellence of the sciences and the arts is only by virtue of one of three things: the nobility of the subject matter, the profundity of the proofs, or the immensity of the benefits in that science or art, whether these benefits are anticipated or are already present. As for the [science or art] which excels others because of the immensity of its benefits, it is like the religious sciences [*al-'ulūm al-shar'iyyah*] and the crafts needed in every age and by every nation. As for that which excels others because of the profundity of its proofs, it is like geometry [*al-handasah*]. As regards that which excels others because of the nobility of its subject matter, it is like astronomy [*'ilm al-nujūm*]. However, all these three things or any two of them may well be combined in a single science such as metaphysics [*al-'ilm al-ilāhī*].[15]

This passage tells us that there are three fundamental bases of hierarchically ordering the sciences, namely the ethical, the methodological and the ontological. The ethical basis pertains to the various degrees of usefulness of the sciences defined in terms of what they could contribute to the fulfilment of practical human needs, both individual and societal. This ethical basis is implied in al-Fārābī's reference to the many practical benefits of the religious sciences and technology.

Next, the methodological basis has to do with the fact that the methods of discovering truths and of proving truth claims are more vigorous, reliable and thus more perfect in some sciences than in others. And this particular basis is implied in al-Fārābī's example of geometry as a science which is superior to many other sciences on account of the profundity of proofs (*istiqṣā' al-barāhīn*) it employs. Among Muslim philosopher–scientists, as was the case among their Greek predecessors and even among the founders of modern science like Descartes, the rigour of geometrical proofs was generally admired as perfect.

Finally, there is the ontological basis. This basis arises from the fact that existents are hierarchically ordered. Some beings are more perfect than others on the scale of existence. There is, to borrow Arthur Lovejoy's expression, a "great chain of being" in the universe. When these beings of different degrees of perfection, or of "nobility" if we were to use al-Fārābī's terminology, are investigated and studied in the different sciences, it results in the corresponding sciences having different degrees of excellence.

Al-Fārābī mentions specifically astronomy as an example of a science which is considered more excellent than many other sciences when these are evaluated according to the ontological criterion. Astronomy fulfils the criterion of having a noble subject matter because it studies the most perfect of bodies, namely celestial bodies. Al-Fārābī argues that celestial bodies have the finest and most excellent of whatever they have in common with terrestrial bodies. They have the best of shapes, which is the spherical and the best of visible qualities, which is light. Further, their motion is the best of possible motions, which is circular.

Although there is general agreement among the philosopher–scientists on the ontological criterion for dividing philosophy into theoretical and practical, and for further dividing theoretical philosophy into natural science, mathematics and metaphysics, they do not approach the problem of conceptualizing the ontological criterion in the same way. The differences in their approaches are most visible when it comes to the question of establishing the domains of natural science and mathematics and of delineating a clear boundary between them.

We have noted the fact that al-Kindī hardly discusses the nature of mathematical objects. He does not explain what is meant precisely by the expression "associated with matter" when referring to the class of immaterial entities that have the property of being associated with matter. We know that we can speak of this "association with matter" at different levels and as occurring in different modes. It is possible to distinguish, for example, between the property of possible association with any kind of matter and the property of necessary association with a specific kind of matter.

Let us consider the status of shape, the very example al-Kindī has given of immaterial entities that have the property of being associated with matter. Is there a distinction between shapes considered as mathematical objects and shapes that are treated as objects of natural science? Al-Kindī has left this question unanswered. It was al-Fārābī who first attempted to define mathematical objects in terms of their special kind of relationship with matter. He specifies them as "things that can be comprehended and conceived irrespective of any material".[16] If, for example, the square is considered a mathematical object, it is because this shape or figure can be associated at the level of concrete things with different kinds of matter and yet it can be comprehended without reference to the specific matter to which it is joined.

In the extramental world of concrete things, we can find square objects made of wood, metal, paper and many other kinds of materials. Mathematics investigates the squareness of these square objects without being concerned with the materials out of which they are made. Squareness is an existent that can be comprehended and conceived irrespective of any material. It therefore satisfies the definition of mathematical objects as given by al-Fārābī. What then constitutes the entire world of mathematical objects? Al-Fārābī defines mathematics as the science whose subject matter is comprised of the genus of numbers and magnitudes. By magnitudes he means the geometrical entities, namely lines, surfaces and solids.

In his famous classification of the sciences given in a treatise entitled *Iḥṣā' al-'ulūm* ("Enumeration of the Sciences"), he divides mathematics into seven branches. The branches are arithmetic, geometry, optics, astronomy, music, science of weights and engineering or science of ingenious devices. No one before al-Fārābī had ever given a classification of mathematics as comprehensive as this. This division raises interesting questions concerning the subject matter of mathematics and the problem of the relationship between mathematics and natural science.

What this sevenfold division of mathematics implies is that there are mathematical sciences which deal with physical bodies or concrete things as well. For example, optics deals with physical light and vision, astronomy with heavenly bodies such as the planets, and music with sound. How does al-Fārābī justify his consideration of these three sciences as well as the science of weights and the science of ingenious devices as branches of mathematics when he has defined mathematics as the science whose subject matter is comprised of numbers and magnitudes and has also stated that mathematics "does not inquire into them as being in materials"?[17] Why are these sciences more worthy to be considered as mathematical sciences rather than as natural sciences?

Al-Fārābī's justification may be summarized as follows. It is true that mathematics comprises the genus of numbers and magnitudes, but these entities are known to exist either as abstract or as concrete quantities. As abstract quantities, that is as pure numbers and magnitudes, they exist in the human mind as intelligibles that have been stripped of their accidental attributes and material attachments. As concrete quantities, they exist in or are associated with various kinds of material objects.

Al-Fārābī's mathematics deals with numbers and magnitudes not only as pure and abstract quantities but also as entities which inhere in other beings. These "other beings" range from the celestial bodies, which he considers to fall outside the domain of natural science, to the natural bodies studied by natural science. Thus when he says that mathematics does not enquire into numbers and magnitudes as being in materials he must be referring to that part of mathematics which deals with pure quantities, namely theoretical arithmetic and theoretical geometry. However, as far as his other branches of mathematics are concerned, they study natural bodies only in so far as these bodies possess the mathematical "properties of measurement and orderly proportions, composition and symmetry" by virtue of the fact that either numbers or magnitudes or both are inherent in them.

For al-Fārābī, the most fundamental of all mathematical objects are pure numbers, followed next by pure magnitudes. For this reason, he considers theoretical arithmetic and theoretical geometry to be the roots and foundations of all the sciences. His approach to the problem of defining the domain of mathematics is to start with pure numbers and magnitudes, which constitute its central domain, and then to investigate their presence in various kinds of things and how their presence results in those things acquiring such mathematical properties as measurement, orderly proportion, composition and symmetry.

On the basis of this investigation, al-Fārābī comes to the conclusion that there are beings in which numbers and magnitudes are inherent essentially. What he means is that number and magnitude enter into the very definitions of these beings. This class of beings include light and the phenomena of vision, the celestial bodies and melodies. To say that numbers and magnitudes enter into the very definitions of these beings is to say that their true natures can be known only mathematically. In this sense, these beings can be considered to attain the status of mathematical entities, and accordingly optics, astronomy and music are to be regarded primarily as mathematical sciences.

In al-Fārābī's description of the various sciences, optics, which he considers to be a subdivision of theoretical geometry, is said to be concerned with the mathematical properties of light and vision; astronomy with the mathematical forms and properties of the heavens and also of planet earth, including its climatic zones; and music with mathematical proportions which characterize melodies and musical compositions. Al-Fārābī is reaffirming here the Pythagorean idea of music as being essentially mathematical. As discovered by Pythagoras, the underlying nature of musical scales is mathematical. The definition of music as the science of proportions was generally accepted by Muslim philosopher–scientists.

It seems that even in the case of the remaining mathematical sciences – science of weights and mechanics (mechanical technology or engineering) – although these sciences are concerned with material things in which numbers and magnitudes are not inherent essentially but in which they enter into certain relations with their physical properties, al-Fārābī sees greater justification in treating them as mathematical sciences than as branches of physics. More specifically, he regards them as applied mathematics. His rationale is that the main basis of existence of the two sciences is the application of arithmetic and geometry to certain kinds of physical problems.

In other words, the two sciences are viewed as having branched out of arithmetic and geometry, primarily the latter. This view was maintained by later classificationists of sciences like Quṭb al-Dīn al-Shīrāzī (d. 712/1311) when he categorized the two as minor branches of mathematics in contrast to arithmetic and geometry which he described as its major branches.[18] Al-Fārābī's science of weights deals with the principles of measurement of weights, the production of the balance as a scientific instrument for such a kind of measurement and the principles of movements of weights. All the principles in question are basically mathematical in nature.

His science of ingenious devices deals with "ways to make all the things happen whose 'modes of existence' were stated and demonstrated in theoretical mathematics". It employs mathematical principles in the design, construction and operation of various kinds of mechanical devices, gadgets and automata. The dimensions of the various parts of these engineering products and their interrelationships are based upon those mathematical principles. Moreover, such physical principles as the hydrostatic, aerostatic or mechanical that are embodied in these devices are usually defined in mathematical terms. For all these reasons, both the science of weights and mechanics have been included among the mathematical sciences.

There is a certain Pythagorean tendency in al-Fārābī's approach to the problem of defining the domain of mathematics. His approach presupposes the idea that numbers and magnitudes permeate the whole universe and that this permeation comes from above. This leads him to investigate numbers and magnitudes in their various modes of existence, and the corresponding mathematical properties, from their metaphysical existence in the cosmic mind (the active intellect) to their mental existence in individual human minds, and finally down to their concrete existence in natural bodies as well as artificial bodies produced through human will and art.

Al-Fārābī's delineation of the scope and position of the mathematical sciences found wide and lasting acceptance in Islamic science. What makes his conception of mathematics still relevant today is the fact that there are contemporary scientists who contend that the universe revealed by twentieth-century science is very much mathematical in the sense he has defined it. In the words of the British physicist, James Jeans, "the universe now appears to be mathematical . . . the mathematics enters the universe from above instead of from below".[19]

Similarly, we still find relevant today al-Fārābī's idea of mechanical engineering as a mathematical science and the inclusion by Quṭb al-Dīn, about four centuries later, of several more engineering sciences as minor branches of mathematics in his classification of the sciences. Today, engineering sciences are no longer considered as branches of mathematics. However, it is interesting to note that, in modern engineering circles, engineering is usually described in terms of the application of mathematical processes to the solution of physical problems. This means that, even in the modern conception of engineering, it is hardly possible to define it without making explicit reference to mathematical elements. Our modern world has not succeeded in offering a more satisfactory solution to the problem of the epistemic relation between mathematics and engineering than what has been presented in traditional Islamic philosophy of science.[20]

Perhaps the best attempt at distinguishing between the objects of mathematics and those of metaphysics on the one hand and between the objects of mathematics and those of natural science on the other came from Ibn Sīnā. In this attempt[21] Ibn Sīnā defines the ontological criterion underlying the distinctions between the three classes of objects of theoretical philosophy in terms of differences in their relations with either motion or matter, both in the human mind and in extramental reality. He understands "associations with motion and matter" as having one and the same meaning.

In the introductory part or *Isagoge* of his philosophical masterpiece, *Kitāb al-shifā'*, perhaps the largest encyclopedia of knowledge ever written by an individual, Ibn Sīnā distinguishes the subject matters of natural science, mathematics and metaphysics from one another as follows:

> The various kinds of sciences therefore either (a) treat the consideration of the existents inasmuch as they are in motion, both in cognitive apprehension [*taṣawwuran*] and in subsistence, and are related to materials of particular species; (b) treat the consideration of the existents inasmuch as they separate from materials of a particular species in cognitive apprehension, but not in subsistence; or (c) treat the consideration of existents inasmuch as they are separated from motion and matter in subsistence and cognitive apprehension.
>
> The first part of the sciences is natural science. The second is the pure mathematical science, to which belongs the well-known science of number, although knowing the nature of number inasmuch as it is number does not belong to this science. The third part is divine science [i.e. metaphysics]. Since the

> existents are naturally divided into these three divisions, the theoretical philosophical sciences are these.[22]

In Ibn Sīnā's ontological scheme, the three fundamental classes of existents are: those that are necessarily unmixed with motion and matter; those that are necessarily mixed with motion and matter; and those that can mix with motion and matter but which can also have an existence separated from them. He mentions God and the soul as examples of existents belonging to the first group, which constitute the objects of metaphysics alone. The second class of existents, examples of which mentioned by him are humanity, horseness and squareness, is studied by natural science and mathematics. As for the third class of existents, Ibn Sīnā gives the examples of individual identity, unity, plurality and causality. It is this last group of existents which had been very little explored by Ibn Sīnā's predecessors as far as their status as the subject matters of the theoretical philosophical sciences is concerned.

With Ibn Sīnā came the clarification that all the three theoretical sciences share between them this last group of existents as objects of their inquiry. Although these existents can mix with motion and matter, they are treated as objects of metaphysical inquiry when they are regarded "inasmuch as they are the things they are", that is, when they are regarded in abstraction completely separate from matter as such. But when these existents are considered in their association with matter, then, like the second class of existents which are necessarily mixed with motion and matter, they become objects of inquiry of mathematics and natural science.

Ibn Sīnā, however, has a way of distinguishing between the objects of these two sciences. They are treated as mathematical objects if they can be apprehended by the mind without looking at the specific matter and motion with which they are associated in the extramental world. Otherwise, they will be regarded as objects of natural science. Taking from Ibn Sīnā's own set of examples, existents like unity, plurality and causality are said to be investigated in natural science when that unity is considered inasmuch as it is an individual substance like fire or air, that plurality considered inasmuch as it is, for instance, the four elements (i.e. fire, air, water and earth), and that causality considered inasmuch as it is warmth or coldness. However, these same existents are viewed as objects of mathematics when that unity refers to the numerical one and that plurality refers to quantitative numbers greater than one on which we can perform arithmetical operations like addition, subtraction, multiplication, division, determination of square roots, cubing and so on.

These arithmetical operations themselves, which Ibn Sīnā calls "the states of a number regarded inasmuch as an accidental thing that has no existence except in matter has occurred to them"[23] form part of the world of mathematical objects. And finally, unity, plurality and causality will be investigated as objects of metaphysics when they are considered in total abstraction from matter. With specific reference to number, Ibn Sīnā states clearly in the passage quoted earlier that there is an aspect of it, namely, "the nature of number inasmuch as it is number", which lies outside the domain of mathematics proper. Although he did not say in which science this meta-mathematical aspect of number is investigated, it is quite clear from his whole discussion that he considers it to be an object of metaphysical knowledge.[24]

Two other examples given by Ibn Sīnā help to clarify further the distinctions he makes between the objects of natural science, mathematics and metaphysics. Both squareness and the form of humanity, says Ibn Sīnā, cannot exist without matter, but whereas the former is a mathematical object, the latter is an object of natural science. This is because no special kind of matter is constitutive of the mathematical object and squareness clearly satisfies that condition. It is possible to know what squareness is without one having to pay attention to specific square objects or to some state of motion. In contrast, asserts Ibn Sīnā, one cannot understand the form of humanity or "man" without understanding that man is composed of flesh and bones.

The second example is the intellect. Ibn Sīnā maintains that the intellect in itself is a separate substance and is, therefore, an object of metaphysical inquiry. In fact, all Muslim philosopher–scientists maintain that celestial Intelligences, or what the Qur'ān calls angels, are intellects (*'uqūl*) that can have an existence separated from matter and motion. But these intellectual substances can also mix with matter and motion as one finds in human beings. It is when this intellectual substance is considered inasmuch as it is in the soul, which in the Peripatetic perspective is a principle of motion, that it becomes an object of natural science. The intellect as it exists in the individual human soul is a principle of motion of the body. This example helps to explain why Ibn Sīnā and his Peripatetic school of philosophy treat psychology as a branch of natural science.

The ontological foundation of science established by al-Fārābī and Ibn Sīnā founds a secure place in the subsequent history of Islamic philosophy and science. Distinguished philosophers and scientists from among his later successors reaffirmed the truth and legitimacy of this foundation and accepted it as an integral part of the paradigm of Islamic science. In his popular encyclopedic work, *Durrat al-tāj* ("Pearls of the Crown"), modelled after Ibn Sīnā's *Kitāb al-shifā'* but written in the Persian language during the later part of the ninth/thirteenth century not long after the destruction of Baghdad and many other neighbouring centres of learning at the hands of the Mongols, Quṭb al-Dīn al-Shīrāzī, one of the leading scientists in the history of Islam, reproduced what must have been generally accepted definitions of mathematics and natural science well before his time.

Quṭb al-Dīn defines mathematical objects as "those which cannot exist except in association with matter but which can be known without reference to matter".[25] He gives as examples numbers, squares, triangles, spheres and circles. As for the objects of natural science, he defines them as "those which are not separate from matter and which cannot be known except in association with matter". These are the natural substances: minerals, plants and animals. The different branches of natural science deal with one or more aspects of these three natural kingdoms.

It is not just the scientists and mathematicians who accepted these definitions and the ontological foundation on which these definitions are based. Even al-Ghazzālī (d. 515/1111), the greatest representative of the philosophical school of *kalām* (dialectical theology) and the most famous Muslim critic of Peripatetic philosophy, defended the legitimacy of mathematics and natural science on both philosophical and religious grounds. His classification of mathematics and natural science[26] is similar to the ones given by al-Fārābī and Ibn Sīnā except for slight variations in his enumeration of the natural sciences, especially with respect to the position of the hidden (*khafiyyah*) or occult (*gharībah*) sciences. While Ibn Sīnā had included sciences like oneiromancy (*ta'bīr*), theurgy (*nayranjiyyāt*) and natural magic (*ṭalismāt*) among the branches of natural science, al-Ghazzālī had placed them among the metaphysical sciences. The interesting point here is the fact that Ibn Sīnā the scientist and al-Ghazzālī the theologian both maintained that, ontologically speaking, there is a basis for accepting the reality of the hidden or occult sciences, although they might have questioned the pursuit of some of these sciences on ethical and moral grounds.

The difference between al-Ghazzālī and the philosopher–scientists in their classifications of mathematics and natural science is insignificant, as similar variations can also be found among the philosopher–scientists themselves. Al-Fārābī has excluded from his classification not only the hidden or occult sciences but also disciplines like medicine, alchemy and agriculture. With Ibn Sīnā, medicine and alchemy appear among the natural sciences, while with Quṭb al-Dīn all the three sciences were treated as minor branches of natural science. In excluding these sciences from his classification of philosophy, al-Fārābī was motivated not by ontological but rather by methodological considerations. It has been shown that al-Fārābī's classification of philosophy is limited to the syllogistic arts or sciences.[27] He had omitted the sciences in question from his list of the philosophical sciences as he considered them to be non-syllogistic.[28]

Taken as a whole, however, al-Ghazzālī's classification of mathematics and natural science clearly shows that he accepted the ontological foundation of science established by the Peripatetic philosophers. His quarrel with them is not over the issue of the legitimacy and usefulness of science but over something else which he had itemized into twenty philosophical issues in his famous work *Tahāfut al-falāsifah* ("The Incoherence of the Philosophers"). He even defended their scientific methodology based primarily on the concept of the demonstrative proof (*al-burhān*) while reminding them of its limitations when it comes to the domain of religious and metaphysical truths, and rejecting their theory of causality since in his view there is no necessary connection between that theory and the demonstrative (scientific) method. Al-Ghazzālī reproached those Muslims who opposed science just because it has been ascribed to the philosophers (*falāsifah*).

In the western lands of Islam, the same can be said of the Andalusian jurist, theologian and historian and philosopher of religion, Ibn Ḥazm (d. 454/1064). Like al-Ghazzālī, he accepted the legitimacy of the mathematical and natural sciences as scientific disciplines on both ontological and methodological grounds. In some ways, he was even more positive than al-Ghazzālī in his attitude towards science and philosophy, partly perhaps because, unlike his younger contemporary from Persia, he did receive a relatively broad formal education in logic and science, especially in medicine.[29] In his work *Risālat al-tawāqif ʿalā shāriʿ al-najāh bi-ikhtiṣār al-ṭarīq* ("Treatise for Setting Up the Way of Salvation in a Brief Manner"), Ibn Ḥazm praises philosophy as

> a good and lofty science because it contains the knowledge of all the world in all aspects pertaining to genera, species, individual substances, and accidents. It also enables the individual to arrive at the scientific proof without which nothing can be certain, and which discerns what is believed to be a proof from what is not. The usefulness of this knowledge is great for discerning realities from non-realities.[30]

Late classifications of the sciences such as those of the famous historian Ibn Khaldūn (d. 808/1406) and Shams al-Dīn al-Āmulī written during the ninth/fifteenth century after the numerous branches of Islamic science had undergone centuries of development and attained their full maturity further confirm the immutability of the fundamental ontological truths on which that science had been based. They also confirm the remarkably broad intellectual consensus reached by the various schools of thought in Islam concerning those ontological truths. Within this unity, however, there have been differences among the scientists themselves as well as between them and the religious authorities pertaining to the epistemic status and the scientific character of some of the sciences like astrology, alchemy, the science of interpretation of dreams and the occult sciences.

There were even a few attempts aimed at a critical re-examination of the position of particular individual sciences that have been traditionally considered as branches either of mathematics or of natural science.

The most significant of these attempts, particularly from the point of view of the modern philosophy of science, was the one made by Ibn al-Haytham (d. 430/1039) to take a fresh look at optics. In modern science, optics is considered one of the physical sciences whereas in Islamic science, ever since al-Fārābī reproduced for Muslims Proclus' classic statement on the subject matter of Greek optics, it has always been treated as a mathematical science. The significance of Ibn al-Haytham's fresh examination of the position of optics as a scientific discipline lies in the fact that he was the first to have transformed that science into an interdisciplinary field of study and explicitly acknowledged the nature of that science as such.

In his *Kitāb al-manāẓir* ("Book of Optics"), which has come to be acknowledged by present-day historians of science as the most complete and most advanced work on optics since Ptolemy's treatise on the subject, and also in his few other optical writings, Ibn al-Haytham presented optics as a composite science. If optics were to develop into a truly complete science of vision, he says, then it must combine mathematics and natural science. Optics depends on natural science because "vision is the activity of one of the senses and these belong to the natural things". It also involves the mathematical sciences because "sight perceives shape, position, magnitude, movement and rest" and all these things are investigated by the mathematical sciences.[31] In his attempt to place optics on new foundations, Ibn al-Haytham broadened its scope by redefining its subject matter so as to include all mathematical, physical and psychological existents pertaining to vision.

The synthetic character of its subject matter demands a corresponding synthesis in its methodology. Thus Ibn al-Haytham speaks of a complete scientific investigation in optics as being composed of two distinct modes of inquiry, namely a physical inquiry into the nature of light, or of transparency or of the ray, and a mathematical inquiry into their modes of behaviour. Ibn al-Haytham's idea of a composite science does not involve the questioning of the ontological basis of either mathematics or natural science. Rather, it raises the interesting question of the possible existence of a science whose subject matter is comprised of phenomena which involve the objects of investigation of several distinct disciplines. With Ibn al-Haytham, optics was no longer just a mathematical science nor simply a natural science. Rather, it was a synthesis of the two sciences. However, optics continues after him to be considered a mathematical science by most Muslim authorities.

METHODOLOGY OF ISLAMIC SCIENCE

Islamic intellectual tradition upholds the idea of the hierarchy and unity of knowledge and of modes of knowing. There are many sources and forms of knowledge, and there are many ways of knowing. In Islam, all possible avenues to knowledge are duly recognized. Each avenue is accorded a legitimate place and function within the total epistemological scheme furnished by the revealed teachings of the religion. This has been the general view of Muslim scholars regardless of whether they are scientists, philosophers, theologians or Sufis.

Observation and experimentation, logical thinking, mathematical analysis and even rational interpretation of sacred Books, not just of Islam but of all humanity, all have their legitimate roles to play in the scientific enterprise of traditional Muslim scientists. If we look at the scientific treatises of famous scientists like Ibn Sīnā, al-Bīrūnī, Naṣīr al-Dīn al-Ṭūsī and Quṭb al-Dīn al-Shīrāzī such as those dealing with astronomy, geology, medicine and cosmology, we will find them arguing not just on the basis of empirical and rational data but also on the foundation of revealed data. Far from generating theoretical conflicts that defy solutions, these different types of data, on the contrary, serve to complement and strengthen each other.

Ibn al-Haytham, for example, presented the principle which says, "Everything whose nature is made subject of inquiry must be investigated in a manner conformable to its kind."[32] Following this general principle, which, of course, was already known to and observed by Muslim scholars before Ibn al-Haytham, they came to hold the view that each discipline is characterized by a particular mode of enquiry, which can be either simple or composite. However, this broad agreement aside, there are points of contention between the different intellectual schools, much more so here in matters pertaining to methodology than in those pertaining to ontology.

Muslim Peripatetic philosophers and scientists have often referred to themselves as "men of logic and demonstration" (*ahl al-manṭiq wa'l-burhān*). In their logical works they usually speak of a type of proof or reasoning which is not unique to science but which is common to all the philosophical sciences, including metaphysics. The technical term they use to refer to this type of proof is *al-burhān*, which means "demonstration". This method of demonstration may be described as their "scientific method", which is not to be equated with the modern scientific method since the former connotes a far wider meaning. The demonstrative method or proof is that method or proof by means of which one obtains new knowledge that is true and certain. In other words, the demonstrative method necessarily leads to rational or intellectual certainty.

This method is distinguished from other methods by the fact that it employs syllogisms or logical reasonings that make use of premisses that are "true, primary and necessary". The certain nature of this category of premisses, which may consist of empirical data provided by the senses or rational (intellectual) data furnished by intuition, revelation, logical reasoning or even spiritual experience, means that the conclusions will necessarily be true and certain knowledge, and this is what makes the demonstrative proof the most scientific of all proofs.

Philosopher–scientists take great pride in being associated with this method. Al-Fārābī, for example, maintains that this method is characteristic of the philosophical sciences alone and that it is on account of this method that these sciences must be considered superior to the religious sciences which at best employ dialectical proofs. Theologians like al-Ghazzālī deny the demonstrative method its competence to establish or arrive at the certainty of metaphysical truths, although in the domain of science itself they acknowledge the usefulness and excellence of this method. Interestingly, al-Kindī also speaks of the limitations of this method when he says that "we ought not to seek a demonstrative finding in the apprehension of every pursuit for not every intellectual pursuit is found through demonstration, since not everything has a demonstration".[33]

The concept of demonstrative method is a broad one. It is still possible to analyse it into its different components, namely the physical or empirical method, the mathematical method and the metaphysical method. The mathematical method, for example, would make use of premisses that are constituted of mathematical data regardless of the source from which they are drawn. Thus while in theory all philosopher–scientists acknowledge the possibility of various modes of knowing and inquiry, and accept the method of demonstration as the most scientific of all inquiries, in practice each philosopher–scientist may show a flair for certain types of demonstration. With al-Kindī, mathematics is the chief instrument of demonstration to the extent that even in medicine he made use of the mathematical method.[34] In his theory of the compound remedies, he based the efficacy of these remedies, like the effect of music, upon geometrical proportion.

With Ibn Rushd, demonstration is achieved primarily through physical or empirical inquiry. Thus in his *Kitāb al-kulliyyāt* he criticized strongly al-Kindī's use of "the arts of arithmetic and music" in the art of medicine. With Ibn al-Haytham, both physical and mathematical inquiries play an equally important role in his demonstrative or scientific method.

In contrast to the Peripatetic philosopher–scientists who emphasize logic and demonstration, the Hermetic–Pythagorean scientists and philosophers, who also played an important role in Islamic science, adopted a methodological approach that is based primarily upon a metaphysical and symbolic interpretation of things. This is the kind of approach used for example by Jābir ibn Ḥayyān in alchemy and by the Ikhwān al-Ṣafā' in the various mathematical sciences. Certain elements of this method are also to be found in the scientific methodology of those scientists whom we usually identify with the Peripatetic school such as Ibn Sīnā.

AIMS AND ROLE OF SCIENCE

It is over the question of the aims and role of science in relation to both individual and social needs that there has been perhaps the least consensus among the different intellectual schools of Islam. All of them acknowledge the usefulness of science. However, they differ in their views concerning the extent of that usefulness. Jurists and theologians generally maintain that science is useful only in so far as it serves as a tool for understanding and implementing the Divine Law. This view was much emphasized by scholars like Ibn Ḥazm and al-Ghazzālī. In his *The Book of Knowledge*, al-Ghazzālī describes many branches of science such as medicine, astronomy and arithmetic as praiseworthy intellectual sciences or as *farḍ kifāyah* sciences in the sense of being indispensable for the welfare of this world. Medicine is necessary for the life of the body, and arithmetic for daily transactions and the division of legacies and inheritances.[35]

In another work, *Deliverance from Error*, al-Ghazzālī maintains that the mathematical sciences are purely quantitative or exact sciences which "do not entail denial or affirmation of religious matters". It is quite clear that he does not see any role for mathematics in spiritual and metaphysical matters. The Ikhwān al-Ṣafā' took a different intellectual stand. For them, numbers and geometrical figures, when seen as qualities and symbols, are not neutral with respect to spiritual truths but rather lend support to them. They affirmed the view of Pythagoras that "the knowledge of numbers and of their origin from unity is the knowledge of the Unity of God". Further, "the knowledge of properties of numbers, their classification and order is the knowledge of the beings created by the Exalted Creator, and of His handiwork, its order and classification".[36]

Peripatetic philosopher-scientists also recognized the role of science beyond its usefulness in practical and technological matters. They emphasized the idea that the theoretical philosophical sciences are pursued first of all for the sake of the rational soul. Science as a branch of theoretical philosophy is therefore useful in the quest for the perfection of the soul, which is a necessary condition for happiness in this world and in the life hereafter. According to Ibn Sīnā, "the purpose in theoretical philosophy is to perfect the soul simply by knowing".[37] In general, they maintain that through science people can fulfil many of their rational and intellectual needs, like the needs for causality and rational certainty.

NOTES

1 Martin Plessner, "The Natural Sciences and Medicine", in J. Schacht and C. E. Bosworth (eds), *The Legacy of Islam* (Oxford, 1979), 2nd ed.: 428.

2 That ancient, pre-Islamic authorities, primarily Greek, are cited, invoked or quoted in abundance in works attributed to Jābir is well known. But, added to all these, a recent study of Jābir's *Book of Stones* announces the discovery of a Jābirian translation of Aristotle's *Categoriae* which is "totally and significantly independent of Isḥāq's text". See Syed Nomanul Haq, *Names, Natures, and Things: the Alchemist Jābir ibn Ḥayyān and his Kitāb al-Aḥjār* (*Book of Stones*) (Dordrecht, London and Boston, 1994).

3 S. H. Nasr, *An Introduction to Islamic Cosmological Doctrines* (Boulder, 1978), 2nd ed. 14.

4 This treatise is found in *Rasā'il al-Kindī al-falsafiyyah*, ed. M. 'A. H. Abū Rīdah (Cairo, 1950–3), 2. Discussions of al-Kindī's classification of the sciences may be found in G. N. Atiyeh, *Al-Kindi: The Philosopher of the Arabs* (Rawalpindi, 1966): 32–40; and L. Gardet, "Le Problème de la philosophie musulmane", in *Mélanges offerts à Etienne Gilson* (Paris, 1959): 261–84.

5 See Alfred L. Ivry, *Al-Kindī's Metaphysics: a Translation of Ya'qūb ibn Isḥāq al-Kindī's Treatise "On First Philosophy"* (Albany, 1974): 55.

6 See his "On the Definition and Description of Things", in Abū Rīdah, *op. cit.*: 173.

7 Ivry, *op. cit.*: 55.

8 *Metaphysics*, 1.3.9836.2.

9 Ivry, *op. cit.*: 59.

10 Ivry, *op. cit.*: 62. (Cf. *Rasā'il*, 1: 108.)

11 *Rasā'il*, 2: 10.

12 Ivry, *op. cit.*: 65.

13 See Majid Fakhry, *A History of Islamic Philosophy* (New York, 1983), 2nd ed.: 73.

14 I have discussed these criteria in great detail in my book *Classification of Knowledge in Islam: a Study in Islamic Philosophies of Science* (Kuala Lumpur, 1992).

15 Al-Fārābī, *Risālat fī faḍīlat al-'ulūm wa'l-ṣinā'āt* ("Treatise on the Excellence of the Sciences and the Arts"). My translation is based on the Arabic text in F. Dieterici, *Al-Farabi's philosophische Abhandlungen* (Leiden, 1980): 105.

16 *Al-Farabi's Philosophy of Plato and Aristotle*, trans. and with an introduction by M. Mahdi (Ithaca, 1969): 18.

17 *Ibid.*: 19.

18 On Quṭb al-Dīn's classification of the sciences, see O. Bakar (1992): chapter 11.

19 James Jeans discussed at length the theme of the scientific picture of the universe as being essentially mathematical in nature in his *The Mysterious Universe* (Cambridge, 1931).

20 Cf. Donald R. Hill's remarks on the mechanical engineering of Ibn al-Razzāz al-Jazarī (flourished *c.* beginning of the seventh/thirteenth century) in his translation with annotations of the latter's *The Book of Knowledge of Ingenious Mechanical Devices* (Dordrecht and Boston), 1974): 279.

21 Ibn Sīnā deals with the ontological basis for the division of theoretical philosophy into natural, mathematical and metaphysical sciences in several of his works. See, for example, both the logical (*al-madkhal*) and metaphysical (*ilāhiyyāt*) parts of his masterpiece of Peripatetic philosophy, *Kitāb al-shifā'* ("The Book of Healing" rendered as *Sufficientia* in Latin); see also his treatise *Fī aqsām al-'ulūm* ("On the Division of the Sciences").

22 Translated by Michael E. Marmura in his "Avicenna on the Division of the Sciences in the *Isagoge* of his *Shifā'*", *Journal for the History of Arabic Science*, 4(1 & 2) (1980): 246.

23 Marmura, *op. cit.*: 245.

24 This view accords fully with the belief generally held in traditional Islamic philosophy of mathematics that numbers exist on three levels of reality: (1) as archetypes in the Divine Intellect and, therefore, as metaphysical objects, (2) as abstract or "scientific" entities in the human mind, and (3) as concrete quantities in material things. See S. H. Nasr (1976): 88.

25 See Bakar, *op. cit.*: 252.

26 For the classification in question, see his *al-Risālat al-laduniyyah* ("Presential Knowledge") trans. into English by M. Smith in *Journal of the Royal Asiatic Society* (1938), part 2: 177–200 and part 3: 353–74; also his *Kitāb al-'Ilm* ("The Book of Knowledge"), trans. N. A. Faris (Lahore, 1962). I have systematized and synthesized the two classifications to produce a more detailed classification. See Bakar, *op. cit.*: chapter 9.

27 See Bakar, *op. cit.*: chapters 3 and 5.

28 On the distinction between syllogistic and non-syllogistic arts, al-Fārābī writes: "The syllogistic arts are those which, when their parts are integrated and perfected, have as their action thereafter the employment of syllogism, while the non-syllogistic arts are those which, when their parts are integrated and perfected, have as their action and end the doing of some particular work, such as medicine, agriculture, carpentry, building, and the other arts which are designed to produce some work and some actions." See D. M. Dunlop, ed. and trans., "Al-Fārābī's Introductory *Risālah* on Logic", *The Islamic Quarterly*, vol. 3 (1956–7): 231–2.

29 Ibn Ḥazm's teachers in medicine include the Jewish physician Ismā'īl ibn Yūnus, the leading Muslim authority on surgery al-Zahrāwī, and Ibn al-Kattānī, a prominent natural scientist. It was Ibn al-Kattānī, however, who exerted the greatest influence on Ibn Ḥazm's scientific training. Some sources attributed as many as ten medical works to Ibn Ḥazm. On Ibn Ḥazm's education in science and philosophy, see A. G. Chejne, *Ibn Ḥazm* (Chicago, 1982). 37–41.

30 *Ibid.*: 152.

31 See *Ibn al-Haytham: Optics*, trans. with introduction and commentary by A. I. Sabra (London, 1989), 1: 4.

32 *Ibid.*, 2: 4.

33 Ivry, *op. cit.*: 65–6.

34 See Nicholas Rescher, *Studies in Arabic Philosophy* (Pittsburgh, 1967): 5–6; also T. J. de Boer, *The History of Philosophy in Islam*, trans. E. R. Jones (London, 1903): 100.
35 Faris, *op. cit.*: 37.
36 Nasr, *Science and Civilization in Islam*: 155.
37 See Marmura, *op. cit.*: 241.

SELECT BIBLIOGRAPHY

Bakar, Osman (1991) *Tawḥīd and Science: Essays on the History and Philosophy of Islamic Science* (Kuala Lumpur and Penang).
— (1992) *Classification of Knowledge in Islam: a Study of Islamic Philosophies of Science* (Kuala Lumpur).
Ivry, Alfred L. (1974) *Al-Kindi's Metaphysics: a Translation of Ya'qub ibn Isḥaq al-Kindī's Treatise "On First Philosophy"* (Albany).
Gillispie, C. (ed.) (1970–) *Dictionary of Scientific Biography* (New York).
Hourani, G. F. (ed.) (1975) *Essays on Islamic Philosophy and Science* (Albany).
Nasr, S. H. (1968) *Science and Civilization in Islam* (Cambridge, Mass.).
— (1976) *Islamic Science: an Illustrated Study* (London).
— (1978) *An Introduction to Islamic Cosmological Doctrines* (Boulder).
Schacht, J. and Bostworth, C. E. (eds) *The Legacy of Islam* (Oxford), 2nd ed.

CHAPTER 54

Mysticism

Mahmud Erol Kiliç

Classical Muslim thought generally seems to regard the meaning of the word *philosophia* only in the sense of its second term *sophia*, distinguishing not only a literary difference between the two terms but also a difference in meaning and reference. Thus *philosophia*, the study of divine wisdom, is understood as *sophia*, divine wisdom in itself. This distinction emphasizes the necessity of the spiritual receptivity of the seeker rather than his mere conceptual comprehension. Since God is al-Ḥakīm (The Wise), the source of all wisdom, a *ḥakīm* (theosopher) is one who receives and participates in divine wisdom. Therefore to study *ḥikmah* (theosophy) is to undertake a journey towards God; towards divinity; in other words, to al-Ḥakīm. The Qur'ān says, "He unto whom the wisdom [*ḥikmah*] is given he truly had received abundant good" (2: 269). While this verse clearly states that wisdom is *given* by God and *received* rather than acquired by humanity, it also indicates that such wisdom is accessible to those prepared to receive it, those who undertake the journey towards Divine Perfection.

As we consider the following definitions of wisdom by some major Islamic figures of philosophy and gnosis, we shall see that they contain an essentially initiatic and esoteric meaning. For example, al-Kindī says:

> Philosophy is the knowledge of the reality of things within man's possibility, because the philosopher's end in his theoretical knowledge is to gain truth and in his practical knowledge to be in accordance with truth . . . philosophy is to act like God's action.[1]

Al-Kindī goes on to tell us that the soul is a light from God, which when detached from the limitations of the body is able to know everything and therefore nothing is hidden from it. When ancient sages realized that it was not possible to attain to the true nature of things (*ḥaqā'iq al-ashyā'*) through the senses or by reasoning, their asceticism brought them to the point where the knowledge of the unseen could be revealed to them, and they then attained to the mystery of creation.[2] "Philosophy is man's knowing himself . . . the art of arts."[3] Al-Fārābī defines philosophy as "comprehension of Being",[4] and Ibn Sīnā as "to know the true nature of things as much as one possibly can".[5] Still, there is a distinction to be made between the *falāsifah* of the Peripatetic school and the gnostics and Illuminationists. For example, Ibn 'Arabī defines *ḥikmah* succinctly as *taṣawwuf* (Sufism)[6] and also as "knowledge of the special knowledge".[7] Suhrawardī says:

> Those who have not yet detached themselves from the limitation of the body and made themselves available to undertake a spiritual journey cannot be regarded as *ḥakīm* . . . Do not pay any attention to the ideas of the materialists who pretend to be philosophers; *the issue is greater than they think*.[8]

Suhrawardī makes his mystical concern explicit when he says that Peripatetics "are those who do not depend upon initiatic experience but upon their reasoning in their quest for knowledge".[9]

Ibn Sīnā, about whom it has been said that he came to the gnostic path after having been affected by the powerful gaze of the Sufi master Abū Yūsuf al-Hamadānī in the streets of Hamadan, is not at all rationalistic in his view of the soul and intellect. He says:

> *Al-nafs al-nāṭiqah* [the human soul] is empty in terms of intelligible forms. When it contacts the active intellect these forms pour into it and it eventually becomes the abode of the forms. All the intelligibles [*ma'qūlāt*] which are at once potential and veiled have been actualized by the illumination of the Active Intellect. When the soul contacts the Active Intellect and because of its nature participates in the Active Intellect's process of knowing, then naturally it can receive something from the Active Intellect according to its pureness. The soul receives the reflection of the First Being through the participation of the celestial world. Mystical knowledge is the continuation and perhaps the more advanced stage of natural rational knowledge. What distinguishes mystical knowledge from natural rational knowledge is not its forms but its objects . . . The revelation of the unseen [*ghayb*] can occur in intense thought. But sometimes it can come within the experiences of a gnostic [*'ārif*].[10]

Ibn Sīnā also observes in another text that "When an initiate [*sālik*] practises enough ascetic discipline and spiritual effort, his or her soul and secret [*sirr*] becomes a mirror which reflects the Real [*al-Ḥaqq*]."[11]

Although we could present numerous examples indicating the mystical and initiatic nature of wisdom, the preceding passages sufficiently prove that many Islamic thinkers who possessed the authentic tradition, even some who were Peripatetics, penetrated to the esoteric core of Islam. Even some of the so-called Peripatetics became very sympathetic to the initiatic path of knowledge in the later period of their lives. We have a striking example in the communication between Abū Sa'īd Abi'l-Khayr and Ibn Sīnā. It is said that Abū Sa'īd wrote to Ibn Sīnā, inviting him to "Come to the true path, a path of knowledge, come to true Islam!" Ibn Sīnā responded, "*Āy bi kufr-i ḥaqīqī wa barāy az islām-i majāzī*" ("You should come from metaphorical Islam to a true infidelity!"). Upon reading these words, the Shaykh was overwhelmed by ecstasy and said, "During my seventy years of worship I have never experienced such a joy as for this response." It is this Ibn Sīnā who travelled through the "Stages of the Gnostics" (*Maqāmāt al-'ārifīn*) to attain the Oriental wisdom and become a real theosopher.

These examples illustrate that it is possible to state that the true Islamic philosophy is essentially a mystical philosophy. Any difference which arises is that between the approaches of the theoretical and initiatic ways of life. Regarding the attainment of knowledge, there are two groups: the possessors of theoretical knowledge, namely the *falāsifah*; and the possessors of real knowledge and *maqām*, namely Sufis (gnostics) and *muḥaqqiqūn*, the true *ḥakīms* of Islam.

The ontological position of those who possess *ḥāl* (spiritual state) is always higher than of those who possess *qāl* (conceptual knowledge). However, there are those who do not endorse the stages of *qāl* as possession of any metaphysical grade at all. The real difference between the two groups is that, while the possessors of *ḥāl* have their referent in vertical knowledge and experience, the possessors of *qāl* make their reference horizontal experience and rational and historical information. Real philosophers "are not those who would report any statements of the sages or the statement of others. In our works we set down only the result of revelation and dictates of the Truth to us."[12]

According to Ibn 'Arabī, who represents the gnostics rather than the *falāsifah*, spiritual travellers, that is individuals engaged in the search for metaphysical knowledge, are of two groups. The first group travels toward God with their thought (*afkār*) and rationality. They inevitably stray from the road, because they accept only the guidance of their own thinking. They are the philosophers and those who follow a corresponding course (*mutakallimūn*). The other group of those who travel are the messengers and prophets and the chosen saints. It is the possession of real knowledge that distinguishes one group from the other.

> The sciences of reason derived from thinking contain an element of changeability, because they follow the temper [*mizāj*] of thinking in the intelligent individual. He considers only the sensible matters which may have existence in his imagination and

> accordingly are his evidence. The result is that the theories with respect to one and the same thing differ or one and the same investigator differs with respect to the same things at different times, because of differences in temper and mixture and combinations in their state of being. Thus their statements differ with respect to one and the same thing and with respect to basic principles upon which they construct their details. In contrast, directly inspired and legislative knowledge possesses one and the same taste, even if the perception of this taste differ.[13]

A contemporary Muslim gnostic also explains the "Oriental Wisdom" almost one thousand years after Shaykh al-Ra'īs ibn Sīnā, demonstrating that this concept is not geographical or national, but vertical, illuminative and metaphysical:

> To comprehend universal principles directly, the transcendent intellect must itself be of the universal order; it is no longer an individual faculty, and to consider it as such would be contradictory, as it is not within the power of the individual to go beyond his own limits . . . Reason is a specifically human faculty but that which lies beyond reason is truly "non-human"; it is this that makes metaphysical knowledge possible, and that knowledge is not a human knowledge. In other words, it is not as man that man can attain it, but because this being that is human in one of its aspects is at the same time something other and more than a human being. It is the attainment of effective consciousness of supra-individual states that is the real object of metaphysics, or better still, of metaphysical knowledge itself . . . in reality the individuality represents nothing more than a transitory and contingent manifestation of the real being. It is only one particular state among the indefinite multitude of other states of the same being . . . Such is the fundamental distinction between "self" and "I", the personality and the individuality . . . so the individuality . . . is bound by personality to the principal centre of being by this transcendent intellect . . . Theoretical knowledge, which is only indirect and in some sense symbolic, is merely a preparation, though indispensable, for true knowledge. It is, moreover, the only knowledge that is communicable, even then only in a partial sense. That is why all statements are no more than a means of approaching knowledge, and this knowledge, which is in the first place only virtual, must later be effectively realized . . . there is nothing in common between metaphysical realization and the means leading to it . . . [for example] concentration harmonizes the diverse elements of human individuality in order to facilitate affective communication

> between this individuality and higher states of being. Moreover, at the start, these means can be varied almost indefinitely, for they have to be adapted to the temperament of each individual to his particular aptitudes and disposition. Later on the differences diminish, for it is a case of many ways that all lead to the same end; after reaching a certain stage, all multiplicity vanishes . . . it is from this human state, itself contingent, that we are at present compelled to start in order to attain higher states and finally the supreme and unconditioned state . . . This realization of integral individuality is described by all traditions as the restoration of what is called a primordial state . . . [this] second state corresponds to the supra-individual but still conditioned states, though their conditions are quite different from those of the human state. Here the world of man, previously mentioned, is completely and definitely exceeded . . . by the world of forms in its widest meaning. . . . Nevertheless, however exalted these states may be when compared with the human state, however remote they are from it, they are still only relative, and that is just as true of the highest of them. Their possession is only a transitory result, which should not be confused with the final goal of metaphysical realization; this end remains outside being, and by comparison with it everything else is only a preparatory step. The highest objective is the absolutely unconditioned state, free from limitation; for this reason it is completely inexpressible . . . In this Unconditioned State all other states of being find their place.[14]

Muslim gnostics and Sufis claim that, since the hierarchical status of being requires a hierarchical status of knowing, then it is natural to envisage that there are different degrees of qualitative knowledge corresponding to different stages of ontological Being. And, according to the Sufis, a person who possesses the higher stages is regarded as a guide for those in the lower stages. The knowledge that belongs to the higher stages of reality is possible only through revelation. It is not the rational soul of the *falsafah* but the illuminated soul of the gnostic or Sufi which is capable of real metaphysical knowledge. Unlike the systematic logic of the Peripatetics, this metaphysical knowledge can be conveyed to the unilluminated only through the language of symbolism. For this reason we can regard the *Mathnawī* of Rūmī, some of Ibn 'Arabī's writings, Rūzbihān's *Shaṭḥiyyāt*, Mawlānā Jāmī's *Salāmān and Absāl*, the *Dīwān* of Shaykh Ghālib and other works of symbolic mysticism as philosophy according to its definition by the gnostics.

However, the perspective of the *philosophia perennis* does not consider it relevant to distinguish between Islamic philosophers who are involved in Sufism and Sufis who are involved in philosophy. Both are able to understand the one and the same Reality according to their degree of approximation to It. In this sense, every seeker of the Truth is classified according to his or her correspondence with the Centre. Those who are close to the Centre are regarded as more similar to it than those who are far from the Centre. Since ontological status reflects epistemological standing, it is not surprising that the knowledge of one individual should be more esoteric and universal and another more exoteric and particular. The travellers of the esoteric path to Truth in the meta-philosophical domain are called *walī*, *mutaṣawwif*, *muḥaqqiq* and *'ārif*, according to their standing. Al-Ghazzālī, who himself travelled these intellectual stages, presents a similar classification in *The Niche for Lights*.

According to him, the soul, in its upward sevenfold way to union with pure Deity, is at every stage stripped of these veils, the dark one first and then the bright ones. After that the naked soul stands face to face with naked Deity, with Absolute Being, with an unveiled Sun, with unadulterated Light. These veils are various according to varieties of the natures which they veil from the one Real.

Al-Ghazzālī grades not only souls but also systems according to their proximity to Absolute Truth in the order of logic and the mathematical sciences and the sciences of Being. The most respected are the sciences of Being which deal not only with contingent beings but with Necessary Being in regard to its Names and Attributes.

> You should know that intellectual sciences are holistic in their content, and from which theoretical knowledge issues. It is both theoretical knowledge and intellectual knowledge that form Sufi knowledge. There are many aspects of Sufi knowledge, such as *ḥāl*, *waqt*, *shawq*, *wajd*, *sukr*, *ṣaḥw*, *iṯhbāt*, *maḥw*, *faqr*, *walāyah* and *irādah*. *Ḥikmah* can be attained only through the given knowledge. Those who do not reach that stage cannot be named "sage" [*al-ḥakīm*], since wisdom is a gift of God.[15]

Specific and very important to the Muslim gnostics is the dynamic and active "being" in the hierarchical structure called the Muḥammadan Reality (*al-ḥaqīqat al-muḥammadiyyah*), considered the first manifestation of Supreme and Unconditioned Being. As the first manifestation, the Muḥammadan Reality is thus also the highest locus of knowledge. According to the great Sufi 'Ayn al-Quḍāt Hamadānī, the esoteric knowledge of the Muḥammadan Reality is an epistemological stage which can lead to Divine knowledge.

> There are three stages in the knowledge of the Truth. The first is the knowledge of God's action and his command which can be gained through the soul. The second is the knowledge of Attributes of God which can be attained through the

Muḥammadan Soul [*al-Nafs al-muḥammadiyyah*]. The third is the knowledge of the Godhead [*al-dhāt al-ilāhiyyah*] which is beyond any description. The grace of a person who possesses such knowledge is always hoped for. The Prophet Muḥammad said, "Whoever has seen me has seen the Truth." Therefore those who do not know themselves cannot know the Prophet Muḥammad and whoever does not know him cannot know God. If one wants to know God in the deep sense, what one has to do is to make one's own soul a mirror and to see the soul of Muḥammad; through the soul of Muḥammad only one would be able to know God Himself. Jāmī says:

> This world is a mirror, all things through the Truth exist.
> In the mirror Muḥammad, God is seen to persist.

One needs to acquire the knowledge of God in this world because what you receive by knowledge today is to be seen tomorrow. Jāmī says:

> Wisdom of Greece itself is a passion and inclination.
> But the wisdom of believers is a command of the Prophet.[16]

As a traveller traverses each stage step by step, he or she is said to become a person of each particular stage who has the knowledge of that stage. A person of each particular stage remains in ignorance of the knowledge of the stage above. Certain Sufi masters teach the secret knowledge of the stages to those qualified by their inherent capacity to receive wisdom. Although the method of training differs from master to master, most of the Ottoman Sufi masters trained their candidates according to the following schema.

Knowledge descends from the upper stages to the lower. The recognition of the descending gradation of knowledge which establishes the ascending stages of wisdom is very important, itself constituting to the first knowledge. In their journey of the purification of the soul, the travellers toward Reality arrive first at the stage of the Lower Soul (*al-Nafs al-ammārah*), and then ascend in order through the Inspired Soul (*al-Nafs al-mulhamah*), the Soul at Peace (*al-Nafs al-muṭma'innah*), the Pleased Soul (*al-Nafs al-rāḍiyyah*), and the Being-Pleased Soul (*al-Nafs al-marḍiyyah*). The final stage in the purification of the soul is the Perfected Soul (*al-Nafs al-kāmilah*).

After passing through the degrees of the purification of the soul, the traveller begins the stage of the purification of the spirit (*rūḥ*). In this stage of purification the traveller reaches first the inner centres of the Heart (*qalb*), then the Spirit (*rūḥ*), Secret (*sirr*), Secret of Secret (*sirr al-sirr*), Arcane (*khifā*), and finally the Most Arcane (*akhfā*). The Most Arcane is directly receptive to Divine Reality, which illuminates the purified traveller. An illuminated person is therefore one who has passed through the stages of the self, the thorough cleansing of the Heart, the emptying of the Secret and the Illumination of the Spirit. According to the traditional perspective, only one of this degree can be called a theosopher, a philosopher or a sage.

According to Muslim gnostics, a sage is one who has passed through the various stages, also described in the following manner:

First stage. In this stage the abode of the spiritual traveller is lowliness; the invocation is "There is no god but God"; and the direction of travelling is "progress towards God"; the state is that of alternating spiritual optimism and pessimism. The realm of the traveller is that of sense perception.

Second stage. In this stage the abode of the spiritual traveller is blaming; the invocation is *Allāh*, the esoteric meaning of which is "There is no aim but Allah." The direction of travelling is "progress to God"; and the state is "contraction and expansion" (*qabḍ wa basṭ*). The realm is the Isthmus (*'ālam al-barzakh*). In this stage love for this world begins to disappear. The degree of certainty is certainty by knowledge (*'ilm al-yaqīn*).

Third stage. In this stage the abode of the spiritual traveller is inspiration. The invocation is *Hū*, the esoteric meaning of this invocation is "There is none to be loved but Allah." The direction of journeying is "progress within God". The state is that of giving up everything. The realm is the realm of Majesty (*'ālam al-haybah*). At this stage the traveller seeks only the love of God. He or she hears the invocation of every thing and of every creature, knows what is inside the heart, and has many secrets here. He or she becomes a place of manifestation of God's Action and Attributes, whose knowledge is composed of certainty by vision (*'ayn al-yaqīn*).

Fourth stage. In this stage the abode of the spiritual traveller is confidence and peace. The invocation is *Ḥaqq*, the esoteric meaning of which is "There is none but Allah." The journeying is the "journey with God". The state alternates between spiritual drunkenness and soberness. The realm is that of omnipotence (*'ālam al-jabarūt*). The love for God is increased. He or she witnesses God everywhere in everything, and undergoes the second unveiling (*fatḥ al-mubīn*); however, the veil over things is not yet completely raised.

Fifth stage. In this stage the abode of the spiritual traveller is pleasing and satisfying. The invocation is *Ḥayy*, the esoteric meaning of which is "There is none but Allah, there is no aim but Allah, there is none to be loved but Allah." The state is the full absorption (*fanā'*) of the human qualities in the Qualities of God and His Attributes. The journeying is the "journey in God" (*sayr fi'Llāh*), and the realm is the realm of Divinity (*'ālam al-Lāhūt*). He or she is located in the Secret of Secrets (*sirr al-asrār*). In this state he or she knows by direct tasting rather than inspiration. Here he or she is one loved by God.

Sixth stage. In this stage the abode of the spiritual traveller is Being Pleased (*Marḍiyyah*). The invocation is *Qayyūm*. The state is establishing (*tamkīn*) and astonishment (*ḥayrah*). The journeying is the "journey from God", and the realm is the realm of the Visible *'ālam al-shahādah*. In this stage the manifestations of the Names of God begin to replace the manifestation of the actions of God. Here the love of God informs the love of God's creatures. Although he or she lives among the creatures, he or she is always with God. This stage is also called "The Grand Vicegerent": one who returns from unity to multiplicity in order to awaken the people. The traveller can attain to this stage through his or her own effort and conduct, but they do not suffice to pass beyond it. Only Divine Grace can attract the traveller from the sixth to the seventh stage.

Seventh stage. In this stage the abode of the spiritual traveller is perfection. The invocation is *Qahhār*. The journeying is the "Journey for God" (*sayr bi'Llāh*). The state is subsistence (*baqā'*). The realm is the "realm of unity in multiplicity and multiplicity in unity". The degree of certainty is certainty by truth (*ḥaqq al-yaqīn*). This stage is also called *aḥadiyyah*, *jam' al-jam'*, *'amā'*, *yaqīn* and by other terms. This is the beginning of the stage of the inner kingdom where all actions as well as inactions are worship. The breathing is power and favour, the face is ease, the words and actions are wisdom. He or she has become a real philosopher, and only one who has reached this stage has the right to be called really a sage (*sophos*). Sainthood is the end of this sevenfold journey. At the completion of the stages of annihilation, essence and manifestation are one in the seeker after Truth and Reality. The beatitude of "as if it were not" is conferred at this station.[17]

Shaykh al-Akbar ibn 'Arabī, himself one of the real sages of Islam, defines the sage or "possessor of wisdom" (*al-ḥakīm*), whether God or human, as "one who does what is proper for what is proper is proper".

> Wisdom is the hallmark of the perfect friends of God, possessed in its fullness only by the "People of Blame" [*malāmiyyūn*], the highest of the perfect men. Since wisdom puts things in their proper places, it rules over *tartīb*, that is, arrangement, order and hierarchy . . . The name "Wise" arranges affairs within their levels and places the things within their measures. It is the perfect combination of knowledge and practice. The name "Wise" has a face toward knowing [*al-'ilm*] and a face toward the governing [*al-mudabbir*]. The gnostics give each thing its due, just as God gives each thing its creation. The distinguishing feature of the gnostics is that they verify that which distinguishes the realities. This belongs only to those who know the order of God's wisdom

> in affairs and who "give each thing its due . . . Know that the wisdom [*al-ḥikmah*] in all things and in every single affair belongs to the levels, not to entities. The most tremendous of the levels is the Divinity, while the lowest of the levels is servanthood . . . So verify, my friend, how you serve your Master! Then you will be one of the men of knowledge who are "deeply rooted in knowledge" [Qur'ān 3: 7], the divine sages [*al-ḥukamā' al-ilāhiyyūn*], and you will attain the further degree and the highest place along with the messengers and prophets![18]

The capability to witness unity in multiplicity indicates the perspective unique to a man of wisdom such as Ibn 'Arabī himself:

> O, you considering the study of the branch of knowledge [that is gnosis] which is the prophetic knowledge inherited from the prophets (may God bless them all), you should not be veiled when you find an idea that has been mentioned by the true Sufi [which has been] also mentioned by a philosopher or a *mutakallim*, or any other thinkers from any branch of knowledge and accuse such a true Sufi of being a rationalistic philosopher just because the philosopher spoke about and believed in the same idea. And do not accuse him of copying the philosophers, or say that he has no religion, just as the philosopher has no religion. Refrain from so doing . . . It does not necessarily follow that all his knowledge is false. This is perceived in the simple intellect [*'aql*] of every intelligent person. Your objection to the Sufi in this case led you away from knowledge, truth and religion on to the path of the ignorant, the liars and slanderers, those who suffer lack of intellect and religion, and the people of corrupt consideration and deviation.[19]

From our discussion we can conclude that, according to the perspective of the *sophia perennis*, Islamic philosophy in its entirety amounts to different explanations proceeding from different degrees of one and the same Reality. As we have shown, the Divinity makes himself known in descending gradation from Subtlety (*laṭāfat*) down to Density (*kithāfat*), from the Hidden (*al-bāṭin*) to the Manifest (*al-ẓāhir*). As Divine Knowledge and the nature and structure of that knowledge are revealed in descending gradation, so does the knowledge of the possessors of knowledge ascend along the same line, beginning with the merely rational and proceeding to the intellectual, and inward from the exoteric to the esoteric. This inward journey to the esoteric knowledge of Divine Reality constitutes *taṣawwuf*, and he who attains to it is a gnostic, sage or Sufi (*al-ḥakīm*). Since real knowledge is ultimately bestowed only upon those who are prepared to receive it, mysticism or *taṣawwuf* is a central theme in classical Islamic philosophy and philosophy on the highest level is not separated from mysticism.

Chism-i sar bā chism-i sirr dar jang būd
Ghālib āmad chism-i sirr ḥujjat namūd.

(The eyes of the head with the eyes of the inner secret quarrelled.
No need to prove that the eyes of the inner secret became victorious.)

Mawlānā Jalāl al-Dīn Rūmī

NOTES

1 al-Kindī, *Rasā'il al-Kindī al-falsafiyyah*, ed. Abū Rīḍah (Cairo, 1950), i: 124.
2 *Ibid.*: 274.
3 *Ibid.*: 173.
4 al-Fārābī, *al-Jam' bayn ra'yay al-ḥakīmayn*, ed. A. Nader (Beirut, 1968): 80.
5 A. M. Goichon, *Lexique de la langue philosophique d'Ibn Sīnā* (Paris, 1938): 281–2.
6 Ibn 'Arabī, *al-Futūḥāt al-makkiyyah* (Beirut, 1970), 2: 296.
7 *Ibid.*: 259.
8 Shihabuddin Suhrawardī, *al-Talwīḥāt*, ed. Henry Corbin (Istanbul, 1945): 113.
9 *Ibid.*: 111.
10 Ibn Sīnā, *al-Ishārāt wa'l-tanbīhāt*, ed. S. Dunyā (Cairo, 1958,) 3; 251.
11 Ibn Sīnā, *al-Najāt*, ed. al-Kurdī (Tehran, n.d.): 268.
12 Ibn 'Arabī, *op. cit.*, 2: 432.
13 *Ibid.*, 1: 333.
14 René Guénon, "Oriental Metaphysics", in *The Sword of Gnosis*, ed. J. Needleman (London, 1986): 47, 49, 51.
15 Al-Ghazzālī, *Risālat al-laduniyyah*, ed. M. al-Kurdī (Cairo, 1910): 22–31.
16 'Ayn al-Qūḍāt Hamadānī, *Zubdat al-ḥaqā'iq* (Tehran, 1962): 35.
17 This schema was originally laid out by Sayyid Yahyā al-Shīrwānī al-Bāquwī and developed by Ottoman Sufi masters under the title *aṭwār-i sab'ah*.
18 Ibn 'Arabī, *op cit.*, 3: 69.
19 *Ibid.*, 1: 32.

(We would like to thank Adnan Aslan for his help in the preparation of this chapter. (O. L. and S. H. N.))

SELECT BIBLIOGRAPHY

Chittick, William C. (1981) "Mysticism Versus Philosophy in Earlier Islamic Philosophy", *Religious Studies*, 17: 87–104.
— (1989) *The Sufi Path of Knowledge* (New York).
Corbin, Henry (1993) *History of Islamic Philosophy* (London).
Guénon, René (1986) "Oriental Metaphysics", in *The Sword of Gnosis*, ed.

D. J. Needleman (London).
Khan, Khaja (1981a) *The Philosophy of Islam* (New Delhi).
—— (1981b) *Studies in Tasawwuf*, (Delhi).
Morewedge, Parwiz (1971) "The Logic of Emanationism and Sufism in the philosophy of Ibn Sīnā", *Journal of the American Oriental Society*, 91 and 92.
—— (1982) "A Philosophical Interpretation of Rūmī's Mystical Poetry", in *The Scholar and the Saint* (London).
Nasr, Seyyed Hossein (1979) *Three Muslim Sages* (Delmar).
—— (1989) *Knowledge and the Sacred* (New York).
—— (1991) *Sufi Essays* (Albany).
Netton, Ian (1989) *Allah Transcendent* (London).
Rosenthal, Franz (1988) "Ibn 'Arabī between 'Philosophy and Mysticism' ", *Oriens*, 31.
Schuon, Frithjof (1976) *Esoterism as Principle and as Way* (London).

CHAPTER 55

Ethics

Daniel H. Frank

Islamic ethics is to be found in an enormous range of materials from Qur'ānic exegesis to *kalām*, from philosophical commentaries on Aristotle to Sufi mystical texts. One might present an historical overview, perhaps subdivided by type of theory. The most recent, comprehensive work on the subject proceeds in just such a manner. Fakhry (1991) divides Islamic ethics into four parts – scriptural morality, theological ethics, philosophical ethics and religious ethics – as he presents his version of the story. I propose, however, to proceed in a rather different manner, eschewing the history of ideas in favour of a more selective approach which will highlight in some detail the views of some major Muslim philosophers on a single philosophical problem: the nature of the human good and its relation to the political order. This problem is without doubt the most important one in the ethical/political tradition in which one must locate the Muslim philosophers, namely the Greek moral philosophical tradition. It is to this latter, thus, that one must turn to set the grounds for the later medieval Muslim elaborations.

THE GREEK BACKGROUND

In understanding ethics as primarily a discussion about the human good, about happiness and its achievement, one needs to understand that this is already a particular way of approaching the subject. It is not the only way. One might be concerned with the grounding and subsequent establishment of a criterion for evaluating particular (types of) action, rather than with what constitutes the best human life overall. Or one might be concerned with metatheoretical discussions about the nature of ethical discourse, rather than with the development of a certain ethical disposition or moral outlook. In general, one might view ethics as a theoretical rather than practical enterprise. But to so view it is not to do ethics in the "Classical" way. For Aristotle, ethics is a practical science, and this means that it subserves a practical end, namely how to live well and, thereby, to achieve the human good. One tends to describe a work like the *Nicomachean Ethics* as a work in ethical *theory*, but we need to understand that for Aristotle the treatise is not a theoretical work, at least in *his* sense. For him, it is treatises such as *Physics*, *De caelo* and the various biological works which are theoretical works, devoted to knowledge for its own sake. But in ethics "we are inquiring not in order to know what virtue is, but in order to become good" (*NE*, 1103b27–8). The goal which a science serves defines its nature. And given this, Aristotle's division of the sciences does not allow for ethics and political philosophy to be construed as theoretical sciences. Even when the goal is theoretical perfection, ethics and political philosophy are eminently practical sciences, subserving a practical end, knowledge for the sake of achieving happiness.

The ultimate practicality of ethics, the signature of Greek moral philosophizing, was accepted throughout the medieval period. Supported by similar, not identical, divisions of the sciences, Avicenna (Ibn Sīnā), Maimonides and Aquinas all viewed ethics as a species of practical science. And their major questions in ethics are those of their great Greek predecessors. Indeed, there were some particular issues, such as the relation of religion to philosophy, which were of no obvious relevance to the pagan philosophers. But even such issues were discussed by the medieval philosophers with reference to Greek philosophical categories and, furthermore, were addressed *solely* to those who had some philosophical training.

To understand, then, the Islamic contribution to the discussion of the human good, we must first get a sense of the Greek background to the discussion. It was Socrates who initiated philosophical reflection about the human good, and it was because of his life (and death) that Plato began to memorialize his "teacher" in dialogues. For present purposes, the most important dialogue concerned with the *summum bonum* is the *Republic*. This great dialogue, known throughout the medieval period in Islam from al-Fārābī to Averroes (Ibn Rushd), pits Socrates against two youthful opponents who want Socrates to defend the life devoted to justice, appearances notwithstanding. In due course, the defence reveals that the truly just individual is a philosopher, one who, unlike the mass of people, has an awareness of and an abiding commitment to non-sensible, transcendent realities. The philosopher is thus opposed to the worldly masses, both in terms of epistemological insight as well as the resultant *modus vivendi*. But such attachment to non-sensible, supramundane realities would seem to entail a disengagement of the philosopher from the world and humanity at large, and from the political order. And so a deep and abiding problem emerges. What argument can be used to induce the philosopher, the pre-eminently happy individual, to take part in politics? Plato has an argument in *Republic*, 7 (519ff.), to my mind a not very convincing one, which is intended to motivate the philosopher to return to the "cave", to the political realm. But for present purposes, what is important to note is that *argument* is needed to convince the philosopher to return. By itself, philosophical contemplation and the life devoted to such activity seemingly entail no moral or political concern. So we have for the first time in Western thought a thoughtful articulation of the nature of the human good and whether or not it is commensurable with morals and politics.

In passing from Plato to Aristotle, we are passing from a more synoptic thinker to one less so, from a hedgehog to a fox. Aristotle was the first to draw the relevant distinctions between the different types of *epistēme* (knowledge or science), between theoretical, practical, and productive knowledge. For him, learning how best to live was the primary subject of the practical science of ethics. Given the eminently practical nature of the subject for Aristotle, one might expect such an anti-theorist moral philosopher to plump for a most "practical" life, in our sense of the term, as paradigmatic. Indeed, the reader (the student) is not disappointed for the bulk of the *Nicomachean Ethics*. Therein Aristotle outlines a view of human excellence, based upon human nature, which includes prominently the exercise of the moral virtues, virtues such as courage, temperance, and liberality. The human good is seemingly to be construed in quite "practical" terms. The contrast in views concerning the human good between Plato and Aristotle would seem to be marked. Whereas the former locates the human good in a life given over to philosophical contemplation and only secondarily (and hesitatingly) to moral and political activity, Aristotle seems to favour the practical over the theoretical. But such a conclusion on Aristotle's behalf is too quick. In the final book of the *Nicomachean Ethics*, such a view is no longer in place. In chapters 7 and 8 of book 10, Aristotle clearly rank-orders the life devoted to *theoria* (philosophical contemplation) over the life devoted to moral and political virtue. On grounds such as self-sufficiency, continuity of activity and pleasure (of a sort), *theoria* is the clear victor over the activity of moral virtue. In the final analysis, the vaunted difference between the "other-worldly" Plato and the "realist" Aristotle comes to little.

Now this is not to suggest that the contemplative ideal entails a monastic existence, far from the madding crowd. Aristotle is clear that we cannot be happy without family, friends and so forth; even Socrates carried forth his activity squarely within the *polis*. Nevertheless, such "material" aspects of human happiness are (merely) enabling conditions for the possibility of attaining the (true) human good.

Before we turn to some Muslim philosophers who were decisively influenced by this Greek conception of human flourishing, we should note a corollary that follows from the aforementioned conception of human flourishing. Given that happiness consists in rational contemplation, an activity of the highest intellectual order, human happiness turns out to be the attainable prize of but a few. Only the intellectual elite, according to both the Platonic and Aristotelian models, can be truly happy; only they can flourish in the highest degree. For those incapable of such feats of ratiocination, a secondary degree of human flourishing is possible. But even here, it should be noted, a certain elitism is evident, for to be able to engage in (Aristotelian) moral virtue, a level of material well-being is required for success. One cannot be liberal without adequate funds, and so forth. In sum, the Greek conception of human flourishing is manifestly aristocratic in its intent. Whether excelling in the highest of the intellectual virtues or in moral and political activity, (true) human happiness is open to some, closed to many.

Thus, we have in Plato and Aristotle an intellectualist version of the human good, with (1) varying discomfort about its connectedness to moral and political life, and (2) an unambiguous elitist propensity. As we turn to some of the Muslim philosophers, I suggest we bear these points in mind. We shall see how they creatively adapt Classical Greek views to their own time and place. The Muslim philosophers to be discussed are al-Fārābī, Ibn Bājjah (Avempace), Ibn Ṭufayl and Averroes.

ISLAMIC DISCUSSIONS OF THE HUMAN GOOD

Al-Fārābī

It is hardly surprising that al-Fārābī (259/872–339/950), an avid student of both Plato's *Republic* and Aristotle's *Nicomachean Ethics*, should be influenced by his Greek predecessors for his own discussions of the human good. Note that I have used the plural "discussions of the human good", for, as Galston (1990) has recently pointed out, al-Fārābī has disparate views of the human good in different works. Indeed, his views run the spectrum from identifying the human good with political activity, to identifying it with theoretical activity alone, to, finally, identifying it with some sort of combination of the two. I think it is fair to say, however, that the latter two are the most prominent in the extant works. And perhaps this is as it should be, given the influence of his Greek predecessors.

We have then in al-Fārābī, generally speaking, two competing views of human happiness, an exclusively theoretical one in *al-Madīnah al-fāḍilah* ("On the Perfect State") and *al-Siyāsah al-madaniyyah* ("The

Political Regime"), and one which attempts in Platonic fashion to wed philosophy and politics in *Taḥṣīl al-sa'ādah* ("The Attainment of Happiness"). The former view suggests that human felicity is to be identified with the activity of that part of the rational soul which is separate or, at any rate, separable from the body. Ṣuch activity in its highest aspect takes the form of *ittiṣāl*, conjunction with the active intellect, this latter a transcendent entity and the proximate source for the possibility of human intellection.

I cannot here dwell upon the nature of such conjunction, but shall merely note that, in those places where *ittiṣāl* is strongly underscored as true human felicity, al-Fārābī thereby adopts a wholly apolitical conception of the human good. Such a view of the human ideal carries with it a (Greek-inspired) intellectual elitism, which allows true happiness to but a very few. Indeed, al-Fārābī's elitism shines through when (in e.g. *Siyāsah*: 56) he strongly distinguishes religion and philosophy, and asserts that the majority of men pursue an imagined (merely apparent) happiness, and not a theoretically grounded one. For al-Fārābī, famously, religion is an image of true wisdom, of philosophy. The former deals with (mere) images in the form of stories and parables, and such "phenomena" are the means whereby the mass of humanity achieves such happiness as it is capable of. And though al-Fārābī grants the mass of humanity a share in happiness, via religion, it is clear that he reserves his praise for the few, the philosophers. Philosophy stands to religion for al-Fārābī, as philosophical insight stands to the unenlightened beliefs of the non-philosophers for Plato.

But, as noted, there is another human ideal for al-Fārābī. For all of his preference for the theoretical, apolitical ideal, he announces in *Taḥṣīl al-sa'ādah* that:

> when the theoretical sciences are isolated and the possessor does not have the faculty for exploiting them for the benefit of others, they are defective philosophy. To be a truly perfect philosopher one has to possess both the theoretical sciences and the faculty for exploiting them for the benefit of all others according to their capacity. Were one to consider the case of the true philosopher, he would find no difference between him and the supreme ruler. For he who possesses the faculty for exploiting what is comprised by the theoretical matters for the benefit of all others possesses the faculty for making such matters intelligible as well as for bringing into actual existence those of them that depend on the will. *The greater his power to do the latter, the more perfect is his philosophy.* Therefore, he who is truly perfect possesses with sure insight, first, the theoretical virtues, and subsequently the practical.
>
> (*Sa'ādah*: 39, trans. Mahdi; my emphases)

This passage is as important as it is clear. Contra the theoretical ideal which we noted above, this passage presents a more "well-rounded" picture of the philosopher as prophet and of philosophy as prophecy. Whereas the previous picture paid no attention to the importance, indeed necessity, of "translating" theory into practice, this portrait sees such an important link between the two that it literally defines (true) philosophy as enlightened political rulership. Reminiscent of Plato, the true philosopher and the supreme ruler are, or ought to be, one.

Although this model of the human ideal is I think incommensurable with the wholly theoretical one, there is at least one point of agreement. We noted the inherent intellectual elitism of the theoretical paradigm, but one cannot deny that it is in place here in this picture of the Islamic supreme ruler. Although he returns to the cave and takes his place in the world, it is only he (the prophet) who has the requisite capacity to ground leadership upon theoretical foundations. In this sense, then, there is a deep underlying unity in al-Fārābī's thinking about human happiness and its possible achievement by humankind at large.

We cannot canvass al-Fārābī's views on the human good more on this occasion, but we should note that he is an excellent point of departure. All subsequent philosophical reflections on the human good in medieval Islam are indebted to him. He is arguably the most Platonic of medieval Muslim philosophers, in so far as he often sees the pressing need to make philosophy and politics commensurable. And critical reactions to his views may be due to the less settled state of philosophy and philosophers in subsequent generations.

Ibn Bājjah (Avempace) and Ibn Ṭufayl

As we turn from East to West and proceed through some two centuries, we come to two Spanish–Muslim thinkers whose particular conclusions concerning the human good stand in marked contrast to those of al-Fārābī. Contra al-Fārābī, who, as we have seen, often equates happiness with prophecy and, thereby, includes moral and political activity in the human good, both Ibn Bājjah (d. 533/1138–9) and Ibn Ṭufayl (d. 580/1185), each in his own way, strongly suggest the incommensurability of philosophy and politics. For them, the human good consists in philosophical (theoretical) activity alone. If one is to speak in Platonic terms, for both Ibn Bājjah and Ibn Ṭufayl, the return to the cave is so dangerous and fraught with posssible misunderstanding that the would-be happy individual is well advised to live in isolation, and in Ibn Ṭufayl's allegorical tale *Ḥayy ibn Yaqẓān* such isolation is quite literally depicted.

Ibn Bājjah, in his *Tadbīr al-mutawaḥḥid* ("The Governance of the Solitary"), addresses himself to the philosopher in the imperfect society, the "real" world. Such men are isolated "weeds" (*nawābit*) as Ibn Bājjah denominates them. They don't fit into their society. Whereas Plato faced the problem of the relationship of the philosopher to the *perfect* (virtuous) state and, as noted, concluded that the philosopher must return, albeit reluctantly, to the cave, Ibn Bājjah is not concerned with an ideal world and thus is not faced with one duty-bound to return to society. Ibn Bājjah's weeds exist *in spite of* the society they inhabit, and thus "they will possess only the happiness of an isolated individual" (*Tadbīr*: 11, trans. Berman). In this regard, they are rather like the Platonic philosopher (Socrates) eternally at odds with his society, of whom Plato says, "he is like a man who takes refuge under a small wall from a storm of dust or hail driven by the wind, and seeing other men filled with lawlessness, the philosopher is satisfied if he can somehow live his present life free from injustice and impious deeds, and depart from it with a beautiful hope, blameless and content" (*Republic*, 6.496d–e; trans. Grube). For both Plato and Ibn Bājjah (and, to be seen, Ibn Ṭufayl), the agenda and set of priorities of the philosopher and of real existent states are at odds. As a result, the philosopher must live in isolation, at least to the extent of not sharing in any way the goals of the state in which he dwells. For Ibn Bājjah, the weed dwells among men, but perfects himself by virtue of perfecting his spiritual nature, dissociating himself from "those whose end is corporeal and those whose end is the spirituality that is adulterated with corporeality" (*Tadbīr*: 78, trans. Berman).

Ibn Ṭufayl's allegorical tale *Ḥayy ibn Yaqẓān* may well be read and understood as an elaboration on the thought of his predecessor, Ibn Bājjah. As noted, Ibn Bājjah finds philosophy and politics incommensurable, with the result that the philosopher must live "apart" from the mass of humankind. This is precisely the lesson which Ḥayy, the protagonist of Ibn Ṭufayl's tale, learns, except that in his case the "apart", the solitude, is not metaphorical. Ḥayy learns that for his well-being and, equally importantly, for the well-being of humankind as a whole, he must live apart, physically distant, for in trying to persuade even the best amongst people on the basis of true (philosophical) wisdom "they recoiled in horror from his ideas and closed their minds . . . [And] the more he taught, the more repugnance they felt" (*Ḥayy ibn Yaqẓān*: 150, trans. Goodman). As a result of such dismal failure the reclusive Ḥayy returns whence he came, realizing that the compassion, born of inexperience, which impelled him from his island was woefully misplaced. Realizing that "most men are no better than unreasoning animals" (153), he departs from the political realm to seek wisdom.

The lesson Ḥayy has so painfully learned is that only a few can be truly happy, made so by philosophy; only a few can perceive the truth unveiled. For the others, the many, the truth must be veiled in the stories and parables of the law. The elitism is apparent. Only the philosopher can ascend to the illuminative mysteries, and, having attained these truths, he must learn the painful lesson that they cannot be communicated to the world at large. Philosophy and politics are incommensurable, indeed to the detriment of both philosopher and non-philosopher, for the former must live in isolation and the latter cannot be enlightened. Quite contrary to al-Fārābī, for whom philosophy was defective if untranslatable, Ibn Ṭufayl (and Ibn Bājjah) are less exercised by the non-practical nature of philosophy. For them, pessimists as they are, humankind cannot be transformed. As a result, human happiness must be found in isolation.

So far, then, we have seen the Muslim philosophers take different sides on the issue of the commensurability of philosophy and politics, with al-Fārābī being most optimistic (Platonic) in the matter, Ibn Bājjah and Ibn Ṭufayl considerably less so. But all are agreed that theoretical wisdom stands at the apex of human achievement, and in it resides human felicity. In such a belief the medieval Muslim philosophers join company with their Greek predecessors. Both Plato and Aristotle are likewise in agreement about the theoretical nature of the human good. As a result, the issue for all concerned, as moral and political thinkers, seems to be the elitist implications of the view. If only a few can achieve true happiness, what *unites* the community?

Averroes

Averroes (d. 595/1198) comes toward the end of the philosophical tradition we are discussing. A commentator on both Plato and Aristotle, Averroes is in many ways reminiscent of al-Fārābī. Al-Fārābī, Ibn Bājjah and Ibn Ṭufayl all discuss the human good and its relation to the political realm. But only al-Fārābī does not give in to despair. Though he believes only a very few can achieve the highest good, al-Fārābī is insistent that such an ideal must serve a political end, and if not, is defective. Averroes, for his part, seems to share the view that the philosopher must find a way to serve the community. In his *Commentary on Plato's Republic*, actually a paraphrase of it, Averroes asserts quite straightforwardly that "the best perfection" (64:26) is to participate as a philosopher *in* a society which appreciates such a person. Indeed, for Averroes, like al-Fārābī and his (Averroes') Jewish counterpart, Maimonides, such enlightened rulership is the mark of the prophet. And prophecy in this sense of enlightened leadership is the ideal. For Averroes, this ideal is in fact grounded in the law. His famous *Faṣl al-maqāl* ("The Decisive Treatise") makes abundantly clear that the law obligates those capable of so doing to study philosophy (*Faṣl al-maqāl*: 1–2), and given that the law was given to ensure the well-being of the *entire* community, including those (non-philosophers) in need of instruction, the obligation to study philosophy must perforce have a *practical* application.

What makes Averroes so important and quite unique in the story being told is his desire to ground philosophy and its study in the law. As bound by the law the philosopher lives as a prophet among people, and by virtue of his excellence in philosophical wisdom he is *obligated* to rule. The necessity which enjoins him to rule provides a rather neat conclusion to the entire issue before us. In Plato, we noted a hesitation in the philosopher's return to the cave. Overwhelmed by the beauty and order of his intellectual vision, it is difficult to motivate the philosopher to return to the political realm. Seemingly, on *philosophical* grounds the marriage between philosophy and politics cannot be consummated. But perhaps there are other grounds.

For Averroes, there are. And this is why the law is so crucial to his theorizing, much more so than to the theorizing of any of the other Muslim thinkers we have discussed. It is only the law which can provide the grounds, the argument why the philosopher should return to the cave. Left to his own devices, Averroes seems to suggest, self-interest will prevail and the philosopher will jib at returning. This is hardly to suggest, as some theologians think, that in fact Averroes must have secretly believed that self-interest must prevail and that, as a result, philosophy and politics do not mix. For this overlooks the manifest fact that Averroes was a Muslim, not a heretic. For him, the law was binding, and it enjoins the study and practice of philosophy for all capable *for the benefit of the entire community*.

The human good, then, for Averroes is really no different from that of his predecessors. It entails the study of philosophy. He is as much an elitist as any of the other thinkers discussed. But the twist which he gives his discussion of the *summum bonum* is its inherently legal status. In achieving the human good one *must* return to the cave. The Platonic worry about the incommensurability of philosophy and politics is obviated.

SELECT BIBLIOGRAPHY

Primary sources

al-Fārābī, *al-Madīnah al-fāḍilah* ("On the Perfect State"), ed. R. Walzer (Oxford, 1985).

—— *al-Siyāsah al-madaniyyah* ("The Political Regime"), ed. F. Najjar (Beirut, 1964).

—— *Taḥṣīl al-saʿādah* ("The Attainment of Happiness"), ed. and trans. M. Mahdi (Ithaca, 1969).

Averroes, *Averroes' Commentary on Plato's Republic*, ed. E. I. J. Rosenthal (Cambridge, 1969).

—— *Averroes on Plato's Republic*, trans. R. Lerner (Ithaca, 1974).
—— *Faṣl al-maqāl* ("The Decisive Treatise"), ed. G. Hourani (Leiden, 1959).
—— *Tahāfut al-tahāfut* ("The Incoherence of the Incoherence"), ed. M. Bouyges (Beirut, 1930).
—— *Averroes' Tahāfut al-tahāfut*, trans. S. Van Den Bergh (Leiden, 1954).
Ibn Bājjah (Avempace), *Tadbīr al-mutawaḥḥid* ("The Governance of the Solitary"), ed. M. Asín Palacios (Madrid and Granada, 1946).
Ibn Ṭufayl, *Ḥayy ibn Yaqẓān*, trans. L. E. Goodman (Los Angeles, 1983).
Medieval Political Philosophy: a Sourcebook, eds R. Lerner and M. Mahdi (Ithaca, 1963).

Secondary sources

Butterworth, C. E. (ed.), *The Political Aspects of Islamic Philosophy: Essays in Honor of Muhsin S. Mahdi* (Cambridge, Mass., 1992).
Fakhry, M., *Ethical Theories in Islam* (Leiden, 1991).
Galston, M., *Politics and Excellence: The Political Philosophy of Alfarabi* (Princeton, 1990).
Leaman, O., *Averroes and his Philosophy* (Oxford, 1988).

CHAPTER 56

Aesthetics

Salim Kemal

In keeping with the traditional exegetical and normative method of Qur'ānic and philological sciences, early aesthetic thought in Islam pursued a validation that may be called "argument by example and illustration". In this mode, critics advanced an account of the nature of poetry by examining the grammatical and philological rules present in works that were accepted as models of good poetry. They do refer to the different mental states of subjects, the play of different causal factors or the play of imagination, but these remain dependent on linguistic factors.

In *al-Bayān wa'l-tabyīn* al-Jāḥiẓ explains *isti'ārah* as calling one thing by the name of something else because of a similarity between two terms based on their contiguity and resemblance.[1] He maintains that it concerns single words or stylistic devices,[2] and warrants its legitimacy by analysing its linguistic structure.[3] Ibn Qutaybah proposes that *majāz* or figurative language underpins poetry, and in *Ta'wīl mushkil al-qur'ān* explains the term through such linguistic terms as *isti'arah, tamthīl*, inversion, omission and repetition.[4]

Tha'ālibī, in *Qawā'id al-shi'r*,[5] analyses the transference of meaning in *isti'ārah* in terms of mental imagery,[6] which he explains through the language poets use to articulate imagery. Similarly, when in *Kitāb al-badī'* Ibn al-Mu'tazz sets out seventeen apparently new figures, his radical innovation is tempered by the facts that, firstly, earlier writers had already set out nine of these figures while in the other eight he proposes distinctions already present, if inadequately identified, in established and exemplary instances,[7] and, secondly, that he explains the figures by reference to the grammatical and philological rules governing their use.[8]

In *al-Muwāzanah buyn shi'r Abī Tammām wa'l-Buḥturī* al-Āmidī argues that, since the purpose of discourse is to communicate something, if the borrowed word or phrase is not useful it also lacks justification and cannot claim to be aesthetic.[9] In order to preserve the inter-subjective validity of poetic discourse, he says, firstly, we cannot make poetic comparisons by using *isti'ārah* that are far-fetched and, secondly, we must use familiar and traditional personification[10] because, thirdly, the audience must be able to grasp the point of any similarity. Otherwise putative poetic discourses become simply subjective, idiosyncratic and incapable of general appreciation.[11] In a parallel move, in *al-Wasāṭah bayn al-mutanabbī wa-khuṣūmih* al-Qāḍī al-Jurjānī treats *isti'ārah* as part of "the perfection of the artistic treatment" and of the creative ability of the poet,[12] which makes it a fundamental element of aesthetic discourse,[13] as contrasted with literal or cognitive expression.

In addition to the linguistic analysis of works, critics argue that the evaluation of poetic discourse must refer to the soul's response – the calm and peace it evokes or the antipathy it causes.[14] Thus in *Kitāb al-badī'* Ibn al-Mu'tazz distinguishes the presence of *isti'ārah*, which makes the use of language agreeable or disagreeable, and shows that language is figurative rather than literal,[15] from the deployment or absence of *kināyah* and *ta'rīḍ*, which make literary discourse beautiful or ugly. Similarly, al-Āmidī validates the communicable meaning of poems by relying on (analogy) *qiyās* with accepted usages but insists on *ijmā'* or agreement in subjects' responses to explain their aesthetic value.

In this context, the critics' analysis of the same examples provides a body of exemplary cases which establish what is good poetry. Analysis displays what their value consists in, why newer works are also good so far as they use these or analogous rules, and how members of the audience can appreciate the work and come to agree, by having for themselves, in response, feelings of calm and peace[16] as factors that beautify.

With theorists like Ibn Fāris, al-Tha'ālibī and Ibn Rashīq, the philological character of their discussions consciously stems from issues raised in Qur'ānic exegesis.[17] In any case, these critics relied on the linguistic exegetical method because that was a guarantee of validity. This grammatical analysis competed with another in which aesthetic validity had a distinctive logical cast. The principal representatives of this approach are the Aristotelian philosophers al-Fārābī, Ibn Sīnā (Avicenna) and Ibn Rushd (Averroes). Grammar to them was limited to examining the rules of a particular language; by contrast logic examined the rules for reasoning generally.

Al-Fārābī considers the logical nature of poetic discourses in at least five texts: *The Canons of Poetry*, *Kitāb al-shi'r*, *Catalogue of the Sciences*, *The Introductory Risālah on Logic* and *The Philosophy of Aristotle*. These see poetry as a distinctive "imaginative syllogistic proof by example" and argue that poetic discourse is rationally acceptable because we can analyse the syllogistic form lying at its basis.[18] In this al-Fārābī relies on Aristotle's definition of a syllogism as a "discourse in which, certain things being posited, something other than what is posited follows of necessity from their being so".[19]

The imaginative nature of poetic discourse is crucial to its distinction from other syllogisms. In the *Catalogue of the Sciences* al-Fārābī explains that poetic discourse brings to mind an image or imagined representation that lacks truth value yet, at a prerational but ratiocinative level, still has an effect upon us. Something happens to us "through the imaginative creation [representation, *takhyīl*] which takes place in our soul".[20] We "create an illusion" to a "circumstance or characteristic . . . of the object one speaks about".[21] We associate things in imagination that do not themselves have this association, for example the span of a day and the span of a life, thereby constituting poetic similes and comparisons that give objects and events new meanings.

In the *Canons* al-Fārābī refers these constructions of imagination to the form of proof by example, which is a subset of arguments by analogy. Poetic similes are like examples that work by associating two objects that resemble each other in some respect, say because both possess a property *P*, and extrapolating that, since they possess property *P* in common, both must also possess another property, *Q*. This extrapolation has the form of a syllogism so far as acceptance of the first association generates a disposition to accept the second. Here imagination has the power to construct the association of representations which are present in examples and poetic similes and comparisons. It supplies the middle or enabling premiss that may be universal but only imagined *or* that associates elements so closely that they carry as much force of conviction for subjects as universal premisses do. The association between a day and a life seems so right that we infer for the life characteristics that we would normally associate only with the day, perhaps thinking of old age as the evening of a life, in which the restfulness felt at the end of a day spent in hard work is the relevant similarity. Other associations are also possible here, too, but the important thing is that for the comparison to be meaningful it must have rules, and al-Fārābī explains the latter as having this form of an argument by example.

The inference secures our acquiescence as if it were a legitimate and warranted syllogism because once we find plausible and concede the initial representation of day and life we also accept the resulting association of evening and old age. The warrant for this plausibility is our ready acceptance of the imaginative construct. And al-Fārābī suggests that we assess poets by their insight in making optimally remote but maximally convincing comparisons in their discourse.

There are problems with al-Fārābī's theory. Firstly, the acceptance of the imaginative construct remains subjective and arbitrary. It is merely psychological, being dependent on how easily representations generate a conviction that may vary from subject to subject. It cannot then so much secure agreement as obtain it only in those contingent cases where subjects' psychology coincides. Secondly, examples neither yield nor rely on propositions that are generally applicable elsewhere; yet if poetic discourse is constituted by arguments by example and, if the premisses of these arguments cannot be justified in the standard way by deriving them from other generalizations or categories, then all we can do is simply accept or reject the premisses, where the psychological basis of such acceptance or rejection remains unjustified. But this arbitrariness of poetic syllogisms renders arbitrary the poetic discourse it sustains, and denies its legitimacy. Legitimacy implies an expectation we can have of how any subject *must* respond; but, because their success depends ultimately on a contingent and variable psychological conviction, arguments by example do not satisfy such expectations. Thirdly, arguably al-Fārābī does not clearly explain the relation between aesthetic value and the logical form of the poetic syllogism. He mentions pleasure as a part of this value but gives little indication of how it gains validity.

These weaknesses in al-Fārābī's theory find some resolution in the work of Ibn Sīnā. Relying on Aristotle's conception of demonstrative syllogisms Ibn Sīnā argues for the formal role of pleasure in constituting poetic syllogisms and for their moral value. He presents his theory in numerous works, including the *Commentary on Aristotle's Poetics, Remarks and Admonitions: Logic*, and *Kitāb al-qiyās*.

For Ibn Sīnā poetic syllogisms are "composed of imagined propositions", or "premisses [having] a certain disposition and composition".[22] Poetic and literary utterances have a logical form which follows the pattern of demonstrative reasoning although, unlike demonstrative syllogisms, poetic ones use "premisses inspired by emotion" – our imaginative assent to a poetic syllogism being due to the pleasure and wonder which we feel in response to understanding and thereby appreciating the harmony of its elements.

For Aristotle and Ibn Sīnā logical necessity is obvious and primitive: it is expressed in the first figure syllogistic, which consists of four perfect and self-evident conclusions, and lacks and does not need any more basic underlying principles to justify its validity. Logicians test the validity of statements, arguments and examples of informal reasoning by seeing whether these are reducible to the first figure without loss of meaning and sense. If they are not, then they involve meanings and connotations that are unruly, and their acceptability is merely a matter of the psychology of a subject rather than of the rules for rational thought.

However, a defence by reference to primitiveness and obviousness, even if it works for demonstration, need not work for poetic syllogisms. Meanings in poetic statements are cumulative and synthetic; their nuances and connotations depend on complex constructions and will be lost on being translated into simpler first figure terms. Thus, their meanings seem irretrievably non-rational. Their openness to infinite interplay, embodied in their complex construction, suggests an irreducibility to first figure terms which, in turn, means that the validity of their syllogism cannot be tested: consequently their acceptance would depend on the psychology of the subject rather than the rules of rational thought.

To answer this doubt, Ibn Sīnā relies on a proposal with a long history that predates his work and is usual even in contemporary thought: the construction of meanings in figurative language involves a relation between terms that, when it is harmonious, occasions pleasure. This proposal blunts the threat of incoherence and psychologism contained in the possibility of an infinite interplay. The occurrence of pleasure from understanding the meanings of terms shows that the mix of terms is not infinite because a harmony between an infinite number of elements is an implausible event: harmony presupposes some sense of a whole, of elements held in a known relation and found to have a harmony. The possibility of an infinite number of elements would disrupt any claim to harmony by always leaving open the possibility of unruly elements. The presence of pleasure and harmony suggests a meaningful order – that meanings are not open to the infinite interplay that threatens incoherence.

Ibn Sīnā limits the interplay of meanings also through the theme guiding the deployment of figurative language. These themes include tragedy, satire[23] and the motifs usual to Arabic poetry such as the *nasībah*, the caravan site and journey, and so on. The themes, once established, will exhaust all figurative language. However, they are open to rational argument and defence: perhaps one theme becomes outdated or there is need for a new "post-tragic epic" form, and so on. In any case, the theme and the pleasure in an harmony of terms provide for a meaningful order and relation of terms in poetic discourse.

By this account, it is important to note, pleasure is a part of the formal structure of the poetic syllogistic, being essential to the validity of the syllogistic because it establishes which meanings are relevant by restricting the interplay of associations to the ones that form a harmonious relation. The feeling is not a factor added externally or arbitrarily, but shows how poetic syllogisms work. They show that poetic discourse is rule-governed; and while it cannot claim the certainty of demonstrative arguments, its emotive and ratiocinative quality is still valid because it is a pleasure in a harmonious relation of terms with given meanings.

The role of feeling also shows that the formal validity of poetry involves an essential reference to the subject and its participation in the aesthetic activity and also bars morally unjustifiable content from poetry. This may be made clearer as follows.

Poetic discourse imitates the subject in that it treats the subject as the end of the process of production of aesthetic discourse because its experience of pleasure forms the ultimate ground for appreciating a poem. Only the occurrence of this feeling will validate aesthetic discourse. A subject appreciates a work when he or she has the appropriate feeling, not when someone else does so. Agreement can only be *given* by the particular subject, who thus becomes crucially important to the success of poetic discourse.

If subjects must *give* assent, then, by implication, evil poems cannot be aesthetically valuable. This needs explanation. Ibn Sīnā follows Aristotle in thinking of virtue as a balanced individual; he also adds that just political relations are partnerships "*only* achieved through *reciprocal* transactions" between individuals: when they contain a balance between individuals.[24] Moreover, the existence of a community is necessary for individual existence, for we recognize ourselves as human beings only through interaction with others like ourselves.[25] An unjust or evil society, then, excludes individuals from reciprocal transactions, especially, perhaps, when they maintain a balanced and virtuous individual life. As an imbalance, evil mis-stresses some parts of ourselves over others, and cannot account for the qualities whose possession makes us virtuous human beings.

By this argument, an evil poem would be morally imbalanced *and* procure an aesthetically pleasing harmony between terms. Yet this remains impossible. Pleasure has to be given by a subject; however, the partial stresses in the evil poem connotes a divisive society that excludes the virtuous individual and moral mean. But those people excluded by the evil poem are also the ones who must appreciate it and constitute its aesthetic value by grasping its meaning and *giving* assent. To find the evil poem beautiful, not only would they have to thwart their own participation in the community just when they gave assent to a poem, but their assent would also be vacuous because they are excluded by the society subtended by the poem. Yet only their pleasurable response can validate the claim that the evil poem is beautiful. In other words, the poem's aesthetic value cannot be constituted except through their participation, yet if their participation is serious, it will restore the balanced community. In a parallel move, we may argue that an evil poem, even if found beautiful by the evil community (assuming that there can be such a thing), will not be beautiful in any serious sense because its aesthetic value has not been tested, so to speak, since the criteria for distinguishing the community are not defeasible. In either case, poetic discourse that is structured by the kind of syllogistic Ibn Sīnā proposes will also have moral connotations.

Perhaps the most important next development of this theory of logical poetical validity occurs with Ibn Rushd, whose *Commentary on the Poetics* harks back over the intervening presence of al-Ghazzālī to reappropriate the tradition begun by al-Fārābī and Ibn Sīnā.[26] Firstly, in texts such as *On the Harmony of Religion and Philosophy* and in *Kitāb al-kashf 'an manāhij al-adillah*, Ibn Rushd considers metaphors in their scriptural use, arguing that we must consider the meanings of metaphors in the context of a search for truth. Truth and knowledge provide the most secure community because they can claim and sustain subjects' agreement. Only when the standard ways of arriving at truth prove inadequate, and in order to grasp the meanings contained in metaphors and allegories, do we use those criteria for explaining metaphorical meanings.

To examine the force, scope and validity of metaphors Ibn Rushd turns to the *Poetics*. His underlying concern for truth is not always clear, for he often distinguishes metaphors in "scriptural texts" from poetry;[27] but that cannot be the whole story. If poetic statements are implausible,[28] exaggerated,[29] incoherent,[30] loose[31] and some other cognates of truth, they will lack validity, he maintains, thus suggesting that truth is vital to poetic validity. We might explain this as follows.

As the structure of a poem or story is made up of such events, actions and character development, then any implausibility in it in this regard occurs as an incoherence in the depiction of events, actions and character. But such incoherence has other implications, for where a story is implausible because it misrepresents or fails to explain the actions, motivations and development of its characters, there we will find incoherence in the structure of the work. The story will be disrupted in the sense that the sequence of events will appear inconsistent, ambiguous or unexplained in some measure at some point in the structure of the story. But this fault in the structure has yet other consequences, for it means that the work lacks cohesion or unity because the actions and events fail to follow the order of a plausible story. The implausibility of actions and events, which is seen in the incoherence of the depicted sequence of events and actions, leads us to doubt the unity of the sequence of events. But the latter make up the structure of the story. Moreover, "unity" or "harmony" is an aesthetic criterion also; so that its absence is a reason for finding a work aesthetically unsatisfactory. Accordingly the aesthetic evaluation of a work by reference to the presence or absence of harmony or unity is explained ultimately by the truths embodied in the actions and events depicted in the story. It suggests why we will find the story better aesthetically if it gives us a better understanding of its truths at the same time as the sequence of its events has a harmonious unity in the structure of the story. And the depth of a story will clearly be better the more truths it makes available. Thus the more successful the harmony of elements of our deeper access to the truth – that is, the deeper the truth and the more diverse the elements held in harmony in the story – the better we shall think it aesthetically. In other words, its truth is essential to the aesthetic character and value of the story; and this yields what we wanted to infer: the aesthetic value of a work, far from precluding it from gaining access to the truth, depends on such access.

A similar situation holds in poetry. We can argue that where a poem is less than truthful – where it is implausible, exaggerated, one-sided, incoherent, etc. – there it is shallow and lacks unity. Thus a poem which misrepresents love is shallow and unlikely to satisfy anyone possessing or wanting a deeper understanding and experience of the subject – whether this understanding is philosophical, dialectical or native to the masses. The poem will not be generally admired and will fail to generate a common response because it does not get at the real matter of love. Further, by contrast with that better understanding, where a poem's structure depends on a superficial understanding of love, there we will find it incoherent, because it is implausible, and therefore lacking in unity and so ill-constructed. The untruthfulness of the poem, then, determines its lack of unity, and so renders it aesthetically inadequate.

These references to truth allow Ibn Rushd to affirm the close relation between truth and beauty. Moreover, he can hold that moral approbation depends on getting closer to the truth and will of God. Consequently, he can argue, as a part of the logical *organon* of philosophy, poetry will bring us closer to God in its distinctive way and so will possess a commensurate value. Poetics tells us of the sorts of demands we may make of each other on the basis of the truth-seeking and affective validity of poetry. Now Ibn Rushd maintains that we must use our reason; and we may suppose that moral justifications are open to rational examination. As Ibn Rushd also contends that rational philosophical justification and religion are equally capable of truth, the rational, philosophical justification of morality and revealed imperatives also give us insight into God's demands of subjects. Thus, as poetry is truthful and a part of philosophy, and as philosophy gives us insight into God's demands of subjects, the claim is that poetry too shares in this enterprise. Consequently, the demands we make of each other on the basis of poetic validity tell us also of the relation between human beings and God which poetry sustains. It tells us of the conception of human being which Ibn Rushd thinks is appropriate to Islam.

NOTES

1 Al-Jāḥiẓ, *al-Bayān wa'l-tabyīn*, ed. A. M. Hārūn (Cairo, 1948–50), 4 vols, 1: 153ff.
2 Heinrichs (1977): 29f.
3 Al-Jāḥiẓ, *al-Bayān*: 153; Heinrichs (1977): 26.
4 *Ta'wīl mushkil al-qur'ān*, ed. A. Sakr (Cairo, 1954): 15–16.
5 Ed. 'Abd al-Tawwāb (Cairo, 1966), p. 57.
6 See Heinrichs (1977): 32–3, where he argues that "the meaning borrows a

mental representation" which for Tha'ālibī constitutes *isti'ārah* as a matter of borrowing "the mental image of the camel, and thus contains all the properties of the camel from which the appropriate ones can be selected to establish the [relevant] analogy".

7 For example, his discussion of *ḥusn al-khurūj min ma'nā ilā ma'nā* at 60ff., which borrows from Tha'ālibī, and of *ḥuṣn al-ibtidā'ah* at 75ff. – i.e., at the end of the book. Ibn al-Mu'tazz, *Kitāb al-badī'*, and Bonebakker, cited below.
8 *Kitāb al-badī', passim.*
9 *Al-Muwāzanah bayn shi'r Abī Tammām wa'l-Buḥturī*, ed A. Sakr (Cairo, 1961, 1965), 1: 135.
10 *Ibid.*: 223, 250–9, 254.
11 *Ibid.*: 250–9.
12 Fourth ed., ed. A. M. al-Bajjāwī and M. A. F. Ibrāhīm (Cairo, 1966): 33, 35–9, 164.
13 *Ibid.*: 319.
14 *Ibid.*: 320.
15 Al-Mu'tazz, *Kitāb al-badī'*, the tropes are discussed throughout the book.
16 Al-Qāḍī al-Jurjānī *al-Wasāṭah bayn al-Mutanabbī wa-khuṣūmih*, 4th ed. by M. A. al-Bījāwī and M. A. Ibrāhīm (Cairo, 1966), p. 320.
17 See Heinrichs (1977): 45ff and 53–5.
18 *Canons of Poetry*, 115, in Cantarino 5, (1970), hereafter abbreviated as *Canons*.
19 Aristotle, *Prior Analytics*, 1, 24b 16
20 *Catalogue of the Sciences*, 118, trans. in Cantarino (1970).
21 *Canons*, 116.
22 *Remarks and Admonishments*: *Logic*, 148.
23 Commentary: 66–8.
24 *Healing: Metaphysics*, 10.110 (italics added).
25 *Healing: Metaphysics*, 10.
26 Ibn Rushd, *Commentary on the Poetics of Aristotle*, trans. and ed. C. W. Butterworth (Princeton, 1988). The issue of Ibn Rushd's conception of the relation between truth and poetry is treated by Mansour Ajami, *The Alchemy of Glory: the Dialectic of Truthfulness and Untruthfulness in Medieval Arabic Literary Criticism* (Washington DC, 1988): 57ff. I think the latter does not give sufficient weight to the tendencies in Ibn Rushd's commentary that militate towards associating truth and poetry positively, and instead, too often, takes the commentator at his apparent word and maintains that truth and poetry are incompatible. See also George F. Hourani, *On the Harmony of Religion and Philosophy: a translation with Introduction and Notes of Ibn Rushd's Kitāb faṣl al-maqāl, with its appendix (Damima) and an extract from Kitab al-kashf 'an manāhij al-adilla* (London, 1976). A fuller translation of the *Kitāb al-kashf* is provided by Jamil Ur-Rehman, *Averroes' Philosophy and Theology* (Baroda, 1921).
27 Ibn Rushd, *Commentary on the Poetics of Aristotle*: 77–8, 92–4, 135, etc.
28 *Ibid.* For example at 83 Ibn Rushd suggests that "false invention" is not part of the poet's activity.
29 *Ibid.*: 84–6: Ibn Rushd criticizes those who in eulogy "exaggerate in praising."
30 *Ibid.*: 82–3, where he argues for a single purpose for poems.
31 *Ibid.*: 81–2, where Ibn Rushd suggests that explanations must be well organized and short.

SELECT BIBLIOGRAPHY

Black, D. (1990) *Logic and Aristotle's Rhetoric and Poetics in Medieval Arabic Philosophy* (Leiden).

Cantarino, V., (1970) *Arabic Poetics in the Golden Age, Selection of Texts Accompanied by a Preliminary Study* (Leiden). This book contains translations of extracts from a number of writers on poetics together with a useful introductory study of the concepts at work in their analyses.

Gelder, G. J. H. (1974) *Beyond the Line, Classical Arabic Literary Critics on the Coherence and Unity of the Poem*, (Leiden). Contrary to some received opinions that Arabic poetics had no strong regard for the unity of a poem, the author analyses examples to show that unity and coherence were important features of works of poetry and crucial to their analysis.

Heinrichs, W. (1977) *The Hand of the North Wind: Opinions on Metaphor and the Early Meaning of isti'āra in Arabic Poetics* (Wiesbaden).

Ibn Rushd (1977) *Jawāmi' li-kitāb Arisṭūṭālis fi'l jadal wa'l-khaṭābah wa'l-shi'r*, ed. and trans. C. Butterworth as *Averroes' Three Commentaries on Aristotle's "Topics", "Rhetoric" and "Poetics"* (Albany).

Ibn Sīnā (1974) *Avicenna's Commentary on the* Poetics *of Aristotle, A Critical Study with an Annotated Translation of the Text* by Ismail M. Dahiyat (Leiden).

Kemal, S. (1991) *The Poetics of Alfarabi and Avicenna* (Leiden). Examines the philosophical justifications for poetic validity given by these writers.

CHAPTER 57

Law

Norman Calder

Western scholarship (even when written by Muslims) has rarely presented Islamic law in such a way as to demonstrate its values rather than the values of the observer. It is legal practice in the Western sense (which admittedly corresponds to the special concerns of some Muslim jurists) that dominates the standard introductions to the subject: Schacht (1950), Linant de Bellefonds (1956) and Fyzee (1964). Certain features of Muslim juristic discourse, those perhaps which are most revealing of its nature and its intentions, are in such works disregarded in favour of a search for practical rules (certainly present, but strangely hard, sometimes, to find).

The problem may be exemplified by reference to two excellent works of scholarship which appeared in the late 1980s. Nabil Saleh, in his *Unlawful Gain and Legitimate Profit in Islamic Law*, pursues an aim which he shares with many modern Muslims, namely that of "reasserting *Sharī'ah* as a valid and sensible corpus of commercial and civil laws" (1986: 4). What he wants to achieve is "a financial system based on Islamic ethics", the subject matter of his final chapter. What stands in his way, and it does stand in his way, is the tradition of Muslim juristic writing. He goes through it honourably; but its variation, its complexity, its extravagant exploration of detail, its constant citation of different authorities, its apparent irrelevance, sometimes, to practice, its cunning and witty accommodation, sometimes, to practice: all these things make his task difficult, and will alert his readers to the fact that "a valid and sensible corpus of laws" is not quite what these jurists had in mind. Baber Johansen's book *The Islamic Law on Land Tax and Rent* (1988) centres on a set of legal concepts which were exploited by (amongst others) the Ottoman jurist Ibn Nujaym (970/1563), in Egypt, as an expression of his opposition to certain government tax-collecting initiatives. (These were justified in turn by a different manipulation of the same concepts.) Johansen's depiction of development, juristic manipulation and social consequence is revealing, but revealing of something that is particularly interesting to Western scholarship, namely the use of the law in a political situation.

Ibn Nujaym did indeed produce a treatise which had direct relevance to the politics of his day. But when he transferred the arguments of that treatise to his great compendium of the law, *Al-Baḥr al-rāʾiq*, the nature of the arguments changed. First, they took their place as a tiny part of the whole that is the law (by no means an insignificant message), and, second, they ceased to have an immediate activist import. They became a part of the tradition. They were thus of course preserved and might be used again, but, in their new context, they had become an element in a pattern, a pattern constituted primarily by citations from earlier authorities. (What a Muslim law-book characteristically reveals is the tradition.) In cases of established dispute, Ibn Nujaym may have had preferences, but his literary procedure was such as to open up to his readers what the tradition had discovered, through a pattern of argument and counter-argument that represented centuries of juristic effort and juristic debate. The concepts of the law were explored through the tradition's provision of scholarly analysis.

The centripetal (if rather distant) focus of scholarly comment was revelation. That consideration suggests a preliminary definition of Islamic law: it is a hermeneutic discipline which explores and interprets revelation through tradition. The last two words of that definition are the most important. For the most obvious shaping factor, in any work of Islamic law, is its engagement with the past of a particular tradition, and its loyalty to it. So much is this true that the tendency of the following pages will be to modify that definition, and suggest rather that Islamic law is a discipline that explores tradition, and uses tradition to discover (and limit) the meanings of revelation.

No one would deny that the explorations of the law were intended to influence, and might be used sometimes to control, practice; but the great exponents of the tradition would not, I think, admit that their work was valueless just because no one paid (practical) attention to it. The impulse to explore the law was (also) for its own sake, as an act of piety complete in itself, and so intrinsically a part of the religious perceptions of the Muslim community, that they hardly gave it (what the modern analyst has none the less to discover) explicit articulation.

The connotations of the phrase "Islamic law" are in part a product of Western perceptions and have been introduced now to Muslim societies through linguistic calques like Arabic *al-qānūn al-islāmī*. There is no corresponding phrase in pre-modern Muslim discourse. There, the two terms which expressed the commitment of the Muslim community to divine law were *fiqh* and *Sharīʿah*. The first of these is the easier to define.

It always refers to the human, and more or less academic, activity of exploration, interpretation, analysis and presentation of the law, whether this takes place in books, in schools, in the mind or in formal response to a specific question. It is possible to write *fiqh*, to teach and study it, to think (about) it and to manipulate and apply its concepts. *Sharī'ah*, on the other hand, is a word whose connotations are divine. It can be used very loosely and broadly to refer to the Muslim religion, because it is God's religion. It connotes God's law even when the details of the law are unknown or immaterial. It inspires loyalty and commitment in a way that the word *fiqh* does not. In a very narrow and specific sense it can refer to God's law as an ideal: that which is somehow contained within revelation, that which the *fuqahā'*, practitioners of *fiqh*, are trying to find through their explorations and analyses. And it is sometimes used to denote the same things as are denoted by the word *fiqh* (books of *fiqh*, books of *Sharī'ah*), but with that added sense of religious loyalty which comes from its association with God and truth. In modern academic analysis of Islamic law, the word *Sharī'ah* is of little use: what we can study and describe is always *fiqh*.

Fiqh is most obviously available to us as a tradition of literature, though, behind this, there is a tradition of thought and of education, and some kind of aspiration to social control. There are two major types of *fiqh* literature, that known as *furū' al-fiqh* (branches) and that known as *uṣūl al-fiqh* (roots). The former sets out, or appears to set out, concepts and rules that relate to conduct, and arguments about them. Its headings are purity, prayer, fasting, alms, pilgrimage (the essential acts of worship, *'ibādāt*, and invariably the first five books of a work of *furū'*) and then such topics as warfare, marriage, divorce, inheritance, penalties, buying and selling, judicial practice, etc., in variable order. The whole is a conceptual replica of social life, not necessarily aspiring to be either complete or practical, but balanced between revelation, tradition and reality, all three of which feed the discussion and exemplify the concepts. The literature of *uṣūl* identifies the divinely revealed sources of the law (Qur'ān and *Sunnah*), auxiliary sources (like consensus – *ijmā'*), and the hermeneutic disciplines which permit the complex intellectual cross-reference between revelation, tradition and reality which is exemplified in a work of *furū'*. The hermeneutic disciplines are historical and biographical (related to abrogation and to the reliability of those who transmit *Sunnah*), linguistic, rhetorical and logical. The linguistic and rhetorical sciences were in the developed tradition finely articulated, and presented usually under simple antithetical headings: command and prohibition, general and particular, absolute and qualified, metaphor and truth, etc. The application of logic to revelation usually meant analogy (*qiyās*) and was variously developed by different schools and individuals. The Shi'ite tradition was inclined to reject analogy as a systematic means to develop the law, but shows a corresponding complexity in the application of other types of rational argument. Books of *uṣūl* characteristically culminate in a discussion of *ijtihād*, a term implying the exercise of the utmost effort to discover a particular item of the law through application of the hermeneutic rules (Calder (1983 and 1989); Hallaq (1984 and 1986)). It is probably true that the literature of *furū'* is larger than the literature of *uṣūl*, and more characteristic. (In the present chapter, and for reasons of space alone, the last two sections will be devoted exclusively to *furū'*.)

There is a third type of literature which has a role in the public presentation of Divine Law. It is that known as *ṭabaqāt* or "generations". Biographical in form, diachronic in organization, such books demonstrate the continuity of the tradition and the moral and intellectual status of its participating scholars. Their message is theological, though about history; it is that the lives and works of individual scholars derive meaning and significance from their place within an ongoing tradition of juristic thought. This is in fact the ubiquitous message of Islamic juristic literature: individual jurists are not engaged in a private dialogue with revelation, they are the heirs to a tradition. The discovery of meaning in revelation depends on conformity to that tradition. The *ṭabaqāt* literature defends, and of course defines, the tradition.

The five major schools of Islamic jurisprudence, the four Sunni schools (Ḥanafī, Mālikī, Shāfi'ī and Ḥanbalī) and the Imāmī (Twelver) Shi'ites, have expressed themselves through the same three literary types. A broad formal description of the works produced within one school (or tradition) will suffice (to a degree) for all, in spite of the many points of detail that mark their differences. All traditions also produced some specialist treatises and monographs, which can usually be accommodated within the three broad literary types identified above.

The *ṭabaqāt* literature has another, perhaps more prosaic, function. Books of this type vary from the extremely schematic list of names, dates, formal virtues, teachers, students and books produced which is the minimal requirement, to great sequences of anecdotes which, collected and juxtaposed on artistic principles, are intended to educate. (The *Ṭabaqāt al-shāfi'iyyat al-kubrā* of al-Subkī – a Shāfi'ī jurist, d. 771/1370 – is an example of the latter type.) The education, reflecting the artistic impulse which works through contrived juxtaposition and variation, is miscellaneous, but is mostly about the law. Truths about the law which find academic, formal, complex articulation in works of *furū'* or *uṣūl* are rendered here through anecdote, sometimes witty, through poetic citations, through the recognition of scholar-heroes, through wondrous resolutions of tricky problems and through a vocabulary of description which carries subtle (or not so subtle) messages about the aims of the tradition.

Abū Ḥanīfah (150/767) was in the mosque one day, surrounded by a group of students who were shouting and arguing. "What, can't you keep them quiet in the mosque?" muttered an irritable passer-by. "Leave them," said Abū Ḥanīfah, "for only thus will they learn *fiqh*." The historicity of the story is immaterial; its message is about the nature of the law – something to be argued about. The same Abū Ḥanīfah was holding a session one day in Mecca, when he was approached by a man from Khurasan. "I am owner of considerable wealth," said the man, "and I have a son. I am inclined to provide him with a wife and to set him up in comfort. But I fear he will divorce her and so squander my wealth. I could buy him a slave-girl and provide him thus with a household, but he might free her and so again squander my wealth. What shall I do?" "Take him to the slave-market," said Abū Ḥanīfah, "and when a particular girl catches his eye, buy her for yourself, and then marry her to him. If, then, he divorces her, she returns to your ownership; and if he frees her . . . well, he can't, for she is yours." The teller of this story was delighted not just by the reply but by the immediacy of Abū Ḥanīfah's response (Dhahabī: 21, 22).

No conclusions may be drawn from this about marriage practice and family problems in third/ninth-century Khurasan. The story is a show-case for the exploration of concepts. It is generated by the dual system of acquisition of rights to legitimate sexual intercourse in Islamic law: marriage and slavery. A master has rights to intercourse with a slave-girl, unless she is married to another; he may in appropriate circumstances transfer those rights to another; only the owner of a slave can set her free; etc. The story can be explained by listing the relevant rules of law. It was preserved and valued because the legal concepts here set to work are embedded in a narrative fragment which has an earthy humour, and because they are neatly manipulated as a display of skill.

In developed Islamic societies (say, from the fifth/eleventh century onwards, but also before this) the only formal, public system of education had as its major components the teaching of revelation and the teaching of the law, that is the schools of law. There were ancillary disciplines, and various means of secular and private education, but most educated members of Muslim society had as their primary currency of cultural exchange the concepts of the law. Through these they shared their leisure time, and created conversation, wit and public display; and through these they were able to analyse their society and their religion, to express their personal and their public piety and to devise various modes of social control. *Fiqh* was a multi-functional discipline. In the way that it possessed the lives of Muslims, it was challenged and in the end complemented only by the structures of Sufism. These two disciplines, at an intellectual and a practical level, were the primary modes of Muslim self-realization prior to the modern period. They could, without lack of piety, be experienced as humorous or serious.

There were of course differences of approach within schools and across schools. The Ḥanafī school in particular enjoyed the law, willingly explored its concepts through hypothetical cases and far-fetched problems and lent itself to cunning contrivances (*ḥīlah*) which exploited the letter of the law in order to uncover its tolerant spirit (or not, as the case may be). All the traditions did this to some degree, the Ḥanbalīs being perhaps the most conservative and piously serious; and all were aware of the dangers of these attractions. The Mālikīs polemically frowned on the Ḥanafī predilection for hypothetical cases, but acknowledged the temptations even as they preserved (created?) the following story. An Iraqi (i.e. Ḥanafī) asked Mālik (179/795) about a man who had sexual intercourse with a dead chicken, which then produced an egg, out of which came a chick; is it permitted for him to eat the flesh of the chick? Mālik's recorded reply is remarkably mild, all things considered (al-Qāḍī 'Iyāḍ (1967): 150–1).

Islamic law, in the thousand years or so of its cultural dominance, was the product of a highly sophisticated civilization. It was intimately related to an educational system which was more or less homogeneous throughout all pre-modern Muslim societies. Its long-term flourishing was due to the inherent flexibility of a conceptual structure which served to describe revelation, tradition and society. If the main aim of the structure was religious, indeed theological (an articulation of the hermeneutic relationship between the ongoing Muslim community and the ever more distant moment of God's direct intervention in human affairs), that does not exhaust the social functions it served. These might be explained in terms of the cultural needs of a sophisticated society, and probably cannot be explained in terms of the historical origins of Islamic law. None the less explanations in terms of origins have been characteristic both of the Muslim tradition and of the Western scholarly tradition.

The distant origins of Islamic law are strictly inaccessible, in the sense that they belong to a period for which we have no written records. The earliest surviving juristic texts are a number of works ascribed to named authorities of the late second/eighth and early third/ninth centuries. These works already show distinct school orientations, covering three major (and several minor) traditions, the Ḥanafī, the Mālikī and the Shāfi'ī. Literary evidence for the existence of a Ḥanbalī school of law is hardly available before the latter part of the third/ninth century, and for an Imāmī Shi'ite school, the early part of the fourth/tenth. If the Muslim tradition has a historical theory (and it might be more accurate to say that the Muslim tradition offers a schematic paradigm whose function is educative) it is as follows. The words and deeds of the Prophet (his *Sunnah*) were preserved, in the form of discrete anecdotes (*Ḥadīth*), which were transmitted orally through the generations. These were the source of juristic discussion which was eventually transformed, via the notably creative contributions of Abū Ḥanīfah, Mālik, Shāfi'ī, Ibn Ḥanbal and, for the Shi'ites, such figures as the Imām Ja'far al-Ṣādiq, into the legal schools we now know. Development within the schools is acknowledged, e.g. by generalized reference to early scholars and later ones (*al-mutaqaddimūn, al-muta'akhkhirūn*), but never explored. Each school is concerned to demonstrate that its tradition can be harmonized with revelation (which is not the same thing as asserting that *Ḥadīth* are in fact, historically, the source of tradition). Historical considerations are almost entirely irrelevant to the aims of Muslim juristic writing.

By contrast, Western scholarship has amongst its foremost achievements Joseph Schacht's *The Origins of Muhammadan Jurisprudence* (1950). (The epithet is justified perhaps by the Muhammadocentric nature of Muslim juristic discourse.) His key observation is simply that the earliest legal texts (especially those of the Ḥanafī tradition) are not notably interested in relating law to Prophetic *Ḥadīth*, whereas later texts (especially those attributed to Shāfi'ī – 204/820) argue systematically that Prophetic *Ḥadīth* are the only justification for juristic rules. Islamic law, he thought, emerged in local Muslim communities as a discursive presentation of local custom (which may well have been thought of as Prophetic), and was only later transformed into a hermeneutic discipline requiring constant cross-reference between rule and *Ḥadīth*, i.e. between law and revelation (for *Ḥadīth*, like Qur'ān, is part of the revelation and quantitatively by far the greater part). A corollary of Schacht's theory is that much, indeed the bulk, of *Ḥadīth* material will be found to be the result of a search for justification, either of the pre-existent schools of law or of those who opposed them. This is perhaps confirmed by the fact that the literary production of *Ḥadīth* collections is mostly posterior to the life of Shāfi'ī, the earliest collection of great authority being that of Bukhārī (256/870).

Historically this means that the Muslim community was, from the late second/eighth to the early fourth/tenth centuries, engaged in a process of self-definition which was intensely focused on the components of and the relations between revelation (Qur'ān and *Ḥadīth*) and the various legal traditions. The literary witness to this process, according to Western scholars, was a number of juristic texts ascribed to early masters, an indeterminately large body of Prophetic *Ḥadīth*, and – perhaps – the canonical text of the Qur'ān (Wansbrough 1977). The stress on community creativity required by this model of historical development has been found theologically repugnant by many Muslims. It is none the less likely to be (broadly) true, and might not be intransigent to some developments of traditional theology. When the situation stabilized, so did the existential task. The Muslim community was committed to a number of divergent juristic traditions which, through polemical debate, had acquired a common sense of methodological purpose. That was the foundation of

Islamic law: a set of legal traditions more or less mutually self-recognizing (the Imāmī Shi'ites never quite fully integrated) and committed to the task of justifying tradition (and developing it) by reference to revelation. The literary products of the formative, pre-Classical period, though held in great veneration, are not the greatest achievements of the traditions. In spite of an insistence (not just Western) on the terminology of decline, the great achievements of Islamic jurisprudence are probably spread fairly evenly from the mid fourth/tenth to the thirteenth/nineteenth centuries.

The literature of *furū'* may be analysed as displaying two major types: *mukhtaṣar* and *mabsūṭ*, the former term designating an epitome or digest of the law, the latter an expansum or broad exploration of the law's details. The terms are given by the tradition, where they figure frequently as the titles of specific books: the *Mukhtaṣar* of Marwazī (Ḥanafī, 334/946), *al-Mukhtaṣar al-nāfi'* by 'Allāmah al-Ḥillī (Shī'ī, 726/1325), the *Mabsūṭ* of Muḥammad ibn Ḥasan al-Ṭūsī (Shī'ī 460/1067) or of Sarakhsī (Ḥanafī, 483/1090). They are also used by Muslim writers as I use them here, to designate types of literature. Even when the terms are not used, the typology is explicitly recognized and its components successfully indicated. Of the Yemeni scholar Ibn al-Muqri' (838/1434) it is recorded that he produced a work known as the *Irshād*. "It is a precious book on Shāfi'ī *furū'*, elegant in expression and sweet in diction, extremely concise and dense with meaning. He himself wrote a commentary on it, in which he flew to the circumambient horizons" (Shawkānī (1929), i: 43). Shawkānī's contrast between the *Irshād* and its commentary indicates precisely what I have in mind by distinguishing *mukhtaṣar* and *mabsūṭ*.

The earliest *mukhtaṣars* were produced in the fourth/tenth century. The four major Sunni schools all produced at least one significant *mukhtaṣar* in this period. They are generally useful works, not notably refined. Some of them (say, the Ḥanafī *mukhtaṣars* of Ṭaḥāwī (321/933) and Marwazī (334/946)) have survived only because they were incorporated into later and more important commentaries (*mabsūṭ*). Some have a functional adequacy which has secured for them centuries of practical (educative) use, notably the *Risālah* of the Mālikī scholar Ibn Abī Zayd al-Qayrawānī (386/996). The Shi'ah produced no similar work earlier than the *Nihāyah* of Ṭūsī, whose late date reflects the relatively late emergence of the Imāmī Shi'ah both as a definitive sectarian group and as a group committed to the normative Muslim discipline of the law. These early *mukhtaṣars* are significant in at least three different ways. Firstly, they are the product of authors who were consciously aiming at analytic control of their material, presentational elegance and some formal artistry. They were successful only to a degree but the sense of authorial personality and achieved personal control is of considerable importance. Secondly, and in some degree of contrast, these works are summaries of a school achievement and express a school loyalty. They rise above the polemical difficulties and the methodological complexities of third/ninth century debate to state the basic programme of concepts and rules which define their school, their tradition, their loyalty. Thirdly, they are functional: they serve the needs of a curriculum, being clearly intended as primers for students, and requiring elucidation and explication from teachers. These are the forerunners of a literary tradition, intimately associated with an educational programme and a social elite whose members, sharing their knowledge of the law, were enabled to analyse, enjoy and give formal religious dignity to the society they lived in.

The genre of *mukhtaṣar* was fundamentally educative. Such works explained the basic concepts and structures of the law, while giving only hints as to how these could be applied or explored. Initially, writers aimed only at a classical elegance of exposition. Their works are marked by restraint and by sufficiency. Their concerns were to choose and to exemplify the basic concepts in order to create a vehicle that would successfully convey its educative message. Meticulous organization and careful recourse to divisions and subdivisions were prerequisites for successful literary production within the genre. It was a limited genre. The concepts of the law did not change through the centuries (though their application might). The (theologically guarded) sanctity of tradition ensured that the production of a single masterpiece, in Classical format, would dominate subsequent efforts, sometimes for centuries. Within the Ḥanafī tradition, the neatly decisive work of Qudūrī (428/1037) lent in various degrees elements of form, order, structure and locution to the succeeding masterpieces of Mawṣilī (683/1284), Nasafī (710/1310, or 701) and Shurunbulālī (1069/1659). Those who were trained in the discipline, who already knew the law, would find pleasure in such works in recognizing the formal skills of the writer, attested through neat deployment, subtle shifts in order, conceptual density and uncluttered precision.

Qudūrī, in his *Mukhtaṣar*, began his section on alms (*zakāt*) thus:

> *Zakāt* is mandatory for the free man who is Muslim, mature and sane; if he owns a minimum quantity of goods, with exclusive ownership; and if he has had them for a year. Children, the insane, and slaves who are buying their own freedom are not subject to *zakāt*. One who is in debt for a sum that equals the value of his possessions is not subject to *zakāt*.

Shurunbulālī, in his *Nūr al-īḍāḥ* offers the following:

> *Zakāt* is the transfer of specified wealth to a specified person. It is incumbent on the free man who is Muslim, subject to divine

> command, and owner of a minimum quantity of goods, whether in the form of coinage, metal, ornaments or vessels; or in the form of trade goods whose value is equal to the minimum quantity; if he is free of debt and after provision of his basic needs; the minimum quantity being of goods which are productive, or potentially so.

Clause by clause the concept of *zakāt* attracts layers of qualification which become densely suggestive of the problems that attend on God's command. It is highly unlikely for most Muslims, most of the time, that their actual performance of this duty conformed to this type of approach. A practical casualness is not at all incompatible with the conceptual search for qualified meaning and precise significance that is articulated by these carefully juxtaposed clauses. The grammatical and terminological density of the originals is weakened in the translations, which involve about twice as many words as are used in the Arabic texts. A careful reading however should induce some consciousness of how the later text has grown out of, and in some degree, away from, the first. The reader should be aware of the increased specificity, the thorough concretenes of "coinage, metal, ornaments, vessels", etc., and the neat placing of "provision for his basic goods". It is entirely appropriate to feel dissatisfied with "trade goods whose value is equal to the minimum quantity" (should it not be "equal to or greater than"?), and then to consider that the missing words would really, perhaps, be superfluous – as nothing at all should be in this kind of work. Between the first text and the second the law has not changed. What has bothered and interested the jurists is their ability to catch the law in a network of words. The syntactic disjuncture that places the final clause in Shurunbulālī's text is conveyed in Arabic by a variation in adjectival agreement which compels admiration for its marriage of concision and complexity. It is precisely this that the jurists wanted to achieve.

Clearly the genre lent itself to mannerism. With the passage of time, it inspired numerous masterpieces of structural, conceptual and syntactic dexterity that dazzle the reader as they invite him or her to share and delight in the writer's virtuoso mastery of a discipline. The mannerist works, unlike the "Classical" ones, do not have the immediate aim of explaining and elucidating the law; they are quite as likely to hide it, in order to entice the reader into that recreative exercise that consists in unpacking the meanings that have been meticulously – but never with recourse to vagueness or generalization – embedded in the intricate texture of language. One of the most successful such works (not in fact unduly tortuous) is the *Mukhtaṣar* of the Mālikī scholar Khalīl ibn Isḥāq (776/1374). From the time of its production till the thirteenth/nineteenth century, it dominated the Mālikī schools of North Africa and was universally recognized as a jewel.

> *Zakāt* is mandatory / on the specified minimum / of flocks / subject to ownership / and the passing of a year / both complete / whether provided with fodder / or working / or product of breeding / but not of coupling with wild beasts; / increase is included / though before the year by only a day / but not on less [than the minimum] . . .

"Woven on a magician's loom" said Ibn Ḥajar al-ʿAsqalānī (852/1448), trying to convey this work's patterned complexity (1966, 2: 175). The style is (part of) the message, and it should not be disregarded in a search merely for the rules. (These can be learnt elsewhere, and cannot be easily learnt from Khalīl.) Such books say that the law is a delight and a pleasure, and that it is a tortuous and inextricable mystery; they create perplexity and the joy of achieved understanding; they lead the mind away from the messy and the mundane to at least a momentary vision of perfection; and they are witty. The last quality seems inherent in the distancing effect of any virtuoso performance, and owes much to the ironic gap that opens between life and its consciously contrived juristic image.

For centuries young Muslims, aspiring to be educated, had to learn such books off by heart. It might now be lamented that this was a sacrifice of young and enquiring minds. But this was also, potentially at least, an invaluable cultural provision, and, if the text remained in the mind as a recourse, it was a constantly available solace and pleasure.

The multi-volume *mabsūṭ*, by contrast with the slim *mukhtaṣar*, is easy to recognize: their authors, like Ibn al-Muqri', "fly to the circumambient horizons". They multiply the details of the law. They may even (though it is not the most characteristic feature of these books) find the opportunity to relate the concepts of the law to the particular circumstances of their time.

Marwazī, Ḥanafī author of an early *mukhtaṣar*, distinguished between legitimate governors and "outlaws" (*khawārij*). If the former collected *zakāt*, while providing the people with adequate military protection, the duty of the people to pay *zakāt* was thereby accomplished. If, however, the outlaws despoiled the people of their goods, while claiming it was *zakāt* (but in fact using the ill-gotten goods for ill-advised ends), the duty of the people *vis-à-vis* God was not accomplished, and they should repeat their distribution of *zakāt*. This was hardly a friendly rule for the people, who, in the last case, were first despoiled, then had to pay their religious duties! Marwazī however may not have had "real" consequences in mind (he derived his rules in any case from the books before him). Engaging the concept *zakāt* with the additional concepts of governors and outlaws was a heuristic device, permitting exploration of the significance of *zakāt*.

The later jurist Sarakhsī, in his *Mabsūṭ*, a commentary on Marwazī, managed to free the people from their double burden.

> As to the collections made by the sultans of our time, these tyrants . . . Marwazī did not deal with them. Many of the religious leaders of Balkh promulgate the ruling, with regard to these governors, that payment is required a second time, in order to fulfil the duty due to God, as in the case of land attacked and conquered by outlaws. This is because we know that they do not distribute the collected wealth as it should be distributed . . . The more valid view is that these illegitimate collections fulfil for the owners of wealth the duty of *zakāt* – as long as they formulate, at the moment of paying, the intention of giving alms to them [i.e. to the unjust sultans]. This is because the wealth that they possess is the property of the Muslims, and the debts they owe to Muslims are greater than their own wealth. If they returned to the Muslims what they owe them, they would possess nothing. Accordingly they have the status of the poor [and are therefore legitimate recipients of *zakāt*].
>
> (Sarakhsī (1986), 2: 180)

This is a *ḥīlah* (a juristic contrivance), and a joke. At least a quiet smile is appropriate on recognizing how Sarakhsī exploits the idea of debt to render the luxurious tyrants into the category of the poor, who are the rightful recipients of *zakāt*. Here he has clearly an eye on reality, and has arranged (and developed) his concepts for the achievement of particular ends. The development of the law by the discovery of new conceptual distinctions (tyrants, added to governors and outlaws) and by the acknowledgement of dispute (*ikhtilāf*) is characteristic of how the traditions, all of them, expanded.

Development in this sense, however, relating the concepts of the law to the particularities of the day, could be only a small part of any given book. In many works of *furū*ʿ it is impossible to detect any responses that are particular to a given time and place. Formally such works are timeless. They have two major structural components. The first is the set of concepts that constitute the law. These are explored through the contrasting effects of terminological density and casuistic extravagance. The implicatory richness of a highly technical vocabulary is unravelled by making it work through cases, which may be hypothetical or practical, highly imaginative or trivially stereotyped. The casuistry is heuristic, a device for exploration, and it would, accordingly, be quite wrong to read such works as if they had immediate practical ends (though they sometimes did, and always contained that potential). The time-bound origins of a particular ruling are cancelled. The multiplicity of rulings thrown up by the tradition, or devised by the individual jurist, become a means to discover the facets through which a legal concept is revealed. Where the tradition offers dispute (*ikhtilāf*), it too becomes a device to achieve a finer and more qualified perception of what a concept implies.

The second structural component of a *mabsūṭ* is revelation and justificatory argument. These are always integrated to some extent in a *mabsūṭ*, but it is a matter of tradition and individual taste how much they are expanded and developed. Both concepts and revelation are theoretically static (in spite of some real development, at least of the former). This literary tradition too, therefore, in time, developed characteristics which might be described as mannerist. To attempt here a history of so large and long a tradition would be vain. The major illustration offered here is taken from the *Muhadhdhab* of the Shāfiʿī jurist, Shīrāzī (476/1083), a work emphatically Classical.

In the following passage, Shīrāzī considers the question how the owner of "hidden" goods (differing from "manifest" goods, flocks or crops, in not being easily accessible to government inspection) should organize the distribution of his *zakāt*. Paragraph division and numbering are mine, but the neatness of the fit is Shīrāzī's. Note how every paragraph is constituted by a rule and the argument which justifies the rule; how the *ikhtilāf* of paragraphs 2.0–2.3 is unresolved.

Chapter on the distribution of alms

1.1 It is permissible for the owner of wealth to distribute *zakāt* on hidden goods by himself. Hidden goods are gold, silver, trade goods and precious stones. This ruling is based on the *ḥadīth* from ʿUthmān, that he said in the month of Muḥarram, This is the month of your *zakāt*, so he who has a debt, let him pay his debt, then let him pay *zakāt* on the remainder of his wealth.

1.2 It is permissible for him to appoint an agent to distribute on his behalf. This is because *zakāt* is a claim on wealth, and it is permissible to appoint an agent to execute it, as with debts between men.

1.3 It is permissible that he pay his *zakāt* to the Imām. This is because the Imām is the representative of the poor. His status is like that of a guardian to an orphan.

2.0 On the question which is the best mode of conduct, there are three views.

2.1 The best mode of conduct is that the owner of wealth should distribute his *zakāt* by himself. This is the evident meaning of the text [i.e. the *ḥadīth* quoted at paragraph 1.1]. Further he is secure in respect of his own paying, but not secure in respect of anyone else paying.

2.2 The best mode of conduct is that he should pay the Imām, whether the Imām is just or unjust. This is because of what is related concerning Mughīrah ibn Sha'bah. He said to a client of his, who had the stewardship of his property in Ṭā'if, What do you do about alms on my property? The client replied, "Some of it I distribute directly as alms, and some of it I give to the authorities." Mughīrah asked what he knew about the latter portion. The client explained, "They buy land and marry women with it." Mughīrah said, "Pay it to them; for the Prophet of God commanded us to pay them." Another reason: the Imām is more knowledgeable about the poor and the extent of their need.

2.3 Amongst our companions there are some who say that if the Imām is just, payment to him is the best mode of conduct, but if he is unjust, then distribution by the owner of the wealth is best. This is because of the Prophet's words, He who asks for it as it should be, let him be given it; he who demands more than he should, let him not be given it. Further, the donor is secure in paying it to a just Imām, but is not secure in paying it to an unjust Imām, for the latter may spend it on his own desires.

(Shīrāzī (1959), 1: 175)

In the *ikhtilāf* of 2.0–2.3 there are three foci of concern: *zakāt* as a personal duty to God, *zakāt* as a communal duty implemented by the Imām and *zakāt* as a functional provision for the poor. The three "best modes of conduct" can be analysed as resulting from the elevation, in sequence, of each of these considerations to a dominant position. Shīrāzī has effectively shown his readers how the Shāfi'ī tradition (his "companions") understood (in this context) the concept of *zakāt*, and how this understanding can be justified by arguments of revelation, of reason and of analogy. If the "best modes of conduct" emerged into the tradition because they were responses to particular situations (as is not unlikely), it is precisely that particularity that has been removed, so rendering the casuistry exploratory and not practical. In the distribution of *zakāt* it is necessary to consider the duty to God, the rights and duties of the governor and the legitimate expectations of the poor. The message is perhaps that no one of these considerations unequivocally overrides the others. This is an abstract analysis of concepts and should not be mistaken for a set of practical rules. If, anywhere in Shīrāzī's work, we could learn anything about, say, the actual practice of his governors (and I think we can't), it would be an accident, and would not represent a part of his purpose in producing this book.

In a *mabsūṭ* then, the concepts of the law are explored, often by varying one or several items in a "case" which, at a given point, reveals the significance of the concept. The result of course is that many different concepts are explored at once in a dense reticulation of argument. Here, in order to illuminate the concept of *zakāt*, Shīrāzī relates it to the concept of "agent" (*wakīl*) (1.2) and to the concept Imām (1.3), and that in turn to the concept of guardianship of orphans. Fully alert readers should begin to ask themselves about the significance of these judgments and might formulate further questions, or cases, which could illuminate the relationship between God, the individual (his or her agent, etc.), the Imām, the poor, etc. It is precisely this multifaceted and more or less hypothetical exploratory activity that constitutes the bulk of a work of *furū'*.

There is none the less a distinguishable third component which is also constitutive of the material contents of a *mabsūṭ*. It is the tradition itself. The exploration of concepts and the relating of concepts to revelation is achieved through tradition, In the passage from Shīrāzī above, we are not to imagine that he himself devised the three "best views"; they were given to him by the tradition, here the Shāfi'ī tradition. His role was to organize and present them in the neat schematic manner that permits the reader to perceive and register their implications. (That this role was creative is not denied.) Often the role of tradition is rendered explicit by reference to named authorities. In the early centuries of juristic writing, the named authorities are likely to be, almost exclusively, the founding fathers of the school tradition, Abū Ḥanīfah and his two pupils dominate the Ḥanafī tradition, Shāfi'ī, Mālik and Ibn Ḥanbal the other Sunni schools. For each of the last three it is commonplace to find that they had two or more opinions about legal problems, or that one of their pupils or colleagues had a well-defended alternative view, worth preserving. A multiple set of authorities and judgments was a prerequisite, for it permitted a concept to be viewed from a number of angles, so engendering complexity (a jurist's delight), and opening up different possibilities of development. The Shi'ite tradition too, when it began to produce juristic literature, called upon a constellation of authorities, as well as a large and diverse set of *ḥadīth* from the Imāms.

With the passage of centuries, the quantity of tradition, the juristic literature itself, became immensely greater than the quantity of revelation. The symbolic importance of the latter was not diminished, but its place in the literature of the law became, necessarily, (even) smaller. Within the school traditions this was not perceived as a problem, though it did prompt, on occasion, fundamentalist reactions, amongst those who felt that revelation rather than tradition should be the immediate source of rules. The prime example of fundamentalist reaction is Ibn Ḥazm, the Literalist (Goldziher 1971), but the tendency recurred from time to time, within various schools, its most notable later representative being the Ḥanbalī Ibn Taymiyyah. Generally, however, inside the schools, the meaning of revelation was discovered through tradition. There is no doubt about the priority of the latter: the first loyalty of a jurist was to his school which alone revealed (!) to him the meaning of revelation (!). The theological implications of that fact can hardly be overstated.

In literary terms, the theological argument was expressed through a number of devices. In addition to those mentioned above, the most obvious is, perhaps, the use of commentary, supercommentary and gloss. These layered texts (increasingly present as the tradition got older) are in part product of a teaching device, in part reflect a delight in the contrasting effects of epitome and expansion, but mostly are a theological affirmation of commitment to tradition. The content of some early *mukhtaṣar*, embedded within a contemporary *mabsūṭ*, are thereby asserted to be identical with the full complexity of the law as it was understood in the later period. Serving the same purpose was the device of jigsaw puzzle composition. Ibn Nujaym's *Al-Baḥr al-rā'iq* is an example. The text of this work is created out of larger or smaller fragments derived (and acknowledged) from the whole tradition of Ḥanafī juristic writing. Explicit authorial intervention is reduced to a minimum and always takes the form of commentary on a citation. What might interest a Western scholar, the chronological order of these things, is quite disregarded. Though there is no doubt that Ibn Nujaym's complex manipulation of the tradition created something new (if only, sometimes, in form, for that too is part of the message), his methodology was designed to affirm the timelessnes of his conceptual explorations. Cut into the tradition at any point and the whole complexity of the law is there.

The law is a timeless structure of concepts, justified by reference to revelation, and fully present, at least by implication, in any articulation within the tradition, whether in a *mukhtaṣar* or in a *mabsūṭ*. Understanding of the law is achieved through understanding of tradition, not through independent or personal assessment of the meaning of revelation. A deeper understanding of the law (always the same as a greater delight in the law) can be achieved through consideration of the implications of *ikhtilāf* and the possibilities of conceptual subdivision. Direct response to revelation or to reality, though always possible, and sometimes detectable, are not particularly characteristic of how the law as a whole develops. With regard to many aspects of social reality, the juristic traditions are marked not by their aspiration to control and understand reality but by abnegation and indifference to development. Jurists, for example, never considered it their business to analyse the real problems faced by real governments in the creation of administrative and financial systems that would work. The efforts made in that direction were few (e.g. by Māwardī *et al.*, see Lambton (1981)), the achievements limited and the results largely disregarded by the mainstream of all the juristic traditions (Calder 1986). In spite of some remarkable exceptions, the jurists on the whole preferred to analyse the concepts and problems they inherited, rather than to take on or create new ones (Imber 1982). And they continued to analyse inherited concepts and problems even when these had no bearing on the practical life of ordinary Muslims. No Muslim who studied *fiqh* would fail to learn the taxonomy of camels (in the archaic and frozen vocabulary of the tradition), and the arithmetic of how to distribute *zakāt* on camels, no matter how little the personal need to know this. Knowledge counted. Shawkānī tells us, with evident admiration, that Ibn al Muqri', on one occasion, considered the implications of the dispute within the Shāfi'ī tradition as to the use of sun-warmed water for ablutions: his heads of analysis reached thousands (Shawkānī (1979), 1.43). There may be exaggeration here, but the point is important: a jurist merits praise when he takes a single given problem or concept of the law and by minute analysis reveals its implications, its thousands (!) of facets. The diamond-cutting analogy is not inappropriate, for the effect of (good) juristic prose is one of crystalline clarity and of dazzling virtuosity.

I have said above that *fiqh* is a multi-functional discipline. It is not too difficult to concede that its primary function is theological, though it is not now easy to recover the theological message of these works. Modernist and fundamentalist Islam has lost the taste, and denies the priorities of traditional writing on the law. Sayyid Quṭb (executed 1966), informal spokesman for the Muslim Brothers in Egypt, and widely acknowledged for his Qur'ān commentary, on numerous occasions expressed what many Muslims now feel, namely that the tradition has somehow failed them. "The *Sharī'ah*," he says, "has been revealed in order to be implemented, not to be known, to be studied, and to be changed into culture in books and treatises" (Quṭb (1971), 1: 746). The observation is pertinent because it acknowledges (correctly) that this, or something like it, is what the tradition did. There, again and again, the stress falls on the need to explore the law in order to know it better, and on the need to create elegant and self-consciously artistic literary forms that will reflect the law's complexity. Whereas the pre-modern writers affirm that tradition controls understanding of revelation, modernist Islam tends to say the opposite, that revelation is a means to get rid of the (burdensome and irrelevant) complexities of a tradition which, perhaps, it is implied, has not served the community well. In the course of the thirteenth/nineteenth century, and largely as a result of Islam's confrontation with Western culture, the tradition had been interrupted, and its message lost. The tenuous continuation of the pre-modern juristic tradition was perhaps less tenuous amongst the Shī'ah, where it provided the concepts that inspired the jurists' intervention in the Iranian Revolution of 1978. Generally, however, the emergence of secular education systems and the divergence of the intellectual elite of Muslim societies to other (and frequently more pressing) matters has ensured that the law (or rather *fiqh*, for the inspirational power of *Sharīʿah*, a concept potentially devoid of detail or specificity, has increased) does not dominate society as it once did.

Quṭb's remark shows that he thinks the *Sharīʿah* (*sic*) exists to be implemented. That stress on loyalty and action, prior to (even independent of) exploratory thought, is part of an activist programme to which he was committed, but it has reverberations throughout modernist Muslim writing, and has affected the perceptions of Western scholars. F. M. Denny is not the only observer to imagine that Islam is better characterized as a religion of orthopraxy than as a religion of orthodoxy (Denny (1985): 98). This is not true, and was traditionally denied by Muslim jurists and theologians. For them, the definition of a Muslim, and the possibility of salvation, depended on faith, not works. For the whole of the Sunni tradition there was no dispute that faith (alone) guaranteed salvation. Works of course were important; Muslims might be punished, according to some temporarily, in Hell, for their failures to conform to God's law (though they might, even then, be saved through the intercession of their Prophet). In practical life, even the simplest, and absolutely undisputed, parts of the law (say, to pray five times a day) are today (and were undoubtedly in the past) often disregarded by some Muslims who, though acknowledging their error, are not (as far as the casual observer can tell) unduly disturbed by their sins, nor rendered doubtful in their conviction of salvation. A Muslim did not have to be a qualified jurist to perceive the law as an ideal.

These remarks, and the general tenor of this chapter, are not intended to deny that the law, and all writing on the law, was expected, in some degree, to influence practice. No jurist was ever oblivious to the fact that conceptual exploration of the law, or theological affirmations about the importance of tradition, had implications for daily life. And every jurist acknowledged his duty, as a member of the learned elite, to provide explicit and unqualified guidance in respect of particular problems that were brought to him by the populace at large. If the jurist Shīrāzī was approached by one who explained his financial circumstances, and enquired about payment of *zakāt*, Shīrāzī would not then sit back to consider the possibilities of the law; he would, as a *mujtahid*, recognize the need to provide an answer. The need to make the law work, to some degree, was universally recognized, and generated bodies of literature distinct from those described in this chapter. Juristic responses to particular questions generated the literature of *fatāwā* (responsa). That literature has its own complexity, which cannot be discussed here. Some parts of the law were more than others integrated into the administrative structures of Islamic society, notably the office of the *qāḍī* and all that appertained to it. Monographs were produced in such fields in which the stress was less on exploring the law, more on the provision of practical advice and rules of expedient conduct. There was even a small and marginal genre of monographs on the structures of government, little though these, on the whole, attracted the attention of the tradition. Many jurists however participated in government (while many others refused to do so) and tried to create some kind of link between the structures of the law and the structures of practical administration.

But practice, in whatever area or form, could never be more than a clumsy, partial and imperfect realization of the divine command. A fuller (if perhaps still inadequate) expression of that command could be achieved in literature. The literature of the law is an exploration of God's self-revelation to and within a particular human society. In all its forms, aspects and implications it is about a divinely sanctioned social order and the (consequent?) possibilities of human social integration. It is not a description of "real" society, nor the provision of a corpus of sensible, practical rules; it is at least the transformation of these things into a theological argument. As much for modern Muslims as for modern academics the task of mastering that literature and translating its implications into an idiom suited to (soon) the fifteenth/twenty-first century is one that has hardly begun. The cultural complement to juristic literature, with its stress on society, is, within Islam, Sufi literature, which provides a corresponding stress on the private devotional life of individuals. It is in the integration of these two structures that most Muslims – including the jurists, who were frequently also mystics – have, historically, found self-realization as Muslims.

BIBLIOGRAPHY

Al-'Asqalānī, Aḥmad ibn Ḥajar (852/1448) (1966) *Al-Durar al-kāminah*, 5 vols, ed. M. S. Jād al-Ḥaqq (Cairo).

Calder, Norman (1983) "*Ikhtilāf* and *ijmā'* in Shāfi'ī's *Risāla*", *Studia Islamica*, 58: 55–81.

—— (1986) "Friday Prayer and the Juristic Theory of Government: Sarakhsī, Shīrāzī, Māwardī", *Bulletin of the School of Oriental and African Studies*, 49(1): 35–47.

—— (1989) "Doubt and Prerogative: the Emergence of an Imāmī Shī'ī Theory of *ijtihād*", *Studia Islamica*, 70 (1989): 57–78.

Denny, F. M. (1985) *An Introduction to Islam* (London and New York).

Al-Dhahabī, Muḥammad ibn Aḥmad Abū 'Abd Allāh (748/1347) (1947) *Manāqib al-Imām Abī Ḥanīfah*, eds M. Z. al-Kawtharī and A.-W. al-Afghānī (Hyderabad and Cairo).

Fyzee, A. A. A. (1964) *Outlines of Muhammadan Law*, 3rd ed. (Calcutta).

Goldziher, Ignaz (1971) *The Ẓāhirīs: Their Doctrine and Their History*, trans. and ed. Wolfgang Behn (Leiden).

Hallaq, Wael B. (1984) "Was the Gate of *ijtihād* Closed?", *International Journal of Middle Eastern Studies*, 16: 3–41.

—— (1986) "On the Origins of the Controversy about the Existence of *mujtahids* and the Gate of *ijtihād*", *Studia Islamica*, 63: 129–41.

Imber, Colin (1982) "*Zina* in Ottoman Law", in *Contribution à l'histoire économique et sociale de l'Empire Ottoman*, Collection Turcica (Louvain), 3: 61–92.

'Iyāḍ, al-Qāḍī (1967) *Tartīb al-madārik wa taqrīb al-masālik li-ma'rifat a'lām madhhab Mālik*, 4 vols, ed. A. B. Mahmoud (Beirut and Tripoli).

Johansen, Baber (1988) *The Islamic Law on Land Tax and Rent* (Exeter Arabic and Islamic series) (London, New York and Sydney).

Khalīl ibn Isḥāq (776/1374) *Al-Mukhtaṣar*, in Muḥammad al-Khurashī, *Sharḥ mukhtaṣar al-khalīl*, 8 vols (Beirut, n.d.; reprint Cairo, 1900).

Lambton, A. K. S. (1981) *State and Government in Medieval Islam: an Introduction to the Study of Islamic Political Theory: the Jurists* (Oxford).

Linant de Bellefonds, Y. (1956) *Traité de droit musulman comparé*, 3 vols (Paris and The Hague).

Al-Qudūrī, Aḥmad ibn Muḥammad Abu'l-Ḥusayn (428/1037) (1957) *al-Mukhtaṣar* or *al-Matn*, 3rd ed. (Cairo).

Quṭb, Sayyid (1971) *Fī ẓilāl al-qur'ān*, 8 vols (Beirut).

Saleh, Nabil (1986) *Unlawful Gain and Legitimate Profit in Islamic Law* (Cambridge Studies in Islamic Civilisation) (Cambridge).

Sarakhsī, Muḥammad ibn Abī Sahl Abū Bakr (483/1090) (1986) *al-Mabsūṭ*, 30 vols (Cairo, 1906; reprinted Beirut, 1986).

Schacht, Joseph (1950) *The Origins of Muhammadan Jurisprudence* (Oxford).

—— (1964) *An Introduction to Islamic Law* (Oxford).

Al-Shawkānī, Muḥammad ibn 'Alī (1250/1834) (1929) *Al-Badr al-ṭāli' bi-maḥāsin man ba'd al-qarn al-sābi'*, 2 vols (Cairo).

Al-Shīrāzī, Ibrāhīm ibn 'Alī Abū Isḥāq (476/1083) (1959) *al-Muhadhdhab fī fiqh al-Imām al-Shāfi'ī*, 2 vols (Beirut).

Al-Shurunbulālī, Ḥasan ibn 'Ammār (1069/1659) (1900) *Nūr al-īḍāḥ*, in Aḥmad ibn Muḥammad al-Ṭaḥāwī, *Ḥāshiyyah 'alā marāqī al-falāḥ sharḥ nūr al-īḍāḥ* (Bulaq).

Wansbrough, John (1977) *Quranic Studies: Sources and Methods of Scriptural Interpretation* (London Oriental Series, 31) (Oxford).

VIII

Later transmission and interpretation

CHAPTER 58

Medieval Christian and Jewish Europe

John Marenbon

With the occasional exception (such as Leibniz, who annotated Maimonides' *Guide of the Perplexed*), Christian philosophers from the seventeenth century onwards have neglected medieval Islamic and Jewish philosophy. By contrast, from the late twelfth to the sixteenth century, Islamic and Jewish thinkers were among the most important influences on scholastic philosophers and theologians. The first two sections below will survey the extent of this influence by showing which works were translated and how much they were read; later sections will consider some individual examples of influence in a little more detail.

THE TRANSLATIONS[1]

Philosophers of the Latin Middle Ages depended on translations for their knowledge of Islamic and Jewish thought. Although scientific works had been put into Latin earlier, translations of philosophy from the Arabic were first made in Toledo in the second half of the twelfth century, by Dominic Gundisalvi (or Gundissalinus), a canon of the cathedral there. Gundissalinus translated with the help of Arabic speaking assistants, one of whom is named as Avendeuth, a Jewish philosopher, identified by some with Abraham ibn Daoud, author of *The Sublime Faith* (Avicenna (1968–72): 91–103; d'Alverny (1989)). Gundissalinus and his helpers put into Latin the sections on the soul (*De anima*) and on metaphysics from the *Book of Healing* by Ibn Sīnā ("Avicenna" for the Latins), and were probably responsible for versions of a little of the logic and some of the *Physics* (d'Alverny (1961): 285). The same team, or members of it, also translated the *De scientiis* and *De ortu scientiarum* by al-Fārābī

("Alfarabi"); the *Fons vitae* by the Jewish philosopher Solomon ibn Gabirol ("Avicebron"/"Avencebrol") and probably an abbreviated version of Isaac Israeli's *Liber de definitionibus*. Probably from this milieu came the translation of one of the versions of al-Kindī's *De intellectu*, of the *Liber introductorius in artem logicae demonstrationis* wrongly attributed to al-Kindī, of the *Intentions of the Philosophers* (known as the *Summa theorice philosophiae*) by al-Ghazzālī ("Algazel"); and also perhaps the translation of Alfarabi's *De intellectu*. At the same period in Toledo, Gerard of Cremona, who concentrated for the most part on putting Arabic versions of Aristotle into Latin, translated the complete text of Isaac Israeli's *Liber de definitionibus*, works by al-Kindī (*De somno et visione*, probably *De quinque essentiis* and perhaps *De ratione* – a version of *De intellectu*), made another version of Alfarabi's *De scientiis* and put into Latin the *Liber de causis*, an Arabic compilation based on the *Elements of Philosophy* by the fifth-century Greek Neoplatonist Proclus.

The writings of Ibn Rushd ("Averroes") were not translated until a little later. In the 1220s, probably in Sicily, Michael Scotus produced Latin versions of Averroes' great commentaries on the *De anima*, *Metaphysics*, *Physics* and *De caelo*, of the middle commentaries on the *De generatione et corruptione* and *Meteorologica* 4 and perhaps of some of his epitomes (Gauthier (1982): 331–4). At much the same date, probably in France, a translation was made of Maimonides' *Guide of the Perplexed*. Executed with considerable freedom, the version was based neither on the Arabic original nor the earliest translation by Samuel ibn Tibbon, but rather on a looser though more stylish Hebrew version made by Jehudah al-Ḥārisī. Although this translation is anonymous, internal evidence suggests that it was made by a learned Jew in collaboration with a Latin-speaking Christian (Kluxen 1954).

By about 1230, then, the Islamic and Jewish philosophical works which were to be most important for Christian thinkers had already been translated. Over the following decades a few additions were made. Hermannus Alemannus, who worked in Toledo, made Latin versions of Averroes' middle commentaries on the *Ethics* (perhaps 1240) and the *Poetics* (1256); Johannes Gunsalvi of Burgos, helped by a Jew called Solomon, translated more of Avicenna's *Book of Healing* between 1274 and 1280: further parts of the *Physics*, and sections 2 (*De caelo et mundo*), 3 (*De generatione et corruptione*), 4 and 5 (d'Alverny (1961–72): 286–7). And, at some time in the thirteenth century – no more precise dating is possible – the middle commentaries by Averroes on Porphyry's *Isagoge*, and Aristotle's *Categories*, *De interpretatione*, *Prior* and *Posterior Analytics* were translated: the first two definitely, and the other three probably, by a certain William of Luna.

Not all the translations available to medieval scholars have survived. This is strikingly the case with regard to Alfarabi, whose great commentary (otherwise lost) on the *Posterior Analytics* was certainly translated, and perhaps also commentaries by him on the *Ethics* and *Physics* (Salman (1939); Grignaschi (1972)). No doubt evidence of other lost translations will be uncovered by future researches.

From this survey it is clear that the works of Islamic (though not Jewish) philosophy translated into Latin were in almost every case closely related to the study of Aristotle. That this was not a matter of chance but a reflection of Christian thinkers' interests is illustrated by an apparent exception to the rule. Averroes' *Destruction of the Destruction* was in fact translated early in the fourteenth century by the Jew Calonymos ben Calonymos for Robert the Wise, King of Naples. But the translation remained almost unknown (de Libera (1991): 110, 369).

AVAILABILITY AND USE

The earliest Christian writer to make use of Avicenna was his translator, Gundissalinus. Gundissalinus had the mentality of a compiler rather than an original thinker or a careful synthesizer. His *De processione mundi* ("On the Coming-forth of the Universe"), borrows from Avicenna, but also uses material from Avencebrol and Boethius (a late antique Christian thinker), and his *De anima* ("On the Soul") uses the same combination of authors and has an explicitly Christian conclusion. An even odder mixture is found in an anonymous work of the early thirteenth century, *De causis primis et secundis* ("On Primary and Secondary Causes"), which brings together Avicenna's *Philosophia prima*, the *Liber de causis* and the *Periphyseon* of John Scotus Eriugena, a ninth-century Christian Neoplatonist (cf. Jolivet 1988). By then, Avicenna was already important in the University of Paris. Indeed, the earliest writers there who seem to display a knowledge of Aristotle beyond his logic turn out to be much more familar with Avicenna. For example, John Blund's treatise on the soul (*De anima*, *c.* 1200) makes passing references to Aristotelian texts but follows Avicenna in the main lines of its argument. Even in the 1230s or early 1240s, William of Auvergne spent most of his energies in his *De anima* attacking Avicenna's views which, despite his direct acquaintance with Aristotle's texts, he consistently attributed to Aristotle himself (Marenbon (1991): 53–6, 109–10).

Closer familiarity with Aristotle's own texts and the availability of Averroes' detailed commentaries on them deprived Avicenna of his pre-eminent position, but his *De anima* and, especially, his *Philosophia prima* remained enormously influential, helping to shape the metaphysics of both Aquinas and Duns Scotus (see the following section). The many manuscripts of the Latin Avicenna from the fourteenth and fifteenth centuries show that he continued to be studied in the late Middle Ages (d'Alverny 1961–72).

Averroes came into use in the university of Paris in the 1220s, despite the prohibition at this stage on the study of many Aristotelian works and their commentaries in the Arts Faculty (Gauthier 1982). When, in the 1250s, an Aristotelian curriculum was adopted by the Arts Faculties in Paris and Oxford, Averroes' detailed commentaries proved invaluable aids for the masters there. To the end of the Middle Ages and later, Averroes continued to play this part, uncontroversially providing scholars with the detailed help they needed to follow Aristotle's arguments. Just as Aristotle was called simply the "Philosophus", so Averroes was the "Commentator". Even in the Renaissance, when scholars reacting against the humanist emphasis on style wished to grasp the substance of Aristotle's thought, they turned to Averroes for help, as is illustrated by the 1520–2 Giunta edition of Aristotle's works, which brought together the best translations of Aristotle with more of Averroes' commentaries than had previously been collected (Schmitt 1979). In addition to this uncontroversial role, Averroes is often seen as the inspiration behind a distinctive (and perhaps heterodox) movement of thought: Latin Averroism (see below).

Algazel's fortune was closely tied to Avicenna's, of whose work his *Intentions* was taken to be an epitome. The fact that Algazel summarized the work of Avicenna and other philosophers only the better to attack it (in his *Destruction* – which was not translated into Latin) was generally ignored if not exactly unknown (Salman 1939). Avencebrol was used by his translator, Gundissalinus (see above), and in his *De universo*, written in the 1230s, William of Auvergne held him in high esteem, and conjectured that, despite his Arab name, he must be a Christian. However, Avencebrol's theory of universal hylomorphism – everything except God is a compound of matter and form – earned him sharp criticism from later scholastics, such as Albert the Great and Thomas Aquinas. None the less, the occasional writer, such as Vital du Four (*c.* 1260–1327) was ready to support him (Bertola (1953): 187–99; Wippel (1982): 408–10).

Maimonides's *Dux perplexorum* was first seriously studied by Albert the Great in the 1240s. The work was an important influence on Aquinas (see below). Duns Scotus occasionally refers to Maimonides, but makes little use of him; and most of the later scholastics ignored him entirely (Guttmann (1908): 140–208; Kluxen (1986)). But there was one important exception. Maimonides had a profound influence on Meister Eckhart (1260–1327), who repeated his arguments that positive attributes cannot be ascribed to God, even by analogy (Koch 1928).

AVICENNA AND LATIN METAPHYSICS IN THE THIRTEENTH CENTURY[2]

Although Islamic writers were seen by the Latin Scholastics almost exclusively as guides to interpreting Aristotle, their writings were far more than merely neutral instruments for transmitting the thought of another. Aristotle is a writer many of whose central texts have never received a single, generally accepted interpretation. Avicenna and Averroes provided their Latin readers with ways of reading Aristotle, which in many cases they would never have derived from the Aristotelian texts alone. These (often conflicting) interpretations set the framework for their discussions, nowhere more obviously than with regard to the *Metaphysics*.

Both Avicenna and Averroes had sought a coherence and definite purpose in Aristotle's chaotic and often inconclusive treatise. What, they asked, is the subject of the work? Avicenna argued that, since no branch of knowledge can demonstrate the existence of its own subject, and since the existence of God is demonstrated in metaphysics, the subject of metaphysics is not God, but being as being. By contrast, Averroes, who held that the existence of God was demonstrated in physics, considered that being in its first instance, the Prime Mover or God, was the subject of metaphysics. Thirteenth-century Christian thinkers, although aware of Averroes' position, tended to follow Avicenna here (Wippel (1982): 385–92). But there was an important difference. For them the question about the subject of metaphysics was linked to an even more important problem: what is the relationship between the study of God in metaphysics and the study of God on the basis on revelation?

Avicenna provided a starting-point not just for the definition, but for the content of metaphysical discussion. In his *Metaphysics*, Avicenna (1977–83: 43–8) distinguished between God, the one necessary being, and all other beings which are merely possible. In the case of possible beings, Avicenna (following Alfarabi) distinguished existence (*esse*: whether the thing in fact exists) from essence (what sort of thing it is). In Algazel's account (1933: 30–1), this distinction is taken to mean that existence is an accident of essence. From William of Auvergne onwards, the distinction played an important part in Western metaphysics and theology. Aquinas was among those who accepted a real distinction between essence and existence. However, he firmly rejected any notion that existence is an accident, and he transformed Avicenna's idea by seeing essence as potency and existence as act. Essence and existence are thus complementary, in the same way as matter and form (in composite things); and everything depends for its existence on God, who is pure act, and in whom alone essence and existence are the same.[3]

Duns Scotus (who taught at the turn of the fourteenth century, and was probably the thinker most influential for the next hundred years) rejected the real distinction between essence and existence. Yet his discussion of being was even more deeply marked than Aquinas' by the teaching of Avicenna. Scotus applied to being Avicenna's idea that something (for example, horse) can be considered neutrally, as neither singular nor universal. He explicitly, though perhaps wrongly, attributed the resulting position – "that being [*ens*] is said in the same meaning [*per unam rationem*] of all that it is said of" – to Avicenna.[4] This theory of the "univocity" of being is a fundamental element in Scotus' thinking, contrasting with Aquinas' theory of analogy, and shaping both his proofs of God's existence and his analysis of objects in the world and their cognition (Gilson (1952): 84–115).

LATIN AVERROISM?[5]

Aquinas directed his brief treatise *On the Unity of the Intellect against the Averroists* against masters at Paris who held the view (derived, they and Thomas considered, from Averroes) that there is only one "possible intellect" for all men. One of those attacked is usually identified as Siger of Brabant (*c.* 1240–84), an arts master who certainly did at one stage propose the view attacked by Aquinas. Siger's name is often coupled with that of his contemporary in the Faculty of Arts, Boethius of Dacia, whose works advocate a sharp division between the field of the arts, which are based on reasoning from self-evident premisses, and theology, which is based on revelation. Historians used commonly to call the ideas of Siger, Boethius and some of their anonymous contemporaries "Latin Averroism". But this description has been challenged: the arts masters were rather, it is argued, "radical" (or "integral") "Aristotelians" (Van Steenberghen 1977; 1978). What did the characteristic positions of Siger, Boethius and their colleagues owe to Averroes?

Whether Averroes himself really supported the unity of the possible intellect is arguable (Gomez Nogales 1976); but, in the 1250s, theologians such as Bonaventure and Albert the Great decided that this was Averroes' position – previously he had been regarded as championing the position that there is an active and potential intellect united in each individual human soul (Gauthier 1982). The theologians raised Averroes' supposed view only in order to refute it. Siger's innovation was to present it as correct, or at least as the correct reading of Aristotle. Boethius of Dacia's wish to emphasize the autonomy of reason within its own domain has no *direct* link with Averroes. In part, it may derive simply from Boethius' position as a master in the Faculty of Arts, the concern of which was exclusively the use of reason without revelation. In part, however, it may be an *indirect* result of Averroes' interpretation of Aristotle. No one doubted that the unity of the possible intellect was a position incompatible with Christian doctrine, since no place is left for individual immortality and heavenly reward or punishment. What, then, was the Christian thinker to say, if he was none the less convinced that this Averroistic interpretation was in accord with Aristotle's intentions? In his *De anima intellectiva* (*c.* 1273), Siger of Brabant tackled exactly this problem by insisting that his job is simply to expound his text, whether or not what Aristotle says is in fact true (1972: 70.11–15).

The characteristic ideas of Siger of Brabant and Boethius of Dacia did not exercise much influence on their immediate successors, probably owing to their inclusion (often distorted) in a set of condemnations issued by the Archbishop of Paris in 1277 (cf. Hissette 1977). But in the early fourteenth century, John of Jandun (1285/9–1328) championed the view that Averroes' supposed interpretation (unity of the possible intellect) is the correct reading of Aristotle, and combined it with a sharp division between the realms of philosophy and theology (cf. Schmugge 1966). His writings were widely read, and an "Averroism" in his mould was adopted in the following decades by scholars in Bologna and Padua, in Erfurt in the late fourteenth century, and Krakow in the mid fifteenth (Kuksewicz 1978). In sixteenth-century Italy, Averroes' supposed views continued to be an important element in discussions of intellect and the soul. Despite wider knowledge of Averroes' works – for instance, Agostino Nifo (1469/70–1538) commented on the *Destruction of the Destruction*) – Renaissance Averroism continued to be influenced by Siger of Brabant and John of Jandun.

"Latin Averroism", then, appears to have combined an interpretation (possibly incorrect) of *one* of Averroes' doctrines (which was taken not as true but as a correct reading of Aristotle), with a view about faith and reason based on the implications of this view. Although it would have been impossible without Averroes, its development was determined not so much by his philosophy as by the internal tensions of thought in the Christian universities.

MAIMONIDES AND AQUINAS[6]

Maimonides' influence on Aquinas was of a different kind from that of Averroes or Avicenna: less pervasive than theirs, but, in the well-defined areas to which it was limited, often far stronger, far less transformed by St Thomas' own thoughts. A striking instance is Aquinas' presentation of the reasons why it was necessary for God to have given in revelation a number of truths also graspable by reason alone (Synave 1930). As this example suggests, Aquinas tended to turn to Maimonides not for help with understanding Aristotle, but when there was a problem about the relation between a philosophical (often Aristotelian) position and doctrine which Jews and Christians held in common. Another such area was the question of the eternity of the world.[7]

Jews and Christians believe not merely that the world is created but that it had a beginning in time. By contrast, Aristotle held that it was eternal. How should Jewish and Christian philosophers react? Already, in the sixth century, John Philoponus, a Greek Christian, had tackled the problem by devising a series of arguments which ingeniously attempt to use Aristotelian principles to demonstrate the very position which Aristotle himself denied – that the world had a beginning. Many of these arguments were adopted by the *mutakallimūn* in Islam, and by Christian theologians contemporary with Aquinas, such as Bonaventure. Maimonides rejected these arguments, and in this (including some of his counter-arguments) he was followed by Aquinas. Moreover, on closer examination, Aquinas' position turns out to be even nearer to that of his great Jewish predecessor. Consider the following propositions:

(1) The world had no beginning in time (i.e. is eternal)
(2) It is possible to demonstrate (1)
(3) It is possible to demonstrate not-(1)
(4) (1) has been demonstrated
(5) not-(1) has been demonstrated

On a straightforward reading of the Latin translation of the *Guide*, such as Aquinas would have made,[8] Maimonides denies (1) in accord with Jewish teaching; and he also explicitly denies (2) and (3) (and so, by consequence, (4) and (5)). Aquinas, too, throughout his works denies (1)–(5). Maimonides also believed that Aristotle himself, whilst holding (1) and, of course, denying (3), also denied (2). His evidence was a passage in the *Topics* where Aristotle gives the eternity of the world as an example of a question for which there is no demonstrative proof on either side. In most of his works Aquinas followed Maimonides in this view.[9] Only towards the end of his life, when Aquinas wrote his detailed commentary on the *Physics*, did he acknowledge that Aristotle held (4) – he believed *he* had demonstrated the eternity of the world – and therefore (2). In this late period, too, an important new element emerges in Aquinas' thought. In his brief *De aeternitate mundi* (probably 1270 or 1271), Aquinas devotes his attention to establishing:

(6) It is possible that (1)

Why was it only in this late work that Aquinas asserted (6)? One historian (Weisheipl (1983): 268–70) has linked the development to Aquinas' realization that Maimonides was wrong to think that Aristotle denied (2). But it is more plausible to see it as a result of a shift in the focus of Aquinas' interest (cf. Wippel (1981): 37). (6) is quite unlike (2)–(5). They are all statements about what man can *demonstrate*, that is what, using self-evident premisses and reason, he can show to be the case; (6) is, rather, a statement about what might absolutely be the case in the nature of things. Until his late years, Aquinas had usually viewed the issue of the eternity of the world in the terms of Maimonides, as a problem about the limits of human reasoning. In his *De potentia* (1265–60), he had already placed the problem in the context of divine possibilities, as the subject of that work invited; but he had not felt confident enough to assert (6). In the *De aeternitate mundi*, however, he argues that, given God's omnipotence, it will be possible for him to create something eternal, so long as there is no incompatibility between being created and being eternal; and he proceeds to show that the two notions are indeed compatible. This interest in God's absolute power has little to do with Maimonides, and is rare in St Thomas' own work; but it anticipates the concerns of Christian theologians in the three decades which followed Aquinas' death. It would add a further twist to the complex story of Islamic and Jewish influence on Christian thought were the elements which inspired the new interest in absolute possibilities to include the very arguments of the *mutakallimūn* as set forth by Maimonides in order to refute them.

NOTES

1 For editions of the Latin translations, see Marenbon (1991): 194–7; and add: al-Fārābī, *De scientiis*, trans. Gundissalinus in al-Fārābī (1954); trans. Gerard of Cremona in al-Fārābī (1953); *Liber exercitationis ad viam felicitatis* in al-Fārābī (1940); complete (uncritical) edition of the *Destruction of the Philosophers* in Latin translation: al-Ghazzālī (1506); logical books from the *Destruction* in al-Ghazzālī (1965); al-Kindī, *De somno et visione, De quinque essentiis, De intellectu* (both translations) in al-Kindī (1897); Averroes, *Destructio destructionum*: Averroes (1497); Maimonides, *Dux seu director dubitantium vel perplexorum* in Maimonides (1520) = the early thirteenth-century translation made from the Hebrew of al-Ḥārisī (Wolfgang Kluxen is preparing a critical edition of this translation). For a bibliographical survey of secondary material, see Daiber (1990).

2 Two valuable, concise introductions to thirteenth-century metaphysics are Wippel (1982) and de Libera (1989): 69–97. Many of their conclusions are followed here.

3 Cf. *Summa theologiae*, 1.q.3, a.4; *Summa contra Gentiles*, 1.22; 2.54.

4 *Quaestiones subtilissimae in Metaphysicas*, 4.q.1; cf. Ordinatio of Sentences commentary 2.d.3, pars 1.q.1, nn. 29–34.

5 A balanced survey of this problem is given by Nardi (1949).

6 Dienstag (1975) reprints many of the most important articles on this subject and provides full bibliography; see also Pines (1976) and Dunphy (1983).

7 For background, see Sorabji (1983): 191–283; for a careful presentation of Aquinas' views through the course of his career, see Wippel (1981).

8 Some interpreters have suggested that Maimonides' real, concealed view about the creation and non-eternity of the world was not that of Jewish teaching; but see Dunphy (1989).

9 See *Topics*: 1.11; *Guide*: 2.15; Aquinas, *In 2 Sententias*, d.1, q.1, a.5; *Summa theologiae* 1.q.46, a.1; cf. Weisheipl (1983): 265–6.

BIBLIOGRAPHY

Accademia dei Lincei (1979) *L'Averroismo in Italia* (Rome) (Atti dei Lincei, 40).

Avicenna (1968–72) *De anima*, ed. S. van Riet, 2 vols (Louvain and Leiden).

—— (1977–83) *Liber de philosophia prima sive scientia divina*, ed. S. van Riet, 3 vols (Louvain and Leiden).

Averroes (1497) *Destructio destructionum philosophiae Algazelis* (Venice) – with commentary by Nifo (reprinted Lyons, 1517, 1529, 1542).

Bertola, E. (1953) *Salomon ibn Gabirol (Avicebron): Vita, opere e pensiero* (Padua).

Daiber, H. (1990) "Lateinische Übersetzungen arabischer Texte zur Philosophie und ihre Bedeutung für die Scholastik des Mittelalters", in J. Hamesse and M. Fattori (eds) *Rencontres de cultures dans la philosophie médiévale* (Louvain-la-neuve and Cassino): 203–50.

d'Alverny, M.-T. (1961–72) "Avicenna Latinus", *Archives de l'Histoire Doctrinale et Littéraire du Moyen Age* 28: 281–316; 29: 217–33; 30: 221–72; 31: 271–86; 32: 259–302; 33: 305–27; 34: 315–43; 35: 301–35; 36: 243–80; 37: 327–61; 39: 321–41.

—— (1989) "Les Traductions à deux interprètes: d'arabe en langue vernaculaire et de langue vernaculaire en latin", in G. Contaime (ed.) *Traduction et Traducteurs au Moyen Age* (Paris).

de Libera, A. (1981) *La Philosophie médiévale* (Paris).

—— (1991) *Penser au moyen âge* (Paris).

Dienstag, D. I. (ed.) (1975) *Studies in Maimonides and St Thomas Aquinas* (New York).

Dunphy, W. (1983) "Maimonides and Aquinas on Creation: a Critique of their Historians", in Gerson (1983): 361–79.

—— (1989) "Maimonides' Not-so-secret Position on Creation", in E. I. Ormsby (ed.), *Moses Maimonides and his Time* (Washington, DC).

al-Fārābī (1940) "Le 'Liber exercitationis ad viam felicitatis' d'Alfarabi", ed. D. Salman, *Recherches de Théologie Ancienne et Médievale*, 12: 33–48

—— (1953) ed. *Al-Farabi Catálogo de las Ciencias*, A. G. Palencia (Madrid).

—— (1954) *Domingo Gundisalvo: De scientiis*, ed. M. Alonso Alonso (Madrid and Granada).

Al-Ghazzālī (1506) *Logica et philosophia Algazelis arabis*, photomechanical reproduction, with introduction by C. H. Lohr (Frankfurt).

—— (1933) *Algazel's Metaphysics: a Mediaeval Translation*, ed. J. T. Muckle (Toronto).

—— (1965) C. H. Lohr, "*Logica Algazelis*: Introduction and Critical Text", *Traditio*, 21: 223–90.

Gauthier, R. A. (1982) "Notes sur les débuts (1225–40) du premier averroisme", *Revue des Sciences Philosophiques et Théologiques*, 66: 321–74.

Gerson, L. P. (ed.) (1983) *Graceful Reason: Essays . . . presented to Joseph Owens. CSSR* (Toronto).

Gilson, E. (1952) *Jean Duns Scot: Introduction à ses positions fundamentales* (Paris).

—— (1969) "Avicenne en occident au moyen âge", *Archives d'Histoire Doctrinale et Littéraire du Moyen Age*, 34: 89–121.

Gomez Nogales, S. (1976) "Saint Thomas, Averroes et l'Averroisme", in Verbeke and Verhelst (1976): 161–77.

Grignaschi, M. (1972) "Les Traductions latins des ouvrages de logique arabe et l'abrégé d'Alfarabi", *Archives d'Histoire Doctrinale et Littéraire du Moyen Âge*, 39: 41–89.

Guttmann, J. (1908) "Der Einfluss der maimonidischen Philosophie auf das christliche Abendland", in W. Bacher, M. Brann and D. Simonsen (eds), *Moses ben Maimon: sein Leben, seine Werke und sein Einfluss* (Leipzig): 135–230; pp. 175–204 are reprinted in Dienstag (1975): 222–51.

Hissette, R. (1977): *Enquête sur les 219 articles condamnées à Paris le 7 mars 1277* (Louvain).

Jolivet, J. (ed.) (1978) *Multiple Averroes* (Paris).

—— (1988) "The Arabic inheritance", in P. Dronke (ed.), *A History of Twelfth-century Western Philosophy* (Cambridge): 113–48.

Al-Kindī (1897) *Die philosophischen Abhandlungen des Ja'qub ben Ishaq Al-Kindi*, ed. A. Navy (Münster).

Kluxen, W. (1954) "Literaturgeschichtliches zum Lateinischen Moses Maimonides", *Recherches de Théologie Ancienne et Médiévale*, 21: 23–50.

—— (1986) "Maimonides and Latin scholasticism", in S. Pines and Y. Yovel (eds), *Maimonides and Philosophy* (Dordrecht, Boston and Lancaster): 224–32.

Koch, J. (1928) "Meister Eckhart und die jüdische Religionsphilosophie des Mittelalters", *Jahres-Bericht der Schlesischen Gesellschaft für vaterländische Kultur*, 101: 134–48, reprinted in his *Kleine Schriften*, 1 (Rome, 1973): 349–65.

Kuksewicz, Z. (1978) "L'Influence d'Averroes sur des universités en Europe centrale: l'expansion de l'averroisme latin", in Jolivet (1978): 275–86.

Maimonides (1520) *Dux seu director dubitantium vel perplexorum*, (Paris; photomechanical reprint: Frankfurt, 1964).

Marenbon, J. (1991) *Later Medieval Philosophy (1150–1350): an Introduction*, 2nd ed. (London).

Nardi, B. (1949) *s.v.* "Averroismo", in *Enciclopedia Cattolica* (Vatican City), 2: 524–30.

Pines, S. (1976) "Saint Thomas et la pensée juive médiévale: quelques notations", in Verbeke and Verhelst (1976): 118–29.

Salman, D. (1939) "The Medieval Latin Translations of Alfarabi's Works", *The New Scholasticism*, 13: 245–61.

Schmitt, C. B. (1979) "Renaissance Averroism Studied through the Venetian Editions of Aristotle–Averroes", *Accademia dei Lincei* (1979): 121–42.

Schmugge, L. (1966) *Johannes von Jandun (1285/9–1328)* (Stuttgart).

Siger of Brabant (1972) *De anima intellectiva, De aeternitate mundi*, Commentary on *De anima*, 3, ed. B. Bazán (Louvain).

Sorabji, R. (1983) *Time, Creation and the Continuum: Theories in Antiquity and the Early Middle Ages* (London).

Synave, P. (1930) "La Révélation des vérités divines naturelles d'après Saint Thomas d'Aquin", in *Mélanges Mandonnet*, 1 (Paris): 327–70, reprinted in Dienstag (1975): 290–333.

Van Steenberghen, F. (1977) *Maître Siger de Brabant* (Louvain).

—— (1978) "L'Averroisme latin au XIIIe siècle", in Jolivet (1978): 283–6.

Verbeke, G. and Verhelst, D. (eds) (1976) *Aquinas and the Problems of his Time* (Leuven and The Hague) (Mediaevalia Lovaniensia, ser. 1, 5).

Weisheipl, J. A. (1983) "The Date and Context of Aquinas's *De aeternitate mundi*", in Gerson (1983): 239–71.

Wippel, J. F. (1981) "Did Thomas Aquinas Defend the Possibility of an Eternally Created World? (The *De aeternitate mundi* Revisited), *Journal of the History of Philosophy*, 19: 21–37.

—— (1982) "Essence and Existence", in N. Kretzmann, A. Kenny and J. Pinborg (eds), *The Cambridge History of Later Medieval Philosophy* (Cambridge): 385–410.

CHAPTER 59

Modern Western philosophy

Catherine Wilson

According to a commonly held view of relations between Islamic culture and the Latin West, the Arabic philosophers absorbed, preserved, and retransmitted Greek thought, notably the legacy of Plato and Aristotle, to Europe during the Middle Ages, thereby ensuring the continuity of the Western philosophical tradition. Though helpful as a starting-point, this curiously teleological account is misleading in three ways. Firstly, the reception of Aristotle and Plato amongst the Arabs was not a matter of mere custodianship but of opposition and transformation. Secondly, in light of this fact, European philosophers from the seventeenth century onwards were increasingly concerned with separating original Aristotelian doctrines – the *pentimento* – from Arabic overpainting, a concern which had a political and religious as well as a scholarly basis. Thirdly, one aspect of the Arabic contribution to European philosophy was the heightened standard of philosophical discourse. The "Socratic rationalism" and logocentrism which is supposed to characterize European thought, whether or not it sprang from Greek soil, acquired its characteristic intensity and precision in the Muslim countries between the ninth and thirteenth centuries.

We will need to distinguish in this brief survey between, on one hand, the reception of Arabic works by medieval philosophers who had access only to manuscripts and, on the other, the dissemination of Arabic philosophy in the age of print. Among the items which first reached a scholastic audience in Europe following the beginning of the Crusades in the early twelfth century were translations of al-Fārābī's logical works and Avicenna's (Ibn Sīnā's) commentaries on Aristotle's *De anima* by Johannes Hispanensis (*fl.* 1133–53); translations of al-Fārābī, Geber, and of other astronomical, medical, and mathematical works undertaken by Gerard of Cremona (1114–87); Michael the Scot's translations of Averroes' (Ibn Rushd's) commentaries on Aristotle's *Metaphysica*,

De anima, *De generatione et corruptione*, *Ethics* and *Poetics*, and other works on sensation, meteors and cosmology; and Avicenna's *Sufficientia* by Antonius Frachantianus Vicentius. The *Fons vitae* of Avicebron (Ibn Gabirol), though not strictly speaking an Arabic work, was translated by Gundissalinus, and Maimonides' *Guide of the Perplexed* was also known to scholars.[1] Also transmitted through the Arabs were two pseudo-Aristotelian works of considerable influence, the so-called *Theology of Aristotle*, actually extracted from Plotinus, and the *Liber de causis*, derived from Proclus, whose emanationist metaphysics provided a rival picture to creation *ex nihilo* up to the seventeenth century. These newly introduced works provided analytical discussions of questions of existence, modality, providence, causation, creation, the soul and freedom and the nature of God and religious truth which define the subject matter of medieval Scholastic philosophy and indeed metaphysics generally up until the time of Christian Wolff. Indeed, Kant's quotational discussion of the antinomies of pure reason,[2] whose status as soluble problems he denies, might be seen as the last trace of Arabic influence, had not analytic philosophy enjoyed a renaissance in the twentieth century.

The second phase of reception, which has been subject to less investigation, occurred when Latin translations were edited and brought into print in the late fifteenth and the sixteenth century. This process was not, however, comprehensive and tended to favour scientific and medical works over speculative thought. Where al-Kindī is represented by only a few works on meteors, medicine and pharmacology, al-Fārābī is almost absent. His *De intellectu* and *De intelligentiis* are printed with Avicenna's main writings and an edition of *De scientiis* (Paris, 1638) is said to exist. For the most part, Avicenna is represented in his medical works, especially his *Canon*, his chemistry and natural magic. Significant editions of philosophy include his *Opera* printed in 1500, and a collection of his main writings translated by Spagna and Gundissalinus, including the *Logica*, the *Sufficientia*, *De caelo et mundo*, *De animalibus* (Venice, 1508) and a translation of Alpago, the *Compendium de anima* (Venice, 1546). Al-Ghazzālī has no independent listings in the *World Catalog* between 1490 and 1600 and only one non-philosophical listing from 1600 to 1700. Averroes' commentaries on Aristotle's *Physics*, *Posterior Analytics*, *De caelo*, *De generatione et corruptione*, *De anima* and *Metaphysics* are fairly well represented before 1600, often bound together with Aristotle's own works. Al-Ghazzālī's *Incoherence of the Philosophers* was translated into Latin as the *Destructio philosophiae* and published in Padua in 1497; it was reprinted in Venice in 1527 and 1562. The *Incoherence of the Incoherence*, or *Destructio destructionum*, Averroes' response to it, which reproduces the original text, becomes a well-read edition of 1529 edited by Agostino Nifo. Maimonides' publication history is steadier.[3] *De idolatria liber* draws the attention of Gerard Vossius and is printed in 1641,

1668 and 1700. Popkin has argued that it was frequently edited and cited, reaching even Puritan theologians at Harvard and Yale.[4] The *Guide of the Perplexed* appears in Latin translations of 1520, 1629, and 1641 and 1642, though it does not seem to have been popular between 1700 and 1800.

The appearance in print of these texts coincided with the beginning of the decline of their direct influence, for print induced, as Eisenstein argued, a retreat from textual modes of knowledge, a reaction against Scholasticism and the commentary tradition.[5] The indexes of the early modern philosophers, who do not habitually name their sources in any case, are largely silent when it comes to the Arabs, and the publication record drops off sharply in the 1600s. Averroes boasts no new editions from 1600 to 1800, except an English *Averroeana* of 1695 and 1707, a "Letters from an Arabian philosopher", dealing with matters "philosophical, physiological, Pythagorical, and medicinal".[6] Bayle, who wrote a long article on Averroes in his *Historical and Critical Dictionary*, obviously had not read him.[7]

Nevertheless, the study of the positive and negative reception of Arabic philosophy in the early modern period sheds valuable light on its formation. This is so for several reasons. First, the Arabs had changed the presuppositions of Greek philosophy by exhaustively considering Platonism and Aristotelianism *vis-à-vis* a monotheistic creator religion, thereby ensuring its relevance for Christian philosophy. Second, in the form of "Averroism" – whose relation to the teaching of the historical Averroes is admittedly problematic – it delivered a robust and intriguing heresy existing side by side with the Christian doctrine of personal immortality. Third, despite their lack of citations and explicit references, early modern authors drew on striking examples and argument forms which were passed down from the Arabic commentaries and which, together with the thematizations which carried over from medieval to modern philosophy, reveal a surprising unity in what might almost be called the Euro-Arab tradition. After surveying some of the main currents of direct transmission to the medievals, this chapter will discuss direct and indirect readings and their incorporation in Descartes, Spinoza, Leibniz, Malebranche and Hume.

MEDIEVAL PHILOSOPHY

The relation of Islamic philosophy to theology has both parallels and differences with the relation of philosophy to Christian doctrine in the Middle Ages. Islam is a monotheistic creator religion, but, unlike Christianity, whose doctrines were formulated in Patristic writings, it is without official creeds and dogmas which facilitate the definition of heresy.

The tension between philosophy as derived from the Greeks and theology appeared at several points nevertheless in Arabic philosophy. Averroes in his *Decisive Treatise* (*Kitāb faṣl al-maqāl*), and to some extent in his commentary on the *Poetics* of Aristotle, argued for the harmony of religion and philosophy. He found it possible to do so however only by asserting that scripture must be interpreted allegorically where it conflicts with reasoning by demonstration and by distinguishing between privileged knowledge reserved for philosophers and doctrinal and literal adherence to the Qur'ān appropriate for the masses.[8] Roger Bacon refers frequently to Averroes, Avicenna and Algazel (al-Ghazzālī),[9] and Jeremiah Hackett has argued that the *Decisive Treatise* furnished the model for Roger Bacon's *Opus maius*, composed around 1266, sent to Pope Clement VI and secretly circulated but published only after a long delay.[10] The doctrine of "double truth", that philosophical truth can appear to be inconsistent with but does not actually contradict revelation, which therefore need not be interpreted in restricted fashion, is decisively rejected by St Thomas. It poses however an increased temptation for philosophers influenced by Cartesian rationalism, and is a focus of concern in Bayle's *Letters to a Provincial*, Leibniz's *Theodicy* and a host of lesser works dealing with the intrinsic reasonableness or paradoxicality of Christianity. A related issue is the problem of equivocal language: is the language adequate for human affairs capable of referring to God and his characteristics, or does He transcend not only the world but language as well?: the problem is discussed by Maimonides, and following his lead, St Thomas,[11] and later Spinoza.[12] Spinoza's scandalous *Tractatus Theologico-Politicus*, like his later *Ethics*, which proves that happiness consists in the wisdom and independence of the philosopher rather than the fulfilment of a religious task, defends privileged philosophical knowledge and regards the Bible as an ethically persuasive work rather than a repository of truth and is perhaps a descendant of the *Decisive Treatise* as it is of Boethius' Averroist *Consolation*.[13] Meanwhile, medieval Christian philosophy took its argumentative apparatus – the apparatus it would use in defending the reasonableness of Christian doctrine – from the Arabic literature. Al-Fārābī's distinction between existence and essence and his theory of contingency organizes philosophical reflection down to the time of Sartre. Such questions as: Does God know only universals or particulars as well? Does His providence extend to individuals? Was the world created in time? Is there causal necessity in nature? are debated in uniform terms for the next three centuries. God's omnipotence, his power to do even what is logically impossible, was maintained by Ibn Ḥazm, defended by Descartes and rejected by Leibniz. The identity of indiscernibles, a key notion in Leibniz's metaphysics, is also discussed in the *Incoherence*, in connection with the problem of creation, as it is in Leibniz's correspondence with Samuel Clarke. The philosophers, al-Ghazzālī says, had sought to prove the eternity of the world by "saying that times are equivalent so far as the possibility that the Divine Will could attach to them is concerned, for what differentiates a given time from an earlier or later time . . . what differentiates one of the two possibles from the other for connection with the eternal Will?" Al-Ghazzālī rejects the proof but accepts the premiss: a man between two cups of water, he says, cannot take one unless he perceives a difference between them: "he can only take the one he thinks more beautiful or lighter or nearer to his right hand if he is right handed, or act from some such reason, hidden or known. Without this the differentiation of the one from the other cannot be imagined."[14] This problem surfaces in the medieval literature as the problem of "Buridan's ass". The problem of intrinsic and extrinsic definition, whether individuals must differ in the matter to be different or can be distinguished by external relations, is also discussed.[15]

Other major readers of Arabic philosophy included Albertus Magnus, Robert Grosseteste, John of Jaundun and Paul of Venice. Though, according to Gilson, there was no "Latin Avicennism" corresponding to Latin Averroism, Avicenna's *Metaphysics* furnished a theological cosmology more elaborate – and perhaps even more "Platonic" – than that of the *Timaeus*. The Christian philosophers from William of Auvergne to St Thomas desired to preserve the notion of the creation of an inferior by a superior and in some cases the notion of intermediary Intelligences, but to avoid Avicenna's emanationism which blurred the distinction between creator and created and his necessitarianism.[16] St Thomas refereed each of the by now well-formulated problems which forced Augustinian doctrine to face conflicting philosophical intuitions and arguments, and he did so with an eye directly on the Arabs, as any annotated edition of his works shows. He also seems to have employed Maimonides' *Guide*, with its delivery of the doctrine of the theological sect of the *mutakallimūn*, whom he calls the *loquentes*, or the speakers of doctrine, in the *Summa contra gentiles*. To their extreme voluntarism he opposes a specifically knowable Christian divine being and a dependent, but still operational, Aristotelian nature.[17] At the same time he attacks the major errors of Averroism.

AVERROISM AND THE AVERROIST HERESY

Averroes' comments on Aristotle's *Metaphysics* and *De anima* were especially troubling to Christian readers. Averroism came to stand for the doctrines of the eternity of the world, the unity of the active intellect (based on the difficult passage in Aristotle's *De anima*, 3.5.430a18), denial of demons and the possibility of attaining perfection in this life, and so for a counter-Christian tradition in Scholasticism. "Arabic" commentary was banned in Paris in 1210 and 1215, later permitted with censorship in 1231 and officially inserted into the curriculum in 1255.[18] The result was a flowering at the University of Paris from 1260–77 due to Siger de Brabant and Boethius, and a reaction. Bonaventure criticized Averroist doctrines in 1268; this was followed by the condemnations of Averroist and other heretical propositions of 1270 and 1277 by Bishop Tempier, who pronounced against the doctrine of double truth. Thomas Aquinas wrote his influential *Tractatus de unitate intellectus contra Averroistas* sometime between 1269 and 1272, central to his effort to produce a marriage of Aristotle and Christianity which would rationalize Christianity without confounding dogma.

The task of separating Aristotle from his commentators and recovering the pristine doctrine became an important one from this point onwards. Legend and invective attached to the name of Averroes. Duns Scotus refers to "that accursed Averroes" and his "fantastic conception, intelligible neither to himself nor to others [which] assumes the intellective part of man to be a sort of separate substance united to man through the medium of sense images". Averroes' person, he thought, is "nothing more than a kind of irrational animal which excels the other animals by reason of an irrational sensitive soul that is more excellent than other souls".[19] The scandalous but fictional book *De tribus impostoribus* (Moses, Christ, Mahomet) was ascribed to him, and the separation begun by St Thomas of the good Aristotle from the bad commentator worked to his detriment. "Aristotle is not very religious but his interpreter Averroes is thoroughly impious," Du Plessis de Mornay was still saying in 1581.[20] Meanwhile, a theological literature calumnating Mahomet and decrying Islam enjoyed distinguished contributors from Martin Luther in 1542 to Hugo Grotius in 1676, relieved only somewhat by less polemical texts on manners, mores, monuments and Turkish military history. In the philosophical arena, we observe that Leibniz was still concerned in the *Theodicy* of 1710 about Averroism and the absorption of the individual's soul at death into an ocean of souls identical with God. The "*monopsychites*", Leibniz argued, influenced Spinoza through the Kabbalah, and Spinozism, married as it was to Cartesian rationalism, he found an exceptionally dangerous version of the heresy.[21] It was defended in his own time, Leibniz reported, by the freethinker M. de Preissac and, according to Gabriel Naude's letters, it was still popular in Italy in the late 1620s through the influence of Pomponazzi, who only pretends to dispute it in his *On the Immortality of the Soul,* and of Cremonini, the teacher of Galileo. Cesalpinus and Cardan had both regarded the world as having a single soul, with passive intelligence divided up into individual men, and Vanini, the unfortunate atheist burned at the stake in 1600, presented himself as a student of Averroes. Leibniz detected a profound undercurrent flowing through history: the Spanish neo-Scholastic Molina, the

German quietists, Erhard Weigel, and Queen Christina of Sweden were targets of suspicion in his *Reflections on the Doctrine of a Single Universal Spirit.*[22] On Renan's account Averroism was given life by the theological orthodoxy which opposed it, but died with the rise of science and thereby created a victory for orthodoxy. By 1630, Italy was in the grip of reaction.[23] This was Leibniz's analysis too: "The corpuscular philosophy," he says, speaking knowledgeably of the Paduan Aristotelians, "appears to have extinguished this excessively peripatetic sect."[24]

Avicenna's Neoplatonic doctrine of creation by emanation portrayed the creation of the world as an outpouring or expression of the divine, rather than a materialization *ex nihilo.* Like the doctrine of the single universal spirit it was theologically heterodox, and attacked as such by al-Ghazzālī, but an important focus of interest to Christian medievals nevertheless. Arguably, it is a feature of St Thomas's theory of creation, where it arrives via Avicenna's *Metaphysica* and the *Liber de causis,* and traces have been argued to persist in Leibniz's picture of God as containing all possibilities within himself and of the monads of his *Monadology* as "outflashings" of the divine.[25]

ATOMISM AND CAUSATION: MALEBRANCHE, LEIBNIZ, HUME

Atomisms of matter, space and time entered Arabic philosophy from India not, as might have been expected, from the Greeks. These ontologies were adopted by the philosophers of the *kalām* against the Aristotelian doctrines of form and matter, substances and natures, and they provided the foundations for occasionalism and a theory of continuous recreation which set the absolute power of God in the place of Greek natural necessity, essence and causal efficacy. It is an unexplored question to what extent the revival of atomism in mid seventeenth-century Europe might have been affected by the clear formulation given e.g. by Maimonides in the *Guide* in addition to the popularity of Epicurus and Lucretius. The theologians, Maimonides says, considered the senses deceptive, both because they were subject to error, illusion and distortion and because they miss the subtlety of nature.[26] They

> thought that the world as a whole . . . is composed of very small particles that, because of their subtlety, are not subject to division. The individual particle does not possess quantity in any respect. However, when several are aggregated, their aggregate possesses quantity and has thus become a body . . . All these particles are alike and similar to one another, there being no difference between them in any respect whatsoever . . .

> [G]eneration consists in aggregation, and corruption in separation.[27]

There is a void to permit motion, accidents are superadded to atoms and do not last during two units of time. The course of nature and all that we regard as natural law, is a habit of God's.[28] Any sequence of events which we can imagine to happen could in fact happen.

Much better understood are the Arabic sources of the occasionalist doctrines of the seventeenth century. Al-Ghazzālī, in the *Incoherence of the Philosophers*, attacks natural necessity in favour of absolute omnipotence of God. Each of two things, he says, has its own individuality and is not the other,

> neither the existence nor the non-existence of the one is implied in the affirmation, negation, existence and non-existence of the other – e.g. the satisfaction of thirst does not imply drinking, nor satiety eating, nor burning contact with fire, nor light sunrise, nor decapitation death, nor recovery the drinking of medicine, nor evacuation the taking of a purgative, and so on for all the empirical connexions existing in medicine, astronomy, the sciences and the crafts. For the connexion in these things is based on a prior power of God to create them in a successive order.[29]

Averroes argues against this that:

> True knowledge is the knowledge of a thing as it is in reality. And if in reality there only existed, in regard both to the substratum and to the Agent, the possibility of two opposites, there would no longer, even for the twinkling of an eye, be any permanent knowledge of anything, since we suppose the agent to rule existents like a tyrannical prince who has the highest power, for whom nobody in his dominion can deputize, of whom no standard or custom is known to which reference might be made.[30]

According to those who have studied the transmission of the problem, the doctrine that natural necessity is incoherent and the substitution of a doctrine of continuous creation reaches Descartes and Malebranche through St Thomas, who, for his part, endorses Averroes' position against the *mutakallimūn*, and the sixteenth-century neo-Scholastic Suarez. From Malebranche, who expounds occasionalism in *Elucidation XVI* to his *Search After Truth* (1675), and in numerous other locations including the *Dialogues on Metaphysics* (1699), the doctrine passes to Hume, who converts the habits of God to the habits of men in his analysis.[31] It is also rediscovered by Leibniz, who finds the doctrines of the *loquentes* in book 2, chapter 73 of Maimonides, which he reads in a

Venice edition of 1629 some time between 1678 and 1695.[32] Breaking from Malebranche, Leibniz rejects occasionalism and voluntarism eloquently in numerous works, notably *De ipsa natura* of 1695. Atomism and the continuum problem were particular concerns of Leibniz, and one might wonder whether the singly quantityless atoms of the *mutakallimūn* which aggregate to form substances are related to the unextended monads, whose aggregates, on some versions of the *Monadology*, are visible and tangible bodies.[33]

PHILOSOPHICAL AUTOBIOGRAPHY AND SUBJECTIVITY: DESCARTES

According to V. V. Naumkin, it has definitely been established that Descartes read al-Ghazzālī's works.[34] Which might have been relevant for him? Al-Ghazzālī wrote a short spiritual autobiography describing how his venture into the "vast ocean" of sects and doctrines from his adolescence onward left him distressed at conflicting and uncertain beliefs. "The thirst for knowledge was innate in me from an early age; it was like a second nature on my part implanted by God . . . No sooner had I emerged from boyhood than I had already broken the fetters of tradition and freed myself from hereditary belief."[35] He then reflected as follows: "The search after truth being the aim which I propose to myself, I ought in the first place to ascertain what are the bases of certitude."[36] Certitude is, he says, "the clear and complete knowledge of things, such knowledge as leaves no room for doubt nor possibility of error and conjecture".[37] Certain knowledge is impervious to doubt: no experience, he says, could make him believe that three is more than ten. At first it seemed to him that sense-perceptions and necessary principles satisfied his criteria; however, some considerations persuaded him that sense-experience was not certain; stars look as large as a piece of gold but are far bigger than the earth. Yet he puzzled whether, as reason overrules sense, something higher might not overrule reason:

> a reflection drawn from the phenomenon of sleep deepened my doubt. "Do you not see," I reflected, "that while asleep you assume your dreams to be indisputably real? Once awake you recognize them for what they are – baseless chimeras, Who can assure you then of the reliability of notions which, when awake, you derive from the senses and from reason?" In relation to your present state they may be real, but it is possible also that you may enter upon another state of being which will bear the same relation to your present state as this does to your condition when asleep.[38]

He remained, al-Ghazzālī says, in a state of doubt for two months, finally delivered by God: "I owed my deliverance not to a concatenation of proofs and arguments, but to the light which God caused to penetrate into my heart – the light which illuminates the threshold of all knowledge." He is disenchanted by the exact sciences, which, associated with naturalism and materialism, bear a taint of impiety, and Sufism shows him that he must forsake his attachment to worldly things. The parallel with Descartes' *Discourse on Method* and the first two books of the *Meditations* is unmistakable; so too is the divergence: Descartes's natural light leads not to fideism but to the exact sciences.

Whether Descartes' famous dualism, which constituted a bold and controversial departure from the prevailing Scholastic hylomorphism, was inspired by Arabic sources is a matter for speculation. Part of al-Ghazzālī's attack on natural necessity involves the point that there is no necessary connection between external events and immediate sensory experience; perception requires the assistance of God. This point is developed both in the sceptical portions of the *Meditations* and later in Malebranche's doctrine of vision in God, in the *Search after Truth*.[39]

Some attention has focused on the celebrated "flying man argument" of Avicenna, a thought-experiment intended not so much to prove as to drive home awareness of the immateriality of the soul in the one who performs it, much as Descartes' experiments in doubt are supposed to elicit knowledge of the self as an immaterial thinking thing. The Mu'tazilite and Ash'arite schools which Avicenna challenges on this point were materialists on the subject of personal identity. "Most people," he reports, "and many of the speculative theologians have thought that the human being is this body and that everyone refers to it when saying 'I'. This is a false belief, as we shall show."[40] The refuting experiment is described (in one of three versions) as follows:

> The one among us must imagine himself as though he is created all at once and created perfect, but that his sight has been veiled from observing external things, and that he is created falling in the air or the void in a manner where he would not encounter air resistance, requiring him to feel, and that his limbs are separated from each other so that they neither meet nor touch. He must then reflect as to whether he will affirm the existence of his self.
>
> He will not doubt his affirming his self existing, but with this he will not affirm any limb from among his organs, no internal organ, whether heart or brain and no external thing. Rather, he would be affirming his self without affirming it for length, breadth, and depth . . .
>
> Hence the one who affirms has a means to be alerted to the

> existence of his soul as something other than the body – indeed, other than body – and to his being directly acquainted with [this existence] and aware of it.[41]

The textual parallels with Descartes are suggestive; unfortunately his knowledge of Avicenna's text has not been established.[42]

PROVIDENCE AND OPTIMALITY

Theodicy was a topic handled at length in Islamic philosophy, and it is again to al-Ghazzālī that we owe a clear formulation of the best of all possible worlds doctrine later associated with Leibniz and Wolff: "There is not in possibility anything more wonderful than what is."[43] This position raised both difficulties – was it an infringement of God's power? – and problems of interpretation. The sect of the Mu'tazilah had held that good and evil are independent of God's will, while the *mutakallimūn* had adopted the voluntarist position, that God is absolutely free in his creation of good and evil. These stances provided two different approaches to defending the rightness of the actual. For the Mu'tazilah, the task was to show that, despite appearances, the world conforms to humanly acceptable criteria of goodness. For the Ash'arites, as goodness was determined by God's arbitrary and inscrutable will, the task was to humble and reconcile oneself to things as they are. The subject, as Eric Ormsby notes, is one left largely undiscussed by the medievals, reemerging as a topic with Malebranche, Leibniz, Hume, Kant and Schopenhauer.[44] But it was treated at length by Maimonides, and evidence is strong that Leibniz's reading of Maimonides – and indeed Pierre Bayle's – was critical in making it a focus of attention in his *Theodicy*. Maimonides argued at length in the *Guide of the Perplexed* that the perception of evil in the world results from people's anthropocentric supposition that Nature was made for them; they suppose that their personal sorrows implicate the whole of the universe. Bayle attacked Maimonides in the *Letters to a Provincial*; Leibniz defended him:

> Maimonides is right in saying that if one took into account the littleness of man in relation to the universe, one would comprehend clearly that the predominance of evil, even though it prevailed among men, need not on that account occur among the angels, nor among the heavenly bodies, nor among the elements and inanimate compounds, nor among many kinds of animals . . . so also on consideration of the metaphysical good and evil which is in all substances, whether endowed with or devoid of intelligence . . . one must say that the universe, such as it actually is, must be the best of all systems.[45]

Leibniz appears to have borrowed liberally from the passages in the *Guide* which argue that evil in the world is an appearance produced by limited perspective and subjective wishes; his notes mention the Ashʿarite and Muʿtazilite positions on the divine will and divine justice. Elsewhere in his writings, he protests against the moral and intellectual voluntarism of Descartes, later against the voluntarism of Samuel Clarke, defending choice, perfection and pre-established harmony in terms reminiscent of the old debates.

MAGIC, IMAGINATION AND IRRATIONALISM

Most recent commentators have focused on the argumentative structure of Arabic rationalism. But the influence of the Arab and Jewish thought on the occult philosophy of the Renaissance, and on the pair of religious deviations of the mid seventeenth century – quietist mysticism and chiliasm – is not to be overlooked. Leibniz, for example, characterized the quietists of his day as Averroist-inspired. In his attacks on sectarian enthusiasm, the Cambridge Platonist Benjamin Whichcote comments, "Among Christians, those, that pretend to be *Inspired*, seem to be Mad: among the *Turks*, those, that are Mad, are thought to be Inspired."[46] Maimonides' discussion of prophecy and imagination in the *Guide*, which Spinoza hearkens to in his *Tractatus theologico-politicus*, forms one current of influence; another can be found in the literature addressing kabbalism.[47]

With magic and sympathetic action there are important relations to be traced in the dissemination of the occult philosophy, along with alchemy, astronomy and medicine, into the Latin West. Avicenna's claim in book 4.4 of the *Liber de anima* that the imagination could operate at a distance in another body than its own, for example through the evil eye, was approved and developed by numerous later writers on magic, including Albertus Magnus, Paracelsus and H. C. Agrippa,[48] and his suggestion that the Intelligences which move the heavenly bodies confer the powers of prophecy and miracle-working is adopted by Marsilio Ficino.[49] Indeed, the theory of the imagination was a particular strength of Islamic philosophy. Pascal's frightened man on a narrow plank who exemplifies the root irrationality Pascal found in humankind and which he took to dispel its claim to self-sufficiency and importance is found in Montaigne and in St Thomas, but earlier in al-Ghazzālī, and originally in Avicenna's *Psychology* and the *Book of Directions and Remarks*.[50]

Locke and Berkeley's man-born-blind-and-made-to-see makes his appearance in al-Gazzālī's *Incoherence*,[51] and no doubt much of what we think of as empiricism – a reaction to Scholastic modes of argument and theological rationalism – might appear as originally interwoven with the latter in medieval Islamic philosophy. Particular mention should be made in this connection of the book of Ibn Ṭufayl (d. 1185), *Ḥayy ibn Yaqẓān*, the story of a solitary infant born or suddenly appearing on a desert island who, by observation and exercise of native reason, attains to religious and metaphysical truth in the absence of all social exchange. The story was translated into Latin by Edward Pococke the Younger in 1671 as *Philosophicus autodidacticus, sive epistola . . . qua ostenditur quomodo ex inferiorum contemplatione ad superiorum notiam ratio humana ascendere possit,* and enjoyed numerous editions and translations in European languages afterwards. Its relationship to philosophical speculation about the roles of experience versus innate ideas in the emergence of abstract thought and to the innateness of religious concepts has attracted some attention.[52]

NOTES

1 On early manuscripts and printed books and their translators, consult Moritz Steinschneider (1956).

2 Immanuel Kant, *Critique of Pure Reason*, A406/B433ff.

3 He enjoys forty-seven *World Catalog* listings from 1490 to 1600, fifty-two between 1600 and 1700.

4 See Richard H. Popkin (1988): 216–29.

5 Elizabeth Eisenstein, *The Printing Press as an Agent of Change*, 2 vols (Cambridge, 1979). Nicholas Rescher in a fine survey article (1966) stresses however their immediate importance in the fifteenth and sixteenth centuries.

6 Avicenna drops from 150 entries in the *World Catalog* between 1490 and 1600 to twenty-four between 1600 and 1700. Averroes' listings in the same periods drop from seventy-four to two.

7 After the sharp drop, the publication curve for Islamic philosophy picks up again in the mid nineteenth century with the development of modern textual scholarship; the interest at this point is mainly historical and philological rather than philosophical.

8 Jeremiah Hackett (1988): 101.

9 Though, according to Gilson, medieval philosophers were not familiar with al-Ghazzālī's *Incoherence*, knowing only his earlier summary of the doctrines of al-Fārābī and Avicenna which he later tries to refute. Etienne Gilson (1955): 216.

10 Hackett (1988).

11 David B. Burrell (1988): 37–48.

12 Harry Austryn Wolfson (1958): 1, 317.

13 On the problem of esoteric and exoteric writing and the philosopher's position with respect to religion, see George F. Hourani (1961). On parallels between Spinoza's position on biblical interpretation and the handling of "contradictions" and the Islamic and Jewish traditions, see Roger Arnaldez (1978): 151–73.

14 Al-Ghazzālī, *The Incoherence of the Philosophers* (*Tahāfut al-falāsifah*) in *Averroes's Tahāfut al-tahāfut* (*The Incoherence of the Incoherence*), trans. S. Van Den Bergh

(London, 1954): 19. Cf. Leibniz, *5th Letter to Clark*, "One must not say, as the author does here, that God created things in what particular space and at what particular time he pleased. For all time and all spaces being in themselves perfectly uniform and indiscernible from each other, one of them cannot please more than another," trans. in Leibniz (1969): 707.

15 *Incoherence of the Incoherence*: 14.

16 See Gilson (1955): 373; 410.

17 St Thomas Aquinas, *Summa contra gentiles*, 3.69.

18 Stuart MacClintock (1967).

19 "The Spirituality and Immortality of the Human Soul", in Duns Scotus (1962): 138.

20 Phillipe Mornay (1581); see the classic study of Ernest Renan (1925).

21 According to Arnaldez (1972: 151), "One cannot detect any definitive sign of direct knowledge of Arabic thought in Spinoza's work, and . . . it is impossible under these conditions to speak of a real influence." He does not rule this out however; see, e.g., his comparison of Spinoza's third category of knowledge and Arabic mysticism and determinism (1972: 169ff.).

22 1702, reprinted in Leibniz (1967): 554–60. Leibniz often presented the monadology as a bulwark against monopsychism. He admitted the idea of a universal intellect had attractions, but believed that it should be interpreted in Augustinian fashion – God is the light of every soul. Cf. his *Discourse on Metaphysics* (1686) (Leibniz (1969): 321) and his argument in the fragment *De realitate accidentium* (*c.* 1688) Akademie Vorausedition, *Sämtliche Schriften und Briefe* (Münster, 1988) (7: 1608), which also treats Spinoza as an Averroist who believed that everything is a transitory mode of God.

23 Renan (1925): 116.

24 Leibniz (1985): no. 11, p. 81.

25 See Daniel Fouke (1994).

26 Moses Maimonides, *The Guide of the Perplexed*, trans. Shlomo Pines (Chicago, 1963), 1. 73: 213.

27 *Ibid.*: 197.

28 "When we, as we think, dye a garment red, it is not we who are by any means the dyers; God rather creates the color in question when in the garment when the latter is in juxtaposition with the red dye, which we consider to have gone over to the garment." *Ibid.*: 201.

29 *Incoherence*: 316. A similar argument was given by Sextus Empiricus and was used by Galen to justify the "empiricist" approach in medicine. On Sextus versus al-Ghazzālī as a source for Hume, see Leo Groarke and Graham Solomon (1991).

30 *Incoherence*: 325. See on the dispute, Barry S. Kogan (1985).

31 James Frederick Naify (1975).

32 His notes are printed in the Akademie Vorausedition Fasz. 10 (Münster, 1991): 2678–91. See Lenn E. Goodman (1980).

33 One early solution Leibniz considers to the problem of the continuum is the doctrine of the "leap" ascribed to al-Naẓẓām (see Majid Fakhry (1983): 215) which a body makes in passing from *A* to *C* avoiding *B*, *Sämtliche Schriften und Briefe* (Berlin, 1980), 6(3): 559–64.

34 This is proved, he says, by a note in the Cartesian collection of the Bibliothèque Nationale of Paris (Naumkin (1987): 124 n. 1).

35 *The Confessions of al-Ghazzali*, trans. Claude Field (Lahore, n.d.): 13–14. Cf. Descartes, *Discourse on Method* "I have been nourished on letters since my childhood, and since I was given to believe that by their means a clear and certain knowledge could be obtained of all that is useful in life, I had an extreme desire to acquire instruction . . . But so soon as I had achieved the entire course of study at the close of which one is usually received into the ranks of the learned, I entirely changed my opinion . . . [A]s soon as age permitted me to emerge from the control of my tutors, I entirely quitted the study of letters" (1932, 1: 83–6).
36 Al-Ghazzālī, *Confessions*: 14.
37 *Ibid.*: 15.
38 *Ibid.*: 18–19. Cf. Descartes, "I have often in sleep been deceived by similar illusions, and in dwelling carefully on this reflection I see so manifestly that there are no certain indications by which we may clearly distinguish wakefulness from sleep that I am lost in astonishment" (*Meditation I*, (1932): 146).
39 "It may happen to any of us that there should be in his presence birds of prey and flaming fires and immovable mountains and enemies equipped with arms, without his seeing them, because God had not created in him the faculty of seeing them." (*Incoherence*: 323).
40 See Michael Marmura (1986).
41 *Ibid.*: 387. The reference is to Avicenna's *Psychology* (part of the *al-Shifā'*): 13, 9–20. Cf. Descartes, *Meditation II*: "I suppose then that all the things I see are false; I persuade myself that nothing has ever existed of all that my fallacious memory represents to me. I consider that I possess no senses; I imagine that body, figure, extension, movement and place are but fictions of my mind . . . [But] I myself, am I at least not something? . . . I was persuaded that there was nothing in all the world, that there was no heaven, no earth, that there were no minds, nor any bodies: was I not then persuaded that I did not exist? Not at all" (1932: 150). The flying man appears too in the well-read Hume: "Suppose . . . a man to be supported in the air, and to be softly conveyed along by some invisible power; tis evident he is sensible of nothing, and never receives the idea of extension, nor indeed any idea, from this invariable motion: Even supposing he moves his limbs to and fro, this cannot convey to him that idea. He feels in that case a certain sensation or impression, the parts of which are successive to each other, and may give him the idea of time. But certainly are not dispos'd in such a manner, as is necessary to convey the idea of space or extension" (1978: 1.2.5).
42 On the problem see Arnaldez (1972); G. Furlani (1927).
43 Eric Ormsby (1984): 32.
44 *Ibid.*: 1ff.
45 *Theodicy*, no. 263. Cf. Maimonides, *Guide of the Perplexed*, 3.12, pp. 441ff. and Leibniz's *Aus Maimonides Dux Perplexorum*, Vorausedition, Fasz. 10: 2685–6.
46 Benjamin Whichcote (1969), no. 1182, p. 336. Locke too, according to Thomas Lennon, *The Battle of the Gods and Giants* (Princeton, 1992): 276, read Paul Ricaut's popular *L'Etat present de l'empire ottoman*, and commented on Turkish enthusiasm.
47 Kalman P. Bland (1991) On millenarianism as a stimulus to Jewish studies, see Richard Popkin (1990).

48 Van Den Bergh, *Incoherence*: 175.
49 D. P. Walker (1975): 162.
50 "When a man walks on a plank between two walls over an empty space, his imagination is stirred by the possibility of falling and his body is impressed by this imagination and in fact he falls, but when this plank is on the earth, he walks over it without falling" (*Incoherence*: 314). Cf. Montaigne, *Essays*, 2.1; St Thomas, *Summa theologia*, 3.103; on its transmission, see Van Den Bergh, *Incoherence*: 174. Pascal's knowledge of Islamic philosophy, according to Henri Gouhier, was obtained at least in part through the influential *Pugio fidei ... adversus Mauros et Judaeos* (1278) of Raymond Martin, edited in 1651 and reprinted several times thereafter.
51 *Incoherence*: 317. Such a man will not guess at the role of light but will think "that the actual perception in his eyes of the forms of visible things is caused by the opening of his eyelids".
52 Rescher (1966): 155 observes the powerful interest it awoke in the Quakers on its appearance. (George Fox, however, had earlier joined in the cultural–religious polemic against "the Turk".) Cf. the references to Vaihinger on Condillac in Furlani (1927): 65. Its probable influence on Defoe's *Robinson Crusoe* (1700) is also argued for by Rescher (1966): 156.

BIBLIOGRAPHY

Arnaldez, R. (1972) "Un precedent avicennien du 'Cogito' cartesien?", *Annales Islamologiques*, 2: 341–9.

—— (1978) "Spinoza et la pensée arabe", in *Actes du Colloque Spinoza Paris 1977, Revue de Synthese 89–91* (Paris): 151–73.

Bland, K. P. (1991) "Elijah del Medigo's Averroist Response to the Kabbalahs of Fifteenth-century Jewry and Pico della Mirandola", *Journal of Jewish Thought and Philosophy*, 23–51.

Burrell, D. B. (1988) "Aquinas's Debt to Maimonides", in *A Straight Path: Studies in Medieval Philosophy and Culture* (Washington, DC): 37–48.

Descartes, R. (1932) *Discourse on Method*, in *Philosophical Works*, 2 vols, trans. E. S. Haldane and G. R. T. Ross (Cambridge).

Duns Scotus (1962) *Selected Writings*, trans. and ed. A. Wolter (Edinburgh).

Fakhry, M. (1983) *A History of Islamic Philosophy* (New York).

Fouke, D. (1994) "Emanation and the Perfections of Being: Divine Causation and the Autonomy of Nature in Leibniz", *Archiv für Geschichte der Philosophie*, 76(2): 168–94.

Furlani, G. (1927) "Avicenna et il *Cogito, ergo sum* di Cartesio", *Islamica*, 3: 53–72.

Gilson, E. (1955) *History of Christian Philosophy in the Middle Ages* (New York).

Goodman, L. E. (1980) "Maimonides and Leibniz", *Journal of Jewish Studies*, 31: 214–36.

Gouhier, H. (1984) *Blaise Pascal Commentaires* (Paris).

Groarke, L. and Solomon, G. (1991) "Hume's Account of Cause", *Journal of the History of Ideas*, 52: 645–63.

Hackett, J. (1988) "Averroes and Bacon on the Harmony of Religion and Philosophy", in *A Straight Path: Studies in Medieval Philosophy and Culture* (Washington, DC): 98–112.

Hourani, G. F. (1961) *Averroes on the Harmony of Religion and Philosophy* (London).

Hume, D. (1978) *Treatise*, 2nd ed., ed. P. H. Nidditch and L. A. Selby-Bigge (Oxford).

Kogan, B. S. (1985) *Averroes and the Metaphysics of Causation* (Albany).

Leibniz, G. W. (1969) *Philosophical Papers and Letters*, trans. and ed. L. E. Loemker (Dordrecht).

—— (1970) *Sämtliche Schriften und Briefe*, ed. Deutsche Akademie der Wissenschaften, (repr. Berlin).

—— (1985) *Theodicy*, ed. A. Farrer, trans. E. M. Huggard (LaSalle).

MacClintock, S. (1967) "Averroism", in *Encyclopedia of Philosophy*, ed. P. Edwards (New York), 1: 224.

Marmura, M. (1986) "Avicenna's Flying Man in Context", *Monist*, 69: 383–93.

Mornay, P. (1581) *De la vérité de la religion chrestienne contre les athées, épicuriens, payens, juifs, Mahumédistes & d'autres infidèles* (Antwerp).

Naify, J. F. (1975) *Arabic and European Occasionalism* (Ph.D. dissertation, (San Diego).

Naumkin, V. V. (1987) "Some Problems Related to the Study of Works by al-Ghazzali", in *Ghazzali, la raison et le miracle* (Paris).

Ormsby, E. (1984) *Theodicy in Islamic Philosophy* (Princeton).

Popkin, R. H. (1988) "Newton and Maimonides", in *A Straight Path: Studies in Medieval Philosophy and Culture* (Washington, DC): 216–29.

—— (1990) *Sceptics, Millenarians and Jews* (Leiden).

Renan, E. (1925) *Averroes et l'Averroisme* (Paris).

Rescher, N. (1966) "The Impact of Arabic Philosophy on the West", in *Studies in Arabic Philosophy* (Pittsburgh): 147–58, orig. publ. in *Islamic Quarterly*, 10: 3–11.

Steinschneider, M. (1956) *Die Europäische Übersetzungen aus dem Arabischen bis mitte des 17. Jahrhunderts* (Graz).

Thomas Aquinas (1975) *Summa contra gentiles*, trans. A. C. Pegis *et al.* (Notre Dame).

Walker, D. P. (1975) *Spiritual and Demonic Magic* (Notre Dame).

Whichcote, B. (1969) *Moral and Religious Aphorisms*, ed. C. A. Patrides, *The Cambridge Platonists* (Cambridge).

Wolfson, H. A. (1958) *The Philosophy of Spinoza* (New York).

CHAPTER 60

The poetic medium: a case study

Branko Aleksić

It is interesting to note Averroes' effect on literature – from the medieval poetry of Guido Cavalcanti and Dante Alighieri, the two most distinguished representatives of the Italian "New School", through a single line by their English follower Geoffrey Chaucer, and up into the twentieth century in the writings of the American Ezra Pound (translator and interpretator of Cavalcanti), the Argentinian Jorge Luis Borges, the Lebanese Adonis and the French Jean-Pierre Faye.

At the time of the great upsurge of Arab poetry in Andalusia, through Provence and up to Italy – where the Florentine *dolce stil nuovo* school of poetry was created – Guido Cavalcanti (*c.* 1250–1300) defined the nature of love in the canzone "Donna mi prega" (seventy-five lines), using the philosophical terms of the *Great Commentary* of Ibn Rushd (Averroes) through whom Aristotle's *Metaphysics* was reinstated in the Western tradition, as well as the *Middle Commentary* on the *De anima* – works that Dante was also familiar with. Aristotle, "the metaphysician" of Averroes, "explains the cause of animated substance" (Averroes (1984): 70), while the poet Cavalcanti, Dante's friend, searched for the cause of love: its force ("sua potenza"), its movement ("movimento"), the form of its condition and state ("suo stato si formato") and its constant changes (Cavalcanti (1960): 524–8). The distinctive attraction of this transference, "the possible intellect" – the concept asserted by Averroes and accepted in Scholastic philosophy from St Thomas Aquinas to Albertus Magnus – is quoted explicitly and paraphrased in Cavalcanti's poem, and that in the sense (along the lines) that Michael Scot translated it into Latin; the possible intellect, the potential intellect as the subject. Cavalcanti offers a definition of love that takes in the possible intellect as in the subject, its place and abode (lines 21ff: "Amore . . . / Ven da veduta forma che s'intende, / che prende – nel possibile intelletto, / come in subietto, – loco e dimoranza"). The cause of love equals the cause of animated substance in Aristotle's *Metaphysics* with a commentary by Averroes (textus 7 etc.). The canzone gives ground to the passage of textus 8 (1,438–15, 1,439,1): "Aristotle says: And since being is elaborated in two manners, all that changes from potential being to actual being" (Averroes (1984): 76). Love fits naturally into this poetic allusion of Cavalcanti to the problem whose generation was resolved by Aristotle, for, in the first book of the *Physics*, that which becomes comes from that which exists potentially, not from that which actually exists. Cavalcanti, as the *ottimo filosofo naturale* (in the words of the Dame in the *Decameron*, 6th day, novel 9), but also as a poet, opts for experience. This is the second decisive stamp of Averroes' lesson. *De naturali philosophia*: Renan in his history assesses the consequence of these words through a fresh religious condemnation. The Council of Paris, which in 1209 fought for the first time against the rise of Arab philosophy, condemned Amaury de Bène, David de Dinant and their disciples, by these words: "Nec libri Aristotelis de naturali philosophia, nec commenta legantur Parisiis publice vel secreto" (Renan (1949): 178). In stating that the essence ("l'esser") of love has its origin in the form of the "possible intellect's" substance, which can be generated and yet remains incorruptible, Cavalcanti demonstrates its nature not as rational but as "that which feels" (line 31: "non razionale – ma che si sente"). We find here again the affirmation of intuitive thought, to which Averroes himself resorts in his polemic work *Tahāfut al-tahāfut* ("Incoherence of the Incoherence", chapter 1,44). As the seat of love, Cavalcanti designates the potential intellect, "the material intellect", "the possible intellect", which in Aristotle (with Averroes' commentary) represents the link with matter, and is related to imagination and memory. With respect to Aristotle's short treatise *De memoria et reminiscentia*, Cavalcanti postulates that the experience of love, by its nature and its cause, belongs to Memory; he is always a poet-philosopher of natural demonstration ("natural dimostramento" – l. 8).

Cavalcanti's poetical and spiritual disciple Dante Alighieri (1265–1321), in his treatise *De monarchia*, offers a direct commentary on Averroes' *De anima*, 3, and references to Averroist cosmological doctrines are detected in Dante's *Convivio*. In a metaphorical way, Dante applies the Averroist theory of collective intellect in his utopia of the "political corpus" governing universally. Dante's "operation adjusted to the human totality and to which this totality is ordered" (*De monarchia*, 1.3, 9), was attacked in the sixteenth century by the Dominican Guido Vernani, as an Averroist theory against the religion of the state (Gilson (1953): 169). Another use of Averroes is found in Dante's *Convivio*, 4.13.8 (the title is based on Plato's *Symposium*): the doctrine of brown lunar stains. Since the heroine of Dante's *Commedia*, Beatrice, discusses the human belief that people see a human figure in these stains, using rare and dense explanations attributed to Ibn Rushd (Nardi (1966): 3-39), canto II of Dante's *Paradiso* (49 ff.) proves, in accordance with the *Convivio*, their common source. Finally, in the first part of the *Commedia*, that poetical summary of the medieval gnosis, the celebrated Islamic interpretator of Aristotle is named next to Avicenna (l. 143), in the concise manner which will remain for centuries as the trade mark in Western civilization: "Averroes, che 'l gran comento feo" (*Inferno*, 4.144) – "Averroes, who made a Great Commentary" – but Dante did not enter into how he made it. It was only seven centuries later that another poet and writer – Jorge Luis Borges – would talk precisely about the problematic way in which Averroes "who, closed within the orb of Islam, could never know the meaning of the terms *tragedy* and *comedy*", still successfully translated Aristotle.

Renan's study of Averroes, which dates from 1851, served for a long time as a source, even in literature. The American poet and critic Ezra Pound (1885–1972), in a long study of his translation of Cavalcanti's "philosophical Canzone", elaborated in 1910–31, quotes Averroes following Renan. The Argentine writer J. L. Borges (1899–1986), inspired by Renan's remark about "Averroes, wanting to imagine what a drama is without ever having suspected what a theater is" (Borges (1964): 155), wrote the paradoxical short story "Averroes' Search". The Lebanese poet Adonis, resident in France, wrote a long poem on Marrakesh and interpretations weaved by space (published originally in Beirut, 1980), and recently accompanied it with a letter on Ibn Rushd and the alliance of poetry and philosophy, dated 1991, on the eight-hundredth anniversary of two Great Treatises by Averroes (1190). At the same time, French writer and essayist Jean-Pierre Faye (b. 1925) composed a long poem, "Le Vivant Ymaginant" on Averroes, where sequences by the philosopher are combined with quotations from Thomas Aquinas as well as William Blake and Georges Bataille. The search for the "moving subject" (Averroes), "or the subject of the moving night" (Bataille) is carried out in philosophy and in poetry, and it can find a final meeting point, resolving the dispute between the two approaches. Since Averroes, with his professional medical background, often used metaphors of spiritual medicine, the English poet Geoffrey Chaucer (*c.* 1343–1400), taking over from the Italian school of Dante, named him as such in his *Canterbury Tales* (General Prologue, l. 433). The philosopher dispenses wisdom (*ḥikmah*, *sophia*); the poet dispenses Eros.

BIBLIOGRAPHY

Adonis (1990) "Marrakech-Fés: L'espace tisse l'interprétation" (Paris) (trans. from the Arabic, "The Book of Five Poems", Beirut, 1980).

Averroes (1984) *Grand Commentaire de la Métaphysique d'Aristote,* Livre *Lam–Lambda,* trans. from the Arabic (Liège).
Borges, J. (1964) "Averroes' Search", in *Ficciones* (Buenos Aires, 1944); English trans.: *Labyrinths: Selected Stories and Other Writings* (London and New York).
Cavalcanti, G. (1960) "Rime", in *Poeti del Duecento,* 2, ed. Gianfranco Contini (Milan and Naples).
Dante (1957) *Divina Commedia* (Milan and Naples).
—— (1979) *Opere minori* (Milan and Naples).
Faye, J.-P. (1991) "Le Vivant Ymaginant", in *Actes du Colloque Averroès* (Paris), Review "Internationale de l'Imaginaire", 17–18: 123–5.
Gilson, E. (1953) *Dante et la philosophie* (Paris).
Nardi, B. (1966) *Saggi di filosofia dantesca* (Florence).
Pound, E. (1960) "Cavalcanti", in *Make It New* (1934), repr. in *Literary Essays of Ezra Pound* (London): 149-200.
Renan, E. (1949) "Averroès et l'averroisme" (1852), and "Averroès" (1861) in *Oeuvres complètes,* ed. M. Calman-Levy (Paris).
Vossler, C. (1904) *Die philosophischen Grundlagen zum "süssen neuen Stil" des Guido Guinizelli, Guido Cavalcanti und Dante Alighieri* (Heidelberg).

(Harry Gilonis assisted in the preparation of this section.)

IX

Islamic philosophy in the modern Islamic world

CHAPTER 61

Persia

Mehdi Aminrazavi

The advent of the "School of Iṣfahān"[1] in the tenth/sixteenth century, and in particular the teachings of its distinguished member Ṣadr al-Dīn Shīrāzī known as Mullā Ṣadrā,[2] was a turning point in the history of Islamic philosophy in Persia. The outpouring during the Ṣafavid dynasty of philosophical activities, which went through a period of decline in the following period, was once again revived by the sages of the Qājār period[3] in the thirteenth/nineteenth century, in particular Mullā 'Alī Nūrī, Mullā Ismā'īl Khājū'ī and Ḥājjī Mullā Hādī Sabziwārī.[4] The philosophical activities in the fourteenth/twentieth century in Iran should therefore be viewed in the light of the influence of the teachings of the grand master of the School of Iṣfahān, Mullā Ṣadrā, and his illustrious commentators and revivers, such as Ḥajjī Mullā Hādī Sabziwārī.[5]

In what follows we will discuss some of those Iranian philosophers who have kept alive the tradition of Islamic philosophy to this day. In doing so we deal with two groups of Iranian philosophers: firstly, those who have had a purely traditional education; secondly, those who are well grounded in Islamic philosophy but have either studied in the West or been familiar with Western modes of thought.

TRADITIONAL PHILOSOPHERS

Following the death of Sabziwārī (1289/1797), Tehran became the most important centre of philosophical activity in Iran and gained further significance when such masters as Mullā 'Abd Allāh and Mullā 'Alī Zunūzī migrated to Tehran to promulgate the teachings of the School of Iṣfahān. In the latter part of the Qājār period in Iṣfahān itself, where Mullā 'Alī Nūrī had been active earlier, philosophy gradually began to wane and, except for Jahāngīr Khān Qashqā'ī, the last notable survivor of the School of Iṣfahān and a remarkable philosopher and mystic and his student Ḥajjī Āqā Raḥīm Arbāb, no other major figure can be mentioned. With the decline of Iṣfahān as the centre of philosophical activity, Tehran became the definite centre where significant work was done on Sabziwārī's interpretation of Mullā Ṣadrā as well as the philosophy of Ibn Sīnā (Avicenna) and Suhrawardī by such figures as the Zunūzī family (Mullā 'Abd Allāh and Mullā 'Alī), Mīrzā Abu'l Ḥasan Jilwah, Mīrzā Mahdī Āshtiyānī, Fāḍil-i Tūnī and Mīrzā Ṭāhir Tūnikābunī, who was also a jurist. Abu'l Ḥasan Jilwah[6] was the only figure among them who wrote against Mullā Ṣadrā, accusing him of taking the Peripatetics' arguments and following the philosophy of Ibn Sīnā himself. Āshtiyānī and Fāḍil-i Tūnī were both attracted to Ibn 'Arabī's philosophical mysticism but also favoured Mullā Ṣadrā. Āshtiyānī, who wrote *Asās al-tawḥīd* and a commentary upon Sabzīwārī's *Sharḥ al-manẓūmah* among other books, trained a number of distinguished students,[7] the most notable of whom is Mahdī Hā'irī. Fāḍil-i Tūnī however, committed himself mostly to the clarification of Ibn 'Arabī's works, in particular his *Fūṣūṣ al-ḥikam*, while he also taught at Tehran University.[8]

Among the philosophers of the last fifty years who have left an indelible mark upon Islamic philosophy in Iran, the following three figures stand out particularly: Sayyid Muḥammad Kāẓim 'Aṣṣār, Sayyid Abu'l-Ḥasan Qazwīnī and Sayyid Muḥammad Ḥusayn Ṭabāṭabā'ī. Sayyid Muḥammad Kāẓim 'Aṣṣār, the oldest of the traditional masters of Islamic philosophy of his generation, was one of the first traditional scholars who went to the West and having studied in France returned then to Najaf for some time. Following his return to Iran, he taught at Tehran University and the Sipahsālār *madrasah*. 'Aṣṣār, who was also a jurist, specialized in the philosophy of Mullā Ṣadrā and Sabziwārī, gnosis (*'irfān*) and theoretical Sufism. 'Aṣṣār's influence upon Islamic philosophy was not so much through his writings as through the training of a number of fine students, among whom one can mention Seyyed Hossein Nasr. Some of his important writings are *'Ilm al-ḥadīth*,[9] and *Waḥdat al-wūjūd wa badā'*[10] and his most important published work, *Thalāth rasā'īl fi'l-ḥikmat al-islāmiyyah*.[11]

Sayyid Abu'l-Ḥasan Rafī'i Qazwīnī,[12] a great scholar of Mullā Ṣadrā was not a prolific author, but had a major influence on the revival and propagation of the "transcendental theosophy" (*ḥikmat al-muta'āliyyah*) of Mullā Ṣadrā. His title as an Ayatollah allowed him greater freedom to teach philosophy which was opposed by some of the jurists. Qazwīnī, who in addition to the religious sciences also knew astronomy and mathematics, wrote *Ittiḥād-i 'āqil wa ma'qūl*, [13] which deals with the doctrine of the unity of the knower and the known, a treatise on the unity of being (*waḥdat-i wujūd*)[14] and a treatise on eternal creation (*ḥudūth-i dahrī*).[15] The most important contribution of Qazwīnī to Islamic philosophy in Iran, however, has again been the training of such outstanding scholars as Sayyid Jalāl Āshtiyānī and Seyyed Hossein Nasr.[16]

Finally, Sayyid Muḥammad Ḥūsayn Ṭabāṭabā'ī,[17] who due to his piety and prolific authorship has gained legendary fame in Iran, should be mentioned. Being a native of Tabriz, "'Allāmah" (the most learned) as he is called, studied philosophy in Najaf with Shaykh Ḥusayn Wāḥid al-'Ayn. Ṭabāṭabā'ī, who resided in Qom, taught mainly the *Shifā'* of Ibn Sīnā and the *Asfār* of Mullā Ṣadrā. He also taught Sufism to a smaller circle of people.

Amongst the more notable works of 'Allāmah Ṭabāṭabā'ī are the twenty-seven volume Qur'ānic commentary *al-Mīzān*, *'Alī wa'l-ḥikmat al-ilāhiyyah*, the new edition of the *Asfār* of Mullā Ṣadrā and two philosophical works written at the end of his life, *Bidāyat al-ḥikmah* and *Nihāyat al-ḥikmah*. Finally, we should mention especially his *Uṣūl-i falsafah wa rawish-i ri'ālizm*[18] with the extensive commentary of his distinguished student Murtaḍā Muṭahharī which was written as a response to the intellectual challenge of the leftist intellegentsia and more especially Marxism, in Iran after the Second World War.

Ṭābāṭabā'ī also carried out a series of annual discussions (1958–78) with Henry Corbin, the outstanding French philosopher and scholar of Islam, in Tehran and Qom. In these meetings various philosophical topics were discussed from a comparative point of view and these discussions became the source of inspiration for a number of younger philosophers. S. H. Nasr, who studied both philosophy and *'irfān* with the 'Allāmah, was the main translator of these sessions in both a linguistic and an intellectual sense.[19]

Among other philosophers of this era who are less known one can mention Muḥammad Ṣāliḥ Ḥā'irī Māzandarānī and Ẓiyā' al-Dīn Durrī both of whom staunchly defended the Peripatetics and remained opposed to Mullā Ṣadrā. In his book *Ḥikmat-i Bū 'Alī*[20] Ha'irī Māzandarānī argued that Mullā Ṣadrā had been inspired by the Peripatetics more than he gave them credit for. Ẓiyā' al-Dīn Durrī wrote extensive commentaries upon the *Asfār* of Mullā Ṣadrā and also argued that Mullā Ṣadrā adopted certain strands of the Peripateticṣ' thought. Durrī mentioned one hundred and three texts which are the foundations of the Ṣadrian philosophy.[21] Also, we should include Mahdī Ilāhī Qūmsha'ī, the author of *Ḥikmat-i ilāhī khāṣṣ wa 'āmm*,[22] Mīrzā Aḥmad Āshtiyānī, well known for his mastery of gnosis and ethics and the author of *Nāma-yi rahbarān-i āmūzish-i kitāb-i takwīn*,[23] 'Abd al-Wahhāb Sha'rānī, the editor of Sabziwarī's *Asrār al-ḥikam* and the *Sharḥ al-tajrīd* of Ḥillī, and finally Muḥammad Taqī Āmulī, the author of *Dūrar al-fawā'id*.[24]

Beside the above figures who composed philosophical treatises, a group of scholars can be named who, although not strictly speaking "philosophers", contributed towards the further enrichment of Islamic philosophy in Iran. Amongst this group can be named Maḥmūd Shahābī who beside his expertise in jurisprudence wrote a fine work on Ibn Sīnā's *al-Ishārāt wa'l-tanbīḥāt*, and a work on logic entitled *Rahbar-i khirad*[25] and Sayyid Muḥammad Mishkāt who wrote numerous short treatises on Ibn Sīnā, Qūṭb al-Dīn Shīrāzī, Ḥillī and Kāshānī. In addition to his scholarship, Mishkāt gathered one of the most valuable libraries on Islamic philosophy and the sciences which he later donated to Tehran University.[26] One should also mention Jalāl Humā'ī, who is best known for his works on literature but also composed one of the most authoritative works on al-Ghazzālī, the *Ghazzālī-nāmah*, and an important work on Mullā Ṣadrā, and Jawād Muṣliḥ who is known for his excellent translation of Mullā Ṣadrā's *Asfār* and *al-Shawāhid al-rubūbiyyah* into Persian. Finally, one can mention a mysterious woman from Iṣfahān who composed a number of works on gnosis and philosophical ethics and who would sign her name as *Yak bānū-yi īrānī* ("a Persian lady" but whose real name was Amīn. She composed a number of works on gnosis and religious sciences, including a major commentary upon the Qur'ān entitled *Makhzan al-'irfān*, two works on eschatology, *Ma'ād yā ākharīn sayr-i bashar* and *Āghāz wa anjām*, and a major philosophical work called *Arba'īn-i hāshāmiyyah*.

Among the next generation of scholars, the most outstanding and prolific figure is Sayyid Jalāl Āshtiyānī who is currently teaching at Mashhad University. Among his major works are *Hastī az naẓar-i falsafah wa 'irfān*, *Sharḥ bar mūqaddamah-yi Qayṣarī dar taṣawwūf-i islāmī*, *Sharḥ-i Ḥāl wa ārā–yi falsafī-yi Mullā Ṣadrā*, an edition of Mullā Ṣadrā's *al-Maẓāhir al-ilāhiyyah*, an edition of Mullā Muḥammad Ja'far Lāhījānī's commentary upon Mullā Ṣadrā's *Mashā'ir*, an edition of Sabziwārī's *Majmūa-yi rasā'il*, a critical edition of Mullā Ṣadrā's *al-Shawāhid al-rubūbiyyah* with the commentary of Sabziwārī, and finally his edition of Mullā Mūḥsin Fayḍ Kāshānī's *Uṣūl al-ma'ārif* with a very long commentary on the philosophy of the school of Mullā Ṣadrā. Perhaps his greatest work, however, has been the editing of an anthology of Islamic philosophy in Persia from Mīr Dāmād to the present with the collaboration of Henry Corbin. All the Classical texts in the anthology have Āshtiyānī's own commentaries and long introductions of great philosophical importance.[27]

Among other traditional philosophers we can mention Miṣbāh Yazdī, who is the author of a two-volume book entitled *Āmūzish-i falsafah*,[28] Jawādī Āmulī and Ḥasan-zādah Āmulī,[29] all of whom teach Islamic philosophy in Qom today. The latter is regarded as the heir to Ṭabāṭabā'ī's chair in philosophy in Qom.

Among the other philosophers of this period, one must name Murtaḍā Muṭahharī,[30] who was a student of 'Allāmah Ṭabāṭaba'ī. Muṭahharī was one of the few traditional scholars to devote a major part of his works to the exposition of Islam for young people. As a result, most of his writings are of a popular nature, although he wrote some works of a highly scholarly nature such as his commentary upon Ṭabāṭabā'ī's *Uṣul-i falsafah wa rawish-i ri'ālīzm*, his edition of Bahmanyār's *Kitāb al-taḥṣīl*, *Khadamāt-i mutaqābil-i islām wa Īrān* in two volumes, and *Sharḥ-i Manẓūma-i Sabziwārī*.[31]

TRADITIONAL PHILOSOPHERS WITH MODERN TRAINING

Among the more prominent Muslim philosophers of the last few decades who have had traditional training and are also at home with Western modes of thought we can name S. H. Nasr, M. Hā'irī, M. Mohaghegh and to some extent A. Fardīd and D. Shayegan.[32] To this list one must also add Henry Corbin, who, although not an Iranian by birth, had made Iran his spiritual home and played an active role on the Iranian philosophical scene. It is by virtue of leaving an indelible mark upon the intellectual landscape of Iran that Corbin should be regarded in any discussion of traditional Islamic philosophy in contemporary Iran.[33]

S. H. Nasr, whose university education was in the West, became further acquainted with Islamic philosophy upon his return to Iran. Amongst the scholars with both traditional and modern training, Nasr is the most prolific. His contributions are numerous, the most important being the introduction of traditional Islamic philosophy to modern educated Iranians, as well as other Muslims, especially at a time when Western rationalistic philosophy had posed a challenge to traditional Islamic philosophy. Nasr should also be credited with making the work of Mullā Ṣadrā and Suhrawardī, in particular his Persian mystical narratives, better known to a wider audience.[34]

One of the greatest achievements of Nasr, however, has been his engagement with modern thought as an Islamic philosopher. The subjects treated by him range from man and nature to traditional cosmology, arts and metaphysics. In his numerous works[35] he has provided a traditional Islamic response to the challenges of the modern world. Some of his works which represent the encounter of traditional Islamic thought and certain strands of modern thought are *Man and Nature*, *Islam and the Plight of the Modern Man* and *The Need for a Sacred Science*. Among the especially philosophically oriented works of Nasr we can mention *Knowledge and the Sacred*, *Three Muslim Sages* and *An Introduction to Islamic Cosmological Doctrine*.[36]

Nasr has not only influenced modern Islamic philosophy in Iran through his works, but his relentless efforts to sponsor conferences and establish centres[37] for the study of Islamic philosophy in the 1960s and

1970s contributed to the spread of Islamic philosophy among the younger intellectuals in Iran.

Mahdī Hā'irī Yazdī, a traditional master of Islamic philosophy, has written extensively on epistemology. Having studied at Qom, he went to Canada and America as the representative of the late Āyatollah Burūjirdī. He studied philosophy at the University of Toronto and, upon his return to Iran, resumed his teaching at Tehran University. He taught for many years in the West.

Hā'irī promulgates an Ibn Sīnan interpretation of Suhrawardī and Mullā Ṣadrā as well as the whole school of *ishrāq*. One of the central concerns of Hā'irī has been to provide an Islamic response to the philosophical questions posed by the Western analytic tradition. His interest in comparative philosophy has made him a unique figure of contemporary philosophy in Iran. Among his major works are *Hiram-i hastī*, *Kāwishhā-yi 'aql-i naẓar-i*, and his latest work, *The Principles of Epistemology in Islamic Philosophy: Knowledge by Presence* with a foreword by S. H. Nasr.[38]

One can also mention Mehdi Mohaghegh, who has taught at Tehran and McGill Universities and is the author of several important works such as *Filsūf-i Ray*.[39] He is also the editor of the *Wisdom of Persia* series, a major scholarly project which has undertaken in-depth studies of various Persian philosophers, and has produced many volumes so far.

Aḥmad Fardīd and Daryush Shayegan are strictly speaking not "Islamic philosophers"; however, they display great interest in Islamic philosophy from a comparative perspective. Fardīd had thorough knowledge of German philosophy but was also well versed in Islamic philosophy.[40] Shayegan, who participated in the circle of 'Allāmah Ṭabāṭabā'ī and Corbin, is more of an independent thinker who has done some interesting work on Shi'ism and Corbin from the modern continental point of view and also on comparative philosophy as far as Islamic and Indian philosophies are concerned. Among his important works are *Hindouisme et Soufisme*, *L'Homme à la lampe magique*, *Le sens du ta'wīl*, *Henry Corbin: la topographie spirituelle de l'Islam iranien*, and his book in Persian, *Āsiyā dar barābar-i gharb*.[41]

Finally, there is Henry Corbin, an exceptionally prolific scholar and philosopher whose early interest in Heidegger was supplemented by his contact with Suhrawardī's *Ḥikmat al-ishrāq* and the whole school of *ḥikmah*. Corbin directed the Institut Franco-Iranien in Tehran for more than twenty years, wrote and edited dozens of books on the tradition of *ḥikmah* in Iran, and spent the last years of his life teaching at the Imperial Iranian Academy of Philosophy. Amongst the major works which he edited are Suhrawardī, *Oeuvres philosophiques et mystiques*, Abū Ya'qūb Sijistānī, *Kashf al-maḥjūb*, Ruzbahān Baqlī Shīrazī, *'Abhār al-'āshiqīn* and Mullā Ṣadrā, *Kitāb al-mashā'ir*. Among the major works he wrote on

Islamic philosophy we can mention *Avicenna and the Visionary Recital, Creative Imagination in the Sufism of Ibn 'Arabī, Spiritual Body and Celestial Earth: From Mazdean Iran to Shi'ite Iran*, and *En Islam iranien*. In addition to these works we must mention what is perhaps his most important contribution to Islamic philosophy, namely the *History of Islamic Philosophy* written in collaboration with S. H. Nasr and O. Yahya, which is the only history of Islamic philosophy to consider fully the later developments of Islamic philosophy in Iran.

One of the most significant contributions of Corbin to the Islamic culture of Iran was to establish a bridge between the pre-Islamic gnostic world view of the Persians and Shi'ite spirituality and philosophy. The philosophical and esoteric aspects of Shi'ite Islam were thoroughly studied by Corbin, whose pioneering work and collaborations with S. H. Nasr and S. J. Āshtiyānī were partly the reason for the revival of the teachings of certain Islamic philosophers in modern Iran.

Among the contemporary younger Iranian philosophers who are currently teaching in Iran, one can mention R. Dāwarī Ardakānī, N. Pourjavādī, Gh. A'wānī, Gh. Ḥaddād 'Ādil and 'A. Surūsh. The works of these philosophers, in particular R. Dāwarī Ardakānī, Ḥaddād 'Ādil and Surūsh, who, following the 1978–9 revolution in Iran, joined the revolutionary process, represent a tension with regard to the direction that Islamic intellectual sciences ought to take. As politically inclined thinkers interested in traditional Islam and its intellectual heritage, they have composed treatises interpreting in different ways the tradition of Islamic philosophy. Among the major works of Dāwarī Ardakānī on traditional Islamic philosophy are *Fārābī: the Founder of Islamic Philosophy* and *The Civil Society of Fārābī*. Surūsh's major works on traditional themes are *Knowledge and Value*, and a short commentary on Mullā Ṣadrā's theory of trans-substantiality of motion entitled *The Restless Substance of the Universe* (*Nahād-i nā ārām-i jahān*).

There are, however, the challenges of the modern world and the difficulties of implementing the *Sharī'ah* in modern Iran. As an attempt to respond to the challenges of the modern world with which they are engaged, these younger philosophers have composed numerous works addressing the encounter between traditional Islam and the modern world. Among Dāwarī Ardakānī's major works in this regard, one can name *Islamic Revolution and the Status of the World, The Present Status of Intellection in Iran* and *The Theoretical Foundation of Western Civilization*. The significant works of Surūsh are *Industry and Human Sciences, Intellectuality and Religiosity* and *Masked Dogmatism*. The above philosophers are now engaged in an intensive discussion concerning the philosophy of law which has been called "*Fiqh-i pūyā wa faqh-i īstā*" (dynamic and static jurisprudence). Using philosophical arguments, the supporters of dynamic jurisprudence argue that the legal codes of the *Sharīʿah* must be reinterpreted within the immutable principles of Islam.

POLITICAL PHILOSOPHERS

Beginning in the 1950s, a number of clerics as well as modernist scholars of Islam began to pay more attention to the political philosophy of Islam which was generally absent in the works of the traditionalists. Some of these scholars were not strictly speaking philosophers or at least not only philosophers, but had traditional training in philosophy. Among the most prominent figures were Ayatollah Rūḥallāh Khumaynī[42] who wrote *Wilāyat-i faqīh* and a number of short treatises on political philosophy in addition to his work *Kashf al-asrār* which is on rituals and prayers. Ayatollah Ṭaliqānī, who offered a leftist interpretation of Islam, is the author of *Partaw'ī az qū'rān*, a commentary upon the Qur'ān, and a book on political economy in Islam entitled *Islam wa mālikiyyat*, both of which became popular in post-revolutionary Iran; and Ayatollah Muntaẓirī, who was more of an activist than a scholar, wrote a number of short treatises on Islamic political philosophy. Murtaḍā Muṭāhharī, whose activities prior to the Iranian Revolution were directed at confronting the domination of Western culture, should also be mentioned. It is for this reason that he undertook the writing of an extensive commentary upon Ṭabāṭabā'ī's work *Uṣūl-i falsafah wa rawish-i ri'ālizm*, which was a response to the challenges of Western intellectual thought.

The second group of political philosophers during this period consists of those who have had some training in the West as well as in Iran and who properly speaking should be called "liberation theologians". Some of the well-known figures among them are 'A. Sharīʿatī, Y. Saḥābī, M. Bāzargān and H. Ḥabībī, who despite their hostile attitude towards traditional Islamic philosophy were engaged in speculative theology to defend the more radical interpretations of Islam. The latter group, whose very outlook is fundamentally different from the traditional Islamic philosophers, have produced a great deal of popular literature which offers a new interpretation of Islam.

Whereas traditional Islamic philosophy emphasizes the implementation of the *Sharīʿah* within society, the modernists rely on the "spirit of Islam" to bring about socio-political change while they question and often reject the relevance of many tenets of traditional Islamic law in the modern world.

A SUMMARY OF THE CENTRAL ISSUES

Later Islamic philosophy in Iran is primarily concerned with such ontological issues as *wujūd* (existence) and *māhiyyah* (quiddity) and epistemology.[43] Whereas the *mashshā'īs* advocate the "principiality" of *māhiyyah*, the *Ishrāqīs* have supported the "principiality" of *wujūd*. Central to the concern of *mashshā'īs* are also such themes as God's knowledge of the world and whether knowledge belongs to the Essence of God or His Attributes. The problem of how multiplicity came from unity and the structure within which this problem is explained (*tashkīk*) is also central to Islamic philosophy.

The Ṣadrian philosophers for whom existence and essence are central have also paid special attention to the unity of the intellect (*'aql*), agent of intellection (*'āqil*) and subject of intellection (*ma'qūl*).[44] It is in this regard that in later Islamic philosophy in Iran ontology and epistemology became intertwined. This is best exemplified in the theory of "knowledge by presence" (*al-'ilm al-ḥuḍūrī*) in which cognition and the presence of one's being are interrelated.[45]

Finally, of some interest is the discussion of change or motion and its philosophical implications. Whereas traditionally motion was perceived to belong to the category of accident, it was Mullā Ṣadrā who argued for the existence of motion in the category of substance. His theory, which came to be known as "trans-substantial motion" (*al-ḥarakat al-jawhariyyah*), has come to be a controversial theory upon which many philosophers such as 'Allāmah Ṭabāṭabā'ī have commented.

Among the other philosophical topics, ethics has been extensively treated. Such a figure as Mīrzā Aḥmad Āshtiyānī developed the kind of spiritual ethics within the context of Sufism that views ethical purity as the salient feature of mysticism.

The tradition of Islamic philosophy rests on the concept of continuity and not change and therefore the philosophical problems treated by Persian philosophers remain the same. What changes, however, is their methods of treatment. It is on the basis of their methodology and not the issues that we can divide them into four different schools.

Firstly, the "Ṣadrians", who are the avid propagators of Mullā Ṣadrā and his school of "transcendental theosophy" (*al-ḥikmat al-muta'āliyah*). The Ṣadrians offer a neo-Ibn Sīnan reading of Islamic philosophy which is at the same time rational and conducive to intellectual intuition. Mullā Ṣadrā's major work, the *Asfār*, is studied not only as his *magnum opus* but also as a source for the history of Islamic philosophy. The thrust of the Ṣadrian school is the "priority" of *wujūd* over *māhiyyah*.[46]

Secondly, the "Ṣadrian–*ishrāqī*" school represents a synthesis of rational knowledge and intellectual intuition. This school is based on a series of principles that are attained through intuition (*al-dhawq*) and therefore are axiomatic. This school maintains that mastery of discursive reasoning is a necessary condition whereas asceticism is also necessary for the intellect to know the true principles of philosophy which Mullā Ṣadrā calls "the Oriental Principles" (*qā'idah mashriqiyyah*). Knowledge, accordingly, is not attained through sense perception or logical deductions (*ḥuṣūlī*) but is obtained through an unmediated mode of cognition between the subject and the object (*ḥuḍūrī*).

Thirdly, Peripatetics (*mashshā'īs*) who follow al-Fārābī, Ibn Sīnā and Ibn Rushd do not take the more intuitive part of the Ṣadrian school seriously; they consider it to belong to the domain of mysticism and not philosophy. Relying on a process of rationalization, attempts have been made to revive Ibn Sīnan philosophy.

Finally, there is philosophical gnosis (*'irfān-i falsafī*), whose propagators adhere to the teachings of Ibn 'Arabī, Qunawī, Fanārī and other members of the Akbarian school. Amongst the more prominent figures of this tradition one can name M. Qumsha'ī and Muḥammad 'Alī Ḥakīm, a mysterious philosopher–gnostic who chose a hermetic life and disappeared from the scene in the 1970s. The pivotal axiom of philosophical gnosis centres on the concept of unity (*tawḥīd*). Various themes such as emanation, the relationship between unity and multiplicity, unity as related to necessity, etc. are all examined in the light of Divine Unity.

One should mentain also the efforts of a number of modern thinkers and translators to develop the philosophical vocabulary drawn from traditional Islamic philosophical terminology for use in dealing with modern philosophy. The delicate task of finding the vocabulary that can represent the philosophical concepts of one linguistic tradition compared to another is a difficult one. This, however, was done in a masterly fashion by such figures as Muḥammad 'Alī Furūghī, Yaḥyā Mahdawī Ghulām Ḥusayn Ṣadīqī, Manūchihr Buzūrgmihr and Aḥmad Ārām.[47]

CONCLUSION

The pivotal point of Islamic philosophy in the last few decades in Iran has been the philosophy of Mullā Ṣadrā and Suhrawardī. During this period there has been an upsurge of interest in the works of these two giants of philosophy and gnosis, and many of their works have been translated from Arabic into Persian as well as the European languages.[48] Also during this era Suhrawardī's Persian mystical narratives as well as his philosophical treatises and their significance have been introduced to the philosophical community at large.[49]

Islamic philosophy, which traditionally was taught exclusively at the *madrasahs* and private circles, became an important part of the educational curriculum of modern universities in addition to research centres and foundations in Iran. Islamic philosophy and *'irfān* continue to flourish and remain an active and integral part of the intellectual life of Iran today.

NOTES

Beside the references that are alluded to in the notes, the author has benefited by two interviews with Seyyed Hossein Nasr and Mahdī Ha'irī Yazdī.

1 For more information on the "School of Iṣfahān" see S. H. Nasr, "the School of Isfahan", in *A History of Muslim Philosophy*, ed. H. M. Sharif (Wiesbaden, 1966), 2: 904–32, and "Spiritual Movements, Philosophy and Theology in the Ṣafavid Period", in *The Cambridge History of Irān*, ed. P. Jackson, (Cambridge, 1969–91), 6: 656–97.

2 For more information on Mullā Ṣadrā and his influence on Islamic philosophy in modern Iran see S. H. Nasr, "Ṣadr al-Dīn Shīrāzi", in *A History of Muslim Philosophy*, 2: 952–61.

3 For more information on Islamic philosophy in the Qājār period see S. H. Nasr, "The Metaphysics of Ṣadr al-Dīn and Islamic Philosophy in Qājār Iran", in C. E. Bosworth and C. Hillenbrand (eds), *Qājār Iran – Political, Social and Cultural Changes 1900–1925* (Edinburgh, 1983): 177–98.

4 For more information on Sabziwārī and his influence on Islamic philosophy see the introduction by Izutsu to *The Metaphysics of Sabzawārī*, trans. M. Mohaghegh and T. Izutsu (New York, 1977): 1–25., and *The Fundamentals of Sabzawārī's Metaphysics*, trans. and ed. M. Mohaghegh and T. Izutsu (1973). See also Nasr, "Sabziwāri", in M. M. Sharif (ed.) *A History of Muslim Philosophy*: 1543–56.

5 For a list of later Islamic philosophers and their biographies see: Manūchihr Ṣadūqī Suhā, *Ḥukamā wa 'urafā-yi muta'akhirīn-ī Ṣadr al-mutā'allihīn* (Tehran, 1980).

6 For more information on Mirzā Abu'l-Ḥasan Jilwah see *ibid.*: 159–72.

7 For more information on Maḥdī Āshtiyānī see the extensive introduction by T. Izutsu in *Sharḥ-i Āshtiyānī bar sharḥ-i manẓūmah* (Tehran, 1973) and *Ḥukamā wa 'urafā-yi*: 64–6.

8 *Ḥukamā wa 'urafā-yi*: 68.

9 Sayyid Muḥammad Kāẓim 'Aṣṣār, *'Ilm al-ḥadīth* (Tehran, 1975).

10 Sayyid Muḥammad Kāẓim 'Aṣṣār, *Waḥdat al-wūjūd wa badā'* (Mashhad, 1971). Critical edition and introduction by Sayyid Jalāl al-Dīn Āshtiyānī.

11 Sayyid Muḥammad Kāẓim, 'Aṣṣār, *Thalāth rasā'il fi'l-ḥikmat al-islāmiyyah* (Tehran, 1961).

12 For more information see S. H. Nasr (ed.), *Mullā Ṣadrā Commemoration Volume* (Tehran, 1961).

13 Sayyid Abu'l-Ḥasan Rafī'i Qazwīnī, *Ittiḥād-i 'āqil wa ma'qūl*; introduction and glossary by Ḥasan Ḥasanzadih Āmūlī (Tehran, 1982).

14 For more information on this see S. H. Nasr, "Mullā Ṣadrā and the Unity of Being", in his *Islamic Life and Thought* (Albany, 1981): 174–80.

15 *Ḥudūth-i dahrī* is a term used by Mīr Dāmād concerning the problem of eternity

(*qidam*) and createdness (*ḥudūth*) of the world. For more information on this see the introduction by M. Mohaghegh to Mīr Dāmād's *Qabasāt* (Tehran, 1989): 11–14.

16 *Ḥukamā wa 'urafā-yi*: 69.

17 For more information on 'Allāmah Ṭabāṭabā'ī see *Yād nāma-yi 'Allāmah Ṭabāṭabā'ī* (Tehran, 1983), introduction S. H. Nasr to his *Shi'ite Islam*, trans. and ed. Nasr (Albany, 1975), and *Kayḥān-i farhangī*, 6(8) (Nov. 1990): 1–16.

18 'Allāmah Ṭabāṭabā'ī, *Uṣūl-i falsafah wa rawish-i ri'ālizm* (Qom, 1953).

19 Among other scholars who participated were D. Shayegan, M. Muṭahharī, B. Furūzānfar, I. Sepahbodi and A. Manāqibī. For more information on these intellectual sessions see D. Shayegan, "The Spiritual Quest of Henry Corbin: From Heidegger to Suhrawardī", Part 1, *Irān-nāmah*, year 7(3) (1989): 479, and D. Shayegan, "Le Sens du Ta'wil", in *L'Herne-Henry Corbin* (Paris, 1981): 84–5; as well as his *Henry Corbin*; and S. H. Nasr, "Henry Corbin Revisited", *Irān-nāmah*, year 9(4) (1991): 665–81. Also, an edited version of these discussions has been published in two volumes.

20 Muḥammad Ṣāliḥ Hā'irī Māzandarānī, *Ḥikmat-i Bū 'Alī*, 3 vols (Tehran, 1956–8).

21 For a brief discussion concerning Durrī and other critics of Mullā Ṣadrā see 'A. Q. Qaraguzlū, "Intiqād bar Mullā Ṣadrā dar 'aṣr-i mā", *Kayhān-i farhangī*, 8(7) (1991): 20–3.

22 Ilāhī Qūmsha'ī, *Ḥikmat ilāhī khāṣṣ wa 'āmm* (Tehran, 1966).

23 Mirzā Aḥmad Āshtiyānī, *Nāma-yi rahbarān-i khirad* (Tehran, 1995).

24 Muḥammad Taqī Āmulī, *Durar al-fawā'id*, 2 vols (Tehran, 1957).

25 Maḥmūd Shahābī, *Rahbar-i khirad* (Tehran, 1961).

26 See *Fiḥrist-i kitābhā-yi ihdā'ī-yi Sayyid Muḥammad Mishkāt* (Tehran, 1957), prepared by M. T. Dānechepazūh. This catalogue is a mine of information for Islamic philosophy provided by Dānechpazūh, who is one of the most outstanding living scholars on Islamic manuscripts, especially those pertaining to philosophy.

27 S. J. Āshtiyānī and H. Corbin, *Anthologie des philosophes iraniens*, 4 vols (Tehran, 1972; 1975). For more information on S. J. Āshtiyānī see his interview in *Kayhān farhangī*, year 2 (1985): 5–18.

28 M. T. Miṣbāḥ Yazdī, *Āmūzish-i falsafah*, 2 vols. (Tehran, 1989).

29 See the extensive commentary and the introduction of Ḥasan Ḥasan-zādih Āmulī to Sayyid Abu'l-Ḥasan Rafī'i Qazwīnī, *Ittiḥād-i 'aqil wa ma'qūl* (Tehran, 1983).

30 M. Muṭahharī, who had joined the Iranian Revolution, was also a member and in fact head of the Revolutionary Council. He was assassinated shortly after the Revolution in 1979.

31 Bahmanyār, *Kitāb al-taḥṣīl*, ed. with commentary by M. Muṭahharī (Tehran, 1971); M. Muṭahharī, *Khadamāt-i mūtāqābil-i islām wa Īrān*, (Tehran, 1976), 2 vols; M. Muṭahharī, *Sharḥ-i manẓūmah*, 2 vols (Tehran, 1982).

32 Nasr in his *Islamic Philosophy in Contemporary Persia: a Survey of Activity During the Past Two Decades* (Research Monograph, no. 3, Middle East Center, University of Utah, 1972), indicates that the following are among the most active philosophers of the last few decades in Iran: "Yaḥyā Mahdawī, Ghulām Ḥusayn Ṣadīqī, Mehdī Mohaghegh, S. H. Nasr, 'Alī Murād Dāwūdī, Sayyid

Abu'l-Qāsim Pūr-Ḥūsaynī, Riḍā Dāwarī, Sayyid Ja'far Sajjādī, Muḥammad Taqī Dānechpazhūh, Aḥmad Fardīd", etc. For a list of contemporary Iranian philosophers see *ibid.*: 8.

33 For more information on Corbin's life and thought see S. H. Nasr (ed) *Henry Corbin Commemoration Volume* (Tehran, 1977). See also D. Shayegan, *Henry Corbin – la topographie spirituelle de l'Islam iranien* (Paris, 1990). For a list of Corbin's works see S. H. Nasr, *ibid.*: 32–3 and *L'Herne – Henry Corbin* (Paris, 1981): 360–543.

34 Suhrawardī, *Oeuvres philosophiques et mystiques* 2, ed. S. H. Nasr (Tehran, 1970).

35 For a complete list of Nasr's works up to his sixtieth birthday see M. Aminrazavi and Zailan Moris, *The Complete Bibliography of the Works of Seyyed Hossein Nasr* (Kuala Lumpur, 1994).

36 S. H. Nasr, *Knowledge and the Sacred* (New York, 1981) and *An Introduction to Islamic Cosmological Doctrine* (Albany, 1993) and *Three Muslim Sages* (New York, 1976).

37 One of the most important centres devoted to the study of Islamic philosophy which Nasr had established was the Imperial Iranian Academy of Philosophy. The Academy had commissioned many interesting projects and undertook the publication of a great number of traditional texts as well as a scholarly journal on published regular basis entitled *Jāvīdān khirad (Sophia Perennis)*. The centre is still very active and operates under the name of the Iranian Academy of Philosophy.

38 M. Hā'irī Yazdī, *The Principles of Epistemology in Islamic Philosophy: Knowledge by Presence* (New York, 1992).

39 M. Mohaghegh, *Fīlsūf-i ray* (Tehran, 1970).

40 Fardīd, who died recently, wrote little but is known especially for his translation of Corbin's *Les Motifs Zoroastriens dans la philosophie de Sohrawardi* (Tehran, 1946).

41 D. Shayegan, *Hindouisme et soufisme* (Paris, 1979); "L'Homme à la lampe magique", in *Mélanges*, (ed.) S. H. Nasr (Paris, 1977); "Le sens du ta'wil", in *L'Herne – Henry Corbin* (Paris, 1981) and *Henry Corbin* (Paris, 1990).

42 It should be noted that Khumayni was also a traditional philosopher who taught gnosis and Mullā Ṣadrā. His love of *'irfān* and philosophy is said to have continued until his death in 1989. It was in 1963 that he turned to politics and wrote treatises of a political nature. He is also the author of a number of works on gnosis and metaphysics including commentaries on some of the traditional texts such as the *Fuṣūṣ* of Ibn 'Arabī.

43 For a very useful analysis of the subject matter see S. H. Nasr, "Existence (*wujud*) and Quiddity (*māhiyyah*) in Islamic Philosophy", *International Philosophical Quarterly*, 29 (116) (1989): 409–34.

44 This view, which is central to the Ṣadrians as well as to Islamic gnosticism (*'irfān*), is referred to as the "Doctrine of the Unity of the Knower and the Known" (*ittiḥād-i 'āqil wa ma'qūl*). See S. A. Qazwīnī, "Ittiḥād-i 'āqil wa ma'qūl", trans. 'Alī Qūlī Qarā'ī, *al-Tawḥīd*, (1950): 85–92.

45 For a complete discussion of the theory of "knowledge by presence" see M. Hā'irī Yazdī, *Epistemology in Islamic Philosophy*, (Albany, 1992). See the preface by S. H. Nasr on Ha'irī and his works.

46 For more information on the Ṣadrian philosophy see S. H. Nasr (ed.) *Mullā Ṣadrā Commemoration Volume* (Tehran, 1961) and *The Transcendental Theosophy of Ṣadr al-Dīn Shīrāzī* (Tehran, 1978); F. Rahman, *The Philosophy of Mullā Ṣadrā* (Albany, 1976); *The Wisdom of the Throne: an introduction to the Philosophy of Mullā Ṣādrā*, trans. James Morris of *al-Ḥikmat al-'arshiyyah* of Mullā Ṣadrā (Princeton, 1981).

47 The works of these figures who were familiar with European philosophers should be regarded as the earliest attempt at comparative philosophy between Islamic philosophy and modern European philosophy. M. A. Fūrūghī's *Sayr-i ḥikmat dar urūpā* and A. Ārām's many translations of European philosophical treatises are among such works.

48 For a translation of Suhrawardī's main works see H. Corbin, *Le Livre de la sagesse orientale* by Shihaboddin Yaḥyā Sohrawardi, traduction et notes par H. Corbin (Paris, 1986). Also, Parvin Peervani's translation of the *Ḥikmat al-ishrāq* into English (forthcoming) should be noted. For translations of Suhrawardī's Persian works see Thackston, *Mystical and Visionary Treatises of Suhrawardi* (London, 1982). For translations of Mullā Ṣadrā see James Morris' translation of the *Ḥikmat al-'arshiyyah* entitled *Wisdom of the Throne* (Princeton, 1981). Also, Mehdī Ḥā'irī Yazdī is currently translating Mullā Ṣadrā's *al-Mashā'ir* under the title *Stages of Wisdom*.

49 In recent years there have appeared numerous articles and books on Suhrawardī. For more information on some of these works see M. Aminrazavi *Suhrawardī's Theory of Knowledge*, (Ph.D. dissertation, Temple University, 1989); M. Bylebyle, *The Wisdom of Illumination: a Study of the Prose Stories of Suhrawardī* (Ph.D. dissertation, University of Chicago, 1976) K. Tehrani, *Mystical Symbolism in Four Treatises of Suhrawardi* (Ph.D. dissertation, Columbia University, 1974); G. Webb, *Suhrawardi's Angelology* (Ph.D. dissertation, Temple University, 1989); H. Zia, *Suhrawardi's Philosophy of Illumination* (Ph.D. dissertation, Harvard University, 1976). Also see S. H. Nasr, "Suhrawardī" in M. M. Sharif (ed.) *A History of Muslim Philosophy*, pp. 372–98; and "Suhrawardī" in his *Three Muslim Sages*, chapter 3: 52–83.

CHAPTER 62

India

Hafiz A. Ghaffar Khan

INTRODUCTION

The Indian subcontinent has been very rich with regard to religion, culture, science, and civilization. It has been the birthplace for various major religions such as Hinduism, Buddhism, Jainism and Sikhism. It also accommodated some alien religions such as Zoroastrianism, Islam and Christianity.

The Indian subcontinent has been the seat of many great civilizations since the Stone Age. The pre-Vedic Dravidian civilization, brought to light by archeological discoveries, equalled and possibly surpassed in splendour the civilizations of ancient Mesopotamia and Egypt. Subsequent to the Dravidian civilization, the Vedic civilization (developed about 1200 B.C. by people of Indo-Aryan stock) was also notable in many respects. The Brahmanic civilization reached its peak during the Mauryan dynasty (322–185 B.C.) founded by Chandragupta. Again it was during this period that Aśoka (273–232 B.C.), the grandson of Chandragupta, extended his kingdom to the farthest corners of the continent. During his rule, Buddhism became the state religion and the Buddhist culture the most prominent in the region. The Mauryan dynasty was followed by the rule of Kushans, the Guptas, the Huns and the Turks in the subcontinent.

But the most powerful and durable civilization which the Indian subcontinent ever experienced was Islamic civilization. Islam as a religion and civilization found its way into the subcontinent, first in 92/711 under Muḥammad ibn Qāsim and then, in 390/1000 under the leadership of Maḥmūd of Ghaznah. It was established in the region gradually and remained as a dominant political, cultural, religious and social force there for more than eight centuries. Islamic civilization reached its peak during the Mughul period and imprinted an indelible mark on Indian civilization and culture as a whole.

In India Islam encountered the Brahmanic and Buddhist cultures and civilizations which were deeply rooted in Hinduism and Buddhism, basically philosophical in nature. In order to cope with this dilemma successfully, the Muslims were obliged to adopt philosophical and dialectical methods for explaining Islamic dogmas and principles. The Muslims, being acquainted with Greek methods, dealt with the situation with ease. A strong philosophical and theological tradition had been established long ago, first in Baghdad and then in Khurasan and Central Asia. The established Islamic intellectual traditions were transmitted into the Indian subcontinent gradually through various channels. Different elements of Islamic society played a significant role in this transmission of the Islamic intellectual tradition into India. For the purpose of our study we will divide this process of transmission into two distinct phases: the pre-Moghul period and the Moghul period.

THE PRE-MOGHUL PERIOD

Before the invasion of India by Maḥmūd of Ghaznah, it was the Ismāʿīlī propagandists who introduced Islamic philosophy in India. In 270/883, the famous Yamanī Ismāʿīlī leader, Abu'l-Qāsim ibn Ḥawshab sent his nephew, al-Haytham, from Yemen as a *dāʿī* (missionary) to Sindh. He was followed by other Ismāʿīlī *dāʿī*s who propagated Ismāʿīlism in the area with great zeal and enthusiasm. In less than a century, they succeeded in converting the local ruler of Multan to Ismāʿīlism. Later on, Jahm ibn Shaybān, an Ismāʿīlī commander, was commissioned to Sindh along with a military force by the Faṭimid ruler of Egypt, and succeeded in gaining control of Multan in 366/977. An Ismāʿīlī state was founded which remained under their influence until Maḥmūd of Ghaznah, the famous ruler of Central Asia, invaded Multan in 401/1010. The Ismāʿīlīs then moved to Mansurah, another stronghold of Ismāʿīlism in Sindh, and established themselves as an organized community.[1]

The Ismāʿīlīs, from the beginning, had based their world view on esoteric teachings. Their radical theological ideas, deeply influenced by Neoplatonic and gnostic teachings, separated them from even the orthodox Shiʿites.[2] They have always been inclined towards philosophical thinking, and whenever they established themselves as a community they developed philosophy and other intellectual disciplines within their circles. So it is easy to presume that during Ismāʿīlī rule in Multan and Mansurah, Sindh (348/960–417/1026) philosophy and other intellectual sciences would have been encouraged.

The Ghaznavids

Maḥmūd of Ghaznah (ruled 388/998–421/1030), the founder of the Ghaznavid dynasty, conquered the western part of India in 412/1021, and appointed Qāḍī Abu'l-Ḥasan Shīrāzī, a Persian official, as governor in Lahore.[3] Thus Lahore became the capital for the newly established state, and replaced Multan and Mansurah as the cultural and intellectual centre of the region. It is because of this achievement that many admirers of Maḥmūd consider him as a munificent patron of the arts and the founder of Muslim culture in the Indian subcontinent.

There is no doubt that Maḥmūd had an antagonistic attitude towards philosophy and the esoteric sciences because of his political and ideological differences with the Ismā'īlīs and their patrons, the Sāmānids. But it is also a fact that he was a great admirer of knowledge and the *'ulamā'*. He tried to gather poets and scholars around him, even by force if necessary. He brought back to Ghaznah whole libraries which fell to him in the course of his conquests of various kingdoms and sultanates, and thus was able to have a valuable collection of books in various disciplines.[4]

As far as his son, Mas'ūd (ruled 421/1031–432/1041) is concerned, he like his father Maḥmūd was a patron of knowledge and the arts. He allowed the growth of philosophy and other intellectual sciences in his kingdom. It is said that when Mas'ūd defeated 'Alā' al-Dawlah, the ruler of Isfahan, some of the philosophical and scientific works of Ibn Sīnā were found in the booty which he preserved in the royal library.[5] He was respectful towards philosophers and poets. During his reign, philosophical thought was transmitted from Ghaznah and Khurasan into India. The Persian secretaries who came to Lahore with the Ghaznavids played a significant role in this elevation of thought. These secretaries brought into India the works of the carly Muslim philosophers such as al-Kindī, al-Fārābī and Ibn Sīnā.

Likewise Sultan Ibrāhīm ibn Mas'ūd (ruled 451/1059–492/1099), and then his son and successor, Mas'ūd III (ruled 492/1099–508/1115), were instrumental in making Lahore the seat of culture and learning. By the time of Shīrzād (ruled 508/1115–509/1115), grandson of Ibrāhīm and viceroy of Lahore, Abū Naṣr Fārsī, a distinguished secretary of Shīrzād, established a *khānqāh* (Sufi commune) which attracted scholars from all over the Muslim world. Because of its cultural and intellectual activities, Lahore was called, at that time, Ghaznayn-khurd ("smaller Ghaznah").[6] Scholars as well as students were provided with ample opportunities for the free exchange of knowledge. Students from throughout the Islamic world visited Lahore and benefited from the intellectual atmosphere of the capital.[7]

The later Ghaznavid rulers continued their patronage and admiration of knowledge and of scholars. They also reconciled themselves with philosophy and other intellectual sciences. Their courts had always been a meeting place for scholars and poets. The greatest philosopher and thinker in the court of Khusraw Malik (ruled 555/1160–582/1186), the last Ghaznavid ruler of India, was Yūsuf ibn Muḥammad al-Darbandī. He was called Jamāl al-falāsifah ("the beauty of the philosophers") because of his profound knowledge of the rational sciences.[8] Similarly Shaykh Ṣafī al-Dīn Gāzrūnī (350/962–399/1007), Shaykh Yūsuf Gardīzī Multānī, Shaykh Ismā'īl Lāhōrī, Salār Mas'ūd Ghāzī and Imām Ḥasan Ṣan'ānī Lāhōrī are personalities of the Ghaznavid period worth mentioning.

Few of the philosophical and intellectual writings of the Ghaznavid period are accessible. The works related to that period available at the present time are mostly in Persian, which replaced Arabic as the *lingua prima*. The Persian *Dīwān* of Abu'l-Faraj Rūnī, for example, was published in Tehran. Mas'ūd Sa'd Salmān composed poetry in Arabic, Hindi and Persian. His Hindi and Arabic poetry has been lost, but the Persian still survives.[9] In prose we have *Kashf al-maḥjūb* ("The Unveiling of the Hidden"), the only work of Shaykh Abu'l-Ḥasan Alī al-Hujwairī known as Dātā Ganj Bakhsh, one of the greatest mystics of the Ghaznavid period.[10] The subject matter of this work is mysticism, its history and principles. It also deals with metaphysical issues such as the theory of knowledge, the Essence and Nature of God, His Attributes, the soul, eschatology, etc.[11]

The Ghūrids

The Ghaznavid rule in India came to an end in 583/1186 when Muḥammad Ghūrī succeeded in getting control of Lahore. He also captured Ajmair, Delhi, Multan and Patnah, and established a strong Muslim empire in India.[12]

The Ghūrids not only maintained the Ghaznavid standard of learning but made remarkable inroads in the field. They established new centres where eminent scholars taught the rational sciences. The founder of the Ghūrid dynasty, Sultan Ghiyāth al-Dīn (ruled 558/1163–599/1203) was a great patron of knowledge and science. Scholars of various schools of thought were welcomed in his court. Many works were dedicated to him, among them the *Mawāqif* of Qāḍī 'Aḍud al-Dīn and the *Laṭā'if* of Imām Fakhr al-Dīn Rāzī are notable.[13]

Sultan Shihāb al-Dīn Muḥammad Ghūrī (ruled 599/1203–602/1206), brother and successor of Sultan Ghiyāth al-Dīn, had also a sympathetic attitude towards the intellectual sciences. His court was a meeting place for the scholars of Islamic learning. Imām Fakhr al-Dīn Rāzī, the most eminent theologian and thinker of the time, was among Muḥammad

Ghūrid's favourites. The Sultan used to attend the weekly sermons or lectures of the Imām with great respect. In 601/1205, when Muḥammad Ghūrī visited India for the last time, Imām Fakhr al-Dīn accompanied him, staying in Lahore for about six months.[14] This was a visit to India of a distinguished Muslim scholar from Central Asia in the Ghūrid period. During his stay at Lahore, the local scholars and students of Islamic sciences benefited from contact with the Imām. Thus intellectual sciences flourished in India during the Ghurid rule under imperial patronage.

The Slaves

These were generals of Muḥammad Ghūrī who were brought from all over Central Asia, often members of ruling families that had been defeated.

Muḥammad Ghūrī was assassinated in 602/1206. His Turkish slave-governor and General, Quṭb al-Dīn Aybak (ruled 602/1206–607/1210), succeeded him and became the sole ruler of the vast Muslim empire in India. Aybak established the empire on a strong basis. The capital was moved from Lahore to Delhi. Delhi then became a centre of intellectual and cultural activities where, under imperial patronage, Islamic sciences flourished. Because of his sympathetic attitude, many prominent scholars such as Ḥasan Niẓāmī and Fakhr-i-Mudabbir dedicated their works to Quṭb al-Dīn Aybak.[15]

Iltutmish (ruled 607/1211–637/1236), the successor of Quṭb al-Dīn Aybak, who had deep interest in mysticism, was also a patron of knowledge and scholars. It was because of his mystical and philosophical inclinations that metaphysical and Sufi literature became popular within intellectual circles. By this time Fāḍil Mu'ayyid Jurjānī had translated *Iḥyā' al-'ulūm*, the famous work of Imām al-Ghazzālī, into Persian and dedicated it to Sultan Iltutmish. Likewise, the *Sirr-i maktūm* of Imām Fakhr al-Dīn Rāzī was translated into Persian at the insistence of Rukh al-Dīn Fayroze ibn Iltutmish.[16] Sultan Iltutmish built two traditional *madrasah*s (religious schools), called Mu'izziyyah and Nāṣiriyyah, in the capital for the teaching of religious and rational sciences. Moreover, a great centre was established at Badayun (India) in the name of his master, Muḥammad Ghūrī.[17]

After Iltutmish, his successors Nāṣir al-Dīn Muḥammad Shah (ruled 644/1246–664/1266) and Sultan Ghiyāth al-Dīn Balbān (ruled 664/1266–686/1287) both encouraged wholeheartedly the cultivation of both the religious and philosophical sciences. The Madrasah-i Fayrūz Shāhī and Nāṣiriyyah were the greatest centres of learning in the region at that time. Nāṣir al-Dīn invited 'Allāmah Quṭb al-Dīn Kāshānī, an eminent philosopher, mystic and theologian, from Persia to Multan and built a *madrasah* for him where the shaykh worked as *shaykh al-jāmi'ah* ("head of the institution").[18]

The most important role in cultivating the sciences during the Ghūrid and Slaves period was played by those scholars and philosophers who migrated to India from Iraq, Iran, Transoxiana, Samarqand, Bukhara and Ghaznah because of the Mongol invasion of those areas. Balbān, the successor of Iltutmish, not only provided shelter for them but also extended to them all possible opportunities and facilities for the teaching of religious and philosophical thought. Thus, speculative philosophy, gnosis and Scholastic theology entered a new phase in the subcontinent. The works of well-known philosophers, mystics and theologians such as Imām al-Ash'arī, Imām Abū Manṣūr al-Māturīdī, Imām al-Ṭaḥāwī, al-Kindī, al-Fārābī, Imām al-Ghazzālī, al-Birūnī and Imām Fakhr al-Dīn Rāzī, along with commentaries on their works, reached India through these immigrants and began to be studied throughout the empire. Balbān assembled, in the capital city, scholars of various schools of thought and made Delhi a seat of intellectual and cultural activities in the Muslim East.[19] A. L. Śrivastava has drawn a brief but an informative sketch of the intellectual activities of the Slaves dynasty:

> When Delhi became the capital of the sultanate (empire) it rivalled Lahore. Here were established a number of *madrasah*s to which Muslim scholars from other countries outside India were attracted as teachers . . . Iltutmish was the first to lay down the foundation of a *madrasah* at Delhi. After the name of Muḥammad Ghūrī he built another center of learning at Badāyūn. During the reign of Nāṣir al-Dīn Muḥammad (ruled 1246–1260 CE), his minister, Balbān founded a *madrasah* and named it Madrasah-i Nāṣiriyyah. The celebrated author of *Ṭabaqāt-i nāṣirī*, Minhāj al-Sirāj, was appointed principal of this *madrasah*. Balbān's court was famous for scholars, theologians, poets and philosophers who had fled from the fury of the Mongol invasion in Central Asia and had taken shelter at Delhi. Two of the most celebrated Indian poets in Persian, named Mīr Ḥasan and Amīr Khusraw, adorned the court of Balbān and enjoyed the patronage of his eldest son, Prince Muḥammad.[20]

The Slaves period has a special significance for metaphysics and mysticism. The two famous Sufi orders, Chishtiyyah and Suhrawardiyyah, reached India during this period. Khwājah Mu'īn al-Dīn Ajmerī (d. 631/1234), founder of the Chishtiyyah order, came to India in 586/1190, but his influence spread mostly during the Slaves dynasty. His successors, Quṭb al-Dīn Bakhtyār Kākī, Bābā Farīd al-Dīn Shakarganj and Niẓām al-Dīn Awliyā', lived during the Slaves' rule. Shaykh Bahā' al-Dīn Zakariyyā' Suhrawardī, founder of the Suhrawardī order in India, and his famous disciple Ḥamīd al-Dīn Nāgūrī, came to India in the early seventh/thirteenth century and established the order there.[21]

As far as mystical and metaphysical writings of that period are concerned, the works of Khwājah Gesūdarāz of the Chishtī order and those of Shaykh Ḥamīd al-Dīn Nāgūrī and Shaykh Ḥusayn Amīr Ḥusaynī of the Suhrawardī order are considered the most valuable. Khwājah Gesūdarāz composed *Asmā' al-asrār, Sharḥ-i risālah-yi qushayrī, Sharḥ-i mashāriq, Khaṭā'ir al-quds, Ma'ārif, Sharḥ-i fuṣūṣ al-ḥikam, Sharḥ-i ādāb al-murīdīn, Sharḥ fiqh al-akbar* and *Ḥawāshī-yi qūt al-qulūb.* Shaykh Ḥamīd al-Dīn Nāgūrī introduced the famous metaphysical and mystical work of his Shaykh, Shihāb al-Dīn Suhrawardī, called *'Awārif al-ma'ārif.* He also wrote *Ṭawāli' al-shumūs* and *Lawā'iḥ*, among the most important works in the field of metaphysics and mysticism. Shaykh Amīr Ḥusayn Suhrawardī wrote *Nuzhat al-arwāḥ, Ṣirāṭ al-mustaqīm, Ṭarab al-majālis* and *Kanz al-rumūz.*[22]

The Khiljīs

In 690/1290, the Khiljīs succeeded in getting control of the Muslim empire in India. The reign of 'Alā' al-Dīn Khiljī (695/1296–715/1316) had particular significance for the cultivation of intellectual sciences. Delhi by that time was called the metropolis of the Muslim East. Scholars of religious sciences, poets, Sufis, philosophers and administrators were well received in his court. Amīr Khusraw (a distinguished poet, philosopher and mystic), Sa'd Manṭiqī (a well-known philosopher), Bārānī (a famous historian) and Niẓām al-Dīn Awliyā' (a notable Sufi and metaphysician) were some of the well-known personalities of that period. Their philosophical, mystical, theological, historical and poetical writings are considered the most precious heritage of the Khiljī period.[23]

'Alā' al-Dīn Khiljī built an important centre of learning called Madrasah-yi ḥawḍ-i khāṣṣ ("School of the special pool") because of its location near the famous pool excavated by the order of the emperor. Branches of the central school were built in almost all the provincial centres where religious and rational sciences were taught under imperial supervision.[24]

Among the noteworthy works of the Khiljī period are *Qirān al-sa'dayn, Miftāḥ al-futūḥ, Khazīnat al-futūḥ, Nūḥ sipihr, Tughluq-nāmah* and the *Dīwān* of Amīr Khusraw; *Fawā'id al-fu'ād* of Amīr Ḥasan; *Malfūẓāt* of Niẓām al-Dīn Awliyā' and *Ṭūṭī-nāmah* of Ḍiyā' Bakhsh.[25]

The Tughluqs

The last ruler of the Khiljī dynasty, Mubārak Shah (ruled 716/1316–720/1320), was killed by one of his confidants, Khusraw Khān, for political reasons. Ghāzī Malik, a frontier general of 'Alā' al-Dīn Khiljī, rebelled against Khusraw Khān and completely destroyed his forces. He seized power under the name of Ghiyāth al-Dīn Tughluq in 720/1320. The Tughluqs then ruled the country for about ninety-six years (720/1320–818/1416).

Sultan Ghiyāth al-Dīn Tughluq, having a strong religious background, was very sympathetic towards Sufis, religious scholars, poets and philosophers. Religious life was visible even in the imperial court, and the emperor himself was very punctual and regular in discharging his religious duties and obligations. He rectified all those religious aberrations which became prevalent during the Khiljī rule. He supported the advancement of knowledge and science through all possible means. That Ghiyāth had great respect for the intellectual sciences is clear from the fact that he appointed Mawlānā 'Ilm al-Dīn, the eminent philosopher and logician of the time, for the training of his son, Muḥammad ibn Tughluq, in philosophy and logic.

This son Muḥammad (ruled 725/1325–752/1351) was a *ḥāfiẓ* (one who knows the Qur'ān by heart). Like his father, he was punctual and regular in discharging his religious duties. He studied logic and speculative philosophy under a distinguished scholar, Shaykh 'Ilm al-Dīn. The famous logician of the Tughluq period, Sa'd Manṭiqī, and the poet of the time, 'Ubayd, had access to the emperor and thus the latter was deeply influenced by the liberal and intellectual ideas of these two thinkers. It was because of this background that the Sultan had always been inclined towards speculative philosophy and used to spend most of his time in studying philosophical works and discussing cogitative and rational issues with other scholars. Narrowly religious scholars as well as Sufis were not well received in his court. By this time the study of intellectual sciences had become prevalent throughout the country, while the study of religious sciences declined and deteriorated.[26] He deputed 'Allāmah Mu'īn al-Dīn to bring Qāḍī 'Aḍud al-Dīn, author of the famous theological and philosophical work *al-Mawāqif*, from Shiraz. But the latter declined to come and, on the insistence of the ruler of Shiraz, preferred to stay there.[27]

The famous Muslim explorer Ibn Baṭṭūṭah came to India during the reign of Muḥammad ibn Tughluq. He was well received by the Sultan as an imperial guest and, later, was appointed the *qāḍī* of Delhi. Afterwards, he was sent to China as an ambassador. This opportunity enabled Ibn Baṭṭūṭah to travel through northern and central India and to visit Malabar, Ceylon, Ma'bar, Bangalah, Arakan, Sumatra and the coastal localities of China.[28]

Fayrūz Shah Tughluq (ruled 752/1351–790/1388), the cousin and successor of Muḥammad Tughluq, continued the tradition of cultivating the rational sciences. In 775/1373, he founded a new city, Junpur, in the eastern part of India after the name of his master (Muḥammad Tughluq). Junpur surpassed even the capital with regard to the study of the intellectual sciences.[29] It was called Delhi-i-thānī (second Delhi) at that time because of its intellectual activities. Shah Jahān (ruled 1037/1627–1069/1658), the great Moghul Emperor, later named it Shīrāz-i Hind. Fayrūz Shah Tughluq built forty mosques and established about thirty new colleges in various parts of the empire. He was also interested in Indian philosophy. Some of the works which were discovered during the conquest of Kangra in 762/1361 were translated into Persian from Sanskrit on his orders.[30]

The period of Ibrāhīm Shah Sharqī (ruled 804/1402–844/1440) was the golden age of Junpur. During his reign, scholars and philosophers of great repute settled in Junpur. Qāḍī Shihāb al-Dīn Dawlatabādī, Sayyid Ashraf Jahāngīr Simnānī, Qāḍī Naṣīr al-Dīn Dihlawī, Shaykh Abu'l-Fattāḥ 'Abd al-Muqtadir, Shaykh Fatḥ Allāh Awdī Anṣārī, Shaykh Khiḍr ibn Ḥasan Balkhī and Sayyid 'Uthmān Shīrāzī were among the distinguished scholars of that time. Significant works were composed in theology, mysticism, logic and philosophy. For instance, Sayyid Ashraf Jahāngīr Simnānī wrote *Sharḥ-i 'awārif al-ma'ārif, Sharḥ fuṣūṣ al-ḥikam, Qawā'id al-qawā'id, Baḥr-i adkhar, Ashraf al-fawā'id, Tanbīh al-ikhwān, Bashārat al-dhākirīn, Mir'āt al-ḥaqīqah, Irshād al-ikhwān, Laṭā'if al-ashrafiyyah* and *Baḥr al-ansāb*. Qāḍī Shihāb al-Dīn Dawlatabādī composed *al-Irshād, al-Baḥr al-mawwāj, al-Miṣbāḥ, Hidāyat al-su'adā', Sharḥ-i Qaṣīdah burdah, Risālah taqsīm al-'ulūm, Jāmi' al-sanā'ī, 'Aqīdat al-shihābiyyah*, and *Risālah mu'āraḍah*.[31]

The Lodhīs

In 816/1413, Maḥmūd Tughluq, the last ruler of the Tughluq dynasty, died and the Sultanate (empire) passed into the hands of the Sādāt who ruled the country for about forty years. In 855/1451, Buhlūl Lodhī (ruled 855/1451–894/1489), founder of the Lodhī dynasty, gained control and became the sole ruler of India. Because of the political changes, the economic and social life of the country was disturbed, yet intellectual activities continued as before. The centres of learning at Delhi, Junpur, Deccan and Kashmir remained open. During the reign of Sikandar Lodhī (ruled 894/1489–932/1517), new educational centres were established and renowned scholars were invited to teach there. In 881/1504, Sikandar Lodhī laid the foundation of a new city, Agra, and made it his capital as well as a seat of learning and culture.[32]

Sikandar Lodhī was inclined towards the intellectual sciences. During his reign, philosophy and other intellectual sciences flourished. He invited Shaykh 'Abd Allāh Tulunbī and his brother Shaykh 'Azīz Allāh Tulunbī, well-known metaphysicians of the time, from Multan to Agra. These two philosophers introduced the systematic study of the intellectual sciences in India. Shaykh 'Azīz Allāh later served as *Shaykh al-jāmi'ah* (director and head) in the famous *madrasah* of Sambhal. Shaykh 'Abd Allāh Tulunbī remained in the capital, where he taught the intellectual sciences for years. More than forty students specialized in the field of philosophy and *ḥikmah* (Islamic theosophy), and they passed on the intellectual tradition to the next generations. He composed many works related to logic and philosophy, of which *Badī' al-mīzān*, a commentary on the famous work on logic, *Mīzān al-manṭiq*, is worth mentioning. It was by his recommendations that *al-Mawāqif* and *Maṭāli'*, the famous theological and metaphysical works of Qāḍī 'Aḍuḍ al-Dīn were included in the syllabus of the educational institutions and thus studied throughout the country. A traditionist and a philosopher of great repute called 'Allāmah Rafī' al-Dīn Shīrāzī (a student of 'Allāmah Jalāl al-Dīn Dawānī and 'Allāmah Sakhāwī) was invited from Shiraz to teach *Ḥadīth*, philosophy and related subjects. The Shaykh, abiding by the imperial invitation, migrated to India where he taught *Ḥadīth* for the rest of his life.[33] The profound knowledge, eloquence and teaching method of Shaykh 'Abd Allāh Tulunbī attracted even the emperor to his lectures on philosophy and *ḥikmah*.[34]

Sikandar Lodhī was also interested in other philosophical traditions. On his insistence, many works of Hindu philosophy were translated into Persian. The Hindus were encouraged to learn the Persian language. People of other traditions were treated equally in education and learning in the *madrasah*s of Mathurah and Narwarl which Sikandar had established. It was also during his reign that the works of later Persian philosophers and thinkers were introduced in India through their students.[35]

THE MOGHUL PERIOD

The ancestors of the Moghuls were patrons of science and knowledge. The culture which Muḥammad Ẓahīr al-Dīn Bābur (889/1483–937/1530), founder of the Moghul dynasty in India, brought to India had flourished long before in Transoxiana and Khurasan. Amīr Taymūr (Tamerlane, d. 807/1405), the predecessor of Bābur, made Samarqand a meeting place for distinguished philosophers, theologians, poets and artists. It was at his court that 'Allāmah Sa'd al-Dīn al-Taftāzānī and Mīr Sayyid al-Sharīf al-Jurjānī, the eminent philosophers and theologians of the time, lived together.[36]

The immediate successors of Taymūr continued the tradition and made many advances in the field of science. Learning centres were established at Herat, where rational and religious studies flourished. Bābur himself grew up in this intellectual environment, and was given the best education available at that time. He eventually transmitted this intellectual and cultural heritage to India after assuming power in 933/1526.[37]

Bābur was succeeded by his son Humāyūn, who was soon defeated and replaced by Sher Khān Sūrī, a famous Afghan leader, in 947/1540. Sher Khān had a profound knowledge of Persian and Arabic literature and he had studied the intellectual sciences at Junpur (one of the greatest learning centres of that time). Having this intellectual background, he gave special attention to the cultivation of philosophical, theological and metaphysical sciences. He founded a *madrasah* at Narnaul, where the curriculum and teaching method of Junpur school were followed. This *madrasah* later became a famous seat of the intellectual sciences.[38]

Humāyūn regained power in 950/1550, with the help of the Persian army. This incident opened a new chapter in cultural activities in India. Distinguished scholars, artists and administrators such as Bayrum Khān, Sayyid 'Alī and 'Abd al-Ṣamad came with him to India from Persia. These scholars brought with them the newly developed philosophical tradition of Persia and introduced it in India.

But the golden age of the intellectual sciences in India begins with Jalāl al-Dīn Akbar, son of Humāyūn, who ruled the country for half a century (961/1556–1014/1606). By that time philosophy and other intellectual sciences dominated even the imperial court. The meetings of the *'Ibādat khānah* (the place of worship which Akbar built within the imperial palace) were eventually devoted to philosophical and theological discussions. Philosophers and scholars of other traditions, particularly Hinduism, Buddhism, Zoroastrianism and Christianity, were also welcomed to participate in the intellectual activities of the court. Mīr Fatḥ Allāh Shīrāzī, Shaykh Mubārak Nāgūrī, his sons Shaykh Abu'l-Faḍl and Shaykh Fayḍī were the eminent exponents of Aristotelian and Illuminationist philosophy and Ibn 'Arabī's gnosis in Akbar's court. Outside the court, there developed learning centres in various parts of the country, among which Delhi, Junpur, Siyalkot, Sirhind, Deccan and Kashmir are worth mentioning.[39]

During the late Moghul period, especially by the time of Jahāngīr and Shah Jahān, philosophical learning continued to flourish. Dārā Shikōh, son and successor of Shah Jahān, had a strong background in Islamic metaphysics and Hindu philosophy. He composed some valuable works which deal with metaphysics and rational philosophy. His *Safīnat al-awliyā'*, *Sakīnat al-awliyā'*, *Risālah ḥaqrnamā*, *Majma' al-baḥrayn* and *Ḥasanāt al-'ārifīn* are of great value. He also translated the Upanishads into Persian under the title *Sirr-i akbar* ("The Great Secret") or *Sirr-i asrār* ("The Secret of the Secrets"). The *Bhagavadgita* and the *Yoga Vaśistha* were also translated into Persian at his insistence.[40] The most important feature of the Moghul period is that by that time there had arisen a theologico-philosophical and metaphysical school of great repute which was of Indian origin. It was really the consequence of the intellectual activities of the past few centuries. Many eminent philosophers, theologians and metaphysicians contributed to the newly established intellectual school. A brief account of a few of the main philosophers of the Moghul period is given below.

Mīr Fatḥ Allāh Shīrāzī

Mīr Fatḥ Allāh Shīrāzī (d. 998/1590) was one of the most outstanding philosophers of his time. He was born in a scholarly Sayyid (descendent from the Prophet) family in Shiraz, Persia. Shiraz at that time was famous for intellectual and religious learning. Mīr Fatḥ Allāh Shīrāzī was provided with the best available education at that time. He studied under distinguished philosophers, theologians and mystics such as Jamāl al-Dīn Maḥmūd, a student of Jalāl al-Dīn Dawānī, Mawlānā Kamāl al-Dīn Shīrāzī, Mawlānā Kurd and the famous philosopher Amīr Ghiyāth al-Dīn al-Manṣūr ibn Mīr Ṣadr al-Dīn al-Dashtakī Shīrāzī.[41]

Upon completing his formal study, Mīr Fatḥ Allāh Shīrāzī started his career as a teacher of the intellectual sciences at Shiraz. He also served as an adviser to the ruler of Shiraz. Then, at the request of 'Ādil Shah, governor of Bijapur, he left Shiraz for India. He worked at Bijapur as an adviser to the ruler as well as principal of the official state school. After the death of 'Ādil Shah, Mīr Fatḥ Allāh Shīrāzī moved to the imperial court in 991/1583 at Akbar's invitation. He was well received in the court and was put in charge of religious affairs and endowments (*awqāf*). Later on, he worked with Rajah Toder Māl to organize the revenue system.[42]

But the most important service of Mīr Fatḥ Allāh Shīrāzī was his educational reform. When Akbar put him in charge of education, he reformed the curriculum on new lines. He not only introduced the works of later Persian scholars such as 'Allāmah Sa'd al-Dīn al-Taftāzānī, Mīr Sayyid al-Sharīf al-Jurjānī, 'Allāmah Jalāl al-Dīn Dawānī, Mīr Ṣadr al-Dīn Shīrāzī and Mīr Ghiyāth al-Dīn Manṣūr Shīrāzī, but made them a necessary part of the curriculum. He also continued teaching in his free time, and numerous students graduated in philosophy under his supervision. He also wrote some valuable commentaries and glossaries on some of the most difficult philosophical and theological works, such as *Sharḥ al-mawāqif* of 'Allāmah Sayyid al-Sharīf al-Jurjānī, *Sharḥ Mullā Jalāl* of 'Allāmah Dawānī and others.[43]

Mīr Fatḥ Allāh Shīrāzī died in Kashmir, during a tour with Akbar, on Jamādī al-Thānī 997/22 January 1589. He was buried in Takht-i Sulayman, a place famous for its beauty.[44]

Shaykh Aḥmad Sirhindī

Shaykh Aḥmad Sirhindī is considered one of the most influential and prominent scholars in the intellectual history of Muslim India. On the basis of his services to the cause of religion, he was given the title of *Mujaddid Alf-i Thānī* ("reformer of the second millennium"). He was born in 971/1564 at Sirhind in a scholarly family. His father, Shaykh 'Abd al-Aḥad, was a theologian and metaphysician, who had studied the intellectual sciences at Junpur.

At an early age, Shaykh Aḥmad first memorized the Qur'ān and then studied the primary books of the religious and intellectual sciences with his father. He was then sent to Siyalkot, a famous seat for learning, to complete his formal study. In Siyalkot, he studied with Shaykh Kamāl al-Dīn, an eminent *muḥaddith* (expert in the traditions). He mastered all the current branches of learning at the age of seventeen.[45]

In 1008/1599, after the death of his father, Shaykh Aḥmad came into contact with Khwājah Muḥammad Bāqī bi'Llāh (970/1563–1012/1603), a celebrated mystic and founder of the Naqshbandī order in India.[46] At the latter's invitation, Shaykh Aḥmad spent a few days in his *khānqāh* (Sufi centre). During his stay, he was deeply influenced by the Khwājah's conduct and spiritual life and was initiated into the order, thus becoming his formal disciple. He stayed with his spiritual master for a few months in order to fulfil the necessary requirements of the order. Finally, he was granted the *khirqah* (Sufi robe) and was permitted to initiate others into the *silsilah* (order).[47]

After the death of the Khwājah, Shaykh Aḥmad made Sirhind his permanent abode and started his mission there. His main concern was to remove all kinds of innovations from the religious life of the Indian Muslims, mostly resulting from Akbar's liberal policy regarding religion. He was anxious to see once again the glory of Muslim orthodoxy in India. To attain his goal, he adopted two means: first, oral instruction and guidance, and, second, writing books and epistles to nobles on various religious topics. The latter approach was more effective and resulted in good relations with some important personalities who later became defenders and champions of orthodoxy within and outside the imperial court.

In 1029/1619, Shaykh Aḥmad was summoned to the court of Jahāngīr (1013/1605–1037/1627) to face charges of innovation and heterodoxy levelled against him. Although he cleared himself from a theological point of view, he was sent to jail for not prostrating before the emperor. During his imprisonment, his piety, constancy, spirituality and influential personality sustained him, and the official circles, including the emperor, were greatly impressed by him. He was released after spending two years in the fort of Gawalior as a prisoner, and was sent back to Sirhind with great respect and valuable gifts.[48]

He spent the last years of his life in seclusion at Sirhind. He died in 1034/1624 and was buried in his native city.

Shaykh Aḥmad Sirhindī's greatest contribution in the field of Islamic thought is his exposition of the concept of *waḥdat al-shuhūd* (unity in consciousness). He severely attacked the well-known metaphysical concept of *waḥdat al-wujūd* (unity of being) of Ibn 'Arabī. For him, the doctrine of *waḥdat al-wujūd* was a subjective experience wherein the mystic and the object of love become identical and where the mystic realizes one overwhelming reality. This state of identity is not a permanent one; it is transient and temporal. The higher state accordingly is that of servitude (*'abdiyyāt*) wherein neither the transcendental nature and infinity of God is degraded nor the contingent and accidental position of man and other creatures is elevated to the realm of transcendence or infinity.[49]

Shaykh Aḥmad Sirhindī also criticized the doctrine of *waḥdat al-wujūd* from the ethical point of view. The "pantheistic" union of God and humanity, for him, negates the idea of human individuality as well as the position as a responsible being before God. It also makes it difficult to evaluate the morals of individuals and thus negates the whole idea of reward and punishment in the hereafter. Furthermore, this conception denies human freedom.[50]

Most of his philosophical, metaphysical and theological thoughts are expounded in his *Maktūbāt* ("Epistles") which have been published in four volumes. Along with this work, he wrote many treatises on various subjects. The following are of great significance: *Risālah tahlīliyyah*, *Risālah fī ithbāt al-nubuwwah*, *Risālah mabda' wa'l-ma'ād*, *Risālah rubā'iyyāt*, *Ta'līqāt-i 'awārif*, *Irshād al-murīdīn* and *Mukāshifāt-i 'Ayniyyah mujaddidiyyah*.[51] Almost all of these works deal with metaphysics and Islamic philosophy and theology.

Mullā 'Abd al-Ḥakīm Siyālkōtī

Mullā 'Abd al-Ḥakīm Siyālkōtī was another notable philosopher, theologian, logician and metaphysician of the Moghul period. He was born at Siyalkot in a well-known family of intellectual repute. He was a later contemporary of Shaykh Aḥmad Sirhindī. By that time Siyalkot was famous for intellectual and transmitted sciences. Mullā 'Abd al-Ḥakīm studied all the branches of philosophy under Shaykh Kamāl al-Dīn, an eminent scholar of his time. He also studied theology under the Shaykh and soon became known as a philosopher.[52]

During the reign of Shah Jahān (ruled 1037/1627–1069/1658), Mullā 'Abd al-Ḥakīm became the most influential scholar in the imperial court. He was granted special awards and prizes for his teaching and religious services in the imperial *madrasah* at the capital. Towards the end of his life, he left the court and returned to his native city, Siyalkot, and devoted his time to teaching and writing. Numerous students studied philosophy and other sciences under him, and later continued the intellectual tradition in India.[53]

Besides being a distinguished teacher, Mullā 'Abd al-Ḥakīm was also a prolific writer. He wrote many valuable glossaries and commentaries on some of the difficult philosophical and theological works. All of his writings were well received by the Muslim scholars within and outside India. His most important works are: *Ḥāshiya-yi sharḥ ḥikmat al-'ayn*, *Ḥāshiya-yi sharḥ al-'aqā'id* of 'Allāmah al-Taftāzānī, *Ḥāshiya-yi sharḥ al-mawāqif* of 'Allāmah al-Jurjānī, *Ḥāshiya-yi sharīfiyyah*, *Ḥāshiya-yi sharḥ-i shamsiyyah* and *Durrat al-thamīnah*.[54]

Mullā 'Abd al-Ḥakīm died in 1067/1656 at Siyalkot and was buried there. His mausoleum still exists on Shaban Road in Siyalkot.

Mullā Maḥmūd Junpūrī Fārūqī

Mullā Maḥmūd Junpūrī ibn Shaykh Muḥammad Junpūrī was another prominent philosopher and metaphysician of Shah Jahān's period. He was born at Junpur in Ramaḍān 1015/1603. His father died before he was twelve. His maternal grandfather Shaykh Shah Muḥammad, a renowned scholar, took him into his care. His early education was completed under the same Shaykh.[55]

For higher study of the intellectual sciences, Mullā Maḥmūd Junpūrī joined the intellectual circle of Ustād al-Mulk Shaykh Muḥammad Afḍal, the well-known rational philosopher of his time. He studied almost all the intellectual sciences under him. For the study of transmitted sciences, he remained a student of Mullā Shams Nūr Bronvī of Junpur. He started teaching while he was under twenty,[56] and soon became a recognized scholar of the intellectual and transmitted sciences.

One thing which distinguishes Mullā Maḥmūd Junpūrī from his Indian contemporary scholars was his attending the circle of Mīr Dāmād, one of the eminent philosophers of Ṣafavid Persia and the foremost teacher of Mullā Ṣadrā. Mullā Maḥmūd Junpūrī attended Mīr Dāmād's lectures on metaphysics and philosophy when the former made a temporary stop at Isfahan while he was on his way to Mecca. The young scholar disagreed with Mīr Dāmād's doctrine of *ḥudūth-i dahrī* (eternal creation). Yet both scholars were deeply impressed by each other.[57]

Mullā Maḥmūd Junpūrī was not a mere speculative thinker; he also had a strong mystical background. There had been a mystical tradition among his paternal and maternal ancestors. He himself was greatly influenced by Miyān Mīr Lāhorī, the famous leader of the Qādiriyyah Order in India at that time.[58] He visited him for the first time in the company of Shah Jahān, then the emperor, and Mullā 'Abd al-Ḥakīm. Miyān Mīr Lāhorī reproached both scholars for their worldly inclinations, particularly the courtly life. He also came in contact with Shaykh Ni'mat Allāh Fayrūzpūrī, a notable Sufi of the Qādiriyyah Order in Bengal. Mullā Junpūrī visited Bengal at Shah Jahān's request for the instruction of Prince Muḥammad Shujā'. Mullā Junpūrī was initiated in the order and was granted *ijāzah* (permission to initiate others in the order). It was a turning point in his life. After that he was completely devoted to teaching, writing and spiritual training.[59]

Mullā Maḥmūd Junpūrī achieved a high social status even during his lifetime. He was considered one of the prominent philosophers and thinkers by his contemporaries. His foremost teacher, Shaykh Muḥammad Afḍal, used to say about him and Mullā 'Abd al-Rashīd Junpūrī (Mullā Maḥmūd's fellow student): "Since the time of 'Allāmah al-Taftāzānī and Mīr Sayyid al-Sharīf al-Jurjānī, no two great scholars of such a high level have come together in one city as Mullā Maḥmūd and Shaykh 'Abd al-Rashīd."

Mullā Maḥmūd Junpūrī died at the age of forty-seven. Despite this short life, he trained numerous students in the field of philosophy and metaphysics. He also composed some original works on logic, theology, metaphysics and speculative philosophy. His *Shams al-bāzighah* is considered one of the most basic works in traditional Islamic philosophy in the subcontinent and the neighbouring countries. It was and continued to be studied along with the *Sharḥ-i hidāyat al-ḥikmat* of Ṣadr al-Dīn Shīrāzī, known as Mullā Ṣadrā, in the traditional *madrasah*s in the eastern Muslim world. The following works of Mullā Maḥmūd Junpūrī are noteworthy: *al-Ḥikmat al-bālighah*, *Shams al-bāzighah*, *al-Farā'id fī sharḥ al-fawā'id*, *Risālat al-dawḥat al-miyādah fī ḥaqīqat al-ṣūrah wa'l-māddah*, *Risālah fi'l-kullī wa'l-juz'ī*, *Risālah irtifā' al-naqīḍayn*, *Risālah fī taḥqīq-i qaḍā' wa qadar* and *Risālah taqsīm-i niswah*.[60]

He died in 1062/1652 while his teacher, Shaykh Muḥammad Afḍal was still alive. The Shaykh was so shocked by the early death of his brilliant student that for forty days nobody saw him smiling. After forty days the master also departed from the temporal world.[61]

Mirzā Muḥammad Zāhid Harawī

Mirzā Muḥammad Zāhid Harawī, son of Qāḍī Muḥammad Aslam, was another distinguished philosopher of the age of Shah Jahān and Awrangzeb (ruled 1069/1658–1119/1707). Moreover, he was the foremost teacher of Shah 'Abd al-Raḥīm, father of Shah Walīullāh. Muḥammad Zāhid's father was *qāḍī al-quḍāt* (chief justice) during the rule of Jahāngīr and Shah Jahān.[62]

During his early years, Mirzā Muḥammad Zāhid studied under his father Qāḍī Muḥammad Aslam and Mullā Muḥammad Fāḍil Badakhshānī. Then he became a disciple of Mullā Ṣādiq Ḥalwā'ī of Kabul, a notable thinker of his day. For the higher study of the intellectual sciences, he went to Turan (Transoxiana) and joined the circle of Mīrzā Jān Shīrāzī, a well-known philosopher in Central Asia, and studied philosophy and other related sciences under him. Later, he studied exegesis of the Qur'ān (*tafsīr*) under the supervision of Mullā Yūsuf Lāhōrī, a student of Mīrzā Jān Shīrāzī. For the study of *fiqh* and *uṣūl al-fiqh*, he remained a student of Mullā Jalāl Lāhōrī.[63] On the completion of his formal study, Mīrzā Muḥammad Zāhid Harawī started teaching at Lahore and soon became renowned as a philosopher and a theologian.

Since his father had been a chief *qāḍī*, Mīrzā Zāhid Harawī also accepted some responsibility at the imperial court. The Emperor Awrangzeb first appointed him as a royal *muḥtasib* (account-general) and then governor of Kabul.

Mirzā Muḥammad Zāhid was a notable scholar of Peripatetic philosophy, *ishrāqī ḥikmah*, Ash'arite and Maturidite theology, and logic. He taught these disciplines privately in his free time. Numerous students mastered the intellectual sciences under his supervision and, in turn, handed over the intellectual tradition successfully to the coming generation. Along with some original works in the field of the intellectual sciences, he also wrote glossaries on 'Allāmah Jalāl al-Dīn Dawānī's commentary on *Hayākil al-nūr* of Suhrawardī Maqtūl, on the *Tajrīd* of Naṣīr al-Dīn al-Ṭūsī, on the *Sharḥ al-mawāqif* of 'Allāmah Mīr Sayyid al-Sharīf al-Jurjānī, on 'Allāmah Dawānī's commentary on *al-Tahdhīb*, and on *Taṣawwur wa'l-taṣdīq* of Quṭb al-Dīn al-Rāzī.[64]

Shah Walīullāh

Quṭb al-Dīn Aḥmad ibn Shah 'Abd al-Raḥīm, known as Shah Walīullāh, is considered the greatest scholar of twelfth/eighteenth-century India. His intellectual contribution is undoubtedly greater than that of any other scholar in the history of Muslim India. It is greater and more important in the sense that it came at the time when the Muslim empire was losing ground, while the Muslims were divided into many factions for numerous reasons. Shah Walīullāh set out to reformulate the religio-intellectual legacy of Islam in order to reorganize the Muslims on the basis of their religion. He gave a new rational interpretation to theological and metaphysical issues which, being in full accordance with the revelation, was more appealing to the contemporary mind. His reconciliatory efforts resolved many controversies among the various factions which had emerged among the Muslims in India.

Shah Walīullāh was born on Wednesday 4 Shawwāl 1114/21 February 1703, at Phult, Delhi. Being a member of a distinguished religious and intellectual family, he was exposed to a highly structured education and spiritual training. Most of his education was undertaken under his father Shah 'Abd al-Raḥīm[65] at Madrasa-yi Raḥīmiyyah (established by the latter), Delhi. He completed his formal study while he was fifteen years old. Afterwards his father initiated him into the famous Naqshbandi order.

After completing his formal education, Shah Walīullāh started teaching at Madrasa-yi Raḥīmiyyah and, after the death of his father in 1131/1719, Shah Walīullāh became the sole leader of the *madrasah*. He taught all the transmitted and rational sciences for about twelve years.

In 1143/1731, Shah Walīullāh left for the *ḥajj* (pilgrimage) to Mecca. He stayed at Mecca and Medina for about fourteen months. This stay at the *ḥaramayn* (the sancturies of Mecca and Medina) provided him with a first-hand knowledge of the various intellectual and juridical schools in Islam and thus universalized his vision. At the end of 1144/1732, he performed *ḥajj* for the second time and then returned home on 14 Rajab 1145/9 July 1726. He spent the rest of his life at Madrasa-yi Raḥīmiyyah in teaching and writing. On 29 Muḥarram 1176/20 August 1762, this prominent scholar of Muslim India died in Delhi and was buried there.[66]

Shah Walīullāh wrote on almost all those subjects which he taught for years. He wrote both in Arabic and Persian. The years of his life between 1145/1732 and 1176/1762 were the most productive in terms of his writings. The exact number of his works is a controversial issue for his biographers. G. N. Jalbānī asserts that more than fifty of his works have been published, while Maẓhar Baqā has given a list of seventy works, including five collections of his letters and epistles. This is a list of those works of Shah Walīullāh which are fully or partially related to philosophy and metaphysics: *Alṭāf al-quds*; *Anfās al-'ārifīn*; *al-Budūr al-bāzighah*; *Fatḥ al-wadūd fī ma'rifat al-junūd*; *Fuyūḍ al-ḥaramayn*; *Hama'āt*; *Hawāmi' Sharḥ ḥizb al-baḥr*; *Ḥujjat Allāh al-bālighah*; *Ḥusn al-'aqīdah*; *al-Intibāh fī salāsil al-awliyā' Allāh wa asānīd wārith rasūl Allāh*; *Kashf al-ghaym 'an sharḥ rubā'iyatayn*; *al-Khayr al-kathīr*; *Lama'āt*; *Lamaḥāt*; *al-Qawl al-jamīl*; *Saṭa'āt*; *Shifā' al-qulūb*; *al-Sirr al-maktūm fī asbāb tadwīn al-'ulūm*; *Surūr al-makhzūn*; *al-Tafhīmāt al-ilāhiyyah*.

Shah Walīullāh's contribution to Islamic philosophy and metaphysics is unique in the sense that he tried to reformulate and reshape these disciplines to be in greater conformity with the teachings of the Qur'ān and *Sunnah*. His rational approach to the controversial issues of metaphysics to a large extent changed the approach of future Muslim metaphysicians and created conformity and harmony among them. His balanced criticism of his predecessors did not cause further controversies. Rather, it was always considered as a sincere attempt of reconciliation. His attempt to reconcile the two apparently contradictory doctrines of *waḥdat al-wujūd* of Ibn 'Arabī and *waḥdat al-shuhūd* of Shaykh Imām Sirhindī is the first effort in the area. Before Imām Sirhindī, the doctrine of *waḥdat al-wujūd* of Ibn 'Arabī was in no way acceptable to the *mutakallimūn* (Muslim theologians). Shaykh Sirhindī, introducing the concept of *waḥdat al-shuhūd*, opened a new factor of controversy even among the Muslin metaphysicians. The exponent of each of these doctrines was aggressively critical of the others. It was Shah Walīullāh whose rational explanation of both the doctrines and their reconciliation resolved the controversy. The positive effect of his reconciliatry efforts was twofold. On the one hand, it brought about harmony between the opposing groups of the metaphysicians; on the other hand it legitimized the doctrine of *waḥdat al-wujūd* among the *mutakallimūn*.

Shah Walīullāh also tried to bring the four schools of law closer to each other. His commentaries on *Muwaṭṭa'* of Imām Mālik called *al-Muṣawwā* (Arabic) and *al-Muṣaffā* (Persian) were written with the same view to finding common orthodox ground for the reconciliation of different schools of law. He also tried to provide common ground and a strong basis for possible harmony and mutual co-operation between the Sunni and Shi'ah. In the same way, Shah Walīullāh's contribution in the field of politics is not surpassed by any other Muslim thinker in the history of Muslim India.

Shah Walīullāh died in 1176/1762. He left behind him a rich intellectual legacy in the form of literary works, of well-trained disciples including his four sons (Shah 'Abd al-'Azīz, Shah 'Abd al-Qādir, Shah Rafī' al-Dīn and Shah 'Abd al-Ghanī) and one of the greatest educational institutions of the time. His reforming mission on political, intellectual and spiritual topics was carried on by his four sons and disciples. They shared the intellectual legacy of their spiritual master with thousands of their students and spiritual disciples who came to them from distant places. They wrote new works on various subjects and added to the legacy of their master. The Madrasa-yi Raḥīmiyyah was the only centre where the affairs of the Indian Muslims were resolved. The students continued the mission even after the centre was destroyed by the British army in 1857.[67]

Ten years after the destruction of the Madrasa-yi Raḥīmiyyah, some of the graduates and spiritual disciples of the family, such as Mawlānā Muḥammad Qāsim Nānotwī, Mawlānā Rashīd Aḥmad Gangōhī, Mawlānā Muḥammad Ya'qūb and Ḥājjī 'Ābid Ḥusayn founded a *dār al-'ulūm* (theological and philosophical seminary) at Deoband. The intellectual tradition of Shah Walīullāh once again made a new start at Deoband under the leadership of his spiritual successors. The Dār al-'Ulūm of Deoband followed strictly the Madrasa-yi Raḥīmiyyah and conformed fully to the method and curriculum prescribed by Shāh Walīullāh. It is through the Dār al-'Ulūm of Deoband that the influence of Shah Walīullāh spread throughout the subcontinent as well as into the neighbouring countries.

Today almost all the religious groups in the subcontinent derive their intellectual inspiration and *sanad* (authority) from Shah Walīullāh. But in most cases only particular aspects of his teachings are emphasized. It is the school of Deoband which has taken up the tradition in full with its universal and balanced nature. His writings are studied not only in the religious *madrasah*s but also in the institutions of modern education.

CONCLUSION

From this account of the transmission of Islamic philosophy into the Indian world we can conclude with four main points.

Firstly, Islamic philosophy developed in India gradually. It was introduced in India, first, by the Ismā'īlī *dā'ī*s (propagandists) during the fourth/tenth century and then it flourished in the country through the centuries under the patronage of orthodox as well as liberal Muslim rulers of India.

Secondly, the intellectual sciences were transmitted into India from Persia, especially the province of Khurasan, Central Asia and Iraq. The most important role in the early transmission of philosophical and metaphysical thought was played by the Sufis. The Persian administrators and secretaries who came to India with the Ghaznavids and Ghurids for governmental affairs in the early centuries and, later, the scholars who fled from their homes in Central Asia, Persia and Iraq in the thirteenth century because of the Mongol invasion in their homeland also shared in the transmission of Islamic learning into the Indian world. These Sufis, administrators and scholars brought with them the works and thoughts of the early philosophers, theologians, Sufis and gnostics into India. *Madrasah*s and institutes were established throughout the country for the teaching of intellectual and religious sciences.

Thirdly, the contribution of these scholars, Sufis and rulers towards the transmission and development of Islamic philosophy and metaphysics in India is colossal in the sense that, if they had not been instrumental in this process, it would have not seen the light of day in that land. They not only introduced the Islamic intellectual sciences in India but also paved the way for its consolidation there. They handed it over successfully to the coming generations who further elaborated it in their writings.

Fourthly, it was, then, during the Mughul period that a systematic philosophical school emerged which was indigenous in the sense that most of its exponents were Indian by birth. In this regard, the efforts and contribution of the later Indian philosophers, such as Mīr Fatḥ Allāh Shīrāzī, Shaykh Aḥmad Sirhindī, Mullā 'Abd al-Ḥakīm Siyālkotī, Mirzā Muḥammad Zāhid Harawī and Shah Walīullāh, have been dealt with in greater detail. The discussion has concluded with a brief account of the process of development and transmission of Islamic philosophy and metaphysics in the Indian world from the time of Shāh Walīullāh up to the present.

NOTES

1 W. Madelung, "Ismā'īliyyah", *Encyclopaedia of Islam*, new ed. (Leiden), 4: 198–99. See also Shaykh Muḥammad Ikram (1986): 30, 338.

2 F. R., "Islām", *Funk and Vegnalls New Encyclopedia*, ed. Roberts Philips, 14: 290.

3 "Towards the end of his reign, Maḥmūd tried to establish a more permanent form of control over the Punjāb, with a division of responsibility there. The military command remained in the hands of Turkish *ghulām* generals, based in Lahore, center of the Muslim *ghāzīs* in India; but at their side was set up a civil administration under a Persian official, the Qāḍī Bu'l-Ḥasan Shīrāzī, of whom the Sultān thought so highly that he had considered him for the Vizierate." For more details see C. E. Bosworth (1973): 76–77.

4 C. E. Bosworth says: "Undoubtedly the courts of Maḥmūd and Mas'ūd at Ghaznah became brilliant cultural centers. According to Daulatshāh, there were four hundred poets, in regular attendance on Maḥmūd, presided over by the laureate, Amir ash-Shu'arā', 'Unsūrī who was himself continuously busy commemorating in verses his master's exploits and campaigns. The polymath of his age, Birūnī, finished his days at Ghaznah, and dedicated his great astronomical treatise, the *Qānūn al-mas'ūdī*, to Mas'ūd, and his book on mineralogy, the *Kitāb al-jamāhir fī ma'rifat al jawāhir*, to his son Mawdūd. In as much as it was Maḥmūd of Ghaznah who brought Birūnī to Ghaznah, the gateway to India, it was he who made possible the *Taḥqīq mā li'l-Hind*." For further details see Bosworth (1973): 131.

5 Shabīr Aḥmad (1967): 23.

6 Shaykh Muḥammad Ikrām (1955): 93.

7 "A large number of seekers after knowledge from all parts of India, the territories of Kashghar, Transoxiana, Iraq, Bukhara, Samarqand, Khurasan, Ghaznah, Herat, etc., benefited by the same. Consequently a new settlement grew up in

the neighborhood of Lahore." See M. A. Ghanī, *Pre-Mughul Persian in Hindustan* (Allahabad, 1941): 194, quoted in Ikram (1964): 34.

8 Aḥmad (1967): 26.

9 Ikrām (1964): 35–6.

10 Shaykh Abu'l-Ḥasan 'Alī Hujwayrī of Ghaznah known as Dātā Ganj Bakhsh (d. 465/1072 C.E.) came to India in 429/1037 with Mas'ūd, son of Sultan Maḥmūd of Ghaznah. He is considered as the founder of *taṣawwuf* in India as well as the most influential saint of his time. He was a renowned scholar of religious sciences, particularly of theology and mysticism. He wrote many valuable works on these subjects. He thought of *taṣawwuf* (Sufism) as a means of inner purification. He died in 465/1072 at Lahore and was buried there. Sultan Ibrāhīm (ruled 450/1057–495/1099), the successor of Mas'ūd, built a mausoleum which still exists. (See M. L. Bāghī (1965): 227.)

11 Ikrām (1964): 36.

12 *Ibid.*: 36.

13 Qāḍī 'Abd al-Raḥmān 'Aduḍ al-Dīn ibn Aḥmad al-Ījī was one of the most celebrated scholars and metaphysicians of the Ghurid period (583/1186–603/1206). *Mawāqif* is one of his important works on theology which he dedicated to Sultan Ghiyāth al-Dīn, the founder of the Ghūrid dynasty. Many commentaries have been written on this work, among which those by Sayyed al-Sharīf al-Jurjānī and 'Allāmah Jalāl al-Dīn Dawānī are worthy to be mentioned. For more details see Mīr Ghulām 'Alī Āzād Bilgrāmī (1971): 193 n. 4.

14 Imām Fakhr al-Dīn Rāzī (543/1148–606/1210), also known as Ibn al-Khaṭīb, is considered one of the greatest intellectual figures in the history of Islamic thought. He wrote about 119 works, mostly on theology, philosophy, natural sciences and logic. His *al-Mabāḥith al-mashriqiyyah* is one of his valuable works, comprising discussions about almost all the intellectual sciences. His commentary on *al-Ishārat wa'l-tanbīhāt* of Ibn Sīnā displays his philosophical understanding. In addition to that, his commentary on the Qur'ān, *Mafātīḥ al-ghayb*, known as *al-Tafsīr al-kabīr*, philosophical in nature, is considered one of the most valuable commentaries on the Qur'ān. Politically, he was attached to the court of Sultan Ghiyāth al-Dīn Ghūrī. After his death, he became one of the favourites of Sultan Shihāb al-Dīn Muḥammad Ghūrī, who had great respect for the Imām. He died at Herat in 607/1210 and was buried there. See Fatḥallā Khulaif (1966): 16.

15 Ikrām (1964): 42.

16 Ikrām (1986): 119.

17 A. L. Śrivastave (1964): 100.

18 A. Rashīd (1969): 155.

19 Śrivastava (1964): 101.

20 *Ibid.*

21 Yūsuf Ḥusayn (1962): 34–7.

22 *Ibid.*, pp. 46–9.

23 Ikrām (1964): 112–14.

24 Śrivastavạ (1964): 101.

25 Ikrām (1964): 115–17.

26 Ikrām (1986): 408.

27 *Ibid.*: 424.
28 *Ibid.*
29 One of Muḥammad Tughluq's names was Jawna (Yavana "foreigner") Shah. In the ninth/fifteenth century Junpur became the centre of the powerful Muslim state. The sultans of Junpur played a significant role in the development of the Islamic culture of the area. For further details about Junpur see Bosworth (1980): 201–2.
30 Rashīd (1969): 157.
31 Qāḍī Āthār Mubārakpūrī (1979): 62–5.
32 Ḥusayn (1962): 76.
33 Ikrām (1968): 455.
34 Ḥusayn (1962): 76–7.
35 Ikrām (1964): 154.
36 *Encyclopaedia of Islam*, new edition, 2: 602.
37 He was a good example of the crucial significance of Persian culture for Islamic life in India.
38 Ḥusayn (1962): 77.
39 Ikrām (n.d.): 162.
40 Ḥusayn (1962): 54.
41 Bilgrāmī (1971): 226.
42 A. 'Abbās Rizvī (1980): 63.
43 Bilgrāmī (1971): 229.
44 *Ibid.*: 228.
45 Ikrām (1964): 167.
46 The Naqshbandī Order was founded by Khwājah Bahā' al-Dīn Pīr Muḥammad Naqshband (718/1317–799/1398) at Bukhara. Khwājah Muḥammad Bāqī bi'Llāh (970/1563–1012/1603), seventh in the line from the founder, introduced the order to India. The Naqshbandīs, from the very beginning, stressed the observance of the *Sharī'ah*. Shaykh Aḥmad Sirhindī, a disciple of Khwājah Bāqī bi'Llāh, gave new momentum to the order by attacking all kinds of innovations. See Ḥusayn (1962): 57.
47 On that occasion, Khwājah Muḥammad Bāqī bi'Llāh said: "Shaykh Aḥmad is . . . rich in knowledge and rigorous in action. I associated with him for a few days, and noticed truly marvellous things in his spiritual life. He will turn into a light which will illumine the world" (for more details see Ikrām (1964): 167).
48 *Ibid.*: 168–9.
49 Ḥusayn (1962): 58.
50 *Ibid.*
51 See Ikrām (n.d.): 243–7.
52 Bilgrāmī (1971): 193.
53 *Ibid.*
54 *Ibid.*: 193–4.
55 Mubārakpūrī (1979): 306–7.
56 Bilgrāmī (1971): 199.
57 Muḥammad Bāqir Damād, better known as Mīr Dāmād, was one of the greatest philosophers and metaphysicians of the Ṣafavid period. His contribution towards the establishment of the theosophical school at Isfahan is greater than any other Persian scholar's. He was the foremost teacher of Mullā Ṣadrā, Sayyid Aḥmad

'Alawī, Mullā Khalīl Qazwīnī and Quṭb al-Dīn Ashkiwarī. Mīr Dāmād composed many valuable works in the field of philosophy and metaphysics, such as *Sharḥ-i najāt, al-Ufuq al-mubīn, al-Ṣirāṭ al-mustaqīm, Qabasāt, Taqdisāt, Jadhawāt* and *Sidrat al-muntahā*. Mīr Dāmād died in Iraq in 1041/1663. For more details see Sayyed Hossein Nasr, "The School of Isfahan", in *A History of Muslim philosophy*, ed. M. M. Sharif (Wiesbaden, 1963), 2: 914–15.

58 The Qādiriyyah Order was founded by Shaykh 'Abd al-Qādir Jīlānī (d. 562/1166). Shaykh Ni'mat Allāh and Makhdūm Jīlānī introduced the order into India in the middle of the ninth/fifteenth century. Miyān Mīr Lāhōrī (957/1550–1044/1635) was a distinguished leader of this order of his time. Dārā Shikoh, a son of Emperor Shah Jahān, was a devoted disciple of Miyān Mīr Lāhōrī. (For more details see M. L. Bāghī (1965): 233.

59 *Ibid.*: 321–2.

60 For more details about his writings and their contents see Mubārakpūrī (1979): 339–59.

61 Bilgrāmī (1981): 91.

62 *Ibid.*: 195–7.

63 Shāh Walīullāh (1974), Urdu trans.: 90.

64 Bilgrāmī (1981): 198.

65 Shah 'Abd al-Raḥīm was born in 1056/1646. At an early age he studied under his elder brother 'Abd al-Riḍā Muḥammad the books of Arabic and Persian grammar and literature, jurisprudence, and the works of Scholastic theology and philosophy up to the level of *Sharḥ al-'aqā'id* of 'Allāmah al-Taftāzānī, *Sharḥ al-Mawāqif* of 'Allāmah al-Sayyid al-Sharīf al-Jurjānī and *Ḥāshiya-yi khiyālī* of 'Allāmah 'Abd al-Ḥakīm Siyālkotī. For more advanced study of the Islamic intellectual sciences, he joined the circle of Mirzā Muḥammad Zāhid Harawī, a well-known theologian, philosopher and metaphysician of the time. After completing his formal study, Shah 'Abd al-Rahīm turned towards spiritual training. In this regard, he visited various saints and renowned scholars, and finally became a spiritual disciple of Ḥāfiẓ Sayyid 'Abd Allāh Akbarābādī, a distinguished *khalīfah* of Sayyid Ādam Benawrī. He fulfilled the requirements of the Naqshbandī order very soon and was granted the *khirqah* (Sufi robe) and *ijāzah* (permission to initiate others into the order). The greatest achievement of Shah 'Abd al-Raḥīm was the establishment and management of the Madrasa-yi Raḥīmiyyah situated in Kotlah Fayroz Shah, in the vicinity of Delhi. In that institution not only Shah Walīullāh was taught and trained but hundreds of students, from far and near studied and quenched their thirst for scientific and spiritual knowledge. This *madrasah* later became a great centre for Shah Walīullāh's intellectual, social and political activities. From this centre, knowledge spread throughout India and even reached neighbouring countries such as Afghanistan, Malaysia and Burma. Shah 'Abd al-Raḥīm died on Wednesday 12 Ṣafar 1131/1718 at the age of seventy-seven, in Delhi, and was buried there. For more details on the subject see Shah Walīullāh (1974): 331.

66 For the biography of Shāh Walīullāh see his autobiography, called *al-Jūz' al-laṭīf fī tarjumat 'abd al-ḍa'īf*, in (1974). Also see Maẓhar Baqā (1973): 55, 59.

67 Barbara Daly Metcalf (1982): 76–9.

BIBLIOGRAPHY

Aḥmad, Bashīr (1967) "Qurūn-e Wusṭā ke Hindustān main Falsafa kā 'Āghāz wa Irtiqā", *Iqbāl Review*, 7(4), (January).
Bāghī, M. L. (1965) *Medieval India: Culture and Thought* (Ambala).
Baqā', M. (1973) *Uṣūl al-fiqh awr Shāh Walī Allāh* (Islamabad).
Bilgrāmī, M. G. A. (1971) *Ma'āthir al-kirām* (Lahore).
Bosworth, C. E. (1973) *The Ghaznavids*, 2nd ed. (Beirut).
— (1980) *The Islamic Dynasties*, 2nd ed. (Edinburgh).
Encyclopaedia of Islam, 1978 new ed. (Leiden).
Funk and Wagnalls New Encyclopedia, ed. L. Bram and N. Dickey (Oxford, 1993).
Ḥusayn, Y. (1962) *Glimpses of Medieval Indian Culture* (Bombay, London and New York).
Ikrām, S. M. (1955) *Cultural Heritage of Pakistan* (Karachi).
— (1964) *Muslim Civilization in India* (New York).
— (1986) *'Āb-i kawthar* (Lahore).
— (n.d.) *Rawd-i kawthar* (Lahore).
Khulaif, F. (1966) *A Study on Fakhr al-Dīn Rāzī and his Controversies in Transoxiana* (Beirut).
Metcalf, B. D. (1982) *Islamic Revival in British India: Deoband, 1860–1900* (Princeton).
Mubārakpūrī, Q. A. (1979) *Diyār-e pūrub main 'ilm awr 'ulamā'* (Delhi).
Rashīd, A. (1969) *Society and Culture in Medieval India* (Calcutta).
Rizvī, A. A. (1980) *Shāh Walī Allāh and His Times* (Canberra).
Shāh Walīullāh (1974) *Anfās al-'ārifīn*, Urdu trans. S. M. Fārooqī al-Qādirī (Lahore).
— *Al-Juz' al-laṭīf fī tarjumat 'abd al-ḍa'īf*, in (1974).
Sharif, M. M. (ed.) (1963) *A History of Muslim Philosophy* (Wiesbaden).
Śrivastava, A. L. (1964) *Medieval Indian Culture* (Jaipur).

CHAPTER 63

Pakistan

M. Suheyl Umar

Pakistan came into existence in 1947.[1] As an heir to the Indo-Muslim civilization that had flourished in the subcontinent since the thirteenth century it inherited, along with other things, the intellectual tradition which manifested itself in the establishment of religious and educational institutions and in the form of various movements, political, cultural, reformist and philosopho-theological. After the introduction of the modern system of education in the Indian subcontinent by the British, the intellectual activity of the Muslims was split into two distinct fields. It perpetuated itself, on the one hand, in the transmission and practice of intellectual sciences taught in the traditional *madrasah* and other centres of esoteric and exoteric learning and, on the other hand, in the newly introduced disciplines of philosophy in the colleges and universities, which included a study of Islamic philosophy in their curriculum, though often in a fragmentary and superficial manner.[2]

The influence of this philosophic activity on the Islamic society at large has, however, always been limited since philosophy, in its modern Western meaning never developed in the Muslim world and whatever influence it exerted always left the heart of the tradition intact.

Taking the word philosophy in its widest and traditional sense one can distinguish its four main branches that exerted their influence on the intellectual and cultural activity of the Pakistani society. These branches are: theoretical philosophy (*falsafah naẓarī*), practical philosophy (*falsafah ʿamalī*), theological thought (*kalām*) and gnosis (*ʿirfān*).

By the turn of the century, interest in the study of intellectual science, even in the traditional *madrasah*s, was on the wane. Moreover theoretical philosophy and Peripatetic thought had rarely found favourable ground in the Sunni world. This lack of interest in theoretical philosophy coupled with a tendency towards gnostic philosophy resulted in a gradual gravitation of almost all higher intellectual activity towards gnosis, which flourished within the bosom of Sufism or *taṣawwuf*. Sufism worked as a centre which attracted and influenced all the strata of Pakistani society through its appeal to different intellectual levels.

Nevertheless, this should not be taken to mean that other branches of Islamic philosophy did not have their influence on Pakistani society. In fact, intellectual activity in Pakistan is more prone to philosophic methodology than could be discerned from its surface. The creation of Pakistan was, in ultimate analysis, based on a concept. National identity also drew its intellectual nourishment from a conceptual basis. Thus Pakistani thinkers more often use the methodology usually associated with philosophy.

Theoretical philosophy (*naẓarī*) has been cultivated, though in a diminished form, both in the traditional *madrasah*s and the departments of philosophy in various colleges and universities, where the subject of Islamic philosophy was introduced soon after the creation of Pakistan. The curricula of the traditional *madrasah*s have included the intellectual sciences especially logic, theology and a philosophy which was a blend of Peripatetic thought, gnosis and theosophy. The scholars trained in these traditional schools of learning have been absorbed in the society every year. Through their influence in society, maintained either from the pulpit or through their circles of teaching, Islamic philosophy has had an indirect influence even on the masses.

No less influential was this branch of Islamic philosophy in the emergence of thinkers and movements which drew their intellectual nourishment from it. Abu'l-A'lā' Mawdūdī was the foremost example of this influence. A translator of Mullā Ṣādrā's *Asfār*[3] in his early days and a student of one of the leading masters of intellectual sciences,[4] Mawdūdī undoubtedly brought his training in Islamic philosophy to bear upon the social, political and theological issues which he discussed in his earlier writings. Even in his later days when his movement had become politicized, his thought continued to exercise a powerful influence on the intellectual activity of the country.

Khalīfah 'Abd al-Ḥakīm[5] was a meeting point of the philosophy taught in the modern universities and the influence of the Islamic intellectual sciences. The impact of practical philosophy could also be discerned in the later movements of reform. Asrār Aḥmad's *Tanẓīm-i islamī*[6] and Ṭāhir al-Qadirī's *Minhāj al-qur'ān*[7] are the foremost examples of this latter-day influence of Islamic philosophy. Whereas the former has laid more emphasis on religious, social and political issues, the latter has incorporated elements of a more philosophic nature among its issues and the resulting literature.

Study of theoretical philosophy (*falsafah naẓarī*) in the traditional schools of learning of Pakistan was constantly on the wane and a general lack of interest in that part of the curriculum was commonplace among the students of intellectual sciences. The study of logic was the only part which survived and even that in a simplified form. Furthermore, in the centres of modern education, theoretical philosophy was mostly confined to an indirect study of the early thinkers and compilation of history. Mention should especially be made of M. M. Sharif's *A History of Muslim Philosophy*[8] and a few other minor works that appeared in the early years of Pakistan's existence. Sharif's work, though slightly outdated now, is still the most comprehensive work in this field. Ẓafar al-Ḥasan undertook a critique of philosophy[9] from the Islamic point of view. His pupil Burhān Aḥmad Farūqī not only elucidated his ideas but also wrote extensively on the theoretical and practical aspects of Islamic philosophy.[10] M. M. Aḥmad was primarily influential as a teacher. He was connected to the gnostic orders himself and combined in his personality the elements of theoretical philosophy and gnosis.

C. A. Qādir was another important figure in the field of theoretical philosophy who not only expounded this branch of philosophy through his works[11] but was instrumental also in establishing and carrying forward the activities of the Pakistan Philosophical Congress.[12] This congress constantly included Islamic philosophy in its agenda and during its yearly gatherings a special session was always held on Islamic philosophy. Proceedings of the Congress manifest the major activity in this field over the last four decades.

Mention should also be made of the establishment of the Iqbal Academy of Pakistan[13] devoted to the study and dissemination of thoughts and ideas of Muhammad Iqbal. It was not simply due to the immense contribution of Iqbal's ideas in the Pakistan movement that so much attention was focused on his thinking presented in his prose writings and his exquisite Urdu and Persian poetry.[14] Apart from being a political thinker and leader, Iqbal was perhaps the most outstanding figure of his times, showing the influence of *kalām*, gnosis and Muslim intellectual sciences as well as of the study of Western philosophy in his personality. He was, in a sense, the epitome of the cumulative influence of the Islamic intellectual heritage on a contemporary mind. This explains the large number of studies, in the form of books and journals, intellectual currents, institutions, thinkers and ideological fermentation that followed in the wake of the creation of Pakistan as well as in the later years and which were undoubtedly steeped in the influence of Iqbal's ideas. We can describe this phenomenon as an indirect influence of Islamic philosophy.

Iqbal was foremost among the champions of a new theology (*'ilm al-kalām*). But *kalām* philosophy was also an essential part of the curriculum of the traditional *madrasahs* of Pakistan. Though also a victim of the detrimental influences of a general lack of interest in the intellectual sciences, *kalām*, however, was not eclipsed to the extent that philosophy, as *falsafah*, for example, was. It not only continued to exercise its influence through the traditional *'ulamā'*, who imbibed its spirit during their years of formal studies, but its influence overflowed, in a sense, in the intellectual activities of the reformers and religious thinkers in varying degrees. A large part of Mawdūdī's writings, works of the Farāhī school of thought and, to a certain extent, that of Ṭāhir al-Qādirī, could be described as an attempt to present the Islamic theological science (*'ilm al-kalām*) in a contemporary idiom. Even among thinkers like Ghulām Aḥmed Parwaiz, who were under the complete sway of Western rationalism, the influence of *kalām* could be discerned to a considerable extent. Special mention should be made of 'Allāmah Ayyūb Dihlawī regarding the influence and impact of *kalām*. His extensive lectures, sermons and writings[15] brought about a flowering of intellectual activity in contemporary society. Thoroughly grounded in all the transmitted (*naqlī*) and intellectual (*'aqlī*) sciences, he was mostly known for his mastery and command over theological reasoning (*kalām*) and his consummate skill at presenting these issues in a lucid and brilliant manner. Some of his expositions could be ranked among the most original contributions to the philosophy of *kalām* in recent times.

Gnosis or gnostic philosophy, as mentioned earlier, flourished in Sufi circles. It also underwent a decline in the sense that it tended more towards moral philosophy or even towards sentimentalism. Nevertheless, the influence of purely gnostic ideas, though in a diminished degree, was ever present in society. It did not often manifest itself in the form of published works, though this aspect was not totally absent from it. One can cite, for example, the publication of the translations of the treatises of 'Abd al-Karīm al-Jīlī, Ibn 'Arabī,[16] etc. as well as the commentaries on *Fuṣūṣ al-ḥikam* etc. by Dhahīn Shah Tājī. It was augmented by the introduction and publication of the works of the traditionalist authors.[17] The process started with the writings of M. Ḥasan 'Askarī,[18] carried on by his disciple Saleem Aḥmed and others in Urdu and English journals and reprints of the works of these authors. Islamic gnostic teachings have had a considerable influence on the highly educated intellectual elite of the society who not only have rediscovered their tradition through these works but also have come face to face with the rich heritage of the sapiential doctrines contained in the intellectual and gnostic aspect of their tradition.

This renewed interest in the more profound and sapiential aspects of the tradition is not altogether unconnected with the influence of gnostic philosophy on literature and art in Pakistan. Here again one finds the perennial wisdom contained in the gnostic philosophy attracting the best minds towards its fold.

The process of Islamization has been also instrumental in highlighting the intellectual aspects of the tradition. We cannot enter into a discussion of its impact here but it can be added that, on its own level, it has been also conducive to revitalizing certain elements of Islamic philosophy.

Almost all the Islamic countries are facing the threat of the modern and postmodern Western civilization. Pakistan is no exception. However, if a genuine revival of the Islamic philosophic or intellectual tradition could materialize, the encounter with the West could be made on a safer and more profound basis.

NOTES

1 For details see 'Ayesha Jalāl, *The Sole Spokesman – Jinnah, the Muslim League and the Demand for Pakistan* (London, 1985); Ch. M. 'Ali *The Emergence of Pakistan* (Lahore, 1988); M. M. Munawwar, *Dimensions of Pakistan Movement*, (Lahore, 1991); S. M. Ikrām, *Modern Muslim India and Birth of Pakistan* (Lahore, 1977); Stanley Wolpert, *Jinnah of Pakistan* (Oxford, 1984).

2 It may be noted that even until recent times the study of Islamic philosophy has been almost exclusively made through Western sources or the works based on these sources written by Muslim scholars.

3 See *Asfār-i-arba'ah*, Urdu trans. (Hyderabad, 1943).

4 During his formative years and the most intensive period of his studies, Mawdūdī was a student of 'Abd al-Salām Niāzī of Delhi, who was renowned for his mastery of the intellectual sciences.

5 See his *Islamic Ideology* (Lahore, 1988) and *The Prophet and his Message* (Lahore, 1980). He also wrote extensively in Urdu and was the editor of the monthly journal *al-Ma'ārif* devoted to religious and philosophical issues.

6 A Lahore-based religious reform movement, influenced by Mawdūdī and adopting more or less the same methodology. However, it limits itself to religious and social issues. Publications, journals, seminars and study circles are its most prominent activities.

7 Another Lahore-based organization. While the *Tanẓīm-i islāmī* appears to be more or less a continuation of Mawdūdī's thought, *Minhāj al-qur'ān* is more akin to sentimentalist religiosity. The activities are similar, with the difference that the latter is also more participative in politics.

8 See M. M. Sharif, *A History of Muslim Philosophy* (Wiesbaden, 1963), reprinted Karachi, 1983.

9 See Ẓafar al-Ḥasan, *Philosophy: a Critique* (Lahore, 1988).

10 See B. A. Fārūqī, *Mujaddid's Concept of Tawḥīd* (Lahore, 1989); *Minhāj al-qur'ān* (Urdu) (Lahore, 1988); *Islām aur musalmānū kay zindā masā'il* (Lahore, 1989).

11 See C. A. Qadir, *Logical Positivism* (Lahore, 1965); *Philosophy and Science in the Islamic World* (London, 1988).

12 See C. A. Qadir, *Quest for Truth* (Lahore, 1985).

13 Established in 1951 through on Act of the Parliament, the Iqbal Academy of Pakistan has published over two hundred books apart from bringing out its quarterly journal in five languages, holding seminars and preparing audio cassettes.

14 See *Kulliyāt-i Iqbāl* (Urdu/Persian) (Lahore, 1990). Also see Annemarie Schimmel, *Gabriel's Wing* (Lahore, 1989); Hafiz Malik, *Iqbal: Poet Philosopher of Pakistan* (New York, 1971).
15 See M. Ayyūb Dihlawī, *Maqālāt-i Ayyūbī*, 3 vols (Karachi, n.d.); *Mas'alā-i-jabr-o-qadr* (Karachi, n.d.); *Tafsīr-i Ayyūbī* (Karachi, 1960).
16 For example, Barkatullāh Farangī Maḥallī (trans.), *Fuṣūṣ al-Ḥikam* (Urdu) (Karachi, n.d.); Dhahīn Shah Tājī (trans.), *Fuṣūṣ al-Ḥikam, Tarjumah, Tanbīhāt wa Tashrīḥāt* (Urdu) (Karachi, 1976); A. Q. Siddiqui (trans.), *Fuṣūṣ al-Ḥikam* (Urdu) (Lahore, n.d.); *Faḍl-i-Mīrān* (trans.), *Insān-i kāmil* (Karachi, 1962); M. Taqī Ḥayder (trans.), *Al-Kahf wa'l Raqīm* (Lahore, 1977).
17 René Guénon, Frithjof Schuon, Titus Burckhardt, Martin Lings, S. H. Nasr, A. K. Coommaraswamy, etc.
18 Especially his posthumously published works, i.e. *Jadīdiyyāt* (Rawalpindi, 1979); *Waqt kī Rāgnī* (Lahore 1979); *Answer to Modernism* (Karachi, 1976). Also see *Riwāyat*, (Lahore, 1983) and *Studies in Tradition* (Karachi, 1992).

CHAPTER 64

The Arab world

Ibrahim M. Abu-Rabiʿ

> It is philosophy that makes man understandable to man, explains human nobility and shows man the proper road. The first defect appearing in any nation that is headed toward decline is in the philosophic spirit. After that deficiencies spread into the other sciences, arts, and associations.
>
> (Jamāl al-Dīn al-Afghānī)[1]

INTRODUCTION

This chapter explores Islamic "philosophical activity" in the Arab world since the late nineteenth century. A convenient overview of the field is provided by Jamīl Ṣalībā's classic article on philosophical production in the modern Arab world.[2] However, any cursory reading of this article and other studies in the field confronts us with a major problem. The problem is a dearth of committed and articulate interpretations of Islamic philosophical thinking in the modern Arab world. Most existing studies are primarily confined to describing tendencies that have had a living presence in the Arab world without shedding enough light on how to treat the philosophical questions at hand theoretically and conceptually. In view of the above, a series of questions may arise. Firstly, how do we define Muslim philosophical thinking in the Arab world over the past century? Secondly, is there a need for a reassessment of the relationship between philosophy and religion in Arab society? And, thirdly, what is the relevance of the Muslim religious and philosophical heritage to modern Arab intellectual history?[3]

Philosophy is by definition a mental human product, and in our case it is part and parcel of modern Arab intellectual history. As such, philosophy is the product of intellectuals who belong to different and often competing intellectual, religious and political camps. In recent years, there has been a significant shift in Western studies of the Muslim world from a course of study emphasizing the role of the elites and the benefits of modernization to a "scholarly concern with the Islamic roots of culture and politics".[4] A parallel shift from liberal, nationalist and secularist philosophies to the Islamic roots of modern Arab philosophy is highly needed. This is an attempt by no means to advocate a reductionist approach in the study of the intellectual history of the modern Arab world but rather to stress the significant role "the Islamic attitude" still plays in shaping Arab philosophy. It is true that the historians of ideas of the modern Arab world have used a variety of methods in studying the complex structure and the salient features of Arab thought, culture and philosophy. But the majority who write on philosophy in the Arab world have followed a dismissive attitude *vis-à-vis* the Islamic roots of philosophical activity.

Most specifically, the renaissance/decline, decadence/renewal and stagnation/revival dichotomies have been used in order to discuss movement and growth in Arab intellectual history.[5] In delineating the main issues and themes of modern and contemporary Arab/Islamic thought, a serious scholar, besides taking note of the diverse data in the field, must consider the question of method or of "correct" interpretation. But the task of the methodological explication of the main themes of Islamic philosophy in the modern Arab world becomes quite difficult in view of the fact that methodological studies of modern Arab/Islamic thought are rare, and, in many instances, are only partially adequate.[6] Hamilton Gibb's observation of 1947 remains, more or less, true in the 1990s: "One looks in vain for any systematic analysis of new currents of thought in the Muslim world."[7] Therefore, one must learn to ask smaller as well as larger questions in order to provide an accurate interpretation of intellectual activity and its reflection of the needs, aspirations and goals of present Arab society. One of these questions is the historicity of this thought. Thought, including the most speculative, abstract and metaphysical, never arises in a vacuum but is organically connected to a set of conceptual, social and historical precedents.

Therefore, it is possible to consider philosophical thinking in the modern Arab world as a reflection of the maturity of thought, consciousness, logic and wisdom that the Arabs have achieved over the centuries. It is true that one has to grapple with the history of philosophy in order to grasp the philosophical issues and problems of the past; but there is no return to the past. It is historically unfeasible to go back to the days of al-Kindī or al-Fārābī or Ibn Sīnā in philosophy. The modern Arab probably need not be an al-Kindī or an al-Fārābī. Their issues belong to a historical and social formation that is different in nature and complexity from that of the present. Yet our learning from this past philosophy is essential, since philosophy, besides being particular and social, can also be universal and abstract.

Our postulate that philosophy is historical leads us to question the state of philosophy in the Arab world on the eve of the Western intervention. Scholars have agreed that both philosophical and theological thinking, far from thriving before the eighteenth and early nineteenth centuries, was in a state of stagnation and decline. Therefore, the first tentative conclusion we may draw is that the reclaiming and revival, if not the genesis, of critical and rational philosophy in the modern Arab world have been mainly due to the military and political catastrophe resulting from the violent encounter between the Arab world and Western colonialism.

Undoubtedly, the traditionalist Arab intelligentsia at the time were alerted to the enormous gaps existing between their Arabo-Islamic culture and the Western one. The answer given by some was not to seek refuge in the past achievements of the ancestors, but to study the Islamic heritage with a critical eye. The Lebanese philosopher Naṣṣīf Naṣṣār argues to that effect and contends that

> In effect the renaissance of the Arab world has never been the resurrection of the medieval Arab world, just as it is not a simple consequence of contact with modern Western civilization. The renaissance of the Arab world signals the entry of the Arab world, after a long period of stagnation, into a new historical period ... This historical phase is distinguished by a confrontation between two civilizations: the Arabo-Islamic civilization of the Middle Ages and the modern Western one. The historian–sociologist should investigate this confrontation at all levels of the social system, economic, political and cultural.[8]

Therefore, philosophical renaissance is still a historical necessity today simply because "the renaissance of philosophy in modern Arab culture is a central problem that indicates the degree of conscience and independence attained by [that] culture".[9] It is true that most philosophical production in the Arab world is that of the history of philosophy and not philosophical thinking itself. But since

> Philosophy has become a central cultural factor; it is necessary that philosophy should liberate itself from the control of the history of philosophy, and that it should ponder living historical issues in a philosophical spirit. In that sense, it seems to us that the basis of spiritual and philosophical renewal in Arab culture should not be the theory of knowledge so much as the theory of the historical being. This theory necessarily implies a theory of knowledge, but above all it implies a theory of socio-historical existence, as well as moral and political action.[10]

Any actual renaissance of philosophy in the modern Arab world, therefore, can succeed only if it is accompanied by a critical perspective. Though critical and philosophical thinking is much more developed in the West than in the contemporary Arab world, "The rights and the tasks of critical thinking for these two types of societies are nevertheless the same."[11] As we shall see later, critical thinking has marked the best-developed Islamic forms of philosophical reflection in the modern Arab world.

BEGINNINGS

The gestation of modern Muslim philosophical activity must be understood against the backdrop of the Arab *Nahḍah* (rebirth, renaissance)[12] of the nineteenth century. *Nahḍah* is

> a vast political and cultural movement that dominate[d] the period of 1850 to 1914. Originating in Syria and flowering in Egypt, the Nahda sought through translation and vulgarization to assimilate the great achievements of modern European civilization, while reviving the classical Arab culture that antedates the centuries of decadence and foreign domination.[13]

Generally speaking, the *Nahḍah* movement stood against the degeneration of Islam, which, according to Gibb, "stayed put – that is it remained fixed in the molds created for it by the scholars, jurists, doctors, and mystics of the formative centuries, and, if anything, decayed rather than progressed".[14]

The modern period of Islamic history, says Smith, "begins with decadence within, intrusion and menace from without; and the worldly glory that reputedly went with obedience to God's law [was] only a distant memory of a happier past".[15] At about this time "Western civilization was launching forth on the greatest upsurge of expansive energy and power vastly accumulated. With them the West was presently reshaping its own life and soon the life of all the world."[16] The *Nahḍah* intelligentsia, therefore, reacted to Islamic decline and theorized on the options for renaissance, while not neglecting Western possibilities for such a renaissance.

One can easily argue that the *Nahḍah* phenomenon is based on a complex epistemological structure, which has both Islamic and Western components. As such, *Nahḍah* was translated by the Arab intellectual pioneers of the nineteenth century into a powerful historical and social movement, and has, consequently, revived a significant number of issues and debates revolving around the Islamic heritage and the challenges of the present; Islam and the question of Arab cultural identity; Islam and the West; the question of women; and the issue of freedom of expression. According to Arkoun, the encounter between the Arab world and the West created new conditions to which Arab and Muslim thought responded by creating new expressions.[17] These expressions represented the new philosophical, socio-cultural, psychological and linguistic orientations of the modern Arab world. In order to understand the background of these new expressions, one must take into account the rise of Western modernity – its nature and contents – and the impact it had on modern Arab/Islamic thought.[18] "The historian of thought," in Arkoun's words, "is bound to go deeper and analyze the relations between material and intellectual modernity."[19]

Arkoun sets forth to explore the impact of modernity on Arab thought and philosophy. He maintains that the Arab world accepted Western modernity and its educational and cultural underpinnings only "slowly and reluctantly". One of the main consequences of the interaction between Arab and Western thought is a new philosophical thinking characterized by criticism, innovation and a futuristic orientation. Arkoun does not reflect much on the present conditions of Muslim philosophical thinking in the Arab world. He none the less calls for a critique of Islamic reasoning as a means of reviving contemporary Arab thought.[20]

The *Nahḍah* thinkers, most notably Ṭaḥṭāwī,[21] Afghānī[22] and ʿAbduh,[23] were confronted with the problem of how to interpret the vast Islamic tradition of Qur'ān, *Ḥadīth* and philosophy in a socio-political and scientific environment dominated by the West. It is to a degree true that these thinkers "lived and acted in an Islamic community that was intellectually still relatively coherent and united",[24] but it is equally true that the premodern notions of Islamic philosophy and religion were inadequate to meet the challenge perpetuated by an aggressive Western world view. The essential question posed by these thinkers was how Muslims can be authentic and modern at the same time. They saw the need for a total revitalization of Islam in the face of encroaching Western culture, since "the attack of the West on the Arab world, aside from its political effects, was also a direct attack against Islam as a religion".[25]

The *Nahḍah* intellectuals attempted to salvage "Islamic Reason" from many centuries of slumber and decadence. They argued for the viability of Islamic reasoning in the modern age, since they believed that Islam was inherently rational. Arming themselves with what they considered to be authentic Islamic criteria for thinking and discourse, they sought to fight both internal Muslim decadence and external Western cultural and political encroachment.[26] Thus, historical continuity with the Islamic tradition was hailed as an answer to historical, cultural and religious rigidity and stagnation.

But, as a matter of fact, two different options presented themselves to and were pursued by the *Nahḍah* thinkers: firstly, the Islamic model, which took its historical shape in the experience of the Prophet and his companions, and whose theoretical foundations are derived from both the Qur'ān and the *Sunnah*,[27] and, secondly, the "Western model",[28] which stressed the ideas of liberalism, rationalism and secularism.[29] Many influential *Nahḍah* thinkers considered the latter model as the cultural expression of Westernization in Muslim lands.[30]

It should be noted, however, that both decadence and colonization brought about a conflict-ridden and often explosive situation in the second phase of the *Nahḍah* which began in the early twentieth century. Theoretically speaking, the problem of the *Nahḍah* can be viewed in terms of three major interrelated components of discourse: doctrinal discourse; philosophical discourse and historical/political discourse.

To begin with, doctrinal discourse concerns the purification of the fundamentals of religion. As Laoust aptly puts it: "No doctrinal reform is possible without return to an original source."[31] Reform or *iṣlāḥ* is the return to the just form of religion, and the affirmation of transcendent truth in a modern setting. This reformist programme has dominated Arab intellectual activity up to the present time. It revolves around the affirmation of "a traditionalist method and language" in a modern setting. Therefore, contemporary Muslim philosophers and intellectuals find themselves face to face with a set of social and historical questions that await a theological answer. It is clear that many Muslim intellectuals remain faithful to their visions of past Muslim history – a vision based on the significant role revelation plays in the process of history. But as a result of the rise of political secularization in the Arab world in the wake of Western colonization, "the reign of the *faqīh*s [jurists and theologians] was substituted, for better or worse, by that of the (technical) experts and the leaders of the masses. This new situation necessitated a new mental attitude and new criteria."[32]

The objective of *philosophical discourse*, as it appears in the early writings of the noted Egyptian philosopher, Shaykh Muṣṭafa 'Abd al-Rāziq,[33] is to show the authenticity of traditional Islamic philosophical discourse, and its relevance to the modern needs of Muslim societies.

The *historical/political discourse* of the *Nahḍah* describes the religion–state relationship. This relationship has undergone many transformations since the nineteenth century. In the first phase of the *Nahḍah* Islam assumed a nationalistic meaning, the purpose of which was to build a strong state able to compete with the West. In the second phase, Islam was expressed by Afghānī, 'Abduh and Riḍā in pan-Islamic terms. The goal was to reinstitute the Muslim *ummah* (community of believers) in the image of the Ottoman Empire. Furthermore, "Islamic fundamentalism"[34] rose in the form of the Muslim Brotherhood movement. Ḥasan al-Bannā, the founder, opted to create an Islamic state. His programme attempted to assert the sacred law in all walks of life. Politics, as a result, dominated philosophy and theology. A rupture between the *'ulamā'*

(Muslim scholars and theologians), as the custodians and defenders of the Classical Sunni tradition, and the Ikhwān, as a mass-based movement, was inevitable. The Ikhwān looked on the *'ulamā'* with great suspicion. In the Ikhwān's view, the *'ulamā'* were upholders of the same *status quo* that the Ikhwān were attempting to abolish. It is not clear, however, whether the Ikhwān's thought should be considered philosophically.

To conclude, any intellectual reflection on the state of the *Nahḍah* in modern Arab/Islamic thought must take into account the present meaning of tradition, the problematic of the state–religion relationship, and the current situation of Islamic culture. By the same token, any economic, political and social analysis of the current state of affairs will be methodologically deficient if a proper treatment of Islam and Islamic culture is lacking.

MUṢṬAFĀ 'ABD AL-RĀZIQ AND HIS SCHOOL

In the above discussion of the philosophical dimension of *Nahḍah* it was suggested that Muṣṭafā 'Abd al-Rāziq (d. 1947) played a major role in focusing the attention of Arab thinkers on the importance of philosophy as a medium of intellectual discourse. Although he is considered a reviver of traditional Islamic philosophy, the rediscovery of philosophy in the Arab world in general, and in Egypt in particular, has been only superficially discussed by scholars. There remains little or no analysis of the role Islamic philosophy plays in modern Arab intellectual life, and of the Azhar's (to which 'Abd al-Rāziq belonged) contributions to it.

In his major work, *Tamhīd li-tārīkh al-falsafat al-islāmiyyah* ("Prolegomena to the History of Islamic Philosophy"), 'Abd al-Rāziq proposes the following: firstly, the Qur'ān, as the sacred book for Muslims, encourages free rational speculation (*naẓar 'aqli ḥurr*); secondly, a literalist interpretation of the Qur'ān is inadequate to portray its rationalistic depth and attitude; thirdly, Islamic rationalism, which is intrinsic to the Islamic revelation, should not be confused with the Greek logic and philosophy that Muslim thinkers adopted and modified, and, fourthly, the Arab race is as capable of philosophy and comprehensive thought as any other people.[35] In this, 'Abd al-Rāziq goes against the grain of nineteenth-century Orientalist thought, one of whose best representatives, Ernst Renan, argued that

> We can not demand philosophical insights from the Semitic race. It is only by a strange coincidence of fate that this race instilled a fine character of power in its religious creations, [for] it never produced any philosophical treatise of its own. Semitic philosophy

> is a cheap borrowing and imitation of Greek philosophy. This should be, in fact, said about Medieval philosophy in general.[36]

Having this thesis in mind, 'Abd al-Rāziq attempts to prove the originality and authenticity of Islamic philosophy by elaborating on the inner theoretical dynamics of Islamic culture and by stressing the strong bond between philosophy on the one hand, and Sufism, *kalām*, jurisprudence and the *Sharī'ah* on the other.[37] His final aim, however, is to prove the compatibility of traditional Islamic philosophy with the rationalism of modern thought.

'Abd al-Rāziq defines philosophy both as the love of wisdom and as a rational method of discourse with which one can comprehend the world and deduce laws by which to govern human society. Furthermore, he postulates that the genesis of Islamic philosophy is to be found in the Qur'ān since it encourages rational research (*baḥth naẓarī*). He also contends that the Qur'ān consists of doctrine and *Sharī'ah*. He defines *Sharī'ah* as a set of rules inspired by doctrine and designed to meet the changing demands of life. In this sense, philosophy is the rational free discussion of the principles of jurisprudence that have a practical aim – to define human behaviour *vis-à-vis* the socio-economic, political and cultural milieu. 'Abd al-Rāziq maintains that after the death of the Prophet, Muslims developed a philosophical system with a double aim in mind: to reflect philosophically on the emerging questions and problems in the nascent Islamic empire, and to defend the doctrines of Islam, especially the doctrine of *tawḥīd* (the oneness of God), against competing non-Islamic philosophies and theologies.[38] This formally established the science of *kalām* in the formative phase of Islam.

'Abd al-Rāziq supports the idea that early Islamic civilization was distinguished by a legal and cultural uniqueness, which mainly stemmed from the historical specificity of Islam then. And, therefore, philosophy took on a legal function and permeated "the science of the principles of jurisprudence" (*'ilm uṣūl al-fiqh*). Thus reasoning about legislation was the cornerstone of all Islamic philosophical and rational investigation: "Any scholar of the history of Islamic philosophy must first investigate *ijtihād* [exercise of reason] from its naive inception as an individual opinion until it became a scientific method of research possessing unique principles and foundations."[39] The different schools of *fiqh* arising during the formative phase of Islam were dependent on *'ilm uṣūl al-fiqh*, and, consequently, a large body of rationalist and legalist literature began to appear in Islam.

The formal wedding in early Islam between philosophy and "the science of the principles of jurisprudence" led to the creation of a novel method of analysis, unknown to the Arabs of the *Jāhiliyyah* (the pre-Islamic period). *Ra'y* (individual opinion), *qiyās* (analogy) and *ijtihād* (exercise of reason) were the blueprint of this method. A student of ʿAbd al-Rāziq, the Egyptian philosopher El-Ehwany maintains that ʿAbd al-Rāziq's method stresses the difference between Islamic jurisprudence, as developed by Shāfiʿī, and Aristotelian logic, adopted by the Muslim philosophers of the formative phase, "The principles of certainty lie in the sayings of God as stated in the Qur'ān. Truth is the conformity of action to these statements, or the statements of the Prophet in his Tradition, or the accord of the community at some time."[40]

ʿAbd al-Rāziq argues that the Prophet used *ra'y* to create laws that were not found in the Qur'ān. Highlighting the role of reasoning in the Prophet's time, ʿAbd al-Rāziq goes against the contention of Joseph Schacht that the Prophet had no reason to alter the customary laws prevailing in Arabia. Though prophetic legislation was brought to an end by the death of the Prophet, ʿAbd al-Rāziq argues that Muslims had to devise new rules – mainly through consensus – that reflected the early Islamic rational activity.

It should be pointed out that ʿAbd al-Rāziq was very loyal to the religious tradition of al-Shāfiʿī, as he was to the Islamic rationalism of Muḥammad ʿAbduh. One wonders why ʿAbd al-Rāziq focused on al-Shāfiʿī's legal philosophy, and not on that of Ibn Mālik, Abū Ḥanīfah or Ibn Ḥanbal, the three other founders of jurisprudence. One possible answer would be that ʿAbd al-Rāziq intended to revive the legal tradition of al-Shāfiʿī, who grew up in Egypt, as a means of dealing with the contemporary problems of Egypt. Ṭaha Ḥusayn corroborates this view by saying that ʿAbd al-Rāziq fell under the influence of al-Shāfiʿī, firstly because "he belonged to the same legal school as did al-Shāfiʿī and considered loyalty to him a debt",[41] and, secondly al-Shāfiʿī's *Risālah* "opened up new scientific horizons that had been closed down to many a Muslim scholar".[42] Also, in the eyes of ʿAbd al-Rāziq, al-Shāfiʿī, in addition to discussing the principles of jurisprudence philosophically, devoted a great deal of time to analysing the dogmas of early Islam.

Shāfiʿī divides the Islamic religious sciences into "the science of the Qur'ān" (*ʿilm al-kitāb*), and "the science of the *Sunnah*" (*ʿilm al-sunnah*). These two gave birth to what ʿAbd al-Rāziq calls the science of the "fundamental principles of religion and law" (*ʿilm al-uṣūl*, i.e., *uṣūl al-dīn*, and *uṣūl al-fiqh*), and the derivative science of the fundamental principles (*ʿilm al-furūʿ*).[43]

To ʿAbd al-Rāziq, the Qur'ān is not solely a book of ethics and morals. It is the basis of all legal, theological and philosophical activity. Primacy goes to faith and reason combined. The Qur'ān is a *bayān* (perspicuous declaration) to the people that prescribes "the rules of metaphysics, nature, humanity, ethics and pragmatism".[44] To ʿAbd al-Rāziq, the Qur'ānic theory of humanity suggests that people are responsible for their actions because they have minds of their own.

Some Muslim theologians, such as Ibn Taymiyyah, discouraged *kalām* for its supposedly heretical nature. 'Abd al-Rāziq, on the other hand, following in the footsteps of al-Ghazzālī and Ibn Khaldūn, maintains that *kalām* provides a rational defence of the main tenets of Islam. Although the Prophet of Islam discouraged arguments that dealt with metaphysics (fearing unnecessary theological arguments and divisions), 'Abd al-Rāziq maintains that the Qur'ān encourages Muslims to comprehend the principles of their religion rationally.

Criticism has been levelled against 'Abd al-Rāziq's "philosophical project" by a number of contemporary Arab thinkers. The Lebanese historian of philosophy Mājid Fakhrī thinks that 'Abd al-Rāziq was wrong in the choice of his title (*Prolegomena to the History of Islamic Philosophy*) since his discussion does not centre on the type of philosophy traditionally understood. Fakhrī argues that, far from being a theoretical introduction or an endeavour to revive philosophy, this is an exclusively historical account of the development of *fiqh* and Islamic *kalām*.[45] On the other hand, the Moroccan philosopher Jābirī claims that 'Abd al-Rāziq fails to show the originality of the Greek-oriented Islamic philosophy since he limits himself to *kalām* and *fiqh*.[46] For his part, the Lebanese Marxist philosopher Ḥusayn Muruwwah argues that 'Abd al-Rāziq's equation of philosophy and religion is a compromising attitude which reflects "the ideological bourgeois attitude, which dominates the activities of other [bourgeois Arab writers'] mental attitudes towards various problems of the modern age".[47]

As mentioned above, 'Abd al-Rāziq's fundamental contribution to modern Arab and Islamic thought is his emphasis upon rationalism, and the inseparable link he posits between rationalism and revelation in Islam. However, one could question whether 'Abd al-Rāziq has contributed in any serious way to the resurgence of Arab/Islamic thought and philosophy. We can perhaps answer this question by comparing 'Abd al-Rāziq with his teacher, Muḥammad 'Abduh. The latter tried to liberate Muslim thought and practices from the shackles of blind imitation by giving reason the upper hand over revelation in solving controversial issues. 'Abd al-Rāziq, on the other hand, attempted to strike a balance between reason and revelation. To him, pure Islamic thought is to be found only in the Qur'ān. Although, generally speaking, both 'Abduh and 'Abd al-Rāziq share the same mission – to recreate the early context of thought in a modern setting – their audience is not the same. 'Abduh's philosophical and educational mission was more intricate and dangerous than that of 'Abd al-Rāziq. 'Abduh did not write for the theologians and the intellectual elite alone; he aimed at correcting those popular beliefs he considered un-Islamic. Another major difference between 'Abd al-Rāziq and 'Abduh lies in their respective attitudes towards Sufism. 'Abduh's negative appraisal of Sufism and its association with Islam's political and cultural decline were not accepted by 'Abd al-Rāziq, who perceived that Sufism had led Muslims to the highest ethical achievements.

Regardless of these differences, both 'Abduh and 'Abd al-Rāziq were in agreement on a number of points. Amīn, for instance, maintains that

> Shaikh Muṣṭafa Abdel-Razek, who was the closest disciple of Muḥammad 'Abduh, thought of putting into practice the principles of his master, who wanted to reconcile Islam with Western civilization. Also Shaikh Abdel-Razek strove resolutely to rejuvenate the old Islamic university which contained more than thirty thousand students coming from all the corners of the earth.[48]

Amin stresses that ethics was promoted at the expense of rationalism in 'Abd al-Rāziq's philosophy. He contends that

> The message of Muṣṭafa Abdel-Razek is therefore a message of moral reform: it cultivates the supreme art, that which forms the soul. Shaikh Abdel-Razek summarizes his philosophy in the words of his master Muḥammad 'Abduh: love in the human world resembles universal attraction in the universe; it maintains society and preserves it from ruin.[49]

In conclusion, it is worth mentioning that no one has done more than 'Abd al-Rāziq to recapture the legal philosophy of al-Shāfi'ī and reinterpret it in a modern setting. 'Abd al-Rāziq's preoccupation with "Islamic rationalism" reflected his concern about the low regard the process of rationalism is accorded in modern Muslim societies.

THE PHILOSOPHICAL LEGACY OF MUṢṬAFĀ 'ABD AL-RĀZIQ

The growth and spread of 'Abd al-Rāziq's Islamic-oriented philosophy must be understood in the context of other trends of philosophical thinking which have been current, especially in Egypt, since the early 1930s. Because of space limitations, I will confine myself to a brief description of the following schools of philosophy.

Ibrāhīm Madkūr's Greek-oriented philosophy.[50] In his early philosophical work, Madkūr discusses the impact Greek philosophy and especially Aristotelian logic had on Muslim philosophers and jurists.

'Uthmān Amīn's "internalist" (juwāniyyah) philosophy.[51] Amīn believes that Islamic spirituality can gain a strong presence in the modern Arab world as a theoretical system as well as a way of life. He agrees with Muṣṭafā 'Abd al-Rāziq that Islamic mysticism is an integral part of Islamic philosophy, and that it is the only power capable of transforming the modern Arab individual.

'Ali Sāmī al-Nashshār's Ash'arite philosophy. Al-Nashshār follows in the footsteps of 'Abd al-Rāziq, and argues that *kalām* in general, and Ash'arite (*Sunni* conservative) *kalām* in particular, developed a unique brand of Islamic philosophical thinking.[52]

'Abd al-Raḥmān Badāwī's existential philosophy.[53] In *al-Zamān al-wujūdī* (Cairo, 1957), Badāwī attempts to apply modern European existential philosophy to Arab society. Badāwī does not believe that Arabs and Muslims possess a genuine philosophical spirit. He contends that "philosophy is the negation of the primal nature of the Muslim soul".[54]

Zakī Najīb Maḥmūd's positivist and empirical philosophy. Maḥmūd's early philosophical works[55] reflected his concern with a positivist and pragmatic philosophy in the mode of William James. His book *The Myth of Metaphysics* calls attention to what Maḥmūd perceived as the needs of Third World societies, especially industrialization and modernization in the image of industrial Western societies. Maḥmūd's approach was not without its detractors. A number of influential Arab–Muslim philosophers criticized positivism vehemently, and argued that its main purpose is to destroy Islamic metaphysics. The Iraqi philosopher 'Allāmah Muḥammad Bāqir al-Ṣadr, for instance, contends that positivist materialism launched a bitter attack against philosophy and its metaphysical subjects. He also argues that "positivism has borrowed a metaphysical notion to complete the doctrinal structure it had established for the purpose of destroying [M]etaphysics".[56]

Aware of its philosophical limitations and non-viability in the modern Arab world, Maḥmūd modified his positivistic philosophical focus by critically examining the Arabo-Islamic heritage as a means of understanding today's malaise. One can notice a clear transition in Maḥmūd's thought in the early 1970s to what might be termed "philosophical liberalism". This is evident from *Tajdīd al-fikr al-'arabī* ("Renewal of Arab Thought"), where Maḥmūd turns to the Arabo-Islamic heritage in order to understand the reasons behind the present backwardness of the Arab world. He argues, firstly, that there is a perceived lack of individual and social freedom in the Arab World, and, secondly, that modern Arab thought is still dominated by the epistemological and intellectual frameworks of the past. The challenge facing the modern Arab world is, therefore, to go beyond an anachronistic type of knowledge that is based on "speech and rhetoric to a new type based on machine and science".[57]

EPISTEMOLOGY AND PHILOSOPHY

In an illuminating piece on the difference between theology and philosophy, Paul Tillich argues that

> epistemology, the "knowledge" of knowing, is a part of ontology, the knowledge of being, for knowing is an event within the totality of events. Every epistemological assertion is implicitly ontological. Therefore, it is more adequate to begin an analysis of existence with the question of being rather than with the problem of knowledge.[58]

Muḥammad ʿĀbid al-Jābirī does not take Tillich's advice, and prefers, instead, to interpret the present problems of Arab and Muslim existence by analysing the cognitive components that have gone into making "the Muslim mind" since the inception of Islam.[59]

What are the benefits of an epistemological critique of the Arab mind – both classical and modern?

Jābirī argues that a thorough deconstruction and critique of "the structure of the Arab mind" is a necessary step towards building a viable Arab future. In *al-Khiṭāb al-ʿarabī al-muʿāṣir* ("Contemporary Arab Discourse"), he maintains that the Arab *Nahḍah* of the nineteenth century did not result in a major epistemological and philosophical breakthrough because of the failure of its representatives to critique the Arab mind itself. Jābirī upholds the Orientalist position that there was a deep decline in the Arab world on the eve of the European intervention.[60]

Jābirī considers the question of decline (*inḥiṭāṭ*) to be one of the main problematics of modern Arab thought and philosophy. He declares that no intellectual trend has been immune from discussing the reasons and nature of this situation. He argues that Muslim thinkers, especially "revivalist" Muslim thinkers, have failed to present a viable alternative to the problem of decline.[61] He further argues that both "the Islamic tendency" and "the liberal Westernized tendency" have not succeeded in diagnosing the intellectual malaise of the Arab world: the former tendency locates the solution in the Islamic past, in the Golden Age, whereas the latter locates it in the European Renaissance, which was the antecedent of European colonialism. In other words, the liberal tendency, according to Jābirī, cannot seek Western philosophical answers to questions and issues arising in the context of the modern Arab world. Finally, Jābirī concludes that the *Nahḍah* discourse in modern Arab thought – be it Islamic, liberal, nationalist or Marxist – is a compromising and self-contradictory one, mainly because it offers ready-made solutions and theses.

Jābirī, like any modern Arab philosopher, is preoccupied with the correct method of investigating and interpreting the intellectual achievements of the Arab world in the last century or so. He contends that the various components that make up the *Nahḍah* discourse, especially the political, Arab nationalist, liberal and Islamic philosophical ones, have paid lip service to the real and fundamental issues and questions facing the Arab world. As a result, "The 'Arab mind' has failed to build up a coherent discourse, which could deal with any of the numerous issues and questions debated in the past one hundred years."[62] Jābirī reaches the grim conclusion that the conceptualizations of the *Nahḍah* discourse were based on prefabricated models that do not necessarily reflect the current social and cultural conditions.

Jābirī inquires, along Foucauldian lines,[63] about the possible relationship between knowledge and power in modern Arab societies. Knowledge is cognition and power is ideology. To understand the deep and complex relationship between cognition and ideology in the modern Arab world, Jābirī begins by analysing the constitutive epistemological principles of what he calls the "Arab mind".[64]

What is the relationship between the cognitive and the ideological? In *Takwīn al-'aql al-'arabī* ("Formation of the Arab Mind"), Jābirī attempts to show that the structure of the Arab mind is different, for instance, from that of the French or Chinese mind. Following in the footsteps of the French epistemologist Lalande, Jābirī draws a distinction between "*la raison constituante*" and "*la raison constituée*".[65] The former is a mental activity that differentiates between principles and consequences, and the latter is defined as the epistemological principles of mind that resist any major change.

Jābirī claims that the Arab mind is "*une raison constituée*". That is to say, it "is a constituted reason: it is the summation of all those principles and rules offered by Arab culture to its adherents as a means of gaining knowledge. In other words, a culture imposes these rules and principles as an epistemological system."[66] Elaborating on the preceding thesis, Jābirī argues that "the Arab mind", which has been formed since the *Jāhiliyyah*, has taken its epistemological shape and depth in the formative phase of Islam, and has thus resisted any later historical and political transformations, especially in the modern period. Jābirī goes on to add that the history of Arab thought is based on three broad epistemological structures: *Jāhiliyyah* epistemology; Islamic epistemology; and *Nahḍah* epistemology. In this classification, Jābirī goes against the grain of many a Muslim thinker who holds firmly to the idea that the Islamic system of knowledge abolished the *Jāhilī* one[67] and that both Islam and *Jāhiliyyah* are mutually exclusive. Jābirī is closer to the ideas of Goldziher and Izutsu, who maintain that Islam, far from abolishing *Jāhiliyyah* thinking, modified its epistemology and directed its world view in an Islamic way. It is interesting to note that, in his analysis of the history of Arab thought, Jābirī subscribes to the notions that explain the evolution of Arab thought linearly and monolithically. And, in that sense, he views the *Nahḍah* problematic as an historical event that can only be understood against the backdrop of pre-Islamic, Islamic and Western epistemologies and world views.

Though there have been some "epistemic ruptures" in the long history of Arab thought, this thought has to be understood as an archeology of knowledge rather than an epistemic mutation. Therefore, there has always been, Jābirī concludes, a strong connection between epistemology and ideology, or tradition and ideology. The Islamic heritage serves several social and political purposes in the modern Arab world. Its utility has been the main source of its strength and longevity.[68]

Jābirī's analysis neglects to mention or give value to the non-literate Arab mind, to folk culture and practices in the Arab world. Whereas the literate Arab mind was formed in the era of *tadwīn* (recording), the same does not apply to folk culture, which is a dominant fact in the Arab world today. Therefore, when we document the *Nahḍah* epoch, we should not neglect the conditions of folk cultures and their eminent contributions to revival.

Jābirī explains that one of the most important steps taken by the literate Arab mind was to build foundations for the Arabic language. Consequently, "After mummification, the Arabic language was frozen . . . But social life can neither be mummified nor frozen."[69] This is the main crisis facing the Arab intelligentsia today since they can write a language that contains elaborate mechanics and linguistic distinctions, thus forcing them to use concepts and terminologies created by their forefathers. Today's Arabic is not equipped with proper linguistic tools to reflect on the colossal historical changes affecting the modern Arab world. Here Jābirī reiterates Abdallah Laroui's thesis on the "anachronism" of the Arabic language: "The *salafī* [traditionalist] imagines that his thoughts are free. He is mistaken: in reality, he is not using language to think within the framework of tradition; rather, it is tradition that lives again through language and is 'reflected' in him."[70] Arabic, as a medium of communication, is ahistorical and unimaginative. Therefore, the first step towards true emancipation comes in the form of freeing the Arabic language from the "epistemological constraints and shackles" of the Grand Ancestors. In turn, this would liberate the Arab intelligentsia from the burden of double thinking. The dichotomy currently present between the traditional and the modern would disappear by the time a new epistemology is created.

Jābirī, following in the footsteps of Schacht[71] and Makdisi,[72] maintains that Iṣlamic civilization is that of *fiqh* (jurisprudence). *Fiqh* was established during the *tadwīn* movement and doubly supported by the *'ulamā'* and the state. The state and its supporters prevented the recording of what they perceived as intransigent material, and therefore, according to Jābirī, the thinkable and unthinkable had to coexist in the Muslim world.[73] Jābirī argues that liberating modern Arab thought from both the language and *fiqh* of the past would restore intellectual rigour and freedom.[74]

TOWARDS AN ISLAMIC PERSONALISM?

Muḥammad 'Azīz Lahbabi's [al-Ḥabābī] philosophy can be summed up as a series of epistemological transitions from personalism to realism and to futurism.[75] Lahbabi's thought is a catalyst of two historical moments, phases, exigencies and conditions. On the one hand, he responds to the challenges of Westernization by accepting a major component of its philosophical expression – personalism.[76] On the other, he is overwhelmed by the concerns of the Muslim world as part of the Third World, and takes an aggressive stand against the West.[77]

Lahbabi's ontology, especially in his early philosophical work, is defined as a web of interaction between man, self and world. Man's awareness of this interaction is what gives him a sense of freedom and destiny. In his view as well as in the view of others who have written on the subject, "a person . . . is a complex unity of consciousness, which identifies itself with its past self in memory, determines itself by its freedom, is purposive and value-seeking, private yet communicating, and potentially rational".[78] To Lahbabi, freedom presupposes responsibility, and responsibility presupposes destiny.[79] Freedom is the freedom of the function or will of man. And here he agrees with Hegel's understanding of the history of the world as "the progress of the consciousness of freedom".[80] Lahbabi's Hegelianism, which is similar to that of the early Marx, stresses the idea that living human beings make their history, and that individuals *per se* are free to function because they possess a complete rational self. Freedom is experienced as deliberation, decision and responsibility. These three elements of freedom constitute man's destiny. The freedom/destiny polarity in Lahbabi's thought is corroborated by the individualization and participation polarity. Lahbabi argues that "the healthy personality is the one which is totally integrated in social life".[81] He further maintains that individuals are distinguished by *telos*, the inner aim, which is the basis of his process of actualization. Participation is essential for the individual, and not accidental. This participation guarantees the relational aspect of human life: humans are related to God and to other beings.

Lahbabi's arguments centre on propositions and concepts that make up "the mental space" of the Western world. He seems here to be more concerned with the crisis of orientation and spiritual malaise in Western societies than he is with the problems of colonization and decolonization. Therefore, in his discussion of being[82] (*être*), Lahbabi is concerned with Western ontology, and its constituent elements.

The term "being" means the whole of human reality: the structure, the meaning and the aim of existence. Lahbabi says that Hegel was the first Western philosopher to give that term "being" a whole philosophical meaning: "Finally, with Hegel, the concept of being is understood for the first time as a dynamic and logical movement of concepts. The human being is thought, and thought cannot be reduced to 'I think.' It [thought] is (to be found) in the wc (think)."[83] Lahbabi is, therefore, immersed in the Hegelian principle of dialectics and vitality. This vitality reflects the inseparable relationship between being and thought, and being and existential freedom. Therefore, one's dynamic interaction with reality is a complex process that leads to continuous self-growth and self-consciousness. One is distinguished from animals by consciousness. In addition to dynamics and form, one is distinguished by vitality and intentionality. Intentionality presupposes an inner aim (*telos*), and *telos* is the source of social dynamics and growth. Intentionality is defined as a human capacity to relate to meaningful structures, to live in universals, to grasp and shape reality. In other words, humans are distinguished by their ability to create technical as well as conceptual tools that relate them to reality in its inclusive sense.

Lahbabi took major strides to apply his personalistic ideas to cultures and civilizations in general. In 1961, he wrote a book on how a national culture, especially the national culture of North Africa, can attain universal principles of action, humanism and dynamism.[84] He contends that a national culture is defined as "a totality of spiritual, intellectual, and material values and forms that are conceived by a nation in the process of its evolution".[85] A national culture can achieve total integration with the world civilization only if its creative energies are translated experientially and existentially. In sum, political independence should lead to the solidification of the national culture, and the vitality of national culture is sought in its contributions to world civilization.

Lahbabi argues throughout his various philosophical works for the revival of the critical spirit in modern Arab and Islamic thought. From this angle, he criticizes the apparent lack of critical philosophical expressions in modern Islamic culture,

> It is unfortunate for the Islamic culture that *ijtihād* has never been respected especially by the *fuqahā'*, who have installed themselves as the protectors of *tashri'* [legislation], and struggled in favour of *taqlīd* [blind obedience to the text]. In other words, they have refused any effort toward personal interpretation or any adaptation of the text to reality. *Taqlīd* is the triumph of the sheep-like spirit. The formalistic and literal spirit has triumphed by neutralizing any spirit of initiative or criticism.[86]

Lahbabi maintains that Sufism has modified the authentic spirit of Islam and has invaded its entire structure. He notes that with Sufism Muslims began to succumb to the various aspects of fatalism (*tawakkul*), dependence, the belief in the precariousness of time, the non-reality of the world and, consequently, the renunciation of this world.[87] Lahbabi considers that the Sufi's retreat from the world has gone in an opposite direction to all cultural and social progress, as well as to the directions of the Qur'ān and the *Sunnah*. Sufism, according to him, occupies only a marginal position in respect to the official religious sciences in Islam: "Because the origin of mysticism is not Islamic, almost all the practices of the Sufis are not Islamic. That is why in the 8th century [AH], the great Muslim thinker Ibn Taymiyyah defined the mysticism of Sufism as an ensemble of *wasāwis* [hallucinations]."[88] Lahbabi's critique of Sufism as an irrational and, implicitly, an irrelevant religious movement appears very clearly in his early writings as a young man enchanted with the scientific and rational contributions of Western civilization. Therefore, in his analysis of Sufism, he argues that it has not been able to produce an adequate and precise language of discourse because its fountainhead is the irrational and unknown.

In addition to the above postulates, Lahbabi proposes that even the modern *salafiyyah* of the Arab world of Jamāl al-Dīn al-Afghānī and Muḥammad 'Abduh has failed to meet the demands of the modern age:

> The *Salafiyyah* can be viewed from two different perspectives: In the first place, it is a movement of purification, of the return to the origins as a means of rejecting all the superstition and myths that have accumulated over the centuries in Islam. In the second place, it is a struggle for the opening of the door of *ijtihād*.
>
> Considering this situation – opening the door of *ijtihād* – the *Salafiyyah* has started to put new interpretations in order to actualize Islam and create an atmosphere of adaptation in the wake of the encounter with the West.[89]

Nevertheless, he goes on to argue that

> we should not blind ourselves to the difficulties and inadequacies facing the *Salafiyyah*. Its promoters, it seems, of the late nineteenth century and the beginning of the twentieth, did not possess, as was necessary, any consciousness of the dynamism of industrial societies, nor did they understand the leading role played by bankers, and technicians in contemporary society.[90]

The modern *Salafiyyah* has thought of religious problems independently of the new context of industrialization – a context of development that created new psychological and social problems, especially amongst the working classes.

In conclusion, Lahbabi applies what he has learned from the philosophies of personalism and existentialism to the modern Muslim world. A transition is made in his thought from speculative thinking to experiential reality. The connection between thought and being has to be translated as dynamism, vitality, responsibility and destiny. Lahbabi is concerned in the current stage of his life with the destiny of Arabs and Muslims. His appraisal of contemporary Muslim culture is based on premisses of rationalization, industrialization, and the creation of a new and efficient intelligentsia. Modern Muslims, in order to survive, have to reappropriate modern culture and its achievements.

ISLAMIC HEGELIANISM?

In his two perceptive studies, *La Personnalité et le devenir arabo-islamique* and *Europe and Islam: Cultures and Modernity*, the Tunisian philosopher Hichem Djait probes into the concerns of what he calls the Arabo-Islamic peronality – its present, its future and its relationship with the West. Djait represents a new brand of Francophone authors and philosophers who are totally immersed in the issues and questions that underlie the Muslim world, and he brings a novel brand of European philosophical insights, especially Hegelian and Existentialist, into his analysis.[91]

As a serious student of cultures, Djait delves into the Islamic heritage as a means of finding answers to his present concerns. He nevertheless turns Islamic religious belief and the inherited Arabo-Islamic culture "into a subject of critical assessment".[92] He argues that Islam, in its Classical age and vigour, was characterized by a high sense of religious and cultural homogeneity and historical consciousness. This was obvious in the writings of the *'ulamā'* and thinkers who ventured to discover the realm of the unknown in the human and social sciences. The elite culture of Islam, Djait tells us, "pursued all the forms of learning, with fierce vigour: history, geography, law, scholastic theology, philosophy, medicine, mathematics. But in the meantime, it was seized and shaken by an underlying force: a fascination with God."[93] However, the obsession with the Divine did not limit itself to the realm of history or that of the secular, in general. It took on a strong scriptural fascination as well.

The Sacred Text (i.e., the Qur'ān) created a long interpretative tradition, which forms the second major tradition in Islam today after the Qur'ān itself.[94] Furthermore, the Sacred Text became the embodiment of the Islamic search for the ideal. Thus a total picture of the majesty that was Islam emerges before our eyes: we are talking about an undeniably theological unity that elevated human culture to the level of the sacred. But the historical continuity of this culture was broken, well before the Western intrusion into Muslim lands.

Therefore, Djait enquires about the theological and cultural homogeneity of the modern Muslim world, and reaches the conclusion that a new terminology, in the form of dialectical epistemology, must be used in order to shed light on the modern situation. Djait sees a historical break-up in modern Islam, and argues for the use of the bipolar concept of historical continuity and discontinuity as a yardstick against which the nature and achievement of the Arab *Nahḍah* are judged. This is a better measure than "the rather hollow dyads of apogee/decline, decadence/ renaissance, Arab/non-Arab, orthodoxy/heterodoxy, not to mention the recent dialectic between tradition and modernity".[95] The multipolar cultural character of modern Islam emerging in the wake of its political and historical break-up destroyed its "living network of human and cultural exchanges, [thus] condemning each region to a solitary existence or to an exclusive dialogue with the past".[96]

To Djait's mind, Islam started to decline when its cultural and political homogeneity was broken down, and that is when Muslims were awakened to a violent encounter with Europe.[97] In a sense, decline means the break-up of the homogeneity that Classical Islam attained. It further means the accentuation of tension between the specific or particular and the universal, between the real and the ideal in Islam. Also, decline means the inability of the '*ulamā*', as the leading intellectual class in Islamic societies, to produce relevant theological knowledge that could be used to offset the rising tide of secular knowledge. Thus we are talking about a fundamental inner mutation in the modern setting of Islam – its cultural and social milieu. This mutation is further accentuated by the political disintegration of modern Islam and by industrial and military weakness. Thus the question arises, can any Islamic movement of thought in the Arab world today salvage the Classical homogeneity of Islam after its historical break-up?

Djait alludes to the lack of philosophical knowledge in modern Islamic resurgence as a popular religious movement, and says that the Islamic movements of today are in an undeniably pitiful and unenviable position. On the one hand, the Islamic resurgence benefited greatly at the mass level from the failure of liberalism, Arab nationalism, Arab socialism and state capitalism; on the other, it has not been able to forge a coherent alliance between knowledge and action, philosophy and movement. On the contrary, Islamic resurgence has had to face an unholy alliance between secular knowledge and power.

The colonial shock has produced in modern Arab society a dialectical situation. The contradiction between the colonizer and the colonized, "produced the bourgeoisie, the petty bourgeoisie and an oppositional intelligentsia".[98] In other words, this encounter has produced a new constellation of power relations that did not exist in the precolonial epoch. One of these changes is that

> the power holder (politician) and the intellectual have become unified in their thinking, especially in the priority they accord praxis over theory, and in the distance they have instituted between reality and truth, or between the true and what is said.

> But, because of his function, the politician, nevertheless, stays as the man of reality, and the intellectual, because of his vocation, stays as the man of truth.[99]

He goes on to argue that

> The major drama of the Arab intellectual rests not only in his witnessing the devaluation that is behind his reason for existence and pride – knowledge and culture – but in being prevented from accomplishing his civilized mission, which is criticism and free speculative thinking. It is even strange to note that the active segment of the Arab intelligentsia has invested its debating power in the notion of social justice, thus neglecting a concept similar in beauty and truth, which is liberty.[100]

From his side, the Egyptian philosopher Ḥasan Ḥanafī, by using some Hegelian and early Marxist categories of analysis, completes Djait's analysis of "theological and cultural homogeneity" by attacking the theologians of Islam. He contends that the traditional function of the *'ulamā'* should be to produce theological works that explain the exigencies and complexities of the modern world. In other words, theology, as is clear in the Qur'ān, has never stood aloof from the social and other problems facing the Muslim individual. It is religious simplification of the complexity of the mundane. But what we see instead is that the theologian "separates his theology from contemporary life, and being the functionary of the state, the theologian or scholar of theology is not a free and engaged thinker".[101] Ḥanafī suggests that a transition is needed from theology to anthroplogy – anthropology being in a general sense the science of humans and their social conditions. Ḥanafī defines theology as "a pure cultural formation, in a certain epoch, produced as the result of the encounter between the revealed text and a new vocabulary presented by other cultures".[102] He prefers anthropology, in a general human sense, to theology for the following reasons: theology is not a science, and as such it lacks a method. Further, it was construed in the form of a defence – of defending Islam rationally against other philosophies and theologies. The premisses and results of theology do not satisfy the rational mind, and they revolve around essence, characteristics, etc. that do not convey a sense of urgency in our contemporary intellectual and cultural life. Lastly, the vocabulary of theology is restrictive and not shared by the entire religious world. Here he refers to the difference between monotheism and other religions, such as Hinduism and Buddhism, that possess a different terminology. For all these reasons, Ḥanafī recommends that theology should be transformed into anthropology since the latter is a human science – the main axis is humanity. He defines this science as "an engaged science, leadership-oriented and militant, in other words, an ideology".[103] The transition from theology to anthropology to ideology is necessary in Ḥanafī's eyes in order to transform human actions. And this is the weakness of the reform movements in Islam since they did not assume this role. To a large extent, "they remained theocentric". He goes on to argue that

> The transformation of theology into anthropology should be integrated into a larger enterprise: the reconstruction of traditional Islamic sciences, their science, culture, and jurisprudence into revolutionary and contemporary actions; the subject matter of ancient philosophy (the existence of God, the creation of the world and the immortality of the soul) to that of human existence of citizens and people; the transformation of the ancient subject matter that concerns the divine essence, to that which concerns man in this world, from the subject matter of ancient mysticism that is concerned about the elevation of the self to that of God to the modern mysticism of romanticism and revolution.[104]

Ḥanafī seems to be frustrated by the lack of creative theological activity amongst the modern *'ulamā'* of the Arab world. He makes a distinction between theology and the sacred. Theology is a human activity. The *'ulamā'* lack a creative interpretation of human existence because of their inability to produce novel formulations of the theological doctrines. They further accept the Classical theological activity as *a priori* and indisputable. In other words, the *'ulamā'* have failed to interpret theology as ontology. "The regimes under whose protection we have lived since World War II, and which are determined to preserve their existence, are mostly dictatorships with complex components. . . . These systems have shown their resistance against downfall. Though coercive, they have been based explicitly on values."[105]

TRADITIONALISM OR HISTORICISM OR MARXISM?[106]

Abdallah Laroui's brand of philosophy cannot be properly termed Islamic, since he maintains that

> philosophy is born, develops, and lives again in polemic. It is not by re-examining old problems with the old terminology that it can save itself from ever-threatening anachronism; it renews itself only by occupying itself with the questions that are the stuff of everyday social practice, and these first appear in the form of critical polemic.[107]

However, its relevance to our present endeavour is derived from Laroui's scathing critique of what he terms "Islamic traditionalism", and its pervasive presence in contemporary Islamic societies. Laroui struggles specifically with the notion of the Islamic tradition *per se*. Though he ends up dismissing the entire theological and philosophical heritage of Islam as obsolete, he maintains that traditional categories of thought still dominate the mental product of a large number of the Arab intelligentsia: "Arab intellectuals think according to two rationales: Most of them profess the traditionalist rationale [*salafī*]; the rest profess an eclecticism. Together, these tendencies succeed in abolishing the historical dimension."[108]

According to Laroui, the real crisis of the traditionalist Arab intelligentsia is to be sought in the "foundations" that give birth to their thought. This mental dependency on and refuge in the past makes the chances of historical consciousness and progress quite remote. What is, therefore, the alternative? Laroui argues that the only means to do away with the traditionalist mode of thinking "consists in strict submission to the discipline of historical thought and acceptance of all its assumptions".[109] Laroui is not quite clear about the real nature of this historical school. Yet his challenge to the functioning categories of the modern Arab mind still awaits an answer. In the words of Hourani, Laroui calls for the adoption of historicism: "that is to say, a willingness to transcend the past, to take what was needed from it by a 'radical criticism of culture, language and tradition', and use it to create a new future".[110] It is true that Laroui brings out a number of important terms that summarize his position on a number of crucial issues. Such terms as hegemony, tradition, historicism and revolution cannot be valued in a historical sense unless they are understood in the context of power dynamics in modern Arab society, and the way this society produces knowledge and culture. One could argue, therefore, on the basis of Laroui's thinking that the real problem facing the modern Arab world is not Westernization, cultural alienation or historical alienation but the preservation of rigid and traditional categories of thought which do not show inner readiness to combat and solve current problems.[111]

Though Laroui's basic aim is "to overcome cultural and intellectual backwardness",[112] his alternative is simplistic at best. He proposes to overcome the past by suggesting its total abolition from the existing memory of Arab society. In other words, far from calling for a critical and engaged reappraisal and reappropriation of the Islamic tradition, in all of its complexity and categories, Laroui calls for the total adoption of Westernization, which should become, in his view, the intellectual problem of the modern Arab people. Therefore, he gives preference to Western political organization, and its technical and scientific activity, and takes them as a measure of progress.[113]

CONCLUDING REMARKS

In spite of his "double criticism" approach, the Moroccan philosopher Abdelkebir Khatībī states that "Contemporary Arab knowledge [including philosophy] cannot, without experiencing a radical rupture, escape its own theological and theocratic foundations which characterize the ideology of Islam and of all monotheism."[114] That the treatment of Islam and the Islamic tradition in modern Arab philosophy is inescapable is clear in liberal, Marxist, nationalist and religious works. The preceding notion is in agreement with the thesis that modern and contemporary Arab philosophy "has not yet been able to establish an independent personality of its own outside the periphery of religion".[115] Therefore, this philosophy, in spite of modern encounters with the West as the "other", has preserved a fundamental historical connection to the medieval Islamic heritage of thought. Consequently, a scholar is compelled to deal with "philosophical production in the modern Arab world" in the context of its historical and cultural specificity. Modern European thought, which broke away from medieval Christian thought, cannot act as the criteria against which one must measure the philosophical contributions of modern Arab society.

Putting the question of continuity aside, this chapter revolves around the richness of contemporary Arab intellectual history. Arab thinkers have been alerted to the need to produce ideas and philosophies that have bearing on present intellectual, social and cultural issues.[116] Since no intelligentsia of any society can be monolithic and dull in terms of its theoretical reflections and ideas, it is taken for granted that the concerns of the Arab intelligentsia are diverse. It could be said that the intellectual life of the twentieth century is more rich and profuse than that of the previous century. This is due to several causes. Firstly, with the end of colonialism and the rise of the independent nation state, new issues came to the fore. Life became more complex and a noticeable shift of emphasis is seen from struggles against colonialism to building the national culture. Secondly, post-colonial Muslim societies have struggled with issues of identity, especially religious identity, and the task of defining the relationship between the nation state and religion, i.e. Islam, became more urgent. Thirdly, the end of official colonialism did not mean the end of Western cultural and scientific influence on the Muslim world. In certain ways, the Western influence upon some Muslim countries increased by leaps and bounds. Today, instead of direct Western military, economic and political hegemony, Muslim societies have to face such issues as Western modernization, modernism, modernity and Westernization. A reconfiguration of these diverse issues and a better definition of the place of religion are two challenging tasks.

The colonial and post-colonial moments in the Muslim world have led to a noticeable erosion in the religious and social position of the *'ulamā'*, as the traditional intelligentsia class in the world of Islam. The function of the traditional *'ālim* is to preserve and transmit religious knowledge.[117] A new type of Muslim intellectual is being born – one who is critical of the *'ulamā'*, and who nevertheless shares more or less the same world view of Islam.

It could be said that the history of modern philosophy in the Arab world is, to a great extent, that "of a certain clash of human temperaments",[118] but it is also the product of historical moments, cultural contradictions and cross-philosophical fertilizations. Modern Arab philosophers are committed and alienated at once. They are committed to the mission of philosophy, which is to give direction and concreteness to thought. However, they are in doubt regarding the method or methods through which to achieve such a mission. We have seen that the ultimate methodological concern of many a philosopher – 'Abd al-Rāziq, al-Nashshār, etc. – is the revival of the *fiqh* methodology and world view. Others have sought methodological directives from Western schools and philosophies. Meanwhile, both groups have called for revival, emancipation, critique, rationalism, equilibrium and philosophical destiny.

One could reasonably argue that philosophy does not permeate Arab society thoroughly and that its presence is "partial and marginal in comparison to that in Western culture or to that in the medieval Arab world".[119] But if we consider philosophy as the reflection of the independence and maturity reached by a culture, the Arab world has come a long way. It is true that the Arab philosopher may have to lead a double and eclectic life reflecting, on the one hand, on his medieval Islamic heritage, and, on the other, attempting to assimilate the Western tradition of philosophy and thought. This process, however, is inevitable, and is not without its difficulties, hazards and deep commitments.

NOTES

1 Jamāl al-Dīn al-Afghānī, "Lecture on Teaching and Learning", in Nikki R. Keddie, *An Islamic Response to Imperialism: Political and Religious Writings of Sayyid Jamāl ad-Dīn al-Afghānī* (Berkeley 1983): 105.

2 J. Ṣalibā, "al-Intāj al-falsafī: al-falsafah 'umūman wa falsafat al-'ulūm'", in Khalil al-Georr *et al.*, *al-Fikr al-falsafī fī ma'at 'ām* (Beirut, 1962): 393–446. Since then, several short studies have appeared: G. Atiyeh, "Another Aspect of Philosophy: Modern Arab Philosophy", in Therese-Anne Druart (ed.) *Arabic Philosophy and the West: Continuity and Interaction* (Washington DC, 1988); S. Binsā'id, "al-Ṭayarāt al-falsafiyah fi'l fikr al-'arabī al-mu'āṣir'", in Ibrāhīm Badrān *et al.* (eds), *al-Falsafah fi'l-waṭan al-'arabī al-mu'āṣir* (Beirut, 1985); J. Charnay, "Courants reformateurs de la pensée musulmane contemporain", in

J. Berque and J. Charnay (eds), *Normes et valeurs dans l'Islam contemporain* (Paris, 1966); J. Charnay, "L'Intellectuel arabe entre le pouvoir et la culture", *Diogènes*, 83 (July–September 1973); A. Chejne, "Intellectual Revival in the Arab World: an Introduction", *Islamic Studies*, 2(4) (1963), 413–37; L. Gardet, "Philosophie arabo-musulmane et philosophie européenne d'aujourd'hui", in I. Madkour (ed.), *Dirāsāt falsafiyyah muhdāt ilā rūḥ 'Uthmān Amīn* (Cairo, 1978): 129–41; A. Ṣubḥī *"Ittijāhāt al-falsafat al-islāmiyyah fi'l waṭan al-'arabī*, 1960–1980", in Ibrāhīm Badrān *et al* (eds), *al-Falsafah fi'l-waṭan al-'arabī al-mu'āṣir* (Beirut, 1985): 101–22. A good bibliography on modern Arab thought is to be found in P. Khoury, *Tradition et modernité: Matériaux pour servir à l'étude de la pensée arabe actuelle* (Münster, 1981).

3 In the course of his comments on what he calls "the problem of Islamic philosophy" facing him as a graduate student at the University of Chicago in the late 1940s, Muhsin Mahdi says: "There was also a more general problem that had to be faced: whether the study of Islamic philosophy or of the philosophic sciences that flourished in Islamic civilization is a legitimate subject for Islamic studies at all. . . . Therefore, the problem of Islamic philosophy became crucial for me: what it is, its relation to the Islamic revelation, its role in Islamic society" (M. Mahdi, "Orientalism and the Study of Islamic Philosophy", *Journal of Islamic Studies*, 1 (1990): 87).

4 E. Burke, III, "Islam and Social Movements: Methodological Reflections", in E. Burke, III and I. Lapidus (eds) *Islam, Politics, and Social Movements.* (Berkeley, 1988): 17.

5 A good example of this method is illustrated in G. Shukrī, *al-Nahḍah wa'l suqūṭ fi'l-fikr al-miṣrī al-ḥadīth* (Beirut, 1976).

6 It was hoped that Issa Boulata's latest work would fill this lacuna. See I. Boullata, *Trends and Issues in Modern Arab Thought* (Syracuse, 1990). See the following critical review of the book: Ibrahim M. Abu-Rabi', "Trends and Issues in Contemporary Arab Thought", *American Journal of the Islamic Social Sciences*, 8(1) (March 1991): 151–66.

7 H. A. R. Gibb, *Modern Trends in Islam* (Chicago, 1947): ix. Gibb claims that the main reason for the decline of Islam and Muslims is the aversion to rationalism in the Muslim world: "The student of Arabic civilization is constantly brought up against the striking contrast between the imaginative power displayed, for example, in certain branches of Arabic literature and the literalism, the pedantry, displayed in reasoning and exposition, even when it is devoted to these same productions. It is true that there have been great philosophers among the Muslim peoples and that some of them were Arabs, but they were rare exceptions. The Arab mind, whether in relation to the outer world or in relation to the processes of thought, cannot throw off its intense feeling for the separateness and individuality of the concrete events. This is, I believe, one of the main factors lying behind that 'lack of a sense of law' which Professor Macdonald regarded as the characteristic difference in the oriental" (*ibid.*. 7). Also, "The rejection of rationalistic modes of thought and of the utilitarian ethic which is inseparable from them has its roots, therefore, not in the so-called 'obscurantism' of the Muslim theologians but in the atomism and discreteness of the Arab imagination" (*ibid.*: 7).

8 N. Nassar, "Remarques sur la renaissance de la philosophie dans la culture

arabe moderne", in N. Nassar, A. Abdel-Malek and Ḥ. Ḥanafī (eds), *Renaissance du monde arabe* (Paris, 1972): 331.

9 *Ibid.*: 332.

10 *Ibid.*: 340–1.

11 M. Arkoun, *La Pensée arabe* (Paris, 1985): 98.

12 See the following on the meanings of *Nahḍah*, deacadence and stagnation: S. H. Nasr, "Decadence, Deviation and Renaissance in the Context of Contemporary Islam", in Khurshid Ahmad and Zafar Ishaq Ansari (eds), *Islamic Perspectives: Studies in Honor of Sayyid Abul A'la Mawdudi* (Leicester, 1980): 35–42. Nasr argues that "The modernists never tire of speaking of nearly every form of activity in the Islamic world as a renaissance, whose Arabic translation, *al-nahḍah*, has become such a prevalent word in contemporary Arabic literature. There is something insidious about the carefree usage of the word renaissance, for it recalls the Renaissance in the West when the re-birth of spiritually deadly elements of Graeco-Roman paganism . . . dealt a staggering blow to Christian civilization and prevented it from reaching its natural period of flowering as a Christian civilization" (*ibid.*: 37). The modernist attitudes that Nasr criticizes are represented by the following: F. Rahman, *Islam and Modernity: Transformation of an Intellectual Tradition* (Chicago, 1982); M. Siddiqi, *Modern Reformist Thought in the Muslim World* (Islamabad, 1982); O. Turan, "The Need of Islamic Renaissance", in M. A. Khan (ed.) *Proceedings of the International Conference* (Islamabad, 1970): 24–31.

13 A. Laroui, *The Crisis of the Arab Intelligentsia: Traditionalism or Historicism?* (Berkeley, 1976): vii. From his side the Tunisian philosopher H. Djait comments on the phenomenon of *Nahḍah* by saying that "It must be acknowledged that the cultural phenomenon of the *Nahḍah* (renaissance) paved the way for both these forms of development by reconstructing the Arab heritage, by restoring the connection to the splendors of an age now given classic status, in a word, by spreading an atmosphere and ideology of renascence. The immediate consequence of this movement, whose vital center lay in Egypt and Syria, was the emergence of a modern Arabic language and literature, hence a re-Arabization by the core of the Middle East" (H. Djait, *Europe and Islam: Cultures and Modernity* (Berkeley, 1986): 137–8.

14 Gibb, *op. cit.*: 1.

15 W. C. Smith, *Islam in Modern History* (New York, 1956): 16.

16 *Ibid.*: 45–6.

17 Arkoun, *op. cit.*: 90.

18 Much has been written about modernity. The following is a select bibliography on the meaning and history of modernism in both the West and Islam.

Modernity and Western thought: P. Ackroyd, *Notes for a New Culture: an Essay on Modernism* (New York, 1976); C. Baudouin, *The Myth of Modernity* (London, 1950); D. Bell, *The Cultural Contradictions of Capitalism* (New York, 1976); P. Berger, *Facing up to Modernity* (New York, 1977); M. Berman, *All That Is Solid Melts Into Air: the Experience of Modernity* (New York, 1982); R. Bernstein, *Habermas on Modernity* (Cambridge, Mass., 1985); J. Collins, *Uncommon Cultures: Popular Culture and Post-modernism* (New York, 1989); H. Foster (ed.), *The Anti-Aesthetic: Essays on Postmodern Culture* (Port Townsend 1983); D. Frisby, *Fragments of Modernity: Theories of Modernity in the Works of Simmel, Kracauer, and Benjamin* (Cambridge, 1985); S. Gablik, *Has Modernism Failed?* (New York, 1984); C. Grana, *Modernity and Its Discontents: French Society and the French Man of Letters in the Nineteenth Century* (New York, 1967); R. Gray, *The Imperative of Modernity: an Intellectual Biography of Ortega y Gasset* (Berkeley, 1989); A. Huyssen, *After the Great Divide: Modernism, Mass Culture, Post-Modernism* (Bloomington, 1986); F. Jameson, "Postmodernism or the Cultural Logic of Late Capitalism", *New Left Review*, (July–August 1984): 53–94; A. Kaplan, *Rocking Around the Clock: Music Television, Postmodernism, and Consumer Culture* (New York, 1987); D. Kolb, *The Critique of Pure Modernity: Hegel, Heidegger and After* (Chicago, 1986); J. Lyotard, *The Post-Modern Condition: on Knowledge* (Minneapolis 1984); S. A. McKnight, *Sacralizing the Secular: the Renaissance Origins of Modernity* (Baton Rouge, 1989); A. Megill, *Prophets of Extremity: Nietzsche, Heidegger, Foucault, Derrida* (Berkeley, 1985); W. Nicholls (ed.), *Modernity and Religion* (Waterloo, 1987); T. Reiss, *The Discourse of Modernism* (Ithaca, 1982); A. Ross (ed.) *Universal Abandon? The Politics of Post-modernism* (Minneapolis, 1988); and G. Vattimo, *The End of Modernity: Nihilism and Hermeutics in Postmodern Culture* (Baltimore, 1989).

Modernity and modern Islamic thought: C. Adams, *Islam and Modernism in Egypt* (London, 1933); Adonis ('Ali Aḥmad Sa'īd), *al-Thābit wa'l mutaḥawwil*, 3 vols (Beirut, 1974–9); J. Ahmad, *The Intellectual Origins of Egyptian Nationalism* (London, 1960); M. Arkoun, *La Pensée arabe* (Paris, 1975); M. Arkoun, *Essai sur la pensée islamique* (Paris, 1973); L. Binder, *Islamic Liberalism: Critique of Development Ideologies* (Chicago, 1988) (see the following critical review of this book by the author: Ibrahim M. Abu-Rabi', "Is Liberalism in the Muslim Middle East Viable? A Critical Essay on Leonard Binder's *Islamic Liberalism: a Critique of Development Ideologies*", *Hamdard Islamicus*, 13(4) (Winter 1989): 15–30); C. Bouamrane, *La Problème de la liberté humaine dans la pensée musulmane* (Paris, 1978); H. Djait, *Le Personnalité et le devenir arabo-islamique* (Paris, 1974); H. Gibb, *Modern Trends in Islam* (Chicago, 1947); Y. Haddad, *Contemporary Islam and the Challenge of History* (Albany, 1982); Ḥ. Ḥanafi, *The Origin of Modern Conservatism and Islamic Fundamentalism in Egypt* (Amsterdam, 1979); H. Ḥanafī, "Des idéologies modernistes à l'Islam revolutionnaire" *Peuples Méditerranéens*, 21 (October–December 1982); A. Hourani, *Arabic Thought in the Liberal Age, 1798–1939* (London, 1970); Ṭ. Ḥusayn, *The Future of Culture in Egypt* (Cairo, 1936); M. 'Imārah, *Tayarāt al-fikr al-islāmī al-ḥadīth* ("Trends of Modern Islamic Thought") (Cairo, 1987); M. Jābirī, *al-Khitāb al-'arabī al-mu'āṣir* ("Contemporary Arabic Discourse") (Beirut, 1982); M. Jābirī, *Ishkāliyyat al-fikr al-'arabī al-mu'āṣir* ("The Problematics of Contemporary Arabic Thought") (Beirut, 1989); F. Jada'āne, *Uṣūl al-taqaddum 'inda mufakirrī al-islām fi'l 'ālam al-'arabī al-ḥadīth* ("Principles of Progress as Viewed by Muslim Thinkers in the Modern Arab World") (Beirut, 1979); M. Lahbabi, *Le Personnalisme musulman* (Paris, 1962); M. Lahbabi, *Le Monde de demain: Le Tiers-monde accuse* (Casablanca, 1980); A. Laroui, *Islam et modernité* (Paris, 1987); S. Mahmassani, "Muslims: Decadence and Renaissance – Adaptation of Islamic Jurisprudence to Modern Social Needs", *The Muslim World*, 44 (1954): 186–201; Z. Maḥmūd, *Tajdīd al-fikr al-'arabī* ("Renewal of Arabic Thought") (Beirut, 1971); R. Martin (ed.),

Approaches to Islam in Religious Studies (Tucson, 1985); F. Rahman, *Islam and Modernity: Transformation of an Intellectual Tradition* (Chicago, 1982); H. Sharabi, *Arab intellectuals and the West: the Formative Years, 1875–1914* (Baltimore, 1974); J. Waardenburg, *L'Islam dans le miroir de l'Occident* (The Hague, 1963); and A. Zein, "Beyond Ideology and Theology: the Search for the Anthropology of Islam", *Annual Review of Anthropology*, 6 (1977): 224–54.

19 Arkoun, *op. cit.*: 93.

20 M. Arkoun, *Essais sur la pensée islamique* (Paris, 1977) and *Pour une critique de la raison islamique* (Paris, 1984).

21 J. Crabbs, *The Study of History in Nineteenth Century Egypt: a Study in National Transformation* (Detroit, 1984).

22 N. Keddie *Sayyid Jamāl al-Dīn al-Afghānī: a Biography* (Berkeley, 1972).

23 On M. 'Abduh, see E. Kedourie, *Afghānī and 'Abduh: an Essay on Religious Unbelief and Political Activism in Modern Islam* (New York, 1962); C. Adams, *Islam and Modernism in Egypt* (New York, 1933); 'U. Amīn, *Mohammad Abduh: essai sur ses idées philosophiques et religieuses* (Cairo, 1944); R. Caspar, "Un aspect de la pensée musulmane moderne: le renouveau du Mo'tazilisme", *Mélanges*, 4 (1957); M. Kerr, *Islamic Reform: the Political and Legal Theories of Muhammad Abduh and Rashid Rida* (Berkeley, 1976); D. Khalid, "Ahmad Amin and the Legacy of Muhammad Abduh", *Islamic Studies*, 9(1) (March 1970); R. Riḍā, *Tārikh al-ustādh al-imām al-shaykh Muḥammad 'Abduh* (Cairo, 1933).

24 M. Mahdi, "Islamic Philosophy in Contemporary Islamic Thought", in C. Malik (ed.), *God and Man in Contemporary Islamic Thought* (Beirut, 1972): 105.

25 S. H. Nasr, *Islam and the Plight of Modern Man* (London, 1975): 90.

26 Concerning this issue see L. Gardet, "De quelle manière s'est ankylosé la pensée religieuse de l'islam", in G. E. V. Grunebaum and R. Brunschwig (eds), *Classicisme et déclin culturel dans l'histoire de l'Islam* (Paris, 1957).

27 According to Laroui, the Arab intellectuals of the nineteenth century posed the question: what is the West? The opposing other – the West – according to Laroui developed two forms of hegemony. In the first instance, the West began to impose its arms, gods, and laws and cultures on the oriental. The indigenous cry against "the imported ideologies of the West" was a last attempt to assert tradition in the face of the invader. Tradition became part of the ideological conflict between East and West. The second form of hegemony, according to Laroui, began with the development of the Industrial Revolution, and attained its apogee in the mid nineteenth century. The world was rounded into final shape, divided among the principal European powers; Asia was said to be sleeping, the East was decadent, and Turkey a sick man.

28 S. Mūsā, *al-Nahḍat al-'urūbiyyah* (Cairo, 1934).

29 S. Mūsā, *Ḥurriyyat al-'aql fī Miṣr* (Cairo, 1947).

30 Muslim travellers to the West in the nineteenth century recorded their fascination with Western culture and civilization. See R. R. al-Taḥṭāwī, *Kitāb takhlīṣ al-ibrīz fī talkhīṣ Bāriz*, in M. 'Imārah (ed.) *Al-a'māl al-kāmilah li-Rifa'ā Rāfi' al-Ṭaḥṭawī* (Beirut, 1973), French trans. A. Louca, *L'Or de Paris: Relation de voyage, 1826–1831* (Paris, 1988). See also S. G. Miller, *Disorienting Encounters: Travels of a Moroccan Scholar in France in 1845–1846: the Voyages of Muḥammad As-Saffar* (Berkeley, 1992).

31 H. Laoust, "Le Réformisme orthodoxe des 'Salafiyya,' et les caractères généraux de son organisation actuelle", *Revue des Etudes Islamiques* (1932) 6: 175–224 (p. 185).
32 M. A. Lahbabi, *Le Personnalisme musulman* (Paris, 1964): 100–1.
33 See our discussion of M. 'Abd al-Rāziq below.
34 On the explication of the term fundamentalism, see D. Eickelman, "Changing Interpretations of Islamic Movements", in W. R. Roff (ed.) *Islam and the Political Economy of Meaning: Comparative Studies of the Muslim Discourse* (Berkeley, 1970); M. Marty and R. S. Appleby (eds) *Fundamentalisms Observed* (Chicago, 1991); Y. Haddad, "Muslim Revivalist Thought in the Arab World: an Overview", *The Muslim World*, (3–4) (July–October 1986); F. Rahman, "Roots of Islamic Neo-Fundamentalism", in P. Stoddard (ed.) *Change and the Muslim World* (Syracuse 1981); W. R. Roff, "Islamic Movements: One or Many?" in W. R. Roff (ed.) *Islam and the Political Economy of Meaning: Comparative Studies of the Muslim Discourse* (Berkeley, 1987); W. Shepard, "Islam and Ideology: Towards a Typology", *International Journal of Middle East Studies*, 19(3) (1987); and J. Voll, "Revivalism and Social Transformation in Islamic History", *The Muslim World*, 76(3–4) (July–October 1986).
35 M. 'Abd al-Rāziq, *Tamhīd li-tārīkh al-falsafat al-islāmiyyah* 3rd ed. (Cairo, 1966): 5.
36 E. Renan, *Averroes et l'Avérroïsme: Essai historique* (Paris 1882): vii–viii.
37 Muslim thinkers of the Classical age attempted this synthesis as well. See L. Gauthier, *Introduction à l'étude de la philosophie musulmane* (Paris, 1923).
38 'Abd al-Rāziq, *op. cit*: 144.
39 *Ibid.*: 123.
40 A. F. El-Ehwany, *Islamic Philosophy* (Cairo, 1957): 140.
41 Ṭ. Ḥusayn, "Le Cheikh Mostafa Abd el-Razeq tel que je l'ai connu", *Mélanges*, 4 (1957): 250.
42 *Ibid.*: 250. Ṭaha Ḥusayn says (*ibid.*: 251) that early Islamic philosophy was as simple as Islam itself because it reflected the liberal spirit of the new religion.
43 For an elaboration on this division, see G. Makdisi, "The Juridical Theory of Shāfi'ī – Origins and Significance of *Uṣūl al-Fiqh*", *Studia Islamica*, 59 (1984): 39.
44 'Abd al-Rāziq, *op. cit.*: 273.
45 M. Fakhrī, "al-Dirāsāt al-falsafiyyat al-'arabiyyah", in *al-Fikr al-falsafī*, ed. F. Ṣarrūf (Beirut, 1962): 256.
46 M. 'A. Jābiri, *al-Khitāb al-'arabī al-mu'āṣir* (Beirut, 1982): 236.
47 H. Muruwwah, *al-Nazaʻāt al-mādiyyah fi'l-falsafat al-'arabiyyah al-islāmiyyah* (Beirut, 1988): 83.
48 'U. Amīn, *Lights on Contemporary Moslem Philosophy* (Cairo, 1959): 115.
49 *Ibid.*: 120.
50 See the following by Madkūr: I. Madkur, *La Place d'al-Farabi dans l'école philosphie musulmane* (Paris, 1938); I. Madkur, *L'Organon d'Aristote dans le monde arab* (Paris, 1938); I. Madkūr, *Fi'l-falsafat al-islāmiyyah: Minhaj wa tatbīquhu* (Cairo, 1968).
51 U. Amīn, *al-Juwāniyyah: uṣūl 'aqīdah wa falsafat thawrah* (Beirut, 1960). See also G. Anawati, "En memoriam: Osman Amine", *Mélanges*, 14 (1980).
52 A. S. al-Nashshār, *Manāhij al-baḥth 'inda mufakkiri'l-islām* (Cairo, 1977);

A. S. al-Nashshār, *Nasha't al-fikr al-falsafī fi'l-islām*, 3 vols (Cairo, 1977).

53 A critique of Badāwī's thought is to be found in: M. A. al-'Ālim, "'Abd al-Rahman Badawi marche-t-il dans une voie sans issue?", *Mélanges*, 8 (1964–6). See also M. A. al-'Ālim, *Ma'ārik fikriyyah* (Cairo, 1970).

54 A. R. Badāwī, *al-Turāth al-yūnānī fi'l-ḥaḍārat al-'arabiyyah* (Cairo, 1962): 111.

55 See the following early works: Z. N. Maḥmūd, *Khurāfāt al-mitāfiziqiyyah* (Cairo, 1953); Z. N. Maḥmūd, *al-Manṭiq al-wadī'ī* (Cairo, 1956) and Z. N. Maḥmūd, *Naḥw falsafah 'ilmiyyah* (Cairo, 1953).

56 M. B. Al-Ṣadr, *Our Philosophy*, trans. S. C. Inati (London, 1987): 69.

57 Z. N. Maḥmūd, *Tajdīd al-fikr al-'arabī* (Beirut, 1976): 239.

58 P. Tillich, *Systematic Theology: Volume One* (Chicago, 1953): 108.

59 M. 'A. Jābirī, *Takwīn al-'aql al-'arabī*; (Beirut, 1988).

60 Jābirī, *al-Khitāb*: 20.

61 In this regard, Jābirī quotes the best representative of modern Islamic revivalism in the Arab world, Sayyid Quṭb who maintains that today's Muslims "are also surrounded by *Jāhiliyyah*, which is of the same nature as confronted during the first period of Islam, perhaps a little deeper. It also appears that our entire environment is seized in the clutches of *Jāhiliyyah*. The spirit of *Jāhiliyyah* has permeated our beliefs and ideas, our habits and manners, our culture and its sources, literature and art, and current rules and laws, to the extent that what we consider Islamic culture, Islamic sources, Islamic philosphy and Islamic thought are all the products of *Jahiliyyah*" (S. Quṭb, *Milestones* (Karachi, 1981): 61).

62 Jābirī, *op. cit.*: 181.

63 See M. Foucault, *Les Mots et les choses* (Paris, 1966) and *L'Archéologie du savoir* (Paris, 1972).

64 J. Charnay, "L'Intellectuel arabe entre le pouvoir et la culture", *Diogènes*, 83 (July–September 1973).

65 J. Lalande, *La Raison et les normes*, (Paris 1963).

66 M. 'A. Jābirī, *Takwīn*: 15.

67 On the Islamic concept of knowledge (*'ilm*) see the following: W. Daud, *The Concept of Knowledge in Islam* (London, 1989); S. Z. Hasan, *Philosophy: a Critique* (Lahore, 1988) and M. H. Yazdi, *The Principles of Epistemology in Islamic Philosophy: Knowledge by Presence* (Albany, 1992).

68 See M. 'A. Jābirī, "Ishkāliyyāt al-aṣālah wa'l-mu'āsarah fi'l-fikr al-'arabī al-ḥadīth wa'l-mu'āṣir", in Sayyid Yassin *et al.*, *al-Turāth wa taḥaddiyyāt al-'aṣr* (Beirut, 1985): 29–58.

69 Jābirī, *Takwīn*: 79.

70 A. Laroui, *The Crisis of the Arab Intelligentsia: Traditionalism or Historicism?* (Berkeley, 1976): 156.

71 J. Schacht, *An Introduction to Islamic Law* (Oxford, 1964).

72 G. Makdisi, "The Juridical Theory of Shāfi'ī – Origins and Significance of Uṣūl al-Fiqh", *Studia Islamica*, 59 (1984).

73 Jābirī draws on Arkoun, who is quoted above.

74 Jābirī's method of deconstruction permeates his total output. See our discussion below.

75 S. Yāfūt, "al-Hājis al-thālith fī falsafat Muḥammad 'Azīz al-Ḥabābī", in I. Badrān *et al.*, *al-Falsafah fi'l-waṭan al-'arabī al-mu'āṣir* (Beirut, 1985): 261.

76 M. A. Lahbabi, *De l'être à la personne: Essai de personnalisme réaliste* (Paris,

1954) and E. Mounier, *Qu'est-ce que le personnalisme?* (Paris, 1961).

77 M. A. Lahbabi, *Le Monde de demain: Le Tiers-monde accuse* (Casablanca, 1980).

78 E. S. Brightman, "Personalism (Including Personal Idealism)", in V. Ferm (ed.), *A History of Philosophical Systems* (New York, 1950): 341.

79 M. A. Lahbabi, *Liberté ou libération* (Paris, 1956).

80 G. Hegel, *Lectures on the Philosophy of World History*, trans. H. B. Nisbet (Cambridge, 1975): 54.

81 Lahbabi, *De l'être*: 16.

82 For a full elaboration of the term "being" in Western philosophical writings, see P. Tillich, *Systematic Theology, Volume One* (Chicago, 1953): 163–210.

83 Lahbabi, *De l'être*: 12.

84 M. A. Lahbabi, *Du Clos à l'ouvert: Vingt propos sur les cultures nationales et la civilization humaine* (Casablanca, 1961).

85 *Ibid.*: 15.

86 M. A. Lahbabi, *Le Personnalisme musulman* (Paris, 1964): 90.

87 Lahbabi's views on Sufism do not stem, in my view, from a real understanding of *taṣawwuf* as an authentic religious science in Islam. The real doctrines of Sufism were developed, to a large extent, against the backdrop of the science of theology (*'ilm al-tawḥīd*) and the tumultuous events of the formative phase of Islam. For a better appreciation of Sufism as an Islamic science, consult the following: Abū Naṣr al Sarrāj, *Kitāb al-luma' fi'l-taṣawwuf* ed. Reynold A. Nicholson, Gibb Memorial Series, 22 (Leiden and London, 1914); A. B. al-Kalābādhī, *al-Ta'rruf li-madhab ahl al-taṣawwuf*, ed. A. J. Arberry (Cairo, 1934), trans. A. J. Arberry, *The Doctrines of the Sufis* (Cambridge, 1935); A.T. al-Makkī, *Qūt al-qulūb fī mu'āmalat al-maḥbūb*, 2 vols (Cairo, 1892–3); A. M. Schimmel, "The Origin and Early Development of Sufism", *Journal of the Pakistan Historical Society* (1958); A. M. Schimmel, *Mystical Dimensions of Islam* (Chapel Hill, 1975); and W. M. Watt, *The Faith and Practice of al-Ghazali* (Chicago, 1982). Al-Ghazzālī (d. 505/1111) attests to the genuine character of Sufism by saying that "Among the things that necessarily became clear to me from my practice of the mystic 'way' was the true nature and special characteristics of prophetic revelation. The basis of that must undoubtedly be indicated in view of the urgent need for it" (*ibid.*: 63).

88 Lahbabi, *op. cit*: 95.

89 *Ibid.*: 99.

90 *Ibid.*: 100.

91 See also H. Djait, *al-Kufa: Naissance de la ville islamique* (Paris, 1991).

92 A. Hourani, *A History of the Arab People* (Cambridge, Mass., 1991): 444.

93 H. Djait, *Europe and Islam: Cultures and Modernity* (Berkeley, 1985): 119.

94 On the metamorphosis of religious tradition and the transmission of religious knowledge from one generation to another, consult E. Shils, *Tradition* (Chicago, 1981).

95 Djait, *op. cit.*: 124.

96 *Ibid.*: 125.

97 See M. Munīr, *al-Fikr al-'arabī fi'l-'aṣr al-ḥadīth* (Beirut, 1973).

98 H. Djait, *Le Personnalité et le devenir arabo-islamique* (Paris, 1974): 163.

99 *Ibid.*: 271.

100 *Ibid.*: 272.

101 Ḥ. Ḥanafī, "Théologie ou anthropologie", in A. Abdel-Malek, A. Belal and Ḥ. Ḥanafī (eds), *Renaissance du monde arabe* (Paris, 1972): 233.
102 *Ibid.*: 235.
103 *Ibid.*: 247.
104 *Ibid.*: 257.
105 *Ibid.*: 273.
106 The term "historicity" or "historicism" is used in two ways. First, it is used by Hegel, Marx and Popper in order to deduce historical patterns or laws on the basis of which future historical events can be predicted. In that task, the conflation of both history and metaphysics is involved. Second, the term is used by Marxists to express how the material foundations of a society can determine the historical stage and evolution of that society. See K. Popper, *The Poverty of Historicism* (New York, 1957). In this work, the term is employed in the first sense. There are certain distinct patterns of the *Nahḍah* according to which we can predict the rise of several theoretical issues in the future Arab world.
107 Laroui, *The Crisis*: 83.
108 *Ibid.*: 153–4.
109 Laroui, *The Crisis*: 154.
110 A. Hourani, *A History*: 445.
111 This is discussed in Sharabi, *Arab Intellectuals* (see n. 18).
112 See Adonis ['Ali Aḥmad Sa'īd], "Reflections on the Manifestations of Intellectual Backwardness in Arab Society", in *Cemam Reports* (Beirut, 1974): especially 25–34.
113 A. Laroui, *L'Idéologie arabe contemporaine, essai critique* (Paris 1977): 19. In addition to Laroui, other Third World Middle East thinkers have pondered the question of tradition and modernity: M. Bennabi, *Islam in History and Society*, trans. A. Rashid (Islamabad, 1988); D. Shayegan, *Qu'est-ce qu'une révolution religieuse?* (Paris, 1991); D. Shayegan, *Le Regard mutilé: Schizophrenie culturelle: pays traditionnels face à la modernité* (Paris, 1989).
114 A. K. Khatibi, "Double Criticism: the Decolonization of Arab Sociology", in H. Barakat (ed.), *Contemporary North Africa: Issues of Development and Integration* (Washington DC, 1985): 14.
15 Atiya, in Druart, *Arabic Philosophy and the West* (see n. 2): 154.
116 See A. El-Kenz, *Algerian Reflections on Arab Crises*, trans. R. W. Stooky (Austin, 1991).
117 See M. Gilsenan, *Recognizing Islam: Religion and Society in the Modern Arab World.* See also D. F. Eickelman, *Knowledge and Power in Morocco: the Education of a Twentieth-Century Notable* (Princeton, 1985) and D. F. Eickelman, "Traditional Islamic Learning and Ideas of the Person in the Twentieth Century", in M. Kramer (ed.) *Middle Eastern Lives: the Practice of Biography and Self-Narrative* (Syracuse, 1991): 35–60.
118 W. James, *Pragmatism: a New Name for Some Old Ways of Thinking* (London, 1913): 6.
119 Nassar, *Remarques* (see n. 8): 340.

CHAPTER 65

Egypt

Massimo Campanini

Philosophical issues are usually neglected when the issues of the Islamic reception and confrontation with the Western world are faced. Most attention is paid to sociology or history or to cultural subjects. But epistemological qualms troubled Muslim thinkers from the very beginning of the reforming path. Egypt can be chosen as a privileged observatory for this kind of question, considering the role it played in the contemporary history of the Arab world.

Liberal and nationalistic thinkers, living in the first decades of the twentieth century when Egypt was more or less openly a British protectorate, showed sometimes a very poor awareness of the potentially destructive contradiction which arises from the mixing of too many different cultures. To be sure, their openmindedness marked a radical transformation and a real change in Egyptian culture and politics, and there is no need to pursue this topic here. It would be enough to remember the names of 'Alī 'Abd al-Rāziq, Aḥmad al-Sanhūrī, and Ṭaha Ḥusayn. Unfortunately, acting as sincere interpreters of a new and changing world, they became the occasionally unconscious upholders of foreign control and intellectual subordination of Egypt. No doubt, colonisation implies a substrate ready to receive the new form, as Malek Bennabi sharply argued; but excitement for outside spiritual – and material – achievements can make intellectuals capable of forgetting their own origin. Ṭāhā Ḥusayn's view, for instance, of Egypt as a sort of failed European country is deeply misguided. Thus, we can understand the warning of the radical Islamist Sayyid Quṭb:

> We should not go to French legislation to derive our laws, or to communist ideals to derive our social order, without first examining what can be supplied from our Islamic legislation which was the foundation of our first form of society. . . . Our

> summons is to return to our own stored-up resources, to become familiar with their ideas, and to proclaim their value and permanent worth, before we have recourse to an untimely servility which will deprive us of the historical background of our life, and through which our individuality will be lost to the point that we will become mere hangers-on to the progress of mankind.[1]

However, we will not speak here only of politics, but firstly of epistemology, even though a judgment about some political issues is obviously implicit.

It is not fortuitous, in my opinion, that Islamic reformism and modernism set up a constructive confrontation with modernity on the basis of a reappraisal of Ibn Sīnā or Ibn Rushd's classic rationalism and especially Mu'tazilite rationalism, which was clearly indebted to its Greek heritage. This is particularly true in Egypt. A long tradition of studies and researches aiming to demonstrate "the revolution of intellect in Arabic philosophy" and its Greek roots enriched Egyptian historiography, from Ibrāhīm Madkūr and 'Abd al-Raḥmān Badawī to 'Āṭif al-'Irāqī.[2]

Muḥammad 'Abduh's *Risālat al-tawḥīd* is a philosophical meditation on anthropology and theology. 'Abduh argued about God's existence and essence in quite Ibn Sīnan (but also Ghazzālian) terms, as the following short passage proves:

> De même que le contingent a besoin d'une cause pour être appelé à l'existence, il en a besoin d'une pour continuer à exister; car nous avons démontré que le contingent n'est pas prédisposé par lui-même à exister et qu'il n'entre dans l'existence qu'à la suite d'une cause efficiente extérieure à lui. . . . Il est évident que l'ensemble des contingences est également contingent, et tout contingent a besoin d'une cause qui lui donne l'existence, donc l'ensemble des contingences a besoin d'un créateur. . . . Ainsi il est prouvé que les contingences qui existent ont une cause efficiente dont l'existence est necéssaire. . . . L'existence de l'être nécessaire est la source de l'existence de tout contingent. . . . Toute perfection de l'existence, qui peut être conçue comme attribut de l'être nécessaire, doit lui être attribué.[3]

Robert Caspar had pointed out Muḥammad 'Abduh's Mu'tazilite outlook many years ago, in particular regarding human freedom of act and will.[4] The novelty of Muḥammad 'Abduh's position did not enable him, however, to join Aḥmad 'Urābī's revolutionary movement in 1882 aiming to overturn the status quo. In this case, a modernistic approach and enlightened attitude did not convince a very independent thinker to choose an uncompromising political position.

Aḥmad Amīn (d. 1954) was actively engaged in Egyptian culture and politics: he was a university professor, Director of the Cultural Centre of the Egyptian Ministry of Education (1945) and later of the Cultural Section of the Arab League (1947). In his major work, *Ḍuḥā al-islām* ("The Morning of Islam"), first published in 1933, he complained about the early disappearance of Mu'tazilism as an irretrievable misfortune for Islam, underlining that

> the Mu'tazilites gave free rein to intellect [*'aql*] in its investigations of all [scientific] problems without setting any bounds. They regarded intellect as the way to truth [*al-ḥaqq*] in its investigation of heaven and earth, God and man, great and little. There is no field which the intellect cannot attain, [because] the intellect was created to know and have knowledge of everything – even what lies behind nature and matter.[5]

Amīn's goal was the revival of Muslim cultural heritage, making of it a way for the intellectual and moral recovery of all Arab and Islamic people. Although he was a somewhat openminded person, he was not fully free from a traditional outlook. Amīn praised the Mu'tazilites for their rationalism and demonstrative skill, but he preferred them to philosophers in the strict sense merely because they are men of faith, while the philosophers are inclined to view religion as not always consistent with rational and theoretical presuppositions.

But besides these "old" modernists, substantially the same positive evaluation of Mu'tazilism arises as a common feature also in Fu'ād Zakariyyah, Zakī Najīb Maḥmūd or Ḥasan Ḥanafī's reflections, even though Western scholarship does not wholly agree about the supposed strict rationalism of the Mu'tazilites.[6]

The influence of Mu'tazilism poses a crucial question: which kind of "rationalism" developed in the Islamic philosophical world? Which kind of "rationalism" should be cultivated in the *contemporary* Islamic philosophical world? Does there exist a unique kind of "Islamic" rationalism? Does it arise in *contemporary* times? Does a reconstruction of Islamic thought suitable for modernity mean or – perhaps better – does it require a reconstruction of its religious dimension? The debate has been particularly alive in Egypt, even though a great deal of comment arose also in other parts (Persia and India) of the Islamic world. It goes without saying that this confrontation with modernity affected Arabic minds as well as other Muslims, and imposed on Arab thinkers the *duty* of answering the Western challenge and discovering – if possible – an even more Arab, more Islamic way of thinking. This led Arab philosophers to a troublesome relationship with their own heritage which they are mostly inclined to consider not appropriate for contemporary issues. It means, moreover, that political claims cannot be obliterated in a larger methodological and philosophical reform grounded on Islamic revivalism, mainly because the reconstruction of politics in theory and of political systems in practice must reckon with the Islamic ideological framework.

It is true that, looking briefly at the eastern Muslim world, an Indian philosopher and poet like Sir Muḥammad Iqbāl (1873–1938) lived his relations with Europe and European (Western) culture more quietly. Neither his mystical nor his theoretical attitudes were completely upset by European (Western) thought. Indeed, he was persuaded that the core of European technical advancement is basically Islamic.[7] Alessandro Bausani stressed more than once that Iqbāl was not an enemy of Europe, albeit he expressed some surprise at the contradiction existing between the Westernizing culture of Iqbāl and his condemnation of democracy. "The *shayāṭīn* (devils) of democracy," Iqbāl writes, "are nowadays the kings of politics: vile earth does not need me any more."[8] This kind of contradiction is unavoidable for an Islamic culture confronting outward categories. Democracy is a revolutionary ideal; it was born from the French Revolution. But Islam did not experience such a revolution.

Perhaps Iqbāl's distinction between a materialistic Europe and a spiritual Orient can be judged hasty or naive, or at least philosophically out of date. But it is quite characteristic that Iqbāl was convinced of a convergence of Bergson's *doctrine de la durée* with the Islamic doctrine of time. Accordingly, Nietzsche would have been ready to accept the mystery of Divine Law moving away from a misunderstood conception of morals learned in corrupted Europe, and he became angry mainly because Europe failed to provide him with suitable moral answers. These – perhaps too open – attempts at "Islamicizing" European (Western) thought can surely be considered from the viewpoint of reformistic modernism, but do they reveal any desire for imitation or flattering of European superiority? In his famous lectures about the reconstruction of religious thought in Islam, Iqbāl was able to stress that

> there is no basic incompatibility between religion and science. Although philosophy can certainly examine the principles of religion, it cannot treat religion as something inferior to it. Religion presents a view of the whole person, while philosophy and science deal just with aspects of the whole.[9]

The superiority of religion over philosophy – and obviously over science – underlines the independence of religion of all external influences. But does this conclusion solve the dramatic contrast between tradition and modernity? Many Arab authors, however, did not recognize this superiority and so damned themselves to bow to the idols of science and progress. Arab–Muslim philosophers often did not succeed in reorientating Islam away from foreign and imported patterns.

If it is not trivial to repeat that a major problem in contemporary Islamic thought is the reconciliation of the urgent necessity of exploiting European progressive ideas in epistemology and scientific research with faithfulness to a past heritage, it is equally worth underlining that this problem was particularly worrying in the *Arab* world and, obviously, in Egypt, where several thinkers nourished a kind of intellectual submission. This is the case of men like Aḥmad Luṭfī al-Sayyid (d. 1963), whose sincere liberalism, inspired by Western philosophical and sociological traditions going back to John Stuart Mill and other similar thinkers, seems to deny an autonomous weight to Islamic heritage. P. Vatikiotis suggests, in quite triumphalist terms, that

> He cannot be credited with any originality of thought; yet he was original in the way he tried to transmit European ideas, and in the manner in which he ventured to use these ideas as the basis for the construction of principles to guide the formation of a modern nation in Egypt. Aḥmad Luṭfī did not provide Egyptians with a metaphysics or an integrated intellectual system. Rather he laid down for them the basic rules for the reasoned criticism of society. Above all, he tried to impress upon his compatriots that a society without a system of values and a set of principles to guide it towards certain goals would remain hopelessly backward. And these could be acquired by modern European education.[10]

If this is true, then we can draw a few negative conclusions as well: firstly, that Islam is lacking in values and principles; secondly, that the repudiation of all the Islamic past and tradition is unavoidable; thirdly, that European education and culture are assumed as meta-historical and not subjected to any sort of criticism. Obviously, Vatikiotis' own view suggests a rather deformed image of Luṭfī al-Sayyid's work. Yet Luṭfī al-Sayyid stands very far from a real Islamic renaissance, if we take European ideas of freedom, nationality and individualism as the only effective path to modernity. It is ironic that the same author, Vatikiotis, charges Islamic modernism and political thought with inconsistency just because it refused to accept Greek rationalism![11]

Indeed, the solutions Egyptian Muslim thinkers put forward are not always satisfying, even when we take a more favourable attitude than Vatikiotis. We can pick out here at least a couple of contrasting trends. On the one hand, some scholars tried to overcome difficulties by discovering a kind of abstract liaison between Islamic and Western (especially Classical) thought. 'Abd al-Halīm Maḥmūd, former Shaykh of Al-Azhar, divided the true value of *falsafah* into theoretical (about God) and ethical investigations. But these values already belong to mature Islamic thought, which he calls more properly *ḥikmah*. *Falsafah* is introductory to *ḥikmah* regarding both intellect (*ʿaql*) and practice (*irtiyāḍ*).[12] It is more or less the same with Iqbāl, but we need to be careful not to forget the *historical* dimension. For instance, in the following passage where Aristotle, al-Kindī and Kant are, so to say, sanctified by the Holy Qur'ān:

> There is no doubt that rational people would agree with Aristotle that "Every order bespeaks the intelligence behind it." Similarly, al-Kindī, the first Muslim philosopher, considered that the evidence of craftmanship in a door, couch or chair, with its design and perfected order, does not reveal its maker any less than the universe reveals its omnipotent Creator . . . Al-Kindī adds that the external manifestations and phenomena that register upon the senses give the clearest indication of the design of the First Planner. . . . The above manner of demonstration is the method which Kant, the greatest philosopher of Germany, declared to be the clearest and strongest proof of the existence of God. It is the way that has been followed by many thinkers from East and West. All these proofs of the existence of God may be summed up in the following verses in the chapter of the Qur'ān called "The Great News":
>
> "Did We not spread the earth as a bed, and raise the mountains as pillars? And did We not create you in pairs and appoint your sleep for a rest, and appoint night as a mantle and the day for your livelihood? And did We not build above you seven mighty heavens . . .?" (78:6)[13]

On the other hand, there is secularism, a more or less strong rejection of original Islamic presuppositions. Unfortunately, the secularism of such a famous person as Fu'ād Zakariyyā'[14] seems to betray the real meaning of Islam: it is absurd to reject the radical tendencies in Islam merely by opposing democracy and political freedom to its inner conservatism. Does there really exist a universal pattern of Westernization? Fu'ād Zakariyyā' argues that the Arab world and its thought decayed for two main reasons: blind deference to tradition (*turāth* and *taqlīd*) and an inability to historicize the past. He writes:

> Nous autres musulmans avons grand besoin de quelqu'un qui nous dise, comme les philosophes de la Renaissance: "Si vous avez devant vous la nature et les problèmes des hommes, pourquoi faut-il que toujours vous reveniez aux textes des ancêtres? Pourquoi faites-vous de la pensée héritée une autorité indiscutable? Pourquoi ne pas affronter les situations nouvelles avec votre raison?
>
> Selon moi, cette incapacité du monde arabe à historiciser

> sa relation au passé constitue la cause première de son sous-développement intellectuel.[15]

Probably, Fu'ād Zakariyyā' is too optimistic regarding the Western attitude to realize rationalism in every field of common life:

> Certes, en Occident aussi, la production scientifique avait pour destinataire initial une petite élite; mais une fois reconnue par celle-ci, elle s'est diffusée peu à peu au sein de couches de plus en plus larges et, sous une forme plus ou moins élaborée, a fini par faire partie du sens commun. Rien de tel dans la *turāth* arabo-musulman: aucun de ses produits n'a accédé à ce statut de culture de masse qui fait que l'on dit par exemple du Français qu'il est cartésien.[16]

If Fu'ād Zakariyyā' is right, all the Western world would be perfect, without racism or dogmatic troubles, in a natural state of paradise, with science solving every problem and granting everyone a happy and affluent life. But hypostatization and mythologization of an assumed absolute truth – either secularism or scientific rationalism – become themselves a kind of *taqlīd*.

Zakī Najīb is more concerned with salvation – or at least a reconsideration – of his Islamic background. He is a "logical positivist", so that it is only natural that he stresses the importance of logic. He claims that Arab Classical thinkers turned their attention to Aristotle's rational solutions immediately after him;[17] meanwhile, he argues, quoting Descartes and Francis Bacon, that Western rationalism was able to develop to a great extent scientific and technological progress[18] – a thing Islam cannot do. Islam remained backward with respect to this astonishing scientific advance for several reasons. First of all, the Islamic world witnessed too many oppressive and autocratic political regimes, where freedom of expression and ideas were forbidden. As an example, the author tells the story of Ibn Ḥanbal and the *miḥnah* under al-Ma'mūn's caliphate.[19] Moreover, too often the (dead) past ruled over the (living) present ("*Sulṭān al-māḍī 'alā'al-ḥāḍir huwa bi-mathābat al-sayṭarah yafriduhā al-mawtī 'alā'al-aḥiyā'*"). Francis Bacon and his doctrine of *idola theatri* (*awhām al-masraḥ*) are used[20] to prove that belief (*al-wahm*) distracted the Muslim from true thought.

After a rather tough condemnation of dead heritage, Zakī Najīb asks a twofold question: how can we connect Arab with Western thought? How can we relate ancient Arab thought to the contemporary?

The most original section of Zakī Najīb's work is when he points out the *dynamism* of reason and philosophy: this dynamism means, from an epistemological point of view, the passage from the known to the unknown, the passage from the past to the present in a comprehensive refoundation of sciences. Zakī Najīb writes: "As to the definition of intellect I wish to note . . ., it is a movement by which I am carried from witness to witnessed, from proof to proven, from premise to consequence . . ., The most important word in this definition is 'movement' [*ḥarakah*]."[21]

Philosophy is the disclosure of secrets, receptiveness of novelty ("*al-falsafah hiya ikhrāj al-asās al-kāminah fī afkārinā*"),[22] so that the greatest goal of intellectual effort must be its encounter with modern science: this is, of course, the goal of Arab intellectual ambitions which started from the very beginning of the last century ("*nasha'at lanā ṣirā'āt fikriyyah jadīdah . . . wa ahammu tilka al-ṣirā'āt al-fikriyyah . . . hiya ṭarīqat al-liqā' allatī nawā'im fihā bayna 'ulūm ḥadīthah*").[23] Obviously, the Arabs' task could be made easier through the renaissance of intellect (*al-'aql*) which moulded the best Classical Muslim culture. Indeed, Muslim thought can go beyond Western achievements; as M. Chartier put it: "la connaissance sensible, cheminant à pas de raison, qui a pour mission de scruter et d'organiser le monde des phénomènes, et une connaissance extra-sensible, qui a un rôle de témoin de ces idéaux sans lequels l'homme perdrait de vue le but ultime de sa vie".[24]

This last conclusion does not prevent secularists from pointing out that the innovation of Zakī Najīb's views consists in their distance from tradition. Celebrating the thinker after his death (Zakī Najīb died in September 1993), Naṣr Ḥāmid Abū Zayd wrote that he was aware of the "living and energetic knowledge of the West against the frozen and stagnant knowledge of *turāth*". In Zakī Najīb's opinion, *turāth* would not be able to solve even one problem ("*al-turāth lā yaḥullu mushkilah wāḥidah min mushkilātinā*") concerning freedom (*ḥurriyyah*) and successful entrance in the epoch of science and industry (*dukhūl fī 'aṣr al-'ilm wa'l-ṣinā'ah*).[25]

Moḥammed Arkoun is perhaps more refined than Zakī Najīb in writing that Islamic thought leaves a large area of shadow in its *impensée.* This "impensée dans la pensée islamique [est] sur tous les mouvements de pensée qui ont accompagné, en Occident, la naissance et l'irrésistible croissance de la civilisation industrielle". Arkoun argues that "on ne peut entretenir un lien vivant avec la *turāth* si l'on n'assume *totalement* la modernité; inversement, on ne peut contribuer de façon originale à travailler la modernité, si l'on continue à confondre *turāth* historique et *turāth* mythologique".[26] This is not the place to discuss Arkoun's thesis thoroughly; while I admit I do not fully agree with him, I suggest that the main fault of thinkers like Fu'ād Zakariyyā' and Zakī Najīb is just the confusion between historical and mythological *turāth*. I know I am going far beyond Arkoun's intentions in pointing to a historical *turāth* which is both rich and constructive: the world of Islam was erected on its basis. Mythological *turāth*, on the contrary, consist of apparently anachronistic rules and impositions many philosophers regarded as oppressive and restricting the free development of Islamic thought. But it is just a mythology, like other mythologies: science, technology and uninterrupted progress (the so-called "magnifiche sorti e progressive", in the words of a sceptical Italian poet, Giacomo Leopardi). In any case, I think that the crisis of contemporary Islamic thought cannot be reduced to a mere crisis of Islamic philosophy, because we must ackowledge that its problem is essentially political and its solution essentially revolutionary, assuming revolution is a radical change of the present situation. We would have to consider in a different light Nasser's political experience, in admitting that the 1967 disaster signified the closure of a whole historical epoch, but also that Nasser's defeat and the failed improvement of social and economic situation in the Arab countries created more scope for an Islamic radical challenge.

Another major negative feature of both Fu'ād Zakariyyā''s and Zakī Najīb's thought lies perhaps in their inadequate awareness of the criticism advanced against the new positivism and scientific objectivity by epistemological anarchism (Feyerabend) and the so-called "weak thought", which means the denial of a strong, metaphysical dominion of being and absolute reason.[27] Feyerabend, on the other hand, argues that unanimity of opinions is appropriate for mythological thought where tyranny and oppression are destroying free scientific research: a real objectivity in knowledge needs a multiplicity of opinions and truths; no one can claim to master any truth, because humanism involves a variety of contending views.[28] In the same new logical positivism (we can think of Wittgenstein), we often discover a very questionable rationalism underlying either the inability of answering philosophical and scientific questions (we must be silent when we cannot speak about something)[29] or the contradictory multiplicity and irreducibility of psychological and linguistic world pictures.[30]

Fu'ād Zakariyyā' and Zakī Najīb were so concerned with establishing a convergence between Arab thought's values and Western ones, coupled with an enthusiastic evaluation of the latter, that they let pass unobserved the most striking difficulties the same Western philosophical tradition found in itself. After Nietzsche no one can accept philosophical statements being sure of asserting, beyond any doubt, epistemological truth and morality.

In Ḥasan Ḥanafī Islamic rationalism finds a phenomenological and anthropological solution which is perhaps the only really "open" version, being "aimed at". We have a sound reference in Husserl's *Krisis des europäischen Wissenschaften und die transzendentale Phänomenologie* and in his theory of phenomenological *telos*. The Italian editor of this important work, Enzo Paci, wrote that "if we admit that truth is reality, [oppressive] apparatuses will win power. If we let unreal truth become in ourselves the life of truth, victory will be of all the men in the world."[31] It means that phenomenological truth alone is our way of improving the social situation and erasing injustice.

Ḥanafī's phenomenological teleology is built on two main aspects: firstly, a new concept of *tawḥīd* intended as the anthropological realization of social justice: God is a principle of equality to whom men are moving in their historical praxis ("*Allāh huwa al-mubda' al-wāḥid al-shāmil alladhī yatasāwā amāmihi jamī' al-'ibād fa'l-shahādah laysat qawlan bal 'amalan wa mu'āraḍah wa thawrah*")[32]; unicity (*tawḥīd*) means the process of unification just as liberty is liberation[33]; and, secondly, the concept of intersubjectivity as pluralization of cultural subjects[34]: against colonialism, exploitation and the double opposition of Orientalism and Westernization, "life in horizontal" means that all the makers of culture and science must claim their right to be acknowledged as active subjects of history. This is why Ḥanafī wrote that

> L'Islam est la religion révolutionnaire par excellence. Le *tawḥīd* est un processus d'unification dans le futur du fait accompli dans le passé. Il veut dire la liberté de conscience, le rejet de la peur, la fin de l'hypocrisie et du dédoublement. "Dieu est grand" signifie la destruction du despotisme. Tous les êtres humains sont égaux et toutes les nations sont égales devant le même principe . . . La vocation de l'homme est de transformer la parole de Dieu, la révélation, comme structure idéale du monde.[35]

Ḥanafī argues that the ancients (*al-qudamā'*) were wrong in seeking to obtain a scientific knowledge of God's Essence, because God is the Absolute (*muṭlaq*) and sciences are accustomed to transform the absolute into the relative ("*al-'ilm mawḍū'uhu wa minhajuhu wa ghāyatuhu taḥwīl li'l-muṭlaq ilā nisbī*").[36] Even though we wish to insist on the relativity of science, this statement does not imply a defeat of reason. Indeed, it is strictly Islamic, because it places God's reality beyond any theoretical grasp. This statement clearly leads to an active transformation of pure philosophy into ethical and anthropological engagement (*'amal*). The same God is praxis: "*Allāh laysa taṣawwuran bal fi'l laysa naẓaran – Logos – bal 'amal – praxis –*".[37]

What is Ḥanafī's philosophical attitude to Westernization? An intriguing historical issue arises here, or rather the issue of historiography and Orientalism. In general, he sharply criticizes historical method when applied to philosophy, on the ground that this method tends to throw doubt on speculation (*naẓar*). Ḥanafī's criticism hits in particular Western Orientalism. Orientalists are not able to give up their "national" (*qawmī*) concept of science, which is obviously "European". Orientalism, for instance, by applying a surreptitious historical method (*minhaj ta'rīkhī*) distorts the thought of men like Suhrawardī, willing to concentrate on his Greek or Indian or anyway external inspirations and so ignoring his Islamic and orthodox background.[38]

In his last important work, *Muqaddimah fī 'ilm al-istighrāb* ("Introduction to the Science of Westernization"), Ḥanafī tries to pave the way for a factual transfer from the illusory knowledge of an alien world (the East) by the "Orientalists" – officiating priests of a transcendental "Orientalism" – to an analogous, equally illusory, knowledge of the West as another alien reality, analysable by "Westernization".[39] Indeed, the main philosophical and ideological problem to overcome is the surreptitious opposition between the *ego* (*anā*) and the *aliud* (*ākhir*), a distinction meaningful only from the point of view of a triumphant and victorious culture over the others (the culture of imperialist Western countries over Africa and Asia for instance), while a real phenomenological perspective implies an intersubjectivity leading to a true transcendence of exploitation and racism.[40]

Secondly, the history of Western philosophy, which Ḥanafī draws from Greek antiquity to contemporary times, shows a progressive decadence and atomization of its coherence. The last stage would be the dissolution of European conscience with the triumph of an irrationalistic mainstream.

In order to demonstrate this assumption, Ḥanafī argues for a cyclical development of history and historical thought, both in the Western world and in the Oriental (and especially Islamic) world, in successive periods of about seven hundred years. In Islam, the first phase went from Hijrah to Ibn Khaldūn, who represented the critical consciousness of Islamic culture at its apogee. After a second phase of decadence corresponding more or less to Ottoman supremacy and failure and subsequent modernization and submission to Westernizing patterns, the fifteenth century of Islam (1400 A.H. corresponds to A.D. 1980) marked the setting forth of a new *nahḍah*. "We are observing," Ḥanafī writes, "the end of the second and the beginning of the third stage, the end of colonialism [*isti'mār*] and the beginning of liberation [*taḥarrur*]. We are contemporaneous to the movements of liberation and we witnessed Arab revolution, along with Palestinian loss."[41] Of course, temporal boundaries must not be kept too strictly, because history is a changing process; but general patterns are clearly discernible.

Comparatively, Western history, which started six hundred or more years before the Muslim era, is now living at the very beginning of decadence entering its third phase. After attaining the peak of power in the nineteenth and twentieth centuries, the Western (but we can say perhaps better "Christian") world is running into a descending parabola coinciding with Islamic awakening and rising. The ideological and philosophical crisis of Western outlook and life is proved by the great hold on common and intellectual minds of nihilism (*falsafāt al-'adam*).

The death of God (*lāhūt mawt al-ilāh*), the death of spirit (*al-mawt fi'l-rūḥ*) in arts and culture "gave expression to a hidden crisis of European consciousness" ("*tu'abbir 'an azmati dafīnah fi'l-wa'y al-ūrubī*").[42] Husserl was aware of this emergency and declared it in his *Krisis*, arguing that the crisis of European sciences is properly the crisis of European humanism ("*azmat al-wa'y al-ūrubī bi'l-insāniyyah*").[43]

In these circumstances, what room is there for the Third World in general and the Islamic world in particular? In the Third World, we have recently experienced national independence and the construction of autonomous economic systems, among which Ḥanafī cites Arabic socialism as a third way between capitalism and Marxist socialism.[44] Indeed, Ḥanafī applies to the Third World a deeper awareness of history, because China and India, Persia, Mesopotamia and Egypt developed in seven thousand years of uninterrupted tradition and civilization.[45] In the new phase of history now starting, however, those cultures and civilizations, which from the Middle Ages moved from East to West, must come back to the East again: this is the promise of a new world.[46]

This analysis underlines the importance of dialogue in a clear distinction of roles and responsibilities. This dialogue must be aware, anyway, that the Islamic mind is seeking a new resolution and probably, when achieved, the new resolution will bring forth a complete *bouleversement* of intellectual outlook and political conditions.

NOTES

1 S. Quṭb, *Social Justice in Islam*, trans. J. B. Hardie (New York, 1980): 15–16.

2 I choose, among the many titles I could quote, I. Madkhur, *L'"Organon" d'Aristote dans le monde arabe* (Paris, 1934), 'Abd al-Raḥmān Badāwī, *Histoire de la philosophie en Islam* (Paris, 1972); 'Ātif al-'Irāqī, *Thawrah al-'aql fi'l-falsafat al-'arabiyyah* (Cairo, 1984).

3 M. 'Abduh, *Risālat al-Tawḥīd: Exposé de la religion musulmane*, trans. B. Michel and M. Abdel Raziq (Paris, 1978): 21–6 *passim*.

4 R. Caspar, "Le Renouveau du Mo'tazilisme", *Mélanges de l'Institut Dominicain d'Etudes Orientale du Caire*, 4 (1957): 141–201.

5 A. Amīn, *Ḍuḥā al-islām* (preface by Ṭaha Ḥusayn) (Beirut, n.d.), 3: 68.

6 See for example C. Bouamrane: "On ne saurait faire tout uniment des Mu'tazilites les 'rationalistes' de l'Islam. . . . Leur visée est d'abord apologétique; ils sont par là d'authentiques *mutakallimūn*. . . . La valeur accordée à la raison ne signifie pas qu'ils lui reconnaissent un droit absolu face à la révélation" (C. Bouamrane and Louis Gardet, *Panorama de la pensée islamique* (Paris, 1984): 42.

7 M. Iqbāl, *The Reconstruction of Religious Thought in Islam* (Lahore, 1989).

8 M. Iqbāl, *Poema Celeste (Jāvēdnamā)*, Italian trans. A. Bausani (Bari, 1965): 301; and see p. 87.

9 Iqbāl, *Reconstruction*: 131.
10 P. Vatikiotis, *The History of Modern Egypt* (London, 1991): 240.
11 P. Vatikiotis, *Islam and the State* (London and New York, 1987): I quote from the Italian translation, *Islam: stati senza nazioni* (Milan, 1993): 69.
12 See 'Abd al-Ḥalīm Maḥmūd, *al-Tafkīr al-falsafī fi'l-islām* (Cairo, 1984).
13 'Abd al-Ḥalīm Maḥmūd, *The Creed of Islam* (London, 1978): 34–5.
14 F. Zakariyyah, *Laïcité ou Islamisme* (Paris and Cairo, 1989).
15 *Ibid.*: 38 and 48.
16 *Ibid.*: 55.
17 Zakī Najīb Maḥmūd, *Tajdīd al-fikr al-'arabī* (Beirut and Cairo, 1982): 313; see also p. 317.
18 *Ibid.*: 23–4.
19 *Ibid.*: 42ff. More or less the same remark in F. Zakariyyah, *Laïcité ou Islamisme*: 49.
20 Zakī Najīb Maḥmūd, *Tajdīd al-fikr al-'arabī*: 51.
21 *Ibid.*: 310.
22 *Ibid.*: 263.
23 *Ibid.*: 269.
24 M. Chartier, "La Rencontre Orient–Occident dans la pensée de trois philosophes egyptiens contemporains", *Oriente Moderno*, 53 (1973): 641.
25 N. H. Abū Zayd in *al-Muṣawwar*, 3598 (24 September 1993): 44–6.
26 M. Arkoun, *Pour une critique de la raison islamique* (Paris, 1984): 59 and 57.
27 See G. Vattimo and P. A. Rovatti (eds) *Il pensiero debole* (Milan, 1983): "la razionalità deve, al proprio interno, depotenziarsi, cedere terreno, non aver timore di indietreggiare verso una supposta zona d'ombra, non restare paralizzata dalla perdita del riferimento luminoso, unico e stabile, cartesiano. 'Pensiero debole' è allora certamente una metafora. . . . E' un modo di dire provvisorio, forse anche contradditorio. Ma segna un percorso, indica un senso di percorrenza: è una via che si biforca rispetto alla ragione-dominio, comunque ritradotta e camuffata. . . . Una via che dovrà continuare a biforcarsi" (p. 10).
28 P. K. Feyerabend, "Against Method", paragraph 3, in M. Radner and S. Winokur (eds) *Minnesota Studies in the Philosophy of Science*, 4 (Minneapolis, 1970): 17–130.
29 L. Wittgenstein, *Tractatus logico-philosophicus*, 1st ed. (London, 1921), paragraph 7.
30 L. Wittgenstein, *Philosophische Untersuchungen* (Oxford, 1953).
31 E. Paci, "Prefazione" to E. Husserl, *La crisi delle scienze europee e la fenomenologia trascendentale* (Milan, 1975): 18.
32 Ḥ. Ḥanafī, *al-Yamīn wa'l yasār fi'l-fikr al-dīnī*, fifth volume of *al-Dīn wa'l-thawrah fī Miṣr* (Cairo, 1989): 54.
33 *Al-Ḥurriyyah taḥarrur* in Ḥ. Ḥanafī, *Min al-'aqīdah ila'l-thawrah* (Cairo, 1988), 3: 380.
34 See my interview with the author, "Per una nuova lettura dell'Islām moderno: intervista ad H. H.", *Islàm: Storia e Civiltà*, vol. 39, (2) (1992): 69–79.
35 Ḥ. Ḥanafī, "Des Idéologies modernistes à l'Islam révolutionnaire", *Peuples Mediterranéens*, 21 (October–December 1982): 12.
36 *Min al-'aqīdah ila'l-thawrah*, 1: 82.

37 *Ibid.*: 88.
38 All these arguments are found in Ḥ. Ḥanafī, *Ḥikmah al-ishrāq wa fī nūmīnūlūjiyā*, included in *Dirāsāt islāmiyyah* (Beirut, 1982): esp. 226–8. But the author deals with them also in his thesis *Les Méthodes d'exégèse: essai sur la science des fondaments de la compréhension ('ilm uṣūl al-fiqh)* (Cairo, 1965): cxli–cl.
39 Ḥ. Ḥanafī, *Muqaddimah fī 'ilm al-istighrāb* (Cairo, 1991).
40 *Ibid.*: 695ff.
41 *Ibid.*: 698.
42 *Ibid.*: 715.
43 *Ibid.*: 718.
44 *Ibid.*: 735.
45 *Ibid.*: 737.
46 *Ibid.*: 768.

CHAPTER 66

Turkey

Mehmet Aydin

HISTORICAL BACKGROUND

It seems that the traditional Turkish attitude to philosophy in general and to Islamic philosophy in particular never freed itself from the influence of al-Ghazzālī's well-known criticism of the *falāsifah*. It was at least partly due to this influence that one can see a theologico-philosophical endeavour which one might loosely name as "the *tahāfut* tradition" – a tradition which was largely based on *Tahāfut al-falāsifah* ("The Incoherence of the Philosophers") and which took little notice of the *Tahāfut al-tahāfut* of Ibn Rushd. This does not mean, however, that al-Ghazzālī's criticism of the *falāsifah* was accepted uncritically.

In the *madrasahs*, *ḥikmah* in its very broad sense was included within the Ottoman educational system. The great Fatih Sultan Mehmed (ninth/fifteenth century), whose keen interest in philosophy, religion, art and education in general is well documented in historical studies, ordered Muṣliḥuddin Muṣṭafa Hocazade and 'Alāuddin 'Alī Ṭūsī to re-examine the main points of the philosophical debate elaborated in al-Ghazzālī's *Tahāfut* and bring some clarification concerning the *falsafah–dīn* (philosophy–faith) relationship. This historical event proves that the Ottoman intellectuals were still very sensitive towards the theological frontiers of Classical Islamic philosophy.

Both scholars took their duties very seriously and each wrote an independent *tahāfut*. Although the one written by Hocazade was considered somewhat deeper and subtler, both *tahāfuts* were well received by the Sultan and the *madrasah* circle.

About a century later Kemāl Paşazade, also known as İbn Kemal (940/1533), wrote a fairly detailed commentary upon the work of Hocazade. This work, which is entitled *Ḥāshiyah 'alā tahāfut al-falāsifah*, is not a mere commentary; it takes all the main arguments of the three *tahāfut*s (al-Ghazzālī's, Ibn Rushd's and Hocazade's), explains them very carefully and puts forward criticisms. There is a study of this work by Ahmet Arslan (Professor of Philosophy at İzmir Ege University). Both this study and the Turkish translation of Kamāl Paşazade's *Ḥāshiyah* were published by the Turkish Ministry of Culture (Ankara, 1987).

Arslan is an ex-student of Mübahat Küyel (Professor of Philosophy at Ankara University), whose pioneering efforts constituted the main source of contemporary interest in the "*tahāfut* tradition". She wrote her doctorate studies on *Üç Tahafüt Bakımından Felsefe Din Münasebetleri* ("The Relations Between Philosophy and Religion from the Point of View of the three *tahāfut*s") and paved the way for the revitalization of the old Turkish interest in the common problems of the *tahāfut*s of al-Ghazzālī and Ibn Rushd. This work, published by Ankara University Press in 1956, still stands as a leading contribution to the study of Islamic philosophy.

There is also a work on Hocazade's *tahāfut* entitled *Ta'liqāt 'alā tahāfut al-falāsifah li Hocazade* by Muḥyiddin Muḥammed Karabağī (d. 1535). Another work with similar content is being studied in Ankara University by Ülker Öktem. This work was written by Mestcizāde 'Abdullah Efendi (1148/1735) and is entitled *al-Masālik fi'l-khilafiyyāt bayn al-mutakallimīn wa'l-ḥukāmā'*.

'Alī Ṭūsī's *Tahāfut*, whose full title is *Kitāb al-ẓuhr [al-Ẓāhirah] fi'l-muḥākamah bayn al-Ghazzālī wa'l-ḥukamā'*, was thoroughly studied and translated into Turkish by Recep Duran, of Ankara University. This work also came out among the publications of the Turkish Ministry of Education in 1980 with the title *Tehafütü'l-felasife (Kitabu'z-Ẓuhr).*

There are more books with similar content written by Ottoman theologians in different periods. When these works are edited and studied, the main contribution of the Turkish "*tahāfut* tradition" to the history of Islamic philosophy will be well documented and thus clearly understood.

In spite of this Classical and modern Turkish interest in some major theological and philosophical problems, Islamic philosophy, especially the metaphysical aspect of it, had never become popular in the Ottoman educational system. As has been pointed out above, the Ghazzālīan suspicion of philosophy has always been kept alive in the intellectual life of the nation.

Fortunately, the situation was quite different with theology (*kalām*). *Tafsīr, Ḥadīth, fiqh* and *kalām* were considered the chief disciplines of "Islamic sciences" (*'Ulūm-i İslamiyye*) and this *kalām* was – perhaps it is needless to point out – the *philosophical* theology of the post-Ghazzālian period: the theological views of Fakhr-al-Dīn al-Rāzī, Sayf al-Dīn al-'Āmīdī and others. It was mainly through this theological channel that philosophical ideas managed to survive in the *madrasah* educational system.

Owing to its direct bearing on theology and jurisprudence, logic had a safe place in that system. A similar position existed for ethics as well. It was studied and taught not as a moral philosophy but as an *'ilm al akhlāq* whose "Islamically acceptable form" was given by al-Ghazzālī in the relevant section of *Iḥyā 'ulūm al-dīn*. Following the path well trodden by such great Persian moral philosophers as Ṭusī, Dawānī and others, the Ottoman thinker Kınalızade 'Alī Efendi (916/1510–980/1572) wrote his *Akhlāq-ı 'alā'ī*, which became a textbook for centuries. The book is interesting and important not because of its contribution to the tradition of *tahdhīb al-akhlāq* but because of its sociological implications for the most brilliant period of the Ottoman history.

While talking of indirect influence, one should not ignore the importance of Ibn 'Arabī's system upon Turkish intellectuals. In this respect, the place of Sadreddin Konevi is very important.

TURKISH STUDIES IN THE AREA OF MANUSCRIPTS

Islamic philosophy proper (falsafah)

Al-Fārābī

"Farabi'nin Bazı Mantık Eserleri" ("Some Logical Works of al-Fārābī: Tawṭī'ah, Fuṣūl, Qiyās al-ṣaghīr"), ed. with Turkish translation and French summary by Mübahat Küyel, *Dil ve Tarih Coğrafya Fakültesi Dergisi*, 16 (3–4) (1958): 165–258.

"Farabi'nin Şerait al-Yakīni" ("Al-Fārābī's Sharā'it al-Yaqīn"), ed. with Turkish translation (and an introduction in French and Turkish) by Mübahat Küyel, *Araştırma*, 1: 195–204.

"Farabi'ye Atfedilen Küçük Bir Eser" ("A Small Treatise Attributed to al-Fārābī"), ed. with Turkish and French translation by Mübahat Küyel, *Araştırma*, 3, (1965) (1967): 57–63.

"Fārābī'nin 'Peri Hermaneias' Muhtasarı" ("The Summary of al-Fārābī's 'Peri Hermaneias'"), ed. with Turkish translation and notes by Mübahat Küyel, *Araştırma*, 4 (1966) (1968): 33–85.

Yaḥyā İbn 'Adī

"Yaḥya b. 'Adi'nin Varlıklar Hakkındaki Makalesi" ("Yaḥya İbn 'Adī's Article on Beings": *Maqālah fi'l-mawjūdāt*), ed. with Turkish translation and notes by Mübahat Küyel, pp. 145–54: Arabic text pp. 155–7.

"Yaḥya b. 'Adi ve Neşredilmemiş Bir Risalesi" ("Yahya İbn 'Adi and one of his Unedited Opuscula"), ed. with Turkish translation and notes by Mübahat Küyel, *Dil ve Tarih Coğrafya Fakültesi Dergisi*, 14(1–2) (1956) pp. 87–102.

Arabic text: *Maqālah fī buḥūth al-arba'ah al-'ilmiyyah 'an ṣinā'at al-manṭiq*, pp. 94, 98.

İbn Sīnā

İbn Sīnā Risaleleri ("Several Opuscula"), ed. with partial French translation by Hilmi Ziya Ülken and Ahmet Ateş (Istanbul, 1953).

Er-Risālah fī-māhiyah al-'ishq ("On the Nature of Love"), ed. with Turkish translation by Ahmet Ateş (Istanbul, 1953).

Islamic theology (kalām)

Al-Ghazzālī

Al-Iqtiṣād fi'l i'tiqād, ed. Hüseyin Atay and İbrahim Agah Çubukçu (Ankara, 1962). Turkish translation by Kemal Işık. *İtikad'da Orta Yol* (Ankara, 1971).

Māturīdī, *İslam Akaidine Dair Eski Metinler* ("Some Old Texts Concerning Islamic Belief"), ed. with Turkish translation by Yusuf Ziya Yörükan (Istanbul, 1953).

Fuzūlī, *Maṭla' al-i'tiqād fī ma'rifat al-mabdā' wa'l-ma'ād*, ed. Muḥammed ibn Tawit al-Tanji (Ankara, 1962). Turkish translation by Esad Coşan and Kemal Isık (Ankara, 1962).

Kadī Iyāz ibn Mūsā, *al-I'lām bi-ḥudūd qawā'id al-Islām*, ed. Muḥammed ibn Tawit al-Tanji (Rabat, 1964).

Sa'duddin Taftāzānī *Sharḥ al-'aqā'id*, ed. with Turkish translation by Süleyman Uludağ (Istanbul, 1980).

es-Subkī, Tacuddin Ebi Nesr Abdulvehhab ibn Ali ibn Abdi'l-kāfi Māturīdī, *Al-Sayf al-mashhūr fī sharḥ 'Aqīdah Abī Manṣūr*, ed. with Turkish translation by M. Saim Yeprem (Istanbul, 1989).

Sufism (taṣawwuf)

Ibn 'Arabī, *Bulghā fil-ḥikmah*, ed. Nihad Keklik (Istanbul, 1966).

al-Baqlī, *Kitāb mashrab bi'l-arwāḥ*, ed. Nazif Hoca (Istanbul, 1974).

Ibn Khaldūn, *Shifā' al-sā'il li-tahdhīb al-masā'il*, ed. Muḥammed ibn Tawit al-Tanjī (Istanbul, 1953). Turkish translation by Süleyman Uludağ (Istanbul, 1977).

Sulamī, *Sülemī'nin risaleleri* ("Some Opuscula of Sulamī"), ed. by Süleyman Ateş (Ankara, 1977).

Sulamī, *Kitab al-futuwwah*, ed. Süleyman Ateş (Ankara, 1981).

Konawī, *Konevi'nin Kırk Hadis Şerhi* ("Commentary on Forty *āḥādith* by al-Konawī"), ed. H. Kamil Yılmaz (Istanbul, 1990).

BIBLIOGRAPHY

Ankara Üniversitesi İlahiyat Fakültesi Yayınları Bibliyoğrafyası, eds Ahmet Koca *et al.* (Ankara, 1978).
Aydın, Mehmet, *Turkish Contribution to Philosophy* (Ankara, 1985).
— "İslam Felsefesi", *Büyük İslam Tarihi*, Çağ Yayınları ed. Kenan Seyithanoğlu (Istanbul 1989): 119–206.
Küyel, Mübahat, *Türkiyede Cumhuriyet Döneminde Felsefe*, (Ankara, 1976).

(Adnan Aslan assisted us with this chapter. (O.L. and S.H.N.))

CHAPTER 67

South-east Asia

Zailan Moris

There are approximately 200 million Muslims in south-east Asia today in the area stretching from southern Thailand, through Malaysia, Singapore, Brunei and Indonesia to the southern Philippines. The Malays constitute the predominant ethnic group of the Muslim population in this part of the world.

The precise date of the introduction of Islam to south-east Asia, or, more specifically, the Malay–Indonesian archipelago, and the place of origin of the Muslims who brought the Islamic religion to this region are not known with certainty, owing to the lack of historical records and data. Consequently, several theses exist on both questions.[1] However, it is evident that by the seventh/thirteenth century there was a definite Muslim presence in north Sumatra[2] and by the eighth/fourteenth century in Trengganu on the north-east coast of Malaysia.[3] In A.D. 1414 the ruler of Malacca embraced Islam and henceforth, until its conquest by the Portuguese in A.D. 1511, Malacca joined Pasai in north Sumatra to become an important centre of Islamic learning and propagation of the Islamic religion throughout the Malay–Indonesian archipelago. After the fall of Malacca, the Muslims moved their centre to Acheh and, like Pasai and Malacca, Acheh very quickly became an important centre of international trade and also of Islam.[4]

The period between the tenth/sixteenth century and the eleventh/seventeenth century witnessed the intense Islamization process of the Malay–Indonesian archipelago, as demonstrated by the tremendous amount of literature produced in the Malay language on a wide range of religious matters covering the fields of Islamic Law (*Sharī'ah*), jurisprudence (*fiqh*), rational theology (*'ilm al-kalām*) and Sufism (*taṣawwuf*).[5] The intense Islamization process which took place during these two centuries is directly related to the presence and activities in Acheh of certain religious scholars or *'ulamā'* from Mecca, Yemen and

Gujerat.[6] These scholars not only brought with them important Islamic texts from their homeland but also taught and held discussions on theology, metaphysics and Sufism. Their intellectual activities and discussions made a tremendous impact on the local Muslim population and were instrumental in the production of a vast amount of writings in Malay on matters related to rational theology, metaphysics and *taṣawwuf*. Among the best examples of such writings and the more profound and philosophical in nature are those of the Sufi poet and metaphysician, Ḥamzah Fanṣūrī (d. *c.* 1000/1600), the Sufi Shaykh, Shams al-Dīn al-Sumātrānī (d. 1040/1630) the Sufi and *'ālim* Nūr al-Dīn al-Rānīrī (d. 1077/1666) and the Sufi saint (*walī*) 'Abd al-Ra'ūf al-Singkelī (d. 1104/1693).[7]

As a result of the fact that Sufism played a dominant role in the Islamization of the Malay–Indonesian archipelago, coupled with the natural predisposition of the Malays, who are more aesthetic than philosophical, there did not develop among the Muslims in south-east Asia a distinct tradition of *falsafah* or *ḥikmah* such as that to be found, for example, in Persia and Andalusia.[8] Philosophical reflections on the nature of reality, the nature and destiny of humanity, the origin and structure of the universe and ethics, for example, are to be found mainly in the writings of the Sufis, the seekers after the veritable experience and knowledge (*ma'rifah*) of God. Metaphysics, cosmology and epistemology can be considered to constitute the doctrinal or theoretical aspect of Sufism and ethics or, more specifically, spiritual ethics and psychology, the practical dimension of *taṣawwuf*. Thus, the following discussion of philosophy in Muslim south-east Asia focuses mainly on the discussions and treatments of subjects of philosophical import and significance, to be found in the writings of the Sufis of the Malay–Indonesian archipelago, especially during the eleventh/seventeenth century in which some of the most outstanding religious writings of this region were produced.

In the eleventh/seventeenth century, there flourished in Acheh a group of Malay Sufis commonly referred to as the Wujūdiyyah, who subscribed to Ibn 'Arabī's doctrine of *waḥdat al-wujūd*, or Unity of Being, and 'Abd al-Karīm al-Jīlī's doctrine of the Universal Man, or *al-insān al-kāmil*.[9] The leading figures of the *Wujūdiyyah* and their greatest exponents were Ḥamzah Fanṣūrī and Shams al-Dīn al-Sumātrānī. Opposed to the teachings of the Wujūdiyyah were the more orthodox Sufis and *'ulamā'*, of whom the most vocal and influential was Nūr al-Dīn al-Rānīrī, who considered the former as heretics (*zindīq*).[10] It is in the mystical writings of Ḥamzah Fanṣūrī and Shams al-Dīn al-Sumātranī and the polemics of Nūr al-Dīn al-Rānīrī against the former that we find some of the most profound expositions and treatments of topics of philosophical import, such as the nature of God – His Essence (*al-Dhāt*), Names and Attributes (*al-asmā' wa'l-ṣifāt*) and Acts (*al-af'āl*) – and His relation with creation or the Universe, the nature of the world (whether it is eternal or created?), the possibility, extent and limits of human knowledge of God and the "World of the Unseen", the nature of the human soul and issues related to its immortality, salvation and perfection.

In his prose works such as the *Sharāb al-'āshiqīn* and *Asrār al-'ārifīn*,[11] Fanṣūrī, the foremost Malay Sufi poet[12] and the first to produce systematic speculative works in the Malay language, discusses his views on the Attributes of God and their relation to the Divine Essence, the manifestation (*tajalliyyāt*) of the Pure Essence of God at the various levels or stages of determination and the relation between God and the created universe. Fanṣūrī's discussion of the indeterminate nature of the Divine Essence which is beyond conception and discourse, the manifestation of the Essence of God in descents (*tanazzulāt*) involving five stages or levels (*martabat*) of determinations and the unity of the being of the Universe and the Being of God reveal the unmistakable influence of Ibn 'Arabī's metaphysical thought.

Another leading exponent of the teachings of the *Wujūdiyyah* was Shams al-Dīn al-Sumātrānī. He was both the "Shaykh al-Islām" of Acheh and the spiritual teacher of the sultan of Acheh at the time of Sultan Iskandar Muda (d. A.D. 1636). Al-Sumātrānī wrote along the same doctrinal line as Fanṣūrī and was the most important commentator on the latter's works. In the *Nūr al-daqā'iq*, which is the first section of a part of a metaphysical work by al-Sumātrānī which has survived,[13] he expounds the doctrine of the seven grades of Being – extending from the Essence of God which is absolutely undetermined to the World of material bodies (*'ālam al-ajsām*) – which had come to characterize and be associated with the *Wujūdiyyah* school; and the esoteric doctrine of the Universal Man. Following 'Abd al-Karīm al-Jīlī, al-Sumātrānī considers the Universal Man as the central and ontologically comprehensive theophany (*tajallī*) or locus (*maẓhar*) of manifestation of the Names and Attributes of Allah. The doctrine of the Universal Man provides the metaphysical basis for the understanding of the famous *ḥadīth* of Prophet Muḥammad: "He who knows himself knows his Lord."

The most influential and intolerant critic of the *Wujūdiyyah* and of Fanṣūrī's and Sumātrānī's teachings in particular, who caused many of the writings of the school to be burnt and some of its members to be persecuted, was the orthodox Sufi and *'ālim*, Nūr al-Dīn al-Rānīrī. Al-Rānīrī criticized and opposed the teachings of the *Wujūdiyyah* on many grounds. However, the most fundamental issue of disagreement between them was the doctrine of the unity of the Being of God and the Universe which underlies much of the metaphysical outlook of the *Wujūdiyyah*.

In his polemical work, *Ḥujjat al-ṣiddīq lī daf' al-zindīq*, al-Rānīrī criticizes (although sometimes inaccurately)[14] the teachings of the *Wujūdiyyah*, especially that of Fanṣūrī and al-Sumātrānī on the relation between God and the Universe. In al-Rānīrī's understanding, Fanṣūrī's identification of the being of the Universe with the Being of God is tantamount to pantheism, which is contrary to Islamic teachings. According to al-Rānīrī, a definite distinction should be made between the contingent being of the Universe and the necessary Being of God. Al-Rānīrī argues that the assertion that the contingent being of the Universe is ultimately reducible to the Being of God logically implies that the Being of God is totally immanent in the being of the Universe, which consequently entails the negation of God's transcendence and the affirmation of the necessary and eternal nature of the being of the Universe.

Besides his polemical works, al-Rānīrī also wrote important texts on Sufism, such as the famous *Bustān al-salāṭīn*, which is a major work consisting of seven books, the first book dealing with the creation of heaven and earth.

In the Malay Islamic world, apart from the speculative writings of the Sufis discussed above, it is also of philosophical significance to mention certain Malay translations, commentaries and adaptations of important Sufi and theological works which enjoyed wide circulation among the Malays and which greatly influenced their religious and philosophical outlook. Noteworthy examples of such works are the Persian text *Tāj al-salāṭīn*[15] which was translated into Malay in the early eleventh/seventeenth century and discusses, among other things, the nature of God, humanity and the world and humanity as the central locus of manifestation of God's Names and Attributes; the Malay translation of the *Sharḥ al-'aqā'id al-nasafiyyah*,[16] which is Sa'd al-Dīn al-Taftāzānī's (d. 791/1388) famous commentary on Abū Ḥafs Najm al-Dīn al-Nasafī's (d. 537/1142) *'Aqā'id*, a comprehensive treatise on the articles of Islamic belief; the *Siyar al-salikīn ilā 'ibadah rabb al-'ābidīn*[17] by 'Abd al-Ṣamad Palimbānī (d. 1190/1776), which is an abridged translation and commentary on Abū Ḥamīd al-Ghazzālī's *magnum opus*, the *Iḥyā' 'ulūm al-dīn*; the *Minhaj al-'ābidīn ilā jannah rabb al-'ālamīn*[18] by Dā'ud ibn 'Abd Allāh al-Pātānī, which is a Malay translation and adaptation of al-Ghazzālī's *Iḥyā'*, *Kitāb al-asrār* and *Kitāb al-qurbān ila'Llāh*; the Malay translation and commentary on the esoteric *Kitāb al-Ḥikam*[19] of the Shadhīlī shaykh Ibn 'Aṭā' Allāh al-Iskandarī; and Kemas Fakr al-Dīn al-Palimbānī's mystical work, *al-Mukhtaṣar*,[20] which is an abridged translation and adaptation of Walī al-Raslān al-Dimishqī's treatise on Divine Unity, *al-Risālah fi'l-tawḥīd*.

The twelfth/eighteenth century witnessed the gradual decline of writings on *taṣawwuf*, especially those of a metaphysical nature, and the situation continued throughout the thirteenth/nineteenth century. In the fourteenth/twentieth century, with the reassertion of Islam in public life in Indonesia and Malaysia,[21] there has been a substantial increase in writings on Islam in general and on Sufism in particular.

Among contemporary Malay intellectuals, the figure who merits mention for his significant contribution and works on matters of philosophical concern and import is Syed Muḥammad Naquib al-Attas. The founder and director of the International Institute of Islamic Thought and Civilization in Kuala Lumpur, Malaysia, which is based on Islamic principles and concepts of knowledge and education, al-Attas has produced numerous works on Islam and Sufism in the Malay world, such as his major work *The Mysticism of Ḥamzah Fanṣūrī* and *The Oldest Known Malay Manuscript: a Sixteenth Century Malay Translation of the 'Aqā'id of al-Nasafī*.

Like many other Islamic thinkers of the fourteenth/twentieth century, two main concerns can be discerned in al-Attas' works: one, a critique of modernism and secularism and their pervasive and negative influence and effects on Muslim life and institutions and, two, an exposition and re-presentation of the Islamic understanding and treatment of certain fundamental aspects of human life and civilization such as religion, knowledge and education, ethics and morality. In his *Islam and Secularism*, al-Attas deals with the problem of secularization and its damaging effect on the Islamic world view which is based on the central doctrine of *al-tawḥid* or the Unity of Allah and the erosion of Islamic values and principles in such important areas as education and ethics. His treatise on *Islam: the Concept of Religion and the Foundation of Ethics and Morality* discusses the Islamic concept of religion and its implications for the ethical life and the Islamic understanding of such concepts as freedom and responsibility, order and justice at the level of the individual and community, and knowledge and salvation. In recent years, al-Attas has written several works on specific topics in Islamic philosophy such as *The Meaning and Experience of Happiness in Islam*, *The Nature of Man and the Psychology of the Human Soul*, *On Quiddity and Essence: an Outline of the Basic Structure of Reality in Islamic Metaphysics* and *Islam and the Philosophy of Science*.

In conclusion it can be stated that Islamic philosophical thought in south-east Asia is closely bound up with Sufism (*taṣawwuf*) and theology (*kalām*), and its development since the intense Islamicization process of the Malay–Indonesian archipelago in the tenth/sixteenth century indicates and reflects not only the particular situation and resources of the Malays and their understanding and interpretation of the Islamic religion but also the kinds of contacts and relations they had with Muslims in the other parts of the Islamic world, particularly the Middle East and India, and the types of works which have reached them and made an impact on their intellectual and religious lives.

NOTES

1 For a comprehensive discussion of this subject, see G. W. J. Drewes (1968): 433–59.

2 According to the Achehnese (Malay) chronicles, Islam was introduced into the northern tip of Sumatra around 506/1112 by an Arab missionary by the name of Sheikh 'Abdallah 'Ārif and became established in the area in 601/1204 when Johan Shah became its first sultan. In addition, Marco Polo, who was visiting north Sumatra in A.D. 1292, observed that the inhabitants were Muslims. S. M. N. al-Attas (1969): 11.

3 A stone inscription dated 702/1302 was discovered at Kuala Berang indicating Muslim settlement in the region. See H. S. Paterson (1924): 252–8.

4 In south-east Asia, Islam came through the channel of trade and missionary activities and there existed a close correspondence between economic prosperity and power and religious achievements. See A. H. Johns (1957): 11.

5 Among these writings is a genre referred to as "*kitāb* literature". They are systematic scholarly treatises written in Malay on *fiqh*, *kalām* and *taṣawwuf* and which draw heavily from Arabic sources and to a lesser extent Persian. It is through this genre of literature that Malay, which was previously a language very much lacking in abstract philosophical concepts and technical vocabulary in such fields as jurisprudence and theology, became transformed into a language capable of expressing and transmitting profound and abstract intellectual concepts and ideas to become the cultural and intellectual language of Islam in the region. See R. O. Winstedt (1958): 113–26; also V. I. Braginsky (Leiden, 1973): 29–43.

6 For the names of these *'ulamā'* and the texts they brought with them and their intellectual activities and interests, see R. Winstedt (1958): 112–13.

7 Several important studies, mainly in the form of doctoral dissertations submitted to the University of Leiden in the Netherlands, have been done on these figures. See, for example, D. A. Rinkes, *Abdoerraoef van Singkel* (1909), J. Doorenbos, *De Geschriften van Hamzah Pansoeri* (1933), C. van Nieuwenhuijze, *Shamsu'l-Din van Pasai* (1945); also S. al-Attas (1970) (originally a doctoral dissertation submitted to the London School of Oriental and African Studies in 1966).

8 During the pre-Islamic period in which the Malays practised Hinduism and later Buddhism, the more intellectual and philosophical dimensions of these religions were neglected in favour of the mythological aspect. For example, there was a preponderance of Malay translations of the epic, romantic and mythological literature of the Hindu religion such as that of the *Mahabharata* and *Ramayana* and hardly of the *Upanishads* or of important Hindu philosophical tracts. Furthermore, the mythological aspects of Hinduism were translated into the skilful art form of the *wayang* or shadow puppet theatre. Similiarly in the case of Buddhism, there did not emerge among the local Malays any Buddhist thinker or philosopher of note or writings on Buddhist philosophy, although in the fourth/tenth and fifth/eleventh centuries Sumatra was an important centre of Buddhism. See al-Attas (1969): 2–10. Also S. T. Alisjahbana (1966a and b).

9 On the Wujūdiyyah and their views, see Johns (1957).

10 Al-Ranīrī wrote two important works *Ḥujjat al-ṣiddīq li daf' al-zindīq* and *Tibyān fī ma'rifat al-adyān*, to refute the teachings of the *Wujūdiyyah* in general and of Ḥamzah Fanṣūrī in particular. For a comprehensive discussion of Rānīrī's refutation, see al-Attas (1966).

11 For a romanized Malay version and English translation of these works, see al-Attas (1970): 2.
12 Ḥamzah Fanṣūrī is well known for his mystical poems (*sh'ir*) which are of great beauty and power and which struck a new note in Malay poetry. See Winstedt (1958): 155–6; also G. W. J. Drewes and L. F. Brakel (1986).
13 Winstedt (1958): 119.
14 On some of al-Rānīrī's errors and inaccurate understanding of Fanṣūrī's metaphysical teachings, see al-Attas (1966): chapter 3.
15 Winstedt (1958): 114–16.
16 See al-Attas (1988).
17 P. Voorhoeve (1960): 92.
18 Winstedt (1958): 126.
19 R. L. Archer (1937).
20 A. H. Johns (1980): 173.
21 See J. Esposito (1987): Introduction.

BIBLIOGRAPHY

al-Attas, S. M. N. (1966) "Rānīrī and the *Wujūdiyyah* of the 17th Century Acheh", *Monographs of the Malaysian Branch Royal Asiatic Society*.
—— (1969) *Preliminary Statement on a General Theory of the Islamization of the Malay–Indonesian Archipelago* (Kuala Lumpur).
—— (1976) *The Mysticism of Ḥamzah Fanṣūrī* (Kuala Lumpur).
—— (1978) *Islam and Secularism* (Kuala Lumpur).
—— (1988) *The Oldest Known Malay Manuscript: A 16th Century Malay Translation of the 'Aqā'id of al-Nasafi* (Kuala Lumpur).
—— (1992) *Islam: the Concept of Religion and the Foundation of Ethics and Morality* (Kuala Lumpur).
Alisjahbana, S. T. (1966a) *Values as Integrating Forces in Personality, Society and Culture* (Kuala Lumpur).
—— (1966b) *Indonesia's Social and Cultural Revolution* (Kuala Lumpur).
Archer, R. L. (1937) "Muhammadan Mysticism in Sumatra", *Journal of the Malayan Branch Royal Asiatic Society*, 15(2).
Braginsky, V. I. (1973) *The System of Classical Malay Literature* (Leiden).
Drewes, G. W. J. (1968) "New Light on the Coming of Islam to Indonesia?", *Bijdragen tot de Taal-, Land-en Volkenkunde*, Deel 124.
Drewes G. W. J. and Brakel, L. F. (1986) *The Poems of Hamzah Fansuri* (Dordrecht).
Esposito, J. (ed.) (1987) *Islam in Asia* (Oxford).
Johns, A. H. (1957) "Malay Sufism", *Journal of the Malayan Branch Royal Asiatic Society*, 3(2).
—— (1980) "From Coastal Settlement to Islamic City: Islamization in Sumatra, the Malay Peninsula and Java", in J. J. Fox, (ed.) *Indonesia: the Making of a Culture* (Canberra).
Paterson, H. S. (1924) "An Early Inscription from Trengganu", *Journal of the Malayan Branch Royal Asiatic Society*, 2(3).
Voorhoeve, P. (1960) "Abd al-Ṣamad al-Palimbānī", *Encyclopaedia of Islam*, 1 (Leiden).
Winstedt, R. O. (1958) "A History of Classical Malay Literature", *Journal of the Malayan Branch Royal Asiatic Society*, 31(3).

X

Interpretation of Islamic philosophy in the West

CHAPTER 68

Orientalism and Islamic philosophy

Oliver Leaman

When Edward Said published his critique of Oriental studies (*Orientalism*, 1978) many of those who wrote on topics connected with the Middle East and its cultures felt that they had to respond to his arguments. He argued that many of the writers on the Middle East had found it difficult to avoid regarding the area and its people as exotic and essentially "other" from the point of view of the West, and that they incorporated colonialist assumptions in their treatment of the cultures of the area. Frequently he points to the negative stereotypes which Western scholars used when describing the people and practices of the region, and he suggests that these have their basis in the very unequal power relations which existed at that time, and indeed continue to exist today, between the West and the Middle East. Then of course one has to take into account the long history of conflict between the European countries and what was regarded as the threatening power of Islam, a conflict which extended over many centuries and which actually resulted in physical conflict on many occasions. Using the tools of the literary theorist, Said showed how difficult as a result was an objective treatment of the Middle East, and he argued that if an accurate picture is to be constructed it must involve an awareness by the writers themselves of the position from which they are writing. That is, they should acknowledge that they are not approaching the issues with complete scientific detachment but that they themselves are part and parcel of an ideological system which is bound to affect how they set about their work. This does not mean that it would be impossible to write accurately and well on the Middle East, but rather that, if such writing is to be possible, the writers must make the effort to understand how what they say and what they examine are aspects of the culture which they inhabit, a culture which is strongly characterized by negative attitudes to different customs and practices.

Said's book led to a lively debate in the world of Islamic studies in general, and many of the inhabitants of that world took great exception to his approach. Others were broadly supportive, and they incorporated what they took to be his message in their work. This is particularly true of some subjects, the study of European paintings of Middle Eastern themes, for example. The analysis of these paintings has been fruitfully deepened by an understanding of the sorts of attitudes towards women and the Middle East which were then current in Western society. Without understanding where the artists were coming from, it might be said, it is difficult to know how to interpret their work. They are not just painting pictures which are on topics that occur to them on a particular occasion. Rather, they are part of a cultural movement which sees people from the Middle East in a certain way, and that way enters into the style and content of the works of art. It is important to grasp the nature of the tradition within which they are working to understand what they are doing.

But it was not only those who wrote on art who took on board many of Said's ideas. His criticisms of historians, literary and cultural historians, analysts of religion and social scientists frequently struck home, and many practitioners in these areas came to reappraise the ways in which they went about their work. They sought to understand, and often challenge, the presuppositions which underlay their approach to their work. When one considers the large numbers of books which have emerged in recent years with titles dealing with "the Muslim mind" or "the Arab personality", perhaps not enough writers have considered the theoretical difficulties of their approach to the Islamic world, since many of these works are premissed on the axiom that there is a basic and deep distinction between Western forms of thought and life and those to be found in the Islamic world. The end of the Cold War and the need to find a new enemy has led to the rediscovery of "the threat of Islam" which has lain below the surface for many centuries in Western culture. Those impressed by the work of Edward Said would find the notion of an Eastern/Western, Christian/Muslim, Us/Them and Same/Other dichotomy running through forms of cultural expression highly problematic, and would seek to challenge it as a starting-point in scholarly work, by contrast with the sort of writing which has become so popular recently as a result of the desperate search by the West for a new bogey to fear and to challenge.

Said does not have much to say about philosophy in his seminal work, but it is clear that his arguments are relevant to the study of Islamic philosophy. The latter is often regarded by the commentators as not being the same as other sorts of philosophy, and so should be studied in diverse ways. Why? Sometimes it is argued that Islam had an enormous impact upon the structure of Islamic philosophy, and so one should not just study the arguments but also analyse the ways in which religious issues pervade those arguments, albeit surreptitiously and not openly. This seems to be a promising line, given that so many of the philosophers themselves make a sharp distinction between what is esoteric (*bāṭin*) and what is exoteric (*ẓāhir*), and often take care to express themselves in ways which will obscure their arguments from those for whom they are not intended. This view of the interpretation of Islamic philosophy has been outlined in the works of Leo Strauss, and his followers have utilized it throughout their approach to the area. Strauss considers a whole range of philosophy to contain a hidden message, one dominated by religious considerations, and he argues in many and varied ways that if we look at the texts in the right sort of way this feature becomes apparent. I have criticized this approach in the past, and its supporters and critics have produced fervent arguments to defend their respective views. What it is interesting to examine here are the Orientalist assumptions of the sort of view which Strauss advocates. The assumption is that Islamic philosophy should not be regarded as philosophy primarily, but more as a code which needs to be cracked in order to discover the opinions of the philosophers. It is seen as a form of literature which disguises the real opinions of its writers, and it is the job of the interpreter to find out what these real opinions are, to pierce the layers of concealment and uncover the genuine beliefs of the author.

It is certainly true that when one does philosophy one is often interested in discovering the real views of the particular philosopher with which one is dealing; but philosophy is far more than just the history of philosophy. The main purpose of philosophy is to understand arguments, and to assess those arguments and construct new arguments around them. The approach which Strauss advocates places the entire emphasis upon the historical aspects of Islamic philosophy. It is as though the philosophy itself is not worth considering as philosophy, so it is more appropriate to consider it as interesting and difficult writing which requires unravelling, a fascinating intellectual problem about understanding the author as opposed to understanding the argument. The latter is not worth doing, since the argument is bound not to be very interesting anyway. Since the Straussians think that Islamic philosophy is basically a vain attempt at reconciling religion with Greek philosophy, and then disguising the author's genuine view that the latter is a better guide to the truth than the former, the arguments are not going to be very interesting. They are going to be predictable and unoriginal. If one is looking for an intellectual problem, then, it will not be found with the argument but rather with the way in which the argument is embedded in a complex form of language which disguises it. Yet when one examines Islamic philosophy one comes across writers who put great effort and care into the logical structure of their argument, and even a cursory glance at those arguments is bound to lead to respect. The philosophers themselves certainly regarded themselves as philosophers, and even those who were hostile to philosophy were concerned to put their objections in language which would fit in with the sort of reasoning which the philosophers used. The notion that one could sweep away all this philosophical output by regarding it as a mysterious form of literature is Orientalism at its worst. It implies that the philosophers in the Islamic world could not really be thought of as philosophers just like philosophers everywhere else, but should be regarded as capable only of a lesser and inferior activity, using philosophical language to present unoriginal views in convoluted ways.

There are many writers on Islamic philosophy who are not Straussians but who adopt a methodology which also appears to rest on Orientalist assumptions. These writers will be more concerned with the analysis of the language of a text than with the meanings to be found in the text. Actually, given the sorry state of manuscripts in the area of Islamic philosophy, there is a great need for careful and scholarly research to try to establish the precise nature of the text in question. This is especially the case when the work is present in a variety of manuscripts which differ from one another, or is in a language other than that in which it was originally written. In that case the original text needs to be constructed out of the available translations, and this is a difficult and time-consuming process. Since much Islamic philosophy also refers to so much outside of itself, to Greek thought, for instance, and to Islam itself, there is a need for commentators to note carefully the sorts of references which the text is making, since readers might otherwise not follow the sort of argument which is being presented. All this sort of work is vital if progress is to be made in our understanding of Islamic philosophy, but it cannot be the end of studying such philosophy. The end, if there is an end, lies in the analysis of the arguments, not as fossils in a museum of the history of ideas but as part and parcel of the development of philosophy. That development consists in the continual examination and analysis of arguments. It is certainly not necessarily the case that the arguments of each succeeding generation of thinkers are superior to earlier arguments, but they are all parts of a tradition, and the key to understanding that tradition lies in understanding the arguments. Those scholars who write on Islamic philosophy as though one could do no more but reconstruct and describe the text are like surgeons whose brilliance makes an operation succeed, only to have the patient die.

There is an approach to Islamic philosophy which might be called Orientalism in reverse. This suggests that the subject can really be understood only by Muslims, since only they are capable of appreciating the religious aspects of the area. Non-Muslims may approach Islamic philosophy to a degree, but they are necessarily limited by their background to a partial view. This might be classified as a type of Orientalism, since it is based upon the presupposition of basic and significant distinctions between Muslims and non-Muslims, between what might be broadly called the "East" and the "West". This is just as problematic as the type of Orientalism which Said identifies. There are clearly differences in looking at a form of cultural expression when one comes from within that culture as compared with being an outsider, but it is not obvious that the former has an advantage over the latter. Insiders may miss just as much as outsiders, albeit different things. Insiders may not notice aspects of the area which appear problematic or interesting to outsiders. It is worth adding that philosophers have a good deal of experience of examining arguments which have been produced within a cultural environment very different from their own. The sorts of religious beliefs held by Plato and Bishop Berkeley, for instance, are very different from the beliefs of many of their modern interpreters, and yet this does not seem to be an obstacle to their comprehension. It is important yet again for us to emphasize that in philosophy it is the arguments which are of most interest, and the actual religious beliefs, or lack of them, of the arguers themselves is not a crucial part of the equation. A whole range of interesting biographical questions could be raised about individual philosophers, and similarly useful observations could be made about the period in which they worked, yet if we are primarily concerned with philosophy and not with the history of ideas these issues are of minor significance.

Yet it might be thought that this is rather too quick, since one of the characteristics of Islamic philosophy is precisely that it is Islamic, that is, primarily religious. If a philosophy is religious, then one perhaps requires criteria for its examination which are distinct from those appropriate to a non-religious form of philosophy. We have to be careful about our use of terms here. When a philosophy is called "Islamic" it is not suggested that everything which is produced under this label directly or indirectly imports religious issues. Quite the contrary. We are talking about philosophy appearing or influenced by the forms of thought current at a particular time in the Islamic world, and as the reader will have seen by even a cursory inspection of some of the chapters in these volumes, many of the philosophers are involved in discussions which have nothing at all to do with religion in the narrower sense of the term. As one would expect with a form of philosophical expression which covers such a long period in time and so many diverse thinkers, there is an immense variety of ideas, themes and arguments. It is a gross over-simplification to try to characterize this variety as being especially wedded to a particular religious perspective, although most of it appeared within a certain religious context. This brings out the radical error in claiming that one needs to share a religious perspective in order to understand what is produced in relation to that perspective. There is no one way in which to study a philosophical tradition, and the only criteria to be employed are those applicable to all philosophy including Christian and Jewish, the criteria of valid demonstration.

The central flaw of Orientalism is that it intrudes on the pursuit of philosophy by illegitimately insisting on just one approach to the understanding of such philosophy. The chief objection here is not so much in the way in which Orientalists interpret texts, although that is bad enough, but more in the idea that there could be just one way of going about such work. This stereotyping of texts goes hand in hand with the stereotyping of ethnic groups, and is just as objectionable. It is to be regretted, then, that the growing influence of the critique of Orientalism which Said produced has yet to have much impact upon the study of Islamic philosophy, by contrast with its effect upon other disciplines in the area of Islamic studies. It reveals how isolated much study of Islamic philosophy remains from the hermeneutic developments in other forms of enquiry.

SELECT BIBLIOGRAPHY

For a very comprehensive bibliography of Western concepts of Islam see N. Daniel, *Islam and the West* (Oxford, 1993). For Islamic views of Jesus and Christianity see N. Robinson, *Christ in Islam and Christianity* (London, 1991). The standard work, of course, is E. Said, *Orientalism* (New York, 1978). A useful bibliography of works on Orientalism in art and society is to be found in J. Thompson, *The East: Imagined, Experienced, Remembered* (Liverpool, 1988) (National Gallery of Ireland and National Museums and Galleries on Merseyside, exhibition catalogue). It is also worth consulting *Fine Material for a Dream . . .?* (Preston, 1992) (Harris Museum and Art Gallery), and J. McKenzie, *Orientalism: History, Theory and the Arts* (Manchester, 1995).

CHAPTER 69

Henry Corbin: his work and influence

Pierre Lory

The work of Henry Corbin extends over different areas of Islamic thought and includes a considerable informative contribution, with editions of texts and doctrinal translations and commentaries. But its significance goes far beyond what is commonly called "Orientalism". Corbin did not seek to display the teaching of the authors he studied in the display cases of a museum of the philosophy of the past. Rather, his aim was to show how far their themes and their presence in the world could illuminate and stimulate intellectual activity at any time, and especially in our own time so often forgetful of its own beginnings.

Born in 1903, Corbin followed a course of philosophy at the Sorbonne from 1919. There he especially attended the courses of Etienne Gilson on the texts of Ibn Sīnā translated into Latin, which made him aware even at this early stage of the importance of angelology in the noetic of this philosopher, and led him to start learning Arabic in 1925. His frequenting of the Ecole des Langues Orientales led him to make the acquaintance of Louis Massignon, an Orientalist with a burning passion for spiritual Islam, and the person who informed him about a text which was to be decisive in his philosophical path, the *Ḥikmat al-ishrāq* of Shihāb al-Dīn Yaḥyā Suhrawardī. It is worth mentioning that Corbin spent much of the 1930s in Germany. There he made the acquaintance of, among others, Rudolf Otto and Martin Heidegger. He was one of the first in France to emphasize the importance of the work of Heidegger and to translate some of it into French. Henry Corbin's interest in German philosophy or in the new Protestant approach of Karl Barth to exegesis took place at the same time as his Islamic investigations, inspired by the same research problems, those of the interpretation of a sacred text and concerning the nature of existence. As part of the mission to the French

Institute in Istanbul in 1940 he was obliged by political and military events to stay there until 1945, finishing off his work there on Suhrawardī. A decisive event for the rest of his life was his trip to Iran in September 1945. The welcome which many important intellectuals and academics provided, and his love for Persian culture, led him to stay in Tehran and resulted in the foundation of the Department of Iranology of the French Institute in the same city.

Appointed in 1954 to the Section des Sciences Religieuses of the Ecole Pratique des Hautes Etudes in succession to Louis Massignon, he split his activities equally between France and Iran. From 1949 he also attended each year the Eranos Circle in Ascona, where he met, among many other intellectuals of the utmost importance, C. G. Jung, M. Eliade and G. Scholem. It is within the context of these meetings that he published a very important part of his work, which he tirelessly continued until the end of his life. Upon retiring from the Sorbonne Corbin became a member of the Iranian Academy of Philosophy founded by S. H. Nasr and taught there until 1978 and the illness which resulted in his death.

Corbin's work is very rich and variegated, and treats the philosophical and spiritual heritage of Islam in three main ways.

SACRED AND HERMENEUTIC WRITING

Henry Corbin undertook a deep reflection on what he called "prophetic philosophy" which is acquired by adherence to a revealed text. Believers – whether Muslim, Christian or Jew – find themselves necessarily in a hermeneutic situation. They seek in the Book for meanings which they discover and test against all that they know and experience in the world. Conversely, the Book will turn around the axes of its own life and will colour its most intimate acts. Hence the facts of one's existence are determined by the act of interpreting oneself, and through this hermeneutic Corbin tried to grasp the basic spirit of some Christian theologians (Luther, Hamann), but especially of Islamic philosophy. This can be particularly observed in the question raised by Shiʿism. After the revelation of the Qur'ān to the Prophet, a new demand was born – to discover the depth of the divine message without altering its outward sense. For those believers who cannot be limited to a literal and agnostic application of the law, there is a need to uncover the hidden, the esoteric (*bāṭin*), which is the inner aspect of what is the apparent meaning (*ẓāhir*). It is to answer this need that we get the mission of the possessor of *walāyah*, that is, the Shiʿite Imām. He does not live in the community of the faithful only in order to guide their exegesis and to be the guarantor of the divine mission. As a receptacle, the bearer of heavenly light, he becomes himself the object of this exegesis. If the Imām is the Perfect Man, the first model of creation, that implies that the Qur'ān, which is the emanation of the first word and divine archetype, both indicates and completely forms the person of the Imām.

A very similar view is found in Sufi gnoseology, where the notion of *walāyah* is entirely separated from the historical figure of the Imāms originating with 'Alī in order to be applied to the invisible hierarchy of saints (*awliyā'; walī* in the singular). The work of Ḥaydar Āmulī in particular (see Corbin (1991), 3) underlines the deep similarities between the fundamental intuitions of the Shi'ite gnosis and the doctrine of the greatest of the Sufi theosophers, such as Ibn 'Arabī (Corbin 1977).

The hermeneutic strategy discussed here is not limited to the mere understanding of the Qur'ānic text. The variety of meanings, the discovery of an internal meaning, can be applied to any conscious act. Some alchemists like Jābir ibn Ḥayyān or Jaldakī (Corbin 1986) discovered a divine image in their laboratory work. The great Sufi Rūzbihān Baqlī saw in the love of feminine beauty the supreme supernatural beauty (Corbin (1991), 3). But this perception itself requires a place and a form for the object perceived, just as it assumes that the hermeneuticist has an organ of metaphysical perception. It is at this point that we need the concept of *'ālam al-mithāl*, the "imaginal world" or the creative imagination, about which Corbin wrote so extensively.

THE IMAGINAL WORLD AND ANGELOLOGY

To make progress in the understanding of the Divine by interpreting the Qur'ān and the world through transcendental exegesis (*ta'wīl*) assumes in effect some intermediary stages of existence between God and human consciousness. For God in Himself is unknowable, indescribable and impenetrable. This leads to the dangerous theological position which Corbin characterizes as the "paradox of monotheism", whereby believers try to describe God using their normal concepts and mental images, but succeed only in making Him out to be rather like the believers themselves. In order to worship this God they fall into an involuntary idolatry. To avoid this pitfall we can refuse all theological or philosophical reflection (as in Ḥanbalism and Ẓāhirism), which leads to a pious agnosticism which says in a legalistic manner, "God has not to be known, but to be obeyed."

Now, the mystics of Islam felt that between our terrestrial domain and the divine Absolute, the universe has stages, distinct worlds which are in correspondence with each other. Immediately higher than the human terrestrial world is the world of angelic beings, equipped with subtle bodies, which is the intermediary world where the spirits take form before becoming events in the terrestrial world, and it is the first paradise where the souls rise after their separation from their bodies. From our life here, each person can have access to the vision of "suspended images" (Ibn 'Arabī) through visions during sleep or while awake, and by intuitions which are for them just signs on their internal journey. It is in order to distinguish these visionary apperceptions from what language commonly calls "imaginary" that Corbin had recourse to the Latin term "imaginal", emphasizing thus both their ontological consistency and their transformational impact and the metamorphosis of the human soul.

Corbin shows how this intermediary world of angelic entities has played an essential role in the development of theosophy in medieval Islam. The cosmology and the noetic of Ibn Sīnā are expressed by a procession in which each "sacred-holy angel" stands in for each of the ten intellects emanating from the Necessary Being (Corbin 1979). It is at this point, as Corbin frequently emphasized, that the negation by Ibn Rushd of this angelic structure marks a rupture which is essential to the history of philosophy, notably in the impact of this "Averroist" philosophy on Latin Europe. The intermediary function of the angel was emptied of meaning by philosophical and theological thought, and believers in the West had to direct their faith towards an immense and incommensurable deity. The world of the prophet and that of the philosopher would in future be separate and virtually independent of each other.

It is Suhrawardī (Corbin (1991), 3) who first described with demonstrative precision the ontological status of this imaginal world, presented under the form of a complex angelology and playing a role in the noetic and interior experience of the mystic. The *'ālam al-mithāl* makes possible the meeting of individual souls with archangelic powers and also creates a space where the path of the philosopher and that of the interpreter of the Qur'ān can come together in a common experience of spiritual life. But it is Mullā Ṣadrā, a passionate reader and commentator on Ibn Sīnā like Suhrawardī and Ibn 'Arabī, who accomplished the most gripping synthesis of "prophetic philosophy" in Islam. Turning back to the Ibn Sīnan perspective, he gave to existence primacy over essence. It is the very act of existing which is in some way the essence of each individual. This act has different states of intensification ("intrasubstantial movement") which cross between the ascending and descending ontological levels where the imaginal world quite naturally finds its place.

SUFFERING GOD AND MYSTIC UNION

All the philosophical enterprise of Ibn Sīnā, Suhrawardī, Mullā Ṣadrā and many other philosophers and theosophers studied by Henry Corbin have only one end: making clear the route to the understanding of the Absolute, towards that experience of union with the One who is the ultimate goal of both the medieval philosopher and the mystic. It is probably in the work of Ibn 'Arabī that we can find the most detailed description of this experience of the Divine, and this is where the majority of the great spiritual thinkers of Islam in the following centuries went to understand their own spiritual lives. For a long time Ibn 'Arabī dwelt on the nature of the origin of instantiation. Unknowable Divine Essence, hidden, wishing to be known, creates the world and people in particular, and calls the latter to re-cognize themselves in their turn under the influence of this creative nostalgia. He also insisted on the individual aspect of the Sufi experience. All believing servants (*'abd*) investigate the consciousness not of the totally unpredictable cosmic God, but of their *rabb*, of their Master, of this particular aspect of the Divine which has been manifested in them and which they have the responsibility to actualize. This aspiration of the servant to encounter and really to become the Master is not a purely mental investigation. It involves all one's being, and shows itself by awakening in the heart of the Sufi a love for God which itself is only a refraction of divine eternal Love (Corbin 1977). However, Corbin did not limit his study to the Sufism of Ibn 'Arabī. He published substantial studies on dozens of other outstanding authorities on mysticism and Islamic theosophy.

CONCLUSION

The legacy of Henry Corbin is of decisive importance, not only for the understanding of a part of Islamic thought previously little known or understood but also because it made the Western public aware of an agenda and a spirituality which had been forgotten or repressed, and which is common to all the "religions of the Book". Believers seek sense in their lives in the comprehension of a revealed message, but they can understand this divine message only in so far as they open themselves up as transcendent subjects.

BIBLIOGRAPHY

Out of more than three hundred titles which are available in *La Bibliographie de Henry Corbin* (Paris: Le Cahier de l'Herne), which was dedicated to him in 1981, we have retained only the most representative works, leaving out articles, prefaces, editions of texts and translations. We have mentioned here only the most recent editions.

En Islam iranien (Paris, 1971–3 and 1991). This comprises four independent volumes. The first deals with imamology of the Twelver Shi'ites and the second with the thought of Suhrawardī. The third and the fourth are a series of studies on Sufism in the Persian language and on the philosophy of Persia up the nineteenth century.

Avicenne et le récit visionnaire (Paris, 1979), trans. W. R. Trask as *Avicenna and the Visionary Recital* (Princeton, 1990). This is an essay on the "Oriental Philosophy" of Ibn Sīnā and an analysis of three symbolic recitals: *Ḥayy ibn Yaqẓān, Recital of the Bird* and *Salāmān and Absāl.*

L'Imagination créatrice dans le soufisme d'Ibn 'Arabī (Paris, 1977), trans. R. Mannheim as *Creative Imagination in the Sufism of Ibn Arabi* (Princeton, 1969). One of the most profound of Corbin's works, dealing with the modalities of knowledge of the divine in Islamic mystical experience.

Corps spirituel et Terre céleste – de l'Iran mazdéen à l'Iran shi'ite (Paris, 1979), trans. N. Pearson as *Spiritual Body and Celestial Earth* (Princeton, 1977). An anthology largely dealing with texts on the imaginal dimension of the world and the body.

L'Homme de lumière dans le soufisme iranien (Paris, 1984) and *The Man of Light in Iranian Sufism,* trans. N. Pearson (London, 1978). A study on the theme of light in the work of many great Persian Sufis.

Temps cyclique et gnose ismaélienne (Paris, 1982), trans. R. Mannheim and J. Morris as *Cyclical Time and Ismaili Gnosis* (London, 1983). On the connection between the metaphysical creation of beings and terrestrial events with some very suggestive comparisons with Mazdaism.

Le Paradoxe du monothéisme (Paris, 1981). A collection of studies on the philosophical consequences of abandoning angelology in monotheist theologies.

Temple et contemplation (Paris, 1981), trans. P. Sherrard as *Temple and Contemplation* (London, 1986). Essays on comparative spirituality on the theme of the Temple, numerical harmonies and colours.

La Philosophie iranienne islamique aux XVIIe et XVIIIe siècles (Paris, 1981). A presentation of the work and thought of the most fruitful Persian philosophers of the period in question.

Face de Dieu, face de l'homme – Herméneutique et soufisme (Paris, 1983). On the spiritual hermeneutics of Islam, with a glance at the elements of the Western tradition.

L'Homme et son ange – Initiation et chevalerie spirituelle (Paris, 1983). Comparison of mystical initiation with contact with the angelic.

L'Alchimie comme art hiératique (Paris, 1986). On alchemy as an approach to understanding the divine in Islamic esotericism.

Philosophie iranienne et philosophie comparée (Paris, 1985). The central themes of philosophical enquiry in medieval Persia.

Histoire de la philosophie islamique (Paris, 1986), (in collaboration with S. H. Nasr and O. Yahya), and *History of Islamic Philosophy,* trans. L. Sherrard (London, 1993). An account of Muslim thought from its origins up to the nineteenth century, with particular attention to Shi'ite theosophy – Twelver and Ismā'īlī – and Sufism.

It is worth pointing to four works dedicated to the thought of Henry Corbin:

Henry Corbin (Paris, 1981). Unedited texts, correspondence and personal accounts, published under the editorship of Christian Jambet.

La Logique des Orientaux – Henry Corbin ou la science des formes (Paris, 1983). Comparison of the Islamic theosophical vision with many leading trends in Western philosophy, by Christian Jambet.

Henry Corbin – la typographie spirituelle de l'Islam iranien (Paris, 1990). A presentation of the unity of Corbin's work, emphasizing its philosophical and spiritual aspects by Daryush Shayegan.

Mélanges offerts à Henry Corbin, ed. S. H. Nasr (Tehran, 1978).

(Translated by O. L.)

CHAPTER 70

Islamic philosophy in Russia and the Soviet Union

Alexander Knysh

This chapter concentrates on the Soviet period because, before the Bolshevik revolution of 1917, studies of Islamic philosophical thought (in contrast to those which focused on the religious, social and political aspects of Islamic civilization) were few and far between. In pre-revolutionary Russia, the study of "Oriental philosophy" occupied a fringe position between "religious studies" and the political and social history of the Muslim world. As in the West, such studies were conducted primarily by philologists. No wonder, then, that Russian Orientalists normally addressed *falsafah* only in passing, as an aside to the treatment of their principal topics, the Muslim religion and *belles lettres*. As exception to the rule, I would cite a brilliant, if concise, study of Persian mystical philosophy by V. Zhukovski, *Chelovek i poznanie u persidskikh mistikov* ("Man and Gnosis in [the Teachings of] Persian Mystics") (St Petersburg, 1895). A thorough and original analysis of Muʿtazilite thought based on rare manuscripts was carried out by P. K. Zhuzé (i.e. Jawzi), a scholar of Syrian–Lebanese background turned Christian missionary (see P. K. Zhuzé, *Muʿtazility: techenie v islame v IX veke* ("The Muʿtazilites: a [Religious] Movement in Islam in the Ninth Century") (Kazan, 1899). Somewhat later the religious and mystical views of ʿAbd al-Wahhāb al-Shaʿrānī were analysed in A. Schmidt, *ʿAbd-al-Wahhāb-ash-Shaʿrānī i ego "Kniga razsypannykh zhemchuzhin"* (ʿAbd al-Wahhāb al-Shaʿrānī and his "Book of Scattered Pearls") (St Petersburg, 1914). Yet all these studies, along with the works of the other outstanding Russian/Soviet Orientalists of the first half of the twentieth century, such as E. Bertels, I. Krachkovski, A. Semenov and V. Barthold, can hardly be described as "philosophical" in the strict sense. Owing to a lack of special philosophical training, these scholars approached *falsafah* as philologists and culturologists par excellence. Their primary goal was to understand Muslim literary works better rather than Muslim theoretical thought.

Under Soviet rule, philosophical discourse in general came to be dominated by the official Marxist–Leninist ideology with its heavy emphasis on the purportedly perennial struggle between "materialism" and "idealism", and the resultant conflict between an unbending religious "obscurantism" fostered by the ruling elites and a more secular "free thinking" associated with the struggle for social equality and intellectual emancipation of the masses. These motifs and the resulting stereotypes became so deeply embedded in the mentality of Soviet scholars that even the cleverest among them could not help paying tribute, wittingly or not, to this rigid ready-made scheme. Only in the 1980s, and especially with the advent of *glastnost* (openness and free speech) and *perestroyka* in 1985, did Russian students of Islamic philosophy, as well as their colleagues in related fields of intellectual endeavour, became cognizant of the inherent biases and pitfalls of the orthodox Marxist approach. Their attempts to remedy the "past transgressions", however, were brought to a halt by an overall collapse of academic publishing and the growing indifference to their studies on the part of the readers who were reduced to bare survival by the economic dislocation of the post-*perestroyka* period.

As Russian academia begins to shake off the stupor induced by the "time of troubles", one may predict that the "revisionist" trend in the Soviet/Russian humanities, which was propelled into prominence by the *perestroyka* mentality, will continue to hold sway over Russian researchers. At this point, however, it is difficult to foretell what concrete forms this "revisionist" stance will take in the long term, and whether or not one should expect a comeback of a revamped Marxist concept of intellectual history some time in the future.

Turning to the concrete studies of Islamic philosophy in the former Soviet Union, I would stress its overriding emphasis on the "rationalist" tradition at the expense of the religious, mythological, mystical, legal, etc. aspects of the Muslim intellectual tradition. Some Muslim thinkers received the lion's share of the scholars' attention, whereas others – including such important figures as Miskawayh, al-Kindī, al-Ash'arī, Abū Bakr al-Rāzī, the Ikhwān al-Ṣafā' and the Mu'tazilites, al-Juwaynī, al-Tawḥīdī, al-Ghazzālī, Suhrawardī al-Maqtūl, Ibn 'Arabī, al-Taftazānī, etc. – were largely (and unjustly) neglected. For a number of reasons (the emergence of nationhood and the resultant "cultural" competition among the Central Asian nation states being among the most important), several Muslim thinkers became the preferred subjects of academic investigation that was sometimes conducted by the entire local institutes of Oriental studies. Among these "lucky ones" were (in order of priority) Ibn Sīnā, al-Fārābī, al-Bīrūnī and – to a somewhat lesser extent – Nāṣir-i Khusraw, Ibn Ṭufayl, Ibn Khaldūn, Ibn Rushd and Naṣīr al-Dīn al-Ṭūsī. Studies devoted to these thinkers – especially the first three of them – are legion.

A few of these are: A. S. Ivanov, *Uchenie al-Farabi o poznavatel'nykh sposobnostyakh cheloveka* ("Al-Fārābī's Doctrine of the Epistemological Faculty of Man") (Alma-Ata, 1977); *Al-Farabi: nauchnoe nasledstvo* ("Al-Fārābī's Scholarly Legacy"), a collection of articles (no known editor) (Moscow, 1975); Zh. M. Abdilin and M. S. Burabaev (eds), *Al-Farabi: Istoriko-filosofskie traktaty* ("Al-Fārābī: Historical and Philosophical Works"), translated from the Arabic (Alma-Ata, 1985); Muhammad Khayrullaev, *Abu Nasr al-Farabi* (Moscow, 1982) (this is just one of at least five books on al-Fārābī written by this prolific Central Asian scholar); Khayrullaev (ed.), *Filosofskoe nasledie narodov Sredney Azii i bo'ba idei* ("Philosophical Legacy of the Peoples of Central Asia and the Struggle of Ideas") (Tashkent, 1988); A. H. Kasimdjanov, *Abu Nasr al-Farabi* (Moscow, 1982). An annotated bibliography on al-Fārābī in Soviet studies can be found in A. V. Sagadeev, "Otechestvennaya literatura ob al-Farabi v god ego 1100-letnego yubileya", *Narody Azii i Afriki* (currently *Vostok*), 6 (1977): 190–7.

Equally vast is the volume of scholarly literature devoted to Ibn Sīnā. Apart from several complete and selected translations (with copious annotations) of his works into Russian, Uzbek and Tajik, mention can be made of the following study of the Shaykh al-Ra'īs: *Ibn Sine (Avitsenne) 1000 let: materialy yubileynykh konferentsiy* ("A Thousand Years Anniversary Since Ibn Sīnā's Birth") (Moscow, 1980). This work faithfully represents the spectrum of approaches to Ibn Sīnā in Soviet Orientalist scholarship and, moreover, furnishes a helpful bibliography.

Al-Bīrūnī's philosophical views are treated in a collective study entitled *Beruni i gumanitarnie nauki* ("Bīrūnī and the Humanitarian Disciplines") (Tashkent, 1972) and a host of other studies of Bīrūnī's *Weltanschauung* produced in the capital of the former Uzbek Soviet Socialist Republic. Ibn Khaldūn's "philosophy of history" was treated in a monograph by S. M. Batsieva, *Istoriko-sotsiologicheskiy traktat Ibn Khalduna "Mukaddima"* ("Ibn Khaldūn's Tract on History and Sociology: The 'Muqaddima'") (Moscow, 1965). She also made a complete Russian translation of the *Muqaddimah* which, unfortunately, remains unpublished.

Of general studies of Islamic philosophy mention should be made of the following: S. N. Grygoryan (ed.), *Iz istorii filosofii Sredney Azii i Irana* ("Notes on the History of Central Asian and Iranian Philosophy") (Moscow, 1960) (contains translations of original Islamic texts, including al-Ghazzālī's *al-Munqidh min al-ḍalāl*, etc.); G. B. Shaymuhambetova, *Araboyazychnaya filosofia srednevekov'ya i klassicheskaya traditsia* ("The Medieval Arabophone Philosophy and the Classic [Greek] Tradition") (Moscow, 1979); E. Frolova, *Problema very i znaniya v arabskoy filosofii* ("The Problem of Faith and Knowledge in Arabic Philosophy") (Moscow,

1983); M. T. Stepaniants, *Musul'manskie kontseptsii v filosofii i politike: XIX–XX vv.* ("Muslim Concepts in Philosophy and Politics: the Nineteenth and Twentieth Centuries") (Moscow, 1982); V. Burov, D. Djohadze *et al.* (eds) *Filosofskoe nasledie narodov Vostoka i sovremennost'* ("The Philosophical Legacy of the Oriental Peoples and the Contemporary World") (Moscow, 1983); *Iz istorii filosofii osvobodivshikhsya stran* ("Towards the History of the Philosophical Traditions of the Liberated [i.e. Third World] Countries") (Moscow, 1983) (collection of articles on the history of Islamic philosophy); N. Kyrabaev, *Sotsyal'naya filosofia musul'manskogo Vostoka: epokha srednevekov'ya* ("Social Philosophy of the Muslim East in the Middle Ages") (Moscow, 1987).

Ismā'īlī philosophy and mystical thought have been treated in many studies, including H. Dodikhudoev, *Filosofia krest'yanskogo bunta* ("The Philosophy of Peasant Uprising" – i.e. Ismā'īlism – *sic*!) (Dushanbe, 1987); B. Ismatov, *Panteistichekaya filosofskaya traditsiya v persidko-tajikskoy poezii IX–XV vv.* ("Pantheistic Strand within the Perso-Tajik Poetry of the 9th–15th Centuries") (Dushanbe, 1986); M. Stepanyants, *Filosofskie aspekty sufizma* ("Philosophical Aspects of Sufism") (Moscow, 1987) English translation 1989); N. Prygarina (ed.), *Sufizm v kontekste musul'manskoy kul'tury* ("Sufism in the Context of Muslim Culture") (Moscow, 1989). A fuller annotated bibliography of Sufi studies in Russia and the Soviet Union can be found in my chapter on Sufism in S. Prozorov, *Islam: Istoriograficheskie ocherki* ("Islam: Studies on Historiography") (Moscow, 1991): 109–207.

Most of the studies listed above, as well as my own, are marred by the typical biases and prejudices of the "ideological" view of religion and philosophy that the Communist Party imposed on the official Soviet academia. They hinge on the obsessive search for "materialist tendencies" in the works of the great Muslim philosophers as well as a disparaging critique of the "bourgeois" and "idealistic" treatment of Islamic history and culture.

Head and shoulders above most of these works stand the studies by Artur Sagadeev, whose *Ibn Rushd (Averroes)* (Moscow, 1973) and *Ibn Sina (Avicenna)*, 2nd ed. (Moscow, 1980) are solid and original contributions to the field. Collective works published under his editorship are also marked by a (relatively) high standard of scholarship and original research rather then the reshuffling of the ideas freely borrowed from Western scholars – a feature that is typical of the many works mentioned in the previous paragraphs. See, e.g., Sagadeev (ed.), *Filosofskaya i obshchstvennaya mysl' stran Azii i Afriki* ("Philosophical and Social Teachings of Asia and Africa") (Moscow, 1981); *Filosofia zarubezhnogo Vostoka o sotsial'noy suchnosti cheloveka* ("Oriental Philosophy on the Social Nature of Man") (Moscow, 1986) (includes Sagadeev's contribution on the philosophical ideas of Ibn Ṭufayl, pp. 54–78). See also his article "Gumanisticheskie idealy musul'manskogo sredenevekov'ya" ("Humanistic Ideals of the Muslim World in the Middle Ages"), pp. 43–62, in an interesting collection, *Chelovek kak filosofskaya problema: Vostok–Zapad* ("Man as a Philosophical Problem: East and West"), ed. N. Kyrabaev (Moscow, 1991).

Sagadeev's lifelong study of Islamic philosophy is summarized in his only major work (aside from a few articles) published in English, namely Taufic Ibrahim and Artur Sagadeev, *Classical Islamic Philosophy* (Moscow, 1990) – a real *tour de force* by the two prominent Russophone experts on Islamic philosophy. Another translation of some Russian works on *falsafah* is M. Stepanyants (ed.), *Muslim Philosophy in Soviet Studies* (New Delhi, 1988). This book includes essays on the Islamic Peripatetic tradition, Ibn Sīnā, Ibn Ṭufayl, Ibn Rushd and Ibn Khaldūn, as well as Rūmī and Muḥammad ʿAbduh.

This is not the place to dwell on the merits and drawbacks of all these works. In general, their scholarly level is inferior to that of their Western counterparts. Furthermore, they are riddled with the stereotypes and biases outlined at the beginning of this chapter. This, however, does not mean they can be indiscriminately brushed aside without even being looked into. Some of the studies of *falsafah* produced in the Soviet Union contain interesting insights and new approaches to the subject which are not to be found in the works of Western Islamicists.

SUPPLEMENTARY BIBLIOGRAPHY

In English

Stepanyants, M. T. (1972) *Pakistan: Philosophy and Sociology* (Lahore).
—— (1988) *Muslim Philosophy in Soviet Studies* (Bangalore).
—— (1994) *Sufi Wisdom* (Albany).

In Russian

Burabavev, M. S., Kenisarin, A. M. and Kurmangalieva, G. K. (1988) *The Problems of Being and Cognition in the Philosophy of al-Farabi* (Alma-Ata).
Dinorshoev, M. (1985) *The Natural Philosophy of Ibn Sīnā* (Dushanbe).
Ibrahim, T. and Efremova, N. (1995) *Muslim Sacred History: From Adam to Jesus* (Moscow).
Ignatenko, A. A. (1989) *In Search of Happiness* (Moscow).
Khayrullaev, M. (1985) *The Cultural Legacy and the History of Philosophical Thought* (Tashkent).
Khazratkulov, M. (1985) *The Philosophical Views of Sadriddin Shirazi* (Dushanbe).
Knysh, A. (1995) *Ibn ʿArabi's "Meccan Revelations": Partial Translations, Commentaries and Bibliography* (St Petersburg).

Kurbanmamadov, A. (1987) *The Aesthetical Doctrine of Sufism (Critical Analysis)* (Dushanbe).
Kyamilev, S. Kh., Levin, Z. I. and Smilyanskaya, I. M. (1987) *Social and Political Ideas in Islam. Past and Present* (Moscow).
Malushkov, V. G. and Khromova, K. A. (1991) *The Search for the Ways of Reformation in Islam: On the Iranian Experience* (Moscow).
Pochta, J. M. (1988) *Islam: the Origins and Present Times* (Moscow).
Smirnov, A. (1993) *The Great Shaykh of Sufism* (*A Sample of Paradigmatic Analysis of Ibn 'Arabi's Philosophy*) (Moscow).
Stepanyants, M. (1994) *Islam in the Philosophical and Social Thought of the Foreign East* (Moscow).

(M. Stepanyants and N. Efremova assisted with the bibliography. (O. L. and S. H. N.))

CHAPTER 71

The possibility of a philosophy of Islam

Shabbir Akhtar

Magic and arguably poetry are arts condemned by the Author of the Qur'ān (2: 102; 26: 224–6). Would academic philosophy of religion have escaped condemnation if the Sacred Text had been revealed in a different age or in a different culture (like, say, Socrates' Greece)?

Ever since the first currents of Hellenic philosophy overwhelmed the simple literalism of the Muslim creed, Islamic "orthodoxy" has never ceased to frown on the power of philosophy to plague its labours. Philosophy, we are told, creates at worst unnecessary doubts and hesitations, and at best mere conjecture and confusion; scripture by contrast, it is said, offers assurances for Paradise. The "orthodox" view prevalent among Muslims, as among orthodox Jews and orthodox Christians, is simple: there is neither the time nor the need for philosophy in a world under the burden of divine nemesis and blessed with the benefits of divine tuition. Does not the book of Allah contain sufficient guidance and education for the faithful student?

Here I intend to explore and refute various religious objections to any philosophical approach to the Muslim faith. I begin with the important if standard religious objection about the essential impiety of philosophical method when applied to revealed conviction. How can the philosopher judge the Word of Allah – one's Lord? Muslim scholars have, from the earliest times, emphasized the Qur'ān's role as final arbiter, as secreting a criterion (*Furqān*; 25: 1; 3: 4) for judgment. Thus, revelation supplies, we are told, a supernatural verdict on humanity and all things natural or human, including human reason (*'aql*). God judges us; we do not judge God or His message. "Is not Allah," asks the Qur'ān rhetorically, "the best of judges?" (95: 8).

Allah is indeed the best of judges. It is of course true – necessarily true – that what God says about us is superior in insight to what we might say about ourselves or God. To say, however, that God's (alleged) revelation should be assessed by use of the normal methods of scrutiny is not to deny the ultimacy or primacy of God's views. It is merely a comment on how to seek to determine what God's views actually are, and the recommendation is that we should use the only apparatus we possess, namely, the methods of reason. (Remember that rejecting the supremacy of reason is one thing; rejecting the importance of reasoning is quite another.)

Related to the first objection is the accusation that reliance on reason in discussions of revealed claims is in effect intellectually idolatrous. The philosopher is an idolater. To obey the voice of reason rather than the revealed commands of scripture is sinful.

This is the most irritating of all the religious objections to rational method. For it is not as though, in the manner of a Faust, one were to sell one's soul in exchange for knowledge, aware of the superior worth of preserving one's soul in order to seek the pleasure of God. Our situation today is hardly that grandiose. At the very least, our alleged intellectual idolatry is unintentional. We are simply ordinary folk caught up in some messy epistemological predicaments in an age of uncertainty. Perplexed people, seeking to know the truth about life before leaving a scene where discordant cries of conflicting views assail them from all sides, are forced to rely upon their intellectual apparatus, modest as that may be for the purpose. Without the discrimination that reason provides, we cannot find our way out of the jungle. How is one to distinguish truth from falsehood – even revealed truth from merely impressive sounding untruth?

Nor is it as though one said, as a Nietzsche would in a defiant mood, "God has his own opinions: I prefer my own." One merely wishes to know what God's views really are. After these are known, it is, for a reasonable person, no longer an open question whether or not such views express an ultimate truth.

Anti-intellectualism runs deep in ordinary religious thought. Nor is it just plain religious folk or even plain religious thinkers who are under its spell. Many sophisticated philosophers believe that systematic rational theorizing about God is due to want of faith.

What are we to make of this? People engage in systematic theology and in philosophy of religion for many different reasons. While it is rare for an atheist to be interested in Christian or Islamic theology proper, there is no shortage of disbelieving philosophers of religion. Now, presumably, the group accused of lack of faith are the believing theologians (isn't a Christian theologian necessarily a Christian believer?) and believing philosophers of religion, and not those who reject faith altogether. The believing theologians would find the charge of lack of faith a curious one:

after all they see themselves as professionally engaged in the service of their faith. Believing philosophers of religion may more plausibly be accused since part of their professional obligation *qua* philosophers requires them to suspend their religious commitments.

It is not easy to make the charge stick. As I understand it, it amounts to saying that, unless believing thinkers and theologians were assailed by doubts about their religious convictions, they would not need the props of academic theology or philosophy in the dark hour of scepticism. But how is this an accusation, even if we accept the foregoing reasoning as sound? Why should it be seen as culpable? We could say that believing writers who suspend their religious convictions temporarily (in the interests of objectivity) are people of "intermittent faith": they sometimes need to think and write like sceptics rather than as mosque- or church-going believers. But to be people of intermittent faith, in this sense, is not the same as being people of "little faith", in the derogatory sense in which this expression is employed in scriptural writings. And it is false to say that people of intermittent faith are people of no faith at all. For such a view would rule out the entire run of ordinary believers from the believing club, leaving only a few of the seminal religious figures (who lived in the heat of active faith and piety day and night) to qualify as genuine believers. Almost all believers have their sceptical moments; believing thinkers or theologians merely seek to cultivate some kinds of sceptical moods as a part of their professional obligation in order to be objective about their religious convictions.

As it happens, the religionist's initial reasoning is itself unsound, inspired as it is by a mistaken view about the nature of faith. It is often said by religious writers that, once faith is proved or conclusively justified, it can no longer be an appropriate candidate for mere belief: one can only have faith where there is uncertainty. But, as the Christian thinker Terence Penelhum has ably shown, faith can incorporate knowledge just as it can incorporate doubts. Faith and knowledge, like faith and uncertainty, can co-exist in religious as in secular contexts. Thus, one can believe what one knows, have faith in what one knows; indeed one can even doubt what one knows or "knows very well". The Classical dichotomy between faith and knowledge, endorsed by such writers as St Thomas Aquinas and by many Muslim and Jewish religious thinkers, is actually untenable. It is surprising that theists should have seen faith as being incompatible with knowledge. After all, many of the seminal religious figures seemed to know that there was a God who cared about humankind and yet they were expected to have faith in him. The Qur'ān presupposes that one can possess knowledge (*'ilm*) while having faith (*īmān*); again, to turn to the Judaeo-Christian tradition, such men as Abraham, Moses and Jesus enjoyed such strikingly intimate relationships with God that one may say they had knowledge of the Divine while simultaneously being faithful. To turn the religious coin, the whole scriptural emphasis on the perversity of rejection presupposes the compatibility of faith and knowledge. The perversity of rejection (*kufr*) can be understood only in terms of people's wilful refusal to have faith in or believe in what they secretly know. The religious opposition to an intellectually sophisticated approach to religious issues is, then, in part the outcome of a misunderstanding about the nature of the life of faith, and of rejection.

At this stage, religionists may shift their ground in the hope of knocking out their opponents in the second round – supposing that all parties survive the opening scuffle. Even granted that the philosophical study of religious faith is religiously permissible, it will be said that it is none the less to be discouraged for various religious reasons. The Qur'ān is addressed to believers, at least in the first instance. ("O you who believe" is a frequent form of address in the sacred volume.) God is concerned to elicit a faithful response, not to make theologians or philosophers of us. The aim of revelation is not to provide us with the truth for truth's sake: the hope is that by knowing the truth we may be liberated from bondage to illusory divinities and attain success (*falāḥ*).

This objection is the outcome of confusing one correct observation with two incorrect inferences. It is true that the aim of the religious life is to find favour in the eyes of our Creator. In that sense, the purpose of revelation is not primarily to satisfy the intellect but rather to show us the way to Heaven; a believer's motives in seeking to learn Allah's purposes from the teaching of the Qur'ān should primarily be practical and devotional rather than academic and controversial. But it does not follow from this correct claim that there is no room for reasoned speculation in the religious life or that the sole purpose of sacred literature is to preach to the converted.

Let me take these last two points in turn. There is both a place and a need for reflection, including detached reflection, about one's religious beliefs and allegiances. In the occasional cool hour, we need to ascertain, as far as it is humanly possible, the objective validity of our faithful convictions. Most of us can and should take off the religious cloak, if only occasionally, and if only to mend it for renewed service. This is the right thing to do given that we wish to live with intellectual integrity in an age of religious and ideological pluralism. Unlike some of the seminal figures of the theistic traditions, hardly any modern believer lives in the heat of an active religiosity day and night. For us, it is both possible and necessary to alternate in the roles of participant and critical spectator.

The Qur'ān is not, to pick up the second point, just a sermon for the faithful. Many of its verses are indeed addressed to or report the actual and normative deportment of believers; all of it was originally vouchsafed to one particular believer, Muḥammad. But none of this could imply that it is the exclusive property of the Muslim club; the document of revelation is the property of all mankind. The author of the Qur'ān has no hesitations about exposing the religious document and its credentials to the scrutiny of the idolaters, the rejectors, the hesitants, the Jews, the Christians and others. Is it too unnatural an extension to encompass the mild gaze of the believing thinker temporarily setting aside religious commitments and putting on the sceptical cloak in the interests of objective study?

The religionist could reply that the Qur'ān (56: 179) itself warns us that "none save the purified shall touch" the revealed Word of God. What are we to make of this? This verse has been variously interpreted. It could mean that the heavenly version of the Qur'ān is inaccessible to those who are impure or it could refer to the Qur'ān in earthly currency being out of the reach of rejectors. The only plausible interpretation is that committed believers should place themselves in a state of ritual physical purity before perusing the Sacred Text: they should perform the necessary ablutions. Such a requirement cannot extend to those who disbelieve the Scripture's inspiration and claims. Any other interpretation is problematic. Muslims could argue that the Qur'ān should be inaccessible to non-Muslims and thus erect a high barricade of religious exclusivism. They could argue that rejectors are "impure"; and it is a short step from here to suggest that those whose orthodoxy is suspect are also impure even though they claim to be believers.

Patient religionists may feel that we have failed to get to the heart of the matter. Islam is not, they retort, some kind of spectator sport: one has to be a submitter to God's Will in heart and mind, in order to have any real idea about the whole thing. Submission to God's Will (i.e. Islam) must include intellectual submission. Can the rejector, or the detached scholar, really understand the quality of total submission, itself rooted in intellectual humility, that the Muslim faith demands? It is impossible, it will be said, to have a purely theoretical interest in Islam, for either one genuinely understands it and then rejects it out of perversity (since to understand all is here to embrace all) or else one simply fails to understand it. And how can the outsider or the thinker who suspends commitment to Islam even comprehend the faith and its scripture as momentous realities that secrete an immediate normative significance for all of us in this life?

Admittedly, one needs some imaginative sympathy with the religious ideal if one is to avoid serious misunderstanding, even a complete failure of understanding. However, sympathy with any religious ideal – though preferably a monotheistic one – usually suffices. (Certainly, it need not be a specifically Muslim ideal.) And most sceptics and secularists do have a participant's understanding of religious belief and practice: they were brought up in religious, including quite pious, homes.

The antipathy to detachment is inspired by the correct observation that to recognize the availability of religious knowledge is also partly to recognize the importance of pursuing it, indeed implementing it through a course of practical religious devotion. One cannot fully grasp the truth about the nature of religious belief without also realizing that it characteristically inspires specifically religious responses to reality. The religionist is mistaken, however, in concluding that one must be a religious believer in order to understand what religious belief is.

What, then, is the role of independent reason in the interpretation of scriptural claims? What is the true office of reason in theology? The Qur'ān itself implies an optimistic assessment of the potential of human intellect (*'aql*); people are constantly invited to think in order that they may believe. But, in the final analysis, faith has decisive priority over reason: faith defines the offices, power and the limits of reason in matters theological. The predominant view among Muslim theologians today as in the past is the view called "fideism" in Christian thought: an intellect unenlightened by God's grace cannot judge faith while an intellect enlightened by God's grace can only judge faith favourably. Faith does not stand in need of rational justification; it is indeed, in religious domains, the arbiter of reason and its pretensions.

The primacy of faith is as much a feature of orthodox Islamic thought as of orthodox Christian thought. The Qur'ān does frequently invite us to ponder the signs of Allah in nature, society and the self. But the reality of Allah Himself is fully accessible only to faith – a faith that is itself a gift of grace. After all Allah is in the first instance the subject of faith and loving obedience, not of rational enquiry or purely discursive thought. Unaided human reason is inferior in status to the gift of faith. Indeed, reason is useful only in so far as it finds a use in the larger service of faith. For the orthodox believer, faith is a gift of grace, to be embraced on the authority of no less an authority than Allah Himself: *credere Deum Deo* (I believe in God on God's own authority) is the slogan.

The problem of the role of independent reason in the interpretation of religious claims brings us to the central issue. The disquiet is about the delicacy of combining a faithful fealty to Islamic convictions with an endorsement of free enquiry about their epistemological status. Can a Muslim, under the tuition of scripture, see the issue of the truth of Islam as an open one?

It is difficult to deny the irreducible tension involved in the making of two disparate commitments: one to the primacy of faith, the other to the primacy of reason. One way to effect an admittedly temporary armistice between faith and reason is to draw a distinction between the philosophy of religion, on the one hand, and theology proper, on the other. Now, the philosophy of religion is in effect the rational examination of theological issues without reference to the authority of any revealed dictum; theology, however, integrally relies on a supranatural authority. The philosophy of religion treats all types of religion and religious faith as its domain, not presupposing the privileged position of any type but aiming at discovering what religious truths, if any, are implied by the psychology, sociology and history of religion. Theology, however, simply starts with the faith of some particular religion, the Jewish or Christian, for example, and expounds that faith while accepting the central tenets of the religion in question as revealed or otherwise authoritatively grounded truths.

If we accept the legitimacy of this distinction, then the believing philosopher of religion will, in his or her philosophical capacity, seek exemption from the normal religious strictures on any criticism of the allegedly revealed bases of faith. The theologian may, however, work and think securely within the ambit of faith. Institutionally, faithful philosophers of religion may conscientiously teach the normal Western university syllabus while their theologically inclined co-religionists would most appropriately teach in a seminary (*madrasah*) set up by the religious authorities.

The Qur'ān itself does not outlaw free enquiry. But it would be self-indulgent to read into its verses any celebration of free enquiry in the modern sense of the term. There are no specifically Islamic reasons for encouraging Muslims to undertake any unduly critical study of their basic religious convictions. Indeed, free enquiry has always been a debatable concept in the *madrasah*: what is the point of free enquiry if one already has the truth?

There remains a final question. What are the basic presuppositions of a philosophy of Islam? There are, I believe, at least three basic assumptions, each controversial, which any philosophy of religion must necessarily make.

Firstly, one needs to assume that religious belief is not *sui generis*: it can be subsumed under a subsection of belief in general in the same way as historical or political or moral belief. Secondly, it has to be assumed that even if religious belief is indeed a special gift of grace, it is at another level simultaneously a purely human conviction whose content is subject to ordinary appraisal and scrutiny. Thus, even if it is true that authentic revelation is the only source of true religious ideas, the thinker may still reasonably assess the truth and plausibility of revealed claims once these have appeared on the mortal plane. And, thirdly, I take it that the actual existence of God is not a necessary condition of the very possibility of entertaining belief in God or belief that there is a God. Some religionists have, mistakenly, thought that the very fact that people actually believe in God implies that the human mind is an arena for the direct causal activities of God, Gabriel or the Holy Spirit.

The religionist may, rightly, argue that, in making these assumptions, I have begged the question against an important theological position

– the position one might call "Islamic neo-orthodoxy" or simply "Islamic orthodoxy". But if the philosopher cannot keep all the balls in the air, neither can the religionist. No method, whether religious or philosophical, is fully presuppositionless. The least controversial method is the one nourished by the minimum number of controversial assumptions. But questions are bound to be begged. (Is the trick merely to beg them persuasively?)

In disputes of this kind, it is customary for both parties to contend that the burden of proof is on the opponent. While these arguments about the location of onus are not compelling, they do, if successfully made, indicate a direction of enquiry. In this secular age, the burden of "proof" (or at least of plausibility) is on the believer's shoulders. If in the past men sought to subsume their world under the aegis of revelation, today they seek to interpret revealed dicta through the primacy of the purely human.

We have here a difference in temper, a conflict of loyalties: a religious mentality views scepticism and suspended commitment as being foreign to genuine faith while the secularized mentality seeks exemption from the dogmatic pressures of revealed conviction. These are genuinely opposed moods which cannot be fully reconciled without a retreat from integrity. Philosophy, as an autonomous branch of learning, can at best only indirectly serve religious ends. In the first instance, it has to be in what it takes to be the service of disinterested truth, whether that be religious or secular. Since philosophers cannot conscientiously assume that they, as philosophers, will always arrive at conclusions favourable to their religious convictions, they must part ways with the religionists. Philosophy can only be an apology for truth.

XI

Bibliography

A guide to bibliographical resources

Oliver Leaman

Much Islamic philosophy is not published in the ordinary journals which specialize in philosophy, nor by publishers who have philosophy lists. Publications in English are sometimes noted in *The Philosopher's Index*, but this is not a good guide to the area. Far better for a whole variety of languages is the *Répertoire bibliographique de la philosophie* (Louvain) which in three out of four issues a year contains a section on "philosophie arabo-musulmane". For recent work there is the very useful "The Study of Arabic Philosophy Today" by Charles Butterworth, in the *MESA Bulletin*, 18 (July and December 1983), parts 1 and 2: 8–24, 161–72), which has also been published with an appendix covering 1983–7 in T.-A. Druart (ed.), *Arabic Philosophy and the West: Continuity and Interaction* (Washington DC 1988): 55–116, and the appendix (1983–7): 117–40. In the 1987 issue of the *Bulletin de Philosophie Médiévale* (edited by the Société Internationale pour l'étude de la Philosophie Médiévale, Louvain), 29: 24–47 G. Anawati published a "Bilan des études sur la philosophie médiévale en terre d'Islam, 1982–1987", and this has been updated by Thérèse-Anne Druart and Michael Marmura in the 1990 edition of the *Bulletin*, 32, to cover 1986–9 (pp. 106–35). This is updated in *Bulletin*, 35 (1993). The best source of bibliographies on individual thinkers is in books dealing with them, but two important sources should be mentioned here. For Ibn Rushd (Averroes) there is P. Rosemann, "Averroes: a Catalogue of Editions and Scholarly Writings from 1821 Onwards", *Bulletin*, 30 (1988): 153–215, and for Ibn Sīnā (Avicenna) there is the masterly J. Janssens, *An Annotated Bibliography on Ibn Sīnā (1970–1989) Including Arabic and Persian Publications and Turkish and Russian References* (Leuven 1991): xxviii–358.

Those journals which specialize in Islamic themes often carry articles and reviews of Islamic philosophy, as do those concerned with issues in religion and Semitic studies in general. There are even some journals such as *Arabic Sciences and Philosophy* (Cambridge University Press) which are specifically concerned with historical aspects of Islamic philosophy, and the general range of intellectual journals in the Islamic world will often have articles on this topic. The books in the series *Islamic Philosophy, Theology and Science*, edited by Hans Daiber and David Pingree and published by Brill, usually have extensive bibliographies. Some publishers have quite extensive list of books on Islamic philosophy, in particular Routledge, State University of New York Press, Oxford University Press and other leading English-language publishers, while European publishers often do bring out the occasional book in the area. There are no series devoted exclusively to Islamic philosophy, though, and books tend to be grouped with others dealing with general issues relating to Islam and its culture.

There is a range of publications which deal with references to articles and books in a variety of languages. The *Geschichte des arabischen Schrifttums* is useful in this respect, especially volumes 1 (1967) and 9 (1984). This is edited by F. Sezgin and published by Brill of Leiden. They also publish *A Greek and Arabic Lexicon*, the first fascicule of which appeared in 1992, and it is edited by G. Endress and D. Gutas. The *Quarterly Index Islamicus* (Cambridge) provides extensive lists of current books, articles and papers on Islamic subjects, and is compiled by G. Roper. The *Geschichte der arabischen Literatur*, ed. Carl Brockelmann (Leiden, 1937–43), with its supplements, is useful. The main scholarly effort in the area is the second edition of the *Encyclopaedia of Islam*, which appears in fascicules, and which has sections on philosophy of considerable length and excellent quality. The first edition is available, and has interesting information on philosophers and concepts. As one might expect, the various histories and encyclopedias which deal with the Islamic world have sections on philosophy. There are useful bibliographies in the journals *Muslim World Book Review*, *Hamdard Islamicus*, *The Muslim World*, *The Middle East Journal*, *MESA (Middle East Studies Association) Bulletin* and *Le Monde Arabe la Recherche Scientifique* which appear on a regular basis.

The study of Islamic philosophy has the unusual feature that many of the raw materials, the manuscripts themselves, have not been edited, printed or even catalogued. There are a great number of manuscripts in Middle Eastern libraries about which very little is known, and the study of the documents in libraries throughout the world has been pursued only slowly by a relatively small number of scholars. Editions are frequently being improved by later discoveries, and work which was thought to have been completely lost is sometimes discovered. Attribution of authorship sometimes changes as new facts come to the surface, and it becomes easier to date works as more are analysed and prepared for publication. Texts which have not been printed were copied by hand, and one is very reliant upon the skill of the copyist for the accuracy of this work. Although many of the copyists were very careful in their work, it is inevitable that some problems crept in and that sometimes copyists replaced an original term which they did not understand with another which they thought fitted the context better. Some of these copies did not survive in the best physical condition, so it is clear that the scholar who deals with such manuscripts has a very slow and difficult task to undertake. To add to the problems, some manuscripts survive only in translation, so the scholar has to try to work out what the original text was like by examining the translation, and when one considers that the original document may not itself have been a perfect copy of the original, the potential for confusion is obvious.

So many of the most important and interesting manuscripts in the area are difficult to read and edit, and much work remains to be done to bring texts to light. This is only the most dramatic aspect of the present state of affairs, though, since many of the surviving documents are in reasonable shape and not difficult to find. The main problem is the paucity of scholars who are capable of dealing with them. In some ways, the research field which is available to those trained in Islamic philosophy is wide open. They are often not in the position of those in other fields of the humanities of discussing texts which have been worked over for many years or even centuries. It is not difficult to find an interesting text, edit it (or make preparatory moves towards this end), translate and discuss parts of it, and point out how the author contributed to the debate of his times in ways which had previously been unacknowledged. As far as texts are concerned, one suffers from an embarrassment of riches.

Why are there not more people who are capable of dealing with such texts? When one considers the skills which are required, it is not difficult to answer this question. The student of Islamic philosophy will need to have a good understanding of a variety of languages which are becoming less prevalent today among those in higher education. If students have a good grasp of Arabic and perhaps Persian, then they will also require an understanding of Greek and perhaps of some of the European languages in which many of the main philosophical ideas may have been comprehensively discussed. If students have a background in modern European languages, then they will need to acquire some linguistic facility in the Classics and in philosophical thought, along with at least Arabic. This is not to suggest that the whole of Islamic philosophy originates with the Greeks, which it certainly does not, and the reader of these volumes will be aware of the very rich and continuing tradition of such thought which is far removed from the principles of Greek philosophy. None the less, it is undeniable that it is important to have an understanding of the basic arguments of the Greek thinkers, since they form such a significant part of the setting of the problems which the philosophers in the Islamic world go on to consider. An equally important form of knowledge is the Islamic sciences, and even Muslims may find that the basic grasp which they have acquired of these through their religious education has not really prepared them for the sophisticated conceptual work of philosophy. Those who are not Muslims will have to try to grasp the principles of the sciences of Islam without seeing them through the conceptual spectacles of their own religion or culture, which is hardly an easy task. There are good reasons, then, for the relative paucity of those who are in a position to study and develop the leading works of Islamic philosophy.

The contributors to these volumes have come from a wide variety of countries and regions of the world, and the place in which one works inevitably has an important effect upon the nature of the approach to the material which is undertaken. The presiding cultural interests will tend to inform the way in which Islamic philosophy is pursued. This is especially the case in the Islamic world, and individual philosophers will be taken up if it is felt that they have a part to play in contributing to current ideas and controversies. One of the exciting features of Islamic philosophy is the variety of hermeneutic approaches which are adopted in its analysis. The field is not homogenous enough for just one approach to dominate the whole area, and unless there are future radical developments it is likely that this state of affairs will continue.

This is an observation which is hardly limited to Islamic philosophy, though. Philosophy as a whole represents a wide gamut of methodological approaches and ideas which frequently display no general agreement as to how to proceed. When one combines the variety of philosophy with the different ways of interpreting Islam and related religions, it is easy to see that the prospect of having any one approach to solving philosophical problems which is going to be accepted by everyone is vacuous. The richness of Islamic philosophy lies precisely in its very diverse ways of addressing conceptual issues. These volumes represent many of these approaches and have set out to respect their variety.

General introductions to Islamic philosophy

Oliver Leaman

Anawati, G. *Etudes de philosophie musulmane* (Paris, 1974).
Armstrong, A. (ed.) *The Cambridge History of Later Greek and Early Medieval Philosophy* (Cambridge, 1970).
Arnold, T. and Guillaume, A. (eds) *The legacy of Islam* (Oxford, 1931).
Badawi, A. *La Transmission de la philosophie grecque au monde arabe* (Paris, 1968).
—— *Histoire de la philosophie en Islam* (Paris, 1972).
Booth, E. *Aristotelian Aporetic Ontology in Islamic and Christian Thinkers* (Cambridge, 1983).
Brinner, W. and Ricks, S. (eds) *Studies in Islamic and Judaic Traditions* (Atlanta, 1986).
Burrell, D. *Knowing the Unknowable God: Ibn Sina, Maimonides, Aquinas* (Notre Dame, 1986).
Butterworth, C. and Kessel, B. (eds) *The Introduction of Arabic Philosophy into Europe* (New York, 1994).
Chahine, O. *Ontologie et théologie chez Avicenne* (Paris, 1962).
Chodkiewicz, M. *Le Sceau des saints: Prophetie et saintété dans la doctrine d'Ibn Arabi* (Paris, 1986).
Corbin, H. *History of Islamic Philosophy* (London, 1992).
Craig, W. *The Cosmological Argument from Plato to Leibniz* (London, 1980).
Davidson, H. *Proofs for Eternity, Creation and the Existence of God in Medieval Islamic and Jewish Philosophy* (New York, 1987).
Druart, T.-A. (ed.) *Arabic Philosophy and the West: Continuity and Interaction* (Washington DC, 1988).
El Amrani-Jamal, A. *Logique Aristotélicienne et grammaire arabe: Etude et documents* (Paris, 1983).
Fakhry, M. *A History of Islamic Philosophy* (New York, 1983).
Gardet, L. *La Pensée réligieuse d'Avicenne (Ibn Sina)* (Paris, 1951).
—— "La Falsafa", in C. Bouamrane and L. Gardet (eds) *Panorama de la pensée islamique* (Paris, 1984).

Genequand, C. "La Philosophie arabe", in *Les Arabes et l'occident* (Geneva, 1982) 51–63.
Gilson, E. *Histoire de la philosophie au Moyen Age* (Paris, 1947).
Goichon, A.-M. *La Distinction de l'essence et de l'existence d'après Ibn Sina (Avicenne)* (Paris, 1937).
Goodman, L. (1991) "Three Enduring Achievements of Islamic Philosophy", in *Culture and Modernity*, ed. E. Deutsch (Honolulu, 1991): 401–29.
Gutas, D. *Avicenna and the Aristotelian Tradition* (Leiden, 1988).
Hallaq, W. and Little, D. (eds) *Islamic Studies presented to Charles J. Adams* (Leiden, 1991).
Hanna, S. (ed.) *Medieval and Middle Eastern Studies: In Honor of Aziz Suryal Atiya* (Leiden, 1972).
Hernández, M. *Historia de la filosofía española: filosofía hispano-musulmana* (Madrid, 1957).
—— *Historia del pensamiento en el mundo islámico*, 2 vols (Madrid, 1981).
Holt, P., Lambton, A. and Lewis, B. (eds) *The Cambridge History of Islam* (Cambridge, 1970).
Horten, M. *Die philosophischen Systeme der spekulativen Theologen im Islam* (Bonn, 1912).
Hourani, G. "The Early Growth of the Secular Sciences in Andalusia", *Studia Islamica*, 32: (1970).
—— *Islamic Rationalism: the Ethics of 'Abd al-Jabbār* (Oxford, 1971).
—— (ed.) *Essays on Islamic Philosophy and Science* (Albany, 1975).
Hyman, A. and Walsh, J. (eds) *Philosophy in the Middle Ages: the Christian, Islamic and Jewish Traditions* (New York, 1967).
Izutsu, T. *Ethico-religious Concepts in the Qur'an* (Montreal, 1966).
—— *A Comparative Study of the Key Philosophical Concepts in Sufism and Taoism: Ibn 'Arabi and Lao-Tzu* (Tokyo, 1971).
—— *Creation and the Timeless Order of Things* (Ashland, 1994).
Jayyusi, S. (ed.) *The Legacy of Muslim Spain* (Leiden, 1992).
Jolivet, J. *L'Intellect selon Kindi* (Leiden, 1971).
Leaman, O. *An Introduction to Medieval Islamic Philosophy* (Cambridge, 1985).
Lerner, R. and Mahdi, M. (eds) *Medieval Political Philosophy: a Sourcebook* (Ithaca and New York, 1972).
Link-Salinger, R. (ed.) *A Straight Path: Studies in Medieval Philosophy and Culture: Essays in Honour of Arthur Hyman* (Washington DC, 1988).
Mahdi, M. *Al-Farabi's Philosophy of Plato and Aristotle* (Ithaca, 1969).
Marmura, M. (ed.) *Islamic Philosophy and Theology: Studies in Honor of George F. Hourani* (Albany, 1984).
Martin, R. (ed.) *Approaches to Islam in Religious Studies* (Tucson, 1985).
Morewedge, P. (ed.) *Islamic Theological Philosophy* (Albany, 1979).
—— (ed.) *Philosophies of Existence: Ancient and Modern* (New York, 1982).
—— (ed.) *Neoplatonism and Islamic Thought* (Albany, 1992).
Munk, S. *Mélanges de philosophie juive et arabe* (Paris, 1955).
Nardi, B. *Studi di filosofia medievale* (Rome, 1979).
Nasr, S. A. *An Annotated Bibliography of Islamic Science*, 3 vols (Tehran, 1975–94).
—— *Islamic Life and Thought* (Albany, 1981).
—— (ed.) *Islamic Spirituality*, 2 vols (New York, 1987–91).

—— *Ideals and Realities of Islam* (London, 1994).
—— *The Islamic Intellectual Tradition in Persia*, ed. M. Aminrazavi (London, 1995).
Netton, I. *Allah Transcendent* (London, 1989).
Peters, F. *Aristotle and the Arabs* (New York, 1968).
—— *Aristoteles Arabus* (Leiden, 1968).
—— *Allah's Commonwealth: a History of Islam in the Near East 600–1100 AD* (New York, 1973).
—— *God's Created Speech* (Leiden, 1976).
Quadri, G. *La Philosophie arabe dans l'Europe méditerranéenne dès ses origines à Averroës*, trans. R. Huret (Paris, 1947).
Rahman, F. *Prophecy in Islam* (London, 1958).
Rosenthal, E. *Studia Semitica*, vols 1 and 2 (Cambridge, 1971).
Rosenthal, F. *The Classical Heritage in Islam* (London, 1975).
—— *Greek Philosophy in the Arab World* (Aldershot, 1990).
Rudavsky, T. (ed.) *Divine Omniscience and Omnipotence in Medieval Philosophy* (Dordrecht, 1985).
Schimmel, A. *Mystical Dimensions of Islam* (Chapel Hill, 1975).
Sharif, M. (ed.) *A History of Muslim Philosophy* (Wiesbaden, 1963).
Shehadi, F. *Metaphysics in Islamic Philosophy* (New York, 1982).
Sheikh, M. *Studies in Muslim Philosophy* (Lahore, 1974).
Steenberghen, F. *Introduction à l'étude de la philosophie médiévale* (Louvain, 1974).
Stern, S., Hourani, A. and Brown, V. (eds) *Islamic Philosophy and the Classical Tradition: Essays Presented to Richard Walzer* (Oxford, 1972).
Stern, S. *Medieval Arabic and Hebrew Thought*, ed. F. Zimmerman (London, 1983).
Twersky, I. (ed.) *Studies in Medieval Jewish History and Literature* (Cambridge, Mass., 1979).
Von Grunebaum, G. (ed.) *Logic in Classical Islamic Culture* (Wiesbaden, 1970).
Walzer, R. *Greek into Arabic: Essays on Islamic Philosophy* (Oxford, 1962).
Watt, W. *Islamic Philosophy and Theology* (Edinburgh, 1985).
Weisheipl, J. *Nature and Motion in the Middle Ages* (Washington DC, 1985).
Wickens, G. (ed.) *Avicenna: Scientist and Philosopher: a Millenary Symposium* (London, 1952).
Wippel, J. *Medieval Philosophy from St Augustine to Nicholas of Cusa* (New York, 1969).
Wolfson, H. *Crescas' Critique of Aristotle: Problems of Aristotle's Physics in Jewish and Arabic Philosophy* (Cambridge, Mass., 1929).
—— *Philo: Foundations of Religious Philosophy in Judaism, Christianity and Islam* (Cambridge, Mass., 1962).
—— *The Philosophy of the Church Fathers: Faith, Trinity, Incarnation* (Cambridge, Mass., 1970).
—— *The Philosophy of Spinoza* (Cambridge, Mass., 1934).
—— *Religious Philosophy: a Group of Essays* (Cambridge, Mass., 1961).
—— *Studies in the History of Philosophy and Religion*, vols 1 and 2 (Cambridge, Mass., 1973 and 1977).
—— *The Philosophy of the Kalam* (Cambridge, Mass., 1976).

Index of names

Index of terms

accident (*'araḍ*) 240, 423, 554, 909
Active Intellect *see under al-'aql al-fa''al*
adab: as *paideia* 157, 158; as culture 42, 156, 385, 404, 568; *see also* ethics
adīb; as *phronimos* 157, 158
aesthetics 969f; and epistemology 183, 185; and ethics 974; Ibn Rushd and 974–6; Ibn Sīnā and 972–4; and language 969–70; Saadiah Gaon and 708–9; *see also* language, literature
agent, first 167
agent intellect *see under al-'aql al-fa''al*
alchemy 206–7
amīr al-kāfirīn (prince of the unbelievers) 73
amīr al-mu'minīn (prince of the believers) 73
al-amr (will) 112, 125, 616
anthropology 1102–3, 1116
al-'aql (intellect) 28, 31, 81–2, 84, 117, 299, 349, 500, 656, 1046, 1162f; types of 186 *and below*
al-'aql bi'l-fi'l (actual intellect) 186, 239
al-'aql bi'l-quwwah (potential intellect) 186
al-'aql al-fa''al (the Active Intellect or agent intellect) 298, 348, 691, 883; in Christian Europe 1006; term coined by al-Fārābī 244 *n.25;* and emanation 198, 191; and al-Fārābī 185–6, 189, 191, 298, 789, 835, 849; Gabriel as 168, 298, 481 and Gersonides 692, 742, 746; and Ibn Bājjah 299–300; and Ibn Kammūnah 490; and Ibn Miskawayh 253, 254; and Ibn Rushd 340, 857, 1017; and Ibn Sina 28, 239, 298, 792, 836–7, 948; and Ibn Ṭufayl 315, 323; in Illuminationism 481; and *ittiṣāl* 186, 358; and Judah Halevi 720, 722; and Suhrawardī 444, 453
al-'aql al-ḥayūlānī (material intellect) 238, 342
al-'aql bi'l-malakah (habitual intellect) 239, 454
al-'aql al-munfa'il (Passive Intellect) 227
al-'aql al-mustafād (acquired intellect) 186, 191, 239
al-'aql al-naẓarī (the theoretical intellect) 28, 81–2, 238
al-'aql al-qudsī (holy intellect) 454
al-'aql wa'l-naql ('reason and tradition') 81–2 132
Arabic language 898, 899–918
arabic numerals 60, 61, 62
archetypes: 651–2, 654
Aristotelianism *see under* Aristotle
'asabiyyah (group feelings) 354–5, 567
aṣālat al-'aql (primacy of the intellect) 475
aṣālat al-māhiyyah (principiality of essence) 615
aṣālat al-waḥy (primacy of revelation) 475
aṣālat al-wujūd (principiality of existence) 615, 647–8
ashkāl (Platonic forms) 224, 323, 476, 479; *see also* forms
astrology 745f
astronomy 59, 60–1, 295–6, 307, 315, 337, 381, 533, 541, 544, 748–9, 789, 931; astronomical tables 60
atomism: Aristotle and 1019; and causation 1019–21; and *kalām* 53–4, 828, 1019; al-Kindī and 169;